THE **GOLD**

BOOK OF

VENTURE

CAPITAL

FIRMS

Published by Kennedy Information, LLC

Publishers of *The Directory of Executive Recruiters*, Executive Recruiter News, SearchSelect®, *The International Directory of Executive Recruiters*, Consultants News, Global IT Consulting Report, Consulting magazine, *The Directory of Management Consultants*, Human Resource Management News, Investor Relations News and Recruiting Trends

KENNEDY INFORMATION

One Kennedy Place, Route 12 South, Fitzwilliam, NH 03447 USA
Phone: 603-585-3101 Fax: 603-585-9555
E-mail: bookstore@kennedyinfo.com Web: www.kennedyinfo.com
ISBN: 1-885922-31-0
Price: $ 37.95

THE GOLD BOOK OF VENTURE CAPITAL FIRMS

DATABASE EDITORS

Constance Kennedy

Susanne Bussiere

Julie Lombardi

Melony Raitto

Kathy Doyle

Joan Geary

DATABASE MANAGEMENT

Philip Sbrogna

Jennifer Shay

DESIGN/LAYOUT

Sharon Price

Darrell Royter

PRODUCTION

R.D. Whitney

KENNEDY INFORMATION

Giles Goodhead, Chairman

Wayne Cooper, President & CEO

Marshall Cooper, Executive Vice President

David Beck, Group Publisher

Timothy Bourgeois, Vice President

Philip Sbrogna, Vice President

R.D. Whitney, Vice President

Dedicated To:

Marilyn and Norman Cooper

Table of Contents

FOREWORD

If you're interested in tapping into the lucrative venture capital industry, you've come to the right place.

We are proud to present this first edition of Kennedy Information's *The Gold Book of Venture Capital Firms*. Over the past 29 years, we have worked hard to earn a reputation as the premier publisher of directories for businesses and professionals. Some of our best known directories include *The Directory of Executive Recruiters* (also known as "The Red Book") and *The Directory of Management Consultants*. This directory is the result of many of our customers urging us to develop a quality directory of venture capital firms for an affordable price.

In a bookstore, it's sometimes hard to compare the quality of alternative directories. The quality of the directory — the accuracy, currency, and depth of the data, and the robustness of the indexes and cross indexes — is sometimes hard to evaluate until one puts it to the ultimate test and uses it. Whether your goal is to raise capital from a venture capital firm, explore career opportunities with one of these firms or one of their portfolio companies, or to research the key players in the venture capital explosion — put this directory to the test.

We make every effort to obtain up-to-date, accurate information, but do not assume any liability for any errors or omissions and reserve the right to include, eliminate or modify listings at our discretion. We stand by this directory, and all our products, with a 100% satisfaction guarantee.

On behalf of our dedicated team of researchers, data editors, database managers and other professionals, I thank you for putting your trust in Kennedy Information. We will continue to work hard to meet, and hopefully exceed, your expectations and to earn your continued business. Please let us know if you have suggestions for how we can improve this directory. And best of luck in your pursuits. We hope this directory helps you achieve your goals.

Sincerely,

Wayne Cooper
Publisher

How to Use This Directory

Kennedy's Gold Book of Venture Capital Firms has been arranged alphabetically by state. Indexes for alternative access include:

- **Key principal** - Look up the name of a vc professional alphabetically by last name to determine which firm they are with and what page the listing appears on.

- **Industry specialization** - To find a firm concentrating on a particular area of venture capital, consult the master list of industries and search on that heading to find specific firms and page numbers.

- **Preferred stage(s) of financing** - Identify which firms participate in each stage of financing, from seed/startup to first stage/second stage through LBO/MBO and venture leasing. Most firms do several of these, if not all, and will be included under multiple categories.

- **Firm** - Look up the name of a vc firm alphabetically to find what page the listing appears on.

HOW TO READ A LISTING

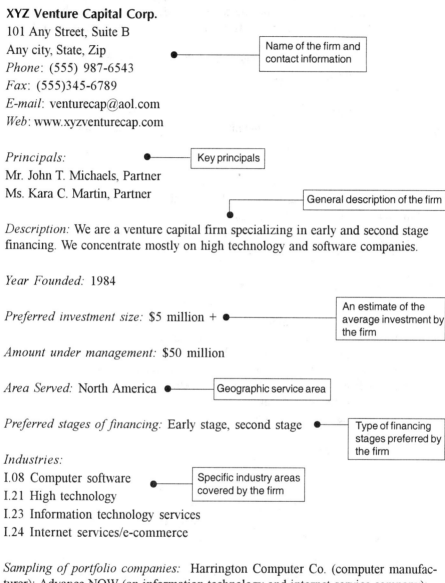

XYZ Venture Capital Corp.
101 Any Street, Suite B
Any city, State, Zip
Phone: (555) 987-6543
Fax: (555)345-6789
E-mail: venturecap@aol.com
Web: www.xyzventurecap.com

Name of the firm and contact information

Principals:

Key principals

Mr. John T. Michaels, Partner
Ms. Kara C. Martin, Partner

General description of the firm

Description: We are a venture capital firm specializing in early and second stage financing. We concentrate mostly on high technology and software companies.

Year Founded: 1984

Preferred investment size: $5 million +

An estimate of the average investment by the firm

Amount under management: $50 million

Area Served: North America

Geographic service area

Preferred stages of financing: Early stage, second stage

Type of financing stages preferred by the firm

Industries:

I.08 Computer software

Specific industry areas covered by the firm

I.21 High technology
I.23 Information technology services
I.24 Internet services/e-commerce

Sampling of portfolio companies: Harrington Computer Co. (computer manufacturer); Advance NOW (an information technology and internet service company); Replicate Fast Inc. (CD and disk replication company)

A sample of companies the firm has invested in

Raising Venture Capital

The venture capital (v.c.) market is red hot. Venture capital firms invested over $12.5 billion in more than 1,800 companies in 1998 alone. And despite the magnitude and growth of these v.c. investments, money is coming into these firms and their funds faster than the venture capitalists can invest the proceeds. The reason is clear: venture capital firms have done well. They have funded some of the most successful companies of our time.

But despite the vast amounts of money that the venture capitalists are looking to deploy, accessing this capital is not guaranteed. Successful fund raising requires several ingredients:

- A compelling idea that satisfies a clear market need
- A strong business plan that lays out a clear, winning strategy
- A management team with the requisite skills
- Targeting the right venture capital firms (who invest in your industry, geography and stage of development)

1. A Compelling Idea

So you've developed a new revolutionary appliance or a leading edge web service. The first thing a savvy venture capitalist (and most of them are savvy) will want to know is "who is the target customer and what is the need that this satisfies?" Too many failed ventures are the result of a technology chasing an application. A cool new technology is not sufficient. It has to do something better, faster or cheaper to have value to customers and get market acceptance. Start with the customer and you're sure to get and stay on the right track.

2. A Strong Business Plan

There are many books that provide advice on writing a winning business plan. The common ingredient is that the plan makes a compelling case for the new business and what competitive advantage(s) the new company will have. Some of the components of a winning business plan include:

- Executive summary: Summarize the highlights of the proposal so that a recipient can get an overview of the opportunity in 5 minutes and determine whether the plan is relevant and interesting enough to read and evaluate.

- The product or service: Describe what the product or service is. Who it is targeted for? What customer need does it fill and how does it do it better than alternatives?

- The market: How big is the target market? What segments comprise this market? What share of market do current alternatives garner and what share is realistic for your firm?

- Competitors: Who are the existing and likely competitors? What advantages do you have over these competitors? How are they likely to respond to your entry? What would their likely reactions mean for the market?

- Operations: How will you produce this product and/or deliver this service? What type of infrastructure and staff is required?

- R&D: What research and development efforts are required to bring your product/service to market? What will be required on an ongoing basis to maintain your technological advantage (if relevant)?

- Sales & marketing: How do you intend to market and sell your product and/or service to your customers? If you will be selling through channels (e.g., wholesalers, retailers), how will you market and sell to and through these channels?

- Management team: What are the backgrounds and credentials of the core management team? Who else do you intend to and need to hire? How do you intend to recruit them?

- Financial projections: Show realistic pro formas with well thought out and justified assumptions. Include a *profit and loss statement, cash flow statement* and *balance sheet* for the startup phase and first 5 years of operation. Also beneficial are a *sources and uses report* (how will you spend the money you are looking to raise) and a *breakeven analysis* (how much volume is required at varying price points to be profitable).

Key Elements Venture Capitalists Look For In A Business Plan

Positives
- Customer need is clear and compelling
- Proprietary technology or other source of competitive advantage
- Experienced manager(s)
- Reasonable financial projections
- Clear marketing/sales strategy
- Appreciation for investor's concerns and needs
- Exit strategy for investors (e.g., sale to strategic acquirer, go public)
- Technology or product focus (vs. customer)

Negatives

- Lack of in-depth customer and competitor knowledge
- Inexperienced management team
- Simplistic financial pro formas (e.g., unrealistic growth or penetration projections)
- Marketing/sales plan that shows weak understanding of channels and purchase process
- Unfocused approach — trying to do too much and not showing clear prioritization

3. A Credible Management Team

This factor is, far and away, the most important variable for a venture capitalist. An outstanding product or service idea, backed by a strong proprietary technology and a superior business plan will not get funded if the venture capital firm doesn't have confidence in the management team. This doesn't mean you have to have your entire team selected, down to the Vice President or Director level (in fact, some venture capitalists would prefer to participate in building out the team); what it does mean is that the venture capitalist must gain confidence in the key person (or people) that will run the business. Relevant experience running a comparable business is the best background, although basic attributes such as intelligence, honesty, industriousness, commitment and communication skills certainly weigh heavily as well.

4. Targeting The Right Venture Capitalist(s)

There are many kinds of venture capitalists who invest in different types of opportunities. We have organized this directory to make it easy to pinpoint the right firms. Some of the most important dimensions are:

- Industry: Many venture capital firms and venture capitalists specialize in a narrow set of industries. Some specialize in semiconductors, others in healthcare devices, biotech or Internet services. Still others invest in "low tech" businesses. We list industry specialties for the majority of firms. Wherever possible, we also list portfolio companies that the firms have invested in. This allows you to determine not only what industries the venture capital firm will consider, but also where they have actually placed their bets to date.

- Geography: Just because a venture capitalist is located in Silicon Valley doesn't mean they only invest in Silicon Valley companies. Some v.c. firms like to invest only in companies that are located near them, while others have a national or global scope. Wherever possible, we list each firm's geographic preference.

- Stage of Development: While some firms like to invest early on, in the infancy of a start-up, others prefer to invest in later stages of development. Here are the key stages of development that we have used to categorize specific firms:

A. Early Stage Financing:

Seed Financing is the initial investment required to prove a concept (e.g., to build a prototype or conduct market research) and qualify for start-up financing.

Startup Financing is what is typically required to build a management team and bring a product (or service) to market.

First Stage Financing is often sought when startup financing is depleted and a young company needs to expand its production, marketing and/or sales capabilities to "ramp up".

B. Expansion Financing:

Second Stage Financing is used by companies that are shipping products (or delivering services) and growing, but need additional sources of funds to fund working capital requirements and grow faster than internally generated cash flow will allow.

Mezzanine Financing is typically used to fund substantial growth and/or expansion of companies that are already up and running and are often at or beyond break-even volumes. Capital to fund a plant expansion or to move into a new geographic market is often categorized into this class of funding.

Bridge Financing is sometimes needed when a company is about to go public within the following year. Bridge financing, as the name implies, is used to get the company to the IPO. Usually, the bridge financing is short term and is paid off with proceeds from the public offering.

C. Acquisitions/ Buyouts:

This type of financing is used to fund the acquisitions or buyouts of existing businesses that are up and running. Many times these are mature businesses that are funded with a large component of debt and a small level of equity capital (leveraged buyouts). The K.K.R. acquisition of RJR/Nabisco was one of the more famous (and largest) examples of this type of transaction.

The purpose of this directory is to help you pinpoint the right venture capitalists for you and to help you prepare to approach them. We hope we can help you succeed.

New Rules for Raising Venture Capital

You may have noticed that venture capital directories keep getting thicker. Money is pouring into venture capital like never before- $12.5 billion in 1998 alone, more than twice the pace set in 1995. Even Wall Street's great bull market pales in comparison.

So, why does is seem so hard to raise financing for your company?

VC's are stretching like never before to gain an edge over the rest of the herd. They are changing their targets and they are changing their tactics. This means that the old conventional wisdom about where to go and how to play the fund raising game has changed.

Here are three trends that will affect which vc's you approach and how you approach them:

1. Make sure the fund still does your type of deal.
Many vc firms have grown so large that they can no longer afford to do small deals. Instead of doling our just $1 million per deal, they need to focus on juggernauts of $10 million or more. This requires a completely different approach to investing - later stage companies, greater financial complexity, slower pacing, lower risk. The upshot for fund-seekers is that you need to ask the right questions: is this venture firm still a true venture firm, or has it migrated up into later stage private equity?

2. Be careful with first time funds.
There are dozens of new funds on the block. Many have sprung up to fill the void left behind as traditional funds evolve into later stage deal focus. Many exist as an outlet for the massive flow of new-found 1990's wealth. And many are led by individuals with strong private equity track records.

On the other hand, there are a good number of "boot-strap" venture capital start-ups out there. Although their money is as "green" as everyone else's, their lack of experience and solid financial backing can sometimes cause problems. Watch out for funds with "soft-circled" limited partners - they have an uncanny way of drying up the day before a close.

Watch out too for vc's who don't have a history of co-investing with their peers - a vc's personal network can be a lifesaver for your fledgling company. Don't get me wrong - first time funds can be a fabulous way to break into the vc scene. Just be sure that the due diligence goes in both directions.

3. Consider strategic co-investors.
Historically, vc's have tried to avoid strategic "corporate-style" investment partners.

This is because strategic investors are viewed as willing to forgo purely financial gains in order to reap ulterior strategic benefits.

But competition has prompted many vc's to bring something to the table besides just money. And they have learned that side by side deals with the right strategic partners can make for a win-win proposition.

For example, Capital One, whose core business is credit cards, has partnered with several vc's to lend its database marketing skills to the venture capital process. Aspiring portfolio companies that come looking for just money are presently surprised to find that they can in addition gain access to technology and operations help and a management team savvy in mass customer acquisition.

Entrepreneurs should target both vc's and strategic co-investors who "get" their business model. As well as improving your odds of raising funds, you can also expect to benefit from helpful Board members, vital operating relationships, higher quality follow-on investors and better valuations as a result.

While it may not always seem like it, the old mantra that there's no shortage of money has never been truer. The current vc marketplace is hungry and is investing. Armed with good business plans, credible management teams are getting funded.

George Overholser is VP, New Business Development, Capital One Services, Inc., Boston, MA

Entrepreneurial Venture Candidates:
A Recruiter's Perspective

The venture capital world is one of the hottest markets for job seekers looking for a new challenge. It provides individuals with an entrepreneurial spirit the opportunity to be involved on the ground floor of cutting-edge innovation. Venture capitalists are continuously searching for experienced senior management to lead new ventures and start-ups. The difficulty for recruiters and companies seeking senior management talent often lies in their own ability to assess the skills of a potential candidate. Does this individual have the ability and skills to start, build, grow, and sustain a new venture? Defining what the senior management of an early stage company should look like is one of the toughest questions facing the industry today. There is no clear-cut definition of what will make an individual a successful candidate for an entrepreneurial venture. When looking at today's most successful entrepreneurs, it is unlikely to find two individuals who have the same background in terms of education and experience. More often than not, however, all are self starters who have a high energy level and a passion for success. The following overview seeks to define what the marketplace looks for in individuals seeking a senior management position within an early stage company.

Candidates for Entrepreneurial Ventures
In executive search, the role of the recruiter goes beyond evaluating a potential candidate's educational background and work experience. The recruiter must also be able to evaluate the "intangible" characteristics of a candidate.

- Does he/she have the ability to work in an entrepreneurial environment?
- Is he/she a strong leader who can recruit and motivate talented individuals?
- Does he/she have the ability to make the tough decisions?
- Can he/she roll up their sleeves and do what it takes to get the job done?
- Is he/she a quick learner? Does he/she have the ability to evaluate the risks and rewards of an opportunity?
- Does he/she have a proven track record of success in their specific industry?
- Is he/she well recognized and highly regarded by their peers in the industry?
- By recruiting this individual to its organization, will the company gain instant credibility with the financial community, especially Wall Street?

A Proven Record of Success
It is these intangible characteristics that really determine whether or not an individual will be successful in an entrepreneurial environment. The most useful advice for individuals considering an entrepreneurial venture is to make sure you know your strengths and weaknesses in these areas before pursuing any opportunity. Whether it is a recruiter, venture capitalist, private investor, or business partner, they will need to be convinced that not only do you have vision, but that you also

have a solid understanding of what it takes to build a company. Ideal candidates have a proven track record of success in a high-growth, entrepreneurial environment. Strong candidates will have the ability to recruit, develop and motivate top-notch individuals who fortify not only their own strengths and weaknesses, but those of the organization as well. A new venture also needs senior management who can quickly identify and assess target markets for their company's product/service. With a solid business background, you will know how to quickly assess a market and how to best position your company to achieve its maximum potential. You will also be able to identify your competition and know how to keep ahead of them in an extremely competitive market. Not only does the senior management team need to be focused internally, it is imperative that they keep up to date with what is happening in their industry in order to remain ahead of their competition.

Focused Managerial Style

Vital to any new venture is the ability of leadership to demonstrate strong organizational guidance and a focused managerial style. A leader is able to build a team by recruiting competent and skilled individuals for various positions, by motivating them to achieve the goals of the company, by creating appropriate incentives, and by understanding what drives each individual in the organization. New ventures often get to a point where it is difficult to see the light at the end of the tunnel. It is the job of senior management to make sure their team remains focused, motivated and confident that the light at the end of the tunnel is not beyond their reach. At the same time, senior management must also remember to listen to their clients, customers, and employees. By being a strong communicator, you will gain their trust and respect which in turn will only help to facilitate the success of the company. A senior management team that remains focused and driven is crucial to any company's success.

Risk and Salary

After evaluating one's own skills, candidates must then determine whether or not they have the confidence and ability to assume the level of risk often associated with new ventures. It is no secret that running and building a start-up venture is one of the most challenging and daring adventures a businessperson can undertake. There are no guarantees. Those willing to accept the challenge of starting and running a business from the ground floor have typically experienced success early in their careers. They understand the risks, and appreciate the rewards. Recruiters look for people who have the confidence, experience, and willingness to take on this risk. The candidate must not only evaluate where they are in their professional lives, they must also take a look at where they are in their personal lives. Often times joining a new venture requires an individual/family to relocate. It may also mean that an individual needs to take a decrease in his/her current compensation in return for a significant equity stake in the company. Can you and your family afford to take these risks, and at what price?

Recruiting for New Ventures:

Identifying the ideal candidate is often not the most difficult task for a recruiter. The difficulty may lie in actually attracting seasoned talent to a specific venture. Seasoned senior managers know that there can often be obstacles in place that will impede their success. To sell the opportunity, the recruiter needs to be prepared to deal with these questions: Is the founder of the company still involved, and to what degree? Will the senior management team have complete control over the decision-making process? Or, will decisions be made at the board level, and if so, will the CEO be a participating member of that board? Will senior managers have the authority and independence to make executive decisions without interference? In order to be successful, senior management must have the autonomy to run the day-to-day operations of the company and the ability to make tough decisions regarding the company's future. It is often difficult for a founder to give up control of a company to which they have devoted so much time and effort. Individuals stepping into a senior management role must realize this and must assess their ability to work alongside the founder until they have gained his/her trust and respect.

Another factor facing any recruiter trying to find senior management in today's market is compensation. Compensation packages will typically include a base salary and bonus, plus a significant equity stake in the company. In new ventures, candidates seek an equity component that will compensate them long term for the risk they will have to undertake in the short term. Companies must remain competitive in terms of compensation in order to attract top-notch talent to their organization.

A recruiter is retained to find the best talent for a particular situation. But, not every seasoned entrepreneurial leader can fit into every situation. By placing the priority on recruiting a proven senior management team, a venture capital firm is stating that the business will only be successful if it has strong leaders behind it. A company may not have an A+ product, but without a top notch management team, they will not make the grade.

Marketplace Analysis

Today, new ventures are exploding onto the scene and their quest for strong leadership is endless. Recruiters are scouring the marketplace for leaders willing to take on the challenge of a new venture who have the experience, ability and business building skills to take a company to the next level. Top-notch management teams will enhance a company's chance of success. Not all new ventures are successful, so candidates for these roles can ill afford to enter into a situation without questioning the product, business plan, and most importantly, their own skills and level of experience. The entrepreneurial spirit is in everyone; whether an individual has the "intangible" qualities required to build a successful organization is the question that needs to be answered.

Karen Burke and Michael Steiner are principals in the Private Equity Practice at Korn/Ferry International's Boston office

Alabama

Cordova Capital

4121 Carmichael Road, Suite 301
Montgomery, Alabama 36106
(334) 271-6011
Fax: (334) 260-0120

Key contact:
Mr. Ed Adair
Mr. W. A. Williamson, Jr.

Area served: Southeast

Preferred stage of financing: Second stage

Industries:
I.06   Communications
I.08   Computer software
I.12   Distribution
I.13   Education
I.14   Electronics
I.15   Energy/natural resources/utilities
I.18   Financial services
I.29   Medical/medical products
I.31   Real estate

FHL Capital Corporation

600 20th Street North, Suite 350
Birmingham, Alabama 35203
(205) 328-3098
Fax: (205) 323-0001
E-mail: fhl@scott.net

Key contact:
Mr. Edwin W. Finch, III, President/CEO
Mr. Kevin J. Keck, Vice President

1941 Florence Boulevard
Florence, Alabama 35630
(205) 767-5900
Fax: (205) 767-5983
E-mail: lyons@HiWaay.net

Key contact:
Mr. Bill J. Lyons, Jr., Managing Director

Description: Merchant bank engaged in mergers and
acquisitions as principle and agent.

Amount of capital invested: $4 million

Preferred investment size: $1-2 million

Area served: United States

Preferred stage of financing: LBO/MBO

Industries:
I.04   Broadcasting
I.05   Chemicals
I.12   Distribution
I.13   Education
I.14   Electronics
I.22   Industrial products
I.27   Manufacturing
I.36   Transportation

First SBIC of Alabama

16 Midtown Park East
Mobile, Alabama 36606
(334) 476-0700
Fax: (334) 476-0026

Key contact:
Mr. David DeLaney

Area served: Southeast

Preferred stages of financing: Seed, Start up, First
stage, Second stage, Mezzanine, LBO/MBO, Third/
later stage

Industries:
I.19   Generalist

FJC Growth Capital Corporation

200 West Court Square, Suite 340
Huntsville, Alabama 35801
(205) 922-2918
Fax: (205) 922-2909

Key contact:
Mr. William Noojin
Mr. Francisco L. Collazo

Area served: Southeast

Preferred stage of financing: Second stage

Industries:
I.19   Generalist

Hickory Venture Capital

200 West Side Square, Suite 100
Huntsville, Alabama 35801
(256) 539-1931
Fax: (256) 539-5130
E-mail: info@hvcc.com
Web: www.hvcc.com

Key contact:
Mr. J. Thomas Noojin, President
Mr. Monro B. Lanier, Vice President

Mr. John R. Bise, Vice President

Description: We are an equity investor providing cash
and seasoned, at-risk management perspective to
growth capital companies for equity appreciation.
We seek companies with experienced management
teams, defensible market niches and favorable return
potential. Portfolio is diversified, but areas of particular interest are healthcare, software, telecom and e-
commerce.

Preferred investment size: $1-10 million

Amount under management: $25-100 million

Area served: Primarily Southeast, United States

Preferred stages of financing: Start up, First stage, Second stage, Mezzanine, LBO/MBO, Expansion

Industries:
I.01   Aerospace
I.04   Broadcasting
I.06   Communications
I.07   Computer hardware
I.08   Computer software
I.12   Distribution
I.14   Electronics
I.19   Generalist
I.20   Healthcare
I.21   High technology
I.22   Industrial products
I.23   Information technology services

I.24   Internet services/e-commerce
I.26   Life sciences
I.27   Manufacturing
I.28   Media/publishing
I.29   Medical/medical products
I.32   Retail
I.34   Services (business)
I.36   Transportation
I.37   Wholesale

Sampling of portfolio companies: Active Servicers Corp. (geriatric health & day services); All Components, Inc. (memory devices); Enclins, Inc. (minimally invasive surgical devices); Jackson Business Forms Co. (specialty printing); Lumitex, Inc. (engineered lighting); Mesa Solutions (GIS software); Network Performance Systems (network management/performance software); PEI (defense electronics)

Jefferson Capital Fund, Ltd.
1901 6th Avenue North, Suite 1510
Farmingham, Alabama 35203
(205) 324-7709
Fax: (205) 324-7783

Key contact:
Ms. Lana E. Sellers

Area served: Southeast

Preferred stage of financing: LBO/MBO

Industries:
I.05   Chemicals
I.06   Communications
I.12   Distribution

Arizona

Banc One Capital Partners
P.O. Box 71
Phoenix, Arizona 85001
(602) 221-2064
Fax: (602) 221-1470
E-mail: fsvorys@bocc.com

Key contact:
Mr. Fred S. Vorys, Director

Description: We provide mezzanine, venture capital and financial advisory services to middle-market operating companies in connection with mergers and acquisitions, recapitalizations, corporate divestitures and expansion capital. Such financings are typically in the form of subordinated debt with warrants and/or preferred stock.

Amount of capital invested: $170 million

Preferred investment size: $5-8 million

Amount under management: $100-500 million

Area served: United States

Preferred stages of financing: Mezzanine, LBO/MBO, Expansion

Industries:
I.06   Communications
I.11   Consumer products
I.12   Distribution
I.13   Education
I.14   Electronics
I.17   Environmental services/waste management
I.18   Financial services
I.19   Generalist

I.20   Healthcare
I.22   Industrial products
I.27   Manufacturing
I.28   Media/publishing
I.29   Medical/medical products
I.34   Services (business)
I.36   Transportation
I.37   Wholesale

Sampling of portfolio companies: Compaq Computer Co. (computer manufacturer); Metro Airlines, Inc. (regional commuter airlines); Beauty Control (cosmetic manufacturer); Callaway Golf Co. (manufacturer of golf clubs); First Plus Financial Group (financial services); Plains Resources, Inc. (oil & gas exploration); A&W Brands (soft drink manufacturer); Pronet, Inc. (telephone paging services); Dr. Pepper Bottling Co. (soft drink bottler); Enclean, Inc. (environmental services); Community Health Systems (healthcare facilities & services); Railtex, Inc. (railcare leasing); Kemet Electronics (manufacturer electronic capacitors); Matador Petroleum Corp. (oil exploration & production); DeCrane Aircraft Holdings (manufacturer aerospace products); Argyle Television (operator of television stations)

Princeton American Corp.

300 West Clarendon, #210
Phoenix, Arizona 85013
(602) 274-4939
Fax: (602) 954-2633

Key contact:
Mr. Bill Taylor
Mr. Dale Eyman
Mr. Winston McKellar
Mr. David Smith

Area served: United States

Preferred stages of financing: First stage, Second stage, LBO/MBO, Third/later stage

Industries:
I.04   Broadcasting
I.07   Computer hardware
I.08   Computer software
I.14   Electronics
I.15   Energy/natural resources/utilities
I.17   Environmental services/waste management
I.18   Financial services
I.19   Generalist
I.29   Medical/medical products
I.31   Real estate
I.32   Retail
I.34   Services (business)
I.35   Services (consumer)
I.36   Transportation

Solstice Capital

13651 East Camino La Cebadilla
Tucson, Arizona 85749
(520) 749-5713
Fax: (520) 749-4743
E-mail: solcap@aol.com

Key contact:
Mr. Harry George

Description: Our basic strategy is to identify companies which are positioned to capitalize on major change factors. Investing in and helping to foster these companies can yield both economic and social returns. We view being a small fund as an advantage, as investing smaller portions of money can prove to be profitable and early stage companies seeking $1 to 2 million are underserved. Areas of principle investment interest include technology based industries, however, we also invest in non-technical areas.

Amount of capital invested: $4.76 million

Preferred investment size: $1 million

Amount under management: $10-25 million

Area served: United States

Preferred stages of financing: Seed, Start up, First stage

Industries:
I.08   Computer software
I.13   Education
I.17   Environmental services/waste management

I.19   Generalist
I.21   High technology
I.22   Industrial products
I.23   Information technology services
I.24   Internet services/e-commerce
I.27   Manufacturing

Sampling of portfolio companies: Abuzz, Inc. (knowledge management software); Accucom Wireless Services (cellular phone location services); Active Control eXperts (vibration & motion control: smart materials); Avalon Imaging, Inc. (machine vision system for plastic injection molding); Blind Faith Cafe, Inc. (whole-foods restaurant); Connected Corp. (network-based back-up & MIS services to businesses); Continuum Software, Inc. (software tools to create multiprocessor applications); E-Ink Corp. (developer of electronic ink displays); Evergreen Solar, Inc. (manufacturer of photovoltaic materials & cells); Lipton Corporate Child Care (back-up child care services); MoneyStar Communications, Inc. (interactive mutual fund sales & software); Mosaic Technologies, Inc. (solid phase DNA probe & related technology); Optimax Systems Corp. (scheduling software for manufacturing); Pharsight Corp. (planning software for clinical trials); PID, Inc. (batch processing manufacturing control software); Proton Energy Systems, Inc. (manufacturer of hydrogen production equipment); Radnet, Inc. (groupware for corporate intranets); Secure Technologies, Inc. (distance detection products based on radio frequency technology)

Southwest Venture Capital Network

One East Camelback Road, Suite 1100
Box 60756
Phoenix, Arizona 85082-0756
(602) 263-2390

Key contact:
Dr. Carrol de Broekert, Chairman/CEO

Description: Angel network with 44 investors seeking opportunities in the $50,000 - $250,000 range of investment. Serve the states of Arizona, Colorado, Nevada, New Mexico and Utah.

Founded: 1990

Amount of capital invested: $1,319,000

Preferred investment size: $250,000

Area served: Arizona, Colorado, Nevada, New Mexico, Utah

Preferred stages of financing: Seed, Start up, First stage, Expansion

Industries:
I.01   Aerospace
I.02   Agriculture/forestry/fishing/mining
I.03   Biotech/genetic engineering
I.06   Communications
I.09   Construction
I.11   Consumer products
I.12   Distribution
I.14   Electronics
I.15   Energy/natural resources/utilities
I.17   Environmental services/waste management

I.20   Healthcare
I.21   High technology
I.22   Industrial products
I.25   Leisure/hospitality
I.26   Life sciences
I.27   Manufacturing
I.29   Medical/medical products
I.32   Retail
I.34   Services (business)

I.35   Services (consumer)
I.36   Transportation
I.37   Wholesale

Sampling of portfolio companies: Upscale, high end wholesale sports; high technology electronics; food service industry; retail sales; high technology physical systems; technology medical systems

Wasatch Venture Fund
3101 North Central Avenue, Suite 540
Phoenix, Arizona 85012
(602) 212-5568
Fax: (602) 230-1005

Key contact:
Mr. Paul Huleatt

Description: Our objective is to finance businesses with extraordinary management that have developed proprietary products and are capable of creating exceptional growth in sales and profits. We will pursue a people-biased, back to basics, early-stage approach to venture capital investing. We intend to invest in information, communication, software and medical product companies based in Utah, California, Arizona, Nevada and other Western states.

Amount of capital invested: $5 million

Preferred investment size: $1 million

Amount under management: $10-25 million

Area served: United States

Preferred stage of financing: First stage

Industries:
I.06   Communications
I.07   Computer hardware
I.08   Computer software
I.21   High technology
I.23   Information technology services
I.24   Internet services/e-commerce
I.33   Semiconductors

Western America Venture Group
10215 North 100 Place
Scottsdale, Arizona 85258
(602) 661-3906
Fax: (602) 661-8439

Key contact:
Mr. Richard Caron, President

Description: Specialize in capital investment of less than $10 million and invest primarily in the technology and resource sectors. We also take companies public by venturing with sponsoring investment dealers or act as agents for private placement using securities regulation exemptions.

Preferred investment size: Up to $1 million

Amount under management: $25-100 million

Area served: Worldwide

Preferred stages of financing: Start up, First stage, Second stage, LBO/MBO, Expansion, Int'l expansion, Succession buy outs

Industries:
I.02   Agriculture/forestry/fishing/mining
I.03   Biotech/genetic engineering
I.07   Computer hardware
I.11   Consumer products
I.12   Distribution
I.14   Electronics
I.15   Energy/natural resources/utilities
I.16   Entertainment
I.17   Environmental services/waste management
I.20   Healthcare
I.21   High technology
I.22   Industrial products
I.23   Information technology services
I.25   Leisure/hospitality
I.26   Life sciences
I.27   Manufacturing
I.29   Medical/medical products
I.37   Wholesale

Arkansas

Small Business Investment Capital, Inc.
12103 Interstate 30
P.O. Box 3627
Little Rock, Arkansas 72203
(501) 455-6599
Fax: (501) 455-6556

Key contact:
Mr. Hubert Fugett
Mr. Charles E. Toland

California

21st Century Internet Venture Partners

Two South Park, 2nd Floor
San Francisco, California 94107
(415) 512-1221
Fax: (415) 512-2650
E-mail: jennifer@21vc.com
Web: www.21vc.com

Key contact:
Mr. J. Neil Weintraut, Partner
Mr. Peter H. Ziebelman, Partner
Mr. Robert H. Reid, Associate

Description: We are devoted to investing in start up ventures pursuing opportunities born of the internet. Our areas of interest include (but are not limited to) internet- and intranet-related software and tools, internet media and the emerging internet-enabled digital economy.

Preferred investment size: $1-5 million

Amount under management: $25-100 million

Area served: United States

Preferred stages of financing: Seed, Start up, First stage, Second stage

Industries:
I.24   Internet services/e-commerce

Sampling of portfolio companies: AvantGo (an enabler of enterprise applications for the mobile web); CareerBuilder (a creator of an internet/intranet recruiting system); Employease (a provider of internet-based human resource & employee benefits administration services); GreenTree (an online nutrition store & information megasite); IMGIS (an ad syndicator); Vicinity (a geo-enabler of web sites); When.com (a provider of web-based collaborative tools)

Acacia Venture Partners

101 California Street, Suite 3160
San Francisco, California 94111
(415) 433-4200
Fax: (415) 433-4250

Key contact:
Ms. C. Sage Givens, General Partner
Mr. David S. Heer, General Partner
Mr. C. Ted Paff, General Partner
Mr. Brian J. Roberts, Associate

Description: We are a private venture capital fund dedicated to investing exclusively in the healthcare services and the health information technology industries. We invest in all stages of company formation and typically take a lead and active investor role.

Amount of capital invested: $20 million

Preferred investment size: $5-7 million

Amount under management: $25-100 million

Area served: United States

Preferred stages of financing: Seed, Start up, First stage, Second stage, Mezzanine, LBO/MBO, Expansion

Industries:
I.20   Healthcare

Sampling of portfolio companies: Abaton.com, Inc. (medical informatics company providing information & transaction processing services based on intranet & internet technologies); Americaid, Inc. (specialty HMO which provides managed care to Medicaid recipients); InSite Clinical Trials, Inc. (Site Management Organization which provides services to pharmaceutical companies to help them complete clinical trials more quickly & efficiently); Managed Care USA, Inc. (provides insurance & managed care services to the workers' compensation market); Oncology Affiliates, Inc. (provides cancer care through a network of owned & affiliated oncology service providers); PhyCom Corp. (medical informatics company which provides medical management software to risk-bearing healthcare payors & providers); PhyCor Management Corp. (formed to develop Independent Physician Associations); Pioneer EyeCare, Inc. (integrated eye care services company that manages ophthalmic physician practices, develops provider networks & provides managed eye care services to healthcare payors); Psychiatric Solutions, Inc. (integrated behavioral healthcare company that provides a portfolio of mental health services to healthcare payors & self-insured employers); Vida Healthcare, Inc. (specialty managed care company providing full-risk disease management carve-out programs to healthcare payors & self-insured employers)

Accel Partners

428 University Avenue
Palo Alto, California 94301
(650) 614-4800
Fax: (650) 614-4880
E-mail: info@accel.com
Web: www.accel.com

Key contact:
Mr. Jim Breyer, Managing Partner
Mr. Bud Colligan, Venture Partner
Mr. Bruce Golden, Entrepreneur-In-Residence
Mr. Gene Hill, General Partner

Mr. Arthur Patterson, Founding Partner
Mr. Joe Schoendorf, Executive Partner
Mr. Jim Swartz, Founding Partner

Description: We are a venture capital firm dedicated to partnering with outstanding management teams to build world-class companies. In order to meet this challenge with a prepared mind, we focus our activity in just three areas: communications, internet and intranet software and services in technology and healthcare.

Preferred stages of financing: Seed, Start up, First stage, Second stage, LBO/MBO

Industries:
I.06   Communications
I.08   Computer software
I.24   Internet services/e-commerce
I.29   Medical/medical products

Sampling of portfolio companies: Actuate (client/server systems software); AXENT (client/server security); Bright Tiger Technologies (enterprise web server management); Data Everywhere (software to enable virtual warehouses); iPass (global internet roaming & settlement services); Travelling Software (mobile communications applications); Biztravel.com (online travel services); Cybermeals (take-out food delivery via the web); PageMart Wireless (personal communications); Sonnet Financial (discount foreign exchange services); Agile Networks (ATM backbone LAN's); AMCC (communications semiconductors); Centrum (multiprotocol remote access servers); Corsair Communications (cellular fraud detection); GoDigital (low cost ISDN transport); Netopia (internet collaboration tools); Polycom (advanced teleconferencing equipment); Teloquent (software for managing public networking); Vitalink (LAN bridges & routers)

Advanced Technology Ventures

485 Ramona Street, Suite 200
Palo Alto, California 94301
(650) 321-8601
Fax: (650) 321-0934
Web: www.atv-ventures.com

Key contact:
Mr. Jos C. Henkens, General Partner
Mr. Steven N. Baloff, General Partner

Description: Since our founding, we have been a leading force in helping emerging information technology and healthcare companies to grow and prosper. With offices in California's Silicon Valley and along Boston's Route 128 corridor, we are one of the country's preeminent venture capital firms focused solely on technology-related investments.

Founded: 1979

Amount of capital invested: $25 million

Preferred investment size: $2-5 million

Amount under management: $100-500 million

Area served: Europe, United States

Preferred stages of financing: Seed, Start up, First stage

Industries:
I.03   Biotech/genetic engineering
I.06   Communications
I.07   Computer hardware
I.08   Computer software
I.14   Electronics
I.20   Healthcare
I.21   High technology
I.23   Information technology services
I.24   Internet services/e-commerce
I.26   Life sciences
I.29   Medical/medical products
I.33   Semiconductors

Sampling of portfolio companies: Actel Corp. (FPGAs & software design systems); Credence Systems (VLSI test equipment); Cytyc Corp. (Thin prep test replacement for pap smears); Novoste Corp. (King Beta-Cath for treatment of restenosis based on radiation); TranSwitch Corp. (VLSI semiconductor devices for telecommunications); VLSI Technology, Inc. (computer-aided design tools for VLSI engineering); Avicenna Systems-acq. by Synetic (intranet- & internet-based products/services for physicians); AccelGraphics (3-D graphics hardware & software products); RF Micro Devices, Inc. (RF semiconductors for digital wireless communications); California Microwave, Inc. (wireless communications products); CollaGenex Pharmaceuticals,Inc. (innovative medical therapy for periodontal disease); Anthra Pharmaceuticals, Inc. (commercialization of pharmaceuticals based on anthracyclines); Continuus Software, Inc. (configuration management software development tools)

Advent International

2180 Sand Hill Road, Suite 420
Menlo Park, California 94025
(650) 233-7500
Fax: (650) 233-7515
Web: www.adventinternational.com

Key contact:
Mr. John J. Rockwell, Partner
Ms. Gwendolyn M. Phillips, Principal
Mr. Gregory C. Smitherman, Principal

Description: We are one of the world's largest private equity investment firms, with $3 billion under management and more than 90 professionals in Europe, North America, Asia and Latin America. Our goal is to invest in attractive, growth-oriented companies on a global basis and to provide management teams with the support needed to build businesses of significant value.

Founded: 1984

Amount of capital invested: $250 million

Preferred investment size: Over $5 million

Amount under management: >$1 billion

Area served: Asia, Latin America, Central Europe, United States

Preferred stages of financing: LBO/MBO, Expansion

Industries:
I.03   Biotech/genetic engineering
I.04   Broadcasting
I.05   Chemicals
I.06   Communications
I.08   Computer software
I.11   Consumer products
I.14   Electronics
I.15   Energy/natural resources/utilities
I.18   Financial services

I.20   Healthcare
I.22   Industrial products
I.23   Information technology services
I.27   Manufacturing
I.28   Media/publishing
I.29   Medical/medical products
I.32   Retail

Sampling of portfolio companies: deCODE Genetics Inc. (population-based genomics); PT Prima Dian Kalimas (ceramic tiles); Colofon BV (professional & business publisher); Icynene Inc. (sprayable polymer foam insulation); Lightbridge Inc. (outsourcing services for cellular & PCS carriers); New Look Group Ltd. (retailer of women's wear); Zindart Ltd. (die-cast ornaments & toys); OK International Inc. (electronic production tools & equipment); Thai Storage Battery Co. (car & truck batteries); Nelson Hurst PLC (full-line insurance broker); Parmalat Finanziaria SpA (long-shelf-life milk & other food products); Main Street Dental Management Corp. (dental practice management); UroCor Inc. (disease management services for urology); Ionics Inc. (membrane separation & water treatment systems); PT Bintang Kharisma (sports shoes); PolyMedica Corp. (diabetes supplies & consumer healthcare products); Sofamor Danek Group Inc. (spinal fixation devices); McDonnell Information Systems Group PLC (systems integration); WebLine Communications Corp. (internet software enabling call centers to visually interact with customers); Tecnologistica SpA (third-party logistics services)

Alafi Capital Company

P.O. Box 7338
Berkeley, California 94707
(510) 653-7425

Key contact:
Moshe Alafi, General Partner

Preferred stages of financing: Seed, First stage

Industries:
I.03   Biotech/genetic engineering
I.05   Chemicals
I.14   Electronics
I.29   Medical/medical products

Alpine Technology Ventures

20300 Stevens Creek Boulevard, Suite 495
Cupertino, California 95014
(408) 725-1810
Fax: (408) 725-1207
E-mail: kathryn@alpineventures.com
Web: www.alpineventures.com

Key contact:
Dr. Chuck K. Chan, General Partner
Mr. David A. Lane, General Partner

Description: We invest in California-based start-up or early stage information technology companies, preferably those with headquarters in Silicon Valley. This geographic focus allows the partners to offer value-added services and to develop close working relationships with the management teams of the portfolio companies.

Amount of capital invested: $11 million

Preferred investment size: $1-2 million

Amount under management: $25-100 million

Area served: Silicon Valley

Preferred stages of financing: Seed, Start up, First stage, Second stage

Industries:
I.06   Communications
I.07   Computer hardware
I.08   Computer software
I.14   Electronics
I.21   High technology
I.24   Internet services/e-commerce
I.27   Manufacturing
I.33   Semiconductors

Sampling of portfolio companies: Acacia Networks, Inc. (networking equipment); Adicom Wireless, Inc. (wireless telecommunications); Austin-James, Inc. (software for customized products); GWcom, Inc. (wireless telecommunications); Microbar, Inc. (semiconductor manufacturing equipment); Novita Communications, Inc. (software for internet appliances); OPC Technology, Inc. (software for manufacturing semiconductors); PinPoint Software, Inc. (software for network management); ProLinx Labs Corp. (semiconductors packaging); Senté, Inc. (EDA software tools for IC design); Virtual Vineyards (marketing of wines & food on the internet)

Alta Partners

One Embarcadero Center, Suite 4050
San Francisco, California 94111
(415) 362-4022
Web: www.altapartners.com

Key contact:
Mr. Jean Deleage, General Partner
Mr. Daniel Janney, General Partner
Mr. Marino Polestra, General Partner
Mr. Garrett Gruener, General Partner
Mr. Guy Nohra, General Partner
Dr. Alix Marduel, General Partner

Description: Founded in February 1996, we are a venture capital partnership investing in information technologies and life sciences companies. Our partnership combines capital experience with exceptional entrepreneurial talent to achieve investing success.

Founded: 1996

Preferred stages of financing: Start up, First stage, Second stage

Industries:
I.03   Biotech/genetic engineering
I.08   Computer software

I.23   Information technology services
I.26   Life sciences
I.29   Medical/medical products
I.30   New media

Sampling of portfolio companies: Adolor; Akos Biomedical, Inc.; @Backup; Be; CDR Therapeutics; deCode genetics; DyNAvax; Fibex Systems; Hepatix, Inc.; ImproveNet; Kosan Biosciences; MitoKor; netbot; Neuron Data; Prolifix Medical; Retinal Displays; T-Sqware, Inc.; Uros Corp.; WavTrace; XLNT

Altos Ventures

2882 Sand Hill Road #100
Menlo Park, California 94025
(650) 234-9771
Fax: (650) 233-9821
E-mail: info@altosvc.com
Web: www.altosvc.com

Key contact:
Mr. Brendon Kim, General Partner
Mr. Han J. Kim, General Partner
Mr. Ho Nam, General Partner

Description: We are a partnership formed to invest in early stage information technology companies, to partner closely with management, to contribute real value and to build significant companies.

Amount of capital invested: approximately $10 million

Preferred investment size: $1 million

Amount under management: $25-100 million

Area served: United States

Preferred stages of financing: Seed, Start up, First stage, Second stage

Industries:
I.12   Distribution
I.21   High technology
I.23   Information technology services
I.24   Internet services/e-commerce
I.30   New media
I.34   Services (business)

Sampling of portfolio companies: Digital Market (procurement software for production goods); Nonstop Solutions (service & software for demand chain management); Instill (procurement service for the restaurant industry); Evolve (next generation enterprise software); Enwisen (intranet publisher of benefits info); Luna (middleware transaction software); Tacit (smartphone software); Call Connect (call outsourcing for healthcare market); GW Comm (2 way communication infrastructure/technology); Visible (city tour on handheld device); Bluedot (virtual trade show & community); Inquisit (personalized info through email); Greetstreet (e-greetings on internet); Homeshark (mortgage broker on the net); Hearing Science (hearing aid retail center); Big Book (network marketing company); Newfire (3-D platform & tools)

Amerindo Investment Advisors Inc.

One Embarcadero Center, Suite 2300
San Francisco, California 94111
(415) 362-0292
Fax: (415) 362-0533
Web: www.amerindo.com

Key contact:
Mr. Robert Murray, Director of Marketing

Description: We are a minority-owned emerging growth small cap stock manager specializing in leading edge technology-oriented companies including biotechnology and allied small healthcare, electronics and software and companies benefiting from technological advances. Our research team is composed of three portfolio managers and seven analysts. Stock selection is based on original fundamental research, confirmed by technical factors such as price momentum, with an 18 to 24 month time horizon. Portfolios are generally concentrated and contain about 12 to 20 issues when fully invested.

Amount of capital invested: $24,700,000

Amount under management: >$1 billion

Area served: United States

Preferred stages of financing: First stage, Second stage, Mezzanine, Privates

Industries:
I.03   Biotech/genetic engineering
I.06   Communications
I.07   Computer hardware
I.08   Computer software
I.14   Electronics
I.20   Healthcare
I.21   High technology
I.23   Information technology services
I.24   Internet services/e-commerce

Sampling of portfolio companies: Company "A" (operating resource management (ORM) solutions); Company "B" (world wide web & tv programmer & information provider); Company "C" (multicast networking technology)

Applied Technology

1010 El Camino Real, Suite 300
Menlo Park, California 94025
(650) 326-8622
Fax: (650) 326-8163

Key contact:
Mr. Gene Flath

Preferred stages of financing: Seed, Start up, First stage, Second stage

Industries:
I.06   Communications
I.08   Computer software

Asia Pacific Ventures Technology Partners

535 Middlefield Road, Suite 150
Menlo Park, California 94025
(650) 327-7871
Fax: (650) 327-7631
Web: www.apvco.com

Key contact:
Mr. Will Stewart, Partner
Mr. Spencer Tall, Partner
Mr. Pete Bodine, Partner
Mr. Ted Holden, Partner
Ms. Helen Ingerson, Partner
Mr. Jim Hinson, Principal
Ms. Christine Lien Choi, Research Analyst

Description: We are a venture capital firm, funded primarily by large technology corporations, which focuses on investing in seed and early-stage high tech companies with proprietary, leading-edge technologies. Our initial fund was established in 1995 and has invested in data communications, computer hardware/software, educational technology, multimedia technologies, networking, internet infrastructure, PC/TV convergence and semiconductors.

Founded: 1990

Preferred stages of financing: Seed, Start up, First stage

Industries:
I.07   Computer hardware
I.08   Computer software
I.14   Electronics
I.21   High technology
I.24   Internet services/e-commerce
I.33   Semiconductors

Sampling of portfolio companies: WebTV Networks (terminals allow viewers to access the internet over a television set); ComputerLiteracy (on-line computer book retailer); Dynamic Pictures (high-performance 3-D graphics accelerators for workstations & high-end PCs); epiphany (enterprise relationship management systems); Equator (programmable consumer processors serving the PC, consumer & communications markets); Frontier Ventures (venture incubator provides management assistance & access to funding for promising technology start-ups); Impala Linear Corp. (mixed-signal circuits for portable computing & communications); iPass Inc. (worldwide cross-authorization & settlement service to internet service providers); Lexar Media (flash memory products for digital cameras & other consumer electronic devices); NeTpower (high performance Windows NT workstations & servers); NETSchools (portable computers & a wireless LAN for the K-12 education market); One Touch (student response systems for highly interactive distance learning); Packet Engines (gigabit ethernet local area network products); Pluto Technologies (digital video networks & servers, initially for post-production & professional markets); ShareWave (PC/TV convergence technology); Ten North Communications (automation software for independent sales reps); Virtual Headquarters (develops & markets executive intranet solutions); Vision Software (productivity tools to automate the development of strategic client/server applications); Zanza Software (java & web-based tools for real-time, customized database query & reports); 911 Entertainment (enhanced music, video CD's & entertainment website)

Aspen Ventures

1000 Fremont Avenue, Suite V
Los Altos, California 94024
(650) 917-5670
Fax: (650) 917-5677
Web: www.aspenventures.com

Key contact:
Mr. Thad Whalen, General Partner
Dr. David Crockett, General Partner
Mr. Alex Cilento, General Partner
Mr. Stephen Fowler, General Partner

Description: We are a seed and early stage venture capital fund investing in software and data communications companies in the Western United States.

Amount of capital invested: $12 million

Preferred investment size: Up to $3 million

Amount under management: $25-100 million

Area served: West

Preferred stages of financing: Seed, Start up

Industries:
I.06   Communications
I.08   Computer software
I.21   High technology
I.23   Information technology services
I.24   Internet services/e-commerce
I.33   Semiconductors

Sampling of portfolio companies: Adaptive Solutions (neural net development systems & chip sets); Athens Corp. (semiconductor manufacturing equipment); Beyond Software (mainframe servers for the world wide web); Clarity Software (communications applications for the world wide web); Cornerstone Imaging (document image processing subsystems); Ellipsys Technologies (test systems for telecommunications networks); Expersoft (tools for developing enterprise-wide client/server applications); Faraday Electronics (personal computer chip sets); Iband (web page development tools); Insight Development (image processing products for the internet); Instill Corp. (electronic commerce software & network services); Kofax Image Products (document image processing subsystems); Landec Corp. (new class of polymetric materials); Lanquest Group (network & internet testing tools); Media Vision (personal computer multimedia products); Microlinear (mixed signal integrated circuits); Netframe Systems (servers for local area networks); Qualix Group (publisher of client/server management software); Read-Rite Corp. (thin film recording heads for disk drives); Reasoning Systems (software reengineering tools); Sierra Semiconductor (standard cell arrays & custom semiconductors); Thru-Put Technologies (scheduling software for manufacturing companies); Timeline Vista (digital audio products for professional sound editing); Vertex Networks (high-speed networking chip sets); Visqus Corp. (contact recording for hard disks)

Asset Management Associates, Inc.
2275 East Bayshore Road, Suite 150
Palo Alto, California 94303
(650) 494-7400
Fax: (650) 856-1826
Web: www.assetman.com

Key contact:
Mr. Craig C. Taylor, General Partner
Mr. John F. Shoch, General Partner
Mr. Franklin P. Johnson, General Partner
Mr. W. Ferrell Sanders, General Partner
Dr. Douglas E. Kelly, M.D., General Partner

Description: A private venture capital firm founded in 1965, we have raised over $200 million and invested in more than 125 companies. We focus on high-potential, technology-based seed and early-stage companies in the biological and information sciences. Areas of interest include bio-pharmaceuticals, gene and cell therapies, medical devices, diagnostics, research and clinical laboratory instrumentation, healthcare information services, multimedia intranet and internet applications, networking, telecommunications, mobile computing and tools.

Founded: 1965

Amount under management: $100-500 million

Area served: New England, West Coast

Preferred stages of financing: Seed, Start up, First stage

Industries:
I.03   Biotech/genetic engineering
I.06   Communications
I.23   Information technology services
I.24   Internet services/e-commerce
I.28   Media/publishing
I.29   Medical/medical products
I.30   New media

Sampling of portfolio companies: Abaxis; Accel-Graphics; Applied Micro Circuits Corp.; Amgen; Boole & Babbage; Castelle; ChemTrak; Conductus; Her Interactive; IDEC Pharmaceuticals; InPart Design; Latitude; Molecular Dynamics; NeTpower; Nuance Communications; Park Scientific Pharmacy-clics; Pharsight; Red Brick Systems; Remedy Corp.

AT&T Ventures
3000 Sand Hill Road
Building 1, Suite 285
Menlo Park, California 94025
(650) 233-0617
Fax: (650) 854-4923

Key contact:
Mr. Neal M. Douglas

Description: We were founded in 1992 as a venture capital partnership to invest in information technology and service enabling companies in emerging growth markets. Drawing from three funds totaling $348 million, we provide capital to start-up and later stage companies in the following markets: wireless communications, internet, value added networking services, content and local service.

Founded: 1992

Preferred investment size: $1-5 million

Amount under management: $100-500 million

Area served: United States

Preferred stages of financing: Seed, Start up, First stage, Second stage

Industries:
I.06   Communications
I.08   Computer software
I.11   Consumer products
I.12   Distribution
I.23   Information technology services
I.24   Internet services/e-commerce
I.28   Media/publishing
I.30   New media

Sampling of portfolio companies: Amteva Technologies; Audible; Cellnet Data Systems; Digital Generation Systems; E-Stamp; Freegate; IBM; Juniper; Multex; NetObjects; Onlive!; Sentient Networks, Inc.; Transcend Access Systems; Veridicom; WNP Communications; BBN Corp.; CommQuest; Datasonix; Gartner Group (J3 Learning); Solectek

Auerbach Acquisition Associates, LLC
1940 Westwood Boulevard, Suite 208
Los Angeles, California 90025
(310) 575-8720

Key contact:
Mr. Douglas Shooker, Managing Director

Preferred stages of financing: Second stage, LBO/MBO

Industries:
I.06   Communications
I.08   Computer software
I.12   Distribution
I.13   Education
I.15   Energy/natural resources/utilities
I.17   Environmental services/waste management
I.18   Financial services
I.25   Leisure/hospitality
I.28   Media/publishing
I.29   Medical/medical products
I.32   Retail

AVI Capital, L.P.

One First Street, Suite 2
Los Altos, California 94022
(415) 949-9862
Fax: (415) 949-8510
E-mail: vc@avicapital.com
Web: www.avicapital.com

Key contact:
Mr. Brian J. Grossi, General Partner
Mr. Barry M. Weinman, General Partner
Mr. Peter L. Wolken, General Partner
Ms. Helen R. S. MacKenzie, CFO

Description: We are the general partner of a family of
professionally-managed venture capital partnerships
specializing in seed and early-stage investments in
high-technology companies positioned for high
growth segments of the information technologies
market. Formed in 1995, we have been organized as
a Participating Securities SBIC with over $60 million
of capital. Limited partners include U.S. pension
funds, insurance companies, corporations, individuals and college endowment funds.

Founded: 1995

Area served: West Coast

Preferred stages of financing: Seed, Start up, First
stage

Industries:
I.06   Communications
I.08   Computer software
I.23   Information technology services
I.28   Media/publishing

Sampling of portfolio companies: Intraspect (software);
Qualix Group (software); Answer Systems, Inc.
(software); Hyper Parallel (software); PowerUp
(software); Sierra Semiconductor (semiconductors);
Cypress Semiconductor (semiconductors); LGC
Wireless (communications & networking); 3Com
(communications & networking); Grand Junction
Networks (communications & networking); Network
Peripherals (communications & networking); Accel-
Graphics (computers & peripherals); radius
(computers & peripherals); Pinnacle Systems
(computers & peripherals); Bell Microproducts (electronics distribution); Innotech Corp. (electronics
distribution); Analog Design Tools (CAD/CAE);
Rasna Corp. (CAD/CAE); Wire Networks (information services); NetChannel (information services)

Axiom Venture Partners

One Post Street, Suite 2525
San Francisco, California 94104
(415) 434-9999
Fax: (415) 434-0505

Key contact:
Dr. Linda Sonntag, Ph.D.

Preferred stages of financing: First stage, Second stage

Industries:
I.03   Biotech/genetic engineering
I.06   Communications
I.29   Medical/medical products

AZCA, Inc.

100 Marine Parkway, Suite 305
Redwood City, California 94065
(650) 598-9900
Fax: (650) 598-9554
Web: www.azcainc.com

Key contact:
Masazumi Ishii

Preferred stages of financing: First stage, Second stage

Industries:
I.03   Biotech/genetic engineering
I.05   Chemicals

I.06   Communications
I.07   Computer hardware
I.08   Computer software
I.11   Consumer products
I.12   Distribution
I.14   Electronics
I.15   Energy/natural resources/utilities
I.17   Environmental services/waste management
I.25   Leisure/hospitality
I.29   Medical/medical products
I.32   Retail
I.35   Services (consumer)

Baccharis Capital, Inc.

2420 Sand Hill Road, Suite 100
Menlo Park, California 94025
(650) 324-6844
Fax: (650) 854-3025

Key contact:
Mr. Noel Perry
Ms. Mary Bechmann

Area served: Rocky Mountains, West Coast

Preferred stages of financing: Start up, First stage,
Second stage, LBO/MBO, Racapitalizations

Industries:
I.08   Computer software

I.11   Consumer products
I.12   Distribution
I.13   Education
I.15   Energy/natural resources/utilities
I.17   Environmental services/waste management
I.32   Retail

Bangert Dawes Reade Davis & Thom

220 Montgomery, Suite 424
San Francisco, California 94104
(415) 954-9900
Fax: (415) 954-9901

Key contact:
Mr. Dexter Dawes, Chairman

Preferred stages of financing: Second stage, LBO/MBO

Industries:
I.03   Biotech/genetic engineering
I.04   Broadcasting
I.08   Computer software
I.11   Consumer products
I.12   Distribution
I.14   Electronics
I.15   Energy/natural resources/utilities
I.17   Environmental services/waste management
I.28   Media/publishing
I.29   Medical/medical products

BankAmerica Ventures

950 Tower Lane, Suite 700
Foster City, California 94404
(650) 378-6000
Fax: (650) 378-6040

Key contact:
Ms. Carla Perumean

Preferred stages of financing: First stage, Second stage, Expansion

Industries:
I.03   Biotech/genetic engineering
I.06   Communications
I.14   Electronics
I.29   Medical/medical products

Bastion Capital

1999 Avenue of the Stars, Suite 2960
Los Angeles, California 90067
(310) 788-5700
Fax: (310) 277-7582

Key contact:
Mr. William Bron

Description: Finance management buy-outs and growth. Need control. Special knowledge of US minorities market and Mexico.

Area served: North America, South/Central America

Preferred stages of financing: LBO/MBO, Expansion

Battery Ventures

901 Mariner's Island Boulevard, Suite 475
San Mateo, California 94404
(650) 372-3939
Fax: (650) 372-3930

Key contact:
Mr. Kenneth P. Lawler, General Partner
Mr. David A. Hartwig, Associate
Mr. Dennis B. Phelps, Associate
Mr. Robert G. Barrett, Managing Partner

Description: Founded in 1983, we are one of the leading high tech venture capital firms in the nation. We manage four investment funds, the most recent of which totals $200 million, placing us among the largest information technology venture capital funds in the country. Our focused investment approach targets early emerging companies in the communications and software technology markets in the U.S. and abroad.

Founded: 1983

Preferred investment size: $1-20 million

Amount under management: $100-500 million

Area served: United States

Preferred stages of financing: Start up, First stage, Second stage

Industries:
I.06   Communications
I.08   Computer software
I.12   Distribution
I.23   Information technology services
I.24   Internet services/e-commerce

I.27   Manufacturing

Sampling of portfolio companies: Banyan Systems (local area network software); Fax Sav Corp. (digital fax network providing real-time & enhanced fax services to users); Meridian Data, Inc. (CD-ROM network servers & mastering software); Open Port Technology, Inc. (fax routing software); US Robotics (manufacturer of high-speed data communications products); Allegiance Telecom, Inc. (competitive local exchange carrier); AMSC (mobile satellite communications networks); Dial Page, Inc. (specialized mobile radio communications); Phoenix Wireless, Inc. (wireless local loop products & services); Acxiom Corp. (supplier of data & processing services for direct marketing); Answersoft, Inc. (computer telephony integration software products); EZ Access (client server recruiting software for corporate human resource departments & professional services companies); Legent Corp. (systems software primarily for mainframe environments); ProLogic Corp. (client-server banking software); Utopia Technology Partners (client-server internal help desk software); Viewlogic Systems, Inc. (supplier of EDA software tools on PCs & workstations); Infoseek Corp. (internet information search service); Inventa Corp. (enterprise level intranet systems integrator); In Focus Systems, Inc. (liquid crystal display-based projection systems); Stratasys, Inc. (manufacturer of CAD rapid prototyping systems)

Bay Partners

10600 North De Anza Boulevard, Suite 100
Cupertino, California 95014-2031
(408) 725-2444
Fax: (408) 446-4502
E-mail: ndbay@aol.com
Web: www.baypartners.com

Key contact:
Mr. John Freidenrich, Founder
Mr. Neal Dempsey

Description: We are a venture capital firm that works
with entrepreneurs to build indispensable, rapidly
growing companies positioned to compete and win in
increasingly competitive markets.

Founded: 1976

Area served: United States

Preferred stages of financing: Start up, First stage,
Second stage, Mezzanine, LBO/MBO, Expansion, Int'l

expansion, Venture leasing, initial public offering

Industries:
I.06   Communications
I.08   Computer software
I.17   Environmental services/waste management
I.23   Information technology services

Sampling of portfolio companies: Brocade Communications Systems, Inc.; Convoy Corp.; Digital Island;
iCat Corp.; Motiva Software Corp.; Neura Communications; Sonnet Financial, Inc.; Wayfarer Communications, Inc.; WiData; Castelle; CoStar Corp.; E-Mu
Systems, Inc. (creative technologies); IXYS Corp.;
Magellan Systems Corp. (orbital sciences corporation); Netlink (Cabletron Systems, Inc.); Opti-
graphics Corps. (Alpharel, Inc.); Protocol Systems,
Inc.; Red Brick Systems; Spectrian; Traveling
Software, Inc.

Behrman Capital

Four Embarcadero Center, Suite 3640
San Francisco, California 94111
(415) 434-7300
E-mail: kullrich@behrmancap.com

Key contact:
Mr. Darryl Behrman, Managing Partner
Mr. Grant Behrman, Managing Partner
Mr. Elliot Maluth
Mr. William Matthes

Description: We are a private investment firm with $67
million under management (1996). Founded in 1992,
we invest in management buyouts of growth companies in a diverse group of industries: software,
information services, music publishing, healthcare,
light manufacturing. We have invested in over 30
companies. Ninety percent of our investors are institutional investors.

Area served: United States

Preferred stages of financing: First stage, Second
stage, Mezzanine, LBO/MBO

Industries:
I.06   Communications
I.07   Computer hardware
I.08   Computer software
I.14   Electronics
I.20   Healthcare
I.27   Manufacturing
I.29   Medical/medical products

Sampling of portfolio companies: Chappell & Co.
(music publishers); Sanmina Corp. (printed circuit
boards); Ross Systems (financial application
software); 3COM Inc. (LAN systems); Linear Technologies (supplier of linear integrated circuits)

Benchmark Capital

2480 Sand Hill Road, Suite 200
Menlo Park, California 94025
(650) 854-8180
Fax: (650) 854-8183
E-mail: info@benchmark.com
Web: www.benchmark.com

Key contact:
Mr. David Beirne, General Partner
Mr. Bruce Dunlevie, General Partner
Mr. Kevin Harvey, General Partner
Mr. Bob Kagle, General Partner
Mr. Andy Rachleff, General Partner
Mr. Burton McMurty, Special Limited Partner
Mr. Steven Merrill, Special Limited Partner

Description: We are dedicated to being the leading
early stage venture capital firm of the next millen-
nium. Our mission is to help great entrepreneurs
build major enterprises, thereby producing
outstanding returns. To fulfill this mission, our focus
is the relentless pursuit and development of
outstanding entrepreneurs and ideas, continual

service to those entrepreneurs and to the investors
who support the firm, and continuous development
of talent within Benchmark.

Founded: 1995

Preferred investment size: $1-5 million

Amount under management: $100-500 million

Preferred stages of financing: Seed, Start up, First
stage, Second stage

Industries:
I.06   Communications
I.07   Computer hardware
I.08   Computer software
I.24   Internet services/e-commerce
I.33   Semiconductors
I.34   Services (business)
I.35   Services (consumer)

Sampling of portfolio companies: Ariba (operating
resource management software); eShop (internet
electronic commerce tools); Encompass (customized
internet services for consumers); Scient (advanced
technology solutions for the internet); Atmosphere

Networks (access system for carrier services); Ipsilon (IP switches); NetEdge (multiservice access concentrators); Turnstone (telecommunications equipment for CLECs); C-Port Corp. (communications microprocessors); Rambus (high-speed chip-to-chip interface technology); Approach (windows database for non-programmers); Broadbase (departmental data warehousing software); Collabra (groupware produ-

citivity software); Genesys (call center CTI software); Impresse Corp. (intranet software); Pure Atria (automated software quality tools); Unify (client/server application development tools); XA Systems Corp. (data utilities for mainframes); Palm (creator of the PalmPilot); Silicon Solutions (EDA hardware accelerators)

Bentley Capital

592 Vallejo Street, Suite 2
San Francisco, California 94133
(415) 362-2868
Fax: (415) 398-8209

Key contact:
Mr. John Hung

Mr. L. C. Chan
Mr. Louis Leong

Preferred stages of financing: First stage, Second stage

Industries:
I.19   Generalist

Berkeley International Capital Corp.

650 California Street, Suite 2800
San Francisco, California 94108-2609
(415) 249-0450
Fax: (415) 392-3929
E-mail: tfukumoto@berkeleyvc.com
Web: www.berkeleyvc.com

Key contact:
Mr. Arthur I. Trueger, Chairman
Mr. Michael J. Mayer, President
Mr. Robert A. Cornman
Mr. Alan D. Foster
Mr. Troy Y. Fukumoto
Ms. Anne M. Gagnon
Mr. Bernard R. Geiger
Mr. Brett A. Gottlieb
Mr. Bruce A. Keller
Mr. Thomas E. Pallante
Mr. Halsted W. Wheeler

Description: Based in San Francisco, we arrange private placement investments into rapidly growing technology and medical companies. We are a

wholly-owned subsidiary of London Pacific Group Limited, a diversified international administration of over $6 billion.

Preferred investment size: $5-15 million

Preferred stage of financing: Mezzanine

Industries:
I.29   Medical/medical products

Sampling of portfolio companies: Acuson Corp.; Adaptec, Inc.; Advanced Cardiovascular Systems; Altera Corp.; America Online, Inc.; Atmel Corp.; Broderbund Software, Inc.; Cadence Design Systems, Inc.; Cirrus Logic, Inc.; Community Health Systems, Inc.; Cypress Semiconductor Corp.; Idexx Laboratories, Inc.; Integrated Device Technology, Inc.; Linear Technology Corp.; LSI Logic Corp.; Nellcor Inc.; Oracle Corp.; Sequent Computer Systems, Inc.; 3Com Corp.; Ventritex, Inc.

Bessemer Venture Partners

535 Middlefield Road, Suite 245
Menlo Park, California 94025
(650) 853-7000
Fax: (650) 853-7001
Web: www.bessemervp.com

Key contact:
Mr. David J. Cowan, Partner

Description: Providing venture capital to entrepreneurial teams for over two decades.

Founded: 1970

Amount of capital invested: $50 million

Preferred investment size: $500,000-5 million

Amount under management: $100-500 million

Area served: United States

Preferred stages of financing: Seed, Start up, First stage, Second stage, Mezzanine, LBO/MBO, Expansion

Industries:
I.01   Aerospace
I.02   Agriculture/forestry/fishing/mining

I.03	Biotech/genetic engineering
I.04	Broadcasting
I.05	Chemicals
I.06	Communications
I.07	Computer hardware
I.08	Computer software
I.09	Construction
I.10	Consulting
I.11	Consumer products
I.12	Distribution
I.13	Education
I.14	Electronics
I.15	Energy/natural resources/utilities
I.16	Entertainment
I.17	Environmental services/waste management
I.18	Financial services
I.19	Generalist
I.20	Healthcare
I.21	High technology
I.22	Industrial products
I.23	Information technology services
I.24	Internet services/e-commerce
I.25	Leisure/hospitality
I.26	Life sciences
I.27	Manufacturing

I.28   Media/publishing
I.29   Medical/medical products
I.30   New media
I.31   Real estate
I.32   Retail
I.33   Semiconductors
I.34   Services (business)
I.35   Services (consumer)
I.36   Transportation
I.37   Wholesale

Sampling of portfolio companies: Altiga Networks (communications); Cascade Communications (communications); ITC DeltaCom (communica-

tions); Telenet (communications); Atreve Software (internet & intranet); Individual, Inc. (internet & intranet); Mindspring (internet & intranet); American Superconductor (semiconductors/components); Pacific Microsonics (semiconductors/components); Chrysalis (software); Pillar Software (software); Versant (software); Airtech (wireless); P-Com (wireless); Factory Card Outlet (retail & consumer goods); Zany Brainy (retail & consumer goods); Commercial Federal Bank (financial services); Datamedic (healthcare information systems); Focus Healthcare (healthcare services); PerSeptive Biosystems (medical products & devices)

Brantley Venture Partners

1920 Main Street, Suite 820
Irvine, California 92614
(949) 475-4242
Fax: (949) 475-1950

Key contact:
Mr. James R. Bergman, General Partner

Area served: United States

Preferred stages of financing: LBO/MBO, Expansion, Consolidation opportunities

Industries:
I.01   Aerospace
I.05   Chemicals
I.08   Computer software

I.10   Consulting
I.11   Consumer products
I.12   Distribution
I.17   Environmental services/waste management
I.18   Financial services
I.19   Generalist
I.20   Healthcare
I.22   Industrial products
I.23   Information technology services
I.27   Manufacturing
I.28   Media/publishing
I.32   Retail
I.34   Services (business)
I.35   Services (consumer)

Brentwood Venture Capital

11150 Santa Monica Boulevard, Suite 1200
Los Angeles, California 90025
(310) 477-7678
Fax: (310) 312-1868
E-mail: bjones@la.brentwoodvc.com
Web: www.brentwoodvc.com

Key contact:
Mr. G. Bradford Jones, General Partner

1920 Main Street, Suite 820
Irvine, California 92614
(949) 251-1010
Fax: (949) 251-1011
E-mail: blink@brentwoodvc.com
Web: www.brentwoodvc.com

Key contact:
Mr. William J. Link, General Partner

3000 Sand Hill Road, Building 1, Suite 260
Menlo Park, California 94025
(650) 854-7691
Fax: (650) 854-9513
E-mail: jwalecka@brentwoodvc.com
Web: www.brentwoodvc.com

Key contact:
Mr. John L. Walecka, General Partner

Description: We are a private venture investment firm with offices in Menlo Park, Los Angeles and Irvine, California. We invest equity capital in start-up, early stage and emerging growth companies, targeting the information technology and healthcare industry areas.

Amount of capital invested: $60 million

Preferred investment size: $5 million

Amount under management: $100-500 million

Area served: United States

Preferred stages of financing: Start up, First stage

Industries:
I.03   Biotech/genetic engineering
I.06   Communications
I.07   Computer hardware
I.08   Computer software
I.20   Healthcare
I.23   Information technology services
I.24   Internet services/e-commerce
I.29   Medical/medical products
I.33   Semiconductors

Sampling of portfolio companies: Agile Networks, Inc. (provider of multiprotocol intelligent switches that automatically respond to changing business needs); OnStream Networks, Inc. (sells broadband wide-area network & access products); SynOptics Communications, Inc. (sells shared-media hubs for corporate LAN's); Cloudscape, Inc. (develops Java-SQL database products that can be configured to run as a client or server); The Extraprise Group (consulting firm focused on intranet/extranet solutions); Internet Access Financial Corp. (provides banking services over the internet); ISOCOR (develops backbone software for electronic information exchange over the internet & other value added networks); Trading Edge (developers of a trading system focused at the high-yield market); Counstellar Corp. (provides large scale data migration & other data morphosis-type applications); Cross/Z Int'l., Inc. (provides powerful data mining & data warehousing tools); The Dodge

Group, Inc. (provider of client/server financial ledger software); Object Design, Inc. (sells database management systems & related tools for internet, intranet & other applications); Portable Software Corp. (provider of enterprise travel & entertainment expense automation); Vitria Technology, Inc.

(supplies real-time business tools & applications); Aradigm, Inc. (medical devices); Cardiovascular Devices, Inc. (medical devices); Corvascular Surgical Systems (medical devices); Innovations (medical devices); Arris Pharmaceutical Corp. (biotechnology); CombiChem, Inc. (biotechnology)

Burr, Egan, Deleage & Company

One Embarcadero Center
Suite 4050
San Francisco, California 94111
(415) 362-4022
Fax: (415) 362-6178
E-mail: info@bedco.com
Web: www.bedco.com

Key contact:
Mr. Jean Deleage
Mr. Robert F. Benbow
Mr. Timothy L. Dibble

Description: Since the 1970s, our principals have invested in many emerging growth companies helping them to become the large corporations of today. We are a private venture capital firm which has invests in over 200 companies throughout America. With capital under management in excess of $600 million, we are positioned in the top tier of venture capital firms.

Preferred investment size: >$1.5 million

Area served: United States

Preferred stages of financing: Start up, LBO/MBO, Expansion

Industries:
I.06   Communications
I.07   Computer hardware
I.14   Electronics
I.20   Healthcare
I.22   Industrial products
I.23   Information technology services
I.26   Life sciences
I.29   Medical/medical products

Sampling of portfolio companies: Accent (speech recognition productsbased on proprietary algorithms which overcome the limitations of traditional approaches to the problems of speech recognition); Aura Vision (develops audio/video integrated circuits for personal computers); Earthwatch (intends to orbit a constellation of earth imaging satellites which will capture digital pictures of the earth below); JT Storage (established to develop, manufacture & market a family of low-profile, high-capacity disk drives targeted to address the high volume segments of the disk drive industry); Multipoint Networks (designs, manufactures & markets wireless metropolitan-area data networks or wireless MANs); Premisys Communications Holdings (develops & markets multi-function customer premises network access equipment); Stylus Assets (designs, manufactures & markets multi-function products for the small office, home office marketplace); Viewlogic Systems (develops & markets CAE software tools for behavioral simulation); Winchester Design (develops Windows-based mechanical design automation software used for solid modeling in the engineering & manufacturing industries); Abaxis (develops, manufactures & markets a portable blood analysis system for both the human 7 veterinary medical markets); Agouron (pioneer & leader in a powerful approach to drug discovery which enables its scientists rationally to design novel synthetic drugs for a broad range of therapeutic applications); Citation Medical (developed a line of disposable arthroscopes for orthopedic, podiatric & rheumatology in-office procedures); Diatech (radiopharmaceutical company that davelops unique imaging products for the detection of diseases); Inspire Pharmaceuticals (focuses exclusively on non-asthmatic lung disease or chronic obstructive pulmonary disease); Localmed (involved in developing local drug delivery catheters); LXN (formed to develop a new generation diabetes control monitor based on the measurement of protein bound glucose); R2 Technology (developing a medical device which performs a computer aided diagnostic analysis of mammograms to detect breast cancers which might otherwise be missed by radiologists); Vanguard Medica Ltd. (pharmaceutical company in England founded to license pharmaceutical companies & develop these compunds at least until preliminary evidence of safety & efficacy have been demonstrated); Continental Cablevision (develops cable television systems in Ohio); OmniAmerica Communications (created to acquire two FM/FM/AM trombos in Cleveland & Columbus, Ohio & an FM/FM duopoly combo in Jacksonville, Florida)

The Cambria Group

724 Oak Grove Avenue, Suite 120
Menlo Park, California 94025
(650) 329-8600
Fax: (650) 329-8601
E-mail: proposals@cambriagroup.com
Web: www.cambriagroup.com

Key contact:
Mr. Paul L. Davies, III, Managing Principal
Mr. Michael D. Mahre, Principal
Mr. Christopher Sekula, Operating Principal

Description: We invest in and acquire established and profitable manufacturing, distribution and service businesses valued at $3 million to $25 million. Our principals provide the majority of the equity themselves and function as active directors and shareholders, drawing on their personal operating and private equity experience.

Amount of capital invested: $1 million

Preferred investment size: $1-3 million

Amount under management: <$10 million

Area served: North America

Preferred stages of financing: Second stage, Mezzanine, LBO/MBO, Expansion

Industries:
I.01   Aerospace
I.02   Agriculture/forestry/fishing/mining
I.04   Broadcasting
I.05   Chemicals
I.06   Communications
I.11   Consumer products
I.12   Distribution
I.13   Education
I.15   Energy/natural resources/utilities
I.16   Entertainment
I.17   Environmental services/waste management
I.18   Financial services
I.19   Generalist

I.22   Industrial products
I.25   Leisure/hospitality
I.27   Manufacturing
I.28   Media/publishing
I.34   Services (business)
I.35   Services (consumer)
I.36   Transportation
I.37   Wholesale

Sampling of portfolio companies: Cobblestone Golf Group (golf course ownership & management); Crossbow Technology Inc. (manufacturer of sensors & actuators)

Canaan Partners

2884 Sand Hill Road, Suite 115
Menlo Park, California 94025
(650) 854-8092
Fax: (650) 854-8127
E-mail: eyoung@canaan.com
Web: www.canaan.com

Key contact:
Mr. John D. Lambrech
Mr. John Baylan
Mr. Eric Young

Description: Our investment strategy focuses on providing capital for growth and we are comfortable working with entrepreneurial companies across all industry sections: information technology, healthcare and medical and otherwise. In addition, we have the ability to invest in any stage of development, from early through expansion stage, and will actively consider other unique growth-oriented opportunities including private placement in public companies, management led buyouts, recapitalizations and other special situations.

Preferred investment size: $500,000-15 million

Area served: United States

Preferred stages of financing: Seed, Start up, First stage, Second stage, Mezzanine, LBO/MBO, Expansion, Recapitalizations

Industries:
I.11   Consumer products
I.12   Distribution
I.18   Financial services

I.20   Healthcare
I.23   Information technology services
I.29   Medical/medical products

Sampling of portfolio companies: Anadigics, Inc. (gallium arsenide monolithic microwave integrated circuits & digital circuits); The Cerplex Group, Inc. (computer repair & parts outsourcing); Concord Communications, Inc. (network management software); DataMind Corp. (data mining solutions for customer lifecycle applications); Dynamic Pictures, Inc. (3-D graphic cards for windows applications); Integrated Packaging Assembly Corp. (integrated circuit packaging services); Int'l. Network Services, Inc. (data communications network support services); Octel Communications Corp. (voice messaging systems); Silicon Compiler Systems (software tools for VLSI circuit design); StarBurst Communications Corp. (multicast data delivery); TravelNet, Inc. (software for corporate travel expense management); Visigenic Software, Inc. (client/server application software development components & utilities); Advance Paradigm, Inc. (health benefits management); Centocor, Inc. (development of novel therapeutics for cancer & infectious diseases); FLA Orthopedics, Inc. (orthopedic safety products); Praecis Pharmaceuticals, Inc. (peptides-based therapeutics); Capital Markets Assurance Corp. (credit enhancement); Capstone Turbine Corp. (equipment for generating electric power or producing heating & cooling energy); AlarmGuard Holdings, Inc. (residential & commercial alarm installation & monitoring); PETsMART, Inc. (warehouse-sized retailer of pet food & pet supplies)

Cardinal Health Partners

1920 Main Street, Suite 820
Irvine, California 92614
(714) 475-4242
Fax: (714) 475-1950

Key contact:
Mr. James Bergman

Description: We seek investment opportunities spanning the breadth of the trillion dollar healthcare economy. Principals have experience in healthcare services, life sciences, healthcare information technology, and medical products and devices. We will consider investments at any stage of a company's development. Principals have particular expertise in the formation and support of early stage ventures.

Amount of capital invested: $5 million

Preferred investment size: $3 million

Amount under management: $25-100 million

Area served: United States

Preferred stages of financing: Seed, Start up, First stage, Second stage

Industries:
I.03   Biotech/genetic engineering
I.06   Communications
I.20   Healthcare
I.23   Information technology services
I.26   Life sciences
I.29   Medical/medical products

Sampling of portfolio companies: Pointshare (maintain medical intranet & extranet networks for physician alliances); Signature Plastic Surgeons (management services in the area of plastic surgery, ear, nose & throat)

Charter Venture Group

525 University Avenue, Suite 1500
Palo Alto, California 94301
(650) 325-6953
Fax: (650) 325-4762

Key contact:
Mr. A. Barr Dolan

Area served: United States

Preferred stages of financing: Seed, Start up, First stage

Industries:
I.03   Biotech/genetic engineering
I.06   Communications
I.20   Healthcare
I.26   Life sciences

Charterway Investment Corporation

624 South Grand Avenue, Suite 1600
Los Angeles, California 90017
(213) 687-8534
Fax: (213) 689-9108

Key contact:
Mr. Tien Chen, President

Area served: California

Preferred stages of financing: Mezzanine, Expansion

Industries:
I.12   Distribution
I.32   Retail

CIBC Capital Partners

One Post Street, Suite 3550
San Francisco, California 94104
(415) 399-5723
Fax: (415) 399-5761
E-mail: vanness@cibc.com

Key contact:
Mr. W. Denman Van Ness

Founded: 1989

Preferred investment size: $5-15 million

Area served: Canada, United States

Preferred stages of financing: Second stage, Mezzanine, LBO/MBO

Industries:
I.05   Chemicals

I.06   Communications
I.08   Computer software
I.11   Consumer products
I.12   Distribution
I.13   Education
I.14   Electronics
I.15   Energy/natural resources/utilities
I.17   Environmental services/waste management
I.18   Financial services
I.22   Industrial products
I.24   Internet services/e-commerce
I.25   Leisure/hospitality
I.28   Media/publishing
I.29   Medical/medical products
I.32   Retail
I.35   Services (consumer)
I.36   Transportation

Comdisco Ventures

3000 Sand Hill Road
Building 1, Suite 155
Menlo Park, California 94025
(650) 854-9484
Fax: (650) 854-4026
Web: www.comdisco.com/ventures

Key contact:
Mr. Jim Labé, President
Mr. Manuel Henriquez, Managing Director
Mr. Geoff Tickner, Managing Director

Description: We provide a wide variety of financing products to venture capital-backed start-up companies. These include equipment leases and loans, subordinated debt, receivables financing and equity financing.

Amount of capital invested: $167,269,749.97

Amount under management: $500 million -1 billion

Area served: United States

Preferred stage of financing: Start up

Industries:
I.03   Biotech/genetic engineering
I.06   Communications
I.08   Computer software
I.14   Electronics
I.23   Information technology services
I.29   Medical/medical products
I.32   Retail
I.33   Semiconductors
I.34   Services (business)

Sampling of portfolio companies: 3-D Pharmaceuticals (biotechnology/biopharmaceutical); ChemGenics Pharmaceuticals (biotechnology/biopharmaceutical); GenVec (biotechnology/biopharmaceutical); LeukoSite (biotechnology/biopharmaceutical); RedCell (biotechnology/biopharmaceutical); Zynaxis Cell Science (biotechnology/biopharmaceutical); Biocircuits (medical devices & servicers); Microsurge (medical devices & servicers); Arbor Software

(software & computer services); Citrix Systems (software & computer services); HNC Software (software & computer services); Redwood Design Automation (software & computer services); SportsLine USA (software & computer services); Custom Foot (consumer related); PetStuff (consumer related); Automated Compliance Systems (other products & services); Aristacom Int'l. (communications & networking); NetLabs (communications & networking); Adaptive Solutions (computer hardware & semiconductor); Integrated Packaging Assembly (computer hardware & semiconductor)

CommTech International

535 Middlefield Road, Suite 200
Menlo Park, California 94025
(415) 328-0190
Fax: (415) 328-6442

Key contact:
Mr. Gerald Marxman
Mr. Mathew Frazer
Mr. Frank Kocsis

Area served: West Coast

Preferred stage of financing: Seed

Industries:
I.03   Biotech/genetic engineering
I.06   Communications
I.08   Computer software

Compass Technology Partners

1550 El Camino Real, Suite 275
Menlo Park, California 94025-4111
(650) 322-7595
Fax: (650) 322-0588

Key contact:
Mr. David Arscott

Area served: United States

Preferred stages of financing: Mezzanine, LBO/MBO

Industries:
I.04   Broadcasting
I.06   Communications
I.07   Computer hardware
I.08   Computer software
I.11   Consumer products
I.12   Distribution
I.14   Electronics
I.17   Environmental services/waste management
I.29   Medical/medical products
I.33   Semiconductors
I.35   Services (consumer)

Convergence Partners

3000 Sand Hill Road
Building Two, Suite 235
Menlo Park, California 94025
(650) 854-3010
Fax: (650) 854-3015
E-mail: info@convergencepartners.com
Web: www.convergencepartners.com

Key contact:
Mr. Paul Dali, Managing General Partner
Mr. Eric Di Benedetto, General Partner
Mr. Russ Irwin, General Partner

Description: We primarily invest in early stage information technology based companies, with some select later stage investments as well. Our strong international relationships and strategic investors enable the portfolio companies to build valuable relationships in Asian and European markets.

Amount of capital invested: $12.16 million

Preferred investment size: $3 million (average)

Amount under management: $25-100 million

Area served: United States

Preferred stages of financing: Seed, Start up, First stage, Second stage

Industries:
I.06   Communications
I.08   Computer software
I.23   Information technology services
I.33   Semiconductors
I.34   Services (business)

Sampling of portfolio companies: Chameleon Systems (leading edge semiconductor products); Decisive Technology (provider of customer intelligence solutions for real time decision making); Entegrity Solutions (information security provider); Freegate Corp. (integrated internet access systems); IMGIS (ad networks & large web site advertising management solutions); iVillage (online content targeted to areas such as parenting health & the workplace); Magnifi (enterprise class software products for knowledge management); Premier RF (performance enhancements for GSM handsets)

Coral Ventures

3000 Sand Hill Road
Building Three, Suite 220
Menlo Park, California 94025
(650) 854-5227
Fax: (650) 854-4625

Key contact:
Ms. Karen M. Boezi, Venture Partner

Description: We contribute strategic guidance, as well as capital, to transform growing enterprises into market leaders. Because we recognize and understand emerging technologies and market trends, we invest in companies poised to capitalize on opportunities inherent in those trends. We work as a partner to develop a long-term relationship with the company and its management team.

Amount of capital invested: $15 million

Amount under management: $100-500 million

Area served: Worldwide

Preferred stages of financing: Seed, Start up, First stage, Second stage, Mezzanine

Industries:
I.03   Biotech/genetic engineering
I.06   Communications
I.07   Computer hardware
I.08   Computer software
I.14   Electronics
I.20   Healthcare
I.21   High technology
I.23   Information technology services
I.24   Internet services/e-commerce
I.26   Life sciences
I.29   Medical/medical products

Crosspoint Venture Partners

2925 Woodside Road
Woodside, California 94062
(650) 851-7600
Fax: (650) 851-7661
E-mail: partners@crosspointvc.com
Web: www.crosspointvc.com

Key contact:
Mr. John B. Mumford, Managing General Partner
Mr. Rich Shapero, General Partner
Mr. Seth Neiman, General Partner
Mr. Steve Foster, Venture Associate

18552 MacArthur Boulevard, Suite 400
Irvine, California 92612
(949) 852-1611
Fax: (949) 852-9804
E-mail: bhoff@crosspointvc.com
Web: www.crosspointvc.com

Key contact:
Mr. Robert A. Hoff, General Partner
Mr. Donald B. Milder, General Partner
Ms. Barbara Lubash, Venture Partner

Description: We are an initial stage equity investor with focused expertise in three strategic areas: networking and communications, health care and financial services. We have a capital base of approximately $500 million and are sponsored by well respected institutions, pension funds, university endowments, foundations and individuals.

Amount of capital invested: $32 million

Preferred investment size: $1-5 million

Amount under management: $500 million -1 billion

Area served: United States

Preferred stages of financing: Seed, Start up, First stage

Industries:
I.06   Communications
I.08   Computer software
I.20   Healthcare
I.23   Information technology services
I.24   Internet services/e-commerce

Sampling of portfolio companies: ARIBA Corp. (intranet/internet corporate purchasing system for indirect goods & services); Chromatis Networks, Inc. (metropolitan area switching systems); Diamond Lane Communications (network equipment providing high-speed data over telco local loop facilities); Efficient Networks, Inc. (ATM network interface adapters); Foundry Networks, Inc. (high performance LAN equipment); i-Pass Alliance Inc.; NetBoost (network equipment platform for embedded network applications); Relevance (Intranet Knowledge Management software); Sonoma Systems (manufacturer of ATM access concentrators); WiData (wireless communications & enterprise software systems for continuous status of assets); XYLAN Corp. (high-performance switched LAN systems); Expersoft (application development software for distributed computing); Sagent Technology (client/server software system providing data access from data warehouses); TallyUp Software (variable compensation management software); Cornerstone Physicians Corp. (organizes & manages physician groups); MicroVention (devices to treat neurovascular disorders); Pharmadigm (managed care services for patients with catastrophic injuries); Sonus Pharmaceuticals (ultrasound contrast agents); Anytime Access, Inc. (financial institution telemarketing & internet lending services); Arithmos, Inc. (LCD driver circuits to OEM flat-panel display manufacturers)

Dawes Investment Partners, LP

350 Santa Rita Avenue
Palo Alto, California 94301
(650) 323-1334
Fax: (650) 323-4209
E-mail: ddawes@pacbell.net

Key contact:
Mr. Dexter Dawes, General Partner

Description: Venture capital partnership.

Amount of capital invested: $600,000

Preferred investment size: $100,000

Amount under management: <$10 million

Area served: North America

Preferred stages of financing: Seed, Start up, First stage

Industries:
I.02   Agriculture/forestry/fishing/mining
I.03   Biotech/genetic engineering
I.08   Computer software
I.09   Construction
I.12   Distribution
I.22   Industrial products
I.26   Life sciences
I.29   Medical/medical products
I.37   Wholesale

Sampling of portfolio companies: Puffin Designs (software); Meridith Estates Vineyards (wine manufacturing); The Gluers (trade bindery); Avigenics (biotechnology); Rom Tech (software); Fold Pak (folding cartons); Hansvedt Industries (machine tools); Embarcadero Publishing (newspapers); Kurtzweil Educational Systems (software); HF

Protein (biotechnology); Clinicor (medical testing); Placemakers Inc. (home building); Meyers Industries (store fixtures)

Delphi Ventures

3000 Sand Hill Road, Building One, Suite 135
Menlo Park, California 94025-7116
(650) 854-9650
Fax: (650) 854-2961

Key contact:
Mr. David L. Douglass, Partner
Mr. James J. Bochnowski, Partner
Mr. Costa G. Sevastopoulos, Partner

Preferred stages of financing: Seed, Start up, First stage

Industries:
I.03   Biotech/genetic engineering
I.29   Medical/medical products

Sampling of portfolio companies: Biomedicines

Digital Technology Partners (DTP)

50 California Street, 15th Floor
San Francisco, California 94111
(415) 439-5350
E-mail: info@dtpnet.com
Web: www.dtpnet.com

Key contact:
Mr. Dean L. Gardner, Founding Managing Director
Mr. Bashir Wada, CFA, Partner/CFO
Mr. James K. Ho, Partner

Description: An independently managed venture capital firm specializing in the digital convergence industry. We focus on the internet, online services, content providers, interactive multimedia and supporting enabling technologies. Our mission is to enhance the value of our portfolio companies by giving them access to critical knowledge, capital and people. With an in-depth knowledge of the industry, an established network of professionals; and experience in venture capital, business development, research, technology transfer and strategic alliance formation, we aim to be the right partner at the right time.

Preferred stages of financing: Start up, First stage

Industries:
I.10   Consulting
I.24   Internet services/e-commerce
I.30   New media

Sampling of portfolio companies: Internet Finance Corp. (building the premier network of affiliated internet finance sites); Internet Games Corp. (developer & operator of Java based multi-user games & networked game environment on the internet); Electric Classifieds, Inc. (providing the most comprehensive transaction-based online commerce solutions to new media publishers); FireFly, Inc. (provider of products & services for relationship management & advanced personalization); Multivox Technologies, Inc. (develops & markets a unique, patent-pending system enabling individuals to make & pay for telephone calls digitally); New Moon Software, Inc. (developing a family of distributed computing software products enabling Windows 95 & Windows NT applications to efficiently operate on the internet & intranets); Virtual Vegas, Inc. (virtual entertainment worlds in cyberspace & legal wagering & casino gaming on the internet & through broadband networks); Upside Magazine (a business & technology publication covering the people & companies shaping the digital age)

Domain Associates

650 Town Center Drive, Suite 1830
Costa Mesa, California 92626
(714) 434-6227
Fax: (714) 434-6088

Key contact:
Mr. Olav B. Bergheim, Venture Partner
Mr. Arthur J. Klausner, General Partner
Mr. Richard S. Schneider, General Partner

Description: We provide seed and early stage financing and organizational support to technology- and service-based companies focused on life sciences. Specific areas of investment interest include biopharmaceuticals, medical devices, bio-instrumentation, diagnostics, new materials as applied to healthcare, healthcare information systems and services. With demonstrated expertise in technology assessment, strategic planning, operations and finance, we have been involved in the creation and development of more than 75 life science ventures.

Amount of capital invested: $38.5 million

Preferred investment size: $5 million (over multiple financing rounds)

Amount under management: $100-500 million

Area served: United States

Preferred stages of financing: Seed, Start up, First stage

Industries:
I.03   Biotech/genetic engineering
I.05   Chemicals
I.20   Healthcare
I.26   Life sciences

Sampling of portfolio companies: Advanced Corneal Systems (drug therapies to improve eyesight); Athena Neurosciences (drugs vs. Alzheimer's & other neurological diseases); Biomagnetic Technologies (magnetic source imaging instruments); British Biotech (drugs vs. cancer & inflammatory & vascular diseases); Chimeric Therapies (cell processing technologies & services); CoCensys (drugs vs. neurological & psychiatric disorders); Dura Pharmaceuticals (marketing of drugs for respiratory disorders); Fusion Medical Technologies (collagen-based surgical sealants); Genta (antisense-based pharmaceuticals); Gynecare (surgical devices for the treatment of uterine disorders); Inspire Pharmaceuticals (drugs vs. respiratory disorders); La Jolla Pharmaceutical Co. (drugs vs. immune system disorders); MitoKor (drugs vs. loss of mitochondrial function); NPS Pharmaceuticals (drugs vs. endocrine, bone & CNS diseases); PointShare (healthcare intranet/ extranet connectivity solutions); polyGenomics (next-generation positional cloning genomics); ReSound Corp. (advanced hearing aids); Sievers Instruments (instruments to detect/measure chemical compounds); Univax Biologics (plasma-based drugs vs. autoimmune/infectious diseases); Vascular Therapeutics (drugs vs. excessive clotting/bleeding disorders)

Dominion Ventures, Inc.

44 Montgomery Street, Suite 4200
San Francisco, California 94104-4602
(415) 362-4890
Fax: (415) 394-9245
E-mail: mkl@domven.com
Web: www.domven.com

Key contact:
Mr. Michael Lee, President

Area served: United States

Preferred stages of financing: First stage, Second stage, LBO/MBO

Industries:

I.03	Biotech/genetic engineering
I.04	Broadcasting
I.06	Communications
I.07	Computer hardware
I.08	Computer software
I.12	Distribution
I.14	Electronics
I.17	Environmental services/waste management
I.18	Financial services
I.29	Medical/medical products
I.34	Services (business)
I.35	Services (consumer)
I.36	Transportation

Draper Fisher Jurvetson

400 Seaport Court, Suite 250
Redwood City, California 94063
(650) 599-9000
Fax: (650) 599-9726
E-mail: mail@drapervc.com
Web: www.drapervc.com

Key contact:
Mr. Timothy C. Draper, Managing Director
Mr. John H. N. Fisher, Managing Director
Mr. Steve T. Jurvetson, Managing Director
Mr. Larry Kubal, Managing Director
Mr. Warren J. Packard, Associate
Ms. Jennifer Scott Fonstad, Associate

Description: We are the leader in start-up venture capital, having invested in over 150 high-tech companies. In the majority of cases, we are the lead investor for a company's first round of financing. We focus on information technology businesses with enormous market potential. Our role is to help entrepreneurs achieve their maximum potential through team building, partnerships, advice and support, as well as investments.

Preferred stage of financing: First stage

Industries:
I.06   Communications

I.07	Computer hardware
I.08	Computer software
I.23	Information technology services
I.24	Internet services/e-commerce
I.28	Media/publishing

Sampling of portfolio companies: Cybermedia (on-line PC repair & recovery); Interzine (internet sports networks); Kana (desk software for e-mail based support); Direct Stock Market (internet public offerings); planetU (internet coupon & promotion programs); Tumbleweed Software (internet document delivery); Troika Networks (fibre channel system-area-networks); Banyan (local area networks); I-Cube (crossbar switches); Photonic Power (fiber power delivery); Ragula Systems (datacom bandwith enhancement software); Cybermedia (automatic Windows 95 repair & recovery); Group Logic (groupware operating system); Software Emancipation Technology (parametric software modelling); Aegis Marketing (hospital media & communications); Cognigine (next generation logic engines); NeoParadigm Labs (semiconductor IP design house); Sierra Semiconductor (BiCMOS & EEPROM technology); Qume Corp. (controllers & peripherals); Pete's Brewing (very wicked ale)

Draper International

50 California Street, Suite 2925
San Francisco, California 94111
(415) 616-4050
Fax: (415) 616-4060
E-mail: mail@draperintl.com
Web: www.drapervc.com/intl

Key contact:
Mr. William H. Draper, III, Managing Director
Ms. Robin A. Richards, Managing Director

Description: We invest in companies in India & in U.S. companies which are doing business in India. We provide entrepreneurs with the financial, managerial and informational resources needed to elevate Indian projects to a globally competitive level.

Amount of capital invested: $7.5 million

Preferred investment size: $2 million

Amount under management: $25-100 million

Area served: India, United States

Preferred stages of financing: Seed, Start up, First stage, Expansion

Industries:
I.06   Communications
I.07   Computer hardware
I.08   Computer software
I.21   High technology
I.23   Information technology services
I.24   Internet services/e-commerce

Sampling of portfolio companies: CMM Ltd. (entertainment software); Cybermedia (automatic service & support software); Geometric Software (CAD/CAM software); Internet Securities (online financial info.); Mediaway (digital multimedia cataloging); Neta, Inc. (internet customer relationship management); Powertel Boca (telecomputing products distributor); Nirwana (web calendaring applications); Querisoft (security & resource management software); Ramp Networks (LAN-based internet access devices); Savesmart (personlized interactive promotions); Selectica (electronic commerce applications development); SR Research (expert decision support for credit services); Torrent Networking Technologies (gigabit-scaled IP routers for intranets); Yantra (supply-chain execution applications)

DSV Partners

1920 Main Street, Suite 820
Irvine, California 92614
(714) 475-4242
Fax: (714) 475-1950

Key contact:
Mr. James R. Bergman
Mr. Kevin G. Connors

Area served: West Coast

Industries:
I.03   Biotech/genetic engineering
I.05   Chemicals
I.06   Communications
I.07   Computer hardware
I.08   Computer software
I.14   Electronics
I.29   Medical/medical products
I.34   Services (business)
I.35   Services (consumer)

DynaFund Ventures

21311 Hawthorne Boulevard, Suite 300
Torrance, California 90503
(310) 792-4929
Fax: (310) 543-5433
E-mail: thung@dynatec.com
Web: www.dynafundventures.com

Key contact:
Dr. Denny R. S. Ko, General Partner
Dr. James H. Liao, General Partner

Description: We provide promising technology companies with the investment capital and management support they need to grow their businesses. In addition, we also provide a critical competitive advantage to our portfolio companies by offering access to key engineering, manufacturing and marketing resources in the U.S. and Asia through our own business networks and the complementary networks of our U.S. and Asian Limited Partners.

Amount of capital invested: $5 million

Preferred investment size: $1-3 million

Amount under management: $25-100 million

Area served: United States

Preferred stages of financing: Start up, First stage, Second stage

Industries:
I.06   Communications
I.07   Computer hardware
I.08   Computer software
I.14   Electronics
I.15   Energy/natural resources/utilities
I.16   Entertainment
I.21   High technology
I.23   Information technology services
I.24   Internet services/e-commerce
I.30   New media
I.33   Semiconductors

Sampling of portfolio companies: Arcturus Engineering (medical instruments); New Era Communications (wireless telecommunications); Single Chip Systems (RFID tags); Troika Networks (computer networking); eToys (internet commerce); FreeGate Corp. (multi-server gateway); Synctrix (newtwork devices); Xalti (network-on-a-chip)

El Dorado Ventures

2400 Sand Hill Road, Suite 100
Menlo Park, California 94025
(650) 854-1200
Fax: (650) 854-1202
E-mail: shanda@eldoradoventures.com
Web: eldoradoventures.com

Key contact:
Ms. Shanda Bahles
Mr. Gary Kalbach
Mr. Tom Peterson

Description: We are a private venture capital partnership that invests primarily in early stage, technology-based companies located on the West Coast. With a particular focus on information technologies, we have helped entrepreneurs turn start-up ventures into companies of lasting value for two decades.

Area served: West Coast

Preferred stages of financing: Seed, Start up, First stage

Industries:
I.06   Communications
I.08   Computer software
I.14   Electronics
I.23   Information technology services
I.30   New media

I.33   Semiconductors

Sampling of portfolio companies: Access Health; Earthlink Network; Rogue Wave Software; Sun Microsystems

---

Emerald Venture, LLC

15373 Innovation Drive, Suite 100
San Diego, California 92128
(619) 451-1001
Fax: (619) 451-1001
E-mail: invest@emeraldventure.com
Web: emeraldventure.com

Key contact:
Mr. Gerry Simoni, President
Ms. Barbara Connaughy, Senior Business Consultant
Ms. Pamela Taylor, Investor Relations

Description: A venture capital consultiung firm specializing in assisting entrepreneurs seeking capital.

Preferred investment size: $1 million

Amount under management: <$10 million

Area served: Worldwide

Preferred stages of financing: Seed, Start up, First stage, Second stage, Mezzanine, Expansion, Int'l expansion

Industries:
I.01   Aerospace
I.02   Agriculture/forestry/fishing/mining
I.03   Biotech/genetic engineering
I.04   Broadcasting
I.05   Chemicals
I.06   Communications
I.07   Computer hardware
I.08   Computer software
I.09   Construction
I.10   Consulting
I.11   Consumer products
I.12   Distribution
I.13   Education
I.14   Electronics
I.15   Energy/natural resources/utilities
I.16   Entertainment
I.17   Environmental services/waste management
I.18   Financial services
I.19   Generalist
I.20   Healthcare
I.21   High technology
I.22   Industrial products
I.23   Information technology services
I.24   Internet services/e-commerce
I.25   Leisure/hospitality
I.26   Life sciences
I.27   Manufacturing
I.28   Media/publishing
I.29   Medical/medical products
I.30   New media
I.31   Real estate
I.32   Retail
I.33   Semiconductors
I.34   Services (business)
I.35   Services (consumer)
I.36   Transportation
I.37   Wholesale

Enterprise Partners

7979 Ivanhoe Avenue, Suite 550
La Jolla, California 92037
(619) 454-8833
Fax: (619) 454-2489
E-mail: afrenz@ent.com
Web: www.ent.com

12011 San Vincente Boulevard, Suite 330
Los Angeles, California 90049
(310) 476-3000
Fax: (310) 476-3030
Web: www.ent.com

5000 Birch Street, Suite 6200
Newport Beach, California 92660
(714) 833-3650
Fax: (714) 833-3652
Web: www.ent.com

Key contact:
Mr. James H. Berglund, General Partner
Mr. James P. Gauer, General Partner
Mr. Andrew E. Senyei, General Partner
Mr. Charles D. Martin, General Partner
Mr. Andrew J. Chedrick
Mr. Robert Choi
Mr. Paul Vais

Description: We are a Southern California venture capital firm organized to make investments in privately held early stage and emerging growth companies with the potential for exceptional growth and selected leveraged buyouts of established companies in collaboration with superior management teams.

Area served: United States

Preferred stages of financing: Seed, Start up, First stage, Second stage, LBO/MBO, Expansion

Industries:
I.06   Communications
I.07   Computer hardware
I.08   Computer software
I.20   Healthcare
I.23   Information technology services
I.29   Medical/medical products

Sampling of portfolio companies: Backup, Inc. (provides automated, encrypted, offsite backups for PCs over ordinary phone lines as a subscription service); Active Software (software products to enable internet users to evolve from passive browsing to a more interactive, dynamic use environment); All Post, Inc. (provider of video post production & feature film restoration services); Applied Digital Access, Inc. (manufacturer of automated monitoring & test systems for the telephone industry); Corixa Corp. (immunologically smart cell-based vaccines for breast, prostrate & colorectal cancers & infectious diseases including tuberculosis); El Dorado Communications (operates a chain on Spanish language radio stations); Genetic BioSystems, Inc. (manufacturer of scientific instruments); Integrated Neuroscience

Consortium (conducts clinical trials for pharmaceutical & biotech companies developing drugs & devices to treat disorders of the central nervous system); Ligand Pharmaceuticals (powerful new technology for rational drug design & development); McGaw, Inc. (manufacturer of intravenous fluids & administrative devices); On Assignment, Inc. (provider of scientific personnel on temporary assignments); Premier Laboratory Services (clinical laboratory chain); Risk Data Corp. (provider of specialized computer services for workers' compensation application in the insurance industry); Scripps Clinic MSO (medical group consisting of approximately 300 specialists & general practice physicians); Simulation Sciences (industrial plant simulation software); Sonus Pharmaceuticals (contrast agents that dramatically improve medical imaging using ultrasound systems); Speed Control, Inc. (patented gear box configuration for a continuously variable gearing ratio); Vesicare (women's specialty disease management); Wheb Systems. Inc. (optical reading systems for forms centric applications); Xatrix Entertainment (CD-ROM video game technology & location-based entertainment)

Eurolink International

690 Market Street, Suite 702
San Francisco, California 94104
(415) 398-6352
Fax: (415) 398-6355

Key contact:
Mr. Jacques Vallee

Description: We are a private venture capital firm that was founded in 1987 with the mission to invest in and support emerging high technolgy companies located in the United States and Europe. We are based in San Francisco and manage the Euro-America fund family, which operates in both the European and American business cultures. Our most recent fund, Euro-America II, closed earlier this year at $20 million, with $10 million more to be added later in the year.

Founded: 1987

Preferred investment size: $1 million

Area served: Worldwide

Preferred stages of financing: Seed, Start up, First stage, Second stage

Industries:
I.03   Biotech/genetic engineering
I.08   Computer software
I.23   Information technology services

Sampling of portfolio companies: Advanced Systems Products, Inc. (develops & markets products that increase the performance of computers by eliminating I/O bottlenecks); Autogenics Corp. (develops & tests surgical kits that incorporate the patients own tissue in heart valve surgery); Electronics for Imaging, Inc. (designs & markets products that enable digital color copiers & printers to provide high-speed, high-quality & networked color printing); Harmonic Lightwaves Inc. (develops, manufactures & sells fiber optic transmission systems for emerging hybrid fiber coax cable television networks); Integrated Packaging Assembly Corp. (a semiconductor packaging foundry); Isocor (develops, markets & supports off-the-shelf electronic information exchange software products & services); Mercury Interactive Corp. (develops, markets & supports a family of automated software quality products that automate testing & quality assurance for software developers); Objectivity Inc. (provider of distributed object databases for software & equipment manufacturers); Pacific Fiberoptics Inc. (high-speed fiber optic digital transmitter & receiver modules targeting the digital communication market); P-Com Inc. (designs, manufactures & markets short-haul millimeter wave radio systems for use in the worldwide wireless telecommunications market); Sangstat Medical Corp. (develops therapeutic & monitoring products to improve the outcome of organ transplantation); Synaptic Pharmaceutical Corp. (develops a technology called human receptor targeted drug design technology which is used to discover & clone human genes); Ubique Ltd. (design & develops teleconferencing software enabling communications via virtual places on the worldwide web)

Far East Capital Corp.

977 North Broadway, Suite 401
Los Angeles, California 90012
(213) 687-1361
Fax: (213) 626-7497

Key contact:
Mr. Tom Wang, Manager

Area served: West Coast

Preferred stage of financing: Second stage

Finnegan & Associates

405 Via Corta
P.O. Box 1183
Palos Verdes Estates, California 90274
(310) 375-8555
Fax: (310) 378-2766
E-mail: finney8311@aol.com

Key contact:
Mr. R. G. Finnegan, President

Description: Strong technology firm with over two decades in consulting and executive search. The principles have strong operating experience with more than 20 high technology firms.

Amount of capital invested: $250,000

Preferred investment size: $250,000

Amount under management: <$10 million

Area served: United States

Preferred stages of financing: Start up, First stage, LBO/MBO

Industries:
I.06   Communications
I.07   Computer hardware
I.08   Computer software
I.14   Electronics
I.21   High technology

I.24   Internet services/e-commerce
I.34   Services (business)
I.35   Services (consumer)

Sampling of portfolio companies: Avcon Industries; Quintron Systems; P.F.S.-Portfolio Financial Systems; California Linear Systems LLC; Bluenose Internet LLC; Microseptec Inc.; Portrait Labs Inc.

First American Capital Funding, Inc.
10840 Warner Avenue, Suite 202
Fountain Valley, California 92708
(714) 965-7190
Fax: (714) 965-7193

Key contact:
Mr. Chuoc Vota

Area served: California

Preferred stages of financing: First stage, Second stage, Third stage

Industries:
I.29   Medical/medical products

Flynn Venture Capital Corporation
One Flynn Center
825 Van Ness Avenue
San Francisco, California 94109
(415) 673-5900
Fax: (415) 673-6093
E-mail: donaldflynn@compuserve.com

Key contact:
Mr. Donald Flynn, Chairman
Mr. Gregory G. Flynn, President

Description: Private venture capital firm investing in early stage financings primarily in specialty restaurant chains, web sites, communications, horticulture and consumer products in Western United States and Western Canada.

Amount of capital invested: $3 million

Preferred investment size: $50,000-250,000

Amount under management: <$10 million

Area served: North America, Prefer West, Western Canada

Preferred stages of financing: Seed, Start up, First

stage, Second stage

Industries:
I.01   Aerospace
I.02   Agriculture/forestry/fishing/mining
I.03   Biotech/genetic engineering
I.06   Communications
I.16   Entertainment
I.23   Information technology services
I.24   Internet services/e-commerce
I.25   Leisure/hospitality
I.30   New media
I.31   Real estate
I.32   Retail
I.34   Services (business)
I.35   Services (consumer)

Sampling of portfolio companies: World Wrapps, Inc. (specialty restaurant chain); World Wrapps Northwest (specialty restaurant chain); Blue Chalk Cafe, Inc. (casual restaurant chain); Left at Albuquerque (casual restaurant chain); Babycenter, Inc. (web site); E-Call, Inc. (communications); Oregon Bulb & Perennial Farms, Inc. (specialty grower & wholesaler); Great Scott, Inc. (toy company)

Forrest Binkley & Brown
840 Newport Center Drive, Suite 480
Newport Beach, California 92660
(949) 729-3222
Fax: (949) 729-3226

Key contact:
Mr. Greg Forrest, Partner
Mr. Nick Binkley, Partner
Mr. Jeff Brown, Partner
Mr. Doug Wolter, Principal

Description: We target growth opportunities, back exceptional management teams, and design deal structures that align investor and management interests. Our principals believe in the value of partnering, both with members of management and with other investors, ideally those with industry-specific expertise. Our partners have significant experience in successfully co-investing in transactions with other equity groups and have developed strong relationships in the financial community built upon trust and integrity.

Amount of capital invested: $23 million

Preferred investment size: $2-8 million

Amount under management: $100-500 million

Area served: United States

Preferred stages of financing: Start up, First stage, Second stage, LBO/MBO, Expansion

Industries:
I.02   Agriculture/forestry/fishing/mining
I.03   Biotech/genetic engineering
I.06   Communications
I.07   Computer hardware
I.08   Computer software
I.11   Consumer products
I.13   Education
I.14   Electronics
I.19   Generalist
I.20   Healthcare
I.21   High technology
I.22   Industrial products
I.23   Information technology services
I.24   Internet services/e-commerce

I.25 Leisure/hospitality
I.27 Manufacturing
I.29 Medical/medical products
I.32 Retail
I.33 Semiconductors
I.34 Services (business)
I.35 Services (consumer)
I.36 Transportation
I.37 Wholesale

Sampling of portfolio companies: InnoTech, Inc. (developes & markets in-office production systems for the fabrication of multi-focal lenses using proprietary molds & resins); Vista Medical Technologies, Inc. (develops, manufactures & markets proprietary visualization & information systems that enable minimally invasive microsurgical procedures); Trikon Technologies, Inc. (develops, manufactures & markets a broad line of advanced processing systems for semiconductor manufacturing); Golden State Vintners, Inc. (owner/operater of vineyards & contractor of wine processors); Crosman Acquisition Corp. (manufactures recreational airguns & accessories); Comcore Semiconductor (designs, delivers & supports integrated circuits for highspeed local & wide area networking applications); Trega Biosciences, Inc. (a drug discovery company which utilizes combinational chemistry & combinational biology technologies to create novel small-molecule drug candidates); Aastrom Biosciences, Inc. (a cellular therapy medical products company engaged in the research & development of technology to control & expand the human stem cell, its blood progeny & other tissues for cellular therapy & gene therapy); Tekni-Plex, Inc. (manufactures trays for chicken & meat packaging, egg cartons, clamshell containers for fast-food service, moisture impermeable blister packs for prescription drug packaging & closures for over-the-counter medicine bottles); Kane Magnetics Int'l., Inc. (designs & manufactures magnetic systems serving the automotive, industrial & office products markets); Care Tools (designs, develops, markets, implements & supports a comprehensive suite of point-of-care process management tools for providers engaged in integrated care delivery); Dash America, Inc. (designs, manufactures, distributes & sells premium cycling & other sporting goods apparel); StampMaster, Inc. (designs software that allows users to purchase & print US postage online); Epic Solutions (a client/server software company that develops digital imaging & information management systems for the criminal justice, jail management & social service sectors); IAFC, Inc. (Internet Access Financial Corp, creator of the first true Internet Visa credit card, NextCard); Neocrin Co. (a research & development company pursuing cell therapy for the treatment of insulin-dependent diabetes mellitus); Object Automation (designs & develops software products for the industrial automation market); HFSC Holdings, Inc. (Hamilton Funeral Service Centers acquires & operates funeral homes & cemeteries in non-metropolitan markets); CallConnect Communications (provides integrated teleservices solutions for the healthcare industry including physician referral, appointment scheduling & confirmation, pharmaceutical information & patient test results); Mineshare, Inc. (develops & markets a suite of advanced tools for building & distributing an enterprise-wide reporting system utilizing on-line analytical processing technology)

Forward Ventures

9255 Towne Centre Drive, Suite 300
San Diego, California 92121
(619) 677-6077
Fax: (619) 452-8799
E-mail: info@forwardventures.com
Web: www.forwardventures.com

Key contact:
Mr. Standish Fleming, Partner
Mr. Jeffrey Sollender
Dr. Ivor Royston, Partner
Ms. RoseAnn Ignell, CFO

Description: We pursue a mix of early stage portfolio investments focused in biotechnology and healthcare, with an emphasis on "seed" and start-up investments. Our unique strength is our management team with a total of over 30 years of venture investing experience. Over the last decade and a half, we have founded 14 life science and healthcare companies. Our extensive scientific and business networks afford access to a unique investment opportunity stream. Our experience enables us to develop portfolio companies that will provide maximum returns.

Amount of capital invested: $3.6 million

Preferred investment size: $1.5-3 million

Amount under management: $25-100 million

Area served: United States

Preferred stages of financing: Seed, Start up, First stage, Second stage, Mezzanine

Industries:
I.03 Biotech/genetic engineering
I.20 Healthcare
I.26 Life sciences

Sampling of portfolio companies: AriZeke Pharmaceuticals (drug delivery); Dynavax Technologies (vaccine development); Ciphergen (protein screening); CombiChem (combinational chemistry); Corixa (cancer vaccine); First Dental Health (dental network provider); GenQuest (cancer research); Gryphon (protein synthesis); IntensiCare (hospitalist physician practice management); MitoKor (mitochondrial research); Onyx Pharmaceuticals (pharmaceuticals); Sequana/Axys (functional genomics); Triangle Pharmaceuticals (pharmaceuticals); Variagenics (functional genomics); Tandem (medical device)

Foundation Capital

70 Willow Road, Suite 200
Menlo Park, California 94025
(650) 614-0500
Fax: (650) 614-0505

Web: www.foundationcapital.com

Key contact:
Mr. James Anderson, General Partner

Mr. William Elmore, General Partner
Ms. Kathryn Gould, General Partner
Mr. Paul Koontz, General Partner

Description: We are a venture capital firm that invests in start-up enterprise and internet software, communications and networking. technical software and semiconductor industries. We like to work with start-ups in their formative stages and we typically invest $1-4 million. We typically invest in companies located within a 2 hour drive or flight of the Bay Area.

Amount of capital invested: $48.7 million

Preferred investment size: $1-4 million

Amount under management: $25-100 million

Area served: Primarily Northern California or within a 2-hour drive/flight of the Bay Area, United States

Preferred stage of financing: Start up

Industries:
I.06 Communications
I.07 Computer hardware
I.08 Computer software

I.21 High technology
I.24 Internet services/e-commerce
I.33 Semiconductors

Sampling of portfolio companies: Chordiant Software (enterprise & internet software); Commerce One (enterprise & internet software); Eloquent (enterprise & internet software); Financial Engines (enterprise & internet software); Idealab (enterprise & internet software); Interwoven (enterprise & internet software); Onyx Software (enterprise & internet software); Precept Software (enterprise & internet software); Success Factor Systems (enterprise & internet software); Atmosphere Networks (communications & networking); One Touch Systems (communications & networking); Rapid City Communications (communications & networking); Shoreline Teleworks (communications & networking); Wave Span (communications & networking); WiData Corp. (communications & networking); Interactive Simulations (technical software); Internet profiles Corp. (technical software); Monterey Design Systems (technical software); Silicon Valley Networks (technical software)

Fulcrum Venture Capital Corporation

300 Corporate Pointe, Suite 380
Culver City, California 90230
(310) 645-1271
Fax: (310) 645-1272

Key contact:
Mr. Brian Argrett

Area served: West Coast

Preferred stage of financing: LBO/MBO

Industries:
I.06 Communications
I.27 Manufacturing
I.34 Services (business)
I.35 Services (consumer)

Generation Partners

600 Montgomery Street, 39th Floor
San Francisco, California 94111
(415) 646-8620
Fax: (415) 646-8625

Key contact:
Mr. Paul F. Balser, Managing Partner
Mr. John A. Hawkins, Managing Partner
Mr. Mark E. Jennings, Managing Partner
Mr. Lloyd Mandell, Vice President
Mr. Robert M. Pflieger, Vice President
Mr. John S. Schnabel, Vice President/CFO
Mr. Andrew Shinn, Analyst

Description: We are a $165 million private investment firm focused on providing equity capital for growth companies. We target investments between $1 and 20 million in private equity transactions including: buyouts, growth build-ups, expansion capital and information technology venture capital opportunities. Offices are located in New York and San Francisco. Our partners have made over $200 million.

Preferred investment size: $1-20 million

Preferred stages of financing: LBO/MBO, Expansion, Growth build-ups

Industries:
I.04 Broadcasting
I.16 Entertainment
I.18 Financial services
I.22 Industrial products
I.23 Information technology services

I.28 Media/publishing

Sampling of portfolio companies: Rocky Mountain Financial Corp. (savings & loan institution in Wyoming); United New Mexico Financial Corp. (bank holding company in New Mexico); Scientific Games Holdings Corp. (world's leading manufacturer of instant scratch-off lottery tickets); The Carbide/Graphite Group, Inc. (manufacturer of graphite electrodes used in electric arc steel furnaces & calcium carbide used to generate acetylene gas); Kansas City Southern Industries, Inc. (businesses include the Kansas City Southern Railroad, DST Systems & Janus Funds); LVI Environmental Services Group, Inc. (environmental remediation service provider, focused on asbestos & lead paint abatement projects); Seaview Petroleum Co. LP (regional asphalt refinery located in New Jersey); AUNET Corp. (Asia-based commercial internet service provider); AuraVision Corp. (developer of video processor integrated circuits for PCs); Meridian Data, Inc. (designer & manufacturer of CD-ROM servers); PixTech, Inc. (developer of field emission display screens); Inter-Media Capital Partners LP (cable TV operator with properties in Tennessee & Virginia); Muzak LP (provider of business music); The Johnny Rockets Group, Inc. (operator of "Johnny Rockets" restaurants); Jeepers!, Inc. (operator of indoor family entertainment centers); United Retail Group, Inc. (500-store specialty retailer of large size women's apparel); Multipoint Networks, Inc. (manufactures & markets wireless metropolitan area networks); Pacific

Communication Sciences, Inc. (designer, developer & marketer of telecommunications & data communications equipment for digital wireless applications); Premisys Communications, Inc. (designs, manufactures & markets integrated access products for tele-communications service providers); P-COM, Inc. (design, manufactures & markets millimeter wave radios for the worldwide wireless telecommunications market)

Genstar Capital, L.L.C.

950 Tower Lane, Suite 1170
Metro Tower
Foster City, California 94404
(650) 286-2350
Fax: (650) 286-2383

Key contact:
Mr. Richard D. Paterson, Managing Director
Mr. Mark E. Bandeen, Managing Director
Mr. Daniel J. Boverman, Principal
Mr. Jean-Pierre L. Conte, Principal
Mr. Angus A. MacNaughton, Senior Advisor
Mr. Ross J. Turner, Senior Advisor
Mr. John A. (Jack) West, Senior Advisor
Mr. Robert J. Weltman, Associate

Area served: Canada, United States

Preferred stage of financing: LBO/MBO

Industries:
I.05	Chemicals
I.06	Communications
I.12	Distribution
I.13	Education
I.14	Electronics
I.15	Energy/natural resources/utilities
I.17	Environmental services/waste management
I.18	Financial services
I.29	Medical/medical products
I.36	Transportation

Glynn Ventures

3000 Sand Hill Road
Suite 235, Building 4
Menlo Park, California 94025
(650) 854-2215
Fax: (650) 854-8083

Key contact:
Mr. Steve Rosston
Mr. John Glynn
Mr. Daryl Messinger

Preferred stages of financing: Second stage, Third/later stage

Industries:
I.03	Biotech/genetic engineering
I.06	Communications
I.07	Computer hardware
I.08	Computer software
I.14	Electronics
I.29	Medical/medical products
I.34	Services (business)
I.35	Services (consumer)

Leonard Green & Partners, LP

11111 Santa Monica Boulevard, Suite 2000
Los Angeles, California 90025
(310) 954-0444
Fax: (310) 954-0404

Key contact:
Mr. Leonard Green, Partner
Mr. Jonathan Sokoloff, Partner
Mr. John Danhakl, Partner
Mr. Peter Nolan, Partner
Mr. Greg Annick, Partner
Ms. Jennifer Holden Dunbar, Partner

Description: We are a private merchant banking firm which specializes in organizing, structuring and sponsoring management buyouts of established companies. We invest in a wide variety of situations, but have special expertise in consumer oriented businesses and family-owned businesses.

Amount of capital invested: $100 million

Preferred investment size: $25-100 million

Amount under management: $500 million -1 billion

Area served: United States

Preferred stage of financing: LBO/MBO

Industries:
I.01	Aerospace
I.04	Broadcasting
I.06	Communications
I.11	Consumer products
I.13	Education
I.14	Electronics
I.16	Entertainment
I.18	Financial services
I.20	Healthcare
I.22	Industrial products
I.25	Leisure/hospitality
I.27	Manufacturing
I.28	Media/publishing
I.32	Retail
I.34	Services (business)
I.35	Services (consumer)
I.36	Transportation

Sampling of portfolio companies: Twinlab Corp. (manufacturer & marketer of nutritional supplements); Diamond Triumph Auto Glass Inc. (automotive glass repair & replacement); Leslies Poolmart Inc. (specialty retail of swimming pool supplies & products); Centers Holding Inc. (home improvement retail stores); Wavetek Corp. (manufacturer & distributor of electronic test equipment); Liberty Group Publishing, Inc. (publisher of 170 local newspapers/publications); Gart Sports, Inc. (retail sporting goods); Arrow Group Industries (manufacturer of metal storage building kits); Communications & Power Inc. (manufacturer & distributor of various electronic devices); Carr Cottstein Foods Inc. (food & drug retail stores); Big 5 Corp. (retail sporting goods)

Greylock Management Corp.

755 Page Mill Road, Suite A100
Palo Alto, California 94304-1018
(650) 493-5525
Fax: (650) 493-5575
E-mail: paloalto@greylock-ca.com
Web: www.greylock.com

Key contact:
Mr. Roger Evans, General Partner
Mr. Dave Strohm, General Partner
Ms. Chris Surowiec

Description: Our role is to support a company's management team in building a world-class enterprise by acting as a responsible and constructive member of the company's board of directors. This takes on many shapes and forms but includes working to build a management team, facilitating relationships with other companies, helping to set a company's strategic direction and raising additional capital both privately and publicly.

Founded: 1965

Amount under management: $500 million -1 billion

Preferred stages of financing: Start up, LBO/MBO, Expansion, Recapitalizations

Industries:
I.03   Biotech/genetic engineering
I.04   Broadcasting
I.06   Communications
I.08   Computer software
I.11   Consumer products
I.14   Electronics
I.15   Energy/natural resources/utilities
I.20   Healthcare
I.22   Industrial products
I.29   Medical/medical products

Sampling of portfolio companies: ISSCO (graphical analysis/presentation software); Sage Systems, Inc. (computer-aided engineering software); Structural Dynamics Research Corp. (mechanical CAE software); Soft•Switch Inc. (PC e-mail interconnect software); Emotion, Inc. (multimedia networking software); Tenth Planet Explorations (educational software); Duet Technologies (intellectual property infrastructure solutions); Micom (data multiplexer & data PABX products); Xcellenet, Inc. (remote distribution of PC applications): Puma Technology, Inc. (mobile data exchange software); Unwired Planet, Inc. (open platform for wireless internet applications); Argon Networks, Inc. (high speed routers); Inverse Network Technology (provider of tools & data for measuring & analyzing internet performance); Worthington Biochemical (enzymes); Oxford Labs (disposable medical products); American Medical Systems (urology products); BioSurface Technology (medical products to treat tissue damage); CompDent (pre-paid dental health plan); The Frontier Group (long term care); Vivra Specialty Partners (specialty focused physician practice management)

Hallador Venture Partners

740 University Avenue, Suite 110
Sacramento, California 95825-6710
(916) 920-5187
Fax: (916) 920-5188

Key contact:
Mr. Chris L. Branscum
Mr. David Hardie

Preferred stages of financing: Seed, First stage, Second stage

Industries:
I.06   Communications
I.14   Electronics
I.23   Information technology services

Hambrecht & Quist LLP

One Bush Street
San Francisco, California 94104
(415) 576-3300
Fax: (415) 576-3621

Key contact:
Mr. Daniel H. Case, III, Chairman/CEO
Ms. Julie Harshberger
Mr. John D. Halpern
Ms. Abby Adlerman
Ms. Kate Geldens

Description: Our domestic venture capital group manages over $330 million in assets in domestic funds. We include investment professionals and a number of consultants who offer a diversified blend of expertise in our targeted industries and extensive experience in growing entrepreneurial companies.

Our focus areas include the following: information technologies, environmental technologies, branded consumer companies.

Preferred stages of financing: Start up, First stage, LBO/MBO

Industries:
I.03   Biotech/genetic engineering
I.06   Communications
I.07   Computer hardware
I.08   Computer software
I.11   Consumer products
I.14   Electronics
I.17   Environmental services/waste management
I.23   Information technology services
I.29   Medical/medical products

High Tech Ventures Inc.

McAndless Towers 3945 Freedom Circle, Suite 1020
Santa Clara, California 95054
(408) 562-0740

Fax: (408) 562-0744
E-mail: it@ix.netcom.com

Description: We are a proven leader in the formation, funding and staffing of data communications and distributed computing start-ups. Ten years of capital creation has established us as the source for participation in a new technology venture.

Preferred stages of financing: Seed, Start up, First stage

Industries:
I.06   Communications
I.08   Computer software
I.24   Internet services/e-commerce

Sampling of portfolio companies: Wellfleet; Beyond Mail; Collabra; Vermeer; Synernetics; Atria; Watermark; Remedy

Hummer Winblad Venture Partners

2 South Park, 2nd Floor
San Francisco, California 94107
(415) 979-9600
Fax: (415) 979-9601
E-mail: jhummer@humwin.com
Web: www.humwin.com

Key contact:
Mr. John Hummer, Partner
Ms. Ann Winblad, Partner
Mr. Mark Gorenberg, Partner
Mr. Bill Gurley, Partner
Mr. Steve Rehmus, Associate

Description: We were created in 1989 as the first venture capital fund exclusively focused on investing in software companies. Today, we have over $200 million in venture capital under management, all concentrated on funding software companies. We invest in software companies at every stage of development from start-up to mezzanine.

Founded: 1989

Preferred investment size: $2 million+

Amount under management: $25-100 million

Area served: United States

Preferred stages of financing: Start up, First stage, Second stage, Mezzanine

Industries:
I.06   Communications
I.08   Computer software
I.13   Education
I.16   Entertainment
I.24   Internet services/e-commerce

Sampling of portfolio companies: Arbor Software Corp. (enterprise applications); Scopus Technology Group (enterprise applications); Stanford Technology (enterprise applications); Wayfarer Communications (enterprise applications); CoroNet Systems (enterprise systems management); CenterView Software (development tools); Integrity QA Software (development tools); NetDynamics (development tools); PowerSoft Corp. (development tools); Viewpoint Datalabs (development tools); Big Book (internet); GlobalCenter (internet); IMX (internet); NetGravity (internet); Escalade (scientific, engineering); Berkeley Systems (consumer software); Humongous Entertainment (consumer software); T/Maker Co. (consumer software); Central Point Software (desktop applications, utilities); Slate Corp. (desktop applications, utilties)

IAI Ventures, Inc.

505 Hamilton Avenue, Suite 315
Palo Alto, California 94301
(650) 470-1200
Fax: (650) 470-1201
Web: www.iaiventures.com

Key contact:
Ms. Lorraine Fox, General Partner

Area served: Europe, North America

Preferred stages of financing: Seed, Start up, First stage, Second stage

Industries:
I.03   Biotech/genetic engineering
I.06   Communications
I.07   Computer hardware
I.08   Computer software
I.20   Healthcare
I.21   High technology
I.23   Information technology services
I.24   Internet services/e-commerce

I.26   Life sciences
I.29   Medical/medical products
I.33   Semiconductors

Sampling of portfolio companies: AdiCom Wireless (telecom equipment); Alta Berkeley V (early stage - European); Baring Communications (early stage - communications); Communications Ventures II (early stage, communications); CryoCath Technologies (medical devices); E/O Networks (telecom equipment)Exxel Group V (late stage - buy out); Fujant Technologies (telecom equipment) Illumenex (medical devices); InfoScape (software-internet commerce); Lightspeed Int'l. (software-telecom); Protein Delivery (pharmaceuticals); Red Creek Comm. (datacom equipment); Relevance (software); StarTech Seed Fund (early stage); Telecom Partners (early stage); ThemeMedia, Inc. (software); Therics, Inc. (medical devices); XIOTEch Corp. (datacom equipment); Zeus Corporation (datacom equipment)

Idanta Partners, Ltd.

4660 La Jolla Village Drive, Suite 850
San Diego, California 92122
(619) 452-9690
Fax: (619) 452-2013
Web: www.idanta.com

Key contact:
Mr. David J. Dunn, Managing Partner
Ms. Perscilla Faily, General Partner
Mr. Jonathan S. Huberman, General Partner
Mr. John C. Kennedy, Associate
Mr. Mahesh Krishnamurthy, Associate

Description: Founded in 1971, we are a private venture capital partnership with capital in excess of $400 million. Our goal is to be the value added venture partner for entrepreneurs and emerging companies. We work closely with management, providing capital, expertise, resources, and strategic thinking to build successful companies.

Amount of capital invested: $15 million

Preferred investment size: $1-5 million

Amount under management: $100-500 million

Area served: North America

Preferred stages of financing: Seed, Start up, First stage, Second stage

Industries:
I.01 Aerospace
I.03 Biotech/genetic engineering
I.05 Chemicals
I.06 Communications
I.07 Computer hardware
I.08 Computer software
I.11 Consumer products
I.12 Distribution
I.13 Education
I.14 Electronics
I.18 Financial services
I.20 Healthcare
I.21 High technology
I.22 Industrial products
I.23 Information technology services
I.24 Internet services/e-commerce
I.26 Life sciences
I.27 Manufacturing
I.29 Medical/medical products
I.30 New media
I.32 Retail
I.33 Semiconductors
I.34 Services (business)
I.35 Services (consumer)

Sampling of portfolio companies: Boxer Cross, Inc. (semiconductor capital equipment); Cosmederm Technologies (skin anti-irritant technologies); Gatefield Corporation (flash-based field programmable gate arrays); Hyperparellel, Inc. (data mining/ knowledge discovery software & services); Iomega Corporation (removable storage drives); Visionary Design Systems (reseller of mechanical computer aided design software & solutions)

Imperial Ventures, Inc.

9920 South La Cienega Boulevard, 14th Floor
Inglewood, California 90301
(310) 417-5710
Fax: (310) 338-6115

Key contact:
Mr. R. Muelhenbeck
Mr. Chris Hobbs

Area served: West Coast

Preferred stages of financing: LBO/MBO, Third/later stage

Industries:
I.03 Biotech/genetic engineering
I.06 Communications
I.07 Computer hardware
I.08 Computer software
I.14 Electronics
I.29 Medical/medical products

Indosuez Ventures

2180 Sand Hill Road, Suite 450
Menlo Park, California 94025
(650) 854-0587
Fax: (650) 323-5561

Key contact:
Mr. David E. Gold, General Partner
Mr. Guy H. Conger, General Partner
Ms. Nancy D. Burrus, General Partner

Description: Venture capital firm focusing on first round investments on the West Coast. All our investments are technology leveraged.

Amount of capital invested: $7-8 million

Preferred investment size: $1-2 million

Amount under management: $100-500 million

Area served: West

Preferred stages of financing: Start up, First stage, Second stage

Industries:
I.06 Communications
I.07 Computer hardware
I.08 Computer software
I.14 Electronics
I.21 High technology
I.22 Industrial products
I.23 Information technology services
I.29 Medical/medical products

Sampling of portfolio companies: Informix Software (software); Accel Graphics (graphics subsystems); Sierra Semiconductor (semiconductors); Calypte (diagnostic testing); Oceania (computerized patient record software)

Information Technology Ventures, L.P.

3000 Sand Hill Road
Building One, Suite 280
Menlo Park, California 94025
(650) 854-5500
Fax: (650) 234-0130
E-mail: main@itventures.com
Web: www.itventures.com

Key contact:
Dr. Mark Dubovoy, Co-Founder
Mr. Sam H. Lee, Co-Founder
Ms. Virginia M. Turezyn, Co-Founder

Description: Our philosophy is one of active participation in bringing to fruition an entrepreneur's dream. We are often lead investor and hold board seats in most of our portfolio companies. The fact that a number of successful entrepreneurs, backed by our principals in the past, are investors in our funds is a solid indication of our successful partnerships with our entrepreneurs. We look forward to the opportunity to discuss new ideas with entrepreneurs who share our philosophy and vision for success.

Preferred investment size: $5-10 million

Amount under management: $100-500 million

Area served: Prefer West

Preferred stages of financing: Seed, Start up, First stage

Industries:
I.06   Communications
I.08   Computer software
I.14   Electronics
I.23   Information technology services
I.24   Internet services/e-commerce
I.33   Semiconductors
I.34   Services (business)

Sampling of portfolio companies: Adaptive Media, Inc. (provides high quality on-demand audio & video software solutions for mission critical applications throughout the enterprise); Ambit Design Systems, Inc. (provides electronic design automation software for the design of complex, high performance chips); Aurum Software, Inc. (provider of customer relationship management software); Berkeley Networks, Inc. (develops a new generation of multi-gigabit routing switch platforms); Compression, Inc. (provider of integrated product development services designed to improve the productivity & competitive position of its customers); Epigram, Inc. (offers advanced technology & products for high-speed resi-dential networking); Epiphany Inc. (provider of software applications & solutions to drive Enterprise Relationship Management); Exodus Communications, Inc. (provides outsourcing internet data center management services & customized applications for companies); iPrint, Inc. (developed the only electronic commerce environment specifically designed to automate mass market custom printing over the internet); JetCell, Inc. (developing wireless communications equipment); Lightwave Microsystems Corp. (designs & manufactures optoelectronic modules & subsystems for data networking & telecommunications systems); Netcentives, Inc. (provides internet marketers with online promotional tools that effectively drive sales & consumer loyalty); Paragon Management Systems, Inc. (provides supply chain management software including advanced planning & scheduling & related logistics software); Seeker Software, Inc. (develops & markets web applications that allow corporations to implement employee self service & enhance communications); Smart Machines, Inc. (develops & produces next generation direct drive robots for transporting wafers in semiconductor process tools); TeraStor Corp. (designs & manufactures ultra-high capacity, high performance data storage devices based on proprietary magnetic & optical technologies); WAVTrace, Inc. (develops point to multi-point millimeter wave telecommunication systems); WebLine Communications Corp. (develops & markets interactive telebusiness solutions for call centers & inside sales & service organizations); Virtual Silicon Technology, Inc. (developing Silicon-Ready libraries, physical design components & services for complex integrated circuits in 0.25 & 0.18 micron semiconductor process technologies)

InnoCal, L.P.
600 Anton Boulevard, Suite 1270
Costa Mesa, California 92626
(714) 850-6784
Fax: (714) 850-6798
E-mail: eharrison@innocal.com
Web: www.innocal.com

Key contact:
Mr. James E. Houlihan, III, General Partner
Mr. H. D. Lambert, General Partner
Mr. Gerald A. Lodge, General Partner
Mr. Raun J. Rasmussen, General Partner
Mr. Russell J. Robelen, General Partner
Mr. Eric S. Harrison, Associate

Description: We are a private venture capital firm with $75 million of committed capital. Funding is provided exclusively by the California State Teachers' Retirement System. Our investment focus is on early and expansion stage, technology-based businesses that have the potential to be leaders within their respective industries.

Preferred investment size: $2 million

Amount under management: $25-100 million

Area served: California, United States

Preferred stages of financing: Start up, First stage, Second stage, Expansion

Industries:
I.03   Biotech/genetic engineering
I.06   Communications
I.07   Computer hardware
I.08   Computer software
I.14   Electronics
I.20   Healthcare
I.23   Information technology services

Sampling of portfolio companies: Advanced Access (provides logistical outsourcing services to a variety of industries); Cloud 9 Interactive (multimedia publisher); CoCensys (develops & markets drugs for disorders of the central nervous system); Collagenex (pursuing drug therapies for periodontal disease); GeoCities Inc. (develops internet-based themed communities); GigaNet Inc. (high speed interconnects & switches for cluster computing); HiLife Inc. (comprehensicve interactive case management of chronic disease states); Implex (orthopedic implants & specialty materials); Maret (drug therapies to promote wound & burn healing); Medical Data Int'l. (provides business information products for healthcare markets); Medical Delivery Devices, Inc. (a medication infusion device company); Motiva Software Corp. (develops & markets intranet-based product information life cycle management systems); SalesLogix Corp. (develops enterprise-wide sales force automation software); Telescan Systems, Inc. (designs & manufactures interactive merchandising systems for the consumer entertainment industry); Thinque Systems Corp. (develops wireless pen-based customer asset management solutions for the consumer packaged goods industry); Trega

Biosciences, Inc. (combinatorial chemistry for drug discovery & development); Trikon Technologies (manufactures etching equipment for the semiconductor industry); TriVida Corp. (develops & markets predictive data management products for corporate networks); Tycom (precision cutting tools used in the manufacturing of printed circuit boards)

Institutional Venture Partners

3000 Sand Hill Road
Building 2, Suite 290
Menlo Park, California 94025
(650) 854-0132
Fax: (650) 854-5762
Web: www.ivp.vom

Key contact:
Mr. Samuel D. Colella, General Partner
Mr. Reid W. Dennis, General Partner
Ms. Mary Jane Elmore, General Partner
Mr. Norman A. Fogelsong, General Partner
Ms. Ruthann Quindlen, General Partner
Mr. L. James Strand, General Partner
Mr. William P. Tai, General Partner
Mr. T. Peter Thomas, General Partner
Mr. Geoffrey Y. Yang, General Partner

Description: Our partners have a broad range of relevant experiences and successful careers in operating positions as well as in venture capital investing. We are company builders and take a supportive, partnership approach to working with entrepreneurs.

Preferred investment size: $50,000-4 million

Amount under management: $500 million -1 billion

Preferred stages of financing: Seed, Start up, First stage

Industries:
I.03   Biotech/genetic engineering
I.06   Communications
I.08   Computer software
I.20   Healthcare
I.23   Information technology services
I.24   Internet services/e-commerce
I.26   Life sciences
I.29   Medical/medical products
I.33   Semiconductors

Sampling of portfolio companies: Alere Medical, Inc. (devices for automated low cost home monitoring of signs & symptoms of patients with high cost chronic medical diseases, like congestive heart failure); Atmosphere Networks, Inc. (high-speed switching products for the telecommunications access loop); Ensemble Communications, Inc. (LMDS equipment for high-speed wireless broadband access of voice, data & video); Pharmasonics, Inc. (intravascular utlrasound devices to prevent restenosis, lyse blood clots & deliver drugs & genes); Shasta Networks, Inc. (access platform for enabling value add services for internet service providers); Success Factor Systems, Inc. (competency-based human resource software for hiring, job-profiling, employee assessment & organizational planning); Excite Corp. (developing a media navigation service & server software for navigation of the internet); Mpath Interactive, Inc. (providing an on-line interactive service for multiplayer games over the internet); Wavespan Corp. (develops high speed wireless systems for connection from customer premises to internet service); Juniper Networks, Inc. (high performance, next generation routers); Diffusion, Inc. (producer & marketer of products for the internet); Netiva, Inc. (developed a family of products for corporate intranets); Golfweb (develops & maintains an internet based publication & service dedicated to golf on the world wide web); Whistle Communications Corp. (turnkey internet server for medium sized businesses)

International Information Investors

7083 Hollywood Boulevard, Suite 501
Hollywood, California 90028
(213) 460-6304
Fax: (213) 460-6314

Key contact:
Mr. Giles P. Goodhead, Managing Director

Description: We are a private equity group which makes investments in media, publishing and information companies. Our focus is on business to business opportunities.

Preferred investment size: $1-3 million

Amount under management: $10-25 million

Preferred stages of financing: First stage, Second stage, Mezzanine, LBO/MBO, Expansion

Industries:
I.04   Broadcasting
I.10   Consulting
I.13   Education
I.16   Entertainment
I.20   Healthcare
I.24   Internet services/e-commerce
I.28   Media/publishing
I.30   New media
I.35   Services (consumer)

Sampling of portfolio companies: LA 411 (entertainment industry directories); Infosis (custom electronic information services); Media Publishing Int'l. (information products covering media); Kennedy Information (information products covering professional services)

InterWest Partners

3000 Sand Hill Road
Building 3, Suite 255
Menlo Park, California 94025-7112
(650) 854-8585
Fax: (650) 854-4706

Key contact:
Mr. Philip T. Gianos, General Partner
Mr. John E. Zeisler, General Partner

Description: Since our inception we've been investing in entrepreneurs - the people who change the way we live and work either by creating an entirely new product or service business, or by transforming an existing one. With over $600 million in committed capital, we are one of the largest venture capital partnerships in the United States. Our business is helping entrepreneurs convert their ideas and ambitions into reality.

Founded: 1979

Preferred stages of financing: Seed, Start up, First stage, Second stage, Mezzanine

Industries:

I.06	Communications
I.07	Computer hardware
I.08	Computer software
I.11	Consumer products
I.12	Distribution
I.13	Education
I.17	Environmental services/waste management
I.20	Healthcare
I.23	Information technology services
I.24	Internet services/e-commerce
I.26	Life sciences
I.27	Manufacturing
I.29	Medical/medical products
I.32	Retail
I.33	Semiconductors
I.35	Services (consumer)
I.37	Wholesale

Sampling of portfolio companies: Crystal (mixed signal analog integrated chips); Ciena (fiber-optic transmission equipment for wide area networks); Ramp Networks (plug & play internet access for small work groups); J3 Learning (CD-ROM & video based multimedia educational titles); Placeware (real-time, community-based applications); Convex (high performance scientific computer systems); Innovasive Devices (bone anchor systems & related tools); Nanogen (diagnostic systems coupling DNA probes with electronic amplification); Hospital Management Assoc. (small hospital management in the South & Southeast); TheraTx (subacute care & contract rehab services); Kelson Physician Partners (physician practice management focused on large groups in the Northeast); Oacis Healthcare Systems (clinical data repositories & applications); Cubist Pharmaceuticals (new antibiotic drugs to address drug resistant diseases); Glycomed (therapeutic products using carbohydrate related technologies); Coulter Pharmaceutical (monoclonal antibody therapy for non-Hodgkins' lymphoma); Mercator Genetics (genomic discovery leading to diagnostic & therapeutic products); DashAmerica (Pearl Izumi brand of performance apparel for cycling & other sports markets); Artco-Bell (manufacturer of school furniture); Gadzooks (mall based teen clothing stores); Bojangles (quick service restaurant chain with 225 units in the Southeast)

JAFCO America Ventures, Inc.

505 Hamilton Avenue, Suite 310
Palo Alto, California 94301
(650) 463-8800
Fax: (650) 463-8801
Web: www.jafco.com

Key contact:
Mr. Barry Schiffman, President
Mr. Hitoshi Imuta, Chairman
Mr. Todd Brooks, Managing Director

Description: We provide value-added financial services to private technology companies focused on high growth markets. Investing in North America based companies, our portfolio includes more than 60 companies spanning the communications, computing, components, health sciences & services industries. Recent investments in telecommunications and data communications technology and services, enterprise software and internet technologies demonstrate our commitment to help entrepreneurs make their ideas a reality.

Preferred investment size: $3-5 million

Amount under management: $100-500 million

Area served: Asia, Europe, United States

Preferred stages of financing: Seed, Start up, First stage, Second stage, Mezzanine

Industries:

I.03	Biotech/genetic engineering
I.06	Communications
I.08	Computer software
I.11	Consumer products
I.21	High technology
I.23	Information technology services
I.33	Semiconductors

Sampling of portfolio companies: Brocade Communication Systems, Inc. (communications); Clear Communications Corp. (communications); IWC (communications); MMC Networks (communications); OSI (communications); Sentient Networks, Inc. (communications); Adicom Wireless, Inc. (communications); Avanex (communications); AT/Comm (info systems); Net Perceptions (info systems); Sonnet Financial (info services); Equator Technologies (semiconductors); Vivid Semiconductor, Inc. (semiconductors); Single Chip Systems (semiconductors); Lightspan Partnership (software); Com21, Inc. (systems/peripherals); NVidia (systems/peripherals); Calimetrics, Inc. (systems/peripherals)

Kingsbury Associates

3655 Nobel Drive, Suite 490
San Diego, California 92122
(619) 677-0600
Fax: (619) 677-0800

Key contact:
Mr. Tim Wollaeger

Area served: California

Preferred stages of financing: Start up, First stage

Industries:

I.03	Biotech/genetic engineering
I.29	Medical/medical products

Kinship Partners

1900 West Garvey Avenue South, Suite 200
West Covina, California 91790-2653
(626) 962-3562
Fax: (626) 962-0758

Key contact:
Mr. Ed Tuck

Area served: Within 2 hours of office

Preferred stages of financing: Seed, Start up, First stage

Industries:
I.03   Biotech/genetic engineering
I.06   Communications
I.07   Computer hardware
I.29   Medical/medical products
I.32   Retail
I.35   Services (consumer)

Kleiner Perkins Caufield & Byers

2750 Sand Hill Road
Menlo Park, California 94025
(650) 233-2750
Fax: (650) 233-0300

Four Embarcadero Center, Suite 1880
San Francisco, California 94111
(415) 421-3110
Fax: (415) 421-3128

Key contact:
Mr. Brook Byers, Partner
Mr. Frank Caufield, Partner
Mr. Kevin Compton, Partner
Mr. Mike Curry, Partner
Mr. John Doerr, Partner
Dr. Cynthia Healy, Ph.D., Partner
Mr. Will Hearst, Partner
Mr. Vinod Khosla, Partner
Mr. Eugene Kleiner, Founding Partner
Mr. Floyd Kvamme, Partner
Mr. Joe Lacob, Partner
Mr. Bernie Lacroute, Partner
Mr. Jim Lally, Partner
Mr. Doug Mackenzie, Partner
Mr. Ted Schlein, Partner
Mr. Russ Siegelman, Partner
Mr. Tom Perkins, Founding Partner

Mr. Roger McNamee, Integral Capital Partner
Mr. John Powell, Integral Capital Partner

Description: In 1972, we began offering entrepreneurs a broader philosophy of value-added investing: not merely access to capital, but access to people. A partnership with experienced industry leaders who recognize, challenge and even improve on a brilliant idea. We believe that we must earn the right to advise entrepreneurs on a daily basis, by intellectually committing to deliver the best ideas of which we are capable.

Founded: 1972

Preferred stages of financing: Seed, Start up, First stage

Industries:
I.03   Biotech/genetic engineering
I.06   Communications
I.14   Electronics
I.20   Healthcare
I.23   Information technology services
I.26   Life sciences

Sampling of portfolio companies: Genentech; Tandem; Lotus; Compaq; Businessland; Intuit; Macromedia; Sun; Netscape

Kline Hawkes California, LP

11726 San Vicente Boulevard, Suite 300
Los Angeles, California 90049
(310) 442-4700
Fax: (310) 442-4707
E-mail: info@klinehawkes.com
Web: www.klinehawkes.com

Key contact:
Mr. Frank R. Kline, Jr., Managing Partner
Mr. Joseph E. Ferguson, Partner
Mr. Jerome S. Engel, Managing Partner

Description: We provide investors access to investment opportunities in emerging growth and middle market California companies. The typical portfolio company has existing revenues of $2 million to $75 million. The fund, which also has a licensed Small Business Investment Company subsidiary, has available up to $112 million of investment capital, including a $45 million commitment from the California Public Employees' Retirement System (CalPERS).

Amount of capital invested: $20.1 million

Preferred investment size: $3-5 million

Amount under management: $100-500 million

Area served: California

Preferred stages of financing: Second stage, Expansion

Industries:
I.20   Healthcare
I.23   Information technology services
I.34   Services (business)
I.35   Services (consumer)

Sampling of portfolio companies: American WholeHealth, Inc. (health services); Blex, Inc. (medical diagnostics); Campuslink Communications Systems, Inc. (communications systems); Cardiac Mariners, Inc. (medical device); Certus Enterprises, LLC (health services); Coryphaeus Software, Inc. (software); Eos Corp. (electronics); MicroNet Technology, Inc. (disk storage products); RDL Commercial Technologies Corp. (telecommunications); RDL Photonic Integrated Chip Corp. (telecommunications); Sensor Systems, Inc. (information technologies); TranSoft Technology Corp. (digital video); Via Medical (medical device)

Labrador Ventures

400 Seaport Court, Suite 250
Redwood City, California 94063
(650) 366-6000
Fax: (650) 366-6430
Web: www.labrador.com

Key contact:
Mr. Larry Kubal, General Partner
Mr. Stuart Davidson, General Partner

Description: We invest in early stage, private companies pursuing opportunities in information
technology. During the last two years we have
invested in 17 companies, 10 of which are directly
related to the internet. About 2/3 of the time we are
the first professional investors in a company.

Amount of capital invested: $3 million

Preferred investment size: $500,000

Amount under management: $10-25 million

Area served: United States

Preferred stages of financing: Seed, Start up, First
stage

Industries:
I.06   Communications
I.08   Computer software
I.21   High technology
I.23   Information technology services
I.24   Internet services/e-commerce

I.33   Semiconductors

Sampling of portfolio companies: Accolade, Inc.
(computer & video game entertainment software);
Aviva Sport/Mattel (children's sporting goods sold
through traditional toy channels); Citizen1 Software,
Inc. (web information tools for the pharmaceutical
industry); .comfax, Inc. (internet fax service not
requiring computers to send or receive); Claremont
Systems (client/server software implementation
tools); Cypress Research (network fax & telephony
software); Differential Corrections, Inc. (corrective
GPS data subscription service); EDGE Systems (low
voltage home automation & entertainment systems);
GlobalCast Communications (reliable multicast
internet software); Greenway Products (network
marketing of environmentally-friendly products);
HotMail/Microsoft (web based email); inTouch, Inc.
(place-based multimedia information & marketing
systems); MobileSoft (software publishing for the
Newton MessagePad); Nextwave Design Automation
(EDA timing simulation software); Preview Travel
(video travel database, new media travel marketing);
Sonix Technologies (next generation hearing aid
technology); Upside Publishing Co. (technology
business magazine publishing); Vividus, Inc. (multimedia animation authoring tools & content);
Worldview Systems (time-sensitive, destination
information travel database); Zane Interactive (multimedia CD-ROM publisher of educational & reference
titles)

LaiLai Capital Corporation

223 East Garvey Avenue, Suite 228
Monterey Park, California 91755
(626) 288-0704
Fax: (626) 288-4101

Key contact:
Mr. Kenneth Chen

Area served: California

Preferred stages of financing: Seed, Start up, First
stage

Industries:
I.19   Generalist

Lawrence Financial

11661 San Vicente #408
Los Angeles, California 90049
(310) 826-1200
Fax: (310) 826-4424
E-mail: lhurw55555@aol.com

Key contact:
Mr. Lawrence Hurwitz, CEO

Description: Firm provides secured asset based funding
to companies experiencing fast growth (exceeding
normal debt to equity ratios) and companies being re-
structured due to losses.

Amount of capital invested: $100 million

Preferred investment size: $1 million

Amount under management: <$10 million

Area served: United States

Preferred stage of financing: Expansion

Industries:
I.01   Aerospace
I.02   Agriculture/forestry/fishing/mining
I.03   Biotech/genetic engineering

I.04   Broadcasting
I.05   Chemicals
I.06   Communications
I.07   Computer hardware
I.08   Computer software
I.09   Construction
I.10   Consulting
I.11   Consumer products
I.12   Distribution
I.13   Education
I.14   Electronics
I.15   Energy/natural resources/utilities
I.16   Entertainment
I.17   Environmental services/waste management
I.18   Financial services
I.19   Generalist
I.20   Healthcare
I.21   High technology
I.22   Industrial products
I.23   Information technology services
I.24   Internet services/e-commerce
I.25   Leisure/hospitality
I.26   Life sciences
I.27   Manufacturing
I.28   Media/publishing

I.29	Medical/medical products		I.34	Services (business)
I.30	New media		I.35	Services (consumer)
I.31	Real estate		I.36	Transportation
I.32	Retail		I.37	Wholesale
I.33	Semiconductors			

LF International, Inc.

360 Post Street, Suite 705
San Francisco, California 94108
(415) 399-0110
Fax: (415) 399-9222
E-mail: hsiehlfi@aol.com

Key contact:
Mr. Michael Hsieh, President
Mr. Harrison Chang, Vice President
Ms. Mindy Chang, Associate

Description: We are a venture capital firm focused on building consumer product companies that have global marketing and sourcing needs. We specialize in the apparel, toys, fashion accessories, home decor and houseware industries. Through our parent company, Li & Fung Ltd., we provide global sourcing expertise in addition to capital for our investment partners.

Preferred investment size: $1 million

Area served: United States

Preferred stages of financing: First stage, Second stage

Industries:
I.11   Consumer products
I.12   Distribution
I.37   Wholesale

Sampling of portfolio companies: Lewis Galoob Toys (toy); Cyrk Inc. (premium); Wilke Rodriguez (apparel); Danskin (apparel); Santana (apparel); Wood Associates (premium); The Lodge at Harvard Square (apparel); The Original San Francisco Toymakers (toy); Millwork Trading Ltd. (apparel)

Liberty Environmental Partners

220 Montgomery Street, Penthouse 10
San Francisco, California 94104
(415) 834-1600
Fax: (415) 834-1603

Key contact:
Mr. Tim Woodward
Mr. Donald Hichens

Area served: Rocky Mountains, West Coast

Preferred stages of financing: First stage, Second stage

Industries:
I.05   Chemicals
I.12   Distribution
I.15   Energy/natural resources/utilities
I.17   Environmental services/waste management

Magna Pacific Investments

330 North Brand Boulevard, Suite 670
Glendale, California 91203
(818) 547-0809
Fax: (818) 547-9303

Key contact:
David Wong, President

Description: We deal strictly with minorities.

Area served: United States

Preferred stages of financing: Seed, First stage, Second stage, LBO/MBO

Industries:
I.03   Biotech/genetic engineering
I.06   Communications
I.07   Computer hardware
I.08   Computer software
I.14   Electronics
I.27   Manufacturing
I.29   Medical/medical products

Mandeville Partners

12100 Wilshire Boulevard, Suite 705
Los Angeles, California 90025
(310) 442-7880
Fax: (310) 442-7890
E-mail: newbusiness@mandevillepartners.com
Web: www.mandevillepartners.com

Key contact:
Mr. David A. Eisner, Managing Director
Mr. Jonathan D. Lloyd, Managing Director
Mr. Rory S. Phillips, Managing Director
Mr. Peter A. Roussak, Managing Director
Mr. Paul B. Savoldelli, Managing Director
Mr. Sean M. Thorpe, Principal

Description: We are a venture capital, merchant banking and investment group focused principally on businesses in telecommunications, technology and media. Formed in 1995, we bring investment banking and management expertise to both new and existing businesses needing assistance either in raising capital, transitioning from concept to operating reality or expanding to the next level.

Founded: 1995

Area served: South/Central America, United States

Preferred stage of financing: Start up

Industries:
I.06   Communications
I.28   Media/publishing

Sampling of portfolio companies: McCaw Cellular Communications; Cellular Communications, Inc.; Whittaker Corp.; Centennial Cellular; Crowley

Cellular; Caesars World, Inc.; Security Link; Angeles Corp.; OpTel, Inc.; C4 Media; QEI, Inc.; Cable Holdings; EuroDisney; LIVE, Inc.; A&M Records; Fleet Call/Nextel; Dispatch Communications; Vanguard Communications, Inc.; Hal Roach Studios, Inc.; TransGlobal Communications

Marwit Capital, L.L.C.

180 Newport Center Drive, Suite 200
Newport Beach, California 92660
(714) 640-6234
Fax: (714) 720-8077

Key contact:
Mr. Matthew L. Witte, President/CEO
Mr. Chris L. Britt, Principal
Mr. Jeffrey P. Schaffer, Vice President

Description: We supply subordinated debt and equity to established and profitable middle market businesses. Our specialty is long-term mezzanine financing, with typically five to seven years subordinated loans with minority equity participation rights. We prefer to work with expansion or acquisition of existing businesses, mergers, refinancings, IPO's and private placements.

Amount of capital invested: total capital under management: $37.2 million

Preferred investment size: $5 million

Amount under management: $25-100 million

Area served: United States

Preferred stages of financing: Mezzanine, LBO/MBO

Industries:
I.06 Communications
I.08 Computer software
I.12 Distribution
I.20 Healthcare
I.22 Industrial products
I.27 Manufacturing
I.29 Medical/medical products
I.34 Services (business)
I.36 Transportation
I.37 Wholesale

Matrix Partners

2500 Sand Hill Road, Suite 113
Menlo Park, California 94025
(650) 854-3131
Fax: (650) 854-3296
E-mail: info@matrixlp.com
Web: www.matrixpartners.com

Key contact:
Mr. Timothy A. Barrows
Mr. John Boyle
Mr. Paul J. Ferri
Mr. W. Michael Humphreys
Mr. Andrew Marcuvitz
Mr. Andrew Verhalen

Description: We are a prominent venture capital firm with an established investment program focused on early stage software and communications companies. While many venture capital firms are reluctant to invest in start-ups, choosing instead to make late-stage equity investments, we believe that risk provides opportunity. We are devoted to company building and focus exclusively on information technology.

Founded: 1982

Preferred investment size: $2.5-3.5 million

Preferred stages of financing: Seed, Start up, First stage

Industries:
I.06 Communications
I.08 Computer software
I.23 Information technology services

Sampling of portfolio companies: Alteon Networks, Inc. (manufactures & markets high-speed switches & adapters for network computing environments); Apple Computer, Inc. (personal computer products); BancTec, Inc. (electronic check processing equipment for banking industry); Cadia Networks, Inc. (manufactures networking equipment); Cascade Communications Corp. (frame relay data communications products); Cipher Data Products, Inc. (magnetic computer memory equipment); Diffusion, Inc. (extranet information delivery software for business-to-business communications); E-mu Systems, Inc. (full line of high quality music synthesizers); FASTech Integration, Inc. (manufacturing automation software); Grand Junction Networks, Inc. (designs, manufactures & markets cost-effective, high-speed LANs for workgroups); Looking Glass Technologies, Inc. (entertainment software); NETWORKS On-Line, Inc. (on-line database of training seminars & courses); Overland Data, Inc. (computer tape drive subsystems); PSINet, Inc. (commercial internet access provider); Rendition, Inc. (high performance 3-D graphics chip for entertainment applications); Stratus Computer, Inc. (fault tolerant computer systems for transaction processing); Unwired Planet, Inc. (open software platform for wireless access to web-based applications); Vertigo Development Group, Inc. (developer of interactive financial planning & advisory tools & innovative webcasting applications for banks); WaveSpan Corp. (wireless broadband communication systems); XILINX, Inc. (user programmable logic cell arrays)

James A. Matzdorff & Company

9903 Santa Monica Boulevard, Suite 374
Beverly Hills, California 90212
(310) 854-4634

Key contact:
Mr. James A. Matzdorff, President/CEO

Description: We arrange corporate debt financing, refinancings restructurings, recapitalizations and acquisition financing. We do difficult financings, public or private companies, around the country.

Founded: 1977

Preferred investment size: $5 million+

Amount under management: $25-100 million

Area served: United States

Preferred stages of financing: Second stage, LBO/MBO, Expansion, Int'l expansion, Venture leasing

Industries:

I.01   Aerospace
I.02   Agriculture/forestry/fishing/mining
I.03   Biotech/genetic engineering
I.04   Broadcasting
I.05   Chemicals
I.06   Communications
I.07   Computer hardware
I.08   Computer software
I.09   Construction
I.10   Consulting
I.11   Consumer products
I.12   Distribution
I.13   Education
I.14   Electronics
I.15   Energy/natural resources/utilities
I.16   Entertainment
I.17   Environmental services/waste management
I.18   Financial services
I.19   Generalist
I.20   Healthcare
I.21   High technology
I.22   Industrial products
I.23   Information technology services
I.24   Internet services/e-commerce
I.25   Leisure/hospitality
I.26   Life sciences
I.27   Manufacturing
I.28   Media/publishing
I.29   Medical/medical products
I.30   New media
I.31   Real estate
I.32   Retail
I.33   Semiconductors
I.34   Services (business)
I.35   Services (consumer)
I.36   Transportation
I.37   Wholesale

Mayfield Fund

2800 Sand Hill Road, Suite 250
Menlo Park, California 94025
(415) 854-5560
Fax: (415) 854-5712
Web: www.mayfield.com

Key contact:
Dr. Yogen K. Dalal, Ph.D., General Partner
Mr. Kevin A. Fong, General Partner
Mr. A. Grant Heidrich, III, General Partner
Dr. Russell C. Hirsch, M.D., General Partner
Mr. Wende S. Hutton, General Partner
Mr. Erik D. Lassila, Associate
Mr. Michael J. Levinthal, General Partner
Mr. F. Gibson "Gib" Myers, Jr.
Dr. A. Richard Newton, Ph.D., Venture Partner
Mr. George A. Pavlov, General Partner/CFO
Mr. William D. Unger, General Partner
Mr. Wendell G. "Van" Van Auken, III, General Partner

Description: We were co-founded by Tommy Davis, who previously co-founded one of the first venture capital firms, Davis & Rock, in 1961. Tommy Davis brought a solid conviction that the foundation upon which an early stage technology company is built should be a close, effective partnership between venture investors and management. He brought an equal conviction that such a partnership must be based, above all, on mutual trust, mutual confidence and mutual respect. This remains the guiding principle of Mayfield Fund today.

Founded: 1961

Amount of capital invested: more than $1 billion since inception

Preferred stages of financing: Seed, Start up, First stage

Industries:
I.03   Biotech/genetic engineering
I.06   Communications
I.08   Computer software
I.14   Electronics
I.23   Information technology services
I.29   Medical/medical products

Sampling of portfolio companies: Advent Software, Inc.; Alantec Corp.; Arbor Software Corp.; Aspect Telecommunications; InControl, Inc.; Legato Systems, Inc.; Linear Technology Corp.; Millenium Pharmaceuticals; Pure Software; Quantum Corp.; Silicon Graphics, Inc.; 3Com Corp.; VIVUS, Inc.; The Vantive Corp.

McCown De Leeuw & Company

3000 Sand Hill Road
Building 3, Suite 290
Menlo Park, California 94025
(415) 854-6000
Fax: (415) 854-0853

Key contact:
Mr. George E. McCown, Managing Partner
Mr. Robert B. Hellman, Partner
Mr. Steven A. Zuckerman, Partner

Description: Venture capital and banking firm investing its own capital.

Preferred investment size: $5 million

Area served: United States

Preferred stages of financing: Second stage, Mezzanine, LBO/MBO

Industries:
I.11   Consumer products
I.18   Financial services
I.23   Information technology services
I.27   Manufacturing
I.34   Services (business)

Sampling of portfolio companies: SARCOM; ASC Network Corp.

MDS Capital Corporation

2121 North California Boulevard, Suite 290
Walnut Creek, California 94596
(925) 974-3540
Fax: (925) 974-3541
E-mail: markc406@aol.com

Key contact:
Mr. Mark Cochran, Vice President

Description: We are a division of one of Canada's
largest venture capital companies focused exclusively on health care and life sciences investing. Our
primary objective is to build significant realizable
value for our shareholders, as well as for the management and shareholders of its investee companies. We
seek to achieve this by bringing a combination of
capital, operating and financial expertise, as well as a
network of international contacts with the life
science area.

Amount of capital invested: $100 million (Canadian)

Preferred investment size: $3-10 million (Canadian)

Amount under management: $500 million -1 billion

Area served: North America

Preferred stages of financing: Seed, Start up, First
stage, Second stage, Mezzanine

Industries:
I.03   Biotech/genetic engineering
I.20   Healthcare
I.26   Life sciences
I.29   Medical/medical products

Sampling of portfolio companies: Alleix Biopharmaceuticals Inc. (focused on the discovery & development of novel biopharmaceutical products for
tissue repair & inflammation for which existing therapies are inadequate or unavailable); Beaconeye Inc.
(provides laser vision correction facilities & services
for primary eyecare providers with patients seeking
an alternative to eyeglasses & contact lenses & for
ophthalmologists performing photorefractive kerate-
ctomy); Cambridge Neuroscience Inc. (developing
small molecule, neuron-specific, ion channel
blockers as well as recombinant nerve growth factors
for the treatment of acute & chronic neurological
disorders); Diabetogen Inc. (biopharmaceutical
company focused on discovering & developing drugs
for the prevention & treatment of Type 1
diabetes)Exogen Neurosciences Inc. (biotechnology
company focusing on the development of novel medi-
cations for the treatment of nervous system diseases
& disorders); Geminx Biotechnologies Inc.
(Montreal-based company engaged in the discovery,
development & commercialization of novel therapeutics to treat diseases such as cancer, viral infections & neurodegeneration); HRG Health Resource
Group Inc. (Alberta-based company formed to
provide healthcare centres across Canada); ISG Technologies Inc. (designs, manufactures & sells through
original equipment manufactures, imaging software,
medical imaging work stations & tools for image
guided surgery); Mitokor, Inc. (developing novel
diagnostic & therapeutic products that address human
brain diseases using a science that involves a
biosystem comprised of a group of proteins found in
neurons which are critical to the management of their
function); Natraceuticals, Inc. (Toronto-based
company developing & marketing products in the
Canadian vitamin, nutritional supplement & home-
opathy markets); Neuro (NS) Inc. (funds early stage
proof-of-principal companies emerging from the
neuroscience community in Canada); Regenerx Inc.
(founded to make scientific developments in the area
of neuron regeneration & neurofilament research that
are important to a number of neurological disorders);
Stressgen Biotechnologies Corp. (focused on creating
therapeutic & vaccine pharmaceutical products
utilizing stress response proteins); Synapse Technologies Inc. (focused on the diagnostic & therapeutic
effects of a specific protein as it relates to Alzheimer's
disease); Terrapin Technologies, Inc. (developing a
proprietary enabling small molecule drug discovery
technology which provides a platform for both in-
house drug development & technology out-licensing
through multiple strategic coporate partnerships);
Triangle Pharmaceuticals, Inc. (biotechnology
company engaged in the development of new drug
candidates primarily in the antiviral area); T2C2
(focused on early stage seed investments in biotechnology & information technology); Urocor, Inc.
(provider of specialty clinical diagnostic & information services for urologists in the U.S.); Vascular
Therapeutics Inc. (developing proprietary biopharmaceuticals for the prevention, treatment &
management of acute & chronic life-threatening
vascular disorders); Xillix Technologies Corp.
(specializes in the redevelopment of medical imaging
devices for the localizing & detection of early stage
cancers)

Media Venture Partners

111 San Pablo Avenue
San Francisco, California 94127-1535
(415) 661-3818
Fax: (415) 661-2542
E-mail: JAYGARDNER@compuserve.com

Key contact:
Mr. James Gardner, Managing General Partner

Description: A fund specializing in media investments
(no movies). Particular emphasis on supplemental
education for children.

Preferred investment size: $250,000+

Amount under management: $25-100 million

Area served: North America

Preferred stages of financing: Seed, Start up, First
stage, Second stage, LBO/MBO, Expansion

Industries:
I.13   Education
I.16   Entertainment
I.28   Media/publishing
I.30   New media

Medicus Venture Partners

2882 Sand Hill Road, Suite 116
Menlo Park, California 94025-7057
(650) 854-7100
Fax: (650) 854-5700
E-mail: fred@medicusvc.com

Key contact:
Mr. Fred Dotzler, General Partner
Mr. John Reher, General Partner

Description: Our strategic focus is on the early stage
financing of medical companies based in the Western
U.S., particularly in California. Preferred areas of
interest include medical devices, biotechnology,
pharmaceuticals, drug delivery, diagnostic devices,
medical software, medical services and medical
instruments and equipment.

Preferred investment size: $500,000-2 million per round

Amount under management: $25-100 million

Area served: West Coast

Preferred stages of financing: Seed, Start up, First
stage

Industries:
I.03   Biotech/genetic engineering
I.20   Healthcare
I.26   Life sciences
I.29   Medical/medical products

Sampling of portfolio companies: Accumetrics, Inc.
(novel point of care diagnostics for cardiovascular/
hematology markets); Advanced Surgical Intervention, Inc. (single-use device used by gynecologists
& urologists to treat female urinary incontinence);
AGY Pharmaceuticals, Inc. (discovery of genes &
proteins involved in central nervous system disorders
as targets for small molecule therapeutics); Anergen
Corp. (novel biotherapeutics for autoimmune
diseases); Biomedical Ventures (incubator project
with IVP to originate an investment opportunity);
Gastrone Inc. (biomolecules for local treatment of
gastrointestinal disease); Guided Medical Systems
(steerable guiding systems for catheters used by
cardiologists & interventional neuroradiologists);
Hemosphere Inc. (patented microshpere technology
with initial product being an artificial platelet); Inhale
Therapeutic Systems (devices & pharmaceutical
formulations that will allow the delivery of biopharmaceuticals via inhalation); Laparomed Corp. (single
use devices for laparoscopic surgery); Medical Data
Int'l. (healthcare business information); Medical Data
Int'l. (healthcare business information);
MicroVention, Inc. (single use devices for interventional neuroradiology); Molecular Applications
Group (bioinformatics & modeling software for
macromolecules); Novamed (medical device
company); Point Medical (ultrasound contrast agent
& a drug delivery system); SenoRx, Inc. (novel
devices for performing diagnostic & therapeutic
breast biopsies); SmartTalk, Inc. (computer aided
telephony for medical applications); 2C Optics, Inc.
(novel polymer technology with applications in spec-
tacle lenses); Vitaphore Corp. (commercialized a
technology for incorporating antimicrobials into
biodegradable & biocompatible materials); Wellmark
Healthcare Services (in-home rehabilitation of
patients)

Menlo Ventures

3000 Sand Hill Road
Building Four, Suite 100
Menlo Park, California 94025
(650) 854-8540
Fax: (650) 854-7059
Web: www.menloventures.com

Key contact:
Mr. H. DuBose Montgomery, General Partner/
   Managing Member
Mr. Thomas H. Bredt, General Partner/Managing
   Member
Mr. Douglas C. Carlisle, General Partner/Managing
   Member
Mr. John W. Jarve, General Partner/Managing Member
Dr. Michael D. Laufer, General Partner/Managing
   Member
Ms. Sonja L. Hoel, General Partner/Managing Member

Description: We provide long-term capital and
management support to early stage and emerging
growth companies. We look for combinations of
management, capital, products or services and
market opportunity that create the potential for an
exceptional rate of return. Since our inception, we
have organized and managed seven funds with
combined investment capital of $710 million. Institu-
tional investors include pension funds, insurance
companies, corporations, commercial banks and
college endowment funds.

Founded: 1976

Amount of capital invested: $54 million

Preferred investment size: $250,000-6 million

Amount under management: $500 million -1 billion

Area served: United States

Preferred stages of financing: Seed, Start up, First
stage, Second stage, Mezzanine

Industries:
I.06   Communications
I.08   Computer software
I.20   Healthcare
I.23   Information technology services
I.24   Internet services/e-commerce
I.26   Life sciences

Sampling of portfolio companies: Clarify (software);
HNC Software (software); UUnet Technologies
(communications) Ascend Communications
(communications); Infoseek (internet); HotMail
(internet); Endovascular Technologies (medical
devices); Octel (communications); Gilead (medical
devices); Pixus (medical devices); IVAC (medical
devices)

Mentor Capital

1444 Foxworthy Avenue
San Jose, California 95118
(408) 269-3913
Fax: (408) 269-0103
E-mail: chester@mentorcapital.com
Web: mentorcapital.com

Key contact:
Mr. Chester Billingsley, President

Description: We are the acquisition arm of Main Street, AC, Inc., a public company.

Amount of capital invested: $19 million

Preferred investment size: $5 million

Amount under management: $10-25 million

Area served: Canada, United States

Preferred stages of financing: Mezzanine, Expansion

Industries:
I.02   Agriculture/forestry/fishing/mining
I.05   Chemicals
I.09   Construction
I.13   Education
I.18   Financial services
I.22   Industrial products
I.24   Internet services/e-commerce
I.27   Manufacturing
I.31   Real estate
I.37   Wholesale

Sampling of portfolio companies: 11 oil & gas partnership buyouts; 6 ATM partnership buyouts

Merrill Pickard Anderson & Eyre

2480 Sand Hill Road, Suite 200
Menlo Park, California 94025
(650) 854-8600
Fax: (650) 854-0345

Key contact:
Mr. Steven L. Merrill
Mr. James C. Anderson
Mr. Bruce W. Dunlevie
Ms. Kathryn C. Gould
Mr. W. Jeffers Pickard
Mr. Andrew S. Rachleff

Area served: West Coast

Preferred stages of financing: Seed, Start up, First stage, Second stage

Industries:
I.06   Communications
I.07   Computer hardware
I.08   Computer software
I.12   Distribution
I.14   Electronics
I.22   Industrial products

Middlefield Financial Services, Inc.

Two Embarcadero Center, Suite 200
San Francisco, California 94111-3834
(415) 835-1308
Fax: (415) 835-1350

Description: Formed in 1984, we are managed by Middlefield Ventures Limited. Investors include pension funds, insurance companies and other major financial institutions. Since inception, we have focused on identifying and investing in early stage companies with excellent earnings growth potential.

Founded: 1984

Area served: Worldwide

Preferred stages of financing: Seed, Start up, First stage

Industries:
I.18   Financial services

Sampling of portfolio companies: Gravure Int'l. Corp. (major producer of flexible packaging); Morrison Middlefield Resources Ltd.

MK Global Ventures

2471 East Bayshore Road, Suite 520
Palo Alto, California 94303
(650) 424-0151
Fax: (650) 494-2753

Key contact:
Mr. Michael Kaufman

Preferred stages of financing: Seed, First stage

Industries:
I.03   Biotech/genetic engineering

I.06   Communications
I.07   Computer hardware
I.08   Computer software
I.11   Consumer products
I.14   Electronics
I.19   Generalist
I.22   Industrial products
I.29   Medical/medical products
I.35   Services (consumer)

Mohr, Davidow Ventures

2775 Sand Hill Road, Suite 240
Menlo Park, California 94025
(650) 854-7236
Fax: (650) 854-7365
E-mail: bobh@mdv.com
Web: www.mdv.com

Key contact:
Ms. Nancy J. Schoendorf, General Partner
Mr. Jonathan D. Feiber, General Partner
Mr. Derek A. Proudian, General Partner
Mr. George Zachary, General Partner

Description: We are a venture capital firm that invests in early stage, west coast, high technology companies. Located in Menlo Park, California, we manage $375 million in committed capital. We advise entrepreneurs and help them build successful companies. We take an active role in helping entrepreneurs through the stages of creating a complete business.

Founded: 1983

Amount of capital invested: $37 million

Preferred investment size: Approximately 20% of company, usually $3-5 million

Amount under management: $100-500 million

Area served: North America, West of the Rockies

Preferred stages of financing: Seed, Start up, First stage, Second stage

Industries:
I.06   Communications
I.07   Computer hardware
I.08   Computer software
I.14   Electronics
I.21   High technology
I.23   Information technology services
I.24   Internet services/e-commerce
I.33   Semiconductors

Sampling of portfolio companies: Accoustic Imaging; Actuate Corp; Auspex; Avanto Performance Systems; C-ATs; Collabra; Chromatic Research; Employee Managed Care; Interventional Technologies; Invest Tools; Jetstream Communications; Kalpana; nChip; Net Positive; Point Cast; Rocket Science Games; Salutar Sierra Semiconductor; Neurobiological Technologies; Travel Net; ZoMed Int'l

JP Morgan Capital Corp.
101 California Street, 38th Floor
San Francisco, California 94111
(415) 954-4704
Fax: (415) 954-4737
Web: www.jpmorgan.com

Key contact:
Matt Niehaus

Description: We offer clients around the world a full range of integrated capabilities, which include capital raising, strategic advice, market access and asset management. Though we operate in a world that is more complex and faster paced than the one of our founders, our business principles remain those espoused by all three Morgans: integrity, objectivity and judgment.

Industries:
I.03   Biotech/genetic engineering
I.06   Communications
I.08   Computer software
I.11   Consumer products
I.12   Distribution
I.14   Electronics
I.29   Medical/medical products
I.32   Retail

Morgan Stanley Venture Partners
3000 Sand Hill Road
Building 4, Suite 250
Menlo Park, California 94025
(650) 233-2600
Fax: (650) 233-2626
E-mail: msventures@ms.com
Web: www.msventures.com

Key contact:
Mr. Robert J. Loarie, General Partner
Mr. William J. Harding, General Partner
Mr. Scott S. Halsted, General Partner
Mr. Jeffrey J. Booth, Vice President
Mr. John F. Ryan, Venture Associate
Ms. Grace Voorhis, Venture Associate
Mr. Patrick Gallagher, Venture Analyst

Description: We manage a group of funds which invest primarily in later-stage high growth companies, concentrating on the information technology and healthcare industries. Our goal is to help build successful companies, create wealth for entrepreneurs and generate superior returns for our investors.

Preferred investment size: $25 million

Industries:
I.06   Communications
I.08   Computer software
I.23   Information technology services
I.29   Medical/medical products

Sampling of portfolio companies: Anasazi Inc. (provides systems & services solutions to the hospitality & travel industry); Chip Express Corp. (developed a series of unique capabilities that allow customization of gate arrays outside of conventional fabs enabling faster time-to-market, significant flexibility & reduced production-costs); Chromatic Research, Inc. (supplier to the PC & consumer electronics industries with a new type of semiconductor technology for the multimedia age); Commerce One (software company); CSG Systems, Inc. (provider of customer management solutions for the converging communications markets of cable tv, direct broad cast satellite, telecommunications & on-line services industries); Evolving Systems, Inc. (provides software development & systems integration services for the automation of key network operation support systems & business support systems); interWAVE Communications, Inc. (developing low cost, digital micro cellular network equipment for the global marketplace); LioNBridge Technologies (provides a full range of localization services to the information technology industry); Neuron Data, Inc. (application development tools for building dynamically scalable enterprise business solutions); PageMart Wireless, Inc. (paging company); Persistence Software, Inc. (object-to-relational application development systems); Precept Software, Inc. (develops & markets standards-based network video applications for the entire enterprise); SemiPower Systems, Inc. (designs & manufactures highly integrated modules & complete drives for controlling AC induction motors used in a wide variety of applications); TelCom Semiconductor, Inc. (designs, manufactures & sells linear semiconductors); Visioneer, Inc. (develops & markets products that provide the fastest & easiest way to get paper into computers & put that paper to work); Cambridge Heart, Inc. (developing non-invasive diagnostic products for the cardiology marketplace); Cytyc Corp. (develops & markets a sample preparation system for medical diagnostic applications); Enterprise Systems, Inc. (reduces the cost of delivering healthcare by developing, implementing & supporting an integrated suite of resource management software solutions); Intuitive Surgical Instruments, Inc. R2 Technology, Inc. (developed a computer-aided diagnostic system for mammograms)

Morgenthaler Ventures

2730 Sand Hill Road, Suite 280
Menlo Park, California 94025
(650) 233-7600
Fax: (650) 233-7606
Web: www.morgenthaler.com

Key contact:
Mr. Gary J. Morgenthaler, General Partner
Mr. Robert C. Bellas, Jr., General Partner
Mr. Gary R. Little, Partner
Mr. G. Gary Shaffer, Partner
Mr. John D. Lutsi, Management Buyout Team
Mr. Peter G. Taft, Management Buyout Team
Mr. Theodore A. Laufik, Management Buyout Team
Ms. Karen L. Tuleta, Management Buyout Team

Description: We are passionately dedicated to being the most valued partner to world-class entrepreneurs building industry-leading enterprises. We have been an active company builder since 1968, funding more than 150 companies, two-thirds of which are now public entities. We focus on early stage investments in information technology and healthcare as well as later stage management-led buyouts.

Founded: 1968

Preferred investment size: $2-8 million

Area served: United States

Preferred stages of financing: Seed, Start up, LBO/MBO

Industries:
I.03   Biotech/genetic engineering
I.06   Communications
I.08   Computer software
I.14   Electronics
I.20   Healthcare
I.24   Internet services/e-commerce
I.29   Medical/medical products

Sampling of portfolio companies: Amati (ADSL modems); NBX Corp. (IP-based network PBX); Chrysalis (formal verification of IC's); SDRC (mechanical CAD); Illustra (object-relational DBMS); Vision Software (java-based business automation platform); Vivo (video streaming); Apple Computer (personal computers); Endgate (wireless broadband radio modules); Vitesse (gallium arsenide IC's); Athena Neurosciences (pharmaceuticals for neurological diseases); Molecular Applications Group (data mining software for genomics); Ribozyme Pharmaceuticals (RNA-based pharmaceuticals for human disease); Vical (DNA-based pharmaceuticals for human disease); Arbor Health Care (skilled nursing & subacute care centers); Medaphis (business management services for hospitals/physicians); AneuRx (stent grafts for abdominal aortic aneurysms); Embol-X (devices to protect the brain from stroke); NeuroControl (devices for the treatment of neuromuscular disorders)

National Corporate Finance, Inc.

2082 Southeast Bristol, Suite 203
Newport Beach, California 92660
(949) 756-2006
Fax: (949) 756-0611
E-mail: srabago@compuserve.com

Key contact:
Mr. Steven R. Rabago, CEO

Description: We are a merchant banking firm that provides strategic and leadership advisory services and makes direct investments into business in several industries. We particularly like to buy majority interests in family or closely held business that can be used as a platform for other acquisitions. We charge fees and receive equity.

Preferred investment size: $7 million

Area served: West

Preferred stages of financing: LBO/MBO, Expansion, Turnaround

Industries:
I.05   Chemicals
I.06   Communications
I.10   Consulting
I.11   Consumer products
I.12   Distribution
I.13   Education
I.15   Energy/natural resources/utilities
I.17   Environmental services/waste management
I.18   Financial services
I.19   Generalist
I.22   Industrial products
I.23   Information technology services
I.24   Internet services/e-commerce
I.25   Leisure/hospitality
I.26   Life sciences
I.27   Manufacturing
I.28   Media/publishing
I.31   Real estate
I.32   Retail
I.34   Services (business)
I.35   Services (consumer)
I.36   Transportation
I.37   Wholesale

Needham & Company, Inc.

3000 Sand Hill Road
Building Two, Suite 190
Menlo Park, California 94025
(650) 854-9111
Fax: (650) 854-9853

Key contact:
Chad W. Keck, Managing Director

Description: We are a full service New York-based
specialty investment bank, which serves emerging
growth companies and their institutional investors
with equity trading, sales, research and corporate
finance services. Needham Capital Partners II is the
long-term equity investment affiliate of Needham &
Company. The fund is a long-term investor in the
private equities of private "mezzanine" stage companies and smaller public emerging growth companies.
The investment focus is on companies in the technology, healthcare and specialty retail industries.

Preferred investment size: $2-4 million

Amount under management: $100-500 million

Area served: United States

Preferred stages of financing: Mezzanine, LBO/MBO

Industries:

I.06	Communications
I.07	Computer hardware
I.08	Computer software
I.11	Consumer products
I.14	Electronics
I.20	Healthcare
I.21	High technology
I.22	Industrial products
I.23	Information technology services
I.24	Internet services/e-commerce
I.27	Manufacturing
I.29	Medical/medical products
I.32	Retail
I.33	Semiconductors

Sampling of portfolio companies: College Enterprises,
Inc. (operates a chain of retail copying, duplicating,
image processing & communication technology
service stores on college campuses throughout the
country); Obsidian, Inc. (developing an advanced
chemical mechanical polishing tool for semiconductor wafers with demonstrated process advantages
& cost effectiveness); Carrier Access Corp.
(develops, manufactures & markets T-1 digital tele-
communcations access products for local carrier
bypass); Cutter & Buck, Inc. (designs men's
sportswear apparel marketed in golf pro shops, resorts
& upscale specialty stores); Calileo Technology, Ltd.
(designs & markets complex semiconductor devices
for high-performance embedded control systems,
principally in the area of data communications);
IMNET Systems, Inc. (develops, markets, installs &
services electronic information & document
management systems for the healthcare industry &
other document intensive businesses); Lids Corp.
(rapidly growing chain of "category-killer" hat
stores); SeaMED Corp. (designs & manufactures
advanced durable electronic & medical instruments
for medical technology companies); WorldGate
Communications, Inc. (start-up cable service that
allows cable operators to offer low cost, fast & simple
access to the internet); U.S. Vision, Inc. (optical
retailer, sells prescription eyewear, contact lenses,
eye exams & services for fitting custom lenses to
eyeglass frames); JT Storage, Inc. (manufactures
small, high-capacity disk drives); InterVentional
Technologies, Inc. (develops, manufactures &
markets invasive disposable microsurgical devices &
systems for the treatment of cardiovascular disease);
Zydacron, Inc. (designs, manufactures & markets a
family of hardware & software products for low cost,
desktop PC videoconferencing); WaferScale Inter-
gration, Inc. (designs, develops & produces high-
programmable VLSI Products, including an innovative portfolio of programmable microcontroller
peripherals); Ramp Networks, Inc. (develops &
markets connectivity products for small workgroups
that allow such groups to seamlessly connect to the
internet while establishing a local area network); Rise
Technology Co., Inc. (designing high-performance,
low-powered X86-compatible microprocessors);
Patient Infosystems, Inc. (provides patient-centered
healthcare information systems that proactively
collect & analyze information to improve patient
compliance with prescribed treatments); PACE
Health Management Systems, Inc. (develops &
markets advanced clinical software which automates
the recording, storage & management of patient care
information); Digital Arts & Sciences Corp.
(develops & distributes graphically oriented software
for the management of inventories & collections of
objects, where images are an integral element); Rosti
(chain of primarily take-out Italian restaurants that is
expanding out of the Los Angeles area)

New Enterprise Associates

2490 Sand Hill Road
Menlo Park, California 94025
(650) 854-9499
Fax: (650) 854-9397
Web: www.nea.com

235 Montgomery Street, Suite 920
San Francisco, California 94104
(415) 352-1520
Web: www.nea.com

Key contact:
Mr. Frank A. Bonsal, Jr., Founding Partner
Mr. Ryan D. Drant, Associate
Mr. Ronald H. Kase, General Partner
Mr. Charles M. Linehan, Partner

Mr. Thomas C. McConnell, General Partner
Mr. John M. Nehra, General Partner
Mr. Charles W. Newhall, III, Co-Founder/ General
  Partner
Dr. Sigrid Van Bladel, Ph.D., Partner
Mr. Stewart Alsop, Venture Partner
Mr. Peter J. Barris, General Partner
Mr. Robert T. Coneybeer
Ms. Suzanne Hooper
Mr. C. Richard Kramlich, Co-Founder/General Partner
Mr. Arthur J. Marks, General Partner
Mr. Peter T. Morris, General Partner
Mr. Mark W. Perry, General Partner
Mr. Scott D. Sandell
Ms. Nora M. Zietz, Partner/Director of Research

Ms. Nancy Dorman, General Partner
Mr. Lou Van Dyck, CFO
Ms. Ann Wilson, Director of Administration & HR

Description: We are one of the industry's premier venture capital firms. For 19 years we have practiced classic venture capital by investing in early-stage companies and working with management to nurture and build companies of real and lasting value. We are now the leading start-up venture investor in the country.

Founded: 1978

Preferred investment size: $500,000-6 million

Preferred stages of financing: Seed, Start up, First stage

Industries:
I.03	Biotech/genetic engineering
I.06	Communications
I.08	Computer software
I.14	Electronics
I.20	Healthcare
I.23	Information technology services
I.24	Internet services/e-commerce
I.26	Life sciences
I.29	Medical/medical products
I.33	Semiconductors

Sampling of portfolio companies: AnueRx, Inc. (develops, manufactures & markets products for the emerging endovascular surgery market); CaRDiMa, Inc. (medical devices for nonsurgical interventions to study, treat & cure electrophysiological disorders); EndoVasix, Inc. (proprietary technology using sound waves delivered through a small fiber to break up blood clots); Optical Sensors Inc. (fiber optic sensor technologies for diagnostic applications in medical & surgical intensive care situations); Transvascular, Inc. (minimally invasive therapeutic alternatives); AutoImmune, Inc. (pharmaceuticals to treat autoimmune diseases by inducing tolerance to autoantigens); Microcide Pharmaceuticals (antimicrobial agents for human bacterial & fungal infections); Scriptgen Pharmaceuticals (drugs that alter gene expression for the treatment of infectious diseases); ElderHealth, Inc. (adult day care centers & services); Domain Solutions Corp. (develops & sells software solutions that help companies optimize their processes to deliver higher quality products to market faster); Ascend Communications, Inc. (data communication products connecting computers to ISDN); Tripod, Inc. (provides digital services on the internet for college students); Alteon Networks, Inc. (complete gigabit ethernet switching system delivering a 50% increase in server & backbone performance at less than the cost of comparable high speed alternatives); Fibex Systems (integrated, flexible & scaleable access platform for the existing & emerging local exchange services market); Pathnet, Inc. (provides microwave incumbent relocation services required by the emergence of PCS services); Datalogix Int'l. (process manufacturing software for food & chemical industries); Financial Engines, Inc. (uses technology & modern portfolio theory to deliver high quality, objective, consistent & prudent investment advice to the individual investor);ObjectShare, Inc. (object-oriented applications development tools for the client-server market); Giga-tronics, Inc. (microwave & RF signal generation & power measurement instruments); Vitesse Semiconductor Corp. (gallium arsenide digital intetgrated circuits for the computer, telecom & defense electronics markets)

Newtek Ventures

500 Washington Street, Suite 720
San Francisco, California 94111
(415) 986-5711
Fax: (415) 986-4618

Key contact:
Mr. John E. Hall
Mr. Peter J. Wardle

Area served: West Coast

Preferred stages of financing: Seed, First stage

Industries:
I.03	Biotech/genetic engineering
I.06	Communications
I.07	Computer hardware
I.08	Computer software
I.14	Electronics
I.17	Environmental services/waste management
I.29	Medical/medical products
I.34	Services (business)
I.35	Services (consumer)

Norwest Venture Partners

245 Lytton Avenue, Suite 250
Palo Alto, California 94301
(650) 321-8000
Fax: (650) 321-8010
E-mail: phaque@norwestvc.com
Web: www.norwestvc.com

Key contact:
Mr. Promod Haque, Partner
Mr. George J. Still, Jr., Partner
Mr. Kevin G. Hall, Partner
Mr. Ernie C. Parizeau, Partner
Mr. John P. Whaley, Partner

Description: We manage about $1 billion in investment funds and are focused on venture capital investments in emerging growth companies in the information technology sector (enterprise software, internet, communications infrastructure equipment, subscriber based businesses & electronics).

Amount of capital invested: $88 million

Preferred investment size: $5 million

Amount under management: >$1 billion

Area served: United States

Preferred stages of financing: Seed, Start up, First stage, Second stage, Mezzanine

Industries:
I.06	Communications
I.08	Computer software
I.14	Electronics
I.18	Financial services

I.23   Information technology services
I.24   Internet services/e-commerce
I.33   Semiconductors

Sampling of portfolio companies: Brocade Communication Systems, Inc. (fibre channel switching products); PID, Inc. (batch process automation software); Maker Communications, Inc. (programmable communications chips for cell & frame-based internetworking); Quadritek Systems, Inc. (internet name management for the enterprise); Comcore Semiconductor, Inc. (physical layer access chips for high speed data communications); Framework Technologies Corp. (project management application for complex architecture, engineering & construction); Silicon Access Technology, Inc. (design libraries &

compilers for integrated circuit design); Docent, Inc. (internet-based training application software); Annuncio Software, Inc. (enterprise marketing automation software); VIA Internet (international provider of internet services); Verio (nat'l. ISP consolidator); Serviceware (authors resolution content for help desks); BUCA (family style Italian cuisine); Nashoba Networks (token ring switching hubs); Una Mas (freshly prepared Mexican cantina); Telops Management (network element interface management); Implant Center (outsourcer of implant services for semiconductors); First Floor (web-based agent applications); 2800 Corp. (consumer goods); Streamfeeder (specialty machining equipment)

Novus Ventures, LP

20111 Stevens Creek Boulevard, Suite 130
Cupertino, California 95014
(408) 252-3900
Fax: (408) 252-1713
E-mail: ddtompkins@aol.com

Key contact:
Mr. Dan Tompkins
Ms. Shirley Cerrudo

Area served: West

Preferred stages of financing: First stage, Second stage

Industries:
I.06   Communications
I.07   Computer hardware
I.08   Computer software
I.14   Electronics
I.19   Generalist

Nth Power Technologies, Inc.

100 Spear Street, Suite 1450
San Francisco, California 94105
(415) 974-1668
Fax: (415) 974-0608
Web: www.nthfund.com

Key contact:
Ms. Nancy C. Floyd, Managing Partner
Mr. Maurice E. P. Gunderson, Principal
Mr. Mason Willrich, Principal
Ms. Robin R. Galer, Director

Description: We are a venture capital firm dedicated to growing businesses in the energy industry. Our investment philosophy is to provide working capital to entrepreneurs that can capitalize on the exploding need for strategic tools within the deregulating energy industry. Our utility partners are primarily electric and gas utilities who intend to profit financially and strategically by our portfolio companies.

Founded: 1992

Preferred investment size: $2-5 million

Amount under management: $25-100 million

Area served: United States

Preferred stages of financing: Start up, First stage, Second stage

Industries:
I.06   Communications
I.14   Electronics
I.15   Energy/natural resources/utilities
I.17   Environmental services/waste management
I.21   High technology
I.23   Information technology services

Oak Investment Partners

525 University Avenue, Suite 1300
Palo Alto, California 94301
(650) 614-3700
Fax: (650) 328-6345
Web: www.oakinv.com

Key contact:
Mr. Bandel Carano, General Partner
Mr. Fred Harman, General Partner

Description: We are a venture capital organization dedicated to helping new enterprises emerge as tomorrow's industry leaders. We were founded in 1978 and have organized seven partnerships with over $1 billion of capital under management. We have three areas of investment focus: information technology, healthcare and retail. We target experi-

enced, entrepreneurial management teams that are resourceful, disciplined and motivated by appropriate incentives.

Founded: 1978

Preferred investment size: $4-20 million

Preferred stages of financing: Seed, Start up

Industries:
I.06   Communications
I.08   Computer software
I.23   Information technology services
I.33   Semiconductors

Sampling of portfolio companies: Actel (develops, manufactures & markets Field Programmable Gate Array solutions); Cephalon; Compaq Computer Corp. (manufactures & markets advanced PC's for business

& professional use); Filene's Basement; Genzyme; HBO & Co.; Network Equipment Technologies, Inc. (communications equipment which enables the building & management of private backbone networks); Octel Communications Corp. (designs, manufactures & markets voice processing systems that are sold primarily to large corporate customers, telephone companies & other providers of Voice Information Services); Office Depot; Parametric Technology Corp. (develops, markets & supports a family of fully integrated parametric feature-based mechanical design automation software); PETsMART; PictureTel (provides high quality, full-color, full-motion video communications at bandwidths commensurate with the new digital, dial-up telephone services being introduced worldwide); Seagate Technology (manufactures & markets Winchester magnetic rigid disk drives for incorpo-ration in minicomputer & microcomputer systems); Stratus (designs, manufactures, markets & services a family of fault tolerant Continuous Processing Systems for critical on-line transaction processing & communications control); SanDisk Corp. (develops & markets solid state non-volatile memory cards & boards for the laptop & portable PC market, as well as other portable communication devices using sophisticated flash E2PROM technology); Sybase, Inc. (develops & markets SYBASE SQL Server); Synopsys, Inc. (produces synthesis products that are complementary to established computer aided engineering tools & run on a broad range of UNIX platforms including those of SUN Microsystems, Apollo & DEC); Ungerman-Bass; Wellfleet (supplies high-performance, full functionality LAN internet working products & systems); Wholefoods

Omega Ventures
(BancAmerica Robertson Stephens)
555 California Street, 26th Floor
San Francisco, California 94104
E-mail: Omega@rsco.com

Key contact:
Mr. Michael J. Stark, Managing Director
Mr. Sy Kaufman, Managing Director
Mr. Anthony P. Brenner, Managing Director
Mr. Vladimir Jacimovic, Principal

Description: Deriving our name from Omega, the last letter of the Greek alphabet, we intend to be the final investor in a company prior to an acquisition or initial public offering and provide the support and infrastructure to help the emerging growth company prepare for this liquidity event. We are one component of BancAmerica Robertson Stephens' Investment Management Group.

Founded: 1980

Preferred investment size: $3-7 million

Industries:
I.06   Communications

I.08   Computer software
I.14   Electronics
I.26   Life sciences
I.34   Services (business)
I.35   Services (consumer)

Sampling of portfolio companies: Broderbund Software, Inc. (software); Insignia Solutions (software); Voyan Technology (software); Appex (communications); Applied Digital Access, Inc. (communications); Radish Communications, Inc. (communications); Shomiti Systems, Inc. (communications); TeleCruz Technology, Inc. (electronics); CBT Group PLC (business services); J3 Learning Corp. (business services); Abgenix, Inc. (healthcare/life sciences); Balanced Care Corp. (healthcare/life sciences); Cyto Therapeutics, Inc. (healthcare/life sciences); DeVilbiss Health Care, Inc. (healthcare/life sciences); MedicaLogic, Inc. (healthcare/life sciences); CompUSA, Inc. (consumer); Dick's Clothing & Sporting Goods (consumer); Petstuff, Inc. (consumer); Matrix Service Co.; Opta Food Ingredients, Inc.

ONSET Ventures
2490 Sand Hill Road
Menlo Park, California 94025
(650) 529-0700
Fax: (650) 529-0777
E-mail: menlopark@onset.com

Key contact:
Mr. Robert F. Kuhling, Jr., General Partner
Mr. Terry L. Opdendyk, General Partner
Mr. Thomas E. Winter, General Partner
Ms. Darlene K. Mann, Venture Partner
Ms. Susan A. Mason, Associate

Description: We are a venture capital firm that helps entrepreneurs who have unique ideas build productive, profitable companies. We specialize in working with start-ups in information, communications and medical technologies, providing essential guidance and support during the crucial period from concept to company- from the genesis of your idea until it becomes a vital business enterprise.

Founded: 1984

Preferred stages of financing: Seed, Start up, First stage

Industries:
I.06   Communications
I.08   Computer software
I.29   Medical/medical products

Sampling of portfolio companies: Alteon Networks (focusing on the application of gigabit ethernet technology to increase the performance, scalability & availability of servers & multi-server applications in inter/intranet computing environments); Arcot Systems (developing innovative security software solutions for the world wide web); BusLogic (supplier of high-performance SCSI solutions for use in personal computers, workstations & file servers); Clarify (provides client-server software & services to automate & enhance technical support in companies that market complex systems or technology-based products); Euphonix (develops & manufactures computer-based systems to bring digital sound mixing, editing, automation & integration to professional recording studios); Gadzoox Networks (designs, manufactures & markets gigabit connectivity solutions for the server-storage network based on fiber channel standards); ichat (develops software tools & applications enabling real-time communication within internet or corporate intranet world wide web sites); NeTpower (develops computer workstations for high performance applications on Windows NT environments); Packeteer (produces bandwidth management solutions for TCP/IP networks to optimize network bandwidth allocation across users & applications, match content delivery to connection speed & report on customer experience); Pathnet (builds new, high-capacity digital microwave communications networks by partnering with existing utility, railroad & pipeline companies operating private networks); TallyUp Software (developing client-server intranet applications for improving the effectiveness of sales force operations & administration); Voysys Corp. (produces general purpose, OEM-programmable voice computers for voice-processing applications); AngioTrax (develops novel medical devices for cardiac revascularization); Arcturus Engineering (develops sophisticated laboratory instruments to enable genetic research, diagnostics & drug discovery); Cardima (develops electrophysiology mapping & ablation systems for cardiac rhythm disorders); Endocardial Solutions (develops proprietary mapping systems for ventricular arrhythmias); Inhale Therapeutic Systems (develops & manufactures non-invasive pulmonary drug delivery systems in partnership with pharmaceutical companies); LocalMed (develops innovative cardiovascular catheter systems for improved angioplasty outcomes); Penederm (develops & markets novel dermatologic pharmaceuticals using proprietary transdermal drug delivery technology); Spinal Concepts, Inc. (develops & markets a family of novel implant devices for internal spinal fixation which are used in a wide variety of spinal surgeries including the treatment of degenerative disc disease & spinal stenosis)

Opportunity Capital Corp.
2201 Walnut Avenue, Suite 210
Fremont, California 94538
(510) 795-7000
Fax: (510) 494-5439

Key contact:
Mr. J. Peter Thompson

Area served: West Coast

Preferred stages of financing: Second stage, LBO/MBO, Third/later stage

Industries:
I.04   Broadcasting
I.06   Communications
I.20   Healthcare
I.27   Manufacturing
I.29   Medical/medical products

Oxford Ventures
650 Town Center Drive, Suite 810
Costa Mesa, California 92626
(714) 754-5719
Fax: (714) 754-6802
Web: www.oxbio.com

Key contact:
Mr. Edmund Olivier, General Partner

Description: We are an independent venture capital firm that provides equity financing and management assistance to start-up and early-stage, entrepreneurial-driven companies in the bioscience and healthcare industries. Our partners currently manage venture funds with combined committed capital of more than $150 million. Our objective is to generate long-term capital gains for both the investors in the fund and the entrepreneurs that we support.

Amount of capital invested: $25 million

Preferred investment size: $2 million

Amount under management: $100-500 million

Area served: Asia, Europe, United States

Preferred stages of financing: Seed, Start up, First stage, Second stage

Industries:
I.03   Biotech/genetic engineering
I.20   Healthcare
I.26   Life sciences
I.29   Medical/medical products

Sampling of portfolio companies: Argomed, Ltd. (minimally invasive, catheter-based treatment for benign prostate hyperplasia); Arrow Corp. (pharmacy management services company); Biocode, Inc. (immunoassay-based product marking systems to detect counterfeiting & smuggling in pharmaceuticals & consumer & industrial products); BioScreen (qualitative gene expression analysis for drug discovery); Cardiopulmonary Corp. (computer controlled patient ventilators for the intensive care unit); Cellomics (high throughput, cell-based screening systems for drug discovery); Ceres, Inc. (agricultural bioscience); Coelacanth (development & manufacturer of novel building blocks for combinatorial chemistry systems); Cytologix, Inc. (automated slide preparation systems for the pathology laboratory); EVAX Technologies GmbH (bacterial-based vaccines for animal & human diseases); GuideStar Health Systems (managed care company providing insurance products to indemnity insurers); Inkine Pharmaceuticals (pharmaceuticals for treatment of cancer & infectious diseases); Memory Pharmaceuticals (pharmaceuticals to restore long-term potentiation of memory); Micromed Technology (left ventricular assist device for congestive heart failure); NetGenics, Inc. (bioinformatics software to manage genomics research programs); Orchid Biocomputer (nanotechnology-based drug discovery systems); Phase I (high throughput toxicology testing services); Physiome Sciences, Inc. (computer-based, physiological models of human organs for drug discovery & evaluation); Variagenics, Inc. (drug discovery & evaluation based on pharmacogenomics)

Pacific Mezzanine Fund, L.P.

2200 Powell Street, Suite 1250
Emeryville, California 94608
(510) 595-9800
Fax: (510) 595-9801
E-mail: nwb@pacmezz.com

Key contact:
Mr. Nathan W. Bell, Partner
Mr. David C. Woodward, Partner
Mr. Andrew B. Dumke, Partner

Description: We are a provider of mezzanine capital to mid-sized companies seeking expansion, recapitalization or buyout financing in the amounts of $2 - 4 million.

Amount of capital invested: $15 million

Preferred investment size: $3 million

Amount under management: $25-100 million

Area served: United States

Preferred stages of financing: Mezzanine, LBO/MBO, Expansion

Industries:
I.01   Aerospace
I.04   Broadcasting
I.05   Chemicals
I.06   Communications
I.07   Computer hardware
I.08   Computer software
I.11   Consumer products
I.12   Distribution
I.14   Electronics
I.16   Entertainment
I.17   Environmental services/waste management
I.20   Healthcare
I.21   High technology
I.22   Industrial products
I.23   Information technology services
I.24   Internet services/e-commerce
I.27   Manufacturing
I.28   Media/publishing
I.29   Medical/medical products
I.32   Retail
I.34   Services (business)
I.35   Services (consumer)

Sampling of portfolio companies: Dataworks (manufacturing software); Valtron (disk drive repair); Ingredients Int'l. (neutrecutical distribution); Relax the Back (specialty retail); Portrait Displays Inc. (monitor software); JJ Norths (restaurant chain); Guerdom Homes (mobile home manufacturing & sales); Packaging Store (retail mail & shipping); Global Personnel Services (temporary employees & leasing) Pinnacle Respond (ATM management); TTI (wireless cable)

Pacific Mezzanine Investors

610 Newport Center Drive, Suite 1100
Newport Beach, California 92660
(949) 721-9944
Fax: (949) 721-5446

Key contact:
Mr. Robert Bartholomew, Principal
Mr. Schuyler G. Lance, Principal

Description: We are a private junior capital investment firm that manages PMI Mezzanine Fund, LP, a private investment partnership. We invest in all layers of junior capital, including subordinated debt, convertible securities, preferred equity and common equity.

Preferred investment size: $10-20 million

Amount under management: $100-500 million

Area served: North America

Preferred stages of financing: Mezzanine, LBO/MBO, Expansion

Industries:
I.01   Aerospace
I.05   Chemicals
I.06   Communications
I.08   Computer software
I.10   Consulting
I.11   Consumer products
I.12   Distribution
I.13   Education
I.14   Electronics
I.15   Energy/natural resources/utilities
I.16   Entertainment
I.17   Environmental services/waste management
I.18   Financial services
I.19   Generalist
I.20   Healthcare
I.22   Industrial products
I.23   Information technology services
I.25   Leisure/hospitality
I.26   Life sciences
I.27   Manufacturing
I.28   Media/publishing
I.29   Medical/medical products
I.34   Services (business)
I.35   Services (consumer)
I.36   Transportation
I.37   Wholesale

Sampling of portfolio companies: Nebraska Book Co., Inc. (leading used textbook wholesaler & retail operator for the college bookstore industry); Details, Inc. (premier quick-turn, short-run manufacturer of complex circuit boards); Corrections Corp. of America (private corrections management firm); AmeriKing (franchisee of Burger King restaurants); Twin Laboratories, Inc. (manufacturer of vitamins, supplements & sports nutrition products); Sleepmaster, LLC (manufacturer of Serta® brand mattresses & box springs); Applause Enterprises, Inc.; Buttrey Food & Drug (supermarket chain in Montana); Kemet Electronics (manufacturer of capacitors); Carr Gottstein Foods Co. (food retailer in Alaska); The Delfield Co. (supplier of custom food service refrigeration equipment); Velda Farms Inc. (producer & distributor of dairy products in Southern Florida); Smarte Carte, Inc. (operator of airport baggage cart rentals); Save Mart Supermarkets (supermarket chain in Central California); Cable Design Technologies (manufacturer of wire & cable for electronic applications); Suiza Food Holdings, Inc. (dairy in Puerto Rico); Nationwide Care, Inc. (operator of nursing homes in Indiana); Wirekraft (independent manufacturer of wire & harnesses for the automobile & appliance industries); America's Best Contacts & Eyeglasses, LP (discount retailer of eyeglasses & contact lenses)

Pacific Venture Group

16830 Ventura Boulevard, Suite 244
Encino, California 91436
(818) 990-4141
Fax: (818) 990-6556
E-mail: lcrouch@pacven.com
Web: www.pacven.com

Key contact:
Mr. Layton R. Crouch, Managing Partner
Ms. Eve M. Kurtin, Managing Partner

15635 Alton Parkway, Suite 230
Irvine, California 92618
(714) 753-0490
Fax: (714) 753-8932
E-mail: rsabin@pacven.com
Web: www.pacven.com

Key contact:
Mr. Ralph C. Sabin, Managing Partner

3000 Sand Hill Road
Building 1, Suite 275
Menlo Park, California 94025
(415) 854-7000
Fax: (415) 854-7260
E-mail: jslewis@pacven.com
Web: www.pacven.com

Key contact:
Mr. John S. Lewis, Managing Partner

Description: Our objective is to identify, create and invest in business opportunities in healthcare services and information systems that have high growth and profit potential where the managing partners can augment capital investment with their knowledge, insight, experience and vision, and combine these characteristics with similarly inclined entrepreneurs to build a true win-win outcome.

Founded: 1995

Area served: United States

Preferred stages of financing: Start up, LBO/MBO, Turnaround

Industries:
I.20   Healthcare

Sampling of portfolio companies: ACCESS Radiology (provider of teleradiology systems & support services utilizing leading edge compression technologies); Channel Point (internet-based distribution utility that facilitates the marketing of health plans); DAOU Systems, Inc. (healthcare services focused systems company that provides networking services including network management & consulting, systems integration & implementation & outsourcing); Hilife Inc. (technology-enabled supported self care case management company focused on improving chronic disease outcomes through systematic patient monitoring, early intervention & behavior modification); Kelson (physician practice management company acquiring & providing management & practice enhancement services to primary care pediatric physician groups); LTCG (long term care & self insured administration company with TPA, underwriting & sales abilities); MasterCare (managed care workers' compensation insurance company providing services in the states of New Jersey, New York, Pennsylvania & Connecticut); MaterniCare, Inc. (physician practice management company focusing on the full spectrum of women's healthcare needs from adolescence through maturity); Meridian Occupational Healthcare Assocs., Inc. (specialized occupational healthcare company developing an integrated network of on-site & free-standing occupational medicine clinics providing managed care services); Perigon Medical Distribution Corp. (medical supply & distribution company acquiring & providing management services to providers of products & services to physicians, long term care & alternate site providers); Point-of-Care Systems, Inc. (healthcare information data capture system focused on point-of-care data capture for the home healthcare industry); Uniphy Healthcare, Inc (multispecialty physician practice management company acquiring & providing management & practice enhancement services to practice groups in second tier geographical markets); UroTherapies, Inc. (single specialty physician practice management company acquiring & providing management & practice enhancement services to urology physician groups with an emphasis on the deployment of leading edge clinical technologies used in treating urological diseases)

Paragon Venture Partners

3000 Sand Hill Road
Building 1, Suite 275
Menlo Park, California 94025
(650) 854-8000
Fax: (650) 854-7260

Key contact:
Mr. John Lewis
Mr. Robert F. Kibble

Preferred stages of financing: Seed, First stage, Sec-

ond stage, Third/later stage

Industries:
I.06   Communications
I.07   Computer hardware
I.08   Computer software
I.14   Electronics
I.29   Medical/medical products
I.34   Services (business)
I.35   Services (consumer)

Partech International

50 California Street, Suite 3200
San Francisco, California 94111

(415) 788-2929
Fax: (415) 788-6763

Key contact:
Mr. Thomas G. McKinley, Founding Partner
Mr. Vincent R. Worms, Founding Partner
Mr. Philippe Cases
Mr. David L. Sherry, Jr., Portfolio Manager
Mr. Glenn Solomon
Mr. Scott Matson, CFO

Description: Venture capital firm with worldwide experience and focus. Our charter is to make equity investments in pioneering high growth companies at all stages of development from seed to last round as well as in public stage companies. We endeavor to assist companies in their development, with a focus on leveraging our integrated networks in Europe, Asia and the United States.

Founded: 1982

Preferred investment size: $500,000-4 million

Area served: Worldwide

Preferred stages of financing: Seed, Start up, First stage, Second stage, Mezzanine

Industries:
I.06   Communications
I.20   Healthcare
I.23   Information technology services
I.26   Life sciences
I.34   Services (business)

Sampling of portfolio companies: Biolink (medical device); Newfire (VRML technology); Informatica (data warehousing); Star Telecommunications (int'l. telecommunications); Apogee (network management); Breezecom (Israeli wireless communication); Avmax; Biovector Therapeutics; ConsenSys Software; Flamel Technologies; Heartstream; Insite Vision; Lynx Therapeutics; MagiNet; Medicode; Pixtech; Softway Systems; Staffing Resources; Urosurge; Wincap

---

Pathfinder Venture Capital Funds
3000 Sand Hill Road
Building One, Suite 290
Menlo Park, California 94025
(650) 854-0650
Fax: (650) 854-4706

Key contact:
Mr. Eugene J. Fischer
Ms. Barbara L. Santry

Preferred stages of financing: Seed, Start up, First stage, Second stage, LBO/MBO

Industries:
I.06   Communications
I.07   Computer hardware
I.08   Computer software
I.14   Electronics
I.19   Generalist
I.29   Medical/medical products

Patricof & Company Ventures, Inc.
2100 Geng Road, Suite 150
Palo Alto, California 94303
(650) 494-9944
Fax: (650) 494-6751
Web: www.patricof.com

Key contact:
Ms. Janet G. Effland
Mr. George D. Phipps
Mr. Paul A. Vais
Ms. Adele C. Oliva
Mr. Jason K. Yotopoulos

Description: We are a leading international private equity investment firm that together with our international affiliate, Apax Partners, manages over $3.4 billion on behalf of major institutional investors in the U.S. and abroad. With over twenty-five years of direct investing experience, we provide long-term equity financing to build companies. We have a solid reputation as a leader in the industry and as an innovative, value-added investor.

Preferred investment size: $5-25 million

Area served: Worldwide

Preferred stages of financing: Start up, First stage, LBO/MBO, Expansion, Recapitalizations

Industries:
I.06   Communications
I.07   Computer hardware
I.08   Computer software
I.11   Consumer products
I.14   Electronics
I.18   Financial services
I.20   Healthcare
I.22   Industrial products
I.23   Information technology services
I.27   Manufacturing
I.29   Medical/medical products
I.30   New media
I.32   Retail
I.34   Services (business)

Sampling of portfolio companies: Spec Group, Inc. (provides technicians, specialists, programmers & professionals for a wide range of staff augmentation, inspection, training & technical consulting services for utility, industrial, commercial & government customers); Johnny Rockets Group, Inc. (restaurant chain featuring a 1950's diner concept); Protection One, Inc. (provides residential monitoring alarm services); CapMAC Holdings (pioneered the commercial monoline financial guarantee business); RBMG Resource Bancshares Corp. (specialty asset gatherer utilizing a banking depository license in South Carolina); Centocor Inc. (healthcare company specializing in the development & commercialization of therapeutic & diagnostic products to meet critical human healthcare needs); Dura Delivery Systems, Inc. (developed a proprietary drug delivery system called the Dryhaler); Bolder Technologies Corp. (developed a new generation of rechargeable, sealed, lead acid batteries); Biocompatibles plc (commercializes a biocompatible coating material for ophthalmic & medical device coating applications); Atcom (primary provider to telephone companies & others of kiosks allowing public access to the internet; provider of high-speed data ports for travelers who want T-1 access from their laptops); Fore Systems, Inc. (designer, developer & manufacturer of high-performance, networking products based on asynchronous transfer mode technology); Rendition, Inc. (fab-less semiconductor company building integrated 2-D/3-D accelerator chips for PCs); Tessera, Inc. (semiconductor packaging technology company); Audible, Inc. (launched its pocket-sized device that holds up to 2 hours of spoken word audio & can play it back either over a car radio or headphones); Medscape (internet site for healthcare professionals); planet U (on-line consumer promotions, including coupons, rebates & sampling); Sunglass Hut Corp. (mall-based specialty retail concept selling a variety of fashion eyewear); Office Depot (retailer of office supplies); Park 'N View, Inc. (provides cable TV & telephone services to truck drivers in their cabs at truck stops); Xpedite Systems, Inc. (provider of enhanced fax services)

Peregrine Ventures

20833 Stevens Creek Boulevard, Suite 102
Cupertino, California 95014
(408) 996-7212
Fax: (408) 996-7232

Key contact:
Mr. Frank LaHaye
Ms. Helen Smith-MacKenzie

Area served: West

Preferred stages of financing: First stage, LBO/MBO

Industries:
I.03   Biotech/genetic engineering
I.06   Communications
I.08   Computer software
I.14   Electronics
I.29   Medical/medical products
I.34   Services (business)
I.35   Services (consumer)

Positive Enterprises, Inc.

1489 Webster Street, Suite 228
San Francisco, California 94115
(415) 885-6600
Fax: (415) 928-6363

Key contact:
Mr. Kwok Szeto, President

Area served: West Coast

Preferred stages of financing: Start up, First stage, Second stage, Third/later stage

Industries:
I.20   Healthcare
I.27   Manufacturing

Power Project Financing

508 San Anselmo Avenue
Suite 1A, Cheda Building
San Anselmo, California 94960
(415) 721-7012
Fax: (415) 721-7356
E-mail: ppf@slip.net
Web: www.slip.net/~ppf

Key contact:
Mr. Daniel A. Potash, Managing Partner

Description: Financing electric power plants and advising and privatization.

Amount of capital invested: $89 million

Preferred investment size: $25 million

Amount under management: $100-500 million

Area served: Worldwide

Preferred stages of financing: Start up, First stage, Second stage, Energy project finance

Industries:
I.15   Energy/natural resources/utilities
I.17   Environmental services/waste management

Premier Medical Partner Fund L.P.

12225 El Camino Real
San Diego, California 92130
(619) 481-2727
Fax: (619) 481-8919

Key contact:
Mr. Richard P. Kuntz
Mr. Palmer B. Ford

Area served: United States

Preferred stages of financing: Start up, First stage, Expansion, Third/later stage

Industries:
I.03   Biotech/genetic engineering
I.20   Healthcare

Quest Ventures

126 South Park
San Francisco, California 94107
(415) 546-7118
Fax: (415) 243-8514

Key contact:
Mr. Lucien Ruby
Mr. William A. Boeger, III

Area served: West

Preferred stages of financing: Seed, First stage

Industries:
I.03   Biotech/genetic engineering
I.06   Communications
I.07   Computer hardware
I.08   Computer software
I.11   Consumer products
I.14   Electronics
I.29   Medical/medical products
I.34   Services (business)
I.35   Services (consumer)

Recovery Equity Investors, L.P.
901 Mariners Island Boulevard, Suite 465
San Mateo, California 94404
(650) 578-9752
Fax: (650) 578-9842

Key contact:
Mr. Joseph Finn-Egan
Mr. Jeffrey Lipkin

Area served: United States

Industries:
I.06   Communications
I.11   Consumer products
I.12   Distribution
I.15   Energy/natural resources/utilities
I.27   Manufacturing
I.29   Medical/medical products
I.34   Services (business)
I.35   Services (consumer)

Redleaf Venture Management
14395 Saratoga Avenue, Suite 130
Saratoga, California 95070
(408) 868-0800
Fax: (408) 868-0810
E-mail: info@redleaf.com
Web: www.redleaf.com

Key contact:
Mr. John Kohler, Principal
Mr. Russ Aldrich, Principal

Description: We are a seed & early stage fund engaged
with information technology firms developing software solutions for business to business commerce.
We are an operationally oriented investment firm &
take an active role in all of our portfolio.

Amount of capital invested: $5 million

Preferred investment size: $1-2 million

Amount under management: $10-25 million

Area served: Silicon Valley, CA; Portland, OR; Seattle, WA; Vancouver, BC

Preferred stages of financing: Seed, Start up

Industries:
I.06   Communications
I.07   Computer hardware
I.08   Computer software
I.21   High technology
I.24   Internet services/e-commerce

Sampling of portfolio companies: Netgravity (internet
advertising); Wireless Online; Redcreek Communications (data encryption for virtual private nets);
Mediaseek Technologies (educational software for
teachers/parents); Infoscape (java-based tracking &
management applications); Semio (visually-based
information retrieval technology); Moai Technologies (business-to-business auction software)

Redwood Partners
3000 Sand Hill Road, Building 4, Suite 230
Menlo Park, California 94025
(650) 854-8077
Fax: (650) 854-4961
E-mail: jtimmins@rdwd.com

Key contact:
Mr. John Savage, Managing Director
Mr. Jim Timmins, Managing Director

Description: We are a venture firm which concentrates
on information technology companies from startup
through buyouts.

Amount of capital invested: $12 million

Preferred investment size: $5 million

Amount under management: $25-100 million

Area served: North America

Preferred stages of financing: Start up, First stage,
Second stage, Mezzanine, LBO/MBO

Industries:
I.01   Aerospace
I.04   Broadcasting

I.06   Communications
I.07   Computer hardware
I.08   Computer software
I.10   Consulting
I.12   Distribution
I.14   Electronics
I.16   Entertainment
I.17   Environmental services/waste management
I.21   High technology
I.22   Industrial products
I.23   Information technology services
I.24   Internet services/e-commerce
I.27   Manufacturing
I.33   Semiconductors
I.34   Services (business)

Sampling of portfolio companies: OrCAD (EDA
software for PC's); Video 7 (graphics & multimedia
products); Microtec (real time OS software); Artias
(workflow automation software); Magellan
(handheld GPS navigation systems); Mattson (semiconductor processing equipment); Paradigm (fast
SRAMs); Iwerks Enterntainment (high tech theater
systems)

Robertson Stephens-Omega Ventures
555 California Street, Suite 2600
San Francisco, California 94104
(415) 693-3492
Fax: (415) 676-2556
Web: omegaventures.com

Key contact:
Mr. Michael Stark, Managing Director
Mr. Sy Kaufman, Managing Director
Mr. Tony Brenner, Managing Director
Mr. Vladimir Jacimovic, Principal

Description: Late stage venture capital

Preferred investment size: $3-7 million

Amount under management: $100-500 million

Area served: Worldwide

Preferred stages of financing: Second stage, Mezzanine, LBO/MBO, Expansion, Int'l expansion

Industries:
I.03   Biotech/genetic engineering
I.06   Communications
I.07   Computer hardware
I.08   Computer software
I.10   Consulting
I.11   Consumer products
I.12   Distribution
I.13   Education
I.14   Electronics
I.15   Energy/natural resources/utilities
I.17   Environmental services/waste management
I.18   Financial services
I.19   Generalist
I.20   Healthcare
I.21   High technology
I.24   Internet services/e-commerce
I.26   Life sciences
I.27   Manufacturing
I.29   Medical/medical products
I.30   New media
I.33   Semiconductors
I.34   Services (business)
I.35   Services (consumer)

Sampling of portfolio companies: Broderbund Software, Inc. (software); Insignia Solutions (software); Voyan Technology (software); Appex (communications); Metapath Software Corp. (communications); Radish Communications, Inc. (communications); Shomiti Systems, Inc. (communications); TeleCruz Technology, Inc. (electronics); Visioneer Communications, Inc. (electronics); CBT Group PLC (business services); J3 Learning Corp. (business services); MemberWorks Inc. (business services); Abgenix, Inc. (healthcare/life sciences); Balanced Care Corp. (healthcare/life sciences); COR Therapeutics, Inc. (heatlhcare/life sciences); DeVilbiss Health Care, Inc. (healthcare/life sciences); CompUSA, Inc. (consumer); Dick's Clothing & Sporting Goods (consumer); Petstuff, Inc. (consumer); Matrix Service Co. (other)

Arthur Rock & Company

One Maritime Plaza, Suite 1220
San Francisco, California 94111
(415) 981-3921
Fax: (415) 981-3924
E-mail: a.rocksf@prodigy.com

Key contact:
Mr. Arthur Rock
Ms. Katherine Styles

Area served: West Coast

Preferred stages of financing: Seed, First stage, LBO/MBO

Industries:
I.06   Communications
I.07   Computer hardware
I.08   Computer software
I.14   Electronics
I.29   Medical/medical products
I.33   Semiconductors

Rosewood Capital, LLC

One Maritime Plaza, Suite 1330
San Francisco, California 94111-3503
(415) 362-5526
Fax: (415) 362-1192
Web: www.rosewoodvc.com

Key contact:
Mr. Byron Adams, Principal
Mr. Kyle Anderson, Principal
Mr. Doug Valenti, Principal

Description: We are a private equity partnership that invests in consumer-oriented growth companies. We look for small to mid-sized emerging growth companies in the branded consumer products, retail and consumer services sectors, including online commerce.

Amount under management: $100-500 million

Area served: United States

Preferred stages of financing: First stage, Second stage, Mezzanine, Expansion

Industries:
I.11   Consumer products
I.13   Education
I.24   Internet services/e-commerce
I.25   Leisure/hospitality
I.32   Retail

I.35   Services (consumer)

Sampling of portfolio companies: AllApartments.com (internet-based provider of apartment rental searches & related products & services to consumers); Gateway Learning Corp. (developed & markets the popular "Hooked on Phonics"® reading program); Jamba Juice (offers fruit smoothies, juices, healthy foods & related products in a high quality setting); Napa Valley Kitchens (manufacturer & marketer of branded gourmet food products); Noah's New York Bagels (chain of upscale bagel stores located throughout the San Francisco Bay area, Los Angeles & other west coast markets); Rainbow Light Nutritional Systems (manufacturer & marketer of branded products in the fast growing nutritional supplement segment); Rubio's Restaurants (upscale, quick service Mexican restaurant category); Sutton Place Gourmet (sells a variety of specialty foods along with hearty home meal replacement items)

San Joaquin Business Investment Group Inc.

1900 Mariposa Mall, Suite 100
Fresno, California 93721
(209) 233-3580
Fax: (209) 233-3709

Key contact:
Mr. Eugene Waller

Area served: West Coast

Preferred stage of financing: Later stage

Industries:
I.19   Generalist

Sanderling Ventures

2730 Sand Hill Road, Suite 200
Menlo Park, California 94025-7067
(650) 854-9855
Fax: (650) 854-3648

Key contact:
Ms. Marilyn Cornel
Dr. Robert G. McNeil, Ph.D.

Mr. Fred A. Middleton

Preferred stages of financing: Seed, First stage

Industries:
I.03   Biotech/genetic engineering
I.05   Chemicals
I.29   Medical/medical products

Sandton Financial Group

21550 Oxnard Street, #300
Woodland Hills, California 91367
(818) 702-9283

Key contact:
Mr. Lawrence J. Gaiber, President

Description: Venture capital firm. Contact us by telephone prior to mailing your business plan.
Thereafter, we will indicate our interest level to you
in writing.

Preferred investment size: Up to $10 million

Area served: North America

Preferred stages of financing: Seed, Start up, First
stage, Case by case basis

Seacoast Capital Partners, LP

One Sansome Street, Suite 2100
San Francisco, California 94104
(415) 956-1400
Fax: (415) 956-1459
E-mail: jjhol@msn.com

Key contact:
Mr. Jeffrey J. Holland, Partner

Description: We are an investment firm dedicated to
providing mezzanine and equity capital for middle
market companies. Founded by the principals of
Signal Capital Corporation and Itel Corporation, we
are the successor to Signal Capital's merchant
banking group, which successfully invested over
$400 million of capital since 1986. We are
committed to investing across a broad spectrum of
industries from our offices in Boston and San
Francisco.

Amount of capital invested: $50 million

Preferred investment size: $2-6 million

Amount under management: $100-500 million

Area served: Canada, United States

Preferred stages of financing: Mezzanine, Expansion,
Int'l expansion

Industries:
I.01   Aerospace
I.02   Agriculture/forestry/fishing/mining
I.04   Broadcasting
I.05   Chemicals
I.06   Communications
I.08   Computer software

I.10   Consulting
I.11   Consumer products
I.12   Distribution
I.13   Education
I.14   Electronics
I.16   Entertainment
I.17   Environmental services/waste management
I.19   Generalist
I.20   Healthcare
I.21   High technology
I.22   Industrial products
I.23   Information technology services
I.24   Internet services/e-commerce
I.25   Leisure/hospitality
I.27   Manufacturing
I.28   Media/publishing
I.29   Medical/medical products
I.30   New media
I.32   Retail
I.34   Services (business)
I.35   Services (consumer)
I.36   Transportation
I.37   Wholesale

Sampling of portfolio companies: All Seasons Services,
Inc. (vending services); City Sports, Inc. (special
retailing); Community Rehab Centers, Inc. (physical
therapy clinics); Global Personnel Services, Inc.
(temporary staffing); Labor Ready, Inc. (temporary
staffing); Mearthane Products Corp. (specialty manufacturing); Metalico, Inc. (metal recovery company);
Microcom Technologies (electronics distribution);
New England Audio (specialty retailing); Overland
Trading Co. (specialty retailing); Radar Extermi-

nating Co., Inc. (pest control services); Specialty Agricultural Products, Inc. (agricultural products manufacturing)

Sequoia Capital

3000 Sand Hill Road
Building Four, Suite 280
Menlo Park, California 94025
(415) 854-3927
Fax: (415) 854-2977
E-mail: sequoia@sequoiacap.com

Key contact:
Mr. Pierre Lamond, Partner
Mr. Douglas Leone
Mr. Tom Stephenson
Mr. Don Valentine
Mr. Michael Goguen
Mr. Michael Moritz
Mr. Gordon Russell
Mr. Mark Stevens
Dr. Tom McMurray, Ph.D.
Ms. Barbara Russell, Partnership Administrator
Ms. Melinda Dunn, Controller

Description: We don't pretend to know all the answers, but we frequently know someone who might have an answer or can help. That's why we take pains to make sure that all our new investments can benefit from the associations accumulated since we were started in 1972. We and our extensive set of contacts provide a range of support for young, private companies at any stage of their development.

Founded: 1972

Area served: West Coast

Preferred stages of financing: Seed, Start up, First stage

Industries:
I.03 Biotech/genetic engineering
I.06 Communications
I.08 Computer software
I.14 Electronics
I.20 Healthcare
I.24 Internet services/e-commerce
I.29 Medical/medical products
I.33 Semiconductors
I.34 Services (business)
I.35 Services (consumer)

Sampling of portfolio companies: Sierra (communications); Cisco Systems (internetworking); Global Village (remote access); CellNet (wireless); Magellan (wireless); Cohesive (carriers/cable); Auspex (enterprise servers); Yahoo! (internet); Visigenic (intranet); Oracle (databases); Infinity (applications); Tandon (peripherals); Quickturn Design (EDA); Valid Logic (EDA); Flextronics (services); Fusion (medical devices); Regen Biologics (medical devices); Biotrack (diagnostics); Glycomed (biotechnology); Oxford Health (services)

Shad Run Investments

P.O. Box 470730
San Francisco, California 94147
(415) 885-6400
Fax: (415) 929-6286

Key contact:
Ms. Sara Hendrickson

Area served: United States

Preferred stage of financing: Second stage

Industries:
I.06 Communications
I.11 Consumer products
I.18 Financial services
I.34 Services (business)
I.35 Services (consumer)

Sierra Ventures

3000 Sand Hill Road
Building 4, Suite 210
Menlo Park, California 94025
(650) 854-1000
Fax: (650) 854-5593
E-mail: info@sierraven.com

Key contact:
Mr. Jeffrey M. Drazan, General Partner
Mr. David C. Schwab, General Partner
Dr. Petri Vainio, General Partner
Mr. Peter C. Wendell, General Partner
Dr. James B. Tananbaum, Venture Partner

Description: A private venture capital firm, we focus our investments on early stage healthcare, information technology-related companies and service businesses. As active lead investors, we work with entrepreneurs and management teams to originate and build new companies into large and profitable businesses.

Area served: West Coast

Preferred stages of financing: Seed, Start up, First stage, Second stage

Industries:
I.03 Biotech/genetic engineering
I.20 Healthcare
I.23 Information technology services
I.26 Life sciences
I.29 Medical/medical products

Sampling of portfolio companies: Advanced Medicine, Inc. (healthcare); Clinical Partners, Inc. (healthcare); EndoVasix, Inc. (healthcare); GenVec, Inc. (healthcare); Healtheon Corp. (healthcare); Intensiva Healthcare Corp. (healthcare); NovaMed Eyecare Management Corp. (healthcare); RiboGene (healthcare); TherOx (healthcare); VenPro Inc. (healthcare); Active Software, Inc. (information technology); Avatar Solutions Inc. (information technology); Candescent Technologies, Inc. (information technology); DAS Devices, Inc. (information technology); FaxSav, Inc. (information technology); iMarket, Inc. (information technology); Production

Group Int'l., Inc. (information technology); SecureSoft, Inc. (information technology); Terayon Corp. (information technology); Vina Technologies, Inc. (information technology)

Sigma Partners

2884 Sand Hill Road, Suite 121
Menlo Park, California 94025
(650) 854-1300
Fax: (650) 854-1323
Web: www.sigmapartners.com

Key contact:
Mr. Clifford L. Haas
Mr. J. Burgess Jamieson
Mr. C. Bradford Jeffries
Mr. Wade Woodson
Mr. Lawrence Finch

Description: We are a privately held venture capital partnership organized in 1984 to make equity investments in businesses which offer favorable opportunity for significant growth in size and value. We have a history of successful investing in entrepreneurial companies. Currently, we manage four funds with combined capital of over $300 million.

Founded: 1984

Area served: United States

Preferred stages of financing: Seed, Start up

Industries:
I.06   Communications
I.07   Computer hardware
I.08   Computer software
I.23   Information technology services
I.29   Medical/medical products
I.33   Semiconductors

Sampling of portfolio companies: Cerulean Technology, Inc. (communications/networking); Vivo Software, Inc. (communications/networking); Kofax Image Products, Inc. (hardware/peripherals); Paradise Electronics, Inc. (semiconductor related); Datasage, Inc. (software); Frequency Technology, Inc. (software); NetFactory, Inc. (software); Vignette Corp. (software); R2 Technology, Inc. (medical); Chipcom Corp. (communications/networking); OnStream Networks, Inc. (communications/networking); Xyplex, Inc. (communications/networking); Micro Linear Corp. (semiconductor related); Tylan General, Inc. (semiconductor related); Aviva Sport, Inc.; Atria Software, Inc. (software); Personal Training Systems (software); STAC Electronics (software); ElectroScan Corp. (hardware/peripherals); Qualstar Corp. (hardware/peripherals)

Silicon Valley Bank

3003 Tasman Drive
Santa Clara, California 95054
(408) 654-7400
Fax: (408) 727-8728
Web: www.sivb.com

Key contact:
Mr. John C. Dean, President/CEO
Mr. Don Cvietusa

Description: We serve emerging growth and middle-market companies in specific targeted niches, focusing on the technology and life sciences industries, while also identifying and capitalizing on opportunities to serve companies in other industries whose financial services needs are underserved.

Area served: United States

Preferred stages of financing: First stage, Second stage

Industries:
I.03   Biotech/genetic engineering
I.06   Communications
I.08   Computer software
I.14   Electronics
I.23   Information technology services
I.29   Medical/medical products

Sampling of portfolio companies: ACT Networks Inc.; Avanti Corp.; Business Resource Group; Datalogix Int'l. Inc.; Documentum Inc.; Firefox Communications; Global Village Communications; Harmonic Lightwaves; Intelliquest Inc.; Lumysis

William E. Simon & Sons, L.L.C.

10990 Wilshire Boulevard, Suite 500
Los Angeles, California 90024
(310) 914-2410
Fax: (310) 575-3174

Key contact:
Mr. Robert W. McDonald
Mr. Henry J. Brandon
Mr. Michael B. Lenard
Mr. William E. Simon, Jr.
Mr. James R. Worms

Area served: United States

Preferred stages of financing: Second stage, Mezzanine, LBO/MBO

Industries:
I.04   Broadcasting
I.09   Construction
I.11   Consumer products
I.15   Energy/natural resources/utilities
I.16   Entertainment
I.17   Environmental services/waste management
I.22   Industrial products
I.31   Real estate
I.34   Services (business)
I.35   Services (consumer)
I.36   Transportation

SOFTBANK Technology Ventures
333 West San Carlos, Suite 1225
San Jose, California 95110
(408) 271-2265
Fax: (408) 271-2270
Web: www.sbvc.com

Key contact:
Mr. Gary E. Rieschel, Executive Managing Director
Mr. Matthew A. Ocko, Managing Director
Mr. E. Scott Russell, Managing Director
Mr. Ronald D. Fisher, Vice Chairman
Mr. Bradley A. Feld, Managing Director
Mr. Charles R. Lax, Managing Director

Description: We make privately negotiated equity and
equity-related investments in companies attempting
to capitalize on opportunities in digital information
technology, including internet communications,
commerce and content. We are affiliated with SOFT-
BANK Holdings Inc., a subsidiary of SOFTBANK
Corporation.

Founded: 1981

Area served: Worldwide

Industries:
I.08   Computer software
I.24   Internet services/e-commerce
I.35   Services (consumer)

Sampling of portfolio companies: 911 Entertainment
(software & information); Electric Communities
(software & information); Fastparts Inc. (business
services); Fourth Communications Network
(business services); GeoCities (software & information); Internet Profiles Corp. (software & information); SaveSmart (software & information); Third
Age Media Inc. (software & information); VStream
Inc. (communications); Zip2 (software & information)

Sorrento Associates, Inc.
4370 La Jolla Village Drive, Suite 1040
San Diego, California 92122
(619) 452-3100
Fax: (619) 452-7607
Web: sorrentoventures.com

Key contact:
Mr. Robert M. Jaffe, President
Mr. Vince Burgess, Vice President

Description: Provide development and expansion
capital to emerging growth businesses in the
computer, communications, healthcare (medical
devices and biotechnology) and specialty retail
industries in the San Diego and Southern California
region.

Founded: 1985

Preferred investment size: $3-5 million

Amount under management: $100-500 million

Area served: San Diego, United States

Preferred stages of financing: Start up, First stage,
Second stage, Mezzanine

Industries:
I.03   Biotech/genetic engineering
I.06   Communications
I.07   Computer hardware
I.08   Computer software
I.11   Consumer products
I.12   Distribution
I.23   Information technology services
I.24   Internet services/e-commerce
I.26   Life sciences
I.29   Medical/medical products
I.30   New media
I.32   Retail
I.33   Semiconductors

South Bay Capital Corporation
5325 East Pacific Coast Highway
Long Beach, California 90804
(562) 597-3285
Fax: (562) 498-7167

Key contact:
Mr. Ken Okajima
Mr. John Wang

Sprout Group
3000 Sand Hill Road
Building 3, Suite 170
Menlo Park, California 94025
(650) 234-2700
Fax: (650) 234-2779

Key contact:
Mr. Keith Geeslin, General Partner

Description: Venture capital affiliate of Donaldson,
Lufkin & Jenrette with more than $1.8 billion of
aggregate committed capital. Over our 28 year
history, we have made investments in nearly 300
companies whose revenues todat exceed $40 billion.
We invest in all stages (from start ups through

buyouts) in high growth areas such as information
technology, medical products and services, business
services and retail.

Amount of capital invested: $163 million

Preferred investment size: $5-50 million

Amount under management: >$1 billion

Area served: North America, South/Central America

Preferred stages of financing: Seed, Start up, First
stage, Second stage, Mezzanine, LBO/MBO, Expansion

Industries:
I.01   Aerospace

I.03   Biotech/genetic engineering
I.08   Computer software
I.10   Consulting
I.12   Distribution
I.13   Education
I.14   Electronics
I.18   Financial services
I.20   Healthcare
I.21   High technology
I.23   Information technology services
I.24   Internet services/e-commerce
I.26   Life sciences
I.29   Medical/medical products

I.30   New media
I.32   Retail
I.33   Semiconductors
I.34   Services (business)
I.35   Services (consumer)
I.37   Wholesale

Sampling of portfolio companies: Corporate Express (office products, wholesale); Staples (office products, retail); Edison Project (education); SDL (semiconductor laser diodes); Norand (handheld computers); Sequana (genomics); IDEC Pharmaceuticals (biotherapeutics); GTECH (on-line lottery networks)

St. Paul Venture Capital

3 Lagoon Drive, Suite 130
Redwood City, California 94065
(650) 596-5630
Fax: (650) 596-5711
Web: www.stpaul.com

Key contact:
Mr. Patrick A. Hopf, Managing General Partner
Mr. Everett Cox, General Partner
Mr. Frederic Boswell, General Partner
Mr. Brian D. Jacobs, General Partner
Mr. Michael Gorman, Partner
Ms. Nancy S. Olson, General Partner
Mr. James R. Simons, General Partner
Mr. Zenas Hutcheson, General Partner
Mr. Carl Witonsky, Venture Partner
Mr. John Rollwagen, Venture Partner
Ms. Katherine Carney, CFO

Description: We are a rock solid venture capital partnership, built on a foundation of time-honored values with a culture characterized by progressive ideas and strategies. That may not sound dramatically different from some other venture firms, but the differences are in the details.

Founded: 1988

Area served: United States

Preferred stages of financing: Seed, Start up, First stage

Industries:
I.08   Computer software
I.11   Consumer products
I.20   Healthcare
I.23   Information technology services
I.27   Manufacturing
I.29   Medical/medical products
I.32   Retail
I.34   Services (business)
I.35   Services (consumer)

Sampling of portfolio companies: Airgonomics (air-adjustable sofabeds to be marketed by Select Comfort); Command Audio (radio programming on demand); DIVA (movies on demand or supercomputing at $3.95/slice); Flycast (marketplace for buying & selling internet ad space); HeartStent (revascularization medical device); PCI (enhanced communications services for teens); St. Paul Software (enabling software for EDI over the internet); Vivo Software (software tools for applications of streaming media); Biopsys (designs & manufactures products for the diagnosis & treatment of breast cancer); Cardiac Pathways (designs, develops & manufactures products for the therapeutic intervention of electrical problems of the heart); Cardiometrics (develops, manufactures & markets intravascular medical devices to measure blood flow impairment caused by coronary artery disease)

Stream USA

633 Battery Street, Suite 640
San Francisco, California 94111
(415) 399-6558
Fax: (415) 399-6565
Web: www.streamusa.com

Key contact:
Mr. Martino Ajmone Marsan, President
Mr. Alex Nigg, Vice President
Mr. Fabio A. Spinella, Vice President

Description: Our essential goal is to facilitate the introduction of new telecommunications, internet and multimedia products and services to Italy and to foster the growth of the internet and new media market in Italy. We identify and build strategic relationships with internet and new media companies in Silicon Valley; seek to gain an in-depth knowledge of key products, services and technology; help to establish operations and introduce innovative products and services in Italy and Europe.

Area served: Europe, United States

Preferred stage of financing: Int'l expansion

Industries:
I.08   Computer software
I.23   Information technology services
I.24   Internet services/e-commerce
I.28   Media/publishing
I.30   New media

Sampling of portfolio companies: Concentric Network Corp. (provider of virtual private networks & consumer internet access services); Protozoa (real-time, 3-D character animation software company); Efusion (provider of internet application gateways)

Summit Partners

499 Hamilton Avenue, Suite 200
Palo Alto, California 94301
(650) 321-1166
Fax: (650) 321-1188
Web: www.summitpartners.com

Key contact:
Mr. Gregory M. Avis, Managing Partner
Mr. Walter G. Kortschak, General Partner

Description: We understand the challenges of building
a successful company. Since our founding in 1984,
we have been the fastest growing private investment
firm in the country. Our growth has taught us about
the value of hard work and innovation, striving
against odds and following a dream.

Founded: 1984

Preferred stages of financing: Mezzanine, LBO/MBO

Industries:
I.06   Communications
I.08   Computer software
I.18   Financial services
I.20   Healthcare
I.23   Information technology services
I.29   Medical/medical products

Sampling of portfolio companies: Avalon Software
(software); Hyperion Software (software); Protel-
licess (software); Digital Link (networking &
communications); Proteon (networking & communications); A+ Network (communications); Octocom
Systems (communications); CMG Information
Services (information services); Boca Research
(peripherals, systems & components); American
Laboratory Assoc. (healthcare/medical services);
Pediatrix Medical Group (healthcare/medical
services); ImageAmerica (healthcare/medical
services); SteriGenics Int'l. (healthcare/ medical
services); Employee Benefit Plans (managed care);
Arlington (funeral homes consolidation); Wilmar
Industries (catalog maintenance products); Cap Note
Holdings (financial services); Providential Home
Income Plan (financial services); Clean Harbors
(environmental services); PACE Laboratories (envi-
ronmental services)

Sutter Hill Ventures

755 Page Mill Road, Suite A-200
Palo Alto, California 94304-1005
(650) 493-5600
Fax: (650) 858-1854

Key contact:
Mr. David L. Anderson, General Partner
Mr. G. Leonard Baker, Jr., General Partner
Mr. Tench Coxe, CEO
Mr. Paul M. Wythes, General Partner
Mr. William H. Younger, Jr., General Partner
Ms. Cherryl W. Hossack, CFO

Description: Silicon Valley firm established in 1962
working at early stage and start-up levels.

Founded: 1962

Area served: United States

Preferred stages of financing: Seed, Start up, First
stage

Industries:
I.03   Biotech/genetic engineering
I.06   Communications
I.08   Computer software
I.12   Distribution
I.14   Electronics
I.20   Healthcare
I.22   Industrial products
I.27   Manufacturing
I.29   Medical/medical products

TA Associates, Inc.

70 Willow Road, Suite 100
Menlo Park, California 94025
(650) 328-1210
Fax: (650) 326-4933
E-mail: info@ta.com

Key contact:
Mr. Jeffrey T. Chambers, Managing Director
Mr. Michael C. Child, Managing Director
Mr. Kurt R. Jaggers, Managing Director

Description: For nearly three decades, we have
provided equity capital and knowledgeable assistance to talented entrepreneurs to help them pull
ahead of their competition and build companies of
significant value.

Founded: 1968

Preferred investment size: $10-100 million

Preferred stages of financing: Start up, First stage,
LBO/MBO, Turnaround

Industries:
I.03   Biotech/genetic engineering
I.08   Computer software
I.14   Electronics
I.15   Energy/natural resources/utilities
I.17   Environmental services/waste management
I.18   Financial services
I.20   Healthcare
I.23   Information technology services
I.34   Services (business)

Sampling of portfolio companies: Auto Palace
(consumer products & services); Federal Express
(consumer products & services); Jenny Craig, Inc.
(consumer products & services); Smith Alarm
Systems (consumer products & services); AIM
Management Group (financial services); Affiliated
Managers Group (financial services); Keystone
Group (financial services); Mutual Risk Management
(financial services); Boron LePore (healthcare
services); CompDent Corp. (healthcare services);
Copley Pharmaceutical (healthcare services); Gulf
South Medical Supply (healthcare services);
Preferred Payment Systems (healthcare services);
Bachtel Cellular Liquidity, LP (media & communica-
tions); Continental Cablevision, Inc. (media &

communications); Galaxy Telecom, LP (media & communications); TSR Wireless (media & communications); ANSYS, Inc. (software & technology); Axent (software & technology); Hummingbird (software & technology)

TechFund Capital

111 West Evelyn Avenue
Sunnyvale, California 94086
(408) 720-7080
Fax: (408) 720-7090
E-mail: inbox@techfundcapital.com
Web: www.techfundcapital.com

Key contact:
Mr. Kurt Keilhacker, Managing Partner
Mr. Gordon Campbell, Managing Partner
Mr. James Whims, Managing Partner

Description: We are an early stage venture capital firm focused on semiconductors, software and networking technologies.

Amount of capital invested: $20 million

Preferred investment size: $2 million

Amount under management: $100-500 million

Area served: Asia, North America

Preferred stages of financing: Seed, Start up, First stage

Industries:
I.07   Computer hardware
I.08   Computer software
I.24   Internet services/e-commerce
I.33   Semiconductors

Sampling of portfolio companies: Coactive Networks (networking technology); Resonate (software); Veland (software); N*Able (e-commerce); Cobalt Microserver (networking technology); Pico Networks (networking technology); Paraform (software); Adaptivity (software); Multitude (software); Possidon (semiconductors); Quantum 3D (systems)

Technology Crossover Ventures

575 High Street, Suite 400
Palo Alto, California 94301
(650) 614-8200
Fax: (650) 614-8222
E-mail: webmaster@tcv.com
Web: www.tcv.com

Key contact:
Mr. Jay C. Hoag, General Partner
Mr. Richard H. Kimball, General Partner
Mr. Marc S. Tesler, General Partner
Mr. Robert C. Bensky, General Partner/CFO

Description: We focus exclusively on information technology, investing in expansion-stage private enterprises as well as select public situations.

Amount of capital invested: $37.4 million

Preferred investment size: $3-5 million

Amount under management: $100-500 million

Area served: Worldwide

Preferred stage of financing: Expansion

Industries:
I.06   Communications

I.07   Computer hardware
I.08   Computer software
I.14   Electronics
I.16   Entertainment
I.18   Financial services
I.21   High technology
I.24   Internet services/e-commerce
I.28   Media/publishing
I.30   New media
I.33   Semiconductors
I.34   Services (business)

Sampling of portfolio companies: Duet Technologies (provider of electronic design technology & networking software development services for high technology companies); IMX Mortgage Exchange (worldwide immediate access to mortgage origination products via a high speed private network); iVillage Women's Network (humanizing cyberspace & providing a relevant & indispensable online experience for adult women); Lynk Systems (merchant processor of credit & debit card transactions); Smart-Patents (developer of business decision software systems that automate the process of relating patents to protected business & product strategies)

Technology Funding

2000 Alameda de las Pulgas, Suite 250
San Mateo, California 94403
(650) 345-2200
Fax: (650) 345-1797
Web: www.techfunding.com

Key contact:
Mr. Charles R. Kokesh, Managing General Partner
Mr. Gregory George, General Partner
Mr. Frank Pope, General Partner
Mr. Peter F. Bernardoni, Venture Partner
Mr. Thomas J. Toy, Managing Director-Corporate Finance

Ms. Debbie A. Wong, Vice President-Finance & Administration
Mr. Charles E. Freeman, Treasurer
Mr. Jody M. Sherman, Vice President

Description: We are a Silicon Valley-based professional venture capital firm. We pioneered and continue to be the leader in public venture funds. Since 1979, we have raised more than $315 million in capital, financed over 230 emerging growth companies, helped 60 portfolio companies go public and managed 11 separate public funds with over 42,000 individual investors.

Founded: 1979

Preferred investment size: $750,000-2.5 million

Amount under management: $100-500 million

Industries:
I.23   Information technology services
I.29   Medical/medical products

Sampling of portfolio companies: Pilot Networks (ensures you can connect to your company's network securely); WorldRes (allows you to make hotel reservations over the internet); Positive Communications (provides nationwide pager services allowing you to be in contact with your loved ones anywhere in the U.S.); Bolder Technologies (designs more efficient & longer lasting batteries, so you don't have to worry about recharging as often); Lynk Systems (processes transactions when you conduct business on the web); Photon Dynamics (makes it cheaper to develop quality flat panel displays); VOIS (enables you to access internet based information over the phone); Digital Smart Phone (with cellular phone email, net browsing, fax send & receive capabilities); GeoWorks (mobile communications devices)

Technology Partners
1550 Tiburon Boulevard, Suite A
Belvedere, California 94920
(415) 435-1935
Fax: (415) 435-5921
E-mail: jennifer@technologypartners.com

Key contact:
Mr. William Hart, General Partner
Dr. Roger J. Quy, Ph.D., General Partner
Mr. J. E. (Ted) Ardell, III, General Partner

64 Willow Place
Menlo Park, California 94025
(415) 435-1935
Fax: (415) 435-5921
E-mail: jennifer@technologypartners.com

Key contact:
Mr. Ira Ehrenpreis, Partner

Description: We are a private venture capital firm that teams with visionary entrepreneurs to create successful new companies. We principally serve as a lead investor and business advisor to innovative technology-based ventures in major new areas of opportunity, with focus on communications, life sciences, e-commerce, software and services.

Founded: 1980

Amount of capital invested: $12,411,130

Preferred investment size: $1-3 million

Amount under management: $100-500 million

Area served: West

Preferred stages of financing: Seed, Start up, First stage

Industries:
I.03   Biotech/genetic engineering
I.06   Communications
I.07   Computer hardware
I.08   Computer software
I.20   Healthcare
I.21   High technology
I.23   Information technology services
I.24   Internet services/e-commerce
I.29   Medical/medical products

Sampling of portfolio companies: Akashic Memories; Automated Power Exchange (APX); Cell Pathways, Inc.; Cholestech Corp.; Crystal Dynamics, Inc.; E-Loan; Forum Application Software Tech Inc.; ImageX; IRIDEX Corp.; Medwave, Inc.; Mobex Communications, Inc.; Percusurge, Inc.; PixelCraft; RoundBook Publishing, Inc.; Silicon Gaming, Inc.; Spinal Dynamics; Telescan Systems, Inc.; Trimble Navigation Ltd.; Ventritex, Inc.; XyberNET

Technology Venture Investors
2480 Sand Hill Road, Suite 101
Menlo Park, California 94025
(650) 854-7472
Fax: (650) 854-4187

Key contact:
Mr. Won Chung
Mr. Burton J. McMurtry

Area served: West Coast

Preferred stage of financing: First stage

Industries:
I.03   Biotech/genetic engineering
I.06   Communications
I.07   Computer hardware
I.08   Computer software
I.11   Consumer products
I.14   Electronics
I.29   Medical/medical products
I.35   Services (consumer)

Telos Venture Partners
2350 Mission College Boulevard, Suite 1070
Santa Clara, California 95054
(408) 982-5800
Fax: (408) 982-5880
E-mail: srooney@telosvp.com
Web: www.telosvp.com

Key contact:
Mr. Bruce R. Bourbon, General Partner
Mr. Athanasios (AK) Kalekos, General Partner

Description: We invest in early stage, high-tech start-up companies engaged in three markets: information technology, semiconductors and communications. The general partners, with years of operating experience, can significantly accelerate the development of a portfolio company through active involvement with the company's management team.

Amount of capital invested: $10.5 million

Preferred investment size: $1-2 million

Amount under management: $25-100 million

Area served: Israel, United States

Preferred stages of financing: Start up, First stage, Second stage, Mezzanine, Expansion

Industries:
I.06 Communications
I.07 Computer hardware
I.08 Computer software
I.14 Electronics
I.21 High technology
I.23 Information technology services
I.24 Internet services/e-commerce
I.33 Semiconductors

Sampling of portfolio companies: Conduct Ltd. (software company providing system & network managers with unified, coupled solutions for performance monitoring, taking into consideration both system & network issues); CrossRoute Software, Inc. (develops & markets cross-enterprise application software products that connect a company's enterprise systems & business models with those of its key trading partners); DynaChip Corp. (fabless semiconductor company specializing in the marketing & design of very high speed field programmable gate arrays); Integrated Memory Logic, Inc. (supplier of system-level, single chip ASSP solutions that integrate memory & logic in a memory-based fabrication process); Intraspect Software (knowledge management software for the enterprise); iReady Corp. (an intellectual property company); Newfire, Inc. (software products that dramatically reduce the technology risk in interactive 3-D entertainment & education title development by enabling entertainment content developers to quickly & affordably create titles & simulations for CD-ROM & the internet); PDF Solutions, Inc. (provider of holistic yield improvement software & services for the semiconductor industry with a combination of manufacturability simulation & analysis software, supported by proven yield enhancement methodologies); Preview Software (developer of products for distributing software over the web, allowing software publishers to electronically package their applications, including secure encryption, merchandising, try-before-you-buy technology & commerce capabilities); SwitchSoft Systems, Inc. (providers of policy-based network management software solutions to business & information technology managers for use in optimizing network administration, monitoring & provisioning)

Thoma Cressey Equity Partners

600 Montgomery Street
San Francisco, California 94111-2790
(415) 263-3660
Fax: (415) 840-0035
E-mail: tcep@tc.nu
Web: tcep@tc.nu

Key contact:
Mr. William W. Liebeck, Partner

Area served: North America

Preferred stages of financing: LBO/MBO, Expansion

Industries:
I.04 Broadcasting
I.05 Chemicals
I.06 Communications
I.10 Consulting
I.12 Distribution
I.13 Education
I.14 Electronics
I.16 Entertainment
I.17 Environmental services/waste management
I.18 Financial services
I.20 Healthcare
I.22 Industrial products
I.23 Information technology services
I.24 Internet services/e-commerce
I.25 Leisure/hospitality
I.27 Manufacturing
I.28 Media/publishing
I.30 New media
I.34 Services (business)
I.35 Services (consumer)
I.36 Transportation
I.37 Wholesale

Thompson Clive Inc.

3000 Sand Hill Road, Building 1, Suite 185
Menlo Park, California 94025
(650) 854-0314
Fax: (650) 854-0670
E-mail: mail@tcvc.com
Web: www.tcvc.com

Key contact:
Mr. Greg Ennis, Principal

Description: We are an international venture capital group with many years experience of successful investment in privately held companies. We are an independent venture company with offices in London, Paris & Menlo Park.

Preferred investment size: $3 million

Amount under management: $100-500 million

Area served: Europe, United States

Preferred stages of financing: Start up, First stage, Second stage, Mezzanine, LBO/MBO, Int'l expansion

Industries:
I.03 Biotech/genetic engineering
I.06 Communications
I.07 Computer hardware
I.08 Computer software
I.14 Electronics
I.20 Healthcare
I.21 High technology
I.29 Medical/medical products

Three Arch Partners

2800 Sand Hill Road, Suite 270
Menlo Park, California 94025
(650) 854-5550
Fax: (650) 854-9880

Key contact:
Dr. Wilfred E. Jaeger, General Partner
Mr. Mark A. Wan, General Partner
Dr. Thomas J. Fogarty, General Partner
Ms. Barclay Nicholson, Controller

Area served: United States

Preferred stages of financing: Seed, Start up, First stage

Industries:
I.20   Healthcare

Sampling of portfolio companies: Adjacent Surgical (medical device); AneuRx (medical device); Biopsys Medical (medical device); Cardiothoracic Systems (medical device); Emergency Medical Systems (medical device); General Surgical Innovations (medical device); LocalMed (medical device); Perclose (medical device); Prolifix Medical (medical device); Spinal Dynamics (medical device); Trans-Vascular (medical device); Uros (medical device); Acorn Cardiovascular (medical device); Aspect Medical (medical device); Radiant Medical (medical device); Windy Hill Technology (medical device); Intensiva Healthcare (healthcare services); Odyssey Healthcare (healthcare services)

Ticonderoga Capital, Inc.

555 California Street, Suite 4360
San Francisco, California 94104
(415) 296-6343
Fax: (415) 296-8956

Key contact:
Dr. Graham K. Crooke, Partner

Description: We are a private equity investment firm with over $125 million of capital under management. Our professionals collectively have over 40 years of private equity investing experience. Having invested capital in 39 companies since 1991, our professionals have extensive experience investing in and providing strategic assistance to rapidly growing companies.

Amount of capital invested: approximately $12 million

Preferred investment size: $5-10 million

Amount under management: $100-500 million

Area served: North America

Preferred stages of financing: Expansion, Late stage growth

Industries:
I.06   Communications
I.12   Distribution
I.13   Education
I.15   Energy/natural resources/utilities
I.23   Information technology services
I.32   Retail
I.34   Services (business)
I.35   Services (consumer)

Sampling of portfolio companies: Community Rehab Centers (regional outpatient physical & occupational therapy services organization); Professional Dental Assoc. (a dental practice management company which seeks to partner with successful private practice dentists throughout the Eastern seaboard in building practices that deliver exceptional care service & financial performance); UroCor, Inc. (provides diagnostic, therapeutic & information support services to assist urologists in the diagnosis, treatment & prognosis of cancer patients); Boots & Coots (specializes in oil well firefighting & blow-outs); Concho Resources Inc. (acquires oil & gas properties in the Permian Basin of Texas & New Mexico & the onshore Gulf Coast in Texas & Louisiana); Fintube, LP (manufacturer of precision-welded finned tubes & derivative products used by the electric industry in generation plants & by petro-chemical & refining industry processing plants); Interenergy Corp. (diversified energy company which provides natural gas gathering, processing, distribution & marketing services in the Rocky Mountain & Mid-Continent regions); Meenan Oil Co., Inc. (heating oil distributor); Roemer-Swanson Energy Corp. (focuses on three market niches: 1) gas imbalance properties, 2) Section 29 tax credit properties & 3) prospect generation); Willbros Group, Inc. (diversified energy services company providing construction, engineering & specialty services to the oil & natural gas industries); Learningsmith, Inc. (mall-based retailer of educational products with 35 stores nationwide); Lids Corp. (retail chain of stores positioned as "category killer" by offering the widest possible selection of casual headwear); Viking Office Products (mail order direct marketer of office supplies); Int'l. Towers, Inc. (designs, manufactures, erects & services transmission towers for the communications & broadcasting industries related primarily to the introduction of high definition television, cellular telephone, PCS & paging services); Radio Movil Digital Americas, Inc. (provider of specialized mobile radio wireless dispatch communications services to businesses in the major countries of South America); Carr Separations, Inc. (produces centrifugal separation devices); Cornell Corrections, Inc. (develops, acquires & operates private correctional facilities; private prison management company); Sales Staffers Int'l. Inc. (provides an outside source of sales & marketing personnel to help its clients generate sales, increase market share & expand their sales reach into new markets without increasing permanent staff & overhead expenses); Team Bancshares, Inc. (acquires, recapitalizes & manages commercial banks & related assets in Texas); USI Holdings Corp. (consolidator of small, privately-held commercial insurance brokerage & insurance-related financial services firms)

Trammell-Shott Capital Management, LLC

601 California Street, Suite 801
San Francisco, California 94108
(415) 394-7271
Fax: (415) 394-5596

Key contact:
Mr. George Shott, Member

Description: We are focused exclusively on providing liquidity to private & institutional investors through the purchase of secondary positions in venture capital & buyout funds.

Amount of capital invested: $4.5 million

Preferred investment size: $5 million

Amount under management: <$10 million

Area served: Asia, Europe, North America

Preferred stage of financing: Secondaries

Industries:
I.01   Aerospace
I.02   Agriculture/forestry/fishing/mining
I.03   Biotech/genetic engineering
I.04   Broadcasting
I.05   Chemicals
I.06   Communications
I.07   Computer hardware
I.08   Computer software
I.09   Construction
I.10   Consulting
I.11   Consumer products
I.12   Distribution
I.13   Education
I.14   Electronics
I.15   Energy/natural resources/utilities
I.16   Entertainment
I.17   Environmental services/waste management
I.18   Financial services
I.19   Generalist
I.20   Healthcare
I.21   High technology
I.22   Industrial products
I.23   Information technology services
I.24   Internet services/e-commerce
I.25   Leisure/hospitality
I.26   Life sciences
I.27   Manufacturing
I.28   Media/publishing
I.29   Medical/medical products
I.30   New media
I.32   Retail
I.33   Semiconductors
I.34   Services (business)
I.35   Services (consumer)
I.36   Transportation
I.37   Wholesale

Trident Capital

2480 Sand Hill Road, Suite 100
Menlo Park, California 94025
(650) 233-4300
Fax: (650) 233-4333
E-mail: administrator@tridentcap.com
Web: www.tridentcap.com

Key contact:
Mr. Donald R. Dixon, Managing Director
Mr. Stephen M. Hall, Managing Director
Mr. John H. Moragne, Managing Director

11150 Santa Monica Boulevard, Suite 320
Los Angeles, California 90025
(310) 444-3840
Fax: (310) 444-3848

Key contact:
Mr. Rockwell A. Schnabel, Managing Director
Mr. Todd A. Springer

Description: We have made it our business to understand information and business services companies. The markets. The movers. The risks. And the potential. By leveraging our industry expertise and resourceful partners and contacts, we've been able to back- and help build- many exciting companies. Many others are becoming leaders in their emerging markets.

Amount of capital invested: approximately $10 million

Preferred investment size: $5-7 million

Amount under management: $100-500 million

Area served: United States

Preferred stages of financing: Seed, Start up, First stage, Second stage, Mezzanine, LBO/MBO, Expansion

Industries:
I.08   Computer software
I.23   Information technology services
I.24   Internet services/e-commerce
I.28   Media/publishing
I.30   New media
I.34   Services (business)

Sampling of portfolio companies: Avesta Technologies, Inc. (provider of software & consulting services specializing in IT service management & high performance intranet applications); CSG Systems Int'l., Inc. (provider of subscriber management systems & services for cable TV, DBS, telecommunications & on-line services); DAOU Systems, Inc. (provider of network integration services to healthcare organizations); Digital Evolutions, Inc. (provider of digital communications technology & services); Evolving Systems, Inc. (provider of software solutions & systems integration services for the telecommunications industry); Firefly Networks, Inc. (provider of intelligent agent technology for the internet & creator of the personalized entertainment service Firefly); Frisco Holdings (direct marketer of consumables to hospital & medical office x-ray & other imaging departments); Geosystems Global Corp. (provider of geographical information systems & services to the publishing, travel & information industries); Health Quality, Inc. (point-of-care clinical management systems combining electronic medical records & medical "quality" measurement); Internet Profiles Corp. (supplier of software & services for collecting, measuring & analyzing internet usage); Internet Securities, Inc. (provider of economic, political & financial information on emerging markets via the internet); Newgen Results Corp. (provider of customer retention & database management services to the automobile industry); Online Interactive, Inc. (provider of branded on-line marketing & shopping services); Pegasus Systems, Inc. (provider of transaction processing services to the hotel industry worldwide through its three services: TravelWeb, www travel booking site; THISCO, which connects hotel central reservation systems to the global distribution systems; & HCC, which aggregates & distributes travel agent commissions); Platinum Software Corp. (provider of LAN-based & client/ server financial accounting applications); Production Group Int'l., Inc. (provider of global events, entertainment exhibitions & business communication services); Research Holdings, Ltd. (provider of interactive investor communication services); Rezsolutions, Inc. (provider of central reservation systems & related services to the travel & leisure industry); Vality Technology, Inc. (provider of data-quality software tools & re-engineering consulting services); Viant Corp. (provider of consulting & systems integration services solely focused on delivering internet strategy & technology solutions)

Trinity Ventures

3000 Sand Hill Road
Building 1, Suite 240
Menlo Park, California 94025
(650) 854-9500
Fax: (650) 854-9501
E-mail: info@trinityventures.com

Key contact:
Mr. Noel J. Fenton, General Partner
Mr. Lawrence K. Orr, General Partner
Mr. James G. Shennan, Jr., General Partner
Mr. Tod H. Francis, General Partner
Mr. Augustus O. Tai, Principal

Description: We are a privately held, professionally managed venture capital firm with $190 million in committed capital. Founded in 1986, we have invested in over 70 companies. Our professionals invest in early stage companies in three industries: information technology, branded consumer products and services and electronic commerce.

Founded: 1986

Preferred investment size: $750,000-4 million

Industries:
I.06   Communications
I.07   Computer hardware
I.08   Computer software
I.11   Consumer products

I.23   Information technology services
I.24   Internet services/e-commerce
I.32   Retail
I.35   Services (consumer)

Sampling of portfolio companies: Alldata Corp. (CD-ROM-based automotive repair data); BackWeb Technologies Ltd. (internet communications software); Crescendo Communications, Inc. (high performance LAN products); Digital Research, Inc. (operating systems & applications software); Expersoft Corp. (object request broker software); Forté Software, Inc. (client-server software development tools); Front Office Technologies (document management software); Intelligent Interactions Corp. (direct marketing management system); KIVA Software (internet application servers); Requisite Technology, Inc. (universal catalog for desktop requisitioning); Virage, Inc. (image retrieval software); Wall Data, Inc. (PC-host connectivity software); Computer Literacy (computer books); GolfWeb (golf internet site); Marmot Mountain Ltd. (technical outerwear & accessories); P.F. Chang's China Bistro (casual dining chinese restaurants); Smith Sport Optics, Inc. (ski goggles & sport glasses); Sweet Factory, Inc. (candy retailer); World Wrapps Inc. (upscale quick serve restaurants); Digital Market, Inc. (on-line market for electronic components)

Triune Capital

1888 Century Park East, Suite 1900
Los Angeles, California 90067
(310) 284-6800
Fax: (310) 284-3290
E-mail: bradley@earthlink.net

Key contact:
Mr. Brad McManus, Principal

Description: We are a consulting firm that positions qualified emerging growth companies for introduction to the venture capital community, then introduces the company to appropriate funding sources and assists in the funding process.

Amount of capital invested: $10 million

Preferred investment size: $2-5 million

Area served: United States

Preferred stages of financing: Second stage, Mezzanine, LBO/MBO, Expansion

Industries:
I.03   Biotech/genetic engineering
I.06   Communications

I.07   Computer hardware
I.08   Computer software
I.11   Consumer products
I.16   Entertainment
I.17   Environmental services/waste management
I.20   Healthcare
I.21   High technology
I.22   Industrial products
I.23   Information technology services
I.24   Internet services/e-commerce
I.26   Life sciences
I.27   Manufacturing
I.28   Media/publishing
I.29   Medical/medical products
I.30   New media
I.32   Retail
I.34   Services (business)
I.35   Services (consumer)

Sampling of portfolio companies: Pink Dot (retailing); Gridcore (recycling); Core Holdings (healthcare services); Waterman Technologies (entertainment)

U.S. Venture Partners

2180 Sand Hill Road, Suite 300
Menlo Park, California 94025
(650) 854-9080
Fax: (650) 854-3018
Web: www.usvp.com

Key contact:
Mr. William K. Bowes, Jr.
Mr. Irwin Federman
Mr. Winston S. Fu
Mr. Steven M. Krausz
Mr. Lucio L. Lanza
Dr. Jonathan D. Root, M.D.
Mr. Philip S. Schlein
Mr. Philip M. Young

Description: We focus our investment activity in those areas in which we have greatest expertise. Thus, we will invest principally in companies headquartered in the Western United States in three sectors of industry: medical, technology and retail/consumer.

Founded: 1981

Preferred investment size: $500,000-4 million

Amount under management: $100-500 million

Area served: West Coast

Preferred stages of financing: Start up, First stage, Second stage

Industries:
I.03 Biotech/genetic engineering
I.06 Communications
I.08 Computer software
I.11 Consumer products
I.23 Information technology services
I.29 Medical/medical products
I.32 Retail

Sampling of portfolio companies: 3Dfx Interactive; Applied Micro Circuits; MMC Networks; NeoMagic; Check Point Software Technologies; Artisan Components; Sun Microsystems; Advanced Cardiovascular Systems

Union Venture Corp.

445 South Figueroa Street
P.O. Box 3100
Los Angeles, California 90071
(213) 236-4092
Fax: (213) 629-5328

Area served: West Coast

Preferred stage of financing: Growth, spin-offs, acquisitions

Industries:
I.06 Communications
I.15 Energy/natural resources/utilities
I.32 Retail

Vanguard Venture Partners

525 University Avenue, Suite 600
Palo Alto, California 94025
(650) 321-2900
Fax: (650) 321-2902

Key contact:
Mr. Don Wood
Mr. Jack M. Gill, General Partner
Mr. Curtis K. Myers, General Partner

Description: Investment focus is on networking equipment, software, telecommunications and wireless communications companies throughout the U.S.

Founded: 1981

Preferred investment size: $500,000-1 million

Amount under management: $25-100 million

Area served: United States

Preferred stages of financing: Seed, First stage

Industries:
I.03 Biotech/genetic engineering
I.06 Communications
I.08 Computer software
I.14 Electronics
I.29 Medical/medical products
I.34 Services (business)
I.35 Services (consumer)

Sampling of portfolio companies: Ciena; Advanced Fiber Communications; Network Appliance; E/O Networks; Tut Systems; Pluris; Digital Island

VenGlobal Capital Partners, LLC

5201 Great America Parkway, Suite 320
Santa Clara, California 95054
(408) 982-2551
Fax: (408) 982-2558
E-mail: partners@venglobal.com
Web: www.venglobal.com

Key contact:
Mr. Gary Y. Cheng, General Partner
Dr. Phil Mak, General Partner

Description: We target investments in early stage companies in Silicon Valley. Our investment focus is in software and telecommunication. The fund is managed by its general partner, a California limited liability company whose managing members include Gary Y. Cheng and Dr. Phil Mak. As former entrepreneurs in Silicon Valley, they understand the challenges of launching and building a new enterprise in the USA.

Amount of capital invested: $8 million

Preferred investment size: $1.5 million

Amount under management: $10-25 million

Area served: United States

Preferred stages of financing: Seed, Start up, First stage

Industries:

I.06   Communications
I.08   Computer software
I.21   High technology
I.23   Information technology services

Sampling of portfolio companies: Alaris, Inc. (PC video conferencing products); Allayer Technologies Corp. (provides integrated circuits for LAN & fiber optic interface); APEX Semiconductor, Inc. (develops pentium chipset, special DRAM); CondorVision Technology, Inc. (CMOS Area Sensor); Impala Linear Corp. (power management & RF circuit for mobile computing); Meropa, Inc. (ASIC design tool-behavior synthesizer); Network Information Systems, Inc. (intranet security software); SureFire Verifications (ASIC design functional verification software); Symmetry Communications Systems, Inc. (develops wireless data-communication server for GSm & CDMA)

Venrock Associates

755 Page Mill Road, Suite A230
Palo Alto, California 94304
(650) 493-5577
Fax: (650) 493-6443
Web: www.venrock.com

Key contact:
Mr. Anthony Sun, Managing General Partner
Mr. Patrick F. Latterell, General Partner
Mr. Ray A. Rothrock, General Partner
Mr. Terence J. Garnett, Venture Partner

Description: We are the venture capital investment arm of the Rockefeller Family, continuing a tradition of funding entrepreneurs that now spans six decades. Our objective is to create long term value by helping build new high technology companies and industries from the earliest stages.

Preferred stages of financing: Seed, Start up, First stage

Industries:

I.03   Biotech/genetic engineering
I.06   Communications
I.07   Computer hardware
I.08   Computer software
I.14   Electronics
I.24   Internet services/e-commerce
I.26   Life sciences
I.29   Medical/medical products

Sampling of portfolio companies: AdOne (nat'l.classified ad network of newspapers); DIGEX, Inc. (business-to-business internet access & web server management provider); NetScheme Solutions (software for accessing, analyzing & reporting information for heterogenous databases); Banyan Systems (networking software); Ramp Networks (internet access customer premise equipment); Conductus (superconductive electronic devices, circuits & systems for communications, test & instrumentation, digital electronics & sensor applications); Komag (magnetic disk media manufacturer); Datalogix Int'l. (manufacture software for formula-based industries); Structural Dynamics Research Corp. (develops & markets computer-aided design software for mechanical components & systems); Apple Computer (Macintosh PC's & servers); CardioThoracic Systems (a system of specialized surgical instruments & devices to perform CABG surgery without a sternotomy & cardiopulmonary bypass); Mitek Surgical Products/Johnson & Johnson (attachment devices); Biocircuits Corp. (develops & markets a low-cost point-of-care diagnostic instrument to enable physician offices to perform immunoassay tests); ThermoTrex (develops advanced technology in electro-optic & electro-acoustic systems, signal processing, materials technology, lasers & themionic & thermoelectric direct-energy conversion); Rehab Systems/Novacare (rehabilitation services); Centocor (development & commercialization of monoclonal antibody-based products to meet critical human healthcare needs, focusing on four major areas: infectious, cardiovascular & autoimmune diseases & cancer); Ligand Pharmaceuticals (discovery & development of therapeutics based on intracellular receptors for the treatment of human disease); SCRIPTGEN Pharmaceuticals (development of transcription-based drugs that act as inhibitors of gene expression); Vical (develops & markets genetic therapy drugs); Symtx (combinatorial synthesis of materials)

Ventana Global, Ltd.

18881 Von Karman, Suite 1150, Tower 17
Irvine, California 92612
(949) 476-2204
Fax: (949) 752-0223
E-mail: kkitridge@ventanaglobal.com
Web: www.ventanaglobal.com

Key contact:
Ms. Karen Kitridge, Investor Relations
Mr. Scott A. Burri, Investment Manager
Mr. Thomas O. Gephart, Chairman/General Partner

8880 Rio San Diego Drive, Suite 500
San Diego, California 92108
(619) 291-2757
Fax: (619) 295-0189
Web: www.ventanaglobal.com

Key contact:
Mr. Duwaine Townsen, General Partner

Description: Since our beginning, we have sponsored six private growth partnerships totaling over $180 million in funds under management. With a historical focus concentrated on technology investment in the electronics, medical, biotechnology and environmental sectors, the firm has made a total of 71 investments to date. These investments provide immediate access to a collective base of over 200 world class scientists, engineers, physicians and researchers who work with the portfolio companies of our 6 funds.

Founded: 1984

Amount of capital invested: $4.5 million

Preferred investment size: $1 million

Amount under management: $100-500 million

Area served: South/Central America, United States

Preferred stages of financing: Start up, First stage, Second stage

Industries:
I.01   Aerospace
I.03   Biotech/genetic engineering
I.05   Chemicals
I.06   Communications
I.07   Computer hardware
I.08   Computer software
I.14   Electronics
I.15   Energy/natural resources/utilities
I.17   Environmental services/waste management
I.20   Healthcare
I.21   High technology
I.22   Industrial products
I.23   Information technology services
I.24   Internet services/e-commerce
I.26   Life sciences
I.29   Medical/medical products
I.33   Semiconductors

I.34   Services (business)

Sampling of portfolio companies: Advanced Tissue Sciences, Inc. (biotechnology); Canji, Inc. (biotechnology); La Jolla Pharmaceutical Co. (biotechnology); Somatix Therapy Corp. (biotechnology); Fuisz Technologies, Ltd. (biotechnological engineering); Proxima Corp. (computer enhancement products); Consorcio Beta, S.A. de C.V. (environmental); PDGEnvironmental, Inc. (environmental); Safety Storage, Inc. (environmental); CarePartners, Inc. (health services); Medical Imaging Centers of America, Inc. (health services); Escalon Medical Corp. (medical products); MDD, Inc. (medical products); R2 Medical Systems, Inc. (medical products); ETM Entertainment (software applications); United Systems Technology, Inc. (software applications); APTA group, Inc. (solid state/electronics); Dimensional Circuits Corp. (solid state/electronics); SenSys Instruments, Inc. (solid state/electronics); Cellnet Corp. (telecommunications)

Venture Strategy Group

1500 Bryant Street, Suite 510
The Hamm's Building
San Francisco, California 94103
(415) 558-8600
Fax: (415) 558-8686
E-mail: vsgroup@venturestrategy.com

Key contact:
Ms. Joanna Rees Gallanter, Managing Director/Co-Founder
Mr. William B. Rosenzweig, Managing Director
Ms. Rosalia B. Dizon, Manager of Research

Description: We are an early-stage capital and strategy consulting firm serving the needs of marketing-driven growth companies. These are companies in which strong brand identity and superior execution - but not breakthrough technology - are crucial for long-term growth and success. These companies are typically found in the following industries: specialty retailing, restaurants and food retailing, consumer goods and services, direct marketing and catalog retailing, business-to-business services and internet and intranet content.

Preferred stages of financing: Seed, Start up, First stage

Industries:
I.11   Consumer products
I.24   Internet services/e-commerce
I.32   Retail
I.34   Services (business)

I.35   Services (consumer)

Sampling of portfolio companies: Instill Corp. (e-commerce & information services in the foodservice industry); Hearing Science (their goal is to build a nationwide chain of professionally managed hearing centers by acquiring the assets & affiliating operations of existing audiology practices); Jamba Juice (specialty retailer of fresh-blended fruit smoothie drinks); ZAO American Noodle Bar (hip, quick-service version of a traditional Asian noodle shop appealing to upscale, yet mainstream American taste buds); Sweet Charlottes (manufactures old-fashioned, hand-crafted butter toffee); Red Tractor (quick-service, family-oriented themed restaurant concept with a special emphasis on meeting growing demand for high-quality "home meal replacement"); ZOIC (designs, manufactures & markets apparel & accessories for the rapidly growing mountain biking industry); United Media (owner of the syndication & licensing rights to many successful comic strips); Infoseek (internet search engine company dedicated to making information easy to find); FOOZI (nat'l. chain of quality neighborhood food stores with a special emphasis on chef-prepared "home meal replacement"); Home Shark (internet-based provider of value-added information services relating to real estate investment & home mortgage finance); Essential Elements (aromatherapy products based on pure essential oils, including fragrances, lotions & bath salts)

Vertex Management, Inc.

Three Lagoon Drive, Suite 220
Redwood City, California 94065
(650) 591-9300
Fax: (650) 591-5926

Key contact:
Mr. Charles Wu

Area served: United States

Preferred stages of financing: First stage, Second stage, Third stage

Industries:
I.06   Communications

I.08   Computer software
I.14   Electronics
I.34   Services (business)
I.35   Services (consumer)

Vision Capital Management

3000 Sand Hill Road, Building 4, Suite 230
Menlo Park, California 94025
(650) 854-8070
Fax: (650) 854-4961
E-mail: brichardson@visioncap.com
Web: www.visioncap.com

Key contact:
Mr. Dag Tellefsen, Managing Partner
Mr. Dag Syrrist, General Partner
Mr. Brendan Richardson, Senior Associate

Description: We are a trans-Atlantic venture fund.
Investment managers look to leverage the potential
value of technological innovations developed on one
side of the Atlantic by introducing them to key industrial partners and market niches that have been
identified on the other side. We take a very hands on
approach and an active role in the trans-Atlantic
expansion.

Amount of capital invested: $10 million

Preferred investment size: $3 million

Amount under management: $25-100 million

Area served: Worldwide

Preferred stages of financing: Start up, First stage,
Second stage, Mezzanine, Expansion, Int'l expansion

Industries:
I.06　Communications
I.07　Computer hardware
I.08　Computer software
I.10　Consulting
I.11　Consumer products
I.12　Distribution
I.14　Electronics
I.17　Environmental services/waste management
I.18　Financial services
I.21　High technology
I.22　Industrial products
I.23　Information technology services
I.24　Internet services/e-commerce
I.27　Manufacturing
I.30　New media
I.33　Semiconductors
I.34　Services (business)

Sampling of portfolio companies: Artios (CAD/CAM
software for the packaging industry); Metorex (manufacturing quality control); Aeneid (parametric search
applications for wide internet use); SCM Microsystems (smart card & security solutions)

Walden Group of Venture Capital Funds

750 Battery Street, 7th Floor
San Francisco, California 94111-1523
(415) 391-7225
Fax: (415) 391-7262

Key contact:
Mr. Arthur S. Berliner
Mr. George S. Sarlo
Mr. Lip-Bu Tan
Mr. William P. Tai

Area served: Worldwide

Preferred stages of financing: Seed, Start up, First
stage

Industries:
I.03　Biotech/genetic engineering
I.06　Communications
I.08　Computer software
I.14　Electronics
I.33　Semiconductors

Weiss, Peck & Greer Venture Partners

555 California Street, Suite 3130
San Francisco, California 94104
(415) 622-6864
Fax: (415) 989-5108
E-mail: www.wpgvp.com

Key contact:
Mr. Philip Greer, Senior Managing Director/Co-
founder
Mr. Gill Cogan, Managing Director/Director of VC
Ms. Annette M. Bianchi, Principal
Mr. Philip D. Black, Principal
Ms. Jeani Delagardelle, Principal
Mr. Barry F. Eggers, Principal
Ms. Ellen M. Feeney, Principal
Dr. Paul R. Low
Mr. Peter Nieh, Principal
Mr. Christopher J. Schaepe, Principal

Description: We are one of the oldest and most active
venture capital firms in the United States. Since
opening, we have managed $600 million of com-
mitted capital with investments in more than 180
companies. Over time, our mission has remained
unchanged: we serve as lead investors in early and
expansion stage information technology and life
sciences companies managed by entrepreneurs

possessing the vision, energy, commitment and
integrity required to build large, sustainable
enterprises.

Founded: 1971

Preferred investment size: $2-5 million

Area served: United States

Preferred stages of financing: Seed, Start up, First
stage, Second stage, Mezzanine, Expansion

Industries:
I.03　Biotech/genetic engineering
I.06　Communications
I.07　Computer hardware
I.08　Computer software
I.14　Electronics
I.20　Healthcare
I.23　Information technology services
I.26　Life sciences
I.29　Medical/medical products
I.33　Semiconductors

Sampling of portfolio companies: Information
Advantage (business analysis software); KIVA
Software (web-based applications platform);
TimesTen Performance Software (high-performance

database solutions); Bridge Communications (networking products); Ciena (fiber optic telecommunications systems); LightSpeed Int'l. (protocol conversion systems); Xantel (computer-telephony systems); Implant Center (semiconductor ion implantation); Tencor Instruments (semiconductor capital equipment); Adaptec (data flow systems); Chryon (broadcast & video systems); Network Computing Devices (network computers); DoubleClick (web advertising networks); Coulter Pharmaceuticals (cancer therapeutics); Cardiothoracic Systems (devices for less invasive bypass); Orquest (devices for spinal fusion); VidaMed (medical devices for prostate disease); CoreSource (managed healthcare services); Oacis Healthcare (hospital information systems); Protocare (site management organization)

Wells Fargo Equity Capital, Inc.

One Montgomery Street
West Tower, Suite 2530
San Francisco, California 94104
(415) 396-5700
Fax: (415) 765-1569
E-mail: green@wellsfargo.com

Key contact:
Mr. Richard R. Green, Managing Director

333 South Grand Avenue, Suite 1150
Los Angeles, California 90071
(213) 253-3671
Fax: (213) 621-2623
E-mail: swburge@wellsfargo.com

Key contact:
Mr. Steven W. Burge, Managing Director

Description: We provide middle market companies equity and mezzanine capital for management buyouts, recapitalizations, expansion capital and strategic acquisitions. We are an SBIC making $3 to $10 million investments in companies with revenues ranging from $20 to $250 million.

Amount of capital invested: $8.5 million

Preferred investment size: $10 million

Amount under management: $25-100 million

Area served: United States

Preferred stages of financing: LBO/MBO, Expansion

Industries:
I.12 Distribution
I.19 Generalist
I.27 Manufacturing
I.28 Media/publishing
I.32 Retail

Sampling of portfolio companies: Guitar Center, Inc. (music equipment retailer); Pacific Precision Metals (metal stamping manufacturers); DotAble Products (manufacturer & distributor of engineered wood products); Bolder Technologies (manufacturer of batteries, rechargeable batteries); Poore Brothers, Inc. (manufacture & market potato chips); InVision Technologies, Inc. (manufactures & markets explosive detection systems)

Wells Investment Group

100 Clock Tower Place, Suite 130
Carmel, California 93923
(831) 625-6500
Fax: (831) 625-6590
E-mail: scottwells@vcmoney.com
Web: www.vcmoney.com

Key contact:
Mr. Scott Wells, Director
Mr. Jeff Wells, Director

Description: Late stage venture capital. Primarily invest up to $1 million in mezzanine or bridge financing.

Amount of capital invested: $3.5 million

Preferred investment size: $500,000

Amount under management: $10-25 million

Area served: United States

Preferred stages of financing: Second stage, Mezzanine, Bridge loan

Industries:
I.06 Communications
I.08 Computer software
I.11 Consumer products
I.12 Distribution
I.16 Entertainment
I.19 Generalist
I.20 Healthcare
I.23 Information technology services
I.24 Internet services/e-commerce
I.25 Leisure/hospitality
I.28 Media/publishing
I.32 Retail
I.34 Services (business)
I.35 Services (consumer)
I.37 Wholesale

Sampling of portfolio companies: Cellegy Pharmaceuticals; New World Coffee; Isonics; Gateway Data Sciences; DCC Compact Classics; Virtual Mortgage Network; Legacy Brands

Westar Capital

949 South Coast Drive, Suite 650
Costa Mesa, California 92626-1776
(714) 434-5160
Fax: (714) 434-5166

Key contact:
Ms. Johanna Nicole
Mr. John W. Clark
Mr. Dale T. Jabour

Area served: West

Preferred stage of financing: LBO/MBO

Industries:
I.06 Communications
I.11 Consumer products
I.14 Electronics
I.18 Financial services

Western States Investment Group

9191 Towne Centre Drive, Suite 310
San Diego, California 92122
(619) 678-0800
Fax: (619) 678-0900
E-mail: scott@wsig.com
Web: www.wsig.com

Key contact:
Mr. Scott R. Pancoast, Executive Vice President
Mr. William B. Patch, Vice President-Administration
Ms. Susan L. Watson, Director of Finance

Description: We invest in a broad range of businesses, including medical products, telecommunications, software, transportation and electronics. We invest in start-up companies, as well as established businesses, located in the Western United States.

Amount of capital invested: $12 million

Preferred investment size: $1-3 million

Amount under management: $25-100 million

Area served: United States

Preferred stages of financing: Seed, Start up, First stage, LBO/MBO, Expansion

Industries:
I.03   Biotech/genetic engineering
I.06   Communications
I.07   Computer hardware
I.08   Computer software
I.12   Distribution
I.13   Education
I.14   Electronics
I.19   Generalist
I.20   Healthcare
I.23   Information technology services
I.26   Life sciences
I.27   Manufacturing
I.29   Medical/medical products
I.33   Semiconductors

Sampling of portfolio companies: BioQuest (a manufacturer of a patented water-treatment device for sanitizing water in spa, fountain & cooling-tower applications); Epic Solutions (a digital-imaging software company targeting law enforcement & social services markets); Single Chip Systems (a maker of a revolutionary new electronic ID tag with a wide variety of applications); Intelliform Software (a patient advisory software business); Medlyte Diagnostics (an early-stage company seeking to develop a minimally-invasive diagnostic test kit for coronary artery disease); Prisa Networks (an innovator of ultra high-speed computer networking devices); Akos Biomedical (a maker of user-friendly endoscopes & biopsy forceps); Asset Recovery Concepts (an electronic asset reclamation company)

Western Technology Investment

2010 North First Street, Suite 310
San Jose, California 95131
(408) 436-8577
Fax: (408) 436-8625
Web: www.westerntech.com

Key contact:
Ms. Patricia Breshears
Mr. Brian Best
Ms. Natalie Crowley
Mr. Sal Gutierrez
Mr. Ron Swenson
Ms. Linda White

Description: We are focused on expanding productive partnerships between venture capital investors and venture leaders. A pioneer in this separate industry segment, we specialize in asset based financing for venture capital funded companies, both in their start-up and later stages. Our experience working with early stage companies enables us to more effectively finance later stage companies. Consequently, many of our customers are more mature organizations attracted by our highly responsive and competitive services that fill the gap between equity financing and traditional bank lending and leasing. These services are offered nationally to companies representing most all areas of venture investment.

Founded: 1980

Preferred stages of financing: Start up, First stage, Second stage, LBO/MBO, Third/later stage

Industries:
I.03   Biotech/genetic engineering
I.11   Consumer products
I.21   High technology

Sampling of portfolio companies: Actel Corp. (field programmable gate arrays); Banyan Systems (LAN systems); Catalina Marketing (scanner-based grocery coupons); Cor Therapeutics Inc. (biotechnology cardiovascular products); Depotech (drug delivery system); Gene Logic, Inc. (drug discovery system); Idec Pharmaceuticals (drug discovery using monoclonal antibodies); InControl (implantable cardiovascular devices); Infoseek (internet search engine); Integ, Inc. (bloodfree & painfree glucose monitoring device); Komag (thin-film disks & heads); Logic Modeling (advanced hardware modeler); MIPS Computer (RISC microprocessor); NeoMagic (developer of a graphics controller chip for laptops); Photon Dynamics (flat panel display tester); RASNA Corp. (mechanical computer-aided software); Sandisk (mass storage system); StrataCom, Inc. (developer & manufacturer of voice & data packet switches); VeriSign, Inc. (digital authentication & identification); VidaMed (device for treatment of BPH)

Weston Presidio Capital

343 Sansome Street, Suite 1210
San Francisco, California 94104-1316
(415) 398-0770
Fax: (415) 398-0990
Web: www.westonpresidio.com

Key contact:
Mr. Michael P. Lazarus, Managing Partner
Mr. James B. McElwee, General Partner
Mr. Philip W. Halperin, General Partner
Mr. Alan L. Stein, Venture Partner
Mr. Thomas A. Patterson, Principal
Mr. Richard S. Friedman, Principal
Ms. Riki Des Rosiers, Director of Adminstration

Description: We believe that companies are better run
and more innovative when those who manage them
are also significant owners. Typically, we assist our
portfolio companies in the following areas, where
appropriate: negotiating and raising additional debt
or equity financing; recruiting additional management; strategic planning; negotiating and advising on
acquisitions, sales or mergers; accessing strategic or
corporate partners; developing compensation and
incentive programs.

Preferred investment size: $5-50 million

Amount under management: $100-500 million

Area served: Worldwide

Preferred stages of financing: LBO/MBO, Recapitalizations

Industries:
I.11   Consumer products
I.20   Healthcare
I.23   Information technology services
I.27   Manufacturing
I.32   Retail
I.34   Services (business)
I.35   Services (consumer)

Sampling of portfolio companies: AAi. Foster Grant
(provider of optical products & a women's accessories service & distribution company with full-
service programs in over 11,000 stores); Digital
Theater Systems (provider of branded high performance digital audio products to the theatrical &
consumer electronics markets); Learning Curve Int'l.
(developer & marketer of high quality, classic
products for children); Beacon Health Systems
(licensed health management organization providing
small groups, large groups & individual products);
The Pharmasource Group/NCS Healthcare (provides
multifaceted pharmacy services to hospitals,
managed care settings & long-term care facilities);
Physician Health Corp. (provides physician groups
with management services, information systems,
equity partnership opportunities & the capital
necessary to effectively compete in a managed care
environment); Consensus Health Corp. (provides a
delivery system for a select universe of alternative
healthcare services & products to health plans);
Tekni-Plex (manufacturer of packaging materials for
the specialty food & pharmaceutical industries); Star
Manufacturing Int'l. (manufacturer of food service
equipment); U.S. Netting (manufacturer of extruded
plastic netting products for a wide variety of industries & applications ranging from packaging products
to air & water filtration systems); The Coffee
Connection/Starbucks Corp. (sold fresh-brewed
coffees & espresso beverages primarily through its
retail stores in New England); Cucina! Cucina!
(operator of mid-priced, casual Italian restaurants);
The Bagel Group (franchisee of Brugger's Bagels);
Just For Feet (specialty athletic footwear retailer
operating company-owned & franchised stores);
Restoration Hardware (specialty home furnishings
retailer featuring a wide range of distinctive
merchandise that includes furniture, lamps, outdoor
accessories, hardware & unique gift items); Sweet
Factory (operates a chain of retail stores providing
bulk candy in over 200 locations); Casella Waste
Systems (provides integrated non-hazardous solid
waste management services to commercial,
municipal, industrial & residential customers); Forest
Products Int'l. Exchange (operates an on-line trading
platform that facilitates transactions between
producers & distributors of forest products); IC
Works (designs & markets mixed signal, specialty
memory & radio frequency logic semiconductor
devices); PictureWorks Technology (provides PC
application software to the digital imaging industry)

William Blair & Company, LLC

Two Embarcadero Center, Suite 2320
San Francisco, California 94111
(415) 986-1600
E-mail: wmb@wmblair.com
Web: www.wmblair.com

Key contact:
Ms. Ellen Carnahan, Managing Director

Description: Headquartered in Chicago, we are a
privately-held, employee-owned investment banking
firm providing a full range of financing and
brokerage services to quality growth companies and
to institutional and private investors nationally and
internationally. Since our founding in 1935, we have
remained dedicated to achieving outstanding long-
term results for our clients.

Founded: 1935

Preferred investment size: $5-10 million

Area served: Worldwide

Preferred stages of financing: First stage, Second
stage, Mezzanine, LBO/MBO

Industries:
I.03   Biotech/genetic engineering
I.06   Communications
I.07   Computer hardware
I.08   Computer software
I.14   Electronics
I.15   Energy/natural resources/utilities
I.22   Industrial products
I.29   Medical/medical products

Woodside Fund

850 Woodside Drive
Woodside, California 94062
(650) 368-5545
Fax: (650) 368-2416
Web: www.woodsidefund.com

Key contact:
Mr. Vincent Occhipinti, General Partner
Dr. Robert E. Larson, General Partner
Mr. V. Frank Mendicino, II, General Partner
Mr. Charles E. Greb, General Partner

4133 Mohr Avenue, Suite H
Pleasanton, California 94566
(510) 462-0326
Fax: (510) 462-4398
Web: www.woodsidefund.com

Key contact:
Mr. V. Frank Mendicino, II, General Partner

Description: We are a venture capital firm specializing in start up companies. Each partner has founded and built at least one company, resulting in 80 years of entrepreneurial experience, prior to joining the fund. Our limited partners include some of the nation's most sophisticated institutional and individual investors.

Preferred investment size: $1-5 million

Amount under management: $25-100 million

Area served: Northwest, Rocky Mountains, Southwest, West Coast

Preferred stages of financing: Seed, Start up, First stage, Second stage

Industries:
I.03   Biotech/genetic engineering
I.06   Communications
I.07   Computer hardware
I.08   Computer software
I.13   Education
I.14   Electronics
I.15   Energy/natural resources/utilities
I.20   Healthcare
I.21   High technology
I.23   Information technology services
I.24   Internet services/e-commerce
I.28   Media/publishing
I.30   New media
I.33   Semiconductors

Colorado

Boulder Ventures, Ltd.

1634 Walnut Street, Suite 301
Boulder, Colorado 80302
(303) 444-6950
Fax: (303) 449-9699
E-mail: kylevc@wynd.net

Key contact:
Mr. Kyle Lefkoff, General Partner
Mr. Josh Fidler, General Partner
Mr. Lawrence Macks, General Partner

Description: We are a venture capital limited partnership that invests in early stage technology companies in Colorado and the mid-Atlantic region. Our strategy is to purchase significant minority positions in our portfolio companies and to add value to our investments through a close working relationship with head entrepreneurs.

Amount of capital invested: $6 million

Preferred investment size: $2 million

Amount under management: $25-100 million

Area served: United States

Preferred stage of financing: First stage

Industries:
I.03   Biotech/genetic engineering
I.05   Chemicals
I.06   Communications
I.07   Computer hardware
I.08   Computer software
I.20   Healthcare
I.22   Industrial products
I.26   Life sciences
I.29   Medical/medical products
I.30   New media

Sampling of portfolio companies: Genomica Corp. (info systems for life science research); Horizon Organic Dairy, Inc. (organic dairy products); Marketscape, Inc. (web/cd distribution software); Zand Herbal Formulas, Inc. (nutraceuticals); Infobeat, Inc. (stock quotes, news, sports, etc. via e-mail); Qualmark Corp. (environmental stress screening devices/services); SMR Direct Inc. (specialized mobile radio dispatch service); Compatible Systems Corp. (virtual private networking); Pioneer Eyecare Inc. (eyecare services)

Capital Health Venture Partners

2084 South Milwaukee Street
Denver, Colorado 80210
(303) 692-8600
Fax: (303) 692-9656

Key contact:
Mr. Kinney Johnson

Preferred stages of financing: Start up, First stage, Second stage, LBO/MBO, Third/later stage

Industries:
I.03   Biotech/genetic engineering
I.29   Medical/medical products

The Centennial Funds

1428 Fifteenth Street
Denver, Colorado 80202
(303) 405-7500
Fax: (303) 405-7575
E-mail: adamg@centennial.com

Key contact:
Mr. Adam Goldman
Mr. Steven C. Halstedt
Mr. Donald H. Parsons, Jr.
Mr. Jeffrey H. Schutz
Mr. G. Jackson Tankersley, Jr.

Area served: United States

Preferred stages of financing: Seed, Start up, First stage, Second stage

Industries:
I.06   Communications
I.07   Computer hardware
I.11   Consumer products
I.14   Electronics
I.35   Services (consumer)

Columbine Venture Funds

5460 South Quebec Street, Suite 270
Englewood, Colorado 80111
(303) 694-3222
Fax: (303) 694-9007

Key contact:
Ms. Joyce Fandal
Mr. Sherman Muller

Area served: Rocky Mountains, Southwest

Preferred stage of financing: Seed

Industries:
I.03   Biotech/genetic engineering
I.05   Chemicals
I.06   Communications
I.07   Computer hardware
I.08   Computer software
I.15   Energy/natural resources/utilities
I.29   Medical/medical products

Sampling of portfolio companies: Afferon Inc. (pharmaceuticals); ReGenisys (software & information)

Communications Equity Associates, Inc.

4582 South Ulster Street, Suite 402
Denver, Colorado 80237
(303) 694-3090
Fax: (303) 220-8029
Web: www.commequ.com

Key contact:
Mr. J. Patrick Michaels, Chairman/CEO
Mr. Harold Ewen
Mr. Bruno Claude
Mr. George Pollock
Mr. Ming Jung
Mr. Thomas W. Cardy, Executive Vice President
Mr. Scott N. Feuer, Vice President
Mr. Bryan L. Crino, Senior Associate

Description: We have a rich 25-year history of diverse experiences and milestone industry accomplishments which establish us as a worldwide leader. By combining the sophisticated skills of a large Wall Street investment firm with a focus on communications industries, we offer a depth of service that's unparalleled. The experience of our professionals speaks for itself: since our founding, we have completed more than 600 transactions, valued at more than $13 billion. With an extensive network of long-standing relationships and offices on almost every continent, along with our affiliates, we have helped clients in 27 countries successfully pursue their financial and strategic goals.

Founded: 1973

Preferred investment size: No more than 15% of the total fund

Amount under management: $100-500 million

Area served: Worldwide

Preferred stages of financing: LBO/MBO, Growth

Industries:
I.04   Broadcasting
I.06   Communications
I.16   Entertainment
I.23   Information technology services
I.24   Internet services/e-commerce
I.28   Media/publishing

Grayson & Associates, Inc.

Republic Plaza
370 17th Street, 52nd Floor
Denver, Colorado 80202
(303) 592-2203
Fax: (303) 592-1510

Key contact:
Mr. Gerald Grayson
Mr. Donald C. Freeman
Mr. Peter J. Leveton

Preferred stages of financing: First stage, Second stage, Mezzanine, LBO/MBO

Industries:
I.03   Biotech/genetic engineering
I.12   Distribution
I.29   Medical/medical products

Opus Capital

1113 Spruce Street
Boulder, Colorado 80302
(303) 443-1023
Fax: (303) 443-0986
E-mail: dheidrich@opuscapital.com
Web: www.opuscapital.com

Key contact:
Mr. K. Dieter Heidrich, Managing Director
Mr. Daryl F. Yurek, Managing Director
Mr. David C. Seigle, Affiliated Executive
Mr. Robert B. Louthan, Affiliated Executive
Mr. Gene R. Copeland, Affiliated Executive

Description: Our primary focus is on small-cap companies in the communications, software and medical equipment industries. Our clients have an established revenue stream and a well-defined niche in a rapidly expanding market. We emphasize four key areas:

strategic planning, turnaround management, expansion financing and presenting the new company story to the investment community.

Area served: Canada, United States

Preferred stages of financing: Expansion, Strategic planning, turnaround management, presenting company to the investment community

Industries:
I.06   Communications
I.08   Computer software
I.29   Medical/medical products

Sampling of portfolio companies: InfoNow (internet, interactive multimedia & systems engineering); Destron Fearing (electronic & visual identification of animals); Network Express (integrated services digital network); NexStar (state-of-the-art robotics)

Phillips-Smith Specialty Retail Group

102 South Tejon Street, Suite 1100
Colorado Springs, Colorado 80903
(719) 578-3301
Fax: (719) 578-8869
E-mail: msnords@aol.com

Key contact:
Mr. James Rothe, Principal

Description: We are a traditional venture capital firm which invests in retail businesses with the potential to become major regional or national retail chains. We were founded in 1986 by our managing general partners Don Phillips and Cece Smith, executives with successful track records in specialty retailing, restaurants and venture investing.

Founded: 1986

Amount of capital invested: $21.4 million

Preferred investment size: $4-5 million

Amount under management: $100-500 million

Area served: United States

Preferred stages of financing: Seed, Start up, First stage, Second stage, Mezzanine, LBO/MBO, Expansion

Industries:
I.24   Internet services/e-commerce
I.32   Retail

Sampling of portfolio companies: Bookstop (book retailer); A Pea In The Pod (maternity apparel); The Sports Authority (sporting goods superstore); BizMart (office supply superstore); Petsmart (pet supply superstore); Gadzooks (teen apparel retailer); Hot Topic (teen apparel retailer); Canyon Cafes (southwestern restaurants)

SOFTBANK Technology Ventures

P.O. Box E
Eldorado Springs, Colorado 80025
(303) 494-3242
Fax: (303) 494-7642
Web: www.sbvc.com

Key contact:
Mr. Bradley A. Feld, Managing Director
Mr. Ronald D. Fisher, Vice Chairman
Mr. Gary E. Reischel, Executive Managing Director
Mr. Charles R. Lax, Managing Director
Mr. Matthew A. Ocko, Managing Director
Mr. E. Scott Russell, Managing Director

Description: We make privately negotiated equity and equity-related investments in companies attempting to capitalize on opportunities in digital information technology, including internet communications, commerce and content. We are affiliated with SOFT-BANK Holdings Inc., a subsidiary of SOFTBANK Corporation.

Founded: 1981

Area served: Worldwide

Industries:
I.08   Computer software
I.24   Internet services/e-commerce
I.35   Services (consumer)

Sampling of portfolio companies: 911 Entertainment (software & information); Electric Communities (software & information); Fastparts Inc. (business services); Fourth Communications Network (business services); GeoCities (software & information); Internet Profiles Corp. (software & information); SaveSmart (software & information); Third Age Media Inc. (software & information); CStream Inc. (communications); Zip2 (software & information)

Thoma Cressey Equity Partners

370 Seventeenth Street
Republic Plaza, Suite 3800
Denver, Colorado 80202
(303) 592-4804
Fax: (303) 592-4819
E-mail: tcep@tc.nu
Web: tcep@tc.nu

Key contact:
Mr. Robert L. Manning, Jr., Partner

Area served: North America

Preferred stages of financing: LBO/MBO, Expansion

Industries:
I.04   Broadcasting
I.05   Chemicals
I.06   Communications
I.10   Consulting
I.12   Distribution
I.13   Education
I.14   Electronics
I.16   Entertainment
I.17   Environmental services/waste management
I.18   Financial services
I.20   Healthcare
I.22   Industrial products
I.23   Information technology services
I.24   Internet services/e-commerce
I.25   Leisure/hospitality
I.27   Manufacturing
I.28   Media/publishing
I.30   New media
I.34   Services (business)
I.35   Services (consumer)
I.36   Transportation
I.37   Wholesale

Connecticut

Achenbaum Capital Partners, LLC

25 Wildwood Road, Suite 204
Stamford, Connecticut 06903-2111
(203) 322-1933
Fax: (203) 322-4575
E-mail: joe@achenbaumcapital.com
Web: www.achenbaumcapital.com

Key contact:
Mr. Joseph P. Achenbaum, Managing Director

Description: We were founded to provide specialized capital raising and investment banking advisory services to mid-sized companies. We bring a unique blend of extensive experience and relationships with sources of institutional debt and equity capital. We regularly assist our clients in developing strategies, marketing, identifying and negotiating with institutions in order to raise the most cost effective source of funds.

Founded: 1996

Amount of capital invested: $500,000

Preferred investment size: $50,000

Amount under management: <$10 million

Area served: North America

Preferred stages of financing: Mezzanine, Expansion

Industries:
I.02   Agriculture/forestry/fishing/mining
I.04   Broadcasting
I.05   Chemicals
I.06   Communications
I.09   Construction
I.10   Consulting
I.11   Consumer products
I.12   Distribution
I.13   Education
I.15   Energy/natural resources/utilities
I.17   Environmental services/waste management
I.18   Financial services
I.19   Generalist
I.20   Healthcare
I.22   Industrial products
I.27   Manufacturing
I.32   Retail
I.34   Services (business)
I.35   Services (consumer)
I.36   Transportation
I.37   Wholesale

Advanced Materials Partners, Inc.

45 Pine Street
P.O. Box 1022
New Canaan, Connecticut 06840
(203) 966-6415
Fax: (203) 966-8448
E-mail: ampnet@gnn.com

Key contact:
Mr. Warner K. Babcock
Mr. William W. Davison
Mr. Charles G. Pieroth
Mr. Stanley B. Roboff

Founded: 1987

Area served: United States

Preferred stages of financing: Seed, Start up, First stage, Second stage, Special situations, acquisitions

Industries:
I.03   Biotech/genetic engineering
I.05   Chemicals
I.14   Electronics
I.15   Energy/natural resources/utilities
I.19   Generalist
I.22   Industrial products

AO Capital Corp.

80 Field Point Road
Greenwich, Connecticut 06830
(203) 622-6600
Fax: (203) 622-1292
E-mail: baylis11@aol.com

Key contact:
Mr. William S. Zegras, Senior Vice President
Mr. Allen I. Skott, Vice President
Mr. David Cunniffe, Vice President

Description: Private investment firm that seeks to
acquire controlling interests in industrial and
consumer products. Preference for under performing
businesses that require operational attention and
capital, revenues $25 million - $250 million.

Amount of capital invested: $7 million

Preferred investment size: $8 million

Amount under management: $100-500 million

Area served: Europe, North America

Preferred stage of financing: LBO/MBO

Industries:
I.01   Aerospace
I.06   Communications
I.11   Consumer products
I.14   Electronics
I.19   Generalist
I.22   Industrial products
I.23   Information technology services
I.27   Manufacturing
I.33   Semiconductors

Sampling of portfolio companies: Radiac Abrasives Inc.
(industrial grinding wheels manufacturer); Triboro
Electric Company (wired electrical devices manufacturer); Rite Off Inc. (packager of aerosol products);
Markin Tubing LP (small diameter steel tubing manufacturer); AO Sunwear USA, Inc. (metal framed
sunglasses manufacturer); Semicon Precision Industries (refurnish parts for manufacturing of semiconductors); American Optical Corp. (worldwide
opthlomic products & industrial safety products
manufacturer); Walter Karl Companies (direct mail
computer data services & mailing list manager);
Buffalo Metals Inc. (metal fabrication)

Atlantic Coastal Ventures, L.P.

777 Summer Street, Suite 300
Stamford, Connecticut 06901
(203) 325-2522
Fax: (203) 325-1064
E-mail: dgreene@atlanticcv.com
Web: www.atlanticcv.com

Key contact:
Mr. Donald F. Greene, General Partner
Mr. Jerold P. West, Administrative Manager

Description: We invest in a diversified portfolio of
telecommunications companies and related service
companies operating within markets that reflect the
convergence of the computer, telephone, cable,
media and communications, information management and technology, broadcast, satellite and
entertainment industries. We further invest in a
variety of other enterprises to produce competitive
companies in those industries characterized by fragmentation and economic or financial inefficiencies.

Amount under management: $25-100 million

Area served: Atlantic Coast

Preferred stage of financing: Mezzanine

Industries:
I.06   Communications
I.16   Entertainment
I.28   Media/publishing

Sampling of portfolio companies: Citywide Communications, Inc. (broadcast operation); El Dorado
Communications, Inc. (media company); ESR Media
Ventures, LLC (media production company); Davis
Broadcasting, Inc.; Z-Spanish Radio Network, Inc.
(communications company); NTT, Inc. (electronic
parts manufacturer/distributor); Coastal Communications of America, Inc. (pay telephone operator on the
East Coast); Greystone Management, Inc. (franchise
centers)

Axiom Venture Partners, L.P.

CityPlace II - 17th Floor
185 Asylum Street
Hartford, Connecticut 06103
(860) 548-7799
Fax: (860) 548-7797

Key contact:
Ms. Jan Mueller, Administrator

Preferred stages of financing: Start up, First stage,
Second stage

Industries:
I.03   Biotech/genetic engineering
I.06   Communications
I.29   Medical/medical products

Baxter Associates, Inc.

P.O. Box 1333
Stamford, Connecticut 06904
(203) 323-3143
Fax: (203) 348-0622

Key contact:
Mr. Carroll A. Greathouse, President

Founded: 1933

Preferred investment size: $250,000-500,000

Area served: Worldwide

Preferred stages of financing: Seed, Start up, First
stage, LBO/MBO, Special situations

Industries:
I.02 Agriculture/forestry/fishing/mining
I.03 Biotech/genetic engineering
I.05 Chemicals
I.06 Communications

I.08 Computer software
I.12 Distribution
I.15 Energy/natural resources/utilities
I.22 Industrial products
I.29 Medical/medical products

Beacon Partners, Inc.
6 Landmark Square, Suite 408
Stamford, Connecticut 06902
(203) 348-8858
Fax: (203) 323-3188

Key contact:
Mr. Leonard Vignola, Partner
Mr. Larry Gorfinkle, Partner
Mr. James Nixon, Partner
Mr. Frank Brunetta, Partner
Mr. Nat Migida, Partner

Description: We are a management consulting and
investment banking firm. We have worked with
under performing companies for over 21 years. Our
management team provides hands-on assistance,
helping companies overcome barriers to growth and
liquidity crisis to major restructuring of businesses.
Each of our senior partners brings 25 or more years
of diverse experience in key management and advisory roles including CEO, COO, CFO and as
advisors to boards of directors.

Area served: United States

Preferred stages of financing: Start up, First stage,
LBO/MBO, Expansion, Turnaround

Industries:
I.03 Biotech/genetic engineering
I.04 Broadcasting
I.05 Chemicals
I.06 Communications
I.07 Computer hardware
I.08 Computer software
I.11 Consumer products
I.12 Distribution
I.14 Electronics
I.15 Energy/natural resources/utilities
I.17 Environmental services/waste management
I.18 Financial services
I.19 Generalist
I.20 Healthcare
I.21 High technology
I.22 Industrial products
I.23 Information technology services
I.26 Life sciences
I.27 Manufacturing
I.28 Media/publishing
I.29 Medical/medical products
I.32 Retail
I.34 Services (business)
I.35 Services (consumer)
I.36 Transportation
I.37 Wholesale

Brand Equity Ventures
Three Pickwick Plaza
Greenwich, Connecticut 06830
(203) 862-5500
Fax: (203) 629-2019
Web: www.brand-equity.com

Key contact:
Mr. Christopher P. Kirchen
Mr. David S. Yarnell
Mr. Marc A. Singer

Mr. Anubhav Goel

Area served: United States

Industries:
I.11 Consumer products

Sampling of portfolio companies: Ranch *1 (NY
sandwich shops specializing in lunch time take-outs)

Canaan Partners
105 Rowayton Avenue
Rowayton, Connecticut 06853
(203) 855-0400
Fax: (203) 854-9117
E-mail: hrein@canaan.com
Web: www.canaan.com

Key contact:
Mr. Harry T. Rein
Mr. Gregory Kopchinsky
Mr. Stephen L. Green
Mr. Robert J. Migliorino

Description: Our investment strategy focuses on
providing capital for growth and we are comfortable
working with entrepreneurial companies across all
industry sections: information technology, healthcare
and medical and otherwise. In addition, we have the
ability to invest in any stage of development, from
early through expansion stage, and will actively
consider other unique growth-oriented opportunities

including private placement in public companies,
management led buyouts, recapitalizations and other
special situations.

Preferred investment size: $500,000-15 million

Area served: United States

Preferred stages of financing: Start up, First stage,
Second stage, Mezzanine, Expansion, Recapitalizations

Industries:
I.11 Consumer products
I.12 Distribution
I.18 Financial services
I.20 Healthcare
I.23 Information technology services
I.29 Medical/medical products

Sampling of portfolio companies: Cayenne Software,
Inc. (supplier of analysis & design solutions for
commercial & technical application & database

development); Comstream Corp. (KU-band VSAT transceivers & RF modems for satellite); Copper Mountain Networks, Inc. (supplies DSL based products to enable high speed data communications in the local loop); Endura Software Corp. (client/server supply chain management software); Latitude Communications, Inc. (audio-conferencing & voice-processing equipment); Saleslogix Corp. (sales automation software); Success Factor Systems (software applications for managing human assets in corporations); WebFlow (develops software which permits users to collaborate on workgroup tasks via their web browsers independent of their location or hardware platform); Applied Immune Sciences, Inc. (treatment of immune system related diseases through proprietary cell capture & activation technologies); Crop Genetics Int'l. Corp. (disease-free cloned sugar cane, automated planting service, microbial venctors for agchemicals); Delos Women's Health (physician practice management company providing comprehensive healthcare services to women through partnership arrangements with OB/GYN physicians); GenVec, Inc. (gene therapy products); Matrix Pharmaceutical, Inc. (proprietary drug delivery technology for cancer & hyperproliferative diseases); Premier Laboratory Services, Inc. (clinical testing laboratories); Somatix Therapy Corp. (gene therapy & drug delivery systems); Chartwell Reinsurance Co. (property & casualty reinsurance); Onyx Acceptance Corp. (auto finance); The Eicon Group, Inc. (environmental & infrastructure consulting & remediation services); Atlantic Greenhouses, Inc. (regional producer of indoor grown flowers); Garden Fresh Restaurant Corp. (soup, salad & baked goods self-service buffet restaurant)

Cognizant Enterprises

200 Nyala Farms
Westport, Connecticut 06880
(203) 222-4594
Fax: (203) 222-4592
E-mail: vkontogouris@cognizantcorp.com
Web: www.cognizantenterprises.com

Key contact:
Ms. Venetia Kontogouris, President
Mr. Peter Meekin, Vice President

Description: We are a corporate venture capital group focused on investing in information services, technology and business/services companies across a broad span of horizontal and vertical markets. We have $260 million under management and are closely associated with our partner, Trident Capital.

Preferred investment size: $5-8 million; maximum $12 million

Amount under management: $100-500 million

Area served: North America

Preferred stages of financing: Start up, First stage, Second stage, Mezzanine, Expansion

Industries:
I.06   Communications
I.08   Computer software
I.20   Healthcare
I.21   High technology
I.23   Information technology services
I.24   Internet services/e-commerce
I.30   New media

Sampling of portfolio companies: Avesta Technologies, Inc. (network management software); DAOU Systems, Inc. (healthcare systems integration services); Digital Evolution, Inc. (internet consulting services); ESS Software, Inc. (employee self service software); Evolving Systems, Inc. (telecommunications software & services); Firefly Network, Inc. (intelligent agent technology); Health Quality, Inc. (clinical information systems); Internet Profiles Corp. (internet measurement services); Internet Securities (emerging markets information services); Nets, Inc. (electronic commerce); OnLine Interactive, Inc. (online software delivery); Pegasus Systems, Inc. (travel information services); Silicon Valley Internet Partners (systems integration services); Vality Technology, Inc. (data integration tools); Aspect Development, Inc. (component information management systems); Course Technology, Inc. (educational software); Dataware Technologies, Inc. (cd-rom authoring & retrieval software); e data resources (risk assessment software & services); EduServ Technologies, Inc. (student loan information & consulting services); Florists TransWorld Delivery (floral delivery information network); Gartner Group, Inc. (technology research, information & training services); Jostens Learning Corp. (K-12 educational software & services); Market Metrics, Inc. (marketing decision support systems); MAXM Systems (network management software); MediQual Systems, Inc. (healthcare benchmarking software & services); Oacis Healthcare Systems, Inc. (clinical data repository software); OneSource Information Services, Inc. (financial, marketing & business information); Risk Management Services, Inc. (earthquake & windstorm risk assessment systems); SR Research, Inc. (credit risk analysis software); Strategic Mapping, Inc. (GIS software); Stream International, Inc. (software management services); T.R.A.D.E., Inc. (inport/export data & trade statistics); TSI Internaitonal, Inc. (EDI & data mapping software); The WEFA Group, Inc. (economic information services)

Collinson Howe & Lennox, LLC

1055 Washington Boulevard
Stamford, Connecticut 06901
(203) 324-7700
Fax: (203) 324-3636
E-mail: chlmedical.com

Key contact:
Mr. Jeffrey Collinson, Partner
Mr. Timothy F. Howe, Partner
Dr. Ronald W. Lennox, Partner
Ms. Rae Pace-Pittman, Office Manager

Description: A venture capital management firm founded in 1990 with a specialized focus on the medical sector defined broadly to include biotechnology, medical devices and health care services.

Founded: 1990

Amount of capital invested: $75,000

Preferred investment size: $2.5 million

Amount under management: $25-100 million

Area served: North America

Preferred stages of financing: Seed, Start up, First stage, Second stage

Industries:
I.03   Biotech/genetic engineering
I.20   Healthcare
I.26   Life sciences
I.29   Medical/medical products

Sampling of portfolio companies: Genetic Systems Corp., Inc. (infectious diseases & cancer therapies, using monoclonal antibodies); Cambridge Bio Tech Corp. (diagnostics for infectious diseases, particularly for HIV); Nova Pharmaceutical Corp. (neurological disorder therapeutics); Texas Biotechnology Corp. (treatments for acute cardiovascular conditions); Cell Therapeutics, Inc. (biotherapeutics for cancer treatment); Chiroscience, Inc. (chiral pharmaceutical & intermediate development); GelTex Phar-maceuticals, Inc. (non-absorbed pharmaceuticals to eliminate target substances from the gastrointestinal tract); LeukoSite Inc. (treatments for inflammatory & autoimmune diseases); Khepri Pharmaceuticals, Inc. (discovery & development of naturally occurring proteases & their inhibitors as novel therapeutics) DNA Plant Technology Inc. (agricultural-based products); Celgene Corp. (chemicals for pharmaceutical, agricultural, & hazardous waste industries using biotechnology); Mycogen Corp. (biopesticides for control of insects & weeds); Raytel Systems Corp. (heart pacemaker monitoring service & outpatient MRI service); Advanced Rehabilitation Resources, Inc. (management of rehabilitation facilities within hospitals); Clinical Partners, Inc. (managed care for long-duration illnesses, e.g. AIDS); Imagyn Medical, Inc. (devices with women's health focus); Advanced Surgical, Inc. (disposable instruments & equipment for minimally invasive surgery); LocalMed, Inc. (catheters for local drug delivery); Innotech, Inc. (system for low-cost fast manufacture of bifocals at retail dispensing locations)

Connecticut Innovations, Inc.
999 West Street
Rocky Hill, Connecticut 06067
(860) 563-5851
Fax: (860) 563-4877
Web: www.ctinnovations.com

Key contact:
Ms. Pamela Hartley, Director of CT Technology Partnerships
Mr. Victor Budnick, President/Executive Director

Description: The state of Connecticut's investor in high technology, providing risk capital to emerging technology companies in Connecticut and fostering the transfer of research into commercial applications. We currently hold a majority of our investments in: biomedical technology, photonics (applied optics) and information technology.

Amount of capital invested: $9 million

Preferred investment size: $500,000-750,000

Amount under management: $25-100 million

Area served: Focused in Connecticut, United States

Preferred stages of financing: Seed, Start up, First stage, Second stage

Industries:
I.01   Aerospace
I.03   Biotech/genetic engineering
I.05   Chemicals
I.06   Communications
I.08   Computer software
I.14   Electronics
I.15   Energy/natural resources/utilities
I.21   High technology
I.23   Information technology services
I.24   Internet services/e-commerce
I.29   Medical/medical products

Sampling of portfolio companies: Torrington Research Co. (design of proprietary air handling systems); Cyberian Outpost (computer retailers); Proton Energy Systems (hydrogen gas researchers)

Consumer Venture Partners
Three Pickwick Plaza
Greenwich, Connecticut 06830
(203) 629-8800
Fax: (203) 629-2019

Key contact:
Mr. Pearson Cummin
Mr. Christopher P. Kirchen
Mr. David S. Yarnell

Area served: United States

Preferred stages of financing: First stage, Second stage, LBO/MBO

Industries:
I.11   Consumer products
I.32   Retail

Crestview Financial Group
431 Post Road East, Suite One
Westport, Connecticut 06880-4403
(203) 222-0333
Fax: (203) 222-0000

Key contact:
Mr. Norman M. Marland, President
Mr. Robert J. Ready, Vice President

Description: Private venture capital firm investing own capital.

Founded: 1969

Preferred investment size: Over $500,000

Area served: Worldwide

Preferred stages of financing: Seed, Start up, First

stage, Second stage, Mezzanine

Industries:
I.02   Agriculture/forestry/fishing/mining
I.03   Biotech/genetic engineering
I.05   Chemicals
I.06   Communications
I.07   Computer hardware
I.08   Computer software
I.10   Consulting
I.11   Consumer products
I.12   Distribution
I.13   Education
I.14   Electronics
I.15   Energy/natural resources/utilities

I.17   Environmental services/waste management
I.18   Financial services
I.19   Generalist
I.20   Healthcare
I.21   High technology
I.22   Industrial products
I.23   Information technology services
I.24   Internet services/e-commerce
I.25   Leisure/hospitality
I.28   Media/publishing
I.29   Medical/medical products
I.31   Real estate
I.33   Semiconductors

Cullinane & Donnelly Venture Partners

One Century Tower, Suite 1004
New Haven, Connecticut 06510
(203) 772-1440
Fax: (203) 772-3656

Key contact:
Mr. John Cullinane
Mr. James F. Donnelly

Area served: Northeast

Preferred stages of financing: Seed, First stage

Industries:
I.06   Communications
I.17   Environmental services/waste management
I.18   Financial services
I.29   Medical/medical products
I.34   Services (business)
I.35   Services (consumer)

Endeavor Capital Management, LLC

830 Post Road East
Westport, Connecticut 06880
(203) 341-7788
Fax: (203) 341-7799

Key contact:
Mr. Anthony F. Buffa, Managing Partner
Ms. Nancy E. Haar, General Partner
Mr. Ron Reed, General Partner
Mr. Phil Siegel, General Partner

Area served: North America

Preferred stages of financing: First stage, Second stage, LBO/MBO, Expansion

Industries:
I.06   Communications
I.08   Computer software
I.18   Financial services
I.23   Information technology services
I.24   Internet services/e-commerce
I.34   Services (business)
I.35   Services (consumer)

Equity Capital Group

120 Long Ridge Road
Stamford, Connecticut 06927
(203) 357-3100
Fax: (203) 357-4462
Web: www.ge.com/capital/equity

Key contact:
Mr. Michael E. Pralle, President
Mr. Jeffrey H. Coats, Managing Director
Mr. John P. Malfettone, Managing Director
Mr. Steven D. Smith, Managing Director
Mr. Paul A. Gelburd, Managing Director
Ms. Sharon Pipe, Managing Director

Description: We are the private equity arm of GE Capital Services, one of the largest diversified financial services companies and a wholly-owned subsidiary of General Electric Company. We provide creative, flexible solutions by tailoring the investment size and structure of each deal to meet the needs of the individual client. We believe in funding a true business partnership with our clients by opening doors to new opportunities through the GE network.

Preferred investment size: $5-50 million

Area served: Worldwide

Industries:
I.06   Communications
I.11   Consumer products
I.16   Entertainment
I.18   Financial services
I.20   Healthcare
I.22   Industrial products
I.23   Information technology services
I.28   Media/publishing
I.32   Retail
I.34   Services (business)
I.36   Transportation

Sampling of portfolio companies: Endura Software Corp. (develops software solutions focused on the order, distribution & supply chain management processes that help distribution businesses); Numetrix Collaborative Enterprise Network (developer of intelligent solutions for global manufacturers & suppliers of consumer products); TruckLite; autobytel.com; iXL Interactive Excellence; Krause's Custom Crafted Furniture; Preview Travel (online travel service); Wink Communications; FastForms® (a quick, simple & secure process to manage forms delivery electronically through the creation of a central forms repository); The Gemplus Group (provider of plastic & smart card-based solutions); InSight Health; Paradigm Health Corp.; Abpac Inc.

(specialist in advanced BGA packaging); ichat (internet community-building application); Vanguard Automation (provides state-of-the-art placement solutions to the semiconductor industry); BayanTel; Euronet Internet;; Long Distance Int'l. Inc.; Signature Security Group

Howard Industries

136 Main Street
Westport, Connecticut 06880
(203) 227-4900
Fax: (203) 227-3314
E-mail: jdeluca@howardind.com
Web: www.howardind.com

Key contact:
Mr. Peter Howard
Mr. Joe DeLuca
Mr. Sean Leonard

Description: We are a private firm investing in closely held companies and corporate divestitures. We work in partnership with management,offering a long-term commitment to achieve significant growth and build value.

Preferred investment size: $20 million

Amount under management: $100-500 million

Area served: North America

Preferred stages of financing: LBO/MBO, Expansion

Industries:
I.01	Aerospace
I.04	Broadcasting
I.05	Chemicals
I.06	Communications
I.07	Computer hardware
I.09	Construction
I.11	Consumer products
I.12	Distribution
I.13	Education
I.14	Electronics
I.17	Environmental services/waste management
I.20	Healthcare
I.21	High technology
I.22	Industrial products
I.23	Information technology services
I.27	Manufacturing
I.28	Media/publishing
I.29	Medical/medical products
I.33	Semiconductors
I.34	Services (business)
I.36	Transportation
I.37	Wholesale

Insurance Venture Partners, Inc.

31 Brookside Drive, Suite 211
Greenwich, Connecticut 06830
(203) 861-0030
Fax: (203) 861-2745
E-mail: brownbe@imms.com

Key contact:
Mr. Bernard M. Brown, Managing Director

Description: Venture capital intermediary specializing in the insurance industry.

Area served: Worldwide

Preferred stages of financing: Seed, Start up, First stage, Second stage, Mezzanine, LBO/MBO, Expansion, Int'l expansion

JH Whitney & Company

177 Broad Street
Stamford, Connecticut 06901
(203) 973-1400
Fax: (203) 973-1422

Key contact:
Mr. Michael C. Brooks
Mr. Peter M. Castleman
Mr. Brian J. Doyle
Mr. James H. Fordyce
Mr. Jeffrey R. Jay
Mr. William Laverack
Mr. James R. Matthews

Mr. Ray E. Newton, III
Mr. Daniel J. O'Brien
Mr. Benno C. Schmidt
Mr. Michael R. Stone

Preferred stages of financing: Start up, First stage, LBO/MBO

Industries:
I.06	Communications
I.23	Information technology services
I.29	Medical/medical products

New Energy Partners, LP

8 Sound Shore Drive, Suite 100
Greenwich, Connecticut 06830
(203) 629-4447
Fax: (203) 629-4848
E-mail: gvpinc@aol.com
Web: www.new-energy.com

Key contact:
Dr. Daniel J. Cavicchio, Jr.

Description: We invest in leading-edge revolutionary energy technologies that are low cost and pollution free. Technologies must have potential to displace fossil fuels in major segments of the energy industry.

Technologies of interest include new hydrogen energy, cavitation devices and electromagnetic devices that demonstrate significant over-unity effects (more energy out than energy in).

Amount of capital invested: $250,000

Preferred investment size: $1 million

Amount under management: $10-25 million

Area served: North America

Preferred stages of financing: Start up, First stage, Second stage, Mezzanine

Industries:
I.15   Energy/natural resources/utilities

Oak Investment Partners

One Gorham Island
Westport, Connecticut 06880
(203) 226-8346
Fax: (203) 227-0372
Web: www.oakinv.com

Key contact:
Mr. Ed Glassmeyer

Description: We are a venture capital organization dedicated to helping new enterprises emerge as tomorrow's industry leaders. We were founded in 1978 and have organized seven partnerships with over $1 billion of capital under management. We have three areas of investment focus: information technology, healthcare and retail. We target experienced, entrepreneurial management teams that are resourceful, disciplined and motivated by appropriate incentives.

Preferred investment size: $4-20 million

Preferred stages of financing: Seed, Start up

Industries:
I.20   Healthcare

Sampling of portfolio companies: Actel (develops, manufactures & markets Field Programmable Gate Array solutions); Cephalon; Compaq Computer (manufactures & markets advanced PC's for businesses & professional use); Filene's Basement; Genzyme; HBO & Co.; Network Equipment Technologies, Inc. (communications equipment which enables the building & management of private backbone networks); Octel Communications Corp. (designs, manufactures & markets voice processing systems that are sold primarily to large corporate customers, telephone companies & other providers of Voice Information Services); Office Depot; Parametric Technology Corp. (develops, markets & supports a family of fully integrated parametric feature-based mechanical design automation software); PETsMART; PictureTel (provides high quality, full-color, full-motion video communications at bandwidths commensurate with the new digital, dial-up telephone services being introduced worldwide); Seagate Technology (manufactures & markets Winchester magnetic rigid disk drives for incorporation in minicomputer & microcomputer systems); Stratus (designs, manufactures, markets & services a family of fault tolerant Continuous Processing Systems for critical on-line transaction processing & communications control); SanDisk Corp. (develops & markets solid state non-volatile memory cards & boards for the laptop & portable PC market, as well as other portable communication devices using sophisticated flash E2PROM technology); Sybase (develops & markets SYBASE SQL Server); Synopsys, Inc. (produces synthesis products are complementary to established computer aided engineering tools & run on a broad range of UNIX platforms including those of SUN Microsystems, Apollo & DEC); Ungerman-Bass; Wellfleet (supplies high-performance, full functionality LAN internet working products & systems); Wholefoods

OEM Capital

406 Harbor Road
P.O. Box 629
Southport, Connecticut 06490
(203) 255-4230
Fax: (203) 259-4041
E-mail: info@oemcapital.com
Web: www.oemcapital.com

Key contact:
Mr. Ronald J. Klammer, Managing Director
Ms. Sharon M. Kane, Managing Director

Description: Merchant banking firm investing own capital or funds of partners or clients.

Preferred investment size: $3 million

Area served: United States

Preferred stages of financing: Mezzanine, LBO/MBO, Expansion

Industries:
I.06   Communications
I.07   Computer hardware
I.08   Computer software
I.14   Electronics
I.21   High technology
I.23   Information technology services
I.24   Internet services/e-commerce
I.29   Medical/medical products
I.33   Semiconductors

Sampling of portfolio companies: Carpenter Technology Corp. (producer & distributor of specialty metals & fabricated metallic parts); V Band Corp. (supplier of instant access voice communications systems); Crystek Crystals Corp. (manufacturer & value-added reseller high frequency quartz crystals & oscillators which are sold directly to original equipment manufacturers of communications & computer equipment & distributors of electronic components)

Oxford Ventures

315 Post Road West
Westport, Connecticut 06880
(203) 341-3300
Fax: (203) 341-3309
Web: www.oxbio.com

Key contact:
Dr. Alan Walton, General Partner
Mr. Cornelius Ryan, General Partner

Description: We are an independent venture capital firm that provides equity financing and management assistance to start-up and early-stage, entrepreneurial-driven companies in the bioscience and healthcare industries. Our partners currently manage venture funds with combined committed capital of more than $150 million. Our objective is to generate long-term capital gains for both the investors in the fund and the entrepreneurs that we support.

Amount of capital invested: $25 million

Preferred investment size: $2 million

Amount under management: $100-500 million

Area served: Asia, Europe, United States

Preferred stages of financing: Seed, Start up, First stage, Second stage

Industries:
I.03   Biotech/genetic engineering
I.20   Healthcare
I.26   Life sciences
I.29   Medical/medical products

Sampling of portfolio companies: Argomed, Ltd. (minimally invasive, catheter-based treatment for benign prostate hyperplasia); Arrow Corp. (pharmacy management services company); Biocode, Inc. (immunoassay-based product marking systems to detect counterfeiting & smuggling in pharmaceuticals & consumer & industrial products); BioScreen (qualitative gene expression analysis for drug discovery); Cardiopulmonary Corp. (computer controlled patient ventilators for the intensive care unit); Cellomics (high throughput, cell-based screening systems for drug discovery); Ceres, Inc. (agricultural bioscience); Coelacanth (development & manufacturer of novel building blocks for combinatorial chemistry systems); Cytologix, Inc. (automated slide preparation systems for the pathology laboratory); EVAX Technologies GmbH (bacterial-based vaccines for animal & human diseases); GuideStar Health Systems (managed care company providing insurance products to indemnity insurers); Inkine Pharmaceuticals (pharmaceuticals for treatment of cancer & infectious diseases); Memory Pharmaceuticals (pharmaceuticals to restore long-term potentiation of memory); Micromed Technology (left ventricular assist device for congestive heart failure); NetGenics, Inc. (bioinformatics software to manage genomics research programs); Orchid Biocomputer (nanotechnology-based drug discovery systems); Phase I (high throughput toxicology testing services); Physiome Sciences, Inc. (computer-based, physiological models of human organs for drug discovery & evaluation); Variagenics, Inc. (drug discovery & evaluation based on pharmacogenomics)

Power Project Financing
302 Lexington Street
New Haven, Connecticut 06513
(203) 469-0797
E-mail: ddr@compucloz.com

Key contact:
Mr. Henry Korszan, Director-Central Europe

Description: Financing electric power plants and advising and privatization.

Amount of capital invested: $89 million

Preferred investment size: $25 million

Amount under management: $100-500 million

Area served: Worldwide

Preferred stages of financing: Start up, First stage, Second stage, Energy project finance

Industries:
I.15   Energy/natural resources/utilities
I.17   Environmental services/waste management

Prince Ventures
25 Ford Road
Westport, Connecticut 06880
(203) 227-8332
Fax: (203) 226-5302

Key contact:
Mr. James W. Fordyce, General Partner
Mr. Mark J. Gabrielson, General Partner

Mr. Gregory F. Zaic, General Partner
Ms. Marianne Croce, Office Manager

Preferred stages of financing: Seed, Second stage

Industries:
I.03   Biotech/genetic engineering
I.29   Medical/medical products

RFE Investment Partners
36 Grove Street
New Canaan, Connecticut 06905
(203) 966-2800
Fax: (203) 966-3109

Key contact:
Mr. R. Peter Reiter, Jr., Senior Analyst
Mr. James A. Parsons, General Partner
Mr. Howard C. Landis, General Partner
Mr. A. Dean Davis, General Partner

Description: Private equity investment firm investing in later stage, profitable basic manufacturing, distribution and service business with at least $15 million of annual revenues.

Amount of capital invested: $26.5 million

Preferred investment size: $10-15 million

Amount under management: $100-500 million

Area served: United States

Preferred stages of financing: Mezzanine, LBO/MBO, Expansion, Recapitalization & acquisition financing

Industries:
I.05   Chemicals
I.06   Communications
I.07   Computer hardware
I.10   Consulting
I.11   Consumer products
I.12   Distribution
I.14   Electronics
I.17   Environmental services/waste management

I.18 Financial services
I.20 Healthcare
I.22 Industrial products
I.27 Manufacturing
I.28 Media/publishing
I.29 Medical/medical products
I.34 Services (business)
I.35 Services (consumer)
I.36 Transportation
I.37 Wholesale

Sampling of portfolio companies: GMM Holdings (manufactured housing); ProActive Therapy (physical therapy provider); VOCA Holdings (provides services to disabled individuals); Parts Plus Group (after market automotive parts distributor); SECOR Int'l. (environmental consulting); Long Manufacturing (food service equipment manufacturer); METALICO (metals recycling); OK Industries (electronics assembly equipment manufacturer); Great Clips (hair salon franchiser); MARCAP (food service equipment manufacturer); Scandura Holdings (conveyor belt manufacturer)

Saugatuck Capital Company

One Canterbury Green
Stamford, Connecticut 06901
(203) 348-6669
Fax: (203) 324-6995

Key contact:
Mr. Richard P. Campbell, Jr., Managing Director
Ms. Christy S. Sadler, Managing Director
Mr. Owen S. Crihfield, Managing Director
Mr. Frank J. Hawley, Jr., Managing Director

Area served: United States

Preferred stages of financing: LBO/MBO, Expansion

Industries:
I.06 Communications
I.11 Consumer products
I.27 Manufacturing
I.29 Medical/medical products
I.34 Services (business)

Schroder Venture Advisors, Inc.

1055 Washington Boulevard, 5th Floor
Stamford, Connecticut 06901
(203) 324-7700
Fax: (203) 324-3636

Description: Venture capital arm of international merchant bank.

Preferred stages of financing: Start up, First stage, LBO/MBO

Industries:
I.03 Biotech/genetic engineering
I.12 Distribution
I.22 Industrial products
I.26 Life sciences
I.29 Medical/medical products

Technology Crossover Ventures

15 Davenport Farms Lane East
Stamford, Connecticut 06903
(203) 595-9111
Fax: (203) 329-0721
E-mail: mtesler@tvc.com
Web: www.tcv.com

Key contact:
Mr. Marc S. Tesler, General Partner

Description: We focus exclusively on information technology, investing in expansion-stage private enterprises as well as select public situations.

Amount of capital invested: $37.4 million

Preferred investment size: $3-5 million

Amount under management: $100-500 million

Area served: Worldwide

Preferred stage of financing: Expansion

Industries:
I.06 Communications
I.07 Computer hardware
I.08 Computer software

I.14 Electronics
I.16 Entertainment
I.18 Financial services
I.21 High technology
I.23 Information technology services
I.24 Internet services/e-commerce
I.28 Media/publishing
I.30 New media
I.33 Semiconductors
I.34 Services (business)

Sampling of portfolio companies: Duet Technologies (provider of electronic design technology & networking software development services for high technology companies); IMX Mortgage Exchange (worldwide immediate access to mortgage origination products via a high speed private network); iVillage Women's Network (humanizing cyberspace & providing a relevant & indispensable online experience for adult women); Lynk Systems (merchant processor of credit & debit card transactions); Smart-Patents (developer of business decision software systems that automate the process of relating patents to protected business & product strategies)

TSG Capital Group, LLC

177 Broad Street, 12th Floor
Stamford, Connecticut 06901
(203) 406-1500
Fax: (203) 406-1590

Key contact:
Mr. Cleveland A. Christophe, Managing Partner
Mr. Darryl B. Thompson, Partner
Mr. Duane E. Hill, Partner

Mr. Mark D. Inglis, Partner

Description: Private equity firm with focus on media and communications, specialty retail, consumer goods and services, manufacturing with emphasis on the automotive sector. Prefers to invest $10 - 50 million in transactions ranging from $50 - 500 million. Additionally the firm invests in companies whose products serve ethnic markets, including African-American, Hispanics and Asians.

Preferred investment size: $10-50 million

Area served: North America

Preferred stages of financing: LBO/MBO, Expansion

Industries:
I.04   Broadcasting
I.11   Consumer products
I.27   Manufacturing
I.28   Media/publishing
I.32   Retail
I.34   Services (business)
I.35   Services (consumer)

Venad Administrative Services, Inc.
100 First Stamford Place, 3rd Floor
Stamford, Connecticut 06902
(203) 454-0639
Fax: (203) 454-7585
E-mail: jnickse@aol.com

Key contact:
Mr. Philip Chapman
Mr. Jay S. Nickse

Area served: United States

Preferred stage of financing: Second stage

Industries:
I.03   Biotech/genetic engineering
I.08   Computer software
I.14   Electronics
I.29   Medical/medical products

Delaware

Blue Rock Capital
5803 Kennett Pike, Suite A
Wilmington, Delaware 19807-1135
(302) 426-0981
Fax: (302) 426-0982

Key contact:
Mr. Terry Collison, Partner

Description: We make long-term equity only investments in seed stage and early stage companies with proprietary technology or business services in mid-atlantic area (North Carolina to Boston). We will not consider bio-tech, pharmaceutical, medical devices, consumer, retail, real estate or natural resources.

Amount of capital invested: $3 million

Preferred investment size: $1 million

Amount under management: $25-100 million

Area served: United States

Preferred stages of financing: Seed, Start up, First stage

Industries:
I.07   Computer hardware
I.08   Computer software
I.13   Education
I.14   Electronics
I.21   High technology
I.23   Information technology services
I.24   Internet services/e-commerce

Triad Investors Corp.
One Innovation Way, Suite 301
Newark, Delaware 19711
(302) 452-1120
Fax: (302) 452-1101

Key contact:
Mr. Jeffrey Davison, Partner

Description: We invest in early stage information technology, healthcare and advanced materials companies located in the Mid-Atlantic region.

Preferred investment size: $500,000

Amount under management: $10-25 million

Area served: North America

Preferred stages of financing: Seed, Start up, First stage

Industries:
I.03   Biotech/genetic engineering
I.05   Chemicals
I.06   Communications
I.07   Computer hardware
I.08   Computer software
I.11   Consumer products
I.13   Education
I.14   Electronics
I.18   Financial services
I.19   Generalist
I.20   Healthcare
I.21   High technology
I.22   Industrial products
I.23   Information technology services
I.24   Internet services/e-commerce
I.26   Life sciences
I.29   Medical/medical products
I.30   New media
I.33   Semiconductors
I.34   Services (business)
I.35   Services (consumer)

Sampling of portfolio companies: Current Analysis, Inc. (competitive intelligence services); Entek Corp. (chemicals); Communications Systems Technology, Inc. (wireless communications hardware); MDI Instruments, Inc. (medical devices); Intranetics, Inc. (software); Faith Mountain Co. (direct mail);

Netbalance Corp. (enterprise software); Visual Networks, Inc. (telecommunications equipment); Wisdomeware, Inc. (software)

District of Columbia

Allied Capital

1666 K Street NW, Suite 901
Ninth Floor
Washington, District of Columbia 20006
(202) 331-1112
Fax: (202) 659-2053

Key contact:
Mr. Tom Westbrook
Mr. G. Cabell Williams, III
Mr. George C. Williams

Area served: United States

Preferred stages of financing: Second stage, LBO/MBO, Third/later stage

Industries:
I.27   Manufacturing
I.32   Retail

Atlantic Coastal Ventures, L.P.

3101 South Street NW
Washington, District of Columbia 20007
(202) 293-1166
Fax: (202) 293-1181
E-mail: wthreadgill@atlanticcv.com
Web: www.atlanticcv.com

Key contact:
Mr. Walter L. Threadgill, General Partner
Mr. Patrick N. Hall, Associate

Description: We invest in a diversified portfolio of telecommunications companies and related service companies operating within markets that reflect the convergence of the computer, telephone, cable, media and communications, information management and technology, broadcast, satellite and entertainment industries. We further invest in a variety of other enterprises to produce competitive companies in those industries characterized by fragmentation and economic or financial inefficiencies.

Amount under management: $25-100 million

Area served: Atlantic Coast

Preferred stage of financing: Mezzanine

Industries:
I.06   Communications
I.16   Entertainment
I.28   Media/publishing

Sampling of portfolio companies: Citywide Communications, Inc. (broadcast operation); El Dorado Communications, Inc. (media company); ESR Media Ventures, LLC (media production company); Davis Broadcasting, Inc.; Z-Spanish Radio Network, Inc. (communications company); NTT, Inc. (electronic parts manufacturer/distributor); Coastal Communications of America, Inc. (pay telephone operator on the East Coast); Greystone Management, Inc. (franchise centers)

Trident Capital

1001 Pennsylvania Avenue NW, 2nd Floor
Washington, District of Columbia 20004
(202) 347-2626
Fax: (202) 347-1818

Key contact:
Mr. Edward J. Mathias, Special Limited Partner

Description: We have made it our business to understand information and business services companies. The markets. The movers. The risks. And the potential. By leveraging our industry expertise and resourceful partners and contacts, we've been able to back- and help build- many exciting companies. Many others are becoming leaders in their emerging markets.

Amount of capital invested: approximately $10 million

Preferred investment size: $5-7 million

Amount under management: $100-500 million

Area served: United States

Preferred stages of financing: Seed, Start up, First stage, Second stage, Mezzanine, LBO/MBO, Expansion

Industries:
I.08   Computer software
I.23   Information technology services
I.24   Internet services/e-commerce
I.28   Media/publishing
I.30   New media
I.34   Services (business)

Sampling of portfolio companies: Avesta Technologies, Inc. (provider of software & consulting services specializing in IT service management & high performance intranet applications); The Compucare Co. (provider of information systems to healthcare providers & their affiliates); CSG Systems Int'l., Inc. (provider of subscriber management systems & services for cable TV, DBS, telecommunications & on-line services); DAOU Systems, Inc. (provider of network integration services to healthcare organizations); Evolving Systems, Inc. (provider of software solutions & systems integration services for the telecommunications industry); Frisco Holdings (direct marketer of consumables to hospital & medical office x-ray & other imaging departments); Geosystems Global Corp. (provider of geographical information systems & services to the publishing, travel & information industries); Health Quality, Inc. (point-of-care clinical management systems combining electronic medical records & medical "quality" measurement); Internet Profiles Corp. (supplier of software & services for collecting, measuring & analyzing internet usage); Internet Securities, Inc. (provider of economic, political & financial information on emerging markets via the internet); Medicode Inc. (provider of medical information services, databases & software); Online Interactive, Inc. (provider of branded on-line marketing & shopping services); Pegasus Systems, Inc. (provider of transaction processing services to the hotel industry worldwide through its three services: TravelWeb, www travel booking site; THISCO, which connects hotel central reservation systems to the global distribution systems; & HCC, which aggregates & distributes travel agent commissions); Platinum Software Corp. (provider of LAN-based & client/server financial accounting applications); Production Group Int'l., Inc. (provider of global events, entertainment exhibitions & business communication services); Research Holdings, Ltd. (provider of interactive investor communication services); Rezsolutions, Inc. (provider of central reservation systems & related services to the travel & leisure industry); Unison Software, Inc. (provider of UNIX client/server software data center management software); Vality Technology, Inc. (provider of data-quality software tools & re-engineering consulting services); Viant Corp. (provider of consulting & systems integration services solely focused on delivering internet strategy & technology solutions)

Westfinance Corporation
3201 New Mexico Avenue NW, Suite 350
Washington, District of Columbia 20016
(202) 895-1390
Fax: (202) 966-8141

Key contact:
Mr. C. Stevens Avery, II, President

Description: Act as a financial intermediary and do not make direct investments. Capabilities/services include raising capital from private and public sources; business plans; financial advisors, chief executive officer, chief financial officer, valuations.

Preferred investment size: $5 million

Area served: North America

Preferred stages of financing: Start up, First stage, Second stage, Expansion, Will assist start-ups

Industries:
I.03   Biotech/genetic engineering
I.06   Communications
I.08   Computer software
I.11   Consumer products
I.14   Electronics
I.17   Environmental services/waste management
I.18   Financial services
I.20   Healthcare
I.21   High technology
I.26   Life sciences
I.27   Manufacturing
I.29   Medical/medical products
I.31   Real estate
I.32   Retail

Florida

Adventure Capital Corp.
P.O. Box 370531
Miami, Florida 33137
(305) 530-0046
Fax: (305) 350-6826
E-mail: corp@adventurecapital.com
Web: www.adventurecapital.com

Key contact:
Mr. Jeffrey M. Stoller, President
Mr. Al Paer, Vice President

Description: We, with our correspondent relationships, can provide substantial equity and/or debt, as well as provide merger and acquisition, debt restructuring, business planning anf due diligence services for all stages of business, including start-ups.

Amount of capital invested: $100 million+

Preferred stages of financing: Seed, Start up, First stage, Second stage, Mezzanine, LBO/MBO, Expansion, Int'l expansion, Venture leasing

Antares Capital Corporation
P.O. Box 410730
Melbourne, Florida 32941
(407) 777-4884
Fax: (407) 777-5884
E-mail: rpoliner@aol.com

Key contact:
Mr. Randall E. Poliner, President
Ms. Lisa A. Clouse

Description: We are a private venture capital firm investing equity capital in developmental and expansion stage companies and in management buy-out opportunities. Candidates for investment should have good management teams in place, established sales and serve large and growing markets. There is no industry restriction with the exclusion of real estate and mineral exploration projects.

Preferred investment size: $2 million

Area served: Texas, Southeast

Preferred stages of financing: Second stage, Mezzanine, Expansion

Industries:
I.04   Broadcasting
I.05   Chemicals
I.06   Communications
I.07   Computer hardware
I.08   Computer software

I.10   Consulting
I.11   Consumer products
I.14   Electronics
I.16   Entertainment
I.17   Environmental services/waste management
I.18   Financial services
I.19   Generalist
I.20   Healthcare
I.21   High technology
I.22   Industrial products
I.23   Information technology services
I.24   Internet services/e-commerce
I.25   Leisure/hospitality
I.27   Manufacturing
I.28   Media/publishing
I.29   Medical/medical products
I.30   New media
I.32   Retail
I.33   Semiconductors
I.34   Services (business)
I.35   Services (consumer)

Sampling of portfolio companies: AEMT, Inc. (power quality & power conditioning services); BRPH Architects Engineers, Inc. (data communications & network products); Conxus Communications, Inc. (narrowband personal communication system for 2-way & voice paging); Crystal Dynamics, Inc. (game software for high-end platforms); The Email Channel, Inc. (email one-to-one marketing, database, distribution & response management services); Flood Data Services, Inc. (information services for mortgage, banking & other financial companies); Sawgrass Electronics Group, Inc. (hybrid & application specific integrated circuits & related electronics devices); SportsLine USA, Inc. (sports media company providing information, entertainment & merchandise to sports enthusiasts over the world wide web); Stadia Net Sports, Inc. (operates a network providing programming & content directed at captive audiences attending live sporting events)

Avery Business Development Services

2506 St. Michel Court
Ponte Vedra, Florida 32082
(904) 285-6033
Fax: (904) 285-6033

Key contact:
Mr. Henry Avery, President

Area served: North America

Preferred stages of financing: Seed, Start up, First stage, Second stage, Mezzanine, LBO/MBO, Expansion

Industries:
I.05   Chemicals
I.08   Computer software
I.21   High technology
I.29   Medical/medical products
I.34   Services (business)

Sampling of portfolio companies: Macrochem (biotechnology); Perspective Biosystems (biotechnology); US Biomaterials (biotechnology); Flit-It (cooking devices); Triggernet (fishing devices)

C&C Vencap Corporation

11000 Prosperity Farms Road
Palm Beach Gardens, Florida 33410
(561) 776-0277
Fax: (561) 776-9838
E-mail: ccvencaps@msn.com
Web: www.c-cvencap.com

Key contact:
Mr. William Cella, President
Mr. Michael Calandra, Executive Vice President

Description: Our mission is to search for the best opportunities for our investors and to provide the appropriate vehicle for wealth creation. Projects are generally technology driven with emphasis on emerging markets and products. We are commited to continuing to build long term relationships with our clients.

Amount of capital invested: $10 million

Preferred investment size: $1 million

Amount under management: <$10 million

Area served: United States

Preferred stages of financing: Seed, First stage, Second stage, Mezzanine, Expansion

Industries:
I.04   Broadcasting
I.06   Communications
I.07   Computer hardware
I.14   Electronics
I.21   High technology
I.23   Information technology services
I.24   Internet services/e-commerce
I.25   Leisure/hospitality
I.26   Life sciences

Sampling of portfolio companies: Security Identification Systems Corp.; WPCX of Chicago, LLP; WPCW of Philadelphia, GP; WPCR of Boston, GP

Communications Equity Associates, Inc.

101 East Kennedy Boulevard, Suite 3300
Tampa, Florida 33602
(813) 226-8844
Fax: (813) 225-1513
Web: www.commequ.com

Key contact:
Mr. J. Patrick Michaels, Chairman/CEO
Mr. Harold Ewen

Mr. Bruno Claude
Mr. George Pollock
Mr. Ming Jung
Mr. Thomas W. Cardy, Executive Vice President
Mr. Scott N. Feuer, Vice President
Mr. Bryan L. Crino, Senior Associate

Description: We have a rich 25-year history of diverse experiences and milestone industry accomplishments which establish us as a worldwide leader. By combining the sophisticated skills of a large Wall Street investment firm with a focus on communications industries, we offer a depth of service that's unparalleled. The experience of our professionals speaks for itself: since our founding, we have completed more than 600 transactions, valued at more than $13 billion. With an extensive network of long-standing relationships and offices on almost every continent, along with our affiliates, we have helped clients in 27 countries successfully pursue their financial and strategic goals.

Founded: 1973

Preferred investment size: No more than 15% of the total fund

Amount under management: $100-500 million

Area served: Worldwide

Preferred stages of financing: LBO/MBO, Growth

Industries:
I.04   Broadcasting
I.06   Communications
I.16   Entertainment
I.23   Information technology services
I.24   Internet services/e-commerce
I.28   Media/publishing

FCP Investors, Inc./Florida Capital Partners

100 North Tampa Street, Suite 2410
Tampa, Florida 33602
(813) 222-8000
Fax: (813) 222-8001
E-mail: gboken@fcpinvestors.com
Web: www.fcpinvestors.com

Key contact:
Mr. Glenn Oken, Partner
Mr. Jay Jester, Partner
Mr. David Malizia, Partner

Description: We acquire profitable private companies with historical pre-tax profits of at least $2 million, working in partnership with operating managers. We do not provide venture capital for emerging businesses.

Amount under management: $100-500 million

Area served: United States

Preferred stages of financing: LBO/MBO, Recapitalization & industry consolidation

Industries:
I.05   Chemicals
I.11   Consumer products
I.12   Distribution
I.19   Generalist
I.22   Industrial products
I.27   Manufacturing
I.37   Wholesale

Heller & Marsh Capital

1214 North University Drive
Plantation, Florida 33322
(954) 475-8484
Fax: (954) 475-1125
E-mail: info@hellercap.com
Web: hellercap.com

Key contact:
Mr. Michael Heller, President
Mr. Gerald Heller, Executive Vice President
Mr. Michael Gorson, Vice President

Description: We have the ability to finance a wide variety of projects. We direct all clients to the most appropriate sources of capital. For smaller projects, our network of specialists guide entrepreneurs through the SBA loan application process. For larger projects, we represent individual private investor angels who seek to invest in start-up and expanding businesses with outstanding management and profit potential. These private sources of captial provide funding for projects between $1 million and $10 million. We also have relationships with other capital sources for projects that exceed $10 million.

Industries:
I.01   Aerospace
I.02   Agriculture/forestry/fishing/mining

I.03   Biotech/genetic engineering
I.04   Broadcasting
I.05   Chemicals
I.06   Communications
I.07   Computer hardware
I.09   Construction
I.10   Consulting
I.11   Consumer products
I.12   Distribution
I.13   Education
I.14   Electronics
I.16   Entertainment
I.17   Environmental services/waste management
I.18   Financial services
I.20   Healthcare
I.21   High technology
I.24   Internet services/e-commerce
I.25   Leisure/hospitality
I.26   Life sciences
I.27   Manufacturing
I.29   Medical/medical products
I.31   Real estate
I.32   Retail
I.34   Services (business)
I.37   Wholesale

The Melbourne Group, Inc.

1900 South Harbor City Boulevard, Suite 227
Melbourne, Florida 32901
(407) 726-6484

Key contact:
Mr. Stephen Baur, President

Description: Consulting firm evaluating and analyzing venture projects and arranging private placements.

Founded: 1985

Preferred investment size: $1-5 million

Area served: Southeast

Preferred stage of financing: Second stage

Industries:
I.03	Biotech/genetic engineering
I.05	Chemicals
I.06	Communications
I.07	Computer hardware
I.08	Computer software
I.14	Electronics
I.15	Energy/natural resources/utilities
I.22	Industrial products
I.29	Medical/medical products
I.33	Semiconductors

North American Business Development Company, L.L.C.

312 S.E. 17th Street, Suite 300
Ft. Lauderdale, Florida 33316
(954) 463-0681
Fax: (954) 527-0904

Key contact:
Mr. Charles L. Palmer, President

Description: General partner of North American Funds, partnerships of institutional investors with $115 million in equity capital that specialize in acquiring or making substantial investments in small businesses with annual revenues of $5-35 million and developing them into significantly larger enterprises.

Amount of capital invested: $15 million

Preferred investment size: $5-10 million

Amount under management: $100-500 million

Area served: United States

Preferred stages of financing: First stage, Second stage, LBO/MBO, Expansion

Industries:
I.01	Aerospace
I.05	Chemicals
I.06	Communications
I.07	Computer hardware
I.08	Computer software
I.10	Consulting
I.11	Consumer products
I.12	Distribution
I.13	Education
I.14	Electronics
I.19	Generalist
I.20	Healthcare
I.21	High technology
I.22	Industrial products
I.23	Information technology services
I.24	Internet services/e-commerce
I.27	Manufacturing
I.29	Medical/medical products
I.34	Services (business)
I.35	Services (consumer)
I.36	Transportation
I.37	Wholesale

Sampling of portfolio companies: ACR Electronics, Inc. (manufacturer of safety & survival devices for marine, aviation & outdoor recreation markets worldwide); MECC/The Learning Co. (leading developer, publisher & distributor of fun learning software for use by children in school & at home); Gateway Healthcare Corp. (full-line distributor of medical/surgical products to physicians, nursing homes & home healthcare agencies worldwide); AMTEC Precision Products, Inc. (manufacturer of high-volume, close-tolerance machined metal components, principally for automotive & capital equipment markets); J&B Foods Corp. (producer of branded specialty meats & cooked-then-frozen foods serving the institutional foodservice market in the Midwest & Southeast); Polymer Design Corp. (pioneer in rapid-turn-around, low-volume production of complex, high-performance plastic parts using unique liquid resin casting(TM) process); Actown-Electrocor, Inc. (manufacturer of high-voltage, power & surface-mount transformers, solenoids & other industrial coils & chip inductors)

Sigma Capital Corp.

22668 Caravelle Circle
Boca Raton, Florida 33433
(561) 994-2295
Fax: (561) 994-9757

Key contact:
Mr. Alvin S. Schwartz, President

Description: Small venture capital firm; max PE deal 500K; Florida only

Amount of capital invested: $250,000

Preferred investment size: $250,000

Amount under management: <$10 million

Area served: Florida

Preferred stages of financing: First stage, Second stage

Industries:
I.09	Construction
I.11	Consumer products
I.12	Distribution
I.14	Electronics
I.22	Industrial products
I.27	Manufacturing
I.29	Medical/medical products
I.31	Real estate
I.37	Wholesale

South Atlantic Venture Fund, L.P.

614 West Bay Street
Tampa, Florida 33606-2704
(813) 253-2500
Fax: (813) 253-2360

Key contact:
Mr. Donald W. Burton
Ms. Sandra P. Barber
Mr. Drew A. Graham
Mr. W. Scott Miller

Area served: Mid Atlantic, Southeast

Industries:
I.06   Communications
I.11   Consumer products
I.14   Electronics
I.18   Financial services
I.23   Information technology services
I.29   Medical/medical products

Texada Capital Corporation

770 West Bay Street
Winter Garden, Florida 34787
(800) 748-4494
Fax: (407) 656-4825

Key contact:
Mr. Laurie G. Kolbeins, Managing Director
Ms. Bluette N. Blinoff, Managing Director

Description: We are an investment banking firm with a primary focus on clients in the direct response support services industry: telemarketing, direct mail, printing, fulfillment, data base management, electronic transfer and website authoring and management. We offer financial and strategic advisory services for the owners and managers of closely held companies or divisions of public companies.

Amount of capital invested: $500,000

Amount under management: <$10 million

Area served: United States

Preferred stages of financing: Mezzanine, LBO/MBO, Expansion

Industries:
I.06   Communications
I.14   Electronics
I.15   Energy/natural resources/utilities
I.22   Industrial products
I.23   Information technology services
I.24   Internet services/e-commerce
I.27   Manufacturing
I.28   Media/publishing
I.34   Services (business)
I.37   Wholesale

Sampling of portfolio companies: Magnetix Corp. (custom audio duplicator primarily serving spoken word customers: audio books, religious & motivational speakers); Dirextions Division (direct mail & fulfillment company serving the Orlando hospitality & entertainment community); Connextions Int'l., Inc. (inbound & outbound telemarketing company based in Orlando)

Union Atlantic LC

701 Brickell Avenue, Suite 2000
Miami, Florida 33131
(305) 374-0282
Fax: (206) 374-5149
E-mail: lenny@ualc.com
Web: ualc.com

Key contact:
Mr. Leonard Sokolow, President

68 Cayman Place
Palm Beach, Florida 33418
(561) 626-9311
Fax: (206) 374-5149
E-mail: tim@ualc.com
Web: ualc.com

Key contact:
Mr. Timothy Mahoney, Partner

Description: A private merchant banking concern providing investment opportunities to corporations and high net worth individuals through equity investments in emerging companies targeted in the technology sector. We look for strong management teams with commercially available products and services.

Preferred investment size: None

Amount under management: <$10 million

Area served: Europe, North America, South/Central America

Preferred stages of financing: First stage, Second stage

Industries:
I.07   Computer hardware
I.08   Computer software
I.10   Consulting
I.12   Distribution
I.14   Electronics
I.21   High technology
I.23   Information technology services
I.24   Internet services/e-commerce
I.33   Semiconductors

Sampling of portfolio companies: The Concours Group (IT consultancy); Galacticomm (internet software); Advanced Electronics Support Products (computer peripherals); LocalNet Communications (multi-level marketing, technology); Command Software (PC software)

Venture Capital Management Corp.

P.O. Box 372626
Satellite Beach, Florida 32937

(407) 777-1969
E-mail: venturecmc@earthlink.net

Key contact:
Dr. Robert A. Adams, President

Description: Private venture capital firm also offering consulting services to entrepreneurs and young companies. Develops business plans and private placement offering memoranda. Assists with funding efforts and acquisition opportunities.

Preferred investment size: $500,000

Amount under management: <$10 million

Area served: Worldwide

Preferred stages of financing: Start up, First stage

Industries:
I.01   Aerospace
I.03   Biotech/genetic engineering

I.05   Chemicals
I.06   Communications
I.11   Consumer products
I.14   Electronics
I.16   Entertainment
I.18   Financial services
I.20   Healthcare
I.21   High technology
I.22   Industrial products
I.23   Information technology services
I.24   Internet services/e-commerce
I.25   Leisure/hospitality
I.27   Manufacturing
I.29   Medical/medical products
I.31   Real estate
I.34   Services (business)
I.35   Services (consumer)

Georgia

The Acquisition Search Corp.
1150 Lake Hearn Drive, Suite 200
Atlanta, Georgia 30342
(404) 250-3250
Fax: (404) 233-4905

Key contact:
Mr. Roger Orloff, President

Preferred stages of financing: First stage, Second stage, LBO/MBO

Industries:
I.05   Chemicals

I.10   Consulting
I.11   Consumer products
I.12   Distribution
I.13   Education
I.14   Electronics
I.15   Energy/natural resources/utilities
I.18   Financial services
I.25   Leisure/hospitality
I.28   Media/publishing
I.29   Medical/medical products
I.36   Transportation

Alliance Technology Ventures
3343 Peachtree Road NE, Atlanta Financial Center
East Tower, Suite 1140
Atlanta, Georgia 30326
(404) 816-4791
Fax: (404) 816-4891
E-mail: fleming@atv.com
Web: www.atv.com

Key contact:
Mr. Michael Henos, Founding General Partner
Mr. Stephen Fleming

Description: We are an early-stage venture capital firm specializing in life sciences and information technology startups. Our first fund has approximately $35 million under management from major corporate and institutional investors, including Georgia Power, BellSouth, UPS, NationsBank, Emory University and Georgia Tech. We began operations in 1994 and are focusing primarily on opportunities in Georgia and the Southeast.

Founded: 1993

Preferred investment size: $500,000-1 million

Amount under management: $25-100 million

Area served: Southeast

Preferred stages of financing: Start up, First stage, Second stage

Industries:
I.23   Information technology services

I.26   Life sciences

Sampling of portfolio companies: Atherogenics (detection & treatment of coronary artery disease); Discovery Therapeutics (development of novel treatments for Parkinson's Disease & other disorders); Neocrin (development of biohybrid pancreatic tissue transplants as a cure for diabetes); Renalogics (development of novel treatments for kidney disease); Inhibitex (hyperimmune treatments for infectious diseases); RF Micro Devices (design & development of sophisticated integrated circuits for wireless applications); Synchrologic (software components for the development of database applications that are intermittently connected to the network); SportsLine USA (source for sports scores, stats & information on the internet); Video Networks (providing cable operators, ad agencies, rep firms & program providers a powerful new way to transport & manage broadcast video & advertising content); Care Centric Solutions (highly-functional point-of-care clinical information systems for use by healthcare professionals in the patient's home or other non-hospital environment); CIENA

Arete Ventures, Inc.

115 Perimeter Center Place, Suite 640
Atlanta, Georgia 30346
(770) 399-1660
Fax: (770) 399-1664

Key contact:
Mr. George W. Levert

Founded: 1985

Preferred investment size: $500,000-3 million

Area served: United States

Preferred stages of financing: First stage, Second stage, Expansion

Industries:
I.06   Communications
I.15   Energy/natural resources/utilities
I.23   Information technology services
I.24   Internet services/e-commerce
I.35   Services (consumer)

Sampling of portfolio companies: Metricom; Ramp Networks; Evolutionary Technologies

Cordova Capital

3350 Cumberland Circle, Suite 970
Atlanta, Georgia 30339
(770) 951-1542
Fax: (770) 955-7610
Web: www.cordovacapital.com

Key contact:
Mr. Paul R. DiBella
Mr. Christopher J. Valianos, President of Cordova Realty II
Mr. W. A. Williamson
Mr. Robert N. Leslie, Vice President-Finance & Administration
Mr. Frank X. Dalton, Head of Software & IT Investments
Mr. Ralph R. Wright, Jr., Principal
Mr. John R. Runningen, Head of Healthcare Practice Group
Dr. Teo Forcht Dagi, M.D., Head of Cordova Technology Fund
Mr. Charles E. Adair
Mr. Gerald F. Schmidt, President/Co-Founder
Mr. Don B. Stout, CEO of Cordova Realty, Inc.

Description: We are a $160 million Atlanta based venture capital firm formed to invest in small to medium-sized growth companies. We provide bridge equity for real estate projects through our Cordova Realty funds. We are not just about money but in truly assisting entrepreneurs in being successful and significant in their communities and industries.

Founded: 1989

Preferred investment size: $500,000-4 million

Amount under management: $100-500 million

Area served: Southeast

Industries:
I.06   Communications
I.17   Environmental services/waste management
I.18   Financial services
I.20   Healthcare
I.23   Information technology services
I.29   Medical/medical products

Sampling of portfolio companies: CogniTech Corp. (developer of client/server software for sales force automation & opportunity management); InterTech Information Management, Inc. (provider of proprietary Microsoft NT centric imaging & document management software products & services); Systems Techniques (provider of proprietary data warehousing products to help major healthcare entities in the design, re-engineering & integration of information systems); CMG Information Services, Inc.

(internet application software developer focusing on website advertising management, targeted delivery & reporting); Technology Builders, Inc. (reseller of software products focusing in areas such as software quality management & client/server internet tools); Kyrus Corp. (reseller & integrator of retail point of sale systems in the grocery, convenience stores, restaurants & specialty retail industry segments); DentalCare Partners, Inc. (provider of dental practice management services to affiliated dental professional associations); Horizon Medical Products, Inc. (manufacturer & distributor of vascular access products sold to oncologists, surgeons & hospitals); Mantis Corp. (provider of subacute services to healthcare systems including ongoing contract infusion & rehabilitation therapy through nursing facilities); Rehab Assoc., Inc. (provider of physical & occupational therapy services in owned & managed free-standing clinics & hospital departments); Charter Communications Int'l., Inc. (provider of telecommunications products & services to domestic & int'l. markets); Network One (provider of nationwide telecommunications services including long distance, 800, pagers, teleconferencing, calling card/debit card, int'l. & one plus services); Signal Point Systems, Inc. (provider of products & services in support of the telecommunications industry, primarily in the cellular & PCS markets); Investors Financial Group, Inc. (financial services company that provides products including mutual funds, fixed & variable annuities, life insurance products & limited partnerships through independent financial planners); Lynk Systems, Inc. (provider of transaction processing to retail merchants, specializing in providing ATM/point of sale debit card payment services); Nat'l. Action Financial Services, Inc. (financial services company specializing in debt collection & receivables management); USBA, Ltd. (provider of financial services to small & medium-sized banks); Accu-Tech Corp. (distributor of electronic wire, cable & network products to contractors, installers, OEMs & electrical wholesalers); The Step Co. (a manufacturer of sports fitness equipment); Metals Recycling Technologies Corp. (developer of The MRT Process, a patented chemical process that recycles eletric-arc furnace dust, a hazardous waste, into commercial products)

EGL Holdings, Inc.
6600 Peachtree-Dunwoody Road
300 Embassy Row, Suite 630
Atlanta, Georgia 30328
(770) 399-5633
Fax: (770) 393-4825
E-mail: samassaro@eglholdings.com
Web: www.eglholdings.com

Key contact:
Mr. Salvatore A. Massaro, Partner
Mr. Murali Anantharaman, Partner
Mr. David O. Ellis, Partner

Description: A buyout/venture capital firm looking to make equity investments in the Southeastern and Eastern United States. Seeks to acquire controlling interests in businesses, high-tech to no-tech, in partnership with qualified management/ownership groups. Also interested in minority stakes in later stage growth companies in a variety of industries.

Preferred investment size: Expansion: $3 million; $7-10 million

Amount under management: $25-100 million

Area served: United States

Preferred stages of financing: LBO/MBO, Expansion

Industries:
I.05   Chemicals
I.06   Communications
I.07   Computer hardware
I.08   Computer software
I.11   Consumer products
I.12   Distribution
I.14   Electronics
I.19   Generalist
I.20   Healthcare
I.21   High technology
I.22   Industrial products
I.23   Information technology services
I.25   Leisure/hospitality
I.27   Manufacturing
I.29   Medical/medical products
I.34   Services (business)
I.35   Services (consumer)

Sampling of portfolio companies: Zarina Holdings, CV ($25 million world wide manufacturer of automatic swimming pool cleaners); Physician Health Corp. ($95 million physician health care services provider); The Learning Company ($350 million consumer software company) Checkmate Electronics ($35 million manufacturer of P-O-S check readers); Artcraft ($30 million whole sale distributor of fine art supplies); Simione Central ($50 million provider of clinical & financial inormation systems to the home healthcare sector)

First Growth Capital, Inc.
I-75 & GA 42, Best Western Plaza
P.O. Box 815
Forsyth, Georgia 31029
(912) 994-9260
Fax: (912) 994-1280

Key contact:
Mr. Vijay Patel

Area served: United States

Industries:
I.19   Generalist

Gray Ventures, Inc.
3350 Cumberland Circle, Suite 1900
Atlanta, Georgia 30339
(770) 240-1505
Fax: (770) 240-1401
E-mail: bernard@grayventures.com
Web: www.grayventures.com

Key contact:
Mr. Bernard Gray

Industries:
I.08   Computer software
I.23   Information technology services

Sampling of portfolio companies: Accipiter Inc. (software & information); Advanced Charger Technology Inc. (software & information); CogniTech Corp. (software & information); Synchrologic Inc. (software & information)

Miller/Zell Venture Group
4715 Frederick Drive, SW
Atlanta, Georgia 30336
(404) 691-7400
Fax: (404) 699-2189

Key contact:
Mr. H. B. Miller
Mr. Gary Meyers

Preferred stages of financing: Seed, Start up, LBO/MBO

Industries:
I.11   Consumer products
I.32   Retail

Morgenthaler Ventures
3200 Habersham Road
Atlanta, Georgia 30305
(404) 816-0051
Fax: (404) 816-0685
Web: www.morgenthaler.com

Key contact:
Mr. Randy G. Brown, Venture Partner

Description: We are passionately dedicated to being the most valued partner to world-class entrepreneurs building industry-leading enterprises. We have been an active company builder since 1968, funding more than 150 companies, two-thirds of which are now public entities. We focus on early stage investments in information technology and health care as well as later stage management-led buyouts.

Founded: 1968

Preferred investment size: $2-8 million

Area served: United States

Preferred stages of financing: Seed, Start up, LBO/ MBO

Industries:
I.03   Biotech/genetic engineering
I.06   Communications
I.08   Computer software
I.14   Electronics
I.20   Healthcare
I.24   Internet services/e-commerce

I.29   Medical/medical products

Sampling of portfolio companies: Endgate (wireless broadband radio modules); Synernetics (high speed networking); Intrinsa (software component verification); Molecular Applications Group (molecular design software); Think & Do (micro-controller programming); Ingres (relational DBMS); TimesTen (main memory data management); VeriFone (credit card verification); Vivo (video streaming); Evans & Sutherland (graphics & simulation); QuickLogic (field programmable logic arrays); Synopsys (synthesis of IC's); Protogene (biochips for genomic analysis); The Liposome Co. (liposome-based drug delivery); Vical (DNA-based pharmaceuticals for human disease); Managed Health Network (managed mental health preferred provider organization); Pointshare Health Networks (medical intranets for physicians & hospitals); CVIS (intravascular ultrasound medical devices); Embol-X (devices to protect the brain from stroke); Perclose (suture-mediated vascular closure systems)

Noro-Moseley Partners
4200 Northside Parkway NW, Building 9
Atlanta, Georgia 30327
(404) 233-1966
Fax: (404) 239-9280

Key contact:
Mr. Charles D. Moseley, Jr.
Mr. Russell R. French

Mr. Charles A. Johnson
Mr. Jack R. Kelly, Jr.

Area served: Southeast

Preferred stages of financing: Second stage, LBO/ MBO, Third stage

---

North Riverside Capital Corporation
50 Technology Park
Norcross, Georgia 30092
(770) 446-5556
Fax: (770) 446-8627

Key contact:
Mr. Thomas R. Barry

Preferred stages of financing: Second stage, LBO/ MBO

Industries:
I.03   Biotech/genetic engineering
I.06   Communications
I.07   Computer hardware
I.08   Computer software
I.14   Electronics
I.18   Financial services
I.19   Generalist
I.22   Industrial products
I.29   Medical/medical products
I.35   Services (consumer)

Ponte Vedra Ventures
5385 Peachtree Dunwoody Road, #215
Atlanta, Georgia 30342
(404) 303-9861
Fax: (404) 303-9563
E-mail: pvv@mindspring.com

Key contact:
Mr. Henry H. Neely, Associate
Mr. Drew Cassidy, Principal/General Partner

Description: We represent a private investor seeking to make investments in early stage companies with a simple concept. Since July 1996, we have focused exclusively on the Southeastern United States. We seek those entrepreneurs who have the competence,

drive and enthusiasm to succeed through leading a fast growth company. We seek entrepreneurs with a desire to build significant businesses.

Founded: 1996

Preferred investment size: $100,000-500,000

Area served: Southeast

Preferred stages of financing: Seed, Start up, First stage

Industries:
I.20   Healthcare
I.27   Manufacturing
I.34   Services (business)

Renaissance Capital Corporation
34 Peachtree Street NW, Suite 2230
Atlanta, Georgia 30303

(404) 658-9061
Fax: (404) 658-9064

Key contact:
Mr. Larry Edler, President

Description: We are licensed by the Small Business Administration as a Specialized Small Business Investment Company (SSBIC). We focus on businesses located in Georgia and the Southeast with special attention on the Atlanta metro area.

Amount of capital invested: $150,000

Preferred investment size: $300,000

Amount under management: <$10 million

Area served: United States

Preferred stages of financing: Second stage, Mezzanine, LBO/MBO, Expansion

Industries:
I.04	Broadcasting
I.06	Communications
I.09	Construction
I.11	Consumer products
I.12	Distribution
I.14	Electronics
I.16	Entertainment
I.20	Healthcare
I.23	Information technology services
I.27	Manufacturing
I.29	Medical/medical products
I.32	Retail
I.36	Transportation
I.37	Wholesale

Richards, LLC

303 Peachtree Street NE, Suite 4100
Atlanta, Georgia 30308
(404) 572-7200
Fax: (404) 572-7227
E-mail: info@richardsco.com
Web: www.richardsco.com

Key contact:
Mr. James C. Richards, Managing Director
Mr. Carl B. Bachmann, Principal
Mr. Robert W. Heller, Principal

Description: We are a private equity investment firm whose principals understand the business dynamics of the south and are committed to the long-term success of growing companies in the region.

Preferred investment size: $5-10 million

Amount under management: $25-100 million

Area served: United States

Preferred stage of financing: LBO/MBO

Industries:
I.06	Communications
I.11	Consumer products
I.12	Distribution
I.22	Industrial products
I.25	Leisure/hospitality
I.27	Manufacturing
I.34	Services (business)
I.35	Services (consumer)
I.36	Transportation
I.37	Wholesale

Sampling of portfolio companies: Transportation Technologies (creators of a process that enhances the maintenance, refurbishment & repair of truck trailers & sea-going containers); Unarco (invented the shopping cart in 1937 & has remained the world's largest manufacturer of steel shopping carts); Tube-Tex (manufacturer of finishing equipment for circular knit fabric producers); Safemark Corp. (supplier of in-room safes to the lodging industry)

State Street Bank & Trust Company

3414 Peachtree Road, N.E., Suite 1010
Atlanta, Georgia 30326
(404) 364-9500
Fax: (404) 261-4469

Key contact:
Mr. Kent D. Mitchell, Vice President

Description: We make senior loans against cash flow. Compensation is interest rate, fees & warrants. Portfolio is generalist in nature; selective as to management teams.

Founded: 1792

Preferred investment size: $10 million

Area served: United States

Preferred stages of financing: LBO/MBO, Expansion

Industries:
I.03	Biotech/genetic engineering
I.04	Broadcasting
I.06	Communications
I.08	Computer software
I.12	Distribution
I.14	Electronics
I.19	Generalist
I.22	Industrial products
I.23	Information technology services
I.24	Internet services/e-commerce
I.26	Life sciences
I.27	Manufacturing
I.28	Media/publishing
I.29	Medical/medical products
I.34	Services (business)
I.37	Wholesale

Hawaii

Bancorp Hawaii SBIC

P.O. Box 2900
Honolulu, Hawaii 96846
(808) 537-8085

Fax: (808) 521-7602

Key contact:
Mr. Robert Paris

Description: Venture capital subsidiary of Bancorp Hawaii, Inc.

Area served: Hawaii

Preferred stages of financing: Second stage, LBO/MBO

Industries:
I.03   Biotech/genetic engineering
I.06   Communications
I.07   Computer hardware
I.08   Computer software
I.29   Medical/medical products

Pacific Venture Capital, Ltd.

222 South Vineyard Street, PH.1
Honolulu, Hawaii 96813
(808) 521-6502
Fax: (808) 521-6541

Key contact:
Mr. Dexter J. Taniguchi

Preferred stages of financing: First stage, Second stage, Third/later stage

Industries:
I.19   Generalist

Venture Planning Associates

1188 Bishop Street, Suite 1508
Honolulu, Hawaii 96813
(808) 545-7473
Fax: (808) 524-2775
E-mail: capital@ventureplan.com
Web: www.ventureplan.com

Key contact:
Mr. William F. McCready, President/CEO

Description: We provide venture capital consulting services for all phases of business development, from start-ups to IPO's.

Industries:

I.01	Aerospace	I.13	Education
I.02	Agriculture/forestry/fishing/mining	I.14	Electronics
I.03	Biotech/genetic engineering	I.15	Energy/natural resources/utilities
I.04	Broadcasting	I.16	Entertainment
I.05	Chemicals	I.17	Environmental services/waste management
I.06	Communications	I.18	Financial services
I.07	Computer hardware	I.19	Generalist
I.08	Computer software	I.20	Healthcare
I.09	Construction	I.21	High technology
I.10	Consulting	I.22	Industrial products
I.11	Consumer products	I.23	Information technology services
I.12	Distribution	I.24	Internet services/e-commerce
		I.25	Leisure/hospitality
		I.26	Life sciences
		I.27	Manufacturing
		I.28	Media/publishing
		I.29	Medical/medical products
		I.30	New media
		I.31	Real estate
		I.32	Retail
		I.33	Semiconductors
		I.34	Services (business)
		I.35	Services (consumer)
		I.36	Transportation
		I.37	Wholesale

Illinois

ABN AMRO Private Equity

208 South LaSalle Street, Suite 1000
Chicago, Illinois 60604-1003
(312) 855-7079
Fax: (312) 553-6648

Key contact:
Mr. Ken Tyszko
Mr. David L. Bogetz
Mr. Keith Walz

Founded: 1996

Area served: United States

Preferred stages of financing: LBO/MBO, Expansion

Industries:
I.11   Consumer products
I.29   Medical/medical products
I.35   Services (consumer)

Alpha Capital Partners, Ltd.

122 South Michigan Avenue, Suite 1700
Chicago, Illinois 60603
(312) 322-9800
Fax: (312) 322-9808
E-mail: acp@alphacapital.com
Web: www.alphacapital.com

Key contact:
Mr. Andrew H. Kalnow, President
Mr. William J. Oberholtzer, Vice President

Description: We are a venture capital management organization which provides equity financing for promising growth business and buyouts or recapitalizations of established companies. The investment activity of Alpha Capital is concentrated mainly in the greater Midwest. The entrepreneurs whom we have supported have achieved success in a variety of industries.

Founded: 1984

Amount of capital invested: $4,109,377

Preferred investment size: $500,000-3 million

Amount under management: $25-100 million

Area served: Midwest, United States

Preferred stages of financing: First stage, Second stage, LBO/MBO, Expansion

Industries:
- I.01 Aerospace
- I.02 Agriculture/forestry/fishing/mining
- I.03 Biotech/genetic engineering
- I.04 Broadcasting
- I.05 Chemicals
- I.06 Communications
- I.07 Computer hardware
- I.08 Computer software
- I.09 Construction
- I.10 Consulting
- I.11 Consumer products
- I.12 Distribution
- I.13 Education
- I.14 Electronics
- I.15 Energy/natural resources/utilities
- I.16 Entertainment
- I.17 Environmental services/waste management
- I.18 Financial services
- I.19 Generalist
- I.20 Healthcare
- I.21 High technology
- I.22 Industrial products
- I.23 Information technology services
- I.24 Internet services/e-commerce
- I.25 Leisure/hospitality
- I.26 Life sciences
- I.27 Manufacturing
- I.28 Media/publishing
- I.29 Medical/medical products
- I.30 New media
- I.32 Retail
- I.33 Semiconductors
- I.34 Services (business)
- I.35 Services (consumer)
- I.36 Transportation
- I.37 Wholesale

Sampling of portfolio companies: Clear Communications Corp. (software sytems for managing telecom broadband network performance); Color Savvy Systems, Ltd. (systems for precise replication of color); Entek Scientific Corp. (software & systems for preventative maintenance in process industries); LDMI (switch-based reseller of long distance telecommunications); ½ Off Card Shop, Inc. (specialty retailer of discount cards & party supplies); CarCare Enterprises, Co. (Jiffy Lube franchisee for northern half of Chicago area); PetCare Plus, Inc. (specialty retailer selling pet food, supplies & accessories); Vista Restaurants, Inc. (restaurant management company & area franchisee for Perkins); CareCentric Solutions, Inc. (software systems for clinical applications in home healthcare); Cirrus Diagnostics, Inc. (developer of automated immunoassay diagnostic instruments); HealthTech Services Corp. (remote telemonitoring & care system for home healthcare); Origen, Inc. (commercialization of veterinary vaccine technologies from universities); Pioneer Laboratories, Inc. (surgical cable & instruments); Somatogen, Inc. (developer of bioengineered blood & other pharmaceutical products); Citizens Financial Corp. (holding company for data processor serving S&L's); Commercial National Bank (community banking group); Red Arrow Products (manufacturer of smoke flavoring for food products); Sutton Tool Co. (manufacturer of deburring machines & work holding devices); Valley Industries, Inc. (manufacturer of heat transfer parts for refrigerators & freezers); Vapor Systems Technologies (systems for recovery & control of vapors from fuels)

Ameritech Development Corporation
30 South Wacker Drive, 37th Floor
Chicago, Illinois 60606
(312) 750-5083
Fax: (312) 207-1365
Web: www.ameritech.com/products/venture

Key contact:
Mr. Robert A. Schriesheim, Managing Director
Mr. Craig Lee, Director
Mr. Charles Ross, Director
Mr. Greg Smitherman, Director
Mr. Darrell A. Williams, Director
Mr. Michael Pickard, Director
Mr. Mark Ward, Associate

Description: We are a wholly-owned subsidiary of Ameritech Corporation, a $15 billion telecommunications, information management and media company. Our venture capital program is chartered with making strategic equity investments in early and mid-stage communications, content and media ventures that enhance our competitive position. By focusing on markets related to the competencies of Ameritech and its business units, we are able to bring substantive value to our portfolio companies.

Area served: Worldwide

Preferred stages of financing: Start up, First stage, Second stage, Int'l expansion

Industries:
- I.06 Communications
- I.24 Internet services/e-commerce

Apex Investment Partners
233 South Wacker Drive, Suite 9500
Chicago, Illinois 60606
(312) 258-0320

Fax: (312) 258-0592
E-mail: apex@apexvc.com

Key contact:
Mr. Frederick W. W. Bolander
Mr. James Johnson
Mr. Bret Maxwell
Mr. George M. Middlemas

Description: Venture capital funds that serve pension funds, institutional investors and qualified individual investors.

Preferred investment size: Over $1 million

Area served: United States

Preferred stages of financing: Start up, First stage, Second stage

Industries:
I.06   Communications
I.07   Computer hardware
I.08   Computer software

I.11   Consumer products
I.12   Distribution
I.14   Electronics
I.17   Environmental services/waste management
I.22   Industrial products
I.23   Information technology services
I.32   Retail

Sampling of portfolio companies: AccessLine Technologies Inc.; American Communications Services Inc.; American Waste Services Inc.; Applied Digital Access Inc.; Arnold Palmer Golf Management Co.; Concord Communications; Data Critical Corp.; Expressly Portraits; Mothers Work Inc.; Ponderosa Fibers of Pennsylvania; Purecycle Corp.; Security Dynamics Technologies Inc.; Select Comfort Corp.; Steinbrecher Corp.; The Zond Group; Tut Systems; Worldtalk Corp.; Zemex Corp.

Arch Venture Partners

8735 West Higgins Road, Suite 235
Chicago, Illinois 60631
(773) 380-6600
Fax: (773) 380-6606
Web: www.archventure.com

Key contact:
Mr. Steven Lazarus, Managing Director
Mr. Keith Crandell, Managing Director
Mr. Robert Nelsen, Managing Director
Mr. Clinton Bybee, Managing Director

Description: We invest in the development of early stage technology companies which have the potential to grow rapidly into substantial enterprises. We invest primarily in companies we co-found with leading scientists and entrepreneurs, concentrating on bringing to market technological innovations developed from academics and corporate research.

Amount of capital invested: $20 million

Preferred investment size: $1 million

Amount under management: $100-500 million

Area served: United States

Preferred stages of financing: Seed, Start up, First stage

Industries:
I.03   Biotech/genetic engineering
I.05   Chemicals
I.06   Communications
I.07   Computer hardware
I.08   Computer software
I.13   Education
I.14   Electronics
I.20   Healthcare
I.21   High technology
I.23   Information technology services
I.24   Internet services/e-commerce
I.26   Life sciences
I.33   Semiconductors

Sampling of portfolio companies: Adolor Corp. (biopharmaceutical); Appliant Corp. (software); Apropos Corp. (software); Bell Geospace (oil field services); Caliper Technologies Corp. (microfluidics); DeCode Genetics (genomic information); Genvec (gene therapy); Intelligent Reasoning Systems (electronic test equipment); Internet Dynamics (internet software); Nanophase Technologies (ultra fine ceramic materials); New Era of Networks (applications integration software); Optobionics (opto-electronic retinal implants); R2 Technology (computer-aided diagnosis of mammograms); Siliscape (virtual displays); RWT Corp. (manufacturing execution software)

Batterson Venture Partners, LLC

303 West Madison Street, Suite 1110
Chicago, Illinois 60606
(312) 269-0300
Fax: (312) 269-0021
E-mail: bvp@vcapital.com
Web: www.vcapital.com

Key contact:
Mr. Leonard A Batterson, Chairman/CEO
Mr. Peter Fuss, Executive Vice President-Technology
Mr. Frederick E. Jordan, Jr., Venture Manager

Description: Our objective is assisting men and women of ability, integrity and energy to create businesses of lasting value, to those who build them, the society which they support, and the individuals with the vision to have committed their capital to these enterprises. We will place our capital and reputations at risk in these endeavors, contributing our counsel, experience, creativity and time to build a successful enterprise.

Amount of capital invested: $1.3 million

Amount under management: $25-100 million

Area served: United States

Preferred stage of financing: Start up

Industries:
I.21   High technology
I.23   Information technology services
I.29   Medical/medical products

Sampling of portfolio companies: CyberSource (software); Endicor (medical device); Paladin (service)

C3 Holdings, LLC
233 South Wacker Drive
Sears Tower, Suite 5330
Chicago, Illinois 60606
(312) 655-5990
Fax: (312) 655-5999
E-mail: businessdevelopment@c3holdings.com
Web: www.c3holdings.com

Key contact:
Mr. G. Cook Jordan, Jr., Principal

Description: Our principals bring more than a recognized breadth of experience in capital formation, corporate and joint venture acquisitions, dispositions, investment banking and corporate restructurings. We have all operated businesses on a daily basis. While each principal brings a successful past and a unique perspective to the firm, the combination of individual talents into this highly skilled team truly distinguishes our firm. And because the firm takes a partnership approach to business, business owners gain access to the expertise of all our partners.

Area served: Midwest

Preferred stages of financing: LBO/MBO, Add-ons

Industries:
I.05   Chemicals
I.06   Communications
I.11   Consumer products
I.12   Distribution
I.15   Energy/natural resources/utilities
I.18   Financial services
I.20   Healthcare
I.22   Industrial products
I.23   Information technology services
I.27   Manufacturing
I.31   Real estate
I.32   Retail
I.35   Services (consumer)
I.37   Wholesale

Sampling of portfolio companies: After Six Ltd. (marketer & distributor of formal apparel & accessories); American Safety Razor Co. (manufacturer of brand-name & private brand personal care consumer products); Bullitt Beverage Co. (wholesale distributor of malt beverage products); LaPetite Academies, Inc. (provider of child day care); Propane Continental, Inc. (consolidator of retail propane distribution companies); Sealright Co., Inc. (designer & manufacturer of value-added packaging & packaging systems for consumer products); Sylvan Learning Systems, Inc. (provider of supplemental education services & computer assisted testing services); Tom's Foods, Inc. (manufacturer of a full-line of snack foods for distribution in the over-the-counter & vending machine markets); William Noble Rare Jewels (specialty retailer of jewelry & gems); ARR-MAZ Products, LP (specialty chemical producer of processing additives for the mining, fertilizer, asphalt pavement, concrete & metal working fluids industries); Durowal Corp. (ASE manufacturer of hangers & fastening systems used in building construction); Heartland Precision Fasteners, Inc. (manufacturer of precision aerospace parts & fasteners); Redwood Microsystems, Inc. (developer & manufacturer of micro-valves for industrial equipment); Unitog Co. (manufacturer of custom designed uniforms & leading supplier of uniform rental services); Wes-Tech, Inc. (manufacturer of factory automation equipment); Assistive Technology, Inc. (developer & provider of computer software & hardware for the physically challenged); HealthCare Capital Corp. (consolidator of audiology centers); Molecular Geriatrics Corp. (developer of Alzheimers testing models); Myriad Ultrasound Systems Ltd. (developer & manufacturer of ultrasound diagnostic equipment); XTL Biopharmaceuticals Ltd. (product developer for treatment of viral & autoimmune diseases)

The Capital Strategy Management Company
233 South Wacker Drive
Chicago, Illinois 60606-0334
(312) 444-1170

Key contact:
Mr. Eric E. von Bauer, President

Description: We are a venture capital resource to both early and later stage businesses. Both debt and equity investments are structured for the needs of both high and low technology companies. We can also take an active advisory role to insure the achievement of growth objectives.

Preferred investment size: $1-5 million

Area served: Primarily Midwest, Mid-Atlantic

Preferred stages of financing: Seed, Start up, First stage, Second stage, Mezzanine, LBO/MBO, Expansion

Industries:
I.01   Aerospace
I.04   Broadcasting
I.06   Communications
I.07   Computer hardware
I.08   Computer software
I.09   Construction
I.11   Consumer products
I.13   Education
I.14   Electronics
I.15   Energy/natural resources/utilities
I.19   Generalist
I.21   High technology
I.22   Industrial products
I.23   Information technology services
I.24   Internet services/e-commerce
I.27   Manufacturing
I.28   Media/publishing
I.29   Medical/medical products
I.30   New media
I.32   Retail
I.33   Semiconductors
I.34   Services (business)
I.35   Services (consumer)
I.36   Transportation
I.37   Wholesale

CID Equity Partners

2 North LaSalle, Suite 1705
Chicago, Illinois 60602
(312) 578-5350
Fax: (312) 578-5358
E-mail: billh@cidequity.com
Web: www.cidequity.com

Key contact:
Mr. G. Cook Jordan, Jr., General Partner

Description: We are a venture capital firm with offices in Indianapolis, Chicago, Cincinnati and Columbus. Our objective is to invest in companies with potential for substantial value appreciation. Through long-term investments of five to seven years, we develop a partnership, establish a direction for growth, and build the value of each company. While daily operating decisions are the responsibility of management, we play an active role in the strategic direction of the business. The size of the investments are generally between $1 million and $10 million.

Amount of capital invested: $35 million

Preferred investment size: $3-5 million

Amount under management: $100-500 million

Area served: United States

Preferred stages of financing: Seed, Start up, First stage, Mezzanine

Industries:
I.03   Biotech/genetic engineering
I.06   Communications
I.08   Computer software
I.12   Distribution
I.18   Financial services
I.20   Healthcare
I.21   High technology
I.22   Industrial products
I.23   Information technology services
I.24   Internet services/e-commerce
I.27   Manufacturing
I.34   Services (business)

Comdisco Ventures

6111 North River Road
Rosemont, Illinois 60018
(847) 698-3000
Fax: (847) 518-5440
Web: www.comdisco.com

Key contact:
Mr. Jim Labé, President

Description: We provide a wide variety of financing products to venture capital-backed start-up companies. These include equipment leases and loans, subordinated debt, receivables financing and equity financing.

Amount of capital invested: $167,269,749.97

Area served: United States

Preferred stage of financing: Start up

Industries:
I.03   Biotech/genetic engineering
I.06   Communications
I.08   Computer software
I.14   Electronics
I.23   Information technology services
I.29   Medical/medical products

I.32   Retail
I.33   Semiconductors
I.34   Services (business)

Sampling of portfolio companies: Alexon Biomedical (biotechnology/biopharmaceutical); CytoMed (biotechnology/ biopharmaceutical); ImmunoPharmaceutics (biotechnology/biopharmaceutical); Microcide Pharmaceuticals (biotechnology/biopharmaceutical); Pharmacyclics (biotechnology/ biopharmaceutical); Vertex Pharmaceuticals (biotechnology/biopharmaceutical); Adv Interventional Systems (medical devices & services); InControl (medical devices & services); Academic Systems (software & computer services); Cortez Software Int'l. (software & computer services); Gupta Technologies (software & computer services); Simba Technologies (software & computer services); Veritas Software (software & computer services); XachLabs (software & computer services); MNI Interactive (consumer related); Sneaker Stadium (consumer related); The Edison Project (other products & services); Appex (communications & networking); Efficient Networks (communications & networking); Crystal Semiconductor (computer hardware & semiconductor)

Continental Illinois Venture Corp.

231 South LaSalle Street, 7th Floor
Chicago, Illinois 60697
(312) 828-8021
Fax: (312) 987-0887
E-mail: gregory.w.wilson@bankamerica.com
Web: www.civc.com

Key contact:
Mr. Gregory W. Wilson, Managing Director
Mr. Christopher J. Perry, President
Mr. Marcus D. Wedner, Managing Director
Mr. Daniel G. Helle, Managing Director
Mr. Thomas Van Pelt, Managing Director
Ms. Sue C. Rushmore, Managing Director

Description: We are a Bank of America funded private equity investment firm focused on majority or minority investments in established US-based service.

Amount of capital invested: $55 million

Preferred investment size: $15-30 million

Amount under management: $100-500 million

Area served: North America

Preferred stages of financing: LBO/MBO, Expansion

Industries:
I.01   Aerospace
I.04   Broadcasting

I.06   Communications
I.10   Consulting
I.13   Education
I.14   Electronics
I.18   Financial services
I.19   Generalist
I.22   Industrial products
I.24   Internet services/e-commerce
I.27   Manufacturing
I.28   Media/publishing
I.34   Services (business)
I.35   Services (consumer)

Sampling of portfolio companies: Advanced Quick
Circuits, LP (produces complex, multilayered printed
circuit boards, especially for prototype applications);
AMP Holding LP (specialty chemical maunfacturer);
Custom Industries, LP (specialty food ingredients
manufacturer); Duo-Tang, Inc. (manufacturer in the
paper-based report covers & portfolios segment of the
office supplies market); Falcon First Communications, LP (cable MSO); Petersen Publishing Co., LLC
(publisher of special-interest consumer magazines);
Teletouch Communications, Inc. (radio paging
company serving rural markets in the mid-South);
TransWestern Publishing Co., LP (second-largest

publisher of yellow pages in the US); Celutel, Inc.
(telecommunications company); New Vision Television, LP (television stations); Q Media Holding,
Inc. (paging companies); SRDS, LP (publishes directories which are considered by many advertising
agencies to be the "bibles" of their industry); Home
Technology Healthcare, Inc. (focuses on nursing
services & infusion therapy); Saba Medical
Management, LP (acquires & operates medical
device companies); Dynamic Health, Inc. (acquires
acute care hospitals in suburban & rural communities); Marks Bros. Jewelers, Inc. (specialty retailer
of fine jewelry, owns & operates over 110 retail
stores); Land 'N' Sea Distributing, Inc. (wholesale
distributor of marine parts & accessories); UI Video
Holdings, Inc. (Blockbuster Video franchisee); First
Franklin Financial Corp. (sub-prime mortgage
lender); Tangram Partners, Inc. (private equity partnership interested in companies involved in plastic
injection molding, specialty chemicals, printed circuit
board manufacturing, & coiled steel tubing manufacturing); Universal Development Corp. (home-
builder); Sunbelt National Mortgage Co. (residential
mortgage banking firm)

First Analysis Venture Capital

Sears Tower
233 South Wacker Drive, Suite 9500
Chicago, Illinois 60606
(312) 258-1400
Fax: (312) 234-0334
E-mail: fasc@firstanalysis.com
Web: www.facvc.com

Key contact:
Mr. Bret R. Maxwell
Mr. Steven F. Bouck
Mr. Brian D. Boyer
Mr. Brian E. Hand
Mr. Larry Hickey
Mr. Mark T. Koulogeorge
Mr. Mark H. Terbeek

Description: We manage over $400 million in three
families of venture capital funds. Our objective is to
provide capital to develop leading companies in the
following sectors: recycling and natural resource
efficiency, specialty chemicals and materials, maintenance and outsourced services,
telecommunications and information services, industrial and institutional automation, waste
management.

Founded: 1985

Preferred investment size: $1-10 million

Preferred stages of financing: Start up, LBO/MBO

Industries:
I.05   Chemicals
I.06   Communications
I.15   Energy/natural resources/utilities
I.17   Environmental services/waste management
I.23   Information technology services

Sampling of portfolio companies: Ponderosa Fibres of
Pennsylvania Inc. (manufactures post-consumer
recycled pulp for use in high-quality printing &
writing paper); Tetra Technologies Inc. (collects
byproducts from chemical processors & processes

them to create specialty chemicals it sells to a variety
of markets); Zond Corp. (wind-powered electrical
generating industry); NuCo2 Inc. (supplies liquid
carbon dioxide to retail establishments for carbon-
ating & dispensing fountain beverages); Performance
Materials Corp. (manufactures proprietary , carbon-
reinforced thermoplastic materials that are used in the
athletic footwear, podiatric & orthotic markets to
provide high levels of structural strength & stiffness
with minimal weight); F.Y.I. Inc. (provides a variety
of document management services to hospitals &
healthcare institutions, banks & financial institutions,
legal practitioners & corporate clients); Matrix
Service Co. (maintains, modifies & constructs above-
ground storage tanks & refinery & petrochemical
plant process units); Tri-Tek Information Systems &
Services, Inc. (solutions-oriented systems integrator
of computer networking technologies); American
Communications Services, Inc. (provides telecommunications customers with direct access circuits to
interexchange carriers); Dialogic Corp. (open-archi-
tecture call processing components); Security
Dynamics (provides products that protect & manage
access to computer-based information resources);
Dynamic Healthcare Technologies Inc. (provider of
patient-centered healthcare information systems);
Environmental Data Resources Inc. (provides environmental, infrastructure, property & population
information in an intelligent, geo-coded format to
consultants, lawyers & bankers for transaction &
capital investment due diligence); Continental Waste
Industries Inc. (provides integrated waste
management services to more than 175,000 residential, commercial & industrial customers in
concentrated, regional markets); Serrot Corp.
(designs, manufactures & installs lining systems for
the solid waste & mining industries); USA Waste
Services Inc. (provides integrated waste management
services in more than 30 states, Canada, Mexico &
Puerto Rico)

Frontenac Company

135 South LaSalle Street, Suite 3800
Chicago, Illinois 60603
(312) 368-0044
Fax: (312) 368-9520
E-mail: frontenac@frontenac.com

Key contact:
Mr. Rodney L. Goldstein, Managing Partner
Mr. James E. Cowie, General Partner
Mr. James E. Crawford, III, General Partner
Mr. Roger S. McEniry, General Partner
Mr. Paul D. Carbery, General Partner
Mr. M. Laird Koldyke, General Partner
Ms. Darcy J. Moore, General Partner
Ms. Laura P. Pearl, General Partner
Mr. Jeremy H. Silverman, General Partner
Mr. Martin J. Koldyke, Chairman

Founded: 1971

Amount of capital invested: $63.4 million

Preferred investment size: $10-20 million

Amount under management: $500 million -1 billion

Area served: United States

Preferred stages of financing: First stage, Second stage, LBO/MBO, Expansion

Industries:
I.06   Communications
I.08   Computer software
I.11   Consumer products
I.13   Education
I.14   Electronics
I.20   Healthcare
I.22   Industrial products
I.23   Information technology services
I.24   Internet services/e-commerce
I.27   Manufacturing
I.32   Retail
I.34   Services (business)
I.35   Services (consumer)

GTCR Golder, Rauner, LLC

6100 Sears Tower
Chicago, Illinois 60606-6402
(312) 382-2200
Fax: (312) 382-2201
E-mail: info@gtcr.com
Web: www.gtcr.com

Key contact:
Mr. Bruce V. Rauner, Principal
Mr. David Donnini, Principal
Mr. Donald Edwards, Principal
Mr. Joe Nolan, Principal
Mr. Phil Canfield, Principal
Mr. Will Kessinger, Principal
Mr. Edgar Jannotta, Jr., Principal

Description: We invest in consolidating fragmented industries by teaming with leading industry executives to build companies through acquisition and internal growth.

Amount under management: >$1 billion

Area served: United States

Preferred stage of financing: Consolidation of fragmented industries

Industries:
I.06   Communications
I.08   Computer software
I.10   Consulting

I.12   Distribution
I.14   Electronics
I.18   Financial services
I.20   Healthcare
I.21   High technology
I.22   Industrial products
I.23   Information technology services
I.24   Internet services/e-commerce
I.27   Manufacturing
I.28   Media/publishing
I.29   Medical/medical products
I.34   Services (business)
I.35   Services (consumer)
I.36   Transportation

Sampling of portfolio companies: Adra Systems, Inc. (electronics); American Medserve Corp. (health care); Anthony's Manufacturing Co. (industrial); Bulk Logistics, Inc. (information); Corestaff, Inc. (service); Crystal Products, Inc. (healthcare); DeLite Outdoor, Inc. (media); Dimac Corp. (consumer); EG&G Inc. (energy); Ero, Inc. (consumer); Geographic Systems, Inc. (information); Highmark Corp. (consumer); Interspec, Inc. (healthcare); MSP Television of Midland-Odessa (communications); The Newtrend Group Ltd. (electronics); Northern Investment LP II (industrial); Nu-Med, Inc. (healthcare); Physicians Radio Network/Sage Broadcasting (communications); Shape, Inc. (industrial); US Fleet Services, Inc. (service)

Hammond, Kennedy, Whitney & Company, Inc.

333 North Michigan Avenue, Suite 501
Chicago, Illinois 60601
(312) 458-0060
Fax: (312) 458-0072

Key contact:
Mr. Andrew McNally

Description: Founded in 1904.

Founded: 1904

Amount of capital invested: $10 million

Preferred investment size: $2-5 million

Amount under management: $25-100 million

Area served: Europe, North America

Preferred stage of financing: LBO/MBO

Industries:
I.27   Manufacturing

Sampling of portfolio companies: Excel Industries Inc. (automotive supplier); Baldwin Technologies Inc. (printing accessories); Control Devices Inc. (automotive sensor supplier); Maine Tire Int'l. (industrial application tires); Grobet File Co. of America (industrial & jewelry tools); Seneco Printing & Label (labels for the bottling industry); Globe Ticket & Label (event tickets); Horton Emergency Vehicles (ambulances); Morehouse Group (publishing specialty)

Holden Capital & Kinship Partners (Venture Management, Inc.)
400 Skokie Boulevard, Suite 265
Northbrook, Illinois 60062
(847) 291-1466
Fax: (847) 291-1890

Key contact:
Ms. Helen Wilcox
Mr. Michael I. Block, Managing Director

Preferred stages of financing: Seed, First stage

Industries:
I.03   Biotech/genetic engineering
I.06   Communications
I.07   Computer hardware
I.08   Computer software
I.29   Medical/medical products

IEG Venture Management
70 West Madison Street, 14th Floor
Chicago, Illinois 60602
(312) 644-0890
Fax: (312) 454-0369
E-mail: frankblair@aol.com
Web: iegventure.org

Key contact:
Mr. Frank Blair, President

Description: We focus on early-stage, technology based Midwest companies.

Preferred investment size: $500,000

Amount under management: <$10 million

Area served: Midwest

Preferred stages of financing: Seed, Start up, First stage

Industries:
I.01   Aerospace
I.05   Chemicals
I.06   Communications
I.07   Computer hardware
I.08   Computer software
I.12   Distribution
I.14   Electronics
I.15   Energy/natural resources/utilities
I.17   Environmental services/waste management
I.20   Healthcare
I.21   High technology
I.22   Industrial products
I.23   Information technology services
I.26   Life sciences
I.27   Manufacturing
I.29   Medical/medical products
I.33   Semiconductors
I.34   Services (business)
I.36   Transportation

INROADS Capital Partners, L.P.
1603 Orrington Avenue, Suite 2050
Evanston, Illinois 60201
(847) 864-2000
Fax: (847) 864-9692
E-mail: cmoore@inroadsvc.com

Key contact:
Mr. Jerrold B. Carrington, General Partner
Ms. Margaret G. Fisher, General Partner
Ms. Sona Wang, General Partner

Description: We are a professionally managed $50 million venture capital fund providing growth and acquisition capital for small and medium-sized ($10-100 million in annual revenues) businesses.

Amount of capital invested: $5.4 million

Preferred investment size: $1-4 million

Amount under management: $25-100 million

Area served: United States

Preferred stages of financing: Second stage, Expansion

JK&B Capital
205 North Michigan Avenue, Suite 808
Chicago, Illinois 60601
(312) 946-1200
Fax: (312) 946-1103

Key contact:
Mr. David Kronfeld

Industries:
I.06   Communications
I.08   Computer software
I.18   Financial services

LaSalle Capital Group, Inc.
5710 Three First National Plaza
Chicago, Illinois 60602
(312) 236-7041
Fax: (312) 236-0720

E-mail: roccomar@msn.com

Key contact:
Mr. Rocco J. Martino, Partner

Mr. Charles S. Meyer, Chairman
Mr. Tony Pesavento, Partner

Description: Principals in the leveraged acquisition of small and medium-sized companies.

Preferred investment size: $1-3 million

Area served: North America

Preferred stage of financing: LBO/MBO

Industries:
I.11   Consumer products
I.12   Distribution
I.13   Education
I.15   Energy/natural resources/utilities
I.19   Generalist
I.22   Industrial products
I.27   Manufacturing
I.29   Medical/medical products
I.34   Services (business)
I.35   Services (consumer)

Sampling of portfolio companies: Continental Scale Corp. (manufactures a complete line of scales for the medical & consumer markets); Bearing Belt & Chain, Inc. (specialty distributor of heavy rubber conveyor belting); Harris & Mallow, Inc. (manufacturer of decorative wall clocks & indoor electric grills); SealRite Windows, Inc. (manufacturer of wood windows for residential construction & remodeling); SNE Enterprises LP (nat'l. manufacturer of wood windows, doors & related products); Belmor Manufacturing LP (manufacturer of specialty accessories for the heavy duty trucking industry); Wm. E. Wright LP (maufacturer & marketer of decorative ribbon, lace, tape, braid & trimming for use in the retail home sewing/craft industry, as well as in the industrial ribbon market in the U.S. & Canada); Copperfield Chimney Supply, Inc. (specialty catalog supply company serving the chimney sweep trade); Consolidated Industrial Plastics, LP (formed to acquire & consolidate distributors of plastic pipes, valves, fittings & related fabricated components); Goode Furniture Co., LP (formed to acquire furniture manufacturers selling to mass merchandisers); Cherry Tree Toys, Inc. (specialty mail-order distributor of wooden craft kits, hand tools & related supplies for the home hobbyist); Precision Products Group, Inc. (manufacturer in two business segments: 1) specialty springs, 2) wound paper & plastic tubing); Elm Packaging Co., LP (manufacturer of foam polystyrene packaging including hinged-lid take-out containers, plates, bowls, egg cartons & other specialty food service & grocery items); Delta III, Inc. (manufacturer & marketer of high quality pick-up truck tool boxes, running boards & other aluminum truck accessories); Nat'l. Metalwares, LP (integrated manufacturer of tubluar steel components for household & juvenile products & commerical furniture, as well as for sporting goods equipment, lawn & garden equipment & toys); Foxwood Manufacturing & Distributing Co., Inc. (distributor & manufacturer of high quality equestrian products from english & western riding markets); E-Z Int'l., Inc. (marketer of quilting, sewing & crafting notions & "how to do it" books to the retail/home sewing craft market); Alambre Products Corp. (manufacturer of coiled springs focusing on small diameter wire applications requiring precise tolerances); Armstrong Containers, Inc. (manufacturer of paint cans & related containers)

Madison Dearborn Partners, Inc.

Three First National Plaza, Suite 3800
Chicago, Illinois 60602
(312) 895-1000
Fax: (312) 895-1001

Key contact:
Mr. John Canning

Area served: Canada, United States

Preferred stage of financing: LBO/MBO

Industries:
I.06   Communications
I.11   Consumer products
I.12   Distribution
I.15   Energy/natural resources/utilities
I.22   Industrial products
I.29   Medical/medical products

Marquette Venture Partners

520 Lake Cook Road, Suite 450
Deerfield, Illinois 60015
(847) 940-1700
Fax: (847) 940-1724

Key contact:
Mr. Lloyd D. Ruth, General Partner
Mr. James E. Daverman, General Partner
Mr. James R. Simons, Partner

Area served: United States

Preferred stages of financing: Seed, First stage, Second stage

Industries:
I.03   Biotech/genetic engineering
I.06   Communications
I.07   Computer hardware
I.08   Computer software
I.11   Consumer products
I.14   Electronics
I.29   Medical/medical products
I.32   Retail
I.34   Services (business)
I.35   Services (consumer)

Mesirow Financial

350 North Clark Street
Chicago, Illinois 60610
(312) 595-6000
Fax: (312) 595-6211

Key contact:
Ms. Mary Kay Hanevold
Mr. Michael J. Barrett
Mr. Thomas E. Galuhn
Mr. Daniel P. Howell

Mr. William P. Sutter, Jr.
Mr. James C. Tyree

Area served: Midwest

Preferred stages of financing: Second stage, LBO/ MBO

Industries:
I.11   Consumer products

I.12   Distribution
I.18   Financial services
I.19   Generalist
I.27   Manufacturing
I.28   Media/publishing
I.34   Services (business)
I.35   Services (consumer)

North American Business Development Company, L.L.C.

135 South LaSalle Street, Suite 4000
Chicago, Illinois 60603
(312) 332-4950
Fax: (312) 332-1540
E-mail: nabdco@interaccess.com

Key contact:
Mr. Robert L. Underwood, Executive Vice President
Mr. R. David Bergonia, Executive Vice President
Mr. Samir D. Desai, Vice President
Mr. Craig Dougherty, Principal

Description: General partner of North American Funds, partnerships of institutional investors with $115 million in equity capital that specialize in acquiring or making substantial investments in small businesses with annual revenues of $5-35 million and developing them into significantly larger enterprises.

Amount of capital invested: $15 million

Preferred investment size: $5-10 million

Amount under management: $100-500 million

Area served: United States

Preferred stages of financing: First stage, Second stage, LBO/MBO, Expansion

Industries:
I.01   Aerospace
I.05   Chemicals
I.06   Communications
I.07   Computer hardware
I.08   Computer software
I.10   Consulting
I.11   Consumer products
I.12   Distribution
I.13   Education

I.14   Electronics
I.19   Generalist
I.20   Healthcare
I.21   High technology
I.22   Industrial products
I.23   Information technology services
I.24   Internet services/e-commerce
I.27   Manufacturing
I.29   Medical/medical products
I.34   Services (business)
I.35   Services (consumer)
I.36   Transportation
I.37   Wholesale

Sampling of portfolio companies: ACR Electronics, Inc. (manufacturer of safety & survival devices for marine, aviation & outdoor recreation markets worldwide); MECC/The Learning Co. (leading developer, publisher & distributor of fun learning software for use by children in school & at home); Gateway Healthcare Corp. (full-line distributor of medical/surgical products to physicians, nursing homes & home healthcare agencies worldwide); AMTEC Precision Products, Inc. (manufacturer of high-volume, close-tolerance machined metal components, principally for automotive & capital equipment markets); J&B Foods Corp. (producer of branded specialty meats & cooked-then-frozen foods serving the institutional foodservice market in the Midwest & Southeast); Polymer Design Corp. (pioneer in rapid-turn-around, low-volume production of complex, high-performance plastic parts using unique liquid resin casting(TM) process); Actown-Electrocor, Inc. (manufacturer of high-voltage, power & surface-mount transformers, solenoids & other industrial coils & chip inductors)

Penman Partners

333 West Wacker Drive, Suite 700
Chicago, Illinois 60606
(312) 444-2763
Fax: (312) 750-4676

Key contact:
Mr. Kelvin J. Pennington
Mr. Lawrence C. Manson, Jr.
Mr. Gordon J. O'Brien
Mr. Mark D. Schindel

Area served: United States

Preferred stage of financing: LBO/MBO

Industries:
I.11   Consumer products
I.12   Distribution
I.28   Media/publishing
I.29   Medical/medical products
I.32   Retail
I.36   Transportation

Peterson Finance and Investment Company

3300 West Peterson Avenue, Suite A
Chicago, Illinois 60643
(773) 539-0502
Fax: (773) 267-8846

Key contact:
Mr. James S. Rhee

Area served: United States

Preferred stage of financing: Later stage

Industries:
I.19   Generalist

Pfingsten Partners, LLC

520 Lake Cook Road, Suite 375
Deerfield, Illinois 60015
(847) 374-9140
Fax: (847) 374-9150
E-mail: pfingstenpartners@msn.com
Web: pfingstenpartners.com

Key contact:
Mr. Thomas S. Bagley, Senior Managing Director
Mr. John H. Underwood, Managing Director
Mr. John P. McNulty, Associate
Mr. Scott A. Finegan, Associate

Description: We blend senior operating management with financial transaction experience. A key element of our investment activities is the established working relationship between Pfingsten Partners and our Executive Limited Partners, a unique group of mostly retired chief executives and senior officers of major corporations.

Preferred investment size: $10-15 million

Amount under management: $25-100 million

Area served: Midwest, United States

Preferred stage of financing: LBO/MBO

Industries:
I.05   Chemicals
I.11   Consumer products
I.12   Distribution
I.13   Education
I.14   Electronics
I.17   Environmental services/waste management
I.22   Industrial products
I.27   Manufacturing
I.28   Media/publishing
I.34   Services (business)
I.36   Transportation
I.37   Wholesale

Sampling of portfolio companies: American Academic Suppliers, Inc. (nat'l. distributor of educational supplies, teaching aids & furniture & equipment to primary & secondary schools); Barjan Products, LP (nat'l. distributor of automotive, electronic & novelty products to travel centers & other non-truck stop channels such as truck fleets, truck dealers, CB retailers, retail automotive chains, mass merchandisers, convenience stores, grocery stores, electronic distributors, local merchants & jobbers); Hallcrest, Inc. (manufacturer of thermochromic liquid crystal temperature-indicating & temperature-sensitve devices, strips, labels, sheets, inks & chemical formulations for the medical, laboratory, consumer, scientific, industrial, cosmetics & commercial promotions markets); HUEBCORE Communications, Inc. (a business magazine publishing company serving the North American manufacturing & process industries); Park Foods, LP (manufacturer of food & beverage products serving foodservice, in-store bakery, contract packing & private label markets); Woodall Publishing Co. (publisher of recreational vehicle park & campground directories since 1936)

Platinum Venture Partners, Inc.

1815 South Meyers Road
Oakbrook Terrace, Illinois 60181
(630) 620-5000
Fax: (630) 691-0710
E-mail: pvpinfo@platinum.com
Web: www.platinumventures.com

Key contact:
Mr. Michael Santer, Partner
Mr. Bryan Kennedy, Partner
Mr. David Sick, Business Analyst

Description: We make venture capital equity investments in early-stage companies in the areas of information technology, entertainment and educational software, and consumer retail concepts. We are located in Oakbrook Terrace, Illinois, a Chicago suburb and invest in companies in all geographic regions of the country. Our principals have raised over $55 million in capital to invest in or start emerging growth companies. The money raised has been organized into four separate investment pools.

Founded: 1992

Preferred investment size: $500,000-1 million

Amount under management: $100-500 million

Area served: United States

Preferred stages of financing: Seed, Start up, First stage

Industries:
I.08   Computer software
I.10   Consulting
I.21   High technology
I.23   Information technology services
I.30   New media
I.34   Services (business)

Sampling of portfolio companies: BC Equity Funding, LLC (provides capital to current & proposed area developers of Boston Market, Inc.); Blue Rhino Corp. (consumer gas-grill propane cylinder exchange at large format retail centers); House of Blues Entertainment, Inc. (diversified entertainment company: restaurant/clubs, retail, music production, radio & television broadcasting); Il Fornaio America Corp. (multi-service Italian food company with restaurants, production bakeries & retail bakery/cafes located in western U.S.); Market Partners, LLC (provides capital to current & proposed area developers of Boston Market, Inc.); Platinum Entertainment, Inc. (recorded music producer, licenser specializing in gospel, country, blues & adult contemporary formats); Platinum Health Development (developer of high-end day spa & lifestyle centers consolidating all health activities into a single venue); Spinergy, Inc. (high value bicycle components); Andromedia, Inc. (web site traffic monitoring tools & utilities); Cambell Software, Inc. (workforce management software for multi-store retail companies); D-Vision Systems, Inc. (digital video editing software for professional film editors & television producers); Dynasty Technologies, Inc. (client-server application development software); CareWise, Inc. (telephone nursing software & services providing point-of-entry patient triage for healthcare providers); intouch group, inc. (preview services of digital media allowing consumers to sample music, software & videos before purchase via online services & in-store kiosks); Red Flash Internet, Inc. (an internet-based guide to daily programming at leading world wide web sites); Seeker Software, Inc. (develops internet software applications cartridges); Spectrum HoloByte, Inc. (entertainment software publisher & developer specializing in flight simulation, strategy, puzzles & adventure games); TomTec Imaging System, Inc. (advanced ultrasound imaging software & systems for health care, specializing in stress echo systems, 3-D & 4-D ultrasound & image management); Whittman-Hart, Inc. (information technology consulting firm specializing in client/ server, open systems, internet & enterprise technologies); VREAM, Inc. (3-D tools & browsers for the world wide web)

Prince Ventures

10 South Wacker Drive, Suite 2575
Chicago, Illinois 60606
(312) 454-1408
Fax: (312) 454-9125

Key contact:
Ms. Sharon Gray

Mr. Angus Duthie, General Partner

Preferred stages of financing: Seed, Second stage

Industries:
I.34   Services (business)
I.35   Services (consumer)

Sprout Group

520 Lake Cook Road, Suite 450
Deerfield, Illinois 60015
(847) 940-1700

Key contact:
Mr. Scott Meadow, General Partner

Description: Venture capital affiliate of Donaldson, Lufkin & Jenrette with more than $1.8 billion of aggregate committed capital. Over our 28 year history, we have made investments in nearly 300 companies whose revenues today exceed $40 billion. We invest in all stages (from start ups through buyouts) in high growth areas such as information technology, medical products and services, business services and retail.

Amount of capital invested: $163 million

Preferred investment size: $5-50 million

Amount under management: >$1 billion

Area served: North America, South/Central America

Preferred stages of financing: Seed, Start up, First stage, Second stage, Mezzanine, LBO/MBO, Expansion

Industries:
I.01   Aerospace
I.03   Biotech/genetic engineering
I.08   Computer software
I.10   Consulting
I.12   Distribution
I.13   Education
I.14   Electronics
I.18   Financial services
I.20   Healthcare
I.21   High technology
I.23   Information technology services
I.24   Internet services/e-commerce
I.26   Life sciences
I.29   Medical/medical products
I.30   New media
I.32   Retail
I.33   Semiconductors
I.34   Services (business)
I.35   Services (consumer)
I.37   Wholesale

Sampling of portfolio companies: Corporate Express (office products, wholesale); Staples (office products, retail); Edison Project (education); SDL (semiconductor laser diodes); Norand (handheld computers); Sequana (genomics); IDEC Pharmaceuticals (biotherapeutics); GTECH (on-line lottery networks)

Thoma Cressey Equity Partners

6100 Sears Tower, Suite 6100
Chicago, Illinois 60606
(312) 382-2200
Fax: (312) 382-2268
E-mail: tcep@tc.nu
Web: tcep@tc.nu

Key contact:
Mr. Carl D. Thoma, Partner
Mr. Bryan C. Cressey, Partner
Mr. Lee M. Mitchell, Partner
Mr. Robert L. Manning, Jr., Partner
Mr. William W. Liebeck, Partner

Area served: North America

Preferred stages of financing: LBO/MBO, Expansion

Industries:
I.04   Broadcasting
I.05   Chemicals
I.06   Communications
I.10   Consulting
I.12   Distribution
I.13   Education
I.14   Electronics
I.16   Entertainment
I.17   Environmental services/waste management
I.18   Financial services
I.20   Healthcare
I.22   Industrial products
I.23   Information technology services
I.24   Internet services/e-commerce
I.25   Leisure/hospitality
I.27   Manufacturing
I.28   Media/publishing
I.30   New media
I.34   Services (business)
I.35   Services (consumer)
I.36   Transportation

I.37   Wholesale

Trident Capital

190 South LaSalle Street, Suite 2760
Chicago, Illinois 60603
(312) 630-5505
Fax: (312) 630-5502

Key contact:
Mr. Robert C. McCormack, Managing Director
Mr. Christopher P. Marshall

Description: We have made it our business to understand information and business services companies.
The markets. The movers. The risks. And the potential. By leveraging our industry expertise and
resourceful partners and contacts, we've been able to
back- and help build- many exciting companies.
Many others are becoming leaders in their emerging
markets.

Amount of capital invested: approximately $10 million

Preferred investment size: $5-7 million

Amount under management: $100-500 million

Area served: United States

Preferred stages of financing: Seed, Start up, First
stage, Second stage, Mezzanine, LBO/MBO, Expansion

Industries:
I.08   Computer software
I.23   Information technology services
I.24   Internet services/e-commerce
I.28   Media/publishing
I.30   New media
I.34   Services (business)

Sampling of portfolio companies: Avesta Technologies,
Inc. (provider of software & consulting services
specializing in IT service management & high performance intranet applications); CSG Systems Int'l., Inc.
(provider of subscriber management systems &
services for cable TV, DBS, telecommunications &
on-line services); DAOU Systems, Inc. (provider of
network integration services to healthcare organizations); Digital Evolutions, Inc. (provider of digital
communications technology & services); Evolving
Systems, Inc. (provider of software solutions &
systems integration services for the telecommunications industry); Firefly Networks, Inc. (provider of
intelligent agent technology for the internet & creator
of the personalized entertainment service Firefly);
Frisco Holdings (direct marketer of consumables to
hospital & medical office x-ray & other imaging
departments); Geosystems Global Corp. (provider of
geographical information systems & services to the
publishing, travel & information industries); Health
Quality, Inc. (point-of-care clinical management
systems combining electronic medical records &
medical "quality" measurement); Internet Profiles
Corp. (supplier of software & services for collecting,
measuring & analyzing internet usage); Internet
Securities, Inc. (provider of economic, political &
financial information on emerging markets via the
internet); Newgen Results Corp. (provider of
customer retention & database management services
to the automobile industry); Online Interactive, Inc.
(provider of branded on-line marketing & shopping
services); Pegasus Systems, Inc. (provider of transaction processing services to the hotel industry
worldwide through its three services: TravelWeb,
www travel booking site; THISCO, which connects
hotel central reservation systems to the global distribution systems; & HCC, which aggregates &
distributes travel agent commissions); Platinum
Software Corp. (provider of LAN-based & client/
server financial accounting applications); Production
Group Int'l., Inc. (provider of global events, entertainment exhibitions & business communication
services); Research Holdings, Ltd. (provider of interactive investor communication services); Rezsolutions, Inc. (provider of central reservation systems &
related services to the travel & leisure industry);
Vality Technology, Inc. (provider of data-quality
software tools & re-engineering consulting services);
Viant Corp. (provider of consulting & systems integration services solely focused on delivering internet
strategy & technology solutions)

The VenCom Group, Inc.

2201 Waukegan Road, Suite E-200
Bannockburn, Illinois 60015
(847) 374-7000

Key contact:
Mr. James A. Otterbeck, President/General Partner
Mr. Jeffrey S. Hohl, Vice President
Mr. William R. Schlecht, Vice President/General
Counsel
Mr. John D. Stavig, Vice President

Description: We manage private equity investments
specializing in the communications industry. We
combine global communications insights, management experience and capital resources to partner with
businesses seeking to create new markets and to
substantially accelerate their growth.

Industries:
I.06   Communications
I.23   Information technology services
I.24   Internet services/e-commerce
I.30   New media

Sampling of portfolio companies: ComPlus; OnePoint
Communications; Hotelvision; Two Way TV; ODS
Technologies; Visual Properties

William Blair & Company, LLC

222 West Adams Street
Chicago, Illinois 60606
(312) 236-1600
Fax: (312) 236-1042

E-mail: wmb@wmblair.com
Web: www.wmblair.com

Key contact:
Ms. Ellen Carnahan, Managing Director

Description: Headquartered in Chicago, we are a privately-held, employee-owned investment banking firm providing a full range of financing and brokerage services to quality growth companies and to institutional and private investors nationally and internationally. Since our founding, we have remained dedicated to achieving outstanding long-term results for our clients.

Founded: 1935

Preferred investment size: $5-10 million

Area served: United States

Preferred stages of financing: First stage, Second stage, Mezzanine, LBO/MBO

Industries:
I.03	Biotech/genetic engineering
I.06	Communications
I.07	Computer hardware
I.08	Computer software
I.14	Electronics
I.15	Energy/natural resources/utilities
I.22	Industrial products
I.29	Medical/medical products

Wind Point Partners

676 North Michigan Avenue, Suite 3300
Chicago, Illinois 60611
(312) 649-4000
Fax: (312) 255-4820

Key contact:
Mr. Robert Cummings
Mr. Arthur DelVesco
Mr. S. Curtis Johnson, III
Mr. Todd G. Smith

Preferred stages of financing: First stage, Second stage, LBO/MBO

Industries:
I.03	Biotech/genetic engineering
I.06	Communications
I.27	Manufacturing
I.29	Medical/medical products
I.34	Services (business)
I.35	Services (consumer)

Indiana

1st Source Capital Corporation

100 North Michigan Street
P.O. Box 1602
South Bend, Indiana 46634
(219) 235-2180
Fax: (219) 235-2227

Key contact:
Mr. Eugene L. Cavanaugh

Area served: Midwest

Preferred stages of financing: Second stage, LBO/MBO, Third/later stage

Industries:
I.03	Biotech/genetic engineering
I.06	Communications
I.08	Computer software
I.11	Consumer products
I.12	Distribution
I.14	Electronics
I.15	Energy/natural resources/utilities
I.27	Manufacturing
I.29	Medical/medical products
I.36	Transportation

Cambridge Ventures, L.P.

8440 Woodfield Crossing Boulevard, Suite 315
Indianapolis, Indiana 46240
(317) 469-3927
Fax: (317) 469-3926

Key contact:
Ms. Carrie Walkup
Ms. Jean Wojtowicz

Area served: Midwest, within 200 miles of office

Preferred stages of financing: Second stage, Mezzanine, LBO/MBO

Industries:
I.19	Generalist

CID Equity Partners

One American Square, Suite 2850
Indianapolis, Indiana 46282
(317) 269-2350
Fax: (317) 269-2355
E-mail: scot@cidequity.com
Web: www.cidequity.com

Key contact:
Dr. John T. Hackett, Managing General Partner
Dr. John C. Aplin, General Partner
Mr. Kevin E. Sheehan, General Partner

Description: We are a venture capital firm with offices in Indianapolis, Chicago, Cincinnati and Columbus. Our objective is to invest in companies with potential for substantial value appreciation. Through long-term investments of five to seven years, we develop a partnership, establish a direction for growth, and build the value of each company. While daily operating decisions are the responsibility of management, we play an active role in the strategic direction of the business. The size of the investments are generally between $1 million and $10 million.

Founded: 1981

Amount of capital invested: $35 million

Preferred investment size: $3-5 million

Amount under management: $100-500 million

Area served: United States

Preferred stages of financing: Seed, Start up, First stage, Mezzanine

Industries:
I.03   Biotech/genetic engineering
I.06   Communications
I.08   Computer software

I.12   Distribution
I.18   Financial services
I.20   Healthcare
I.21   High technology
I.22   Industrial products
I.23   Information technology services
I.24   Internet services/e-commerce
I.27   Manufacturing
I.34   Services (business)

Concept Development Associates, Inc.

P.O. Box 15245
1408 Lark Drive
Evansville, Indiana 47716-0245
(812) 471-3334
Fax: (812) 477-6499

Key contact:
Mr. Chuck Frary, Chairman

Description: We are a globally-connected venture capital group. We receive and review over 100 projects a day from all over the world. Our group is listed and profiled in most viable databases that deal with venture capital, mergers, acquisitions, buyouts and private equity investments in the U.S. and in international markets.

Amount of capital invested: $2,650,000

Preferred investment size: $1 million

Amount under management: <$10 million

Area served: Worldwide

Preferred stages of financing: Seed, Start up, R&D

Industries:
I.02   Agriculture/forestry/fishing/mining
I.03   Biotech/genetic engineering
I.04   Broadcasting

I.05   Chemicals
I.06   Communications
I.07   Computer hardware
I.08   Computer software
I.10   Consulting
I.11   Consumer products
I.12   Distribution
I.13   Education
I.14   Electronics
I.15   Energy/natural resources/utilities
I.16   Entertainment
I.17   Environmental services/waste management
I.18   Financial services
I.20   Healthcare
I.21   High technology
I.22   Industrial products
I.23   Information technology services
I.24   Internet services/e-commerce
I.25   Leisure/hospitality
I.26   Life sciences
I.27   Manufacturing
I.28   Media/publishing
I.30   New media
I.32   Retail
I.34   Services (business)
I.35   Services (consumer)
I.36   Transportation
I.37   Wholesale

Hammond, Kennedy, Whitney & Company

8888 Keystone Crossing, Suite 690
Indianapolis, Indiana 46240
(317) 574-6900
Fax: (317) 574-7515

Key contact:
Mr. Glenn Scolnik

Description: Founded in 1904.

Founded: 1904

Amount of capital invested: $10 million

Preferred investment size: $2-5 million

Amount under management: $25-100 million

Area served: Europe, North America

Preferred stage of financing: LBO/MBO

Industries:
I.27   Manufacturing

Sampling of portfolio companies: Excel Industries Inc. (automotive supplier); Baldwin Technologies Inc. (printing accessories); Control Devices Inc. (automotive sensor supplier); Maine Tire Int'l. (industrial application tires); Grobet File Co. of America (industrial & jewelry tools); Seneco Printing & Label (labels for the bottling industry); Globe Ticket & Label (event tickets); Horton Emergency Vehicles (ambulances); Morehouse Group (publishing specialty)

InvestAmerica N.D. Management, Inc.

101 Second Street SE, Suite 800
Cedar Rapids, Indiana 52401
(319) 363-8249
Fax: (319) 363-9683

Key contact:
Mr. David R. Schroder, President
Mr. Robert A. Comey, Vice President

Description: We are the general partner and investment advisor for the North Dakota Small Business Investment Company (NDSBIC). NDSBIC is a licensed SBIC and will invest a majority of its capital in later stage companies.

Amount of capital invested: $2.2 million

Preferred investment size: $500,000

Amount under management: <$10 million

Area served: United States

Preferred stages of financing: Mezzanine, LBO/MBO, Expansion

Industries:
I.01   Aerospace
I.02   Agriculture/forestry/fishing/mining
I.03   Biotech/genetic engineering
I.05   Chemicals
I.06   Communications
I.07   Computer hardware
I.08   Computer software
I.09   Construction
I.10   Consulting
I.11   Consumer products
I.12   Distribution
I.13   Education
I.14   Electronics
I.17   Environmental services/waste management
I.19   Generalist
I.20   Healthcare
I.21   High technology
I.22   Industrial products
I.23   Information technology services
I.24   Internet services/e-commerce
I.25   Leisure/hospitality
I.26   Life sciences
I.27   Manufacturing
I.29   Medical/medical products
I.32   Retail
I.33   Semiconductors
I.34   Services (business)
I.35   Services (consumer)
I.36   Transportation
I.37   Wholesale

MW Capital Partners

201 North Illinois Street, Suite 300
Indianapolis, Indiana 46204
(317) 237-2323
Fax: (317) 237-2325

Key contact:
Mr. Thomas A. Hiatt, Managing Director
Mr. D. Scott Lutzke, Managing Director
Mr. H. Garth Dickey

Description: We are a private equity fund established to generate compounded annual returns to our investors of 25% to 30% by investing in a diversified portfolio of investment opportunities in the Midwestern region of the United States. The target size of the fund is $1 million.

Preferred investment size: $2-5 million

Amount under management: $25-100 million

Area served: United States

Preferred stages of financing: First stage, Second stage, Mezzanine, LBO/MBO, Expansion

Industries:
I.06   Communications
I.12   Distribution
I.18   Financial services
I.20   Healthcare
I.21   High technology
I.22   Industrial products
I.23   Information technology services
I.24   Internet services/e-commerce
I.26   Life sciences
I.27   Manufacturing
I.29   Medical/medical products
I.30   New media
I.34   Services (business)

Sampling of portfolio companies: Impath, Inc. (medical information, cancer diagnostics); Bioanalytical Systems, Inc. (contract research for pharmaceutical companies); Power Way, Inc. (software products & services); Alternate Marketing Services (business services); Wes-Tech, Inc. (advanced manufacturing)

Union Atlantic LC

5469 Woodfield Drive
Carmel, Indiana 46033
(317) 846-2400
Fax: (317) 846-1800
E-mail: bobrien@ualc.com
Web: ualc.com

Key contact:
Mr. Robert O'Brien, Partner

Description: A private merchant banking concern providing investment opportunities to corporations and high net worth individuals through equity investments in emerging companies targeted in the technology sector. We look for strong management teams with commercially available products and services.

Preferred investment size: None

Amount under management: <$10 million

Area served: Europe, North America, South/Central America

Preferred stages of financing: First stage, Second stage

Industries:
I.07   Computer hardware
I.08   Computer software
I.10   Consulting
I.12   Distribution
I.14   Electronics
I.21   High technology
I.23   Information technology services
I.24   Internet services/e-commerce
I.33   Semiconductors

Sampling of portfolio companies: The Concours Group (IT consultancy); Galacticomm (internet software); Advanced Electronics Support Products (computer peripherals); LocalNet Communications (multi-level marketing, technology); Command Software (PC software)

Kansas

Child Health Investment Corporation

6803 West 64th Street, Suite 208
Shawnee Mission, Kansas 66202
(913) 262-1436
Fax: (913) 262-1575
Web: www.chca.com

Key contact:
Mr. Ed Kuklenski

Description: We are the investment division of Child Health Corporation of America and we maximize member return by funding new technologies and bringing new products and services to market. We formed innovative relationships with venture capital firms and technology-oriented companies to make investments in pediatric medicine, healthcare services and biological sciences.

Founded: 1985

Area served: United States

Preferred stages of financing: Seed, Start up, First stage

Industries:
I.20   Healthcare
I.29   Medical/medical products

Sampling of portfolio companies: AbTox, Inc. (manufactures sterility assurance equipment & supplies to acute care & industrial markets); Ascent Pediatrics, Inc. (pharmaceutical manufacturer focused in the area of pediatric products); Healthtech Services Corp. (developer of an integrated telecommunication system to monitor home care patients); MDI Instruments, Inc. (develops & markets consumer & professional ear infection screening products); OraVax, Inc. (engages in the discovery & development of oral vaccines); Strategic HealthCare Programs, LLC (develops & markets outcomes software tools & services); Thermo Electron Corp. (manufactures respiratory diagnostic systems & non-invasive gas monitors); Caring Technologies (medical instruments & devices); Periodontix Inc. (pharmaceuticals); Stor Comm (software & information); Q397

Kansas Venture Capital, Inc.

6700 Antioch, Suite 460
Overland Park, Kansas 66204
(913) 262-7117
Fax: (913) 262-3509

Key contact:
Mr. Rex E. Wiggins
Mr. Thomas C. Blackburn

Area served: Midwest

Preferred stages of financing: First stage, Second stage, LBO/MBO, Third/later stage

Industries:
I.19   Generalist

Kentucky

Equal Opportunity Finance, Inc.

420 South Hurstbourne Parkway, Suite 201
Louisville, Kentucky 40222
(502) 423-1943
Fax: (502) 423-1945

Key contact:
Mr. David A. Sattich

Area served: Midwest

Preferred stages of financing: First stage, Second stage, Third/later stage

Industries:
I.19   Generalist

Mountain Ventures, Inc.

P.O. Box 1738
362 Old Whitley Road
London, Kentucky 40743
(606) 864-5175
Fax: (606) 864-5194

Key contact:
Mr. Ray Moncrief

Area served: Southeast

Preferred stages of financing: Seed, First stage, Third/later stage

Industries:
I.19   Generalist

Summit Capital Group, Inc.

6510 Glenridge Park Place, Suite 8
Louisville, Kentucky 40222
(502) 429-4515
Fax: (502) 429-4518

Key contact:
Mr. David Schechter
Ms. Terry A. Chambers

Area served: Canada, United States

Preferred stages of financing: First stage, Second stage

Louisiana

Bank One Equity Investors
451 Florida Street
Baton Rouge, Louisiana 70801
(504) 332-4421
Fax: (504) 332-7377

Key contact:
Mr. Thomas J. Adamek, President
Mr. Michael P. Kirby, Senior Vice President
Mr. W. Stephen Keller, Vice President
Ms. Shelley G. Whittington, Vice President

200 Carondelet Street
New Orleans, Louisiana 70161
(504) 596-0248
Fax: (504) 569-0233

Key contact:
Mr. Steve Keller

Description: We are a bank owned SBIC with $200 million of assets under management. We are affiliated with Banc One Capital Markets, Inc., a subsidiary of Banc One Corporation.

Amount under management: $100-500 million

Area served: United States

Preferred stages of financing: Second stage, Mezzanine, LBO/MBO, Expansion

Industries:
I.04   Broadcasting
I.05   Chemicals
I.06   Communications
I.12   Distribution
I.13   Education
I.15   Energy/natural resources/utilities
I.20   Healthcare
I.22   Industrial products
I.27   Manufacturing
I.28   Media/publishing
I.29   Medical/medical products

Hibernia Capital Corporation
313 Carondelet Street, 16th Floor
New Orleans, Louisiana 70130
(504) 533-5988
Fax: (504) 533-3873
E-mail: thoyt@hiberniabank.com

Key contact:
Mr. Thomas B. Hoyt, President
Mr. John Driscoll, Senior Director
Mr. Chris Nines, Associate

Description: We invest on a national basis in subordinated debt (with equity features), preferred and common stock issued by later stage venture capital companies, buyouts and companies needing expansion capital.

Amount of capital invested: $6 million

Preferred investment size: $3-5 million

Amount under management: $25-100 million

Area served: United States

Preferred stages of financing: Second stage, Mezzanine, LBO/MBO, Expansion

Industries:
I.02   Agriculture/forestry/fishing/mining
I.05   Chemicals
I.06   Communications
I.09   Construction
I.11   Consumer products
I.12   Distribution
I.14   Electronics
I.15   Energy/natural resources/utilities
I.16   Entertainment
I.17   Environmental services/waste management
I.22   Industrial products
I.23   Information technology services
I.27   Manufacturing
I.33   Semiconductors
I.36   Transportation

Sampling of portfolio companies: Alexander Technologies (manufacturer of rechargeable batteries); Mycotech Corp. (agricultural bioscience); Cardinal Services (offshore oil & gas well servicing); Petrocom Inc. (Gulf of Mexico telecommunications)

Source Capital Corporation
455 East Airport
Baton Rouge, Louisiana 70806
(504) 922-7411
Fax: (504) 922-7418
E-mail: request@sourcecap.com
Web: sourcecap.com

Key contact:
Mr. Kevin H. Couhig, President
Mr. Greg M. Naquin, Executive Vice President
Mr. Walter M. Anderson, Senior Vice President
Mr. Paul M. McCown, CFO

2014 West Pinhook Road, Suite 503
Lafayette, Louisiana 70508
(318) 237-3323
Fax: (318) 234-5535

Key contact:
Mr. Jeffrey Benton

2424 Edenborne Avenue, Suite 640
Metairie, Louisiana 70001
(504) 833-1509
Fax: (504) 833-1548

Key contact:
Mr. Aaron Miscenich

1900 North 18th Street, Suite 435
Monroe, Louisiana 71201
(318) 325-6572
Fax: (318) 325-6575

Key contact:
Mr. Randy Garner

400 Travis Street, Suite 306
Shreveport, Louisiana 71101
(318) 222-7010
Fax: (318) 222-9001

Key contact:
Ms. Barbara Wilcox

Area served: United States

Preferred stages of financing: Start up, First stage,
Second stage, Mezzanine, LBO/MBO, Expansion

Industries:
I.03   Biotech/genetic engineering
I.06   Communications
I.11   Consumer products
I.12   Distribution
I.14   Electronics
I.16   Entertainment
I.20   Healthcare
I.25   Leisure/hospitality
I.27   Manufacturing
I.29   Medical/medical products
I.31   Real estate
I.32   Retail
I.34   Services (business)
I.35   Services (consumer)

Maine

North Atlantic Capital Corporation
70 Center Street
Portland, Maine 04101
(207) 772-4470
Fax: (207) 772-3257
E-mail: info@NorthAtlanticCapital.com
Web: www.NorthAtlanticCapital.com

Key contact:
Mr. David M. Coit, President
Mr. Albert W. Coffrin, III, Vice President

Description: We are a fund manager that provides risk
capital to privately owned businesses in the
Norheastern United States. Our investment interests
support established companies seeking growth
through internal expansion or acquisition. We also
finance the recapitalization or ownership changes of
profitable, well established businesses. Investments
range from $1 to 4 million, with the $2 to 3 million
level preferred.

Preferred investment size: $2-3 million

Amount under management: $25-100 million

Area served: Northeast

Preferred stages of financing: Second stage, Mezzanine, LBO/MBO, Expansion

Industries:
I.07   Computer hardware
I.08   Computer software
I.10   Consulting
I.12   Distribution
I.14   Electronics
I.17   Environmental services/waste management
I.19   Generalist
I.21   High technology
I.23   Information technology services
I.27   Manufacturing
I.29   Medical/medical products
I.34   Services (business)

Sampling of portfolio companies: Brunswick Technologies, Inc. (industrial reinforcement fabrics); Casella
Waste Systems, Inc. (solid waste management);
Channel Computing, Inc. (database management
software); Commonwealth Care, Inc. (home
healthcare services); Community Rehab Centers
(physical therapy rehabilitation centers); Contemporary Products, Inc. (home healthcare respiratory
products); Earth's Best, Inc. (organic baby food);
Georgetown Collection, Inc. (direct response
marketer of collectable dolls); IDEXX Laboratories,
Inc. (diagnostic products for veterinary, environmental & food applications); Kitchen Etc. (multi store
discount retailer of dinnerware & cookware); Rowena
Broadcasting, Inc. (AM/FM broadcasting stations);
Steinbrecher Corp. (digital transceivers for cellular
communication industry); Transition Technology,
Inc. (intelligent PC based controllers); Westminster
Craker Co., Inc. (oyster & other specialty crackers);
Keyfile Corp. (integrated document management
software); Ocean Products, Inc. (atlantic salmon
aquaculture); Schiavi Leasing Corp. (modular
classroom leasing); Storage Computer Corp. (high
speed memory storage devices); Verax Corp.
(biotechnology cell culture); Wright Express Corp.
(credit & information services for commercial vehicle
fleet management)

Maryland

ABS Ventures
1 South Street, Suite 2150
Baltimore, Maryland 21202
(410) 895-3895
Fax: (410) 895-3899

Key contact:
Mr. Bruns Grayson

Area served: United States

Preferred stages of financing: Start up, First stage,
Second stage, Mezzanine

Industries:
I.03   Biotech/genetic engineering
I.06   Communications

I.08   Computer software
I.29   Medical/medical products

Anthem Capital, L.P.
16 South Calvert Street, Suite 800
Baltimore, Maryland 21202
(410) 625-1510
Fax: (410) 625-1735

Key contact:
Mr. C. Edward Spiva
Mr. William M. Gust

Area served: Mid-Atlantic

Preferred stages of financing: Seed, First stage, Second stage, Third/later stage

Industries:
I.03   Biotech/genetic engineering
I.06   Communications
I.08   Computer software
I.14   Electronics
I.29   Medical/medical products

Arete Ventures, Inc.
2 Wisconsin Circle, Suite 620
Chevy Chase, Maryland 20815
(301) 652-8066
Fax: (301) 652-8310
E-mail: arete@ari.ari.net

Key contact:
Mr. William T. Heflin
Mr. Todd D. Klein
Mr. Robert W. Shaw
Mr. Jake Tarr

Founded: 1985

Preferred investment size: $500,000-3 million

Area served: United States

Preferred stages of financing: First stage, Second stage, Expansion

Industries:
I.06   Communications
I.15   Energy/natural resources/utilities
I.23   Information technology services
I.24   Internet services/e-commerce
I.35   Services (consumer)

Sampling of portfolio companies: Metricom; Ramp Networks; Evolutionary Technologies

AT&T Ventures
Two Wisconsin Circle, Suite 610
Chevy Chase, Maryland 20815
(301) 652-5225
Fax: (301) 664-8590

Key contact:
Mr. Richard S. Bodman

Description: We were founded in 1992 as a venture capital partnership to invest in information technology and service enabling companies in emerging growth markets. Drawing from three funds totaling $348 million, we provide capital to start-up and later stage companies in the following markets: wireless communications, internet, value added networking services, content and local service.

Founded: 1992

Preferred investment size: $1-5 million

Amount under management: $100-500 million

Area served: United States

Preferred stages of financing: Seed, Start up, First stage, Second stage

Industries:
I.06   Communications
I.08   Computer software
I.11   Consumer products
I.12   Distribution
I.23   Information technology services
I.24   Internet services/e-commerce
I.28   Media/publishing
I.30   New media

Sampling of portfolio companies: Argon; Avesta; City-Search; e.Fusion; First Virtual Corp.; Hybrid Networks; Knology; Nat'l. Transportation Exchange; Netro; PeopleLink; Software.com; TUT Systems; Verisign; Xedia Corp.; America On Line (Redgate Communications); Classic Sports Network; CUC Int'l. (Knowledge Adventure); Echo Logic; Netscape; Spectrum Holobyte

Embryon Capital
7903 Sleaford Place
Bethesda, Maryland 20814
(301) 656-6837
Fax: (301) 656-8056
E-mail: info@embryon.com
Web: www.embryon.com

Key contact:
Mr. William H. Tobey, Partner
Mr. Timothy J. Webb, Partner
Mr. Philip B. Smith, Partner

Description: We provide venture capital to entrepreneurial companies specializing in information technology products and services. We are interested primarily in IT companies active in the following businesses: internet commerce, enterprise management, telecommuncation networking, telemedicine, education and training and space commerce.

Preferred investment size: $250,000-1 million

Area served: Greater Washington, D.C.; Mid-Atlantic, United States

Preferred stages of financing: Seed, Start up, First stage, Second stage

Industries:
I.06   Communications
I.08   Computer software

I.13   Education
I.14   Electronics
I.23   Information technology services
I.24   Internet services/e-commerce
I.30   New media

Grotech Capital Group
9690 Deereco Road, Suite 800
Timonium, Maryland 21093
(410) 560-2000
Fax: (410) 560-1910
E-mail: ajones@grotech.com

Key contact:
Mr. Frank A. Adams, President/CEO
Mr. Stuart D. Frankel, Managing Director
Mr. Patrick J. Kevins
Mr. Dennis J. Shaughnessy, Managing Director
Mr. Hugh A. Woltzen
Mr. J. Roger Sullivan, Jr., Vice President
Mr. Andrew E. Jones, Investment Analyst
Mr. Jeffrey R. Schechter, Director of Finance
Ms. Sharon E. Gogol, Assistant Controller

Description: For more than a decade, we have forged investment partnerships with men and women who have high levels of competence, integrity and energy. The majority of these partnerships are located in the Mid-Atlantic and Southeastern regions of the United States and include investments in companies in the early, emerging and later stages of their growth cycles.

Preferred stages of financing: Seed, Start up, First stage, Mezzanine, LBO/MBO, Expansion

Industries:
I.06   Communications
I.07   Computer hardware
I.08   Computer software
I.11   Consumer products
I.17   Environmental services/waste management
I.24   Internet services/e-commerce
I.29   Medical/medical products
I.32   Retail
I.33   Semiconductors
I.34   Services (business)
I.35   Services (consumer)

Sampling of portfolio companies: A&W Restaurants, Inc. (operates a fast food restaurant chain through 771 franchises in the US & the Asia Pacific markets); CDNow, Inc. (offers 250,000 music-oriented products for sale over the internet); Dentalco, Inc. (an owner/operator of multi-specialty dental sites); Digex, Inc. (provides commercial internet access in major cities throughout the US); Environmental Control Group (full service company removing & disposing of asbestos from commercial buildings); Forensic Technologies Int'l. Corp. (provides forensic engineering, visual communications & project management to law firms, insurance companies, industrial corporations & utilities in the context of litigation & alternative dispute resolutions); LLoyd's Food Products (manufactures & distributes barbecued meat products for institutional & retail customers); Master Power, Inc. (produces & sells production air tools & related service parts & sources certain accessories & other products); Nassau Broadcasting Partners (operates 15 radio stations in New Jersey & Pennsylvania); Network Construction Services, Inc. (provides engineering, furnishing & installation services for telecom, datacom, cable TV & other outside plant facilities, consisting of aerial & underground copper, coaxial & fiber optic networks); Pathnet, Inc. (telecommunications firm established to capitalize on the FCC regulatory action requiring relocation of 2 GHz private microwave users affected by the recent broadband PCS auctions); Phoenix Services, LP (owns & operates the largest dedicated medical waste incineration plant in the US); Pusser's, Inc. (operates a chain of company-owned restaurants & retail stores in waterfront locations in the US & the Caribbean); Quality Software Products Holdings, PLC (designs, develops, markets & supports accounting & procurement software for IBM & IBM compatible mainframe computers); Spectrum Holobyte (develops, publishes & markets high end computer simulation games in North America, Europe & Japan); TESSCO, Inc. (distributor of products to the wireless communications industry); The Regency Corp. (designs, builds & sells single-family & multi-family homes in the Washington, DC, Baltimore & Richmond metropolitan statistical areas); Thunderbird Technologies, Inc. (designs & develops semiconductor technologies for fabless applications); US Vision, Inc. (nationwide processor & retailer of various types of eyeware products); Verity Inc. (develops, markets & supports document management systems for the internet)

H. C. Wainwright & Company, Inc.
400 East Pratt Street
Baltimore, Maryland 21202
(410) 347-3900
Fax: (410) 727-1295
E-mail: kquinn@hcwainwright.com
Web: hcwainwright.com

Key contact:
Mr. Kevin Quinn, Managing Director

Area served: United States

Preferred stages of financing: Seed, Start up, First stage, LBO/MBO

Industries:
I.20   Healthcare
I.21   High technology
I.24   Internet services/e-commerce
I.30   New media

MMG Ventures, L.P.
826 East Baltimore Street
Baltimore, Maryland 21202
(410) 659-7850
Fax: (410) 333-2552
E-mail: tuckerst@erols.com

Key contact:
Mr. Stanley W. Tucker, President
Ms. Catherine D. Lockhart, Principal
Mr. Timothy L. Smoot, Principal
Mr. R. Randy Croxton, Principal

Description: We are a specialized Small Business
Investment Company investing in emerging growth
companies owned and operated by African-Ameri-
cans, Hispanic-Americans and Asian-Americans
with a Mid-Atlantic focus. We will address an unmet
need in the marketplace for providing "patient"
capital to minority businesses. We will primarily
seek investment opportunities in the medical (healthcare services, medical information services), retail,
consumer and business products and services, and
multi-unit franchises and new franchises.

Amount of capital invested: $1,250,000

Preferred investment size: $1 million

Amount under management: <$10 million

Area served: United States

Preferred stages of financing: Start up, Second stage,
Mezzanine, Expansion

Industries:
I.06 Communications
I.07 Computer hardware
I.08 Computer software
I.20 Healthcare
I.21 High technology
I.23 Information technology services
I.24 Internet services/e-commerce
I.29 Medical/medical products
I.32 Retail

Sampling of portfolio companies: Z-Spanish Radio
Network, Inc. (radio broadcasting/communications)

New Enterprise Associates
1119 St. Paul Street (between Biddle & Chase Streets)
Baltimore, Maryland 21202
(410) 244-0115
Fax: (410) 752-7721
Web: www.nea.com

Key contact:
Mr. Frank A. Bonsal, Jr., Founding Partner
Mr. Ryan D. Drant, Associate
Mr. Ronald H. Kase, General Partner
Mr. Charles M. Linehan, Partner
Mr. Thomas C. McConnell, General Partner
Mr. John M. Nehra, General Partner
Mr. Charles W. Newhall, III, Co-Founder/General
Partner
Dr. Sigrid Van Bladel, Ph.D., Partner
Mr. Stewart Alsop, Venture Partner
Mr. Peter J. Barris, General Partner
Mr. Robert T. Coneybeer
Ms. Suzanne Hooper
Mr. C. Richard Kramlich, Co-Founder/General Partner
Mr. Arthur J. Marks, General Partner
Mr. Peter T. Morris, General Partner
Mr. Mark W. Perry, General Partner
Mr. Scott D. Sandell
Ms. Nora M. Zietz, Partner/Director of Research
Ms. Nancy Dorman, General Partner
Mr. Lou Van Dyck, CFO
Ms. Ann Wilson, Director of Administration & HR

Description: We are one of the industry's premier
venture capital firms. For 19 years we have practiced
classic venture capital by investing in early-stage
companies and working with management to nurture
and build companies of real and lasting value. We
are now the leading start-up venture investor in the
country.

Founded: 1978

Preferred investment size: $500,000-6 million

Preferred stages of financing: Seed, Start up, First
stage

Industries:
I.03 Biotech/genetic engineering
I.06 Communications
I.08 Computer software
I.14 Electronics
I.20 Healthcare
I.23 Information technology services
I.24 Internet services/e-commerce
I.26 Life sciences
I.29 Medical/medical products
I.33 Semiconductors

Sampling of portfolio companies: Archimedes Surgical,
Inc. (surgical devices & technologies for minimally
invasive general surgery & vascular surgery); Iotek,
Inc. (drug delivery systems to treat male impotence &
a medical device to treat female incontinence);
Nellcor, Inc. (oximeters & other patient monitoring
instruments & disposable supplies for use in surgery);
Zymark Corp. (laboratory automation systems);
AutoImmune, Inc. (pharmaceuticals to treat
autoimmune diseases by inducing tolerance to
autoantigens); Neocrin (an implantable bioartificial
pancreas for insulin dependent diabetes); Russ Pharmaceuticals (analgesic components covering the full
spectrum of pain); Long Term Care Group (markets
& administers long term care insurance products for
individuals, large employers & government organizations); United Medical Plan (independent practice
association type HOM's); IBAH, Inc. (contract
clinical & development services to the pharmaceutical & biotechnology industries); Bay Networks, Inc.
(multi-protocol internetworking products); Packeteer
(quality of service tools for the internet based on efficient bandwidth management); AdiCom Wireless,
Inc. (wireless local loop products based on CDMA
technology for low cost voice & data services); Fibex
Systems (integrated, flexible & scaleable access
platform for the existing & emerging local exchange
services market); Netrix Corp. (integrated communications switches for voice, data, frame relay & ATM);
Cogit Corp. (delivers marketing automation software
to help marketers continually optimize their customer
relationship & promotion strategies); Mobius

Management Systems, Inc. (electronic document warehouse software for high-volume archiving & retrieval of diverse documents in heterogeneous computing environments); Sherpa Corp. (software for engineering change management & product infor- mation management); Scientific Time Sharing, Inc. (interactive financial applications written in APL); BusLogic Inc. (SCSI host adapters for controlling microcomputer buses)

Spectra Enterprise Associates

1119 St. Paul Street
Baltimore, Maryland 21202
(410) 244-0115

Key contact:
Ms. Nancy Dorman
Mr. Curran W. Harvey

Area served: United States

Preferred stages of financing: Seed, Start up, First stage

Industries:
I.06   Communications
I.07   Computer hardware
I.08   Computer software
I.14   Electronics

T. Rowe Price Associates, Inc.

100 East Pratt Street
Baltimore, Maryland 21202
(410) 345-2000

Key contact:
Mr. Pat Archer
Mr. Douglas O. Hickman
Mr. Terral M. Jordan

Description: Founded in 1937 by Thomas Rowe, Jr., the Baltimore-based investment management firm is one of the nation's leading providers of no-load mutual funds for individual investors and corporate retirement programs. Along with our affiliates, we manage over $135 billion for more than six million individual and institutional accounts.

Founded: 1937

Preferred stages of financing: Second stage, Mezza- nine, LBO/MBO

Industries:
I.03   Biotech/genetic engineering
I.06   Communications
I.07   Computer hardware
I.08   Computer software
I.14   Electronics
I.15   Energy/natural resources/utilities
I.20   Healthcare
I.22   Industrial products
I.28   Media/publishing
I.29   Medical/medical products

TDH

4800 Montgomery Lane, Suite 875
Bethesda, Maryland 20814
(301) 718-7353

Key contact:
Mr. J. B. Doherty, Partner

Description: Our management team has experience in venture capital investing through multiple economic and portfolio cycles. Since our founding, we have consistently applied an investment approach directed towards a diversified portfolio that avoids excessive concentration in any one industry and is balanced among early, later stage and acquisition financings. We prefer to lead our investments and generally invest between $1 mm to 3 mm.

Founded: 1978

Amount of capital invested: $2.5 million

Preferred investment size: Over $1 million

Amount under management: $25-100 million

Area served: Prefer East of the Mississippi, United States

Preferred stages of financing: Start up, First stage, Second stage, Mezzanine, LBO/MBO

Industries:
I.01   Aerospace
I.02   Agriculture/forestry/fishing/mining
I.03   Biotech/genetic engineering
I.04   Broadcasting
I.05   Chemicals

I.06   Communications
I.07   Computer hardware
I.08   Computer software
I.11   Consumer products
I.13   Education
I.14   Electronics
I.18   Financial services
I.20   Healthcare
I.21   High technology
I.22   Industrial products
I.23   Information technology services
I.24   Internet services/e-commerce
I.26   Life sciences
I.27   Manufacturing
I.28   Media/publishing
I.29   Medical/medical products
I.30   New media
I.33   Semiconductors
I.34   Services (business)
I.35   Services (consumer)

Sampling of portfolio companies: Airgas, Inc. (inde- pendent distributor of industrial gases & welding equipment); The Aviation Group, Inc. (contract aircraft operator in the overnight package delivery business, serving Emery & Perolator air couriers); Comsell, Inc./Industrial Training Corp. (develops, programs & markets off-the-shelf interactive programs for applications in industrial & technical skills training); ESPN, The Entertainment Sports Programming Network (all-sports cable tv network created for delivery of programming via satellite); Exogen, Inc. (develops products focused on the biophysical treatment of muscoloskeletal injury &

disease); Intelligent Electronics, Inc. (franchiser of microcomputer hardware & office equipment stores, distributor of products to the stores which trade under the names of Today's Computer Business Centers,

Entre Computer Centers & Connecting Point of America); Staples, Inc. (large format, discount office supply superstore)

Triad Investors Corp.

300 East Joppa Road
Suite 1111
Baltimore, Maryland 21286
(410) 828-6497
Fax: (410) 337-7312

Key contact:
Ms. Barbara Melera, Partner

Description: We invest in early stage information technology, healthcare and advanced materials companies located in the Mid-Atlantic region.

Preferred investment size: $500,000

Amount under management: $10-25 million

Area served: North America

Preferred stages of financing: Seed, Start up, First stage

Industries:
I.03   Biotech/genetic engineering
I.05   Chemicals
I.06   Communications
I.07   Computer hardware
I.08   Computer software
I.11   Consumer products
I.13   Education
I.14   Electronics
I.18   Financial services
I.19   Generalist
I.20   Healthcare
I.21   High technology
I.22   Industrial products
I.23   Information technology services
I.24   Internet services/e-commerce
I.26   Life sciences
I.29   Medical/medical products
I.30   New media
I.33   Semiconductors
I.34   Services (business)
I.35   Services (consumer)

Sampling of portfolio companies: Current Analysis, Inc. (competitive intelligence services); Entek Corp. (chemicals); Communications Systems Technology, Inc. (wireless communications hardware); MDI Instruments, Inc. (medical devices); Intranetics, Inc. (software); Faith Mountain Co. (direct mail); Netbalance Corp. (enterprise software); Visual Networks, Inc. (telecommunications equipment); Wisdomeware, Inc. (software)

Massachusetts

Aberlyn Holding Company

1000 Winter Street
Waltham, Massachusetts 02154
(781) 895-1144
Fax: (781) 895-1645

Key contact:
Ms. Diana Spano

Area served: Europe, North America

Preferred stages of financing: First stage, Second stage, Mezzanine, LBO/MBO, Expansion, Venture leasing

Industries:
I.03   Biotech/genetic engineering
I.20   Healthcare
I.26   Life sciences
I.29   Medical/medical products

Advanced Technology Ventures

281 Winter Street, Suite 350
Waltham, Massachusetts 02154
(781) 290-0707
Fax: (781) 684-0045
E-mail: info@atv-ventures.com
Web: www.atv-ventures.com

Key contact:
Mr. Pieter J. Schiller, General Partner
Mr. Michael E. Frank, General Partner
Ms. April E. Evans, Vice President/CFO

Description: Since our founding, we have been a leading force in helping emerging information technology and healthcare companies to grow and prosper. With offices in California's Silicon Valley and along Boston's Route 128 corridor, we are one of the country's preeminent venture capital firms focused solely on technology-related investments.

Founded: 1979

Amount of capital invested: $25 million

Preferred investment size: $2-5 million

Amount under management: $100-500 million

Area served: Europe, United States

Preferred stages of financing: Seed, Start up, First stage

Industries:
I.03   Biotech/genetic engineering
I.06   Communications
I.07   Computer hardware
I.08   Computer software
I.14   Electronics
I.20   Healthcare
I.21   High technology
I.23   Information technology services

I.24   Internet services/e-commerce
I.26   Life sciences
I.29   Medical/medical products
I.33   Semiconductors

Sampling of portfolio companies: Actel Corp. (FPGAs & software design systems); Credence Systems (VLSI test equipment); Cytyc Corp. (Thin prep test replacement for pap smears); Novoste Corp. (King Beta-Cath for treatment of restenosis based on radiation); TranSwitch Corp. (VLSI semiconductor devices for telecommunications); VLSI Technology, Inc. (computer-aided design tools for VLSI engi-neering); Avicenna Systems-acq. by Synetic (intranet- & internet-based products/services for physicians); AccelGraphics (3-D graphics hardware & software products); RF Micro Devices, Inc. (RF semiconductors for digital wireless communications); California Microwave, Inc. (wireless communications products); CollaGenex Pharmaceuticals,Inc. (innovative medical therapy for periodontal disease); Anthra Pharmaceuticals, Inc. (commercialization of pharmaceuticals based on anthracyclines); Continuus Software, Inc. (configuration management software development tools)

Advent International

101 Federal Street
Boston, Massachusetts 02110
(617) 951-9400
Fax: (617) 951-0566
Web: www.adventinternational.com

Key contact:
Mr. Peter A. Brooke, Chairman
Mr. Douglas R. Brown, President/CEO
Mr. Thomas R. Armstrong, Executive Vice President/COO
Mr. Thomas H. Lauer, Managing Director/CFO
Mr. Nicholas B. Callinan, Managing Director-Emerging Markets

Description: We are one of the world's largest private equity investment firms, with $3 billion under management and more than 90 professionals in Europe, North America, Asia and Latin America. Our goal is to invest in attractive, growth-oriented companies on a global basis and to provide management teams with the support needed to build businesses of significant value.

Founded: 1984

Amount of capital invested: $250 million

Preferred investment size: Over $5 million

Amount under management: >$1 billion

Area served: Asia, Latin America, Central Europe, United States

Preferred stages of financing: LBO/MBO, Expansion

Industries:
I.03   Biotech/genetic engineering
I.04   Broadcasting
I.05   Chemicals
I.06   Communications
I.08   Computer software
I.11   Consumer products
I.14   Electronics
I.15   Energy/natural resources/utilities
I.18   Financial services
I.20   Healthcare
I.22   Industrial products
I.23   Information technology services
I.27   Manufacturing
I.28   Media/publishing
I.29   Medical/medical products
I.32   Retail

Sampling of portfolio companies: Cubist Pharmaceuticals Inc. (discovery & development of antibiotics); Vanguard Medica Group PLC (drug development); Induplex Holdings Inc. (thermal insulation, filter aids & fillers); @Entertainment Inc. (multichannel pay television); Aspen Technology Inc. (computer-aided process engineering software); PT Indolitharge Megahtama (lead monoxide from lead ingots); Advanced Radio Telecom Corp. (broadband wireless carrier); SeaChange Int'l. Inc. (digital video solutions for cable TV); Fantom Technologies Inc. (floor-care products); Abpac Inc. (integrated circuit packaging foundry); Active Power Inc. (flywheel energy storage systems); CardSystem Upsi SA (credit card administrator); Devro Holdings Ltd. (edible sausage casings); Americus Dental Labs Inc. (dental laboratory); AeroGen Inc. (airless spraying device); Brilliant Manufacturing (S) Pte. Ltd. (aluminum base plates for disk drives); 3i/Implant Innovations Inc. (dental implants); Versant Object Technology Corp. (object database management systems); Alta Gestion SA (temporary employment & outsourcing employment services)

American Research & Development Corp.

30 Federal Street
Boston, Massachusetts 02110
(617) 423-7500
Fax: (617) 423-9655

Key contact:
Mr. Francis J. Hughes, Jr., President
Mr. Harold L. Finelt

Area served: Northeast

Preferred stages of financing: Seed, Start up, First stage, Second stage

Industries:
I.06   Communications
I.07   Computer hardware
I.08   Computer software
I.14   Electronics
I.15   Energy/natural resources/utilities
I.22   Industrial products
I.24   Internet services/e-commerce

Ampersand Venture Management Corp.

55 William Street, Suite 240
Wellesley, Massachusetts 02481
(781) 239-0700
Fax: (781) 239-0824
E-mail: info@ampersandventures.com
Web: www.ampersandventures.com

Key contact:
Mr. Richard A. Charpie, Managing General Partner
Mr. Stuart A. Auerbach, General Partner
Mr. Peter D. Parker, General Partner
Mr. Charles D. Yie, General Partner
Mr. Robert A. Charpie, Chairman/Special Partner
Mr. Donald B. Hawthorne, CFO/Partner
Mr. David J. Parker, Partner
Mr. David V. Ragone, Special Partner
Mr. Paul C. Zigman, Partner

Description: We were founded as a spinoff from Paine
Webber, to pursue a differentiated private equity
investment strategy. We were created to focus exclusively on the specialty materials and chemicals
(SMC) industry.

Founded: 1988

Preferred investment size: $2-10 million

Amount under management: $100-500 million

Area served: North America

Preferred stages of financing: Seed, Start up, First
stage, Second stage, LBO/MBO, Expansion

Industries:
I.05   Chemicals

Sampling of portfolio companies: Kroy Building
Products (vinyl fencing); ADFlex Solutions
(polymide-based flexible circuits); INNOVA (digital
radios for wireless communications); Pacific
Communications Sciences, Inc. (wireless communications equipment & systems); Silicon Wave (RF
chip sets for digital cellular radios); Smartflex
Systems (advanced flexible circuit assemblies); Spectrian (power amplifiers for wireless applications);
INCON (industrial instrumentation); MIssbrenner
(textile design & printing); Moldflow (process
software for injection molded parts); Nanodyne
(nanostructured composites for industrial tools);
ACLARA BioSciences, Inc. (microfluidic-based
research products); Alexis (reagents for life science
researchers); AutoCyte (cervical cancer screening
systems); VITEX (viralty inactivated blood
products); Advanced Chemistry & Technology (aerospace adhesives & sealants); Daniel Products Co.
(high performance additives for paints & inks);
Huntington Laboratories (infection control chemicals); Quaichem (high purity molybdenum chemicals); Tomah Products (specialty surfactants)

Applied Technology

One Cranberry Hill
Lexington, Massachusetts 02173
(781) 862-8622
Fax: (781) 862-8367

Key contact:
Mr. Frederick Bamber

Preferred stages of financing: Seed, Start up, First
stage, Second stage

Industries:
I.06   Communications
I.08   Computer software

Argo Global Capital, Inc.

210 Broadway, Suite 101
Lynnfield, Massachusetts 01940
(781) 592-5250
Fax: (781) 592-5230
E-mail: rwwhite@gsmcapital.com
Web: www.gsmcapital.com

Key contact:
Mr. R. W. White, Vice President/Partner
Mr. T. Wooters, Vice President/Partner
Ms. B. Bradin, Vice President/Partner
Mr. H. H. Haight, President/Partner

Description: We are a $137 million fund focused on
investments in wireless technology. One third of the
capital was provided by nine of the world's leading

wireless carriers. Investments are made in companies
located anywhere in the world and at any stage of
their development.

Preferred investment size: $5 million

Amount under management: $100-500 million

Area served: Worldwide

Preferred stages of financing: Start up, First stage,
Second stage, Mezzanine, LBO/MBO, Expansion, Int'l
expansion

Industries:
I.06   Communications

Sampling of portfolio companies: Novatel Wireless
(wireless modem technology); LGC Wireless
(wireless in-building signal distribution)

Atlantic Capital

164 Cushing Highway
Cohasset, Massachusetts 02025
(781) 383-9449
Fax: (781) 383-6040

Key contact:
Mr. Fraser J. Cameron

Preferred stage of financing: First stage

Industries:
I.06   Communications
I.07   Computer hardware
I.08   Computer software
I.11   Consumer products

I.12   Distribution
I.14   Electronics
I.18   Financial services

I.29   Medical/medical products
I.32   Retail
I.33   Semiconductors

Atlas Venture

222 Berkeley Street
Boston, Massachusetts 02116
(617) 859-9290
Fax: (617) 859-9292
E-mail: boston@atlasventure.com
Web: www.atlasventure.com

Key contact:
Mr. Michael Du Cros, Life Sciences Investment Team
Mr. Allan Ferguson, Life Sciences Investment Team
Mr. Barry Fidelman, Information Technology Investment Team
Mr. Jean-François Formela, Life Sciences Investment Team
Ms. Jeanne Larkin Henry, Finance & Administration
Mr. Jean-Yves Quentel, Information Technology Investment Team
Mr. Christopher Spray, Information Technology Investment Team

Description: Partnership of international venture capitalists formed to finance high-technology businesses seeking success in the global economy. Since 1980 we have focused our resources to provide real service to our companies. We concentrate our investments in just two sectors, life sciences and information technology. Each sector has investment teams in Europe and the US with the right mix of financial, operational and technical skills.

Founded: 1980

Amount of capital invested: $40 million

Preferred investment size: $500,000-5 million

Amount under management: $100-500 million

Area served: Europe, East Coast, United States

Preferred stages of financing: Seed, Second stage

Industries:
I.08   Computer software
I.20   Healthcare
I.29   Medical/medical products

Sampling of portfolio companies: Applied Language Technologies Inc. (speech recognition software); Artel Video Systems, Inc. (video transmission & switching products); Cerulean Technology, Inc. (wireless mobile information software); Firefly Network, Inc. (internet based intelligent agent software); FutureTense, Inc. (professional web publishing software); GeoTel Communications Corp. (telecommuncations call routing software); Network Integrity, Inc. (data integrity & availability software); PCs Compleat, Inc. (direct marketing of computers & computer related products); FASTech Integration, Inc. (factory automation software); FirstSense Software, Inc. (applications management software); SolidWorks Corp. (mechanical design automation software); Ascent Pediatrics, Inc. (pediatric pharmaceuticals); Cardima, Inc. (micro catheter devices for mapping & ablation of arrhythmias); CytoMed, Inc. (pharmaceuticals for treatment of inflammatory diseases); Diatide, Inc. (radiopharmaceuticals for nuclear medicine); MediSpectra, Inc. (optical instruments for minimally invasive medical diagnosis); NitroMed, Inc. (pharmaceuticals based on nitrogen monoxide); Transfusion Technologies Corp. (blood separation & processing device); Scriptgen Pharmaceuticals, Inc. (anti-viral & anti-fungal pharmaceuticals); Variagenics, Inc. (novel drug targets based on genetic variance)

Bain Capital Inc.

Two Copley Place
Boston, Massachusetts 02116
(617) 572-3000
Fax: (617) 572-3274

Key contact:
Mr. Geoff Rehnert

BancBoston Capital/BancBoston Ventures

175 Federal Street, 10th Floor
Boston, Massachusetts 02110
(617) 434-2509
Fax: (617) 434-1153
Web: www.bkb.com

Key contact:
Mr. Frederick M. Fritz, President
Ms. Marcia Bates, Managing Director-Healthcare
Mr. Sanford Antsey, Managing Director-Media/Telecom
Mr. Craig Deery, Managing Director-U.S. Private Equity
Mr. Mark H. DeBlois, Managing Director-U.S. Private Equity
Mr. Lee Tesconi, Managing Director-Portfolio Acquisitions
Ms. Cynthia Duda, Managing Director-Insitutional Mgmt.
Mr. Zack Edmonds, Treasurer-Management & Finance

Ms. Christina Novicki, Director of Marketing

Description: We are the private equity and mezzanine investment subsidiary of Bank Of Boston Corporation. We have been active since 1959, when the Bank launched the first SBIC-licensed venture capital firm in the country. Since then, we have broadened our investment capabilities and invested over $1 billion in approximately 300 businesses in North America, Europe and Latin America.

Founded: 1959

Amount under management: $500 million -1 billion

Area served: Asia, Europe, North America, South/Central America

Preferred stages of financing: Mezzanine, LBO/MBO, Expansion, Recapitalizations

Industries:
I.18   Financial services
I.23   Information technology services

I.27   Manufacturing
I.28   Media/publishing

Battery Ventures
20 William Street, Suite 200
Wellesley, Massachusetts 02181
(781) 237-1001
Fax: (781) 996-7788
Web: www.battery.com

Key contact:
Mr. Richard D. Frisbie, Managing Partner
Oliver D. Curme, General Partner
Mr. Thomas J. Crotty, General Partner
Mr. Todd A. Dagres, General Partner
Mr. Howard Anderson, General Partner
Mr. Ravi Mohan, Vice President
Mr. R. David Tabors, Associate
Mr. Morgan M. Jones, Associate
Mr. Scott R. Tobin, Associate

Description: Founded in 1983, we are one of the leading high tech venture capital firms in the nation. We manage four investment funds, the most recent of which totals $200 million, placing us among the largest information technology VC funds in the country. Our focused investment approach targets early emerging companies in the communications and software technology markets in the U.S. and abroad.

Founded: 1983

Preferred investment size: $10-20 million

Amount under management: $100-500 million

Area served: United States

Preferred stages of financing: Start up, First stage, Second stage

Industries:
I.06   Communications
I.08   Computer software
I.12   Distribution
I.23   Information technology services
I.24   Internet services/e-commerce
I.27   Manufacturing

Sampling of portfolio companies: Brooktrout Technology (voice & fax messaging systems); Concord Communications, Inc. (LAN management systems); FlowWise Networks, Inc. (IP switching systems); Focal Communications (competitive local exchange carrier); Network Equipment Technologies, Inc. (intelligent network processors for private T1 digital networks); Radnet Ltd. (ATM switching multiplexor); All City Communications, Inc. (specialized mobile radio & paging communications); General Wireless, Inc. (broadband PCS network); UniSite, Inc. (site management services for wireless communications) XCOM (competitive local exchange carrier); AEC Data Systems, Inc. (distributed facilities maintenance & management software); Atrieva (remote LAN backup software); HNC (neural network software for decision analysis); Phoenix Technologies, Inc. (system software for personal computers); SmartPatents, Inc. (client-server intellectual property asset management software); Witness Systems (call center monitoring software); Instream Corp. (on-line service for the behavioral health industry); VDONet Corp. (software for internet-based video services); Pixelworks, Inc. (distributors & developers of digital computer displays & controllers); Universal Electronics (manufacturer of universal remote controls)

Berkshire Partners
One Boston Place, Suite 3300
Boston, Massachusetts 02108
(617) 227-0050
Fax: (617) 227-6105

Key contact:
Ms. Jeanine H. Neumann, Director-Client Services

Preferred stage of financing: LBO/MBO

Industries:
I.05   Chemicals
I.11   Consumer products
I.18   Financial services
I.29   Medical/medical products
I.35   Services (consumer)

Bessemer Venture Partners
83 Walnut Street
Wellesley Hills, Massachusetts 02181
(781) 237-6050
Fax: (781) 237-7576
Web: www.bessemervp.com

Key contact:
Mr. William T. Burgin, Partner
Mr. G. Felda Hardymon, Partner
Mr. Robert H. Buescher, Partner
Mr. Christopher F. O. Gabrieli, Partner
Mr. David J. Cowan, Partner
Mr. Bruce K. Graham, Partner

Area served: United States

Preferred stages of financing: Seed, Start up, First

stage, Second stage, Mezzanine, LBO/MBO, Expansion

Industries:
I.01   Aerospace
I.02   Agriculture/forestry/fishing/mining
I.03   Biotech/genetic engineering
I.04   Broadcasting
I.05   Chemicals
I.06   Communications
I.07   Computer hardware
I.08   Computer software
I.09   Construction
I.10   Consulting
I.11   Consumer products
I.12   Distribution
I.13   Education
I.14   Electronics

I.15   Energy/natural resources/utilities
I.16   Entertainment
I.17   Environmental services/waste management
I.18   Financial services
I.19   Generalist
I.20   Healthcare
I.21   High technology
I.22   Industrial products
I.23   Information technology services
I.24   Internet services/e-commerce
I.25   Leisure/hospitality
I.26   Life sciences
I.27   Manufacturing
I.28   Media/publishing
I.29   Medical/medical products
I.30   New media
I.31   Real estate
I.32   Retail
I.33   Semiconductors
I.34   Services (business)
I.35   Services (consumer)

I.36   Transportation
I.37   Wholesale

Sampling of portfolio companies: Advantage Schools; Dick's Clothing & Sporting Goods; Domain Home Furnishings; Eagle Hardware & Garden; Factory Card Outlet; Fort James; Hometown Buffet; Multiple Zones; The Sports Authority; Staples; Timothy's Coffees; Zany Brainy; Epix Medical; Gamera Bioscience; OPTA Food Ingredients; PerSeptive Biosystems; Alkermes; ChemGenics Pharmaceuticals (now Millenium); Isis Pharmaceuticals; Oclassen Pharmaceuticals; American Medical Communications; Datamedic; GMIS (now HBOC); Synergy Healthcare; Access Radiology; Allscrips Pharmaceuticals; FemPartners; Focus Healthcare; GMS Dental (now Gentle Dental); Kelson Physician Partners; Meridian Occupational Healthcare Associates; Morgan Health Group; Princeps; ProMedCo; Providers' Assurance; TravCorps; VistaCare

BG Affiliates LLC

470 Atlantic Avenue
Boston, Massachusetts 02210
(617) 556-1400
Fax: (617) 423-8916

Key contact:
Mr. Frank Apeseche, President/CEO
Mr. Matthew Hills, Senior Vice President

Description: We are a private equity investment firm that provides capital to high quality, middle-market operating companies. We develop long-term partnerships with the management team of each company and support them in building their businesses. Our investment interests are in industries as diverse as healthcare, financial services, real estate services, material handling. basic manufacturing and distribution.

Preferred investment size: $2-10 million

Area served: Canada, United States

Preferred stages of financing: Start up, LBO/MBO, Expansion, Acquisitions, growth capital

Industries:
I.18   Financial services
I.20   Healthcare
I.31   Real estate

Sampling of portfolio companies: Harborside Healthcare (integrated healthcare service provider); Berkshire Mortgage Finance (multi-family & healthcare finance); Berkshire Realty Co., Inc. (multi-family REIT); Berkshire Property Management (property management company); K-Bro Linen Systems (specializes in cleaning & renting linen for hospitals, nursing homes & hotels)

Boston Capital Ventures

45 School Street
Old City Hall
Boston, Massachusetts 02108
(617) 227-6550
Fax: (617) 227-3847
E-mail: AWilmerding@bcv.com
Web: info@bcv.com

Key contact:
Mr. H. J. von der Goltz, Partner
Mr. J. J. Shields, Partner
Mr. Alex von der Goltz, Principal
Mr. Alexander Wilmerding, Principal

Description: We manage venture capital partnerships which invest in growth companies. Its partners and principals are experienced professionals who have a diverse range of skills and broad network of domestic and international relationships which have proven invaluable to portfolio companies. The firm typically invests in software, communications, technology and services companies which will generate revenues in the near term.

Preferred investment size: $2-8 million

Amount under management: $100-500 million

Area served: Asia, North America, South/Central America

Preferred stages of financing: Seed, Start up, First stage, Second stage

Industries:
I.06   Communications
I.08   Computer software
I.17   Environmental services/waste management
I.18   Financial services
I.21   High technology
I.23   Information technology services
I.24   Internet services/e-commerce
I.34   Services (business)
I.35   Services (consumer)

Sampling of portfolio companies: Brand Direct Marketing (direct marketing); Conservation Tourism (eco-tourism); Exa Corp. (software); International Cornerstone Group (direct marketing/catalogue); MGC Communications, Inc. (telecom); SCC Communications, Inc. (telecom); Sensitech, Inc. (distribution); Teletrac, Inc. (telecom); 21st Century Telecom Group (telecom); Unisite, Inc. (communications); Vectrix Corp. (transportation solutions); Verio, Inc. (internet)

Boston Millennia Partners L.P.

30 Rowes Wharf
Boston, Massachusetts 02110
(617) 428-5150
Fax: (617) 428-5160
E-mail: marty@millenniapartners.com
Web: www.milleniapartners.com

Key contact:
Mr. Martin J. Hernon, General Partner
Mr. Suresh Shanmugham, Principal
Mr. Robert S. Sherman, General Partner

Description: We are a private equity firm which invests in high growth companies in the healthcare and life sciences, telecommunications and information technology industries. Our investment philosophy is geared towards realizing attractive investment returns while carefully managing risk. We finance talented, hard-working management teams who can build successful high growth companies.

Amount under management: $100-500 million

Area served: United States

Preferred stage of financing: Expansion

Industries:
I.06   Communications
I.11   Consumer products
I.20   Healthcare
I.23   Information technology services
I.26   Life sciences

Sampling of portfolio companies: Brand Direct (consumer)

Burr, Egan, Deleage & Company

One Post Office Square #3800
Boston, Massachusetts 02109
(617) 482-8020
Fax: (617) 482-1944
E-mail: info@bedco.com
Web: www.bedco.com

Key contact:
Mr. Craig L. Burr
Mr. Brian W. McNeill
Mr. William P. Egan

Description: Since the 1970s, our principals have invested in many emerging growth companies helping them to become the large corporations of today. We are a private venture capital firm which has invests in over 200 companies throughout America. With capital under management in excess of $600 million, we are positioned in the top tier of venture capital firms.

Preferred investment size: >$1.5 million

Area served: United States

Preferred stages of financing: Start up, LBO/MBO, Expansion

Industries:
I.06   Communications
I.07   Computer hardware
I.14   Electronics
I.20   Healthcare
I.22   Industrial products
I.23   Information technology services
I.26   Life sciences
I.29   Medical/medical products

Sampling of portfolio companies: Abacus Direct (develops & enhances databases of names to be used by direct mail companies); American Superconductor (develops cost effective manufacturing processes to produce superconducting wire for power & magnet applications); Diva Communications (focused on the use of wireless technology to build telephone infrastructures in rapidly industrializing countries); N Dimension (will develop an interactive CD-ROM & on-line guide to popular entertainment); Pacific Communications Sciences (develops telecommunications systems & products in the multiplexer, mobile communication & vice compression areas); Powersoft (develops & markets the Powersoft Enterprise Series, database-independent, scalable client/server development tools); Sierra Semiconductor (supplier of CMOS mixed analog/digital integrated circuits); Spectrum Assoc. (MRP software & services company which is in the process of introducing a new object-oriented MRP system); Windata (develops & markets wireless, ethernet-compatible local area networks utilizing spread spectrum technology); Acusphere (biomaterials company with very broad patents, technology & marketing opportunities); Cellpro (develops devices & instrumentation for the isolation, purification, growth & delivery of cells to be used for diagnostic & therapeutic purposes); Depotech (drug delivery company engaged in the development & manufacture of sustained-release therapeutic products based on DepoFoam, an injectable, depot drug delivery technology); Innerdyne Medical (developed a line of unique single use devices which permit or improve a physician's ability to access internal organs or vessels in a less invasive manner); Interpore International (main product is a porous hydroxyapatite which is being used for bone repair in orthopedic & oral maxillo-facial surgery); Oravax (biopharmaceutical company, the worldwide leader in the discovery & development of mucosal immune system-based pharmaceutical products for the prevention & cure of human infectious diseases); Terrapin Technologies (pharmaceutical discovery company with a proprietary molecular fingerprinting technology which accelerates the discovery of new drugs with unprecedented speed & specificity); Vesica Medical (designs, manufactures & markets minimally invasive surgical devices for the treatment of female urinary incontinence); Brooks Fiber Properties (competitive access service provider in fifteen to twenty second tier cities, MSA #'s 50-100); Old Dominion Capital (formed to purchase, at a discount, the existing senior debt securities plus warrant & option kickers provided by equipment vendors to small cellular companies); Panache Broadcasting LP (owns & operates talk radio station WWDB-FM in Philadelphia & WTLC-AM/FM serving the black community in Indianapolis)

CB Health Ventures

470 Atlantic Avenue, Suite 902
Boston, Massachusetts 02210
(617) 450-9800
Fax: (617) 450-9749
E-mail: rick@health-ventures.com

Key contact:
Mr. Frederick R. Blume, Manager
Mr. Daniel M. Cain, Manager
Mr. Robert B. Schulz, Manager
Mr. Enrico Petrillo, Manager

Description: We are a group of seasoned professionals investing in early and emerging companies with new products, services or technology addressing large markets in healthcare. We seek to leverage our experience and considerable resources to contribute to the speed of development and market acceptance of our portfolio companies.

Preferred investment size: $2.5-5 million

Area served: Canada, United States

Preferred stages of financing: First stage, Second stage, Mezzanine, Expansion

Industries:
I.03   Biotech/genetic engineering
I.20   Healthcare
I.26   Life sciences
I.29   Medical/medical products

Charles River Ventures

Bay Colony Corporate Center
1000 Winter Street, Suite 3300
Waltham, Massachusetts 02154
(781) 487-7060
Fax: (781) 487-7065
Web: www.crv.com

Key contact:
Mr. Izhar Armony, Principal
Mr. Rick Burnes, Principal
Mr. Ted Dintersmith, Principal
Mr. Don Feddersen, Principal
Mr. Jonathan Guerster, Principal
Mr. Mike Zak, Principal
Mr. Paul J. Conway, CFO
Ms. Vita Spakevicius, Analyst
Ms. Mickey Nobile, Accounting Manager
Ms. Lily Badger, Administrative Assistant
Ms. Karen Christensen, Administrative Assistant
Ms. Anne-Marie Maguire, Administrative Assistant
Ms. Karen Mullen, Receptionist

Description: We are one of the nation's leading early-stage venture capital firms. Founded in 1970 and based in Boston, our mission is to contribute to the creation of significant new enterprises by working in constructive partnership with driven, talented entrepreneurs. Focus is East Coast, communications-related investments.

Founded: 1970

Preferred investment size: $3-5 million

Amount under management: $100-500 million

Preferred stages of financing: Seed, First stage

Industries:
I.06   Communications
I.08   Computer software
I.14   Electronics
I.23   Information technology services
I.24   Internet services/e-commerce

Sampling of portfolio companies: Agile Networks (develops data communications products based on asynchronous transfer mode); Cascade Communications Corp. (manufactures a family of high performance, multi-service wide area network switches); CellCall, Inc. (building a regional mobile communications network offering high quality mobile telephone, fleet dispatch & paging services); C-Port Corp. (developing a programmable multiprocessor whose architecture is optimized for data communications tasks); Sonus Networks (developing carrier-class voice communications equipment); Teloquent Communications Corp. (develops a call center automation software for the management of phone calls in customer service centers); Atreve Software, Inc. (provides management & monitoring solutions for large, high traffic enterprise web sites); Chrysalis Symbolic Design (develops, markets & supports electronic design automation software products used in the design of complex integrated circuits); Epoch Systems, Inc. (assembled & sold on-line backup storage & memory management systems for the NFS/UNIX environment found in workstation networks); MainControl Inc. (develops enterprise-wide network management systems for client/server networks that are distributed across multiple computing platforms but are reliant on IBM mainframes); Parametric Technology Corp. (developer of software for the automation of the mechanical design process); Sitara, Inc. (developing a new class of protocol software that will allow corporate end-users & internet service providers to achieve significant improvements in network performance); Sybase, Inc. (develops & markets a full line of relational database management software products & services for on-line applications in networked computing environments); Abacus Direct Corp. (provides mailing lists to direct marketers through a database it maintains); Excite Corp. (offers a web-based navigation information service for online media); InPart Design, Inc. (provides component data & computer-aided design content on the internet, revolutionizing the way designers search, select & specify standard parts); Amgen Inc. (independent biotechnology company); Aspect Medical Systems, Inc. (developing a non-invasive diagnostic system to measure an anesthetized patient's consciousness level); Odin Technology, Ltd. (developing a small, low cost, portable magnetic resonance image system for monitoring & guiding surgical & other therapeutic procedures); Seragen, Inc. (discoverer & developer of therapeutic products called fusion toxins)

Chestnut Street Partners, Inc.
75 State Street, Suite 2500
Boston, Massachusetts 02109
(617) 345-7220
Fax: (617) 345-7201

Key contact:
Mr. David D. Croll

Preferred stage of financing: Seed

Citizens Capital
28 State Street
Boston, Massachusetts 02109
(617) 725-5633
Fax: (617) 725-5630

Key contact:
Mr. Robert E. Garrow, President/Managing Director
Mr. Daniel P. Corcoran, Jr., Managing Director
Mr. Gregory F. Mulligan, Managing Director
Ms. Glenna M. Hicks, Vice President

Description: We provide subordinated debt and equity
capital to middle market companies to support
growth, acquisitions, management buyouts and
recapitalizations. Investment size is up to $15
million. We also invest as a limited partner in other
private equity partnerships.

Preferred investment size: $3-15 million

Amount under management: $100-500 million

Area served: North America

Preferred stages of financing: Mezzanine, LBO/MBO,
Expansion

Industries:
I.04   Broadcasting
I.05   Chemicals
I.06   Communications
I.07   Computer hardware
I.08   Computer software
I.11   Consumer products
I.12   Distribution
I.14   Electronics
I.17   Environmental services/waste management
I.18   Financial services
I.20   Healthcare
I.21   High technology
I.22   Industrial products
I.23   Information technology services
I.24   Internet services/e-commerce
I.27   Manufacturing
I.28   Media/publishing
I.29   Medical/medical products
I.32   Retail
I.34   Services (business)
I.35   Services (consumer)

Claflin Capital Management Inc.
77 Franklin Street
Boston, Massachusetts 02110
(617) 426-6505
Fax: (617) 482-0016

Key contact:
Mr. Thomas M. Claflin, II
Mr. Lloyd C. Dahmen
Ms. Margaret M. Daniels
Mr. John O. Flender
Mr. Joseph Stavenhagen

Preferred stage of financing: Seed

Industries:
I.03   Biotech/genetic engineering
I.06   Communications
I.07   Computer hardware
I.08   Computer software
I.14   Electronics
I.29   Medical/medical products

CMG Information Services
100 Brickstone Square
Andover, Massachusetts 01810
(978) 684-3600
Fax: (978) 684-3658
Web: www.cmgi.com

Key contact:
Mr. David S. Wetherell, President/CEO
Mr. John A. McMullen, Founder/Managing Principal
Mr. Craig Goldman, President-Cyber Consulting
Services
Mr. Andrew J. Hajducky, CFO/Treasurer
Mr. Hans Hawrysz, President-Planet Direct

Description: We invest in and integrate advanced
internet, interactive media and database management
technologies.

Founded: 1986

Industries:
I.24   Internet services/e-commerce

Sampling of portfolio companies: Engage Technologies, Inc. (provides standards-based, enterprise-
class software system solutions); ADSmart (automated the process of matching a given advertising
compaign to audience specific characteristics corre-
lated to articles or sections in internet sites that belong
to the ADSmart.net internet advertising network);
InfoMation Publishing Corp. (builds best-of-breed
knowledge management applications); Planet Direct
Corp. (next-generation personal web service); Sale-
sLink Corp. (provides fulfillment & turnkey services
to the high-tech, financial services & healthcare
markets); CMG Direct Corp. (provides solutions for
integrating traditional direct marketing with internet
marketing); NaviSite Internet Services Corp.
(provides web hosting & internet server management
to companies that depend on the internet as a critical
business tool); Lycos, Inc. (personal internet guide
company); GeoCities (community on the internet);
KOZ, Inc. (media company); blaxxun interactive, inc.
(provides the software infrastructure for 3-D online
communities); Reel.com, LLC (web-based movie

store); Parable, LLC (internet multimedia tools company); Ikonic, Inc. (consulting & development company that provides the strategy, architecture & implementation services needed to enable some of the world's largest companies to extend their brands & businesses onto the internet); Sage Enterprises, Inc./ PlanetAll (online community that helps members get in touch, & stay in touch, with people & groups important to them); Silknet Software, Inc. (delivers a superior, enterprise-level customer-service software package through the application of new internet technologies); Vicinity Corp. (private-label provider of GeoEnabled (TM) technology, content & services for web publishers & corporate web sites); Softway Systems, Inc. (provider of UNIX system products for Windows NT, built as part of a strategic & source code agreement with Microsoft Corp.)

Comdisco Ventures

One Newton Executive Park
2221 Washington Street, Suite 302
Newton Lower Falls, Massachusetts 02162
(617) 244-6622
Web: www.comdisco.com

Key contact:
Mr. Mark C. M. Grader

Description: We provide a wide variety of financing products to venture capital-backed start-up companies. These include equipment leases and loans, subordinated debt, receivables financing and equity financing.

Founded: 1987

Amount of capital invested: $167,269,749.97

Amount under management: $500 million -1 billion

Area served: United States

Preferred stage of financing: Start up

Industries:
I.03   Biotech/genetic engineering
I.06   Communications
I.08   Computer software
I.14   Electronics
I.20   Healthcare

I.23   Information technology services
I.29   Medical/medical products
I.32   Retail
I.33   Semiconductors
I.34   Services (business)

Sampling of portfolio companies: Cephalon (biotechnology/biopharmaceutical); Focal (biotechnology/ biopharmaceutical); Khepri Pharmaceuticals (biotechnology/biopharmaceutical); Pharmaceutical Peptides (biotechnology/biopharmaceutical); Somatix (biotechnology/biopharmaceutical); Virus Research Institute (biotechnology/biopharmaceutical); Adv. Surgical Intervention (medical devices & services); TomTec Imaging Systems (medical devices & services); Avail Systems (software & computer services); Electric Classifieds (software & computer services); Lightspan Partnership (software & computer services); TimeLine Vista (software & computer services); Visio (software & computer services); Auto Parts Club (consumer related); SportsTown (consumer related); National IPF Company (other products & services); Cascade Communications (communications & networking); Wayfarer Communications (communications & networking); Aspen Peripherals (computer hardware & semiconductors); Power Integrations (computer hardware & semiconductors)

Commonwealth Capital Ventures, L.P.

20 William Street, Suite 225
Wellesley, Massachusetts 02181
(781) 237-7373
Fax: (781) 235-8627
E-mail: mfitz@ccvlp.com
Web: www.ccvlp.com

Key contact:
Mr. Michael T. Fitzgerald, General Partner/Founder
Mr. R. Stephen McCormack, General Partner/Founder
Mr. Jeffrey M. Hurst, General Partner/Founder
Mr. Rob S. Chandra, General Partner

Description: Venture capital/private equity partnership formed to invest in new and established growth companies in the New England region.

Amount of capital invested: $12.5 million

Preferred investment size: $1 million

Amount under management: $100-500 million

Area served: New England

Preferred stages of financing: Seed, Start up, Expansion

Industries:
I.03   Biotech/genetic engineering
I.06   Communications
I.08   Computer software
I.11   Consumer products
I.14   Electronics
I.15   Energy/natural resources/utilities
I.20   Healthcare
I.21   High technology
I.22   Industrial products
I.23   Information technology services
I.27   Manufacturing
I.29   Medical/medical products
I.32   Retail
I.34   Services (business)

Sampling of portfolio companies: Polar Beverages (retail); Cerulean Technology (tech. soft.); Olympus Healthcare(healthcare); Lids (retail); Artel Video Systems (tech.); American Hearing Centers (healthcare)

Commonwealth Enterprise Fund, Inc.

10 Post Office Square, Suite 1090
Boston, Massachusetts 02109

(617) 482-1881
Fax: (617) 482-7129

Key contact:
Mr. Charles Broming, Manager
Mr. Milton Benjamin, Chairman
Mr. Kamal Quadir, Consultant

Description: We invest in early stage ventures owned and lead by women and minorities and which are located in Massachusetts.

Amount of capital invested: $750,000

Preferred investment size: $250,000-300,000

Amount under management: <$10 million

Area served: United States

Preferred stages of financing: Seed, Start up, First stage, LBO/MBO

Sampling of portfolio companies: InTouch Communications, LLC (telecom/paging); Advanced Techcom, Inc. (short-hand microwave, telecom); Infocus Publications, Inc. (specialized publishing); Imagex, Inc. (paper recycling, document security); Mosaic Technologies, Inc. (DNA-based medical diagnostics)

Community Technology Fund
(affiliated with Boston University)
108 Bay State Road
Boston, Massachusetts 02215
(617) 353-4550
Fax: (617) 353-6141
E-mail: rcrawfor@bu.edu
Web: www.geocities.com/wallstreet/2734

Key contact:
Mr. Matthew J. Burns, Managing Director
Mr. Randall C. Crawford

Description: We provide venture capital and management assistance to early stage companies. We primarily focus on those companies located within the Northeast area of the U.S., but will consider investments in companies located throughout the U.S. We typically focus on companies with the photonics and healthcare industries. We are a technology-oriented, early stage venture capital firm and have an affiliation with Boston University. Together we offer a unique intellectual and physical resource base for supporting the development of early stage companies.

Area served: United States

Preferred stages of financing: Seed, Start up, First stage

Industries:
I.03   Biotech/genetic engineering
I.11   Consumer products
I.20   Healthcare
I.29   Medical/medical products

Sampling of portfolio companies: Concord Communications, Inc.; FASTech Integration, Inc.; MicroE, Inc.; Acusphere Inc. (biotechnology); CytoLogix Corp. (medical instruments & devices); NitroMed Inc. (pharmaceuticals); Pharmadyne Inc. (biotechnology); Visualization Technology, Inc. (medical instruments & devices)

Dominion Ventures, Inc.
60 State Street, Suite 2170
Boston, Massachusetts 02109
(617) 367-8575
Fax: (617) 367-0323

Key contact:
Mr. Randy Werner

Area served: United States

Preferred stages of financing: First stage, Second stage, LBO/MBO

Industries:
I.03   Biotech/genetic engineering

I.04   Broadcasting
I.06   Communications
I.07   Computer hardware
I.08   Computer software
I.12   Distribution
I.14   Electronics
I.17   Environmental services/waste management
I.18   Financial services
I.29   Medical/medical products
I.34   Services (business)
I.35   Services (consumer)
I.36   Transportation

Fidelity Capital
82 Devonshire Street - R25C
Boston, Massachusetts 02109
(617) 563-9106
Fax: (617) 476-6097

Key contact:
Ms. Janet New
Mr. Peter Mann
Mr. John J. Remondi
Mr. Neal Yanofsky

Description: Boston base venture capital arm of Fidelity Investments.

Preferred investment size: Over $1 million

Area served: International

Preferred stages of financing: First stage, Second stage, LBO/MBO

Industries:
I.05   Chemicals
I.06   Communications
I.08   Computer software
I.12   Distribution
I.14   Electronics
I.18   Financial services
I.29   Medical/medical products
I.36   Transportation

Fowler, Anthony & Company

20 Walnut Street, 3rd Floor
Wellesley Hills, Massachusetts 02181
(781) 237-4201
Fax: (781) 237-7718

Key contact:
Mr. John A. Quagliaroli, President

Description: VC and buyout firm. All industries except real estate. In operation since 1976. Three professionals.

Founded: 1976

Preferred investment size: $1-20 million+

Area served: Canada, Europe, United States

Preferred stages of financing: Seed, Start up, First stage, Second stage, Mezzanine, LBO/MBO, Expansion

Industries:
I.01   Aerospace
I.02   Agriculture/forestry/fishing/mining
I.03   Biotech/genetic engineering
I.04   Broadcasting
I.05   Chemicals
I.06   Communications
I.08   Computer software
I.09   Construction
I.11   Consumer products
I.14   Electronics
I.15   Energy/natural resources/utilities
I.16   Entertainment
I.17   Environmental services/waste management
I.19   Generalist
I.20   Healthcare
I.21   High technology
I.22   Industrial products
I.23   Information technology services
I.24   Internet services/e-commerce
I.25   Leisure/hospitality
I.26   Life sciences
I.27   Manufacturing
I.28   Media/publishing
I.29   Medical/medical products
I.30   New media
I.32   Retail
I.34   Services (business)
I.35   Services (consumer)
I.36   Transportation
I.37   Wholesale

Sampling of portfolio companies: Restaurant chains/ brand name; Multimedia company; Fasteners; Sports media/entertainment; Automotive; Aerospace/ services; PPM Rollup; Telecommunications services; Environmental services; Medical instrumentation

Gemini Investors LLC

55 William Street, Suite 120
Wellesley, Massachusetts 02181
(781) 237-7001
Fax: (781) 237-7233
E-mail: gmninvest@aol.com

Key contact:
Mr. James J. Goodman, President
Mr. David F. Millet, Managing Director
Mr. Jeffrey T. Newton, Managing Director
Mr. C. Redington Barrett, III, Managing Director

Description: We manage two funds, the most recent with $110 million to invest in established companies (at least 3 years of operations, revenues of $10 million and within one year of profitability) in a wide range of industries, except real estate or lending institutions. We will invest $2 - 6 million per deal, usually in preferred stock or subordinated debt. The 4 GP's collectively have 70+ years of experience in principal investing, operations, investment banking and consulting.

Amount of capital invested: $10 million

Preferred investment size: $3-5 million

Amount under management: $100-500 million

Area served: United States

Preferred stages of financing: Second stage, Mezzanine, LBO/MBO, Expansion

Industries:
I.19   Generalist

Sampling of portfolio companies: Kitchen Etc. (specialty retail); Tutor Time Learning Systems (child care chain); Adventure Entertainment Corp. (family entertainment parks); Sega Gaming Technology (manufacturer of gaming equipment); Arizona Pennysaver Inc. (publishing, shopper newspapers); Luxtec (manufacturer of surgical illumination products); LIDS (specialty retail); Ziro (consumer product manufacturer); Edutrek (education, for profit university); Learningsmith (specialty retail); Dyax (biotechnology); Tristar Industries (industrial parts distributor)

Greylock Management Corp.

One Federal Street
Boston, Massachusetts 02110-2065
(617) 423-5525
Fax: (617) 482-0059
E-mail: boston@greylock.com
Web: www.greylock.com

Key contact:
Mr. Henry McCance, General Partner
Mr. Howard Cox, General Partner
Mr. Bill Kaiser, General Partner
Mr. Bill Helman, General Partner

Mr. Chip Hazard, General Partner
Mr. David Aronoff, Associate
Mr. Bill Nussey, Associate
Mr. Jon Karlen, Associate

Description: Our role is to support a company's management team in building a world-class enterprise by acting as a responsible and constructive member of the company's board of directors. This takes on many shapes and forms but includes working to build a management team, facilitating relationships with other companies, helping to set a company's strategic direction and raising additional capital both privately and publicly.

Founded: 1965

Amount under management: $500 million -1 billion

Preferred stages of financing: Start up, LBO/MBO, Expansion, Recapitalizations

Industries:
I.03 Biotech/genetic engineering
I.04 Broadcasting
I.06 Communications
I.08 Computer software
I.11 Consumer products
I.14 Electronics
I.15 Energy/natural resources/utilities
I.20 Healthcare
I.22 Industrial products
I.29 Medical/medical products

Sampling of portfolio companies: American Management Systems (systems integration services); Pansophic Systems (system software & utilities); Molecular Design Ltd. (databases for chemical research); Ross Systems (financial & manufacturing software); cc: Mail, Inc. (PC e-mail software); C•ATS Software, Inc. (enterprise-wide financial risk management software); Trilogy Development Group, Inc. (enterprise software applications for sales & marketing); Gradient Technologies, Inc. (communications & security software); Sagent Technology, Inc. (data warehouse software); Cygnus Solutions (development tools for microcontrollers); Ascend Communications, Inc. (remote networking solutions); Whitetree Network Technologies, Inc. (ATM networking equipment); Zeitnet Data Systems, Inc. (ATM network interface cards); Maker Communications (high speed ATM chip sets); Biomedical/Resources Int'l. Clinical Labs (clinical labs); Neutrogena (dermatology); Genetics Institute (protein based therapeutics); Rehab Systems (rehabilitation hospitals); Mitotix (cell cycle/proliferation therapeutics); Pharmacopeia, Inc. (small molecule combinatorial chemistry)

Gryphon Ventures

222 Berkeley Street, Suite 1600
Boston, Massachusetts 02116-3748
(617) 267-9191
Fax: (617) 267-4293

Key contact:
Mr. Andrew Atkinson
Mr. William F. Aikman
Mr. Edward B. Lurier

Mr. Arthur M. Vash

Area served: Northeast

Preferred stages of financing: First stage, Second stage

Industries:
I.03 Biotech/genetic engineering
I.05 Chemicals

H. C. Wainwright & Company, Inc.

One Boston Place
Boston, Massachusetts 02108
(617) 227-3100
Fax: (617) 589-9478
E-mail: kquinn@hcwainwright.com
Web: hcwainwright.com

Key contact:
Mr. Kevin Quinn, Managing Director

Area served: United States

Preferred stages of financing: Seed, Start up, First stage, LBO/MBO

Industries:
I.20 Healthcare
I.21 High technology
I.24 Internet services/e-commerce
I.30 New media

Hancock Venture Partners

One Financial Center, 44th Floor
Boston, Massachusetts 02111
(617) 348-3707
Fax: (617) 350-0305

Key contact:
Mr. Kevin S. Delbridge
Mr. Tannis Fussell
Mr. William A. Johnston
Mr. Edward W. Kane
Mr. Frederick C. Maynard

Mr. Ofer Nemirovsky
Mr. Robert M. Wadsworth
Mr. D. Brooks Zug

Preferred stages of financing: Second stage, LBO/MBO, Third/later stage

Industries:
I.06 Communications
I.08 Computer software
I.28 Media/publishing

HarbourVest Partners, LLC

One Financial Center, 44th Floor
Boston, Massachusetts 02111
(617) 348-3707
Fax: (617) 350-0305
E-mail: labraham@hvpllc.com

Key contact:
Mr. Peter Lipson, Investment Analyst
Mr. Ofer Nemirovsky, Managing Director
Mr. Robert Wadsworth, Managing Director
Mr. Bill Johnston, Managing Director

Description: We are one of the largest private equity investment firms in the world, managing assets of approximately $4.5 billion. We invest in three areas including 1) software, with a preference towards enterprise-wide applications, 2) networking equipment and software, and 3) telecommunications and media delivery.

Founded: 1982

Amount of capital invested: $150 million

Preferred investment size: $5-20 million

Amount under management: >$1 billion

Area served: Worldwide

Preferred stages of financing: Second stage, Mezzanine, LBO/MBO, Expansion, Int'l expansion

Industries:
I.04   Broadcasting
I.06   Communications
I.07   Computer hardware
I.08   Computer software
I.21   High technology
I.23   Information technology services
I.24   Internet services/e-commerce

Sampling of portfolio companies: Atlantic Cellular Co., LP (cellular telephone properties); Dial Page, Inc. (alphanumeric messaging pagers); MultiTechnology Corp. (integrated private cable television & telephone company); OneComm Corp. (SMR businesses); Xircom, Inc. (wireless communication devices); Applied Microsystems Corp. (microporcessor test evaluation equipment); LANart Corp. (stackable, switchable data communication hubs for local area networks); RAScom, Inc. (data communications equipment vendor); UUNET Technologies, Inc. (internet access provider); Avid Technology, Inc. (video production software); Marcam Corp. (application software for CIM on IBM computers); SQL Financials Int'l., Inc. (client/server financial applications software); CV Consumer Services Ltd. (video megastores in Hong Kong); Supermarkets Holding, LP (supermarket chains); First Capital Corp. (unregulated lender providing secured working capital financing to small businesses); Coil N.V. (Europe's largest anodizer of aluminum rolled coils); Elifin S.A. (textile rental business); Huestis Machine Acquisition Corp. (equipment for the wire, cable & radiology markets); General Surgical Innovations, Inc. (balloon dissection systems for minimally invasive surgery); PRIZM Pharmaceuticals, Inc. (novel therapeutics for oncologic & ophthalmic indications)

Healthcare Ventures LLC

One Kendall Square, Building 300
Cambridge, Massachusetts 02139
(617) 252-4343
Fax: (617) 252-4342

Key contact:
Mr. John Littlechild, Managing Director
Mr. Mark Leschly, Managing Director

Description: Creation and financing of early stage healthcare and life science companies that have significant growth potential.

Preferred investment size: $5-10 million

Amount under management: $100-500 million

Area served: United States

Preferred stages of financing: Seed, Start up, First stage, Second stage, Mezzanine

Industries:
I.03   Biotech/genetic engineering
I.20   Healthcare
I.26   Life sciences

Sampling of portfolio companies: Dendreon Corp. (biotechnology); Biotransplant, Inc. (biotechnology); Cytomed, Inc. (biotechnology); Diacrin, Inc. (biotechnology); Genetic Therapy, Inc. (biotechnology); Human Genome Sciences, Inc. (biotechnology); Leukosite, Inc. (biotechnology); 3D Pharmaceuticals, Inc. (biotechnology); Magainin Pharmaceuticals, Inc. (biotechnology); Nitromed, Inc. (biotechnology); Osteotech, Inc. (biotechnology); Pharmagene, Inc. (biotechnology); Virus Research Institute, Inc. (biotechnology); Argonex, Inc. (biotechnology); Delsys Pharmaceutical Corp. (biotechnology); VerSicor, Inc. (biotechnology); Diversa Corp. (life sciences)

Heritage Partners, Inc.

30 Rowes Wharf, Suite 300
Boston, Massachusetts 02110
(617) 439-0688
Fax: (617) 439-0689
E-mail: robertaL@wn.net
Web: nmq.com/heritage

Key contact:
Mr. Michel Reichert, Managing General Partner
Mr. Peter Z. Hermann, General Partner
Mr. Michael F. Gilligan, General Partner

Description: We specialize in providing capital in the form of common and preferred stock to private, middle market companies, often in consolidating industries, with sales between $25 and $500 million. We seek investments in mature, successful organizations with strong management teams, focusing on family-owned businesses seeking liquidity, growth capital and/or ownership transition with a conservative capital structure while maintaining control.

Amount of capital invested: $70 million

Preferred investment size: $20-50 million

Amount under management: $500 million -1 billion

Area served: United States

Preferred stage of financing: LBO/MBO

Industries:
I.04   Broadcasting
I.11   Consumer products
I.12   Distribution
I.13   Education
I.14   Electronics
I.20   Healthcare
I.22   Industrial products

I.27   Manufacturing
I.28   Media/publishing
I.29   Medical/medical products
I.34   Services (business)
I.35   Services (consumer)
I.36   Transportation
I.37   Wholesale

Sampling of portfolio companies: Western Parcel Express (business to business ground parcel delivery); Fojtasek (manufacturer, distributor of windows & doors); Natural Science Industries (manufacturer of children's toys/arts & crafts); Jordan's Foods (meat processor & food service distributor); American Tack & Hardware (designer, manufacturer, distributor of switchplates, plant hardware, homeware); IMPAC Group (high-end packaging manufacturer); Cecilware (manufacturer foodservice equipment, namely beverage dispensers); 20th Century Plastics (manufacturer, distributor of polypropylene & vinyl office products, photo storage, CD storage); Fountain View (skilled nursing & assisted living service provider)

High Tech Ventures Incorporated

55 Old Bedford Road, Lincoln North
Lincoln, Massachusetts 01773
(781) 259-4444
Fax: (781) 259-1361
E-mail: webmaster@htventures.com

Description: We are a proven leader in the formation, funding and staffing of data communications and distributed computing start-ups. Ten years of capital creation has established us as the source for participation in a new technology venture.

Preferred stages of financing: Seed, Start up, First stage

Industries:
I.06   Communications
I.08   Computer software

Sampling of portfolio companies: Wellfleet; Beyond Mail; Collabra; Vermeer; Synernetics; Atria; Watermark; Remedy

Highland Capital Partners, Inc.

Two International Place, 22nd Floor
Boston, Massachusetts 02110
(617) 531-1500
Fax: (617) 531-1550

Key contact:
Ms. Kathleen A. Barry, CFO/Senior Vice President
Mr. Robert F. Higgins, Managing General Partner
Mr. Paul A. Maeder, Managing General Partner
Mr. Wycliffe K. Grousbeck, General Partner
Mr. Daniel J. Nova, General Partner
Mr. Burton C. Hurlock, Venture Partner
Mr. Stephen J. Harrick, Senior Associate
Mr. Corey M. Mulloy, Analyst

Description: We attribute our success to our people. We have assembled a team of committed professionals with deep knowledge and sharp instincts. Each year we look for a handful of entrepreneurs and growing businesses in the information technology and healthcare industries who share these same attributes. We provide them with the capital and strategic assistance that they need and a remarkably high percentage of them provide excellent returns for our limited partners.

Preferred stages of financing: Start up, First stage

Industries:
I.20   Healthcare
I.23   Information technology services
I.29   Medical/medical products

Sampling of portfolio companies: Atria Software Inc. (developed & marketed a comprehensive software configuration management system for the UNIX marketplace); CheckFree Corp. (provider of e-commerce processing services & software products); Continental Cablevision (an alternative to off-air television reception in rural areas); The Dodge Group (supplies operation, management & financial accounting software & services to the finance & banking sector); GeoSystems Global Corp. (supplier of geographical information products & services to the information publishing industry in both print & electronic mapping); The MESA Group (develops & markets a work-sharing program for computer networks); Pro CD (a national electronic telephone directory that enables users to access over 100 million US residential & business listings); Quote.com (provides quality financial market data from US & Canadian markets to internet users); SQL Financials (provides mid to large-sized cross industry enterprises with innovative technology that can be implemented, changed & upgraded in a fraction of the time it takes other vendors); Sybase, Inc. (provide customers with the ability to develop & deliver complete information solutions that help to ease rapid business growth); Tessera Enterprise Systems (developer of high-performance solutions for clients' information-based marketing needs); Mitotix, Inc. (developing small molecule drugs to treat cancer, infectious diseases & other cell proliferation disorders); Praecis Pharmaceuticals Inc. (biopharmaceutical company pioneering revolutionary new treatments for prostate cancer); Delos WomensHealth, Inc. (physician practice management company providing comprehensive healthcare services to women through partnership arrangements with OB/GYN physicians); The Morgan Health Group, Inc. (offers a low-cost healthcare plan that is centered around primary care physicians); Odyssey HealthCare, Inc. (provides palliative healthcare-hospice care, to terminally ill patients & their families); Theraphysics Corp. (designs healthcare & workers' compensation solutions for employers, HMOs, insurers & integrated provider organizations); Microsurge, Inc. (developed, manufactured & marketed disposable & re-usable instruments for minimally invasive surgery); Radiant Medical, Inc. (targeting stroke, a very significant emerging neuro-medical device market); SynaPix (developing a 3-D palette for the composition of video special effects)

JAFCO America Ventures, Inc.

1 Boston Place, Suite 3320
Boston, Massachusetts 02108
(617) 367-3510
Fax: (617) 367-3532
Web: www.jafco.com

Key contact:
Mr. Andrew Goldfarb, Managing Principal

Description: We provide value-added financial
services to private technology companies focused on
high growth markets. Investing in North America
based companies, our portfolio includes more than
60 companies spanning the communications,
computing, components, health sciences & services
industries. Recent investments in telecommunications and data communications technology and
services, enterprise software and internet technologies demonstrate our commitment to help
entrepreneurs make their ideas a reality.

Preferred investment size: $3-5 million

Amount under management: $100-500 million

Area served: Asia, Europe, United States

Preferred stages of financing: Seed, Start up, First
stage, Second stage, Mezzanine

Industries:
I.03   Biotech/genetic engineering
I.06   Communications
I.08   Computer software
I.11   Consumer products
I.21   High technology
I.23   Information technology services
I.33   Semiconductors

Sampling of portfolio companies: Ciena Corp. (communications); CommQuest Technologies, Inc. (communications); LightSpeed Int'l., Inc. (communications);
NeoMagic Corp. (communications); Pacific Mono-
lithics, Inc. (communications); Vixel Corp. (communications); Aptis Communications
(communications); Softwire Corp. (communications); AT/Comm (info systems); NetRail (info
services); DynaChip Corp. (semiconductors); Vivid
Semiconductor, Inc. (semiconductors); iReady (semiconductors); FlexiInternational (software); Network
Integrity (software); Cerulean Technology
(software); enCommerce (software); Main Control
(software); RWT Corp. (software); PocketScience
Inc. (systems/peripherals)

Kestrel Venture Management

31 Milk Street
Boston, Massachusetts 02109-5400
(617) 451-6722
Fax: (617) 451-3322
E-mail: jward@kestrelvm.com
Web: www.kestralvm.com

Key contact:
Mr. Edward J. Stewart, III, Partner
Mr. R. Gregg Stone, Partner
Mr. Nuri A. E. Z. Wissa, Partner

Description: We provide equity capital and support to
small companies with exceptional growth prospects.
Since inception, our objective has been to achieve
superior returns for our investors while providing
entreprenuers the opportunity to build significant and
successful businesses. We focus on private investment opportunities in the New England area that are
too large for most individual investors and too small
for the great majority of venture capital firms.

Area served: New England

Preferred stages of financing: Seed, Start up, First
stage, Second stage, Mezzanine, LBO/MBO, Third/
later stage

Industries:
I.06   Communications
I.07   Computer hardware
I.08   Computer software
I.13   Education
I.14   Electronics
I.17   Environmental services/waste management
I.18   Financial services
I.20   Healthcare
I.27   Manufacturing
I.28   Media/publishing
I.29   Medical/medical products
I.32   Retail
I.34   Services (business)

Levy Trajman Management Investment LLC

67 South Bedford Street, 400W
Burlington, Massachusetts 01803
(781) 229-5818
Fax: (781) 229-1808
E-mail: dtrajman@LTMI.com
Web: www.LTMI.com

Key contact:
Mr. Yacov Levy, Managing Partner
Mr. Dan Trajman, Managing Partner

Description: We are an enhanced venture capital firm
offering investors and portfolio companies a new
approach to early-stage venture investment. We
combine prudent capital financing with hands-on
management involvement. Our goal is to reduce risk
and maximize investment returns by carefully
selecting a small number of venture-stage hi-tech-
nology companies that fit a technology and business
model for global business success.

Preferred investment size: $1-3 million

Area served: North America, Israel, Western Europe

Preferred stages of financing: Start up, First stage,
Second stage, Int'l expansion

Industries:
I.06   Communications
I.07   Computer hardware
I.08   Computer software
I.11   Consumer products
I.14   Electronics
I.20   Healthcare

I.21   High technology
I.23   Information technology services
I.24   Internet services/e-commerce

I.29   Medical/medical products
I.30   New media

Massachusetts Capital Resources Company

420 Boylston Street
Boston, Massachusetts 02116
(617) 536-3900
Fax: (617) 536-7930

Key contact:
Mr. Ben Bailey III
Mr. Richard W. Anderson
Mr. Kenneth J. Lavery
Ms. Joan Creamer McArdle
Mr. William J. Torpey, Jr.

Area served: Northeast

Preferred stages of financing: Second stage, LBO/MBO

Industries:
I.08   Computer software
I.19   Generalist
I.29   Medical/medical products

Massachusetts Technology Development Corp. (MTDC)

148 State Street
Boston, Massachusetts 02109
(617) 723-4920
Fax: (617) 723-5983
Web: www.mtdc.com

Key contact:
Mr. John F. Hodgman, President
Mr. Robert J. Crowley, Executive Vice President
Mr. Robert J. Creeden, Vice President
Ms. Kathleen F. Birmingham, Associate
Mr. Mark C. M. Grader, Associate
Mr. William J. Wilcoxson, Associate
Mr. Joseph J. Boyd, Controller
Ms. Karen L. Butts, Director of Administration
Ms. Gail M. Cormier, Executive Assistant
Ms. Esther E. Larson, Administrative Manager
Ms. Marie B. Phaneuf, Public Information Officer
Ms. Mary E. Stack, Accounting & Portfolio Data
   Assistant

Description: We are a leading edge venture capital firm that addresses the capital gap for start-up and expansion of early-stage technology companies operating in the Commonwealth of Massachusetts. We have invested in many of the State's most promising new technology-based companies.

Founded: 1979

Area served: Massachusetts

Preferred stages of financing: Seed, Start up

Industries:
I.06   Communications
I.07   Computer hardware
I.08   Computer software
I.17   Environmental services/waste management
I.22   Industrial products
I.24   Internet services/e-commerce
I.29   Medical/medical products

Sampling of portfolio companies: Rare Earth Medical, Inc. (develops & markets laser products for medical applications)

Matrix Partners

Bay Colony Corporate Center
1000 Winter Street, Suite 4500
Waltham, Massachusetts 02154
(781) 890-2244
Fax: (781) 890-2288
E-mail: info@matrixlp.com
Web: www.matrixpartners.com

Key contact:
Mr. Timothy A. Barrows, General Partner
Mr. John C. Boyle, General Partner
Mr. Paul J. Ferri, General Partner
Mr. W. Michael Humphreys, General Partner
Mr. Andrew Marcuvitz, General Partner
Mr. Andrew Verhalen, General Partner

Description: We are a prominent venture capital firm with an established investment program focused on early stage software and communications companies. While many venture capital firms are reluctant to invest in start-ups, choosing instead to make late-stage equity investments, we believe that risk provides opportunity. We are devoted to company building and focus exclusively on information technology.

Founded: 1982

Preferred stages of financing: Seed, Start up, First stage

Industries:
I.06   Communications
I.08   Computer software
I.23   Information technology services

Sampling of portfolio companies: American Internet Corp. (provides IP network solutions for large private & public data networks); Applix, Inc. (office automation software); Atria Software, Inc. (software configuration management tools); Bridge Communications, Inc. (computer networking equipment); Cascade Communications Corp. (frame relay data communications); Centrum Communications, Inc. (provides remote networking solutions for large organizations with multivendor, multiprotocol computer networks); Clarify, Inc. (software for customer support organizations); Copper Mountain Networks, Inc. (high performance DSL networking solutions); Federal Express Corp. (overnight package delivery); FileNet Corp., Inc. (automated filing system using optical disk technology); Geotel Communications, Inc. (customer premise telephone call routing software); Grand Junction Networks, Inc. (designs, manufactures & markets cost-effective, high speed LANs for workgroups); NetCentric Corp. (provider of enhanced internet services); OnStream Networks, Inc. (design & manufacture of high speed telecommunications products); PSINet, Inc.; (commercial internet access provider); Red Pepper Software Co.

(operations planning & scheduling software for manufacturers); Sandisk Corp. (solid state mass storage systems); Tivoli Systems, Inc. (system administration software for UNIX); VideoServer, Inc. (network system supplier to video conferencing market); Whitetree Network Technologies, Inc. (ATM communications products for LANs)

Media/Communications (M/C) Partners

75 State Street, Suite 2500
Boston, Massachusetts 02109
(617) 345-7200
Fax: (617) 345-7201

Key contact:
Mr. David D. Croll, Managing General Partner
Mr. Stephen F. Gormley, General Partner
Mr. James F. Wade, General Partner
Mr. Christopher S. Gaffney, General Partner
Mr. John G. Hayes, General Partner
Mr. Peter H. O. Claudy, Vice President
Mr. Mark E. Evans, Associate

Description: We are a Boston based investment firm that provides equity financing and strategic guidance to entrepreneurial ventures in the media and telecommunications industries. With an active investment portfolio exceeding $400 million, we and our predecessor TA Communications have long been recognized as one of the most active private equity investors in the media and telecommunications industries. Particular areas of focus for the firm include telecommunications (wired and wireless), telecommunications services, broadcasting, publishing, electronic media and cable television.

Preferred investment size: $5-25 million

Amount under management: $100-500 million

Preferred stages of financing: LBO/MBO, Acquisitions, recapitalizations, internal growth

Industries:
I.04   Broadcasting
I.06   Communications
I.28   Media/publishing

Sampling of portfolio companies: Advent Cellular Systems (telecommunications); BRE Communications, Inc. (telecommunications); CellCall, Inc. (telecommunications); Interstate Cellular (telecommunications); NEXTEL (telecommunications); Teltrust, Inc. (telecommunications); Classis Communications (radio broadcasting); Federal Communications (radio broadcasting); OmniAmerica (radio broadcasting); Sunbelt Communications (radio broadcasting); Trumper Communications (radio broadcasting); Adams Trade Press, Inc. (publishing); Horizon Cablevision (cable television); N-Com Limited Partnership (cable television); United Broadcasting Company (cable television); KBS, Inc. (television broadcasting); Smith Broadcasting (television broadcasting); WTVG, Inc. (television broadcasting); Maximum Protection Industries, Inc. (security monitoring); Mass Communications Corp. (outdoor advertising)

Medical Science Partners

20 William Street, Suite 250
Wellesley, Massachusetts 02181
(781) 237-3772
Fax: (781) 237-3773

Key contact:
Dr. Andre Lamotte, Managing General Partner
Mr. Joseph Lovett, General Partner

Description: Investors in leading edge technologies and novel discoveries in healthcare. Emphasis placed on pharmaceuticals, diagnostics, devices, in vivo imaging, low-cost equipment and healthcare services.

Amount of capital invested: $1.7 million

Preferred investment size: $250,000-2.5 million

Amount under management: $25-100 million

Area served: Worldwide

Preferred stages of financing: Seed, Start up

Industries:
I.03   Biotech/genetic engineering
I.20   Healthcare
I.29   Medical/medical products

Sampling of portfolio companies: Applied Spectral Imaging Ltd. (medical devices); Ascent Pediatrics, Inc. (biotechnology & pharmaceuticals); Cardiac Assist Technologies (medical devices); deCode genetics, inc. (biotechnology & pharmaceuticals); Hybridon, Inc. (biotechnology & pharmaceuticals); Imagyn Medical Technologies (medical devices); Implemed, Inc. (medical devices); Inspire, Inc. (biotechnology & pharmaceuticals); Light Sciences, Inc. (medical devices); Ontogeny (biotechnology & pharmaceuticals); Ophtha-Med, Inc. (medical devices); Pangaea Pharmaceuticals, Inc. (biotechnology & pharmaceuticals); Peptide Therapeutics (biotechnology & pharmaceuticals); Quantum Biotechnologies (services); Resintel (services); Symbiotech, Inc. (diagnostics); Telemed-Canada (services); Telemedicine SA (services); Vanguard Medica Ltd. (biotechnology & pharmaceuticals); WorldCare Int'l. (services)

Monosson Technology Enterprises

20 Overland Street
Boston, Massachusetts 02215
(617) 437-7605
Fax: (617) 437-7601

E-mail: sonny@bfec.com

Key contact:
Mr. Adolf (Sonny) Monosson, Principal

Description: Zero stage venture investment.

Preferred investment size: $500,000

Amount under management: $10-25 million

Area served: United States

Preferred stages of financing: Seed, Start up, Mezzanine, Venture leasing

Industries:
I.02 Agriculture/forestry/fishing/mining
I.03 Biotech/genetic engineering
I.04 Broadcasting
I.05 Chemicals
I.06 Communications
I.07 Computer hardware
I.08 Computer software
I.09 Construction
I.14 Electronics
I.18 Financial services
I.20 Healthcare
I.21 High technology
I.22 Industrial products
I.23 Information technology services
I.24 Internet services/e-commerce
I.27 Manufacturing
I.28 Media/publishing
I.29 Medical/medical products
I.30 New media
I.32 Retail
I.33 Semiconductors
I.34 Services (business)
I.35 Services (consumer)

Needham & Company, Inc.
One Post Office Square, Suite 370
Boston, Massachusetts 02109
(617) 457-0910
Fax: (617) 457-5777
Web: www.needhamco.com

Key contact:
Ms. Margaret S.C. Johns, Managing Director

Description: We are a full service New York-based specialty investment bank, which serves emerging growth companies and their institutional investors with equity trading, sales, research and corporate finance services. Needham Capital Partners II is the long-term equity investment affiliate of Needham & Company. The fund is a long-term investor in the private equities of private "mezzanine" stage companies and smaller public emerging growth companies. The investment focus is on companies in the technology, healthcare and specialty retail industries.

Preferred investment size: $2-4 million

Amount under management: $100-500 million

Area served: United States

Preferred stages of financing: Mezzanine, LBO/MBO

Industries:
I.06 Communications
I.07 Computer hardware
I.08 Computer software
I.11 Consumer products
I.14 Electronics
I.20 Healthcare
I.21 High technology
I.22 Industrial products
I.23 Information technology services
I.24 Internet services/e-commerce
I.27 Manufacturing
I.29 Medical/medical products
I.32 Retail
I.33 Semiconductors

Sampling of portfolio companies: College Enterprises, Inc. (operates a chain of retail copying, duplicating, image processing & communication technology service stores on college campuses throughout the country); Computer Literacy, Inc. (sells computer manuals, training texts & books over the internet to programming professionals); Carrier Access Corp. (develops, manufactures & markets T-1 digital telecommuncations access products for local carrier bypass); Corsair Communications, Inc. (designs, manufactures & markets cellular fraud reduction systems based on RF "fingerprinting" techniques in which each handset is individually identified); DAOU Systems, Inc. (provides software products to healthcare organizations); IMNET Systems, Inc. (develops, markets, installs & services electronic information & document management systems for the healthcare industry & other document intensive businesses); LeCroy Corp. (develops, manufactures & sells signal analyzers, principally high-performance digital oscilloscopes & related products); SeaMED Corp. (designs & manufactures advanced durable electronic & medical instruments for medical technology companies); WorldGate Communications, Inc. (start-up cable service that allows cable operators to offer low cost, fast & simple access to the internet); U.S. Vision, Inc. (optical retailer, sells prescription eyewear, contact lenses, eye exams & services for fitting custom lenses to eyeglass frames); JT Storage, Inc. (manufactures small, high-capacity disk drives); Silicon Magic Corp. (designs embedded memory logic chips for high bandwidth graphic/video PC applications); Cardima, Inc. (develops, manufactures & markets micro-catheter devices for the diagnosis & treatment of cardiac-electrophysical disorders); IMarket Inc. (helps sales & marketing professionals find new customers through its business-to-business marketing tools); Ramp Networks, Inc. (develops & markets connectivity products for small workgroups that allow such groups to seamlessly connect to the internet while establishing a local area network); Rise Technology Co., Inc. (designing high-performance, low-powered X86-compatible microprocessors); Array Microsystems, Inc. (develops & markets high-performance, low-cost video compression chipsets & related support software for use in personal computer-related applications with an emphasis on personal video communication applications); Patient Info-systems, Inc. (provides patient-centered healthcare information systems that proactively collect & analyze information to improve patient compliance with prescribed treatments); Digital Arts & Sciences Corp. (develops & distributes graphically oriented software for the management of inventories & collections of objects, where images are an integral element); Rosti (chain of primarily take-out Italian restaurants that is expanding out of the Los Angeles area)

Norwest Venture Partners

40 William Street, Suite 305
Wellesley, Massachusetts 02181
(781) 237-5870
Fax: (781) 237-6270
Web: www.norwestvc.com

Key contact:
Mr. Ernest C. Parizeau
Mr. Blair P. Whitaker

Description: We manage about $1 billion in investment funds and are focused on venture capital investments in emerging growth companies in the information technology sector (enterprise software, internet, communications infrastructure equipment, subscriber based businesses & electronics).

Amount of capital invested: $88 million

Preferred investment size: $5 million

Amount under management: >$1 billion

Area served: United States

Preferred stages of financing: Seed, Start up, First stage, Second stage, Mezzanine

Industries:
I.06   Communications
I.08   Computer software
I.14   Electronics
I.18   Financial services
I.23   Information technology services
I.24   Internet services/e-commerce
I.33   Semiconductors

Sampling of portfolio companies: Golden Sky Systems, Inc. (reseller of direct satellite TV programming); Xedia Corp. (internet access communication platform with provisions for quality of service); Chordiant Software, Inc. (call center software for complex customer interactions); Health Systems Technologies, Inc. (health information systems for managed care); OnDisplay, Inc. (web integration software for global enterprise); One Touch Systems, Inc. (interactive distance learning systems & software); Kiva Software, Inc. (internet application servers for business critical solutions); Docent, Inc. (internet-based training application software); WebChat Communications, Inc. (internet-based community site); Internet Travel Network, Inc. (internet-based travel reservation system); Arbortext (SGML-based document publishing tools software); Lifetime Fitness (chain of fitness centers); 3Dfx Interactive (high performance graphics chipsets); Metapath Corp. (real time systems for telecommunications providers); Primus Communications (problem resolution tools for help desks); Cadis (part classification & management application); PMT CVD (semiconductor equipment for CVD); B-Tree Verification Systems, Inc. (test & verification for embedded systems); Hawaiian Wireless (SMR cellular service in Hawaii); Petersen Publishing Co. (media publications)

Oxford Ventures

31 St. James, Suite 570
Boston, Massachusetts 02116
(617) 357-7474
Fax: (617) 357-7476
Web: www.oxbio.com

Key contact:
Mr. Jonathan Fleming, General Partner
Mr. Martin Vogelbaum, Principal

Description: We are an independent venture capital firm that provides equity financing and management assistance to start-up and early-stage, entrepreneurial-driven companies in the bioscience and healthcare industries. Our partners currently manage venture funds with combined committed capital of more than $150 million. Our objective is to generate long-term capital gains for both the investors in the fund and the entrepreneurs that we support.

Amount of capital invested: $25 million

Preferred investment size: $2 million

Amount under management: $100-500 million

Area served: Asia, Europe, United States

Preferred stages of financing: Seed, Start up, First stage, Second stage

Industries:
I.03   Biotech/genetic engineering
I.20   Healthcare
I.26   Life sciences
I.29   Medical/medical products

Sampling of portfolio companies: Argomed, Ltd. (minimally invasive, catheter-based treatment for benign prostate hyperplasia); Arrow Corp. (pharmacy management services company); Biocode, Inc. (immunoassay-based product marking systems to detect counterfeiting & smuggling in pharmaceuticals & consumer & industrial products); BioScreen (qualitative gene expression analysis for drug discovery); Cardiopulmonary Corp. (computer controlled patient ventilators for the intensive care unit); Cellomics (high throughput, cell-based screening systems for drug discovery); Ceres, Inc. (agricultural bioscience); Coelacanth (development & manufacturer of novel building blocks for combinatorial chemistry systems); Cytologix, Inc. (automated slide preparation systems for the pathology laboratory); EVAX Technologies GmbH (bacterial-based vaccines for animal & human diseases); GuideStar Health Systems (managed care company providing insurance products to indemnity insurers); Inkine Pharmaceuticals (pharmaceuticals for treatment of cancer & infectious diseases); Memory Pharmaceuticals (pharmaceuticals to restore long-term potentiation of memory); Micromed Technology (left ventricular assist device for congestive heart failure); NetGenics, Inc. (bioinformatics software to manage genomics research programs); Orchid Biocomputer (nanotechnology-based drug discovery systems); Phase I (high throughput toxicology testing services); Physiome Sciences, Inc. (computer-based, physiological models of human organs for drug discovery & evaluation); Variagenics, Inc. (drug discovery & evaluation based on pharmacogenomics)

Palmer Partners L.P.

200 Unicorn Park Drive
Woburn, Massachusetts 01801
(781) 933-5445
Fax: (781) 933-0698

Key contact:
Mr. John Shane
Mr. William H. Congleton
Ms. Alison J. Seavey

Preferred stages of financing: Expansion, Third/later stage

Industries:
I.05   Chemicals
I.06   Communications
I.07   Computer hardware
I.08   Computer software
I.14   Electronics
I.23   Information technology services
I.35   Services (consumer)

A. M. Pappas & Associates

5 Ingraham Road
Wellesley, Massachusetts 02181
(781) 235-7554
Fax: (781) 235-6940
E-mail: nhsiung@ampappas.com

Key contact:
Dr. Nancy Hsiung, Director-Northeast Operations

Description: We are an international venture development company dedicated to accelerating the
development of life science companies, products and
related technologies. We bring together- under one
roof- risk capital and value-added management,
scientific and technical consulting expertise to help
our clients and our portfolio companies turn great
ideas into commercial successes.

Amount of capital invested: $20 million

Preferred investment size: $2 million

Amount under management: $25-100 million

Area served: Worldwide

Preferred stages of financing: Seed, Start up, First
stage, Second stage, Mezzanine

Industries:
I.03   Biotech/genetic engineering
I.26   Life sciences
I.29   Medical/medical products

Sampling of portfolio companies: SciQuest, Inc.
(operates a scientific vendor website); Maize Genetic
Resources (agricultural biotechnology); Ganymede
Software (computer & network software); Coper-
nicus Gene Systems (focuses on developing &
commercializing products for human gene therapy);
GeneLogic (differential display technology to
identify & quantify novel drug targets from nucleic
acid sequences)

Pioneer Capital Corporation

60 State Street
Boston, Massachusetts 02109
(617) 422-4947
Fax: (617) 742-7315
E-mail: info@pioneer-capital.com

Key contact:
Ms. Patricia M. Flaum, CPA, Director of Finance
Mr. Frank M. Polestra, President/General Partner
Mr. Christopher W. Lynch, Vice President/General
Partner
Mr. Leigh E. Michl, Vice President/General Partner
Mr. Christopher W. Dick, Vice President/General
Partner

Description: We are a venture capital firm which
provides early stage, growth, acquisition and recapitalization financing to New England-based
companies in a variety of industries.

Founded: 1980

Area served: New England

Preferred stages of financing: Start up, First stage,
Third/later stage

Industries:
I.06   Communications
I.08   Computer software
I.23   Information technology services
I.24   Internet services/e-commerce

Sampling of portfolio companies: Applied Immune
Sciences; Bertucci's, Inc.; Cardiometrics, Inc.; Chem
Design Corp.; Concord Communications, Inc.
(develops, markets & supports a family of turnkey,
automated, scaleable, software-based performance
analysis & reporting solutions for the management of
computer networks); Hologic, Inc.; Mariner Health
Group; MathSoft; MicroTouch Systems; Network
Engines, Inc. (provider of fault-tolerant, load
balanced clustered application servers); Nabnasset
Corp. (provider of computer telephony integration
software); SyQuest Technologies; TACC Int'l. Corp.
(manufacturer of construction adhesives & sealants);
Viewlogic Systems; Vivid Technologies, Inc.

Robertson Stephens-Omega Ventures

One International Place, 30th Floor
Boston, Massachusetts 02110
(617) 526-7400
Fax: (617) 526-7499

Description: Late stage venture capital.

Preferred investment size: $3-7 million

Amount under management: $100-500 million

Area served: Worldwide

Preferred stages of financing: Second stage, Mezzanine, LBO/MBO, Expansion, Int'l expansion

Industries:
I.03   Biotech/genetic engineering

I.06   Communications
I.07   Computer hardware
I.08   Computer software
I.10   Consulting
I.11   Consumer products
I.12   Distribution
I.13   Education
I.14   Electronics
I.15   Energy/natural resources/utilities
I.17   Environmental services/waste management
I.18   Financial services
I.19   Generalist
I.20   Healthcare
I.21   High technology
I.24   Internet services/e-commerce
I.26   Life sciences
I.27   Manufacturing
I.29   Medical/medical products
I.30   New media
I.33   Semiconductors

I.34   Services (business)
I.35   Services (consumer)

Sampling of portfolio companies: Broderbund Software, Inc. (software); ICVerify, Inc. (software); Voyan Technology (software); Applied Digital Access, Inc. (communications); Metapath Software Corp. (communications); Shomiti Systems, Inc. (communications); TeleCruz Technology, Inc. (electronics); CBT Group PLC (business services); J3 Learning Corp. (business services); MemberWorks Inc. (business services); Abgenix, Inc. (healthcare/life sciences); Balanced Care Corp. (healthcare/life sciences); COR Therapeutics, Inc. (heatlhcare/life sciences); Cyto Therapeutics, Inc. (health care/life sciences); MedicaLogic, Inc. (health care/life sciences); CompUSA, Inc. (consumer); Dick's Clothing & Sporting Goods (consumer); Petstuff, Inc. (consumer); Matrix Service Co. (other); Opta Food Ingredients, Inc. (other)

Seacoast Capital Partners, LP

55 Ferncroft Road, Suite 110
Danvers, Massachusetts 01923
(978) 750-1351
Fax: (978) 750-1301
E-mail: gdeli@seacoastcapital.com
Web: www.seacoastcapital.com

Key contact:
Mr. Gregory A. Hulecki, Partner
Mr. Eben S. Moulton, Managing Partner
Mr. Paul G. Giovacchini, Partner
Mr. Thomas W. Gorman, Partner

Description: We are an investment firm dedicated to providing mezzanine and equity capital for middle market companies. Founded by the principals of Signal Capital Corporation and Itel Corporation, we are the successor to Signal Capital's merchant banking group, which successfully invested over $400 million of capital since 1986. We are committed to investing across a broad spectrum of industries from our offices in Boston and San Francisco.

Amount of capital invested: $50 million

Preferred investment size: $2-6 million

Amount under management: $100-500 million

Area served: Canada, United States

Preferred stages of financing: Mezzanine, Expansion, Int'l expansion

Industries:
I.01   Aerospace
I.02   Agriculture/forestry/fishing/mining
I.04   Broadcasting
I.05   Chemicals
I.06   Communications

I.08   Computer software
I.10   Consulting
I.11   Consumer products
I.12   Distribution
I.13   Education
I.14   Electronics
I.16   Entertainment
I.17   Environmental services/waste management
I.19   Generalist
I.20   Healthcare
I.21   High technology
I.22   Industrial products
I.23   Information technology services
I.24   Internet services/e-commerce
I.25   Leisure/hospitality
I.27   Manufacturing
I.28   Media/publishing
I.29   Medical/medical products
I.30   New media
I.32   Retail
I.34   Services (business)
I.35   Services (consumer)
I.36   Transportation
I.37   Wholesale

Sampling of portfolio companies: All Seasons Services, Inc. (vending services); City Sports, Inc. (special retailing); Community Rehab Centers, Inc. (physical therapy clinics); Global Personnel Services, Inc. (temporary staffing); Labor Ready, Inc. (temporary staffing); Mearthane Products Corp. (specialty manufacturing); Metalico, Inc. (metal recovery company); Microcom Technologies (electronics distribution); New England Audio (specialty retailing); Overland Trading Co. (specialty retailing); Radar Exterminating Co., Inc. (pest control services); Specialty Agricultural Products, Inc. (agricultural products manufacturing)

Seaflower Associates, Inc.

1000 Winter Street, Suite 1000
Waltham, Massachusetts 02154
(781) 466-9552
Fax: (781) 466-9553
E-mail: moot@seaflower.com

Key contact:
Mr. James Sherblom, President

Mr. Alexander W. Moot, Partner/General Manager
Ms. Sheryl Tsaknopoulos, Office Manager

Description: We invest in promising, early-stage biomedical firms. We consider seed and first-round investments in companies in most segments of the biomedical industry, including biotechnology, medical devices, healthcare information technology and healthcare services. Geographically, we will consider investments in New England and in the Great Lakes region. We have offices in Waltham, Massachusetts and near Ann Arbor, Michigan.

Amount of capital invested: $2 million

Preferred investment size: $250,000-2.5 million

Amount under management: $10-25 million

Area served: United States

Preferred stages of financing: Seed, Start up, First stage

Industries:
I.03   Biotech/genetic engineering
I.20   Healthcare
I.26   Life sciences
I.29   Medical/medical products

Sampling of portfolio companies: ACCESS Radiology Corp. (manager of teleradiology networks); Accu-Photonics, Inc. (developing probes for use in near-field scanning optical microscopy); Brock Rogers Surgical, Inc. (developing computer-enhanced laparoscopic systems for use in minimally-invasive surgery); MetaWorks, Inc. (a clinical informatics company providing evidence-based medical information to biopharmaceutical & health care clients); Molecular Geodesics, Inc. (developing novel biomimetic materials for use in biomedical, industrial & military applications); Natura, Inc. (developing improved, natural food ingrediants); MicroPulse, Inc. (commercializing patented patient support surfaces for the prevention & treatment of decubitis ulcers); Synthon Corp. (a chiral chemistry firm providing chiral building blocks to the pharmaceutical industry for use in the synthesis & manufacture of single-isomer drugs); t. Breeders Inc. (biotechnology company developing a novel bioreactor for selecting & expanding rare populations of cells, including stem cells); VisionScope, Inc. (developing novel laparoscopic & endoscopic imaging tools for minimally-invasive surgery)

The Shepherd Group LLC

179 Great Road, Suite 208
Acton, Massachusetts 01720
(978) 266-1859
Fax: (978) 266-0499
E-mail: shepherd@tsgequity.com

Key contact:
Mr. Thomas R. Shepherd, Chairman
Mr. T. Nathanael Shepherd, President
Mr. Sean M. Marsh, Associate
Mr. John S. Surface, Consultant
Mr. Soren L. Oberg, Consultant

Description: We are a private equity investment firm providing early-stage, growth and acquisition financing to venture and middle-market companies. We focus on companies with high-growth potential and unique market-ready quality products and services. We prefer to make investments in companies that have completed the initial conceptual stage of their development and are either collecting revenue from their product or are on the cusp of taking the product to market.

Founded: 1996

Preferred investment size: $500,000-1 million

Area served: New England

Preferred stages of financing: Start up, First stage, LBO/MBO, Expansion, Growth

Industries:
I.08   Computer software
I.24   Internet services/e-commerce
I.34   Services (business)

Sampling of portfolio companies: Andover Advanced Technologies, Inc. (internet publishing & advertising); American Photo Booths, Inc. (digital interactive photo sticker vending machines); Computer Aided Marketing, Inc. (computer database marketing software); Community Resource Systems, Inc. (senior community service provider)

Sigma Partners

20 Custom House Street, Suite 830
Boston, Massachusetts 02110
(617) 330-7872
Fax: (617) 330-7975
Web: www.sigmapartners.com

Key contact:
Mr. Robert Davoli
Mr. Gardner C. Hendrie
Mr. John Mandile

Description: We are a privately held venture capital partnership organized in 1984 to make equity investments in businesses which offer favorable opportunity for significant growth in size and value. We have a history of successful investing in entrepreneurial companies. Currently, we manage four funds with combined capital of over $300 million.

Founded: 1984

Area served: United States

Preferred stages of financing: Seed, First stage, LBO/MBO

Industries:
I.06   Communications
I.07   Computer hardware
I.08   Computer software
I.14   Electronics
I.29   Medical/medical products
I.33   Semiconductors

Sampling of portfolio companies: Argon Technologies (communications/networking); LANart Corp. (communications/networking); World Power Technologies (hardware/peripherals); Rendition, Inc. (semiconductor related); Context Integration, Inc. (software); Edify Corp. (software); Modern Age Books Inc. (software); Poet Software Corp. (software); Vignette Corp. (software); Laser Diagnostic Technologies, Inc. (medical); Bytex Corp. (communications/networking); Global Village Communications, Inc. (communications/

networking); Octel Communications Corp. (communications/networking); Micro Linear Corp. (semiconductor related); Cooperative Solutions, Inc. (software); FileNet Corp. (software); Splash Technology, Inc. (software); Datasonix Corp. (hardware/peripherals); Iris Graphics, Inc. (hardware/peripherals); SuperMac Technology (hardware/peripherals)

SOFTBANK Technology Ventures

10 Langley Road, Suite 403
Newton Center, Massachusetts 02159
(617) 928-9300
Fax: (617) 928-9301
Web: www.sbvc.com

Key contact:
Mr. Charles R. Lax, Managing Director
Mr. Ronald D. Fisher, Vice Chairman
Mr. Gary E. Rieschel, Executive Managing Director
Mr. Bradley A. Feld, Managing Director
Mr. Matthew A. Ocko, Managing Director
Mr. E. Scott Russell, Managing Director

Description: We make privately negotiated equity and equity-related investments in companies attempting to capitalize on opportunities in digital information technology, including internet communications, commerce and content. We are affiliated with SOFTBANK Holdings Inc., a subsidiary of SOFTBANK Corporation.

Founded: 1981

Area served: Worldwide

Industries:
I.08   Computer software
I.24   Internet services/e-commerce
I.34   Services (business)

Sampling of portfolio companies: 911 Entertainment (software & information); Electric Communities (software & information); Fastparts Inc. (business services); Fourth Communications Network (business services); GeoCities (software & information); Internet Profiles Corp. (software & information); SaveSmart (software & information); Third Age Media Inc. (software & information); VStream Inc. (communications); Zip2 (software & information)

Solstice Capital

33 Broad Street, 3rd Floor
Boston, Massachusetts 02109
(617) 523-7733
Fax: (617) 523-5827
E-mail: solcap@aol.com

Key contact:
Mr. Harry George, Managing General Partner
Mr. Henry Newman, General Partner

Description: Our basic strategy is to identify companies which are positioned to capitalize on major change factors. Investing in and helping to foster these companies can yield both economic and social returns. We view being a small fund as an advantage, as investing smaller portions of money can prove to be profitable and early stage companies seeking $1 to 2 million are underserved. Areas of principle investment interest include technology based industries, however, we also invest in non-technical areas.

Amount of capital invested: $4.76 million

Preferred investment size: $1 million

Amount under management: $10-25 million

Area served: United States

Preferred stages of financing: Seed, Start up, First stage

Industries:
I.08   Computer software
I.13   Education
I.17   Environmental services/waste management
I.19   Generalist
I.21   High technology
I.22   Industrial products
I.23   Information technology services
I.24   Internet services/e-commerce
I.27   Manufacturing

Sampling of portfolio companies: Abuzz, Inc. (knowledge management software); Accucom Wireless Services (cellular phone location services); Active Control eXperts (vibration & motion control: smart materials); Avalon Imaging, Inc. (machine vision system for plastic injection molding); Blind Faith Cafe, Inc. (whole-foods restaurant); Connected Corp. (network-based back-up & MIS services to businesses); Continuum Software, Inc. (software tools to create multiprocessor applications); E-Ink Corp. (developer of electronic ink displays); Evergreen Solar, Inc. (manufacturer of photovoltaic materials & cells); Lipton Corporate Child Care (back-up child care services); MoneyStar Communications, Inc. (interactive mutual fund sales & software); Mosaic Technologies, Inc. (solid phase DNA probe & related technology); Optimax Systems Corp. (scheduling software for manufacturing); Pharsight Corp. (planning software for clinical trials); PID, Inc. (batch processing manufacturing control software); Proton Energy Systems, Inc. (manufacturer of hydrogen production equipment); Radnet, Inc. (groupware for corporate intranets); Secure Technologies, Inc. (distance detection products based on radio frequency technology)

The Spray Venture Fund

One Walnut Street
Boston, Massachusetts 02108
(617) 305-4140
Fax: (617) 305-4144

Key contact:
Mr. Kevin Connors, General Partner
Mr. Dan Cole, General Partner
Mr. Paal Gisholt, General Partner
Dr. Danny Sachs, M.D., Principal

Description: We focus and invest in seed and early stage medical technology companies that provide innovative solutions to major unmet clinical needs. Our partners have a unique combination of venture capital, entrepreneurial and industry operating experience which enables us to work closely with founders and CEOs to recruit and build management teams, refine development, patent, clinical and market entry strategies and obtain access to worldwide distribution.

Amount of capital invested: approximately $6 million

Preferred investment size: $2 million

Preferred stages of financing: Seed, Start up, First stage

Industries:
I.03 Biotech/genetic engineering
I.20 Healthcare
I.26 Life sciences
I.29 Medical/medical products

Sampling of portfolio companies: Akos Biomedical (gastrointestinal devices); Acorn Cardiovascular (congestive heart failure); Gamera Bioscience (microfluidics for life sciences & diagnostis); Ekos (ultrasound drug delivery); Galt (female urinary incontinence); Survivalink (automatic external defibrillators)

Still River Fund

100 Federal Street, 29th Floor
Boston, Massachusetts 02110
(617) 348-2327
Fax: (617) 348-2371
E-mail: saalfield@msn.com

Key contact:
Mr. James A. Saalfield, General Partner
Mr. Joseph J. Tischler, General Partner

Description: Classic venture capital fund investing $500,000 - $2 million in informatics, specialty retail and consumer products and medical services and devices.

Amount of capital invested: $4.8 million

Preferred investment size: $500,000-2 million

Amount under management: $10-25 million

Area served: United States

Preferred stages of financing: Seed, Start up, First stage, LBO/MBO

Industries:
I.03 Biotech/genetic engineering
I.06 Communications
I.11 Consumer products
I.12 Distribution
I.13 Education
I.14 Electronics
I.19 Generalist
I.20 Healthcare
I.21 High technology
I.22 Industrial products
I.23 Information technology services
I.24 Internet services/e-commerce
I.26 Life sciences
I.29 Medical/medical products
I.32 Retail

Sampling of portfolio companies: Bus-Tech (mainframe to WAN/LAN connectivity); LIDS (hat retailer); Brand Direct (direct data base marketing); MassTrace (medical devices); eprise (web page management); C2 (genomics)

Summit Partners

600 Atlantic Avenue, Suite 2800
Boston, Massachusetts 02210
(617) 824-1000
Fax: (617) 824-1100
Web: www.summitpartners.com

Key contact:
Mr. E. Roe Stamps, IV, Managing Partner
Mr. Stephen G. Woodsum, Managing Partner
Mr. Martin J. Mannion, General Partner
Mr. Ernest K. Jacquet, General Partner
Mr. Joseph F. Trustey, General Partner
Mr. Bruce R. Evans, General Partner
Mr. Thomas S. Roberts, General Partner
Mr. John A. Genest, General Partner/CFO

Description: We understand the challenges of building a successful company. Since our founding in 1984, we have been the fastest growing private investment firm in the country. Our growth has taught us about the value of hard work and innovation, striving against odds and following a dream.

Founded: 1984

Preferred stages of financing: Mezzanine, LBO/MBO

Industries:
I.06 Communications
I.08 Computer software
I.18 Financial services
I.20 Healthcare
I.23 Information technology services
I.29 Medical/medical products

Sampling of portfolio companies: McAfee Assoc. (software); Simulation Sciences (software); DSET (networking & communications); TGV (networking & communications); CIDCO (communications); Powerwave (communications); Intelliquest (information services); Pharmaco Dynamics Research (information services); HMT Technology (peripherals, systems & components); RasterOps (peripherals, systems & components); Criticare Systems (healthcare/medical equipment); Renal Treatment Centers (healthcare/medical services); United Dental Care, Inc. (managed care); Acurex (aerospace refrigeration); Chromium Graphics (consumer products); Paragon Optical (consumer products); Chase Federal Bank (financial services); Mutual Risk Management (financial services); Organic Waste Technologies (environmental services); Superior Environmental (environmental services)

TA Associates, Inc.

High Street Tower, Suite 2500
125 High Street
Boston, Massachusetts 02110
(617) 574-6700
Fax: (617) 574-6728
E-mail: info@ta.com

Key contact:
Mr. C. Kevin Landry, Managing Director
Mr. P. Andrews McLane, Managing Director

Description: For nearly three decades, we have provided private equity capital and knowledgeable assistance to talented entrepreneurs to help them pull ahead of their competition and build companies of significant value.

Founded: 1968

Preferred investment size: $10-100 million

Preferred stages of financing: Start up, First stage, LBO/MBO, Turnaround

Industries:
I.03   Biotech/genetic engineering
I.08   Computer software
I.14   Electronics
I.15   Energy/natural resources/utilities

I.17   Environmental services/waste management
I.18   Financial services
I.20   Healthcare
I.23   Information technology services
I.34   Services (business)

Sampling of portfolio companies: Auto Palace (consumer products & services); Federal Express (consumer products & services); Jenny Craig, Inc. (consumer products & services); Smith Alarm Systems (consumer products & services); AIM Management Group (financial services); Affiliated Managers Group (financial services); Keystone Group (financial services); Mutual Risk Management (financial services); Boron LePore (healthcare services); CompDent Corp. (healthcare services); Copley Pharmaceutical (healthcare services); Gulf South Medical Supply (healthcare services); Preferred Payment Systems (healthcare services); Bachtel Cellular Liquidity, LP (media & communications); Continental Cablevision, Inc. (media & communications); Galaxy Telecom, LP (media & communications); TSR Wireless (media & communications); ANSYS, Inc. (software & technology); Axent (software & technology); Hummingbird (software & technology)

Ticonderoga Capital, Inc.

20 William Street, Suite G40
Wellesley, Massachusetts 02481
(781) 416-3400
Fax: (781) 416-9868

Key contact:
Mr. Craig A. T. Jones, Managing Partner
Dr. Graham Crooke, Partner
Mr. Peter Leidel, Partner
Mr. James E. Vanderuelden, Principal
Mr. Oliver Haarmann, Principal

Description: We are a private equity investment firm with over $200 million of capital under management. We make equity investments of $4 - 8 million. Though we invest opportunistically across a variety of service sectors, we focus on businesses in the following industry area: 1) health care services, 2) energy, 3) specialty retail & distribution; 4) communication services and 5) other services such as financial, governmental and business services.

Amount of capital invested: $15 million

Preferred investment size: $5-10 million

Amount under management: $100-500 million

Area served: North America

Preferred stages of financing: LBO/MBO, Expansion

Industries:
I.06   Communications
I.10   Consulting
I.11   Consumer products
I.12   Distribution
I.13   Education
I.15   Energy/natural resources/utilities
I.18   Financial services
I.20   Healthcare
I.23   Information technology services

I.32   Retail
I.34   Services (business)
I.35   Services (consumer)
I.37   Wholesale

Sampling of portfolio companies: Community Rehab Centers (regional outpatient physical & occupational therapy services organization); Professional Dental Assoc. (a dental practice management company which seeks to partner with successful private practice dentists throughout the Eastern seaboard in building practices that deliver exceptional care service & financial performance); Boots & Coots (specializes in oil well firefighting & blow-outs); Concho Resources Inc. (acquires oil & gas properties in the Permian Basin of Texas & New Mexico & the onshore Gulf Coast in Texas & Louisiana); Fintube, LP (manufacturer of precision-welded finned tubes & derivative products used by the electric industry in generation plants & by petrochemical & refining industry processing plants); Interenergy Corp. (diversified energy company which provides natural gas gathering, processing, distribution & marketing services in the Rocky Mountain & Mid-Continent regions); Roemer-Swanson Energy Corp. (focuses on three market niches: 1) gas imbalance properties, 2) Section 29 tax credit properties & 3) prospect generation); Willbros Group, Inc. (diversified energy services company providing construction, engineering & specialty services to the oil & natural gas industries); The Big Party Corp. (party supply superstore with store locations in New England & Florida); Learningsmith, Inc. (mall-based retailer of educational products); Lids Corp. (retail chain of stores positioned as "category killer" by offering the widest possible selection of casual headwear); Metal Supermarkets Ltd. (oversees 41 owned or franchised wholesale metal parts distribution centers in Canada, the U.S. & the United Kingdom); Viking Office Products (mail order direct marketer of office supplies); Int'l. Towers, Inc. (designs, manufactures, erects & services transmission towers for the communications & broadcasting industries related primarily to the introduction of high definition television, cellular telephone, PCS & paging services); CapMac Holdings (monoline financial guaranty insurer specializing in structured asset-backed & other taxable obligations); Carr Separations, Inc. (produces centrifugal separation devices); Formica Corp. (designs, manufactures & distributes decorative laminates & other surfacing products through most of the world; produces high pressure laminates); Sales Staffers Int'l., Inc. (provides an outside source of sales & marketing personnel to help its clients generate sales, increase market share & expand their sales reach into new markets without increasing premanent staff & overhead expenses); Team Bancshares, Inc. (acquires, recapitalizes & manages commercial banks & related assets in Texas); USI Holdings Corp. (consolidator of small, privately-held commercial insurance brokerage & insurance-related financial services firms)

TLP Leasing Programs, Inc.

One Financial Center, 21st Floor
Boston, Massachusetts 02111
(617) 482-8000
Fax: (617) 423-2776

Key contact:
Mr. Nicholas C. Bogard, Chairman
Mr. Arthur P. Beecher, President

Description: Our venture leasing program is designed to finance the capital equipment requirements of start-up or emerging growth companies. The typical customer is one that has received its first or second round of VC funding with a promising or proven product. We establish leaselines with our customers which allows them to draw on the line as needed. We provide lease financing to companies in a variety of markets which include telecommunications, information services, software, medical, manufacturing and financial services.

Preferred investment size: $750,000

Amount under management: $25-100 million

Area served: North America

Preferred stage of financing: Venture leasing

Industries:
I.06   Communications
I.07   Computer hardware
I.08   Computer software
I.10   Consulting
I.11   Consumer products
I.13   Education
I.14   Electronics
I.18   Financial services
I.21   High technology
I.23   Information technology services
I.24   Internet services/e-commerce
I.27   Manufacturing
I.28   Media/publishing
I.29   Medical/medical products
I.33   Semiconductors
I.34   Services (business)
I.35   Services (consumer)

Trammell-Shott Capital Management, LLC

One International Place, 31st Floor
Boston, Massachusetts 02110
(617) 790-2960
Fax: (617) 790-2982

Key contact:
Mr. Paul Reese, Member

Description: We are focused exclusively on providing liquidity to private & institutional investors through the purchase of secondary positions in venture capital & buyout funds.

Amount of capital invested: $4.5 million

Preferred investment size: $5 million

Amount under management: <$10 million

Area served: Asia, Europe, North America

Preferred stage of financing: Secondaries

Industries:
I.01   Aerospace
I.02   Agriculture/forestry/fishing/mining
I.03   Biotech/genetic engineering
I.04   Broadcasting
I.05   Chemicals
I.06   Communications
I.07   Computer hardware
I.08   Computer software
I.09   Construction
I.10   Consulting
I.11   Consumer products
I.12   Distribution
I.13   Education
I.14   Electronics
I.15   Energy/natural resources/utilities
I.16   Entertainment
I.17   Environmental services/waste management
I.18   Financial services
I.19   Generalist
I.20   Healthcare
I.21   High technology
I.22   Industrial products
I.23   Information technology services
I.24   Internet services/e-commerce
I.25   Leisure/hospitality
I.26   Life sciences
I.27   Manufacturing
I.28   Media/publishing
I.29   Medical/medical products
I.30   New media
I.32   Retail
I.33   Semiconductors
I.34   Services (business)
I.35   Services (consumer)
I.36   Transportation
I.37   Wholesale

TTC Ventures
(a subsidiary of The Thomson Corp.)
One Main Street, 3rd Floor
East Arcade
Cambridge, Massachusetts 02142
(617) 528-3137
Fax: (617) 577-1715
Web: www.ttcventures.com

Key contact:
Mr. D. Jarrett Collins, Director
Ms. Beth Edwards
Ms. Karin Kissane, Associate
Ms. Mary Reilly, Business Development Manager

Description: We are the venture capital subsidiary of
The Thomson Corporation, one of the largest information publishers in the world. Through our
affiliation with Thomson, we bring much more than
capital to our investments. We help our portfolio
companies accelerate their growth through access to
more than 300 businesses within Thomson. In fact,
we have a full-time professional on staff whose sole
responsibility is to foster relationships between our
portfolio companies and Thomson businesses.

Area served: North America

Preferred stages of financing: Start up, First stage

Industries:
I.08   Computer software

I.13   Education
I.18   Financial services
I.23   Information technology services
I.28   Media/publishing
I.34   Services (business)

Sampling of portfolio companies: Audible, Inc.
(delivers spoken audio via the web for mobile
playback through a hand-held device); Brightware,
Inc. (offers customer-direct application products that
use AI technology to establish the two-way communication required to make the Net a viable marketing
& sales channel); CareerBuilder, Inc. (provides a
complete solution for companies recruiting personnel
over the Web); The EC Company (provides easy-to-
use, cost-effective solutions for business-to-business
e-commerce); Financial Engines, Inc. (develops &
markets impartial Internet-based investment advisory
services for individuals); FutureTense, Inc. (creates
dynamic electronic publishing solutions for the web);
IXL Holdings, Inc. (full-service interactive company
specializing in the creation & management of digital
content); NetGravity, Inc. (online advertising
management solutions); UpShot Corp. (provides a
web-based sales force automation application for
organizations of any size); Virage, Inc. (provider of
products & technologies for visual information
retrieval)

TVM Techno Venture Management
101 Arch Street, Suite 1950
Boston, Massachusetts 02110
(617) 345-9320
Fax: (617) 345-9377
E-mail: info@tvmvc.com
Web: tvmvc.com

Key contact:
Mr. John J. DiBello, Partner
Ms. Patricia Wessling Dane, Controller

Description: We are an international venture capital
firm that provides capital and management assistance
to innovative growth companies in Germany, the
U.S. and throughout Europe. We are focused on
technology-based high growth industries in information technology and the life sciences.

Amount of capital invested: $15 million

Preferred investment size: $1-3.5 million

Amount under management: $100-500 million

Area served: Europe, United States

Preferred stages of financing: Start up, First stage,
Second stage

Industries:
I.03   Biotech/genetic engineering
I.06   Communications
I.07   Computer hardware

I.08   Computer software
I.14   Electronics
I.20   Healthcare
I.21   High technology
I.23   Information technology services
I.24   Internet services/e-commerce
I.26   Life sciences
I.29   Medical/medical products
I.33   Semiconductors

Sampling of portfolio companies: AnswerSoft (telecommunications); Lannet Data Communications (telecommunications); Netrix Systems
(telecommunications); Aspen Technology (computer,
software & networking); Cicorel (computer, software
& networking); Dataware (computer, software &
networking); Fast Multimedia (computer, software &
networking); Novell (digital research); ReGenisys
(computer, software & networking); Viewlogic
(computer, software & networking); Amylin (life
sciences); Curative Technologies (life sciences);
Dura Pharmaceuticals (life sciences); MediGene (life
sciences); Oxford GlycoSciences (life sciences);
Synaptic Pharmaceuticals (life sciences); Atomika
Instruments (advanced materials & capital
equipment); ChemDesign (advanced materials &
capital equipment); LaserSpec Analytik (advanced
materials & capital equipment); Quantum Magnetics
(advanced materials & capital equipment)

Union Atlantic LC
Great Island, 63 Smiths Point Road West
Yarmouth, Massachusetts 02673
(508) 771-3506
Fax: (508) 771-3418

E-mail: bill@ualc.com
Web: ualc.com

Key contact:
Mr. William Coldrick, Partner

Description: A private merchant banking concern
providing investment opportunities to corporations
and high net worth individuals through equity investments in emerging companies targeted in the
technology sector. We look for strong management
teams with commercially available products and
services.

Preferred investment size: None

Amount under management: <$10 million

Area served: Europe, North America, South/Central
America

Preferred stages of financing: First stage, Second stage

Industries:

I.07	Computer hardware
I.08	Computer software
I.10	Consulting
I.12	Distribution
I.14	Electronics
I.21	High technology
I.23	Information technology services
I.24	Internet services/e-commerce
I.33	Semiconductors

Sampling of portfolio companies: The Concours Group
(IT consultancy); Galacticomm (internet software);
Advanced Electronics Support Products (computer
peripherals); LocalNet Communications (multi-level
marketing, technology); Command Software (PC
software)

UST Capital Corporation
40 Court Street
Boston, Massachusetts 02108
(617) 726-7000
Fax: (617) 695-4185

Key contact:
Mr. Arthur F. Snyder

Area served: Northeast

Preferred stages of financing: Seed, First stage

Industries:
I.19   Generalist

The Venture Capital Fund of New England
160 Federal Street, Floor 23
Boston, Massachusetts 02110
(617) 439-4646
Fax: (617) 439-4652

Key contact:
Mr. Richard A. Farrell, General Partner
Mr. Harry J. Healer, Jr., General Partner
Mr. Kevin J. Dougherty, General Partner
Mr. William C. Mills, III, General Partner

Description: We provide equity capital and management assistance to emerging growth-oriented
companies with a focus on early stage companies
technology based primarily in New England.
Emphasis is on information technologies, industrial
technologies, medical technologies and healthcare
services.

Amount of capital invested: $3,950,000

Preferred investment size: $1 million

Amount under management: $25-100 million

Area served: New England, United States

Preferred stages of financing: Start up, First stage,
Second stage

Industries:

I.03	Biotech/genetic engineering
I.04	Broadcasting
I.06	Communications
I.07	Computer hardware
I.08	Computer software
I.14	Electronics
I.20	Healthcare
I.21	High technology
I.22	Industrial products
I.23	Information technology services
I.24	Internet services/e-commerce
I.26	Life sciences
I.28	Media/publishing
I.30	New media
I.33	Semiconductors

Sampling of portfolio companies: Acusphere, Inc.
(contrast agents for medical ultrasound imaging);
Argus Software, Inc. (quality control information
management software for healthcare); Commonwealth Care, Inc. (comprehensive home healthcare
programs); Endius, Inc. (steerable endoscopic
surgical instruments); Extraction Systems, Inc. (gas
filtration systems); Infocellular, Inc. (point-of-sale
software for cellular telephone industry); Inspectron
Corp. (high-speed print imaging inspection systems);
Linguistic Technology Corp. (natural language front
ends for SQL databases); Loudon Telecommunications (operates CATV system in Loudoun County,
VA); Occupational Health & Rehabilitation, Inc.
(system of occupational medicine outpatient clinics);
Panache Broadcasting (operates AM & FM radio
stations in metropolitan areas); Optimax Systems
Corp. (production scheduling software applications);
Riverton Software Corp. (software tools for business
process workflow integration); Sanders Prototype,
Inc. (desktop rapid prototyping 3-D modelling
systems); Transcend Therapeutics (pharmaceuticals
for controlling free radical oxidative damage); Ultra-
cision, Inc. (ultrasonically activated surgical
systems); Thermatrix, Inc. (in-line thermal
processing of hazardous materials)

Venture Management Consultants, LLC
60 Wells Avenue
Newton, Massachusetts 02159
(617) 928-9888
Fax: (617) 964-5318

Key contact:
Mr. Richard Tuch, Partner
Mr. Mark Levine, Partner
Mr. Alfred Ross, Partner

Area served: United States

Preferred stages of financing: Start up, First stage, Second stage, Mezzanine, Bridge

Industries:
I.03   Biotech/genetic engineering
I.06   Communications
I.08   Computer software
I.11   Consumer products
I.16   Entertainment
I.20   Healthcare
I.21   High technology
I.23   Information technology services
I.24   Internet services/e-commerce
I.25   Leisure/hospitality
I.29   Medical/medical products
I.31   Real estate
I.34   Services (business)
I.35   Services (consumer)

Weston Presidio Capital

One Federal Street, 21st Floor
Boston, Massachusetts 02110-2004
(617) 988-2500
Fax: (617) 988-2515
Web: www.westonpresidio.com

Key contact:
Mr. Michael F. Cronin, Managing Partner
Mr. Carlo A. von Schroeter, General Partner
Mr. Kevin M. Hayes, Principal
Ms. Courtney M. Russell, Principal
Ms. Dianne M. Hillyard, CFO
Ms. Laura Jun, Research Assistant

Description: We believe that companies are better run and more innovative when those who manage them are also significant owners. Typically, we assist our portfolio companies in the following areas, where appropriate: negotiating and raising additional debt or equity financing; recruiting additional management; strategic planning; negotiating and advising on acquisitions, sales or mergers; accessing strategic or corporate partners; developing compensation and incentive programs.

Preferred investment size: $5-50 million

Amount under management: $100-500 million

Area served: Worldwide

Preferred stages of financing: LBO/MBO, Recapitalizations

Industries:
I.11   Consumer products
I.20   Healthcare
I.23   Information technology services
I.27   Manufacturing
I.32   Retail
I.34   Services (business)
I.35   Services (consumer)

Sampling of portfolio companies: AAi. Foster Grant (provider of optical products & a women's accessories service & distribution company with full-service programs in over 11,000 stores); Sassaby/ Estee Lauder Cos. (developed, marketed & sold the JANE line of color cosmetics targeted at teenage girls); L. Kee & Co. (markets a broad assortment of coordinated hand crafted home textile products); The Frontier Group (acquires, develops & operates long-term healthcare facilities in New England); The PharmaSource Group/NCS Healthcare (provides multi-faceted pharmacy services to hospitals, managed care settings & long-term care facilities); XyberNET (provides software & connectivity services to the healthcare services & credit insurance industries); NOVA Pb (operates fully integrated lead recycling facility); Star Manufacturing Int'l. (manufacturer of food service equipment); The Lion Brewery (regional brewer specializing in the brewing & bottling of new age sodas, premium beers & Malta); The Coffee Connection/Starbucks Corp. (sold fresh-brewed coffees & espresso beverages primarily through its retail stores in New England before being acquired by Starbucks Corp.); Leeann Chin (operator of quick service & casual dining locations in Minneapolis-St. Paul that feature unique contemporary Chinese cuisine); Guitar Center (retailer of guitars, amplifiers, percussion instruments, keyboards & pro audio & recording equipment); New England Audio/Tweeter, etc./Bryn Mawr Stereo/Hifi Buys (full-service specialty retailer of a broad range of premium consumer electronic products); Petzazz/PETsMART (operated a chain of retail superstores providing discount pet foods, services, supplies & accessories); Wild Oats Markets (operator of natural food supermarkets); Casella Waste Systems (provides integrated non-hazardous solid waste management services to commercial, municipal, industrial & residential customers); Morris Air Corp./Southwest Airlines (regional discount airline); GeoSystems Global Corp. (supplier of maps & mapping-related products, services & technology to companies in the publishing, travel, yellow pages & real estate markets, as well as directly to consumers); Picture-Works Technology (provides PC application software to the digital imaging industry); NeTpower (provides client/server hardware & software systems focused on the Microsoft Windows NT operating system environment)

Zero Stage Capital Company, Inc.

101 Main Street, 17th Floor
Cambridge, Massachusetts 02142
(617) 876-5355
Fax: (617) 876-1248

Key contact:
Mr. Paul Kelley
Mr. Gordon B. Baty
Mr. Luc M. Beaubien
Mr. William Golden
Mr. Jerome Goldstein

Mr. Joseph P. Lombard
Mr. Edward Roberts

Area served: Northeast

Preferred stages of financing: Seed, Start up, First stage, Second stage

Industries:
I.03   Biotech/genetic engineering
I.05   Chemicals

I.06   Communications
I.07   Computer hardware
I.08   Computer software
I.13   Education

I.14   Electronics
I.15   Energy/natural resources/utilities
I.36   Transportation

Michigan

Arbor Partners, LLC
130 South First Street
Ann Arbor, Michigan 48104
(734) 668-9000
Fax: (734) 669-4195
E-mail: jburr@arborpartners.com

Key contact:
Mr. Richard Crandall, Managing Director
Mr. Richard Eidswick, Managing Director
Mr. Donald Walker, Managing Director
Mr. Stephen Swanson, Managing Director

Description: We invest in and assist small companies
in the Michigan area that specialize in software,
hardware and telecommunications. All deals are
syndicated, allowing for rounds up to $10 million. A
second fund is in the works which will not be limited
to Michigan. This should be ready for placement by
11/98.

Amount of capital invested: $1 million

Preferred investment size: $1 million

Amount under management: <$10 million

Area served: United States

Preferred stages of financing: Start up, First stage,
Second stage

Industries:
I.07   Computer hardware
I.08   Computer software
I.23   Information technology services
I.24   Internet services/e-commerce

Sampling of portfolio companies: Blue Gill Technologies (software for electronic bill presentment);
Genitor Corp. (software development tools vendor);
CMS Technologies (vendor of asset tracking/security
devices)

Dearborn Capital Corp.
The American Road
Dearborn, Michigan 48121-1732
(313) 337-8577
Fax: (313) 248-1252

Key contact:
Mr. Mike Kehres

Area served: United States

Preferred stages of financing: Second stage, LBO/
MBO, Third/later stage

Endeavor Capital Management, LLC
317 South Division Street, Suite 49
Ann Arbor, Michigan 48104
(734) 996-3032
Fax: (734) 996-0886
E-mail: ronreed@endeavorcap.com

Key contact:
Mr. Ron Reed, General Partner

Area served: North America

Preferred stages of financing: First stage, Second
stage, LBO/MBO, Expansion

Industries:
I.06   Communications
I.08   Computer software
I.18   Financial services
I.23   Information technology services
I.24   Internet services/e-commerce
I.34   Services (business)
I.35   Services (consumer)

Enterprise Development Fund
425 North Main Street
Ann Arbor, Michigan 48104
(734) 663-3213
Fax: (734) 663-7358
E-mail: edf@edfvc.com

Key contact:
Mr. Hayden H. Harris, General Partner
Mr. Thomas S. Porter, General Partner
Ms. Mary L. Campbell, General Partner

Description: Private venture capital firm whose
mission is to earn superior returns on capital by
making equity investments in start-up, early stage
and emerging growth companies.

Preferred investment size: $1 million

Amount under management: $25-100 million

Area served: Great Lakes Region

Preferred stages of financing: Seed, Start up, First
stage, Second stage, LBO/MBO

Industries:
I.03   Biotech/genetic engineering
I.07   Computer hardware
I.08   Computer software
I.20   Healthcare
I.21   High technology
I.23   Information technology services
I.24   Internet services/e-commerce

I.29   Medical/medical products

Sampling of portfolio companies: Aastrom Biosciences, Inc. (developer of proprietary devices to grow stem cells for therapeutic purposes); Auxein Corp. (proprietary natural compounds to increase plant growth & development); GenVec, Inc. (in vivos gene therapy for the treatment of cancer, cardiovascular & lung diseases); Health Care Solutions, Inc. (provider of comprehensive home health care services); IntraLase Corp. (developer of femtosecond laser for opthalmic surgery); Matrigen, Inc. (developer & marketer of products to stimulate tissue regeneration; initial market is bone growth); Media Station, Inc. (developer & publisher of interactive multimedia titles); OmniLink Corp. (developer & marketer of ISDN connectivity devices); Origen, Inc. (develops & markets genetically engineered vaccines & vaccine development technologies for farm animals); Pacific Biometrics, Inc. (developer of non-invasive medical diagnostic products; diseases of interest: osteoporosis & diabetes); Pixelworks, Inc. (developer & marketer of flat panel displays & proprietary chips for these displays); RWT Corp. (sells manufacturing execution systems for real-time control of discrete manufacturing); Synthon Corp. (developer & marketer of chiral intermediate fine chemicals for the pharmaceutical industry); TherOx, Inc. (provider of medical products for low cost, high efficacy, localized oxygen delivery to diseased, damaged or at-risk cells & organs); Think & Do Software, Inc. (develops network management services to corporate clients); Weston Information Technologies, Inc. (provides network management services to corporate clients)

Seaflower Associates, Inc.
5170 Nicholson Road
Fowlerville, Michigan 48836
(517) 223-3335
Fax: (517) 223-3337
E-mail: gibbons@seaflower.com

Key contact:
Ms. Christine Gibbons, Partner/CFO

Description: We invest in promising, early-stage biomedical firms. We consider seed and first-round investments in companies in most segments of the biomedical industry, including biotechnology, medical devices, healthcare information technology and healthcare services. Geographically, we will consider investments in New England and in the Great Lakes region. We have offices in Waltham, Massachusetts and near Ann Arbor, Michigan.

Amount of capital invested: $2 million

Preferred investment size: $250,000-2.5 million

Amount under management: $10-25 million

Area served: United States

Preferred stages of financing: Seed, Start up, First stage

Industries:
I.03   Biotech/genetic engineering

I.20   Healthcare
I.26   Life sciences
I.29   Medical/medical products

Sampling of portfolio companies: ACCESS Radiology Corp. (manager of teleradiology networks); Accu-Photonics, Inc. (developing probes for use in near-field scanning optical microscopy); Brock Rogers Surgical, Inc. (developing computer-enhanced laparoscopic systems for use in minimally-invasive surgery); MetaWorks, Inc. (a clinical informatics company providing evidence-based medical information to biopharmaceutical & health care clients); Molecular Geodesics, Inc. (developing novel biomimetic materials for use in biomedical, industrial & military applications); Natura, Inc. (developing improved, natural food ingrediants); MicroPulse, Inc. (commercializing patented patient support surfaces for the prevention & treatment of decubitis ulcers); Synthon Corp. (a chiral chemistry firm providing chiral building blocks to the pharmaceutical industry for use in the synthesis & manufacture of single-isomer drugs); t. Breeders Inc. (biotechnology company developing a novel bioreactor for selecting & expanding rare populations of cells, including stem cells); VisionScope, Inc. (developing novel laparoscopic & endoscopic imaging tools for minimally-invasive surgery)

Sloan Enterprises
312 George Street
Birmingham, Michigan 48009
(248) 540-9660
E-mail: sloan.info@sloanenterprises.com

Key contact:
Mr. Jeffrey M. Sloan, Co-Founder
Mr. Richard S. Sloan, Co-Founder

Description: We are dedicated to new business development centered around innovative products, technologies and services. We provide early-stage venture capital, business plan development, identification of operational management, and on-going strategic management in exchange for equity in new ventures across a wide range of industries.

Founded: 1990

Preferred stages of financing: Seed, Start up, First stage

Industries:
I.11   Consumer products
I.23   Information technology services
I.34   Services (business)
I.35   Services (consumer)

Sampling of portfolio companies: Inergi Fitness, LLC (developing & marketing innovative fitness products centered around the philosophy of total body fitness); VetGen, LLC (molecular genetics company specializing in canine & equine genetic disease research & disease detection services); GeneWorks, LLC (advanced transgenics company which manufactures desirable proteins & enzymes for pharmaceutical, industrial, laboratory research & other customer applications)

Wellmax, Inc.

6905 Telegraph Road, Suite 330
Bloomfield Hills, Michigan 48301
(248) 646-3554
Fax: (248) 646-6220

Key contact:
Mr. Jack E. Maxwell, President

Description: We focus on the acquisition of manufacturing or disribution companies (no retailing) located in the Midwest or Florida having sales of $5 to $35 million who meet the criteria set by a half dozen clients.

Area served: United States

Preferred stages of financing: Start up, First stage, Second stage, LBO/MBO

Industries:
I.11   Consumer products
I.12   Distribution
I.17   Environmental services/waste management
I.22   Industrial products
I.27   Manufacturing
I.29   Medical/medical products
I.34   Services (business)
I.36   Transportation
I.37   Wholesale

White Pines Management, L.L.C.

2401 Plymouth Road, Suite B
Ann Arbor, Michigan 48105
(734) 747-9401
Fax: (734) 747-9704
E-mail: IBund@whitepines.com

Key contact:
Mr. Frederick L. Yocum, Chairman
Mr. Ian R. N. Bund, President
Ms. Lois F. Marler, Vice President/CFO

Description: To be an active partner in financing and growing businesses with proven, capable management teams and outstanding prospects for growth. Provide growth capital primarily to midwest and southeast manufacturing and value added services companies with current annual sales of $5 million or more. In return for our capital and active contributions to companies, we expect to earn an above average return.

Amount of capital invested: WPLPI: $4.04 million; PCLP: $3.4 million

Preferred investment size: $1-3 million

Amount under management: $100-500 million

Area served: United States

Preferred stages of financing: Mezzanine, LBO/MBO, Expansion

Industries:
I.03   Biotech/genetic engineering
I.04   Broadcasting
I.05   Chemicals
I.06   Communications
I.07   Computer hardware
I.08   Computer software
I.10   Consulting
I.11   Consumer products
I.12   Distribution
I.13   Education
I.14   Electronics
I.16   Entertainment
I.17   Environmental services/waste management
I.18   Financial services
I.19   Generalist
I.20   Healthcare
I.21   High technology
I.22   Industrial products
I.23   Information technology services
I.24   Internet services/e-commerce
I.25   Leisure/hospitality
I.26   Life sciences
I.28   Media/publishing
I.29   Medical/medical products
I.30   New media
I.32   Retail
I.33   Semiconductors
I.34   Services (business)
I.35   Services (consumer)
I.36   Transportation
I.37   Wholesale

Sampling of portfolio companies: Imagination Publishing, LLC (custom publisher); Organized Living, Inc. (specialty retailer); Quality Communications, Inc. (telecommunications consulting); HealthTech Services Corp. (telemedicine); Anchor Computer Sales, Ltd. (systems integrator); Birch Telecom, Inc. (competitive local exchange carrier); American Endoscopy Services, Inc. (laparoscopic fee for service to hospitals); TransMap Corp. (digital mapping of landscapes); Clinical Site Services Corp. (clinical research site management organization); EFS, Inc. (construction management for school districts); HLM Design, Inc. (architectural & engineering services); First Physician Care, Inc. (physician practice management company); Quality Transportation Services (special education transport services)

Minnesota

Agio Capital Partners I, L.P.

601 2nd Avenue South, Suite 4600
Minneapolis, Minnesota 55402
(612) 339-8408
Fax: (612) 349-4232
E-mail: agiocap@aol.com
Web: www.agio-capital.com

Key contact:
Mr. Kenneth F. Gudorf, President/CEO
Mr. Donald M. Haas, Managing Director
Mr. David J. Raffel, Associate

Description: We are a Minneapolis-based private
investment partnership. We will make equity investments up to $30 million in a wide variety of
manufacturing and service companies, with a
primary focus on management buy-outs.

Amount of capital invested: $6.7 million

Preferred investment size: $2.5 million

Amount under management: $25-100 million

Area served: United States

Preferred stages of financing: Second stage, LBO/
MBO, Expansion

Industries:
I.04   Broadcasting
I.12   Distribution
I.14   Electronics
I.16   Entertainment
I.17   Environmental services/waste management
I.18   Financial services
I.22   Industrial products
I.25   Leisure/hospitality
I.27   Manufacturing
I.28   Media/publishing
I.29   Medical/medical products
I.34   Services (business)
I.35   Services (consumer)
I.37   Wholesale

Sampling of portfolio companies: Tooling for injection
molding; flood insurance services; video game distribution; truck filter guages; bakery waste/animal feed
processor

Capital Dimensions, Inc.

7831 Glenroy Road, Suite 480
Minneapolis, Minnesota 55337
(612) 831-2025
Fax: (612) 831-2945

Key contact:
Mr. Stephen A. Lewis, Vice President
Mr. Dean R. Pickerell, Executive Vice President
Mr. Thomas F. Hunt, Jr., President

Description: SBIC mezzanine lender with investment
experience in radio/TV, specialized food services,
telephone. Targeting established businesses requiring
expansion financing.

Amount of capital invested: $3 million

Preferred investment size: $500,000-5 million

Amount under management: $25-100 million

Area served: United States

Preferred stages of financing: Second stage, Mezzanine, LBO/MBO, Expansion

Industries:
I.04   Broadcasting
I.06   Communications
I.13   Education
I.18   Financial services
I.22   Industrial products
I.27   Manufacturing

Cherry Tree Investment Company

7601 France Avenue South, Suite 225
Edina, Minnesota 55435
(612) 893-9012
Fax: (612) 893-9036

Key contact:
Mr. Dan Albright
Mr. John C. Bergstrom
Mr. Tony Christianson
Mr. Gordon F. Stofer

Area served: Midwest

Preferred stages of financing: Start up, First stage

Industries:
I.08   Computer software
I.11   Consumer products
I.13   Education
I.23   Information technology services
I.29   Medical/medical products

Churchill Capital, Inc.

333 South Seventh Street, Suite 2400
Minneapolis, Minnesota 55402
(612) 673-6633
Fax: (612) 673-6630
Web: www.churchillnet.com

Key contact:
Mr. Barry Lindquist, Senior Vice President

Description: Our $200 million subordinated debt fund
provides both fixed rate all-coupon subdebt with tax-
advantaged interest deferral options and equity-
linked subdebt to U.S. and Canadian companies for a
variety of purposes. Our $188 million ESOP fund
provides subdebt and equity to employee and
management-owned companies.

Amount of capital invested: $119 million

Preferred investment size: $5-15 million

Amount under management: $500 million -1 billion

Area served: Canada, United States

Preferred stages of financing: Mezzanine, LBO/MBO, Expansion, Recapitalizations, acquisitions

Industries:
I.01   Aerospace
I.05   Chemicals
I.11   Consumer products
I.12   Distribution
I.13   Education
I.14   Electronics
I.17   Environmental services/waste management
I.22   Industrial products
I.27   Manufacturing
I.34   Services (business)
I.37   Wholesale

Sampling of portfolio companies: Consumer Products; Industrial Products; Medical/Dental Products; Packaging Products; Aerospace Products; Automotive Products; Building Materials; Distribution; Service Providers

Coral Ventures

60 South 6th Street, Suite 3510
Minneapolis, Minnesota 55402
(612) 335-8666
Fax: (612) 335-8668

Key contact:
Mr. Yuval Almog, Managing Partner
Mr. Peter H. McNerney, General Partner
Ms. Karen M. Boezi, Venture Partner
Mr. William R. Baumel, Venture Partner

Description: We contribute strategic guidance, as well as capital, to transform growing enterprises into market leaders. Because we recognize and understand emerging technologies and market trends, we invest in companies poised to capitalize on opportunities inherent in those trends. We work as a partner to develop a long-term relationship with the company and its management team.

Amount of capital invested: $15 million

Amount under management: $100-500 million

Area served: Worldwide

Preferred stages of financing: Seed, Start up, First stage, Second stage, Mezzanine

Industries:
I.03   Biotech/genetic engineering
I.06   Communications
I.07   Computer hardware
I.08   Computer software
I.14   Electronics
I.20   Healthcare
I.21   High technology
I.23   Information technology services
I.24   Internet services/e-commerce
I.26   Life sciences
I.29   Medical/medical products

The Food Fund

5720 Smetana Drive, Suite 300
Minnetonka, Minnesota 55343
(612) 939-3950
Fax: (612) 939-8106

Key contact:
Mr. John Trucano, Managing General Partner
Mr. Dick Coonrod, General Partner

Description: Focused venture capital fund on the food industry: food manufacturers, food marketers, food equipment, relevant distribution systems.

Amount of capital invested: $700,000

Preferred investment size: $500,000

Amount under management: <$10 million

Area served: North America

Preferred stages of financing: First stage, Second stage

Sampling of portfolio companies: American Specialty Confections, Inc. (markets confections to the specialty retail trade); Aquahealth, Inc. (markets premium water fountain systems); Award Baking International (manufactures & markets gourmet wafers & biscotti); Daily Bread Co., Inc. (manufactures & markets specialized ready-to-bake bread mixes); DeLuca, Inc. (manufactures fresh refrigerated Italian entrees); Hoffman Aseptic Packaging (aseptic contract packaging of shelf stable foods in plastic cups); Keurig, Inc. (manufacturer of a coffee system for fresh brewed single serve coffee); Moline Machinery, Ltd. (manufactures bakery dough processing & handling equipment); Motion Technology, Inc. (manufactures self-venting, fully-automatic deep fry equipment); Mrs. Clark's Foods, Inc. (manufactures private label juices, beverages, sauces & dressings); Orval Kent Foods Co. (manufactures refrigerated prepared salads & fresh fruit products); Packaged Ice, Inc. (markets automatic ice making & bagging systems); Pappy's Foods Co. (manufactures frozen dough, thaw & sell & fresh-bakery products); Stars Beverage Co. (markets soft drinks & New Age beverages); Uncle B's Bakery, Inc. (manufactures & markets both refrigerated & fresh baked bagels)

IAI Ventures, Inc.

601 Second Avenue South, Suite 3800
Minneapolis, Minnesota 55402
(612) 376-2800
Fax: (612) 376-2824
Web: www.iaiventures.com

Key contact:
Mr. David Spreng
Mr. Jeffrey Tollefson
Mr. Tony Daffer
Ms. Lorraine Fox

Description: For more than 15 years, we have worked in partnership with talented entrepreneurs and managers to help build some of America's most successful growth companies. Over time, our mission and focus has remained consistent: to invest in companies managed by entrepreneurs possessing the vision, ability and motivation required to build large, sustainable enterprises.

Amount of capital invested: $45 million

Preferred investment size: $500,000-1 million

Preferred stages of financing: Seed, Start up, First stage, Second stage

Industries:
I.03   Biotech/genetic engineering
I.06   Communications
I.07   Computer hardware
I.08   Computer software
I.20   Healthcare
I.21   High technology
I.23   Information technology services
I.24   Internet services/e-commerce
I.26   Life sciences
I.29   Medical/medical products
I.33   Semiconductors

Sampling of portfolio companies: AdiCom Wireless (telecom equipment); Alta Berkeley V (early stage - European); Baring Communications (early stage - communications); Communications Ventures II (early stage - communications; CryoCath Technologies (medical devices); E/O Networks (telecom equipment); Exxel Group V (late stage - buy out); Fujant Technologies (telecom equipment); Illumenex (medical devices); InfoScape (software-internet commerce); Lightspeed Int'l. (software-telecom); Protein Delivery (pharmaceuticals); Red Creek Comm. (datacom equipment); Relevance (software); StarTech Seed Fund (early stage); Telecom Partners (early stage); ThemeMedia, Inc. (software); Therics, Inc. (medical devices); XIOTech Corp. (datacom equipment); Zeus Corporation (datacom equipment)

Medical Innovation Partners

9900 Bren Road East
Opus Center, Suite 421
Minnetonka, Minnesota 55343
(612) 931-0154
Fax: (612) 931-0003

Key contact:
Dr. Mark B. Knudson
Mr. Timothy I. Maudlin
Mr. Robert S. Nickoloff

Area served: Midwest

Preferred stage of financing: Seed

Industries:
I.03   Biotech/genetic engineering
I.20   Healthcare
I.29   Medical/medical products

Milestone Growth Fund, Inc.

401 2nd Avenue South, Suite 1032
Minneapolis, Minnesota 55401
(612) 338-0090
Fax: (612) 338-1172

Key contact:
Mr. Purne Gurung
Ms. E. Guerrero-Anderson

Area served: United States

Preferred stages of financing: First stage, Third/later stage

Industries:
I.19   Generalist

Northeast Ventures Corp.

802 Alworth Building
Duluth, Minnesota 55802
(218) 722-9915
Fax: (218) 722-9871

Key contact:
Tom Van Hale, Vice President

Area served: Midwest

Preferred stages of financing: Seed, Start up, First stage, Second stage, Mezzanine, LBO/MBO

Industries:
I.19   Generalist

Northland Business Capital

1285 Northland Drive
St. Paul, Minnesota 55120-1139
(612) 681-3023
Fax: (612) 681-3040
E-mail: bks-nbc@minn.net
Web: www.nbcapital.com

Key contact:
Mr. Brian K. Smith, Managing Partner
Mr. Alan R. Thometz, Principal

Description: We are an established private investment partnership affiliated with The Northland Company, a financial services company with assets in excess of $1 billion and a history dating back to the 1800's.

Area served: United States

Preferred stages of financing: Mezzanine, LBO/MBO, Recapitalizations

Industries:
I.06   Communications
I.12   Distribution
I.27   Manufacturing

Northwest Capital

1509 Upper Afton Road
St. Paul, Minnesota 55106
(612) 774-1976
Fax: (612) 774-6356
E-mail: michae90@ix.netcom.com
Web: www2.bitstream.net/~nwf

Key contact:
Mr. Michael Mehsikomer, President
Mr. Christopher Weinberger, Vice President
Mr. Kevin Lynch, Associate

Description: We provide intermediary services for
mergers and acquisitions, finance. Also provide
investment for leveraged build ups.

Preferred investment size: $3 million+

Amount under management: <$10 million

Area served: North America

Preferred stages of financing: Mezzanine, LBO/MBO,
Expansion

Industries:
I.02   Agriculture/forestry/fishing/mining
I.06   Communications
I.11   Consumer products
I.18   Financial services
I.25   Leisure/hospitality
I.27   Manufacturing
I.29   Medical/medical products
I.31   Real estate
I.36   Transportation

Norwest Venture Partners

2800 Piper Jaffray Tower
222 South Ninth Street
Minneapolis, Minnesota 55402
(612) 667-1650
Fax: (612) 667-1660
Web: www.norwestvc.com

Key contact:
Mr. Daniel J. Haggerty
Mr. John P. Whaley

Description: We manage about $1 billion in investment
funds and are focused on venture capital investments
in emerging growth companies in the information
technology sector (enterprise software, internet,
communications infrastructure equipment, subscriber
based businesses & electronics).

Amount of capital invested: $88 million

Preferred investment size: $5 million

Amount under management: >$1 billion

Area served: United States

Preferred stages of financing: Seed, Start up, First
stage, Second stage, Mezzanine

Industries:
I.06   Communications
I.08   Computer software
I.14   Electronics
I.23   Information technology services

I.24   Internet services/e-commerce
I.33   Semiconductors

Sampling of portfolio companies: Brocade Communication Systems, Inc. (fibre channel switching
products); Golden Sky Systems, Inc. (reseller of
direct satellite TV programming); Xedia Corp.
(internet access communication platform with provisions for quality of service); Maker Communications,
Inc. (programmable communications chips for cell &
frame-based internetworking); Quadritek Systems,
Inc. (internet name management for the enterprise);
Comcore Semiconductor, Inc. (physical layer access
chips for high speed data communications);
Framework Technologies Corp. (project management
application for complex architecture, engineering &
construction); Kiva Software, Inc. (internet application servers for business critical solutions);
WebChat Communications, Inc. (internet-based
community site); Via Internet (int'l. provider of
internet services); Verio (nat'l. ISP consolidator);
Intrepid Systems (retail enterprise information
systems); BUCA (family style Italian cuisine); Una
Mas (freshly prepared Mexican cantina); NetObjects
(web site production & management); PMT CVD
(semiconductor equipment for CVD); Extreme
Networks (gigabit Ethernet switching hubs); 2800
Corp. (consumer goods/recapitalization); Petersen
Publishing Co. (media publications); Transition
Systems (decision support for healthcare providers)

Oak Investment Partners

4550 Norwest Center
90 South Seventh Street
Minneapolis, Minnesota 55402
(612) 339-9322
Fax: (612) 337-8017
Web: www.oakinv.com

Key contact:
Ms. Cathy Agee
Mr. Jerry Gallagher

Description: We are a venture capital organization
dedicated to helping new enterprises emerge as
tomorrow's industry leaders. We were founded in
1978 and have organized seven partnerships with

over $1 billion of capital under management. We
have three areas of investment focus: information
technology, healthcare and retail. We target experienced, entrepreneurial management teams that are
resourceful, disciplined and motivated by appropriate
incentives.

Preferred investment size: $4-20 million

Preferred stages of financing: Seed, Start up

Industries:
I.32   Retail

Sampling of portfolio companies: Actel (develops, manufactures & markets Field Programmable Gate Array solutions); Cephalon; Compaq Computer (manufactures & markets advanced PC's for businesses & professional use); Filene's Basement; Genzyme; HBO & Co.; Network Equipment Technologies, Inc. (communications equipment which enables the building & management of private backbone networks); Octel Communications Corp. (designs, manufactures & markets voice processing systems that are sold primarily to large corporate customers, telephone companies & other providers of Voice Information Services); Office Depot; Parametric Technology Corp. (develops, markets & supports a family of fully integrated parametric feature-based mechanical design automation software); PETsMART; PictureTel (provides high quality, full-color, full-motion video communications at bandwidths commensurate with the new digital, dial-up telephone services being introduced worldwide); Seagate Technology (manufactures & markets Winchester magnetic rigid disk drives for incorporation in minicomputer & microcomputer systems); Stratus (designs, manufactures, markets & services a family of fault tolerant Continuous Processing Systems for critical on-line transaction processing & communications control); SanDisk Corp. (develops & markets solid state non-volatile memory cards & boards for the laptop & portable PC market, as well as other portable communication devices using sophisticated flash E2PROM technology); Sybase (develops & markets SYBASE SQL Server); Synopsys, Inc. (produces synthesis products are complementary to established computer aided engineering tools & run on a broad range of UNIX platforms including those of SUN Microsystems, Apollo & DEC); Ungerman-Bass; Wellfleet (supplies high-performance, full functionality LAN internet working products & systems); Wholefoods

Pathfinder Venture Capital Funds

7300 Metro Boulevard, Suite 585
Minneapolis, Minnesota 55439
(612) 835-1121
Fax: (612) 835-8389

Key contact:
Mr. Jack Ahrens, II
Mr. Andrew J. Greenshields
Mr. Brian P. Johnson
Mr. Gary A. Stoltz

Area served: Midwest

Preferred stages of financing: Seed, Start up, First stage, Second stage, LBO/MBO

Industries:
I.06   Communications
I.07   Computer hardware
I.08   Computer software
I.14   Electronics
I.19   Generalist
I.29   Medical/medical products

Piper Jaffray Ventures Inc.

222 South Ninth Street
Minneapolis, Minnesota 55402
(612) 342-5686
Fax: (612) 342-8514

Key contact:
Ms. Kim Osborne
Mr. Buzz Benson
Mr. Gary Blauer

Area served: United States

Preferred stages of financing: Seed, Start up, First stage, Second stage

Industries:
I.08   Computer software
I.29   Medical/medical products

St. Paul Venture Capital

8500 Normandale Lake Boulevard, Suite 1940
Bloomington, Minnesota 55437-3831
(612) 830-7474
Fax: (612) 830-7475
Web: www.stpaul.com

385 Washington Street
St. Paul, Minnesota 55102
(612) 310-7911
(800) 328-2189
Web: www.stpaul.com

Key contact:
Mr. Patrick A. Hopf, Managing General Partner
Mr. Everett Cox, General Partner
Mr. Frederic Boswell, General Partner
Mr. Brian D. Jacobs, General Partner
Mr. Michael Gorman, Partner
Ms. Nancy S. Olson, General Partner
Mr. James R. Simons, General Partner
Mr. Zenas Hutcheson, General Partner
Mr. Carl Witonsky, Venture Partner
Mr. John Rollwagen, Venture Partner

Ms. Katherine Carney, CFO

Description: We are a rock solid venture capital partnership, built on a foundation of time-honored values with a culture characterized by progressive ideas and strategies. That may not sound dramatically different from some other venture firms, but the differences are in the details.

Founded: 1988

Area served: United States

Preferred stages of financing: Seed, Start up, First stage

Industries:
I.08   Computer software
I.11   Consumer products
I.20   Healthcare
I.23   Information technology services
I.27   Manufacturing
I.29   Medical/medical products
I.32   Retail

I.34   Services (business)
I.35   Services (consumer)

Sampling of portfolio companies: Airgonomics (air-adjustable sofabeds to be marketed by Select Comfort); Command Audio (radio programming on demand); DIVA (movies on demand or supercomputing at $3.95/slice); Flycast (marketplace for buying & selling internet ad space); HeartStent (revascularization medical device); PCI (enhanced communications services for teens); St. Paul Software (enabling software for EDI over the internet); Vivo Software (software tools for applications of streaming media); Biopsys (designs & manufactures products for the diagnosis & treatment of breast cancer); Cardiac Pathways (designs, develops & manufactures products for the therapeutic intervention of electrical problems of the heart); Cardiometrics (develops, manufactures & markets intravascular medical devices to measure blood flow impairment caused by coronary artery disease)

Mississippi

Source Capital Corporation

713 South Pear Orchard Road, Suite 100-5
Ridgeland, Mississippi 39157
(601) 952-1958
Fax: (601) 899-5943

Key contact:
Mr. Rand Ray

Area served: United States

Preferred stages of financing: Start up, First stage, Second stage, Mezzanine, LBO/MBO, Expansion

Industries:
I.03   Biotech/genetic engineering

I.06	Communications
I.11	Consumer products
I.12	Distribution
I.14	Electronics
I.16	Entertainment
I.20	Healthcare
I.25	Leisure/hospitality
I.27	Manufacturing
I.29	Medical/medical products
I.31	Real estate
I.32	Retail
I.34	Services (business)
I.35	Services (consumer)

Sun-Delta Capital Access Center, Inc.

819 Main Street
Greenville, Mississippi 38701
(601) 335-5291
Fax: (601) 335-5295

Key contact:
Mr. Howard Boutte, Jr.

Missouri

Baring Private Equity Partners, Ltd.

P.O. Box 12491
St. Louis, Missouri 63131
(314) 993-0007
Fax: (314) 993-0464

Key contact:
Mr. L. E. Klein, Partner

Preferred stages of financing: First stage, Second stage, Mezzanine

Industries:
I.06   Communications
I.12   Distribution
I.14   Electronics
I.22   Industrial products
I.28   Media/publishing
I.29   Medical/medical products

C3 Holdings, LLC

4520 Main Street, Suite 1600
Kansas City, Missouri 64111
(816) 756-2225
Fax: (816) 756-5552
E-mail: businessdevelopment@c3holdings.com
Web: www.c3holdings.com

Key contact:
Mr. Barton J. Cohen, Principal
Mr. D. Patrick Curran, Principal
Mr. Patrick F. Healy, Principal
Ms. Mary Ripka, CFO
Mr. Gregg A. Herman, Associate Director of
    Development

Description: Our principals bring more than a recognized breadth of experience in capital formation, corporate and joint venture acquisitions, dispositions, investment banking and corporate restructurings. We have all operated businesses on a daily basis. While each principal brings a successful past and a unique perspective to the firm, the combination of individual talents into this highly skilled team truly distinguishes our firm. And because the firm takes a partnership approach to business, business owners gain access to the expertise of all our partners.

Preferred investment size: $5-30 million

Amount under management: $10-25 million

Area served: Midwest

Preferred stages of financing: LBO/MBO, Expansion, Add-ons, growth financings

Industries:

I.05	Chemicals
I.06	Communications
I.11	Consumer products
I.12	Distribution
I.15	Energy/natural resources/utilities
I.18	Financial services
I.20	Healthcare
I.22	Industrial products
I.23	Information technology services
I.27	Manufacturing
I.31	Real estate
I.32	Retail
I.35	Services (consumer)
I.37	Wholesale

Sampling of portfolio companies: After Six Ltd. (marketer & distributor of formal apparel & accessories); Applebees Int'l., Inc. (operator & franchiser of casual dining restaurants); Chart Ltd. (wholesale distributor of Adolph Coors & Co. products for northwest Missouri); LaPetite Academies, Inc. (provider of child day care); Sealright Co., Inc. (designer & manufacturer of value-added packaging & packaging systems for consumer products); Sylvan Learning Systems, Inc. (provider of supplemental education services & computer assisted testing services); William Noble Rare Jewels (specialty retailer of jewelry & gems); ARR-MAZ Products, LP (specialty chemical producer of processing additives for the mining, fertilizer, asphalt pavement, concrete & metal working fluids industries); Cook Paint & Varnish Co. (manufacturer of coatings & related products for residential & commercial uses); TSI Holdings, Inc. (consolidator of manufacturers of freestanding & chassis mounted tanks); Assistive Technology, Inc. (developer & provider of computer software & hardware for the physically challenged); Physiologic Diagnostic Services, Inc. (developer & manufacturer of uterine activity monitoring devices); XTL Biopharmaceuticals Ltd. (product developer for treatment of viral & autoimmune diseases); ACR Systems, Inc. (system software provider & integrator to major retail marketing segments); KUSK-TV, Inc. (full-power & low-power television stations in northern Arizona); Radar Control Services, Inc. (developer & provider of Doppler radar-based signal technology for electronic linkage of vehicles); American Auto Funding Corp. (sub-prime used automobile finance); First Business Bank of K.C. (middle market commercial banking institution); Sands Partnership (oil exploration & production); DynaVest Joint Venture (undeveloped real estate joint venture)

Crown Capital Corp.

540 Maryville Centre Drive, Suite 120
St. Louis, Missouri 63141
(314) 576-1201
Fax: (314) 576-1525
E-mail: crown@crown-cap.com

Key contact:
Mr. R. William Breece, Jr., President/Managing
Director

Description: Investment and merchant banking firm. We provide private equity funding for corporate transactions including acquisitions, expansions, management buy-outs, management buy-ins, and recapitalizations. We acquire companies in partnership with corporate managers.

Amount of capital invested: $35 million

Preferred investment size: $5-100 million

Amount under management: $100-500 million

Area served: Asia, North America, South/Central America

Preferred stages of financing: Second stage, Mezzanine, LBO/MBO, Expansion, Int'l expansion

Industries:

I.06	Communications
I.11	Consumer products
I.12	Distribution
I.14	Electronics
I.16	Entertainment
I.17	Environmental services/waste management
I.18	Financial services
I.20	Healthcare
I.22	Industrial products
I.23	Information technology services
I.24	Internet services/e-commerce
I.25	Leisure/hospitality
I.27	Manufacturing
I.29	Medical/medical products
I.31	Real estate
I.34	Services (business)

Enterprise Fund

150 North Meramec
Clayton, Missouri 63105
(314) 725-5500
Fax: (314) 725-1732
Web: www.EnterpriseFund.com

Key contact:
Mr. Joseph D. Garea, President

Description: We are a labour sponsored investment fund corporation making venture capital investments in small-to-medium sized corporations. We are committed to producing superior long-term returns from investments in developing companies, through careful analysis, active participation and prudent diversification within our portfolio.

Area served: Canada

Sampling of portfolio companies: Image Processing Systems Inc. (computer-based quality control vision inspection systems); CleanSoils Ltd. Partnership (hydrocarbon contaminated soil remediation services); Consultronics Ltd. (telecommunication test & simulation equipment); The Nu-Gro Corp. (fertilizers & horticultural supplies); Engineering Interface Ltd.- Tescor Energy Services (building performance contracting)

Gateway Associates, L.P.

8000 Maryland Avenue, Suite 1190
St. Louis, Missouri 63105
(314) 721-5707
Fax: (314) 721-5135

Key contact:
Mr. John McCarthy

Industries:
I.06   Communications
I.07   Computer hardware
I.29   Medical/medical products
I.34   Services (business)
I.35   Services (consumer)

InvestAmerica N.D. Management, Inc.

Suite 2424, Commerce Tower
911 Main Street
Kansas City, Missouri 64105
(816) 842-0114
Fax: (816) 471-7339

Key contact:
Mr. Kevin F. Mullane, Vice President

Description: We are the general partner and investment
advisor for the North Dakota Small Business Investment Company (NDSBIC). NDSBIC is a licensed
SBIC and will invest a majority of its capital in later
stage companies.

Amount of capital invested: $2.2 million

Preferred investment size: $500,000

Amount under management: <$10 million

Area served: United States

Preferred stages of financing: Mezzanine, LBO/MBO,
Expansion

Industries:
I.01   Aerospace
I.02   Agriculture/forestry/fishing/mining
I.03   Biotech/genetic engineering
I.05   Chemicals
I.06   Communications
I.07   Computer hardware
I.08   Computer software
I.09   Construction
I.10   Consulting
I.11   Consumer products
I.12   Distribution
I.13   Education
I.14   Electronics
I.17   Environmental services/waste management
I.19   Generalist
I.20   Healthcare
I.21   High technology
I.22   Industrial products
I.23   Information technology services
I.24   Internet services/e-commerce
I.25   Leisure/hospitality
I.26   Life sciences
I.27   Manufacturing
I.29   Medical/medical products
I.32   Retail
I.33   Semiconductors
I.34   Services (business)
I.35   Services (consumer)
I.36   Transportation
I.37   Wholesale

Kansas City Equity Partners

233 West 47th Street
Kansas City, Missouri 64112
(816) 960-1771
Fax: (816) 960-1777
E-mail: info@kcep.com
Web: www.kcep.com

Key contact:
Mr. William Reisler, Managing Partner
Mr. David Schulte, Partner
Mr. Thomas Palmer, Partner

Description: Private venture capital firm that is
licensed as a small business investment company
with approximately $30 million under management.
We have invested in 19 companies representing early
stage, expansion, buyout and recapitalization transactions. Investments are made primarily in the
Midwest region and range from $500,000 to $2.5
million.

Preferred investment size: $1-1 million

Amount under management: $25-100 million

Area served: United States

Preferred stages of financing: First stage, Second
stage, Mezzanine, LBO/MBO, Expansion

Industries:
I.01   Aerospace
I.06   Communications
I.07   Computer hardware
I.08   Computer software
I.11   Consumer products
I.12   Distribution
I.14   Electronics
I.19   Generalist
I.20   Healthcare
I.21   High technology
I.22   Industrial products
I.23   Information technology services
I.27   Manufacturing
I.29   Medical/medical products
I.30   New media
I.32   Retail
I.34   Services (business)
I.37   Wholesale

United Missouri Capital Corp.

1010 Grand Boulevard
Kansas City, Missouri 64141
(816) 860-7914

Fax: (816) 860-7143

Key contact:
Mr. Noel Shull

Area served: Midwest

Industries:
I.19   Generalist
I.27   Manufacturing

Montana

Montana Science & Technology Alliance
1424 9th Avenue
Helena, Montana 59620
(406) 444-2778
Fax: (406) 444-1585

Key contact:
Ms. Bobbie Pomerow
Ms. Ann M. Welz

Area served: Northwest

Preferred stage of financing: Seed

Industries:
I.19   Generalist

Nebraska

Heartland Capital Fund, Ltd.
11930 Arbor Street, Suite 201
Omaha, Nebraska 68144
(402) 333-8840
Fax: (402) 333-8944
E-mail: HrtlndCptl@aol.com

Key contact:
Mr. Bradley K. Edwards, General Partner
Mr. Patrick A. Rivelli, General Partner
Mr. John G. Gustafson, Vice President

Description: We seek transition stage investments in
    technology related companies located principally in
    the Central and Southwestern U.S.

Area served: North America

Preferred stages of financing: First stage, Second stage

Industries:
I.06   Communications
I.07   Computer hardware
I.08   Computer software
I.12   Distribution
I.14   Electronics
I.21   High technology
I.23   Information technology services
I.24   Internet services/e-commerce
I.33   Semiconductors

World Investments Inc.
World-Herald Square
Omaha, Nebraska 68102-1138
(402) 444-1172
Fax: (402) 345-9115
E-mail: world_investments@prodigy.com

Key contact:
Mr. William E. Conley, President

Description: We are a wholly-owned subsidiary of The
    Omaha World-Herald Company that was formed to
    invest in early-stage and expansion-stage growth
    companies. We seek businesses primarily located in
    the midwest in the information technology, commu-
    nications and marketing services industries. Our
    midwestern location, values and approach make us a
    unique option to businesses in search of capital.

Amount of capital invested: $7.5 million

Preferred investment size: $1-2 million

Amount under management: $25-100 million

Area served: United States

Preferred stages of financing: Start up, First stage,
Second stage, Mezzanine, Expansion

Industries:
I.06   Communications
I.07   Computer hardware
I.08   Computer software
I.14   Electronics

I.16   Entertainment
I.21   High technology
I.23   Information technology services
I.24   Internet services/e-commerce
I.28   Media/publishing
I.30   New media

Sampling of portfolio companies: Election Systems &
    Software (election services & equipment); McCarthy
    Group, Inc. (investment company); Prairie Systems,
    Inc. (enhanced telecommunications services);
    Heartland Capital Fund (venture capital fund); Sitel
    Corp. (teleservices); Data Transmission Network
    (data communications)

Nevada

Venture Planning Associates

2885 South Decatur, Suite 3010
Las Vegas, Nevada 89103
(702) 367-0234
Fax: (808) 524-2775
E-mail: capital@ventureplan.com
Web: www.ventureplan.com

Key contact:
Mr. William F. McCready, President/CEO

Description: We provide venture capital consulting
services for all phases of business development, from
start-ups to IPO's.

Industries:
I.01   Aerospace
I.02   Agriculture/forestry/fishing/mining
I.03   Biotech/genetic engineering
I.04   Broadcasting
I.05   Chemicals
I.06   Communications
I.07   Computer hardware
I.08   Computer software
I.09   Construction
I.10   Consulting
I.11   Consumer products
I.12   Distribution
I.13   Education
I.14   Electronics
I.15   Energy/natural resources/utilities
I.16   Entertainment
I.17   Environmental services/waste management
I.18   Financial services
I.19   Generalist
I.20   Healthcare
I.21   High technology
I.22   Industrial products
I.23   Information technology services
I.24   Internet services/e-commerce
I.25   Leisure/hospitality
I.26   Life sciences
I.27   Manufacturing
I.28   Media/publishing
I.29   Medical/medical products
I.30   New media
I.31   Real estate
I.32   Retail
I.33   Semiconductors
I.34   Services (business)
I.35   Services (consumer)
I.36   Transportation
I.37   Wholesale

New Jersey

Accel Partners

One Palmer Square
Princeton, New Jersey 08542
(609) 683-4500
Fax: (609) 683-0384
E-mail: info@accel.com
Web: www.accel.com

Key contact:
Mr. Carter Sednaoui, Administrative Partner
Mr. Jim Flach, Executive Partner
Mr. John Partridge, Associate
Mr. Jim Swartz, Founding Partner
Mr. Peter Wagner, General Partner

Description: We are a venture capital firm dedicated to
partnering with outstanding management teams to
build world-class companies. In order to meet this
challenge with a prepared mind, we focus our
activity in just three areas: communications, internet
and intranet software and services in technology and
healthcare.

Preferred stages of financing: Seed, Start up, First
stage, Second stage, LBO/MBO

Industries:
I.06   Communications
I.08   Computer software
I.20   Healthcare
I.24   Internet services/e-commerce

Sampling of portfolio companies: Abaton.com
(software to network physician groups); Arbor
Software (decision support software); Bright Tiger
Technologies (enterprise web server management);
Broadbase Information Systems (analytical
datamart); First Floor (shared file software for PC
LAN's); Macromedia (multi-platform authoring
software for multimedia); Remedy (adaptable
software for business processes); Biztravel.com
(online travel services); Fabrik Communications
(business to business internet e-mail services);
iBEAM Broadcasting (data broadcast services);
Sonnet Financial (discount foreign exchange
services); Alantec (intelligent switching hubs);
Broadband Technologies (fiber to the home);
Foundry Networks (communications equipment);
GoDigital (low cost ISDN transport); Omneon Video
Networks (professional video networking); Racotek
(mobile data systems integration); Teleos (enterprise
video networking); Tellium (optical communications
equipment); Vertical Networks (integrated access
equipment)

American Acquisition Partners

175 South Street
Morristown, New Jersey 07960
(973) 267-7800
Fax: (973) 267-7695

Key contact:
Dr. Ted Bustany

Preferred stage of financing: LBO/MBO

Industries:
I.05   Chemicals

I.27   Manufacturing

AT&T Ventures

295 North Maple Avenue
Room 3353C1
Basking Ridge, New Jersey 07920
(908) 221-7061
Fax: (908) 630-1455

Key contact:
Mr. R. Bradford Burnham

Description: We were founded in 1992 as a venture capital partnership to invest in information technology and service enabling companies in emerging growth markets. Drawing from three funds totaling $348 million, we provide capital to start-up and later stage companies in the following markets: wireless communications, internet, value added networking services, content and local service.

Founded: 1992

Preferred investment size: $1-5 million

Amount under management: $100-500 million

Area served: United States

Preferred stages of financing: Seed, Start up, First stage, Second stage

Industries:
I.06   Communications
I.08   Computer software
I.11   Consumer products
I.12   Distribution
I.23   Information technology services
I.24   Internet services/e-commerce
I.28   Media/publishing
I.30   New media

Sampling of portfolio companies: Amteva Technologies; Avesta; CitySearch; e.Fusion; First Virtual Corp.; Home Data; Internet Security Systems; Meigher Communications; Nat'l. Transportation Exchange; Object Design; Physicians On Line; Topometrix; UniSite; Video Networks Inc.; Xedia Corp.; America On Line (Redgate Communications); Classic Sports Network; CUC Int'l. (Knowledge Adventure); Netscape; Spectrum Holobyte

BCI Advisors, Inc.

Glenpointe Centre West
Teaneck, New Jersey 07666
(201) 836-3900
Fax: (201) 836-6368
E-mail: bciadv@mail.idt.net

Key contact:
Mr. Stephen J. Eley
Mr. Hoyt Goodrich
Mr. J. Barton Goodwin
Mr. Matthew E. Gormly, III

Mr. Theodore T. Horton
Mr. Donald P. Remey

Area served: United States

Preferred stages of financing: Second stage, Third/later stage

Industries:
I.06   Communications
I.28   Media/publishing

Capital Express, L.L.C.

100 Plaza Drive
Secaucus, New Jersey 07094
(201) 583-3635
Fax: (201) 583-3634

Key contact:
Mr. Niles Cohen, Managing Member

Description: Private venture capital firm investing our own funds.

Preferred investment size: $250,000-1 million

Amount under management: <$10 million

Area served: United States

Preferred stages of financing: Seed, Start up, First stage, Second stage

Industries:
I.02   Agriculture/forestry/fishing/mining
I.11   Consumer products
I.12   Distribution
I.19   Generalist
I.24   Internet services/e-commerce
I.28   Media/publishing
I.30   New media
I.32   Retail

Sampling of portfolio companies: Mirrotek Int'l., LLC (manufacturer of specialty mirrors, wall decor & novelty items); 1-800 Birthday, LLC (direct marketing-consumer); Forman Interactive Corp. (internet e-commerce); Voxware, Inc. (software); J. Peterman Co., Inc. (catalog company)

Cardinal Health Partners

221 Nassau Street, 3rd Floor
Princeton, New Jersey 08542
(609) 924-6452
Fax: (609) 683-0174
E-mail: johnclarke@cardinalventures.com

Key contact:
Mr. John K. Clarke, Managing General Partner

Mr. Brandon H. Hull, General Partner
Mr. John J. Park, General Partner/CFO
Mr. Morton Collins

Description: We seek investment opportunities spanning the breadth of the trillion dollar healthcare economy. Principals have experience in healthcare services, life sciences, healthcare information technology, and medical products and devices. We will consider investments at any stage of a company's development. Principals have particular expertise in the formation and support of early stage ventures.

Amount of capital invested: $5 million

Preferred investment size: $3 million

Amount under management: $25-100 million

Area served: United States

Preferred stages of financing: Seed, Start up, First stage, Second stage

Industries:
I.03 Biotech/genetic engineering
I.06 Communications
I.20 Healthcare
I.23 Information technology services
I.26 Life sciences
I.29 Medical/medical products

Sampling of portfolio companies: Pointshare (maintain medical intranet & extranet networks for physician alliances); Signature Plastic Surgeons (management services in the area of plastic surgery, ear, nose & throat)

The CIT Group/Equity Investments

650 CIT Drive
Livingston, New Jersey 07039
(973) 740-5181
Fax: (973) 740-5555

Key contact:
Mr. Paul J. Laud
Mr. Colby W. Collier
Mr. Kevin P. Falvey
Mr. Bruce Schackman

Mr. Christopher L. Weiler

Area served: United States

Preferred stages of financing: Second stage, LBO/MBO

Industries:
I.27 Manufacturing
I.29 Medical/medical products

DeMuth, Folger & Wetherill

300 Frank W. Burr Boulevard
Glenpointe Centre East, 5th Floor
Teaneck, New Jersey 07666
(201) 836-6000
Fax: (201) 836-5666
E-mail: dfwmgmt@aol.com

Key contact:
Mr. Donald F. DeMuth, General Partner
Mr. Keith W. Pennell, General Partner
Ms. Lisa Roumell, General Partner
Mr. David C. Wetherill, General Partner

Description: We make active and direct private equity investments in high growth/market niche situations with emphasis on health and business services, consumer services, specialty manufacturing and value added distribution.

Amount of capital invested: $21 million

Preferred investment size: $3-8 million

Amount under management: $100-500 million

Area served: United States

Preferred stages of financing: LBO/MBO, Expansion

Industries:
I.06 Communications
I.08 Computer software
I.11 Consumer products
I.12 Distribution

I.13 Education
I.14 Electronics
I.19 Generalist
I.20 Healthcare
I.22 Industrial products
I.23 Information technology services
I.27 Manufacturing
I.28 Media/publishing
I.29 Medical/medical products
I.34 Services (business)
I.35 Services (consumer)
I.37 Wholesale

Sampling of portfolio companies: APT (specialty filters for the automotive industry); Clear Communications (turnkey services for wireless communications towers); ConsoliDent (dental practice management services); General Rental (equipment rental centers); Great Lakes Health Plan (HMO & healthcare clinics for Medicaid population); Hamilton Funeral Services (funeral services in secondary markets); Matcom Systems (information technology services, primarily to US government agencies); Pathology Consultants of America (pathology practice management services); Peak Medical (skilled nursing & assisted living continuum); Premier Medical Services (healthcare personnel for home & hospital nursing); Spectrascan Health Services (Ob/Gyn practice management services); USB (credit card processing services for mall merchants)

Domain Associates

One Palmer Square
Princeton, New Jersey 08542
(609) 683-5656
Fax: (609) 683-9789
Web: www.domainvc.com

Key contact:
Mr. James C. Blair, General Partner
Mr. Brian H. Dovey, General Partner

Ms. Kathleen K. Schoemaker, Administrative General Partner
Mr. Jesse I. Treu, General Partner

Description: We provide seed and early stage financing and organizational support to technology- and service-based companies focused on life sciences. Specific areas of investment interest include biopharmaceuticals, medical devices, bio-instrumentation, diagnostics, new materials as applied to healthcare, healthcare information systems and services. With demonstrated expertise in technology assessment, strategic planning, operations and finance, we have been involved in the creation and development of more than 75 life science ventures.

Amount of capital invested: $38.5 million

Preferred investment size: $5 million (over multiple financing rounds)

Amount under management: $100-500 million

Area served: United States

Preferred stages of financing: Seed, Start up, First stage

Industries:
I.03   Biotech/genetic engineering
I.05   Chemicals
I.20   Healthcare
I.26   Life sciences

Sampling of portfolio companies: Acea Pharmaceuticals (drugs vs. central nervous system disorders); Athero-Genics (drugs vs. atherosclerosis & related diseases); Biosite Diagnostics (hand-held diagnostics for drugs-of-abuse & cardiology); CareCentric Solutions (point-of-care clinical information systems); Chrysalis Int'l. Corp. (contract research organization); Connetics Corp. (rheumatology & dermatology drugs); Focal (synthetic, absorbable liquid surgical sealants); GelTex Pharmaceuticals (drugs to remove substances from the gastrointestinal tract); Gensia Sicor (multisource injectable drugs); Geron Corp. (drugs vs. cancer & age-related diseases); Imagyn Medical (surgical devices for women's healthcare); Lumisys (instruments to convert medical images into digital format); Microsurge (hand instruments for minimally invasive surgery); Neocrin (immunoprotected cellular transplants vs. diabetes); OncoTherapeutics (cancer immunotherapeutics); Prizm Pharmaceuticals (targeted gene delivery); Sepracor (purified forms of existing drugs); Trega Biosciences (drug discovery based on combinatorial chemistry); UroTherapies (urology-focused physician practice management company); VenPro Corp. (biologically derived venous valves)

DSV Partners

221 Nassau Street
Princeton, New Jersey 08542
(609) 924-6420
Fax: (609) 683-0174

Key contact:
Mr. John K. Clarke
Mr. Morton Collins

Preferred stages of financing: Seed, First stage, Second stage, LBO/MBO

Industries:
I.03   Biotech/genetic engineering
I.05   Chemicals
I.06   Communications
I.07   Computer hardware
I.08   Computer software
I.14   Electronics
I.29   Medical/medical products
I.34   Services (business)
I.35   Services (consumer)

Edelson Technology Partners

300 Tice Boulevard
Woodcliff Lake, New Jersey 07675
(201) 930-9898
Fax: (201) 930-8899
E-mail: harry@edelsontech.com
Web: edelsontech.com

Key contact:
Mr. Harry Edelson, General Partner
Mr. John E. Fox, Partner

Description: We invest corporate funds rather than pension funds. The General Partner provides the Limited Partners with a variety of investment banking services in addition to a "window on technology." Portfolio companies are introduced to corporate partners for potential business mergers or liasons.

Amount of capital invested: $3.5 million

Preferred investment size: $1 million

Amount under management: $100-500 million

Area served: Worldwide

Preferred stages of financing: Seed, Start up, First stage, Second stage

Industries:
I.01   Aerospace
I.03   Biotech/genetic engineering
I.04   Broadcasting
I.05   Chemicals
I.06   Communications
I.08   Computer software
I.11   Consumer products
I.13   Education
I.14   Electronics
I.15   Energy/natural resources/utilities
I.16   Entertainment
I.17   Environmental services/waste management
I.20   Healthcare
I.21   High technology
I.23   Information technology services
I.24   Internet services/e-commerce
I.26   Life sciences
I.28   Media/publishing
I.29   Medical/medical products
I.33   Semiconductors
I.35   Services (consumer)
I.36   Transportation

Sampling of portfolio companies: Alacrity (desktop document management system for personal computers); China Internet (selects & translates business information over the internet & delivers to Chinese & US corporate subscribers); Duck (develops & licenses innovative, video compression solutions for multimedia applications involvig interactive tv, video games, CD-ROM, video conferencing, telecommunications, internet & content applications); EXA (workstation software products for computational fluid dynamics which can replace wind tunnels); GIGA (provides information & analysis to information technology vendors & the rapidly growing IT end user market); Momentum Software (assists companies in becoming more effective & competitive by supporting their mission critical application integration needs); Neormedical Systems (screening of cancers by neural computers); Pointcast (leader in Push Technology for the internet); City Dial Network Services (provides fixed-rate, medium-distance voice & data services in major Canadian cities); Diginet Communications (provides customers & internet subscribers with low priced data communications); Satcom (provides low cost, satellite-based mobile data, global positioning & messaging communications services in Europe); Simpact (designs & manufactures high-performance data communication products that solve today's toughest, mission critical internet problems); Ergenics (processes special purpose hydride material & develops hydride based heat transfer systems for automotive & other applications); Environmental Technology Group (mobile truck service for on-site reprocessing & recycling of industrial solvents); Lithium Technology (develops & manufactures lithium polymer batteries featuring high power density & long life cylce); Membrex (innovative filtration membranes & systems for industrial waste minimization & recycling); Oxford Glycosciences (leader in carbohydrate engineering currently applying its technology to develop drugs for cancer, inflammation & infectious diseases); Portable Energy Products (designs, manufactures & markets advanced rechargeable Sealed Lead-Acid (SLA) batteries, primarily for use in portable computers, instruments & medical devices); Alternative Postal Delivery (national media company providing advertisers with an effective approach in targeting consumers through suburban newspapers); College Enterprises (designs, builds & operates "The Pulse Copy & Technology Center" at universities)

Edison Venture Fund

997 Lenox Drive #3
Lawrenceville, New Jersey 08648
(609) 896-1900
Fax: (609) 896-0066
E-mail: johnm@edisonventure.com
Web: www.edisonventure.com

Key contact:
Mr. John H. Martinson, Managing Partner
Mr. Richard J. Defieux, General Partner
Mr. Gustav H. Koven, General Partner
Mr. Ross T. Martinson, General Partner/CFO
Mr. James T. Gunton, Vice President

Description: Since our formation in 1986, we have invested in more than 75 companies. We usually are the sole or lead venture investor. Multiple invest-ments have been completed in our industry specialties, including computer software, communi-cations and other technologies. Our investments are located primarily in the New York-Washington corridor with concentrations in New Jersey, Pannsyl-vania, Delaware, Maryland and Virginia.

Preferred investment size: $500,000-5 million

Area served: Mid-Atlantic

Preferred stage of financing: Expansion

Industries:
I.06   Communications
I.08   Computer software
I.11   Consumer products
I.13   Education
I.14   Electronics
I.15   Energy/natural resources/utilities
I.17   Environmental services/waste management
I.18   Financial services
I.20   Healthcare
I.24   Internet services/e-commerce
I.28   Media/publishing

Sampling of portfolio companies: Commence (software groupware for customer interactive applications); Dendrite (develops, markets & supports software for electronic territorial management by pharmaceutical sales representatives); Learning Co. (consumer education & entertainment software); Longview Solutions (budgeting, reporting & planning software); Marketing Information Systems (sales automation software, focused on telemarketing appli-cations, primarily in IBM AS/400); Mcorp (hotel property management software, primarily serving mid-sized hotels & military bases); DSET (telecom-munications management network agent tools for managing multi-vendor, multi-platform communica-tions networks); Netscape (internet browser & server software); Procom (telephone answering, voicemail, alpha paging dispatch, order entry & other messaging services); Visual Networks (network test & management equipment for frame relay & ATM WANs)

Geocapital Partners

1 Bridge Plaza
Ft. Lee, New Jersey 07024
(201) 461-9292
Fax: (201) 346-9191
E-mail: investments@geocapital.com
Web: www.geocapital.com

Key contact:
Mr. Stephen Clearman, Partner
Mr. Lawrence Lepard, Partner
Mr. Richard Vines, Partner

Description: We are a leading source of venture capital and buyout financing for the software and informa-tion services industry.

Preferred investment size: $10 million

Amount under management: $100-500 million

Area served: Europe, United States

Preferred stage of financing: Expansion

Industries:
I.08   Computer software
I.21   High technology
I.23   Information technology services

Sampling of portfolio companies: 4-Sight plc (provider of communications solutions for the printing, pre-press & graphic arts industries); Armstrong Laing (developer of activity-based costing & activity-based management solutions); Autoweb.com (provider of internet-based marketing service for new & used car purchasing); Desktalk Systems (provider of measurement & analysis tools for networks); Hospitality Systems (Windows-based point-of-sale systems for the hospitality industry); Interlynx Technology (employee & manager self-service applications to extend human resource management systems); RealSelect (provider of internet-based marketing services for real estate); Storeroom Solutions (provider of outsourced MRO supply solutions); JMW Systems (developer of information technology software & solutions for the trucking & carrier industries)

Healthcare Ventures LLC

44 Nassau Street
Princeton, New Jersey 08542
(609) 430-3900
Fax: (609) 430-9525

Key contact:
Dr. James H. Cavanaugh, President
Mr. William W. Crouse, Managing Director
Mr. John W. Littlechild, Managing Director
Mr. Harold R. Werner, Managing Director
Mr. Mark Leschly, Managing Director

Description: Creation and financing of early stage healthcare and life science companies that have significant growth potential.

Preferred investment size: $5-10 million

Amount under management: $100-500 million

Area served: United States

Preferred stages of financing: Seed, Start up, First stage, Second stage, Mezzanine

Industries:
I.03   Biotech/genetic engineering
I.20   Healthcare
I.26   Life sciences

Sampling of portfolio companies: Dendreon Corp. (biotechnology); Biotransplant, Inc. (biotechnology); Cytomed, Inc. (biotechnology); Diacrin, Inc. (biotechnology); Genetic Therapy, Inc. (biotechnology); Human Genome Sciences, Inc. (biotechnology); Leukosite, Inc. (biotechnology); 3D Pharmaceuticals, Inc. (biotechnology); Magainin Pharmaceuticals, Inc. (biotechnology); Nitromed, Inc. (biotechnology); Osteotech, Inc. (biotechnology); Pharmagene, Inc. (biotechnology); Virus Research Institute, Inc. (biotechnology); Argonex, Inc. (biotechnology); Delsys Pharmaceutical Corp. (biotechnology); VerSicor, Inc. (biotechnology); Diversa Corp. (life sciences)

InnoCal, L.P.

Park 80 West, Plaza One
Saddle Brook, New Jersey 07663
(201) 845-4900
Fax: (201) 845-3388
E-mail: eharrison@innocal.com
Web: www.innocal.com

Key contact:
Mr. James E. Houlihan, III, General Partner
Mr. H. D. Lambert, General Partner
Mr. Gerald A. Lodge, General Partner
Mr. Raun J. Rasmussen, General Partner
Mr. Russell J. Robelen, General Partner
Mr. Eric S. Harrison, Associate

Description: We are a private venture capital firm with $75 million of committed capital. Funding is provided exclusively by the California State Teachers' Retirement System. Our investment focus is on early and expansion stage, technology-based businesses that have the potential to be leaders within their respective industries.

Preferred investment size: $2 million

Amount under management: $25-100 million

Area served: California, United States

Preferred stages of financing: Start up, First stage, Second stage, Expansion

Industries:
I.03   Biotech/genetic engineering
I.06   Communications
I.07   Computer hardware
I.08   Computer software
I.14   Electronics
I.20   Healthcare
I.23   Information technology services

Sampling of portfolio companies: Advanced Access (provides logistical outsourcing services to a variety of industries); Cloud 9 Interactive (multimedia publisher); CoCensys (develops & markets drugs for disorders of the central nervous system); Collagenex (pursuing drug therapies for periodontal disease); GeoCities Inc. (develops internet-based themed communities); GigaNet Inc. (high speed interconnects & switches for cluster computing); HiLife Inc. (comprehensicve interactive case management of chronic disease states); Implex (orthopedic implants & specialty materials); Maret (drug therapies to promote wound & burn healing); Medical Data Int'l. (provides business information products for healthcare markets); Medical Delivery Devices, Inc. (a medication infusion device company); Motiva Software Corp. (develops & markets intranet-based product information life cycle management systems); SalesLogix Corp. (develops enterprise-wide sales force automation software); Telescan Systems, Inc. (designs & manufactures interactive merchandising systems for the consumer entertainment industry); Thinque Systems Corp. (develops wireless pen-based customer asset management solutions for the consumer packaged goods industry); Trega Biosciences, Inc. (combinatorial chemistry for drug discovery & development); Trikon Technologies (manufactures etching equipment for the semiconductor industry); TriVida Corp. (develops & markets predictive data management products for corporate networks); Tycom (precision cutting tools used in the manufacturing of printed circuit boards)

Johnston Associates, Inc.

181 Cherry Valley Road
Princeton, New Jersey 08540
(609) 924-3131
Fax: (609) 683-7524

Key contact:
Mr. Richard G. Horan
Mr. Robert F. Johnston
Mr. Robert B. Stockman

Area served: East Coast

Preferred stage of financing: Seed

Industries:
I.20   Healthcare
I.29   Medical/medical products

Med-Tech Ventures, Inc.

201 Tabor Road
Morris Plains, New Jersey 07950
(973) 540-6212
Fax: (973) 540-2119

Key contact:
Mr. Dennis Thompson
Mr. Fred G. Weiss
Dr. Wendell Wierenga, Ph.D.

Preferred stages of financing: Start up, First stage,
Second stage

Industries:
I.03   Biotech/genetic engineering
I.26   Life sciences
I.29   Medical/medical products

Mentor Capital Partners, Ltd.

1534 Hainesport Road
Mt. Laurel, New Jersey 08054
(609) 802-1788
Fax: (609) 802-1791

Key contact:
Dr. George P. Stasen, Partner

Description: We are a regional diversified venture
capital & private equity firm, working in partnership
with portfolio company management, private or
public, to create exceptional value for its investors.
We employ our capital to "facilitate a leadership role
with company management." It is management's
responsibility to operate the business. We partner
with management to develop the best liquidity
alternatives.

Amount of capital invested: $2.5 million

Preferred investment size: $1 million

Amount under management: $10-25 million

Area served: United States

Preferred stages of financing: Mezzanine, LBO/MBO,
Expansion

Industries:
I.01   Aerospace
I.06   Communications
I.07   Computer hardware
I.08   Computer software
I.11   Consumer products
I.12   Distribution
I.14   Electronics

I.18   Financial services
I.19   Generalist
I.20   Healthcare
I.21   High technology
I.22   Industrial products
I.23   Information technology services
I.24   Internet services/e-commerce
I.27   Manufacturing
I.29   Medical/medical products
I.32   Retail
I.34   Services (business)
I.35   Services (consumer)

Sampling of portfolio companies: AxSys Corp.
(developer & marketer of imaging software for MRI
& CT equipment); College Financial Planning Counselors, Inc. (advisors regarding the financing of
college tuition & through affiliated financial planners
the financing of college costs); CoreCare Systems,
Inc. (provider of mental health & behavioral care
services in Eastern Pennsylvania & Central NJ);
Declaration Holdings, Inc. (provider of administrative services to the mutual fund industry); The
Eastwind Group, Inc. (holding company which
acquires underperforming businesses in manufacturing & technology); JADE Equipment Corp.
(manufacturer of build-to-customer-specification
precision automated assembly equipment); KNF
Corp. (nylon blown film extruder & bag manufacturers serving the aerospace, chemical, medical, food
& electronic industries); North American Cable
Equipment, Inc. (distributor of telecommunication
products sold to satellite, cable television & wireless
industries)

MidMark Capital, L.P.

466 Southern Boulevard
Chatham, New Jersey 07928
(973) 822-2999
Fax: (973) 822-8911
E-mail: mfinlay@midmarkassoc.com
Web: members.bellatlantic.net/~midmark1

Key contact:
Mr. Denis Newman, Managing Director

Mr. Wayne Clevenger, Managing Director
Mr. Joseph R. Robinson, Managing Director
Mr. Matthew W. Finlay, Vice President

Description: We, and our general partner MidMark
Associates, Inc., combine financial resources and
business capabilities to acquire significant ownership

positions in privately and publicly owned middle market companies with the objective to increase the value of those positions over the long term.

Amount of capital invested: $6,180,000

Preferred investment size: $3-5 million

Amount under management: $25-100 million

Area served: United States

Preferred stages of financing: LBO/MBO, Expansion

Industries:
I.01   Aerospace
I.04   Broadcasting
I.05   Chemicals
I.06   Communications
I.11   Consumer products
I.12   Distribution
I.14   Electronics
I.18   Financial services
I.19   Generalist
I.20   Healthcare
I.22   Industrial products
I.23   Information technology services
I.24   Internet services/e-commerce
I.25   Leisure/hospitality
I.27   Manufacturing
I.28   Media/publishing
I.30   New media
I.32   Retail
I.34   Services (business)
I.37   Wholesale

Sampling of portfolio companies: AccTech, LLC (specialized cleaning products & other accessories for computer, telecommunication & related equipment); Buxton Co., LLC (designer, sourcer & marketer of men's & women's wallets, travel kits & other leather accessories); Clearview Cinema Group, Inc. (a chain of community-centered movie theater that target families & value-oriented older audiences); Cook & Dunn Enterprises, LLC (regional paint manufacturer & distributor); Fetco Holding Corp. (designer, sourcer & distributor of branded picture frames to multi-channel markets); Lionheart Industries, Inc. (specialty ferrous foundries & machine shop); Maurice Corp. (a specialty retailer of branded men's casual apparel in smaller towns); Mercury Radio Communications, LLC (operator of four radio stations in Buffalo, NY); MRI Flexible Packaging Co. (high speed flexographic printing company); Santana Ltd. (designer, sourcer & marketer of high quality young men's & boys' casual tops); SPD Technologies, Inc. (develops, manufactures & services circuit breaker protection systems for the Navy & commercial applications); Spring Broadcasting, LLC (operator of nine radio stations in small & medium markets)

Nassau Capital, LLC
22 Chambers Street, Suite 401
Princeton, New Jersey 08542
(609) 924-3555
Fax: (609) 924-8887
Web: www.nassau.com

Key contact:
Mr. Randall A. Hack, Member
Mr. John G. Quigley, Member
Mr. Robert L. Honstein, Member
Mr. Jonathan A. Sweemer, Member
Mr. Curtis A. Glovier, Principal
Mr. William H. Stewart, Principal
Mr. Thomas C. Barnds, Associate

Description: We are an independent firm which invests in private companies and assets on behalf of Princeton University's $5 billion endowment. We presently have a $1 billion pool of capital invested directly in private companies, real estate, and energy-related assets, and in limited partnerships or funds sponsored by others.

Preferred investment size: $10-30 million

Amount under management: >$1 billion

Area served: United States

Preferred stages of financing: Second stage, LBO/MBO, Expansion

Industries:
I.01   Aerospace
I.04   Broadcasting
I.06   Communications
I.08   Computer software
I.11   Consumer products
I.12   Distribution
I.13   Education
I.15   Energy/natural resources/utilities
I.18   Financial services
I.20   Healthcare
I.24   Internet services/e-commerce
I.27   Manufacturing
I.28   Media/publishing
I.29   Medical/medical products
I.31   Real estate
I.32   Retail
I.34   Services (business)
I.36   Transportation

Sampling of portfolio companies: Amerigroup, Inc. (healthcare); Bridge Medical, Inc. (health care); Calendar Broadcasting, Inc. (media); Crown Castle Int'l., Inc. (telecommunications); Decrane Aircraft Holdings, Inc. (aerospace); EW&S Railways, Ltd. (transportation); Favorite Brands Int'l., Inc. (food); KMC Telecom, Inc. (telecommunications); Lightspan Partnership, Inc. (educational software); M-Tec Corp. (manufacturing); Omnicell Technologies, Inc. (health care); Peterson Publishing (media/publishing); Portal Software (internet billing services); Racing Champions Corp. (manufacturing); Rental Service Corp. (equipment leasing); Shape, Inc. (plastics); Signius Corp. (telecommunications); Zany Brainy (retail)

Rutgers Minority Investment Company
180 University Avenue, 3rd Floor
Newark, New Jersey 07102
(973) 353-5627

Fax: (973) 353-1110

Key contact:
Mr. Oscar Figueroa

Area served: Northeast

Preferred stages of financing: First stage, Second stage

Industries:
I.19   Generalist

William E. Simon & Sons, L.L.C.
310 South Street
P.O. Box 1913
Morristown, New Jersey 07962-1913
(973) 898-0290
Fax: (973) 829-0840

Key contact:
Mr. Mark Sellon
Mr. Robert Healy
Mr. Mark J. Butler
Mr. Conor T. Mullet
Mr. J. Peter Simon
Mr. William E. Simon

Area served: United States

Preferred stages of financing: Second stage, Mezzanine, LBO/MBO

Industries:
I.04   Broadcasting
I.09   Construction
I.11   Consumer products
I.15   Energy/natural resources/utilities
I.16   Entertainment
I.17   Environmental services/waste management
I.22   Industrial products
I.31   Real estate
I.34   Services (business)
I.35   Services (consumer)
I.36   Transportation

WM Sword & Company
34 Chambers Street
Princeton, New Jersey 08542
(609) 924-6710
Fax: (609) 924-3890
Web: wmsword.com

Key contact:
Mr. William Sword, Jr., Managing Director
Mr. Allan M. Benton, Managing Director

Description: Investment bank/merchant bank specializing in smaller to mid-sized transactions (up to $100 million in value).

Amount of capital invested: $25 million

Preferred investment size: $5-25 million

Area served: North America

Preferred stages of financing: Second stage, LBO/MBO, Expansion

Industries:
I.02   Agriculture/forestry/fishing/mining

I.04   Broadcasting
I.05   Chemicals
I.06   Communications
I.08   Computer software
I.10   Consulting
I.11   Consumer products
I.13   Education
I.15   Energy/natural resources/utilities
I.16   Entertainment
I.17   Environmental services/waste management
I.18   Financial services
I.19   Generalist
I.20   Healthcare
I.22   Industrial products
I.23   Information technology services
I.24   Internet services/e-commerce
I.26   Life sciences
I.27   Manufacturing
I.28   Media/publishing
I.30   New media
I.34   Services (business)
I.35   Services (consumer)

Technology Crossover Ventures
56 Main Street, Suite 210
Millburn, New Jersey (973) 467-5320
Fax: (973) 467-5323
E-mail: rbensky@tcv.com
Web: www.tcv.com

Key contact:
Mr. Robert C. Bensky, General Partner/CFO

Description: We focus exclusively on information technology, investing in expansion-stage private enterprises as well as select public situations.

Amount of capital invested: $37.4 million

Preferred investment size: $3-5 million

Amount under management: $100-500 million

Area served: Worldwide

Preferred stage of financing: Expansion

Industries:
I.06   Communications
I.07   Computer hardware

I.08   Computer software
I.14   Electronics
I.16   Entertainment
I.18   Financial services
I.21   High technology
I.23   Information technology services
I.24   Internet services/e-commerce
I.28   Media/publishing
I.30   New media
I.33   Semiconductors
I.34   Services (business)

Sampling of portfolio companies: Duet Technologies (provider of electronic design technology & networking software development services for high technology companies); IMX Mortgage Exchange (worldwide immediate access to mortgage origination products via a high speed private network); iVillage Women's Network (humanizing cyberspace & providing a relevant & indispensable online experience for adult women); Lynk Systems (merchant processor of credit & debit card transactions); Smart-

Patents (developer of business decision software systems that automate the process of relating patents to protected business & product strategies)

Technology Management & Funding, L.P.

707 State Road
Princeton, New Jersey 08540
(609) 921-2001
Fax: (609) 497-0998
E-mail: cristaldowning@tmflp.com
Web: www.tmflp.com

Key contact:
Mr. Harry Brener, Chairman/Co-Founder
Peter J. Cossman, Esq., Managing Director
Mr. Michael A. Gort, J.D., Managing Director
Mr. William Z. Marder, Managing Director
Richard Serbin, Esq., Managing Director
Dr. Anthony C. Warren, President/COO/Co-Founder

Description: We accelerate the process of building equity value in emerging high-technology companies, while minimizing investment risk. We bridge the gap between technological innovation and commercialization by establishing partnerships between small technology companies and major corporations. With over 50 companies in our portfolio, we have developed breakthrough technologies ranging from industrial products and biotechnology to software and telecommunications.

Industries:
I.03   Biotech/genetic engineering
I.05   Chemicals
I.06   Communications
I.07   Computer hardware
I.08   Computer software
I.14   Electronics
I.15   Energy/natural resources/utilities
I.27   Manufacturing
I.29   Medical/medical products

Sampling of portfolio companies: NTI Int'l., LLC (FDA-approved surfactant for disinfecting carcasses of cattle, poultry & seafood); Boron Biologicals, Inc. (diagnostic & therapeutic compounds derived by substituting boron for carbon or oxygen in known biomolecules); Aklimate, LLC (non-toxic, cost-effective passivation for metallic surfaces); Quantum Leap Innovations, Inc. (real time behavior based security products for computer telecommunication sectors); Intersignal, LLC (real time adaptive signal discrimination & channel sharing for the communications, entertainment & diagnostic industries); World Flywheel Consortium, Inc. (flywheel energy storage systems); Healthful Beverage Technologies, LLC (coffee-brewing process that extends pot life, removes acid & intensifies flavor); Ultrafast, Inc. (low cost, high precision fasteners & tools for the automotive, aerospace & construction industries); PECT Technologies, LLC (low cost, high voltage piezoelectric carbon fiber actuators); Omniplanar, Inc. (omni-directional bar-code readers); Laser Ablation Systems, Inc. (solvent free radiant energy surface stripping & cleansing); Carbon Composites Int'l., LLC (cost effective process for ultra high strength, lightweight carbon based materials); Environmental Foam Systems, Inc. (high performance ceramic/polymer foam composites); Porodigm, LLC (liquid crystal polymer membranes with engineered porosity); Tissue Harvest, LLC (safer, more efficient skin grafts for burns & wounds); Foam Delivery Systems, LLC (unique non-aqueous foam systems for healthcare, cosmetic products & edible food products); Liquid Tablet, LLC (superior delivery systems for masking the taste of orally administered products); Flexsoft Int'l., LLC (intrinsically correct software automation); KATrix, Inc. (animation of fully intelligent, real time interactive characters for multimedia entertainment, film production & the internet); Cash On Demand, Inc. (low cost, dial-up telecommunications for financial transactions)

The Vertical Group

18 Bank Street
Summit, New Jersey 07901
(908) 277-3737
Fax: (908) 273-9434

Key contact:
Mr. Richard Emmitt

Industries:
I.20   Healthcare
I.29   Medical/medical products

Westford Technology Ventures, L.P.

17 Academy Street, Suite 515
Newark, New Jersey 07102
(973) 624-2131
Fax: (973) 624-2008

Key contact:
Mr. Jeffrey T. Hamilton
Ms. Susan J. Trammell

Area served: Northeast

Preferred stages of financing: Seed, Start up, First stage

Industries:
I.05   Chemicals
I.06   Communications
I.07   Computer hardware
I.08   Computer software
I.14   Electronics
I.23   Information technology services

New Mexico

Arch Venture Partners

1155 University Boulevard SE
Albuquerque, New Mexico 87106
(505) 843-4293
Fax: (505) 843-4294
E-mail: cwb@archventure.com
Web: www.archventure.com

Key contact:
Mr. Clint Bybee, Managing Director

Description: We invest in the development of early
stage technology companies which have the potential
to grow rapidly into substantial enterprises. We
invest primarily in companies we co-found with
leading scientists and entrepreneurs, concentrating
on bringing to market technological innovations
developed from academics and corporate research.

Amount of capital invested: $20 million

Preferred investment size: $1 million

Amount under management: $100-500 million

Area served: United States

Preferred stages of financing: Seed, Start up, First
stage

Industries:
I.03   Biotech/genetic engineering
I.05   Chemicals
I.06   Communications
I.07   Computer hardware
I.08   Computer software
I.13   Education
I.14   Electronics
I.20   Healthcare
I.21   High technology
I.23   Information technology services
I.24   Internet services/e-commerce
I.26   Life sciences
I.33   Semiconductors

Sampling of portfolio companies: Adolor Corp. (biopharmaceutical); Appliant Corp. (software); Apropos
Corp. (software); Bell Geospace (oil field services);
Caliper Technologies Corp. (microfluidics); DeCode
Genetics (genomic information); Genvec (gene
therapy); Intelligent Reasoning Systems (electronic
test equipment); Internet Dynamics (internet
software); Nanophase Technologies (ultra fine
ceramic materials); New Era of Networks (applications integration software); Optobionics (opto-electronic retinal implants); R2 Technology (computer-
aided diagnosis of mammograms); Siliscape (virtual
displays); RWT Corp. (manufacturing execution
software)

Murphree & Company Inc.

1155 University Boulevard SE
Albuquerque, New Mexico 87106
(505) 843-4277
Fax: (505) 843-4278
E-mail: tomsteph@murphco.com

Key contact:
Mr. Thomas J. Stephenson

Description: We are an early stage investor with a
primary focus in the Southwestern U.S-mainly in
Texas, New Mexico and Colorado. Investments are
currently being made through Murphree Venture
Partners IV, L.P.-a $50 million early stage fund
which focuses primarily on high tech opportunities.

Preferred investment size: $1 million

Area served: United States

Preferred stages of financing: Seed, Start up, First
stage

Industries:
I.01   Aerospace
I.03   Biotech/genetic engineering
I.06   Communications
I.07   Computer hardware
I.08   Computer software
I.14   Electronics
I.21   High technology
I.23   Information technology services
I.24   Internet services/e-commerce
I.26   Life sciences
I.29   Medical/medical products
I.33   Semiconductors

Sampling of portfolio companies: Activerse Inc.
(software which creates real-time collaboration over
the internet); Ensyn Technologies Ltd. (creates
biofuel by converting waste wood & wood products
into synthetic oil for energy generation & food additives); E-Stamp Corp. (patented PC-based software/
hardware system to create postage in lieu of stamps or
metering); FFPI Industries Inc. (patented fiber optic/
laser-based sensors to detect changes in pressure,
deflection, temperature & cavitation); MicroOptical
Devices Inc. (VCSEL laser manufacturing utilizing
Sandia-developed intellectual property); ModelOffice Inc. (develops software applications that
provide shortcuts for writing tasks including sample
documents, forms & templates); Physix Inc.
(develops medical software systems to provide handheld solutions for doctors & nurses in lieu of written
charts, prescriptions, etc.) World.hire Inc. (software
for recruiting & screening employment candidates via
corporate intranets & the internet); Wintel Inc.
(scheduling & routing software for mobile field
personnel in industries such as home healthcare,
home repair, utilities, etc.); Adaptive Learning Technologies Inc. (educational software which dynamically modifies itself to best suit a child's learning
style); Journee Inc. (java based software company
developing rapidly-deploying business enterprise
software for the $6 billion ERP market)

Technology Ventures Corporation
1155 University Boulevard SE
Albuquerque, New Mexico 87106
(505) 246-2882
Fax: (505) 246-2891

Key contact:
Mr. Randy Wilson
Mr. Sherman McCorkle

Area served: Southwest

Preferred stages of financing: Seed, Start up, First
stage, Second stage

Industries:
I.19   Generalist

New York

Aberlyn Holding Company
500 Fifth Avenue, Suite 730
New York, New York 10110
(212) 391-7750
Fax: (212) 391-7762

Key contact:
Mr. Lawrence M. Hoffman, Chairman/CEO
Mr. Henry G. Geyer, President
Mr. Andrew Stanhope, Managing Director

Area served: Europe, North America

Preferred stages of financing: First stage, Second
stage, Mezzanine, LBO/MBO, Expansion, Venture
leasing

Industries:
I.03   Biotech/genetic engineering
I.20   Healthcare
I.26   Life sciences
I.29   Medical/medical products

Advanta Partners, LP
712 Fifth Avenue
New York, New York 10019
(212) 649-6900
Fax: (212) 956-3301
E-mail: gneems@advanta.com
Web: www.advanta.com

Key contact:
Mr. Gary Neems, Managing Director

Description: We differentiate ourselves by providing
the knowledge, resources and experience which
comes from industry specialization and the insights
of a strategic partner. Specifically, we are looking for
companies that can benefit from our expertise in
direct marketing, market segmentation, database
management, consumer behavior modeling, transaction processing and electronic commerce.

Amount of capital invested: $25 million

Preferred investment size: $5-25 million

Amount under management: $100-500 million

Area served: United States

Preferred stages of financing: Second stage, LBO/
MBO, Expansion

Industries:
I.08   Computer software
I.18   Financial services
I.23   Information technology services
I.34   Services (business)
I.35   Services (consumer)

Sampling of portfolio companies: HNC Software
(neural network software); Innovative Services of
America (sophisticated inbound teleservices); RMH
Teleservices (high-volume telemarketer); Brightware
(internet-based intelligent software); JDR (accounts
receivable management); Great Expectations (video
dating service); Harmonic Systems (on-line interactive applications for retail chains); Sky Alland
Marketing (relationship marketing firm)

Amerindo Investment Advisors Inc.
399 Park Avenue, 22nd Floor
New York, New York 10022
(212) 371-6360
Fax: (212) 371-6988
E-mail: murray@amerindo.com
Web: www.amerindo.com

Key contact:
Mr. Robert Murray

Description: We are a minority-owned emerging
growth small cap stock manager specializing in
leading edge technology-oriented companies
including biotechnology and allied small healthcare,
electronics and software and companies benefiting
from technological advances. Our research team is
composed of three portfolio managers and seven
analysts. Stock selection is based on original funda-

mental research, confirmed by technical factors such
as price momentum, with an 18 to 24 month time
horizon. Portfolios are generally concentrated and
contain about 12 to 20 issues when fully invested.

Amount of capital invested: $24,700,000

Amount under management: >$1 billion

Area served: United States

Preferred stages of financing: First stage, Second
stage, Mezzanine, Privates

Industries:
I.03   Biotech/genetic engineering
I.06   Communications
I.07   Computer hardware
I.08   Computer software

I.14   Electronics
I.20   Healthcare
I.21   High technology
I.23   Information technology services
I.24   Internet services/e-commerce

Sampling of portfolio companies: Company "A" (operating resource management (ORM) solutions); Company "B" (world wide web & tv programmer & information provider); Company "C" (multicast networking technology)

Arch Venture Partners

45 Rockefeller Plaza, Suite 2520
New York, New York 10020
(212) 262-7260
Fax: (212) 397-1782
E-mail: mjm@archventure.com

Key contact:
Mr. Mark Mendel

Description: We invest in the development of early stage technology companies which have the potential to grow rapidly into substantial enterprises. We invest primarily in companies we co-found with leading scientists and entrepreneurs, concentrating on bringing to market technological innovations developed from academics and corporate research.

Amount of capital invested: $20 million

Preferred investment size: $1 million

Amount under management: $100-500 million

Area served: United States

Preferred stages of financing: Seed, Start up, First stage

Industries:
I.03   Biotech/genetic engineering
I.05   Chemicals
I.06   Communications
I.07   Computer hardware
I.08   Computer software
I.13   Education
I.14   Electronics
I.20   Healthcare
I.21   High technology
I.23   Information technology services
I.24   Internet services/e-commerce
I.26   Life sciences
I.33   Semiconductors

Sampling of portfolio companies: Adolor Corp. (biopharmaceutical); Appliant Corp. (software); Apropos Corp. (software); Bell Geospace (oil field services); Caliper Technologies Corp. (microfluidics); DeCode Genetics (genomic information); Genvec (gene therapy); Intelligent Reasoning Systems (electronic test equipment); Internet Dynamics (internet software); Nanophase Technologies (ultra fine ceramic materials); New Era of Networks (applications integration software); Optobionics (opto-electronic retinal implants); R2 Technology (computer-aided diagnosis of mammograms); Siliscape (virtual displays); RWT Corp. (manufacturing execution software)

Barclays Capital Investors Corp.

222 Broadway, 7th Floor
New York, New York 10038
(212) 412-3937
Fax: (212) 412-6780

Key contact:
Mr. Graham McGahen, President

Preferred stages of financing: Second stage, Mezzanine, LBO/MBO

Industries:
I.03   Biotech/genetic engineering
I.05   Chemicals
I.06   Communications
I.07   Computer hardware
I.08   Computer software
I.11   Consumer products
I.14   Electronics
I.27   Manufacturing
I.29   Medical/medical products
I.32   Retail

Behrman Capital

126 East 56th Street
New York, New York 10022
(212) 980-6500
Fax: (212) 980-7024
E-mail: dbaerga@behrmancap.com

Key contact:
Mr. Darryl Behrman, Managing Partner
Mr. Grant Behrman, Managing Partner

Description: We are a private investment firm with $67 million under management (1996). Founded in 1992, we invest in management buyouts of growth companies in a diverse group of industries: software, information services, music publishing, healthcare, light manufacturing. We have invested in over 30 companies. Ninety percent of our investors are institutional investors.

Founded: 1992

Area served: United States

Preferred stages of financing: First stage, Second stage, Mezzanine, LBO/MBO

Industries:
I.06   Communications
I.07   Computer hardware
I.08   Computer software
I.14   Electronics
I.20   Healthcare
I.27   Manufacturing
I.29   Medical/medical products

Sampling of portfolio companies: Chappell & Co. (music publishers); Sanmina Corp. (printed circuit boards); Ross Systems (financial application software); 3COM Inc. (LAN systems); Linear Technologies (supplier of linear integrated circuits)

Bessemer Venture Partners

1400 Old Country Road, Suite 407
Westbury, New York 11590
(516) 997-2300
Fax: (516) 997-2371
Web: www.bessemervp.com

Key contact:
Mr. Robert H. Buescher, Partner

Description: Providing venture capital to entrepreneurial teams for over two decades.

Amount of capital invested: $50 million

Preferred investment size: $500,000-5 million

Amount under management: $100-500 million

Area served: United States

Preferred stages of financing: Seed, Start up, First stage, Second stage, Mezzanine, LBO/MBO, Expansion

Industries:
I.01   Aerospace
I.02   Agriculture/forestry/fishing/mining
I.03   Biotech/genetic engineering
I.04   Broadcasting
I.05   Chemicals
I.06   Communications
I.07   Computer hardware
I.08   Computer software
I.09   Construction
I.10   Consulting
I.11   Consumer products
I.12   Distribution
I.13   Education
I.14   Electronics
I.15   Energy/natural resources/utilities
I.16   Entertainment
I.17   Environmental services/waste management
I.18   Financial services
I.19   Generalist
I.20   Healthcare
I.21   High technology
I.22   Industrial products
I.23   Information technology services
I.24   Internet services/e-commerce
I.25   Leisure/hospitality
I.26   Life sciences
I.27   Manufacturing
I.28   Media/publishing
I.29   Medical/medical products
I.30   New media
I.31   Real estate
I.32   Retail
I.33   Semiconductors
I.34   Services (business)
I.35   Services (consumer)
I.36   Transportation
I.37   Wholesale

Sampling of portfolio companies: Aptis Communications (communications); Omni Communications (communications); Ungermann-Bass (communications); Extraprise (internet & intranet); VeriSign (internet & intranet); CPort (semiconductors/components); Quantum Effect Design (semiconductors/components); InCert Software (software); Metapath (software); Veritas (software); Celcore (wireless); Triton Networks (wireless); Domain Home Furnishings (retail & consumer goods); Timothy's Coffees (retail & consumer goods); Community First Bankshares (financial services); Arris Pharmaceuticals (biotechnology); Synergy Health Care (healthcare information systems); Allscrips Pharmaceuticals (healthcare services); Providers' Assurance (healthcare services); EPIX Medical (medical products & devices)

Bradford Equities Fund, LLC

1 Rockefeller Plaza, Suite 1722
New York, New York 10020
(212) 218-6900
Fax: (212) 218-6901

Key contact:
Mr. Robert J. Simon, Senior Managing Director
Mr. Thomas L. Ferguson, Managing Director
Mr. Noel E. Wilens, Managing Director

Description: We make controlling equity investments in management-led buyouts of well-managed, niche, profitable industrial manufacturers and distributors with annual revenues between $15 million and $65 million.

Amount of capital invested: $20 million

Preferred investment size: $10 million

Amount under management: $100-500 million

Area served: North America

Preferred stage of financing: LBO/MBO

Industries:
I.01   Aerospace
I.05   Chemicals
I.11   Consumer products
I.12   Distribution
I.19   Generalist
I.22   Industrial products
I.27   Manufacturing

Sampling of portfolio companies: Ampco Metal Inc. (metals); Pamarco Technologies, Inc. (printing equipment & supplies); Paramount Cards, Inc. (greeting cards); Tefco Technologies, Inc. (paper converting); Adco Technologies Inc. (specialty chemicals); Holopak Technologies Inc. (paper converting); The Sunbelt Companies (building materials & supplies); C. R. Gibson (stationery/gift books)

Bristol Capital Management, Inc.

155 East 76th Street
New York, New York 10021
(212) 879-1202
Fax: (212) 879-1150

E-mail: alan.donenfeld@usa.net

Key contact:
Mr. Alan P. Donenfeld, President

Description: We manage the capital requirements of small businesses requiring growth capital. Financings include common equity, preferred stock and subordinated debt. Management involvement is required. We pride ourselves on responding quickly to financing requests.

Amount of capital invested: $5.3 million

Preferred investment size: $3 million

Amount under management: $10-25 million

Area served: United States

Preferred stages of financing: Mezzanine, LBO/MBO, Expansion

Industries:
I.03   Biotech/genetic engineering
I.06   Communications
I.07   Computer hardware
I.08   Computer software
I.11   Consumer products
I.16   Entertainment
I.20   Healthcare
I.21   High technology
I.22   Industrial products
I.23   Information technology services
I.25   Leisure/hospitality
I.26   Life sciences
I.27   Manufacturing
I.28   Media/publishing
I.29   Medical/medical products
I.30   New media
I.34   Services (business)
I.35   Services (consumer)

Sampling of portfolio companies: Materials Communications & Computers, Inc. (systems integration); Agri-Foods International (food technology); Team Entertainment (TV production); Manorgate Telecommunications (UK local & long distance telecom service); Marine Management System (software development & applications)

BT Capital Partners

130 Liberty Street, 25th Floor
New York, New York 10006
(212) 250-5563
Fax: (212) 250-7651

Key contact:
Mr. Doug Brent

Description: Established in 1972 as venture capital unit of Banker's Trust Company. Serve a wide range of industries at second/later round of investment need.

Founded: 1972

Preferred investment size: Over $5 million

Preferred stages of financing: Second stage, LBO/MBO

Industries:
I.11   Consumer products
I.20   Healthcare
I.29   Medical/medical products

William A.M. Burden & Company, L.P.

10 East 53rd Street, 32nd Floor
New York, New York 10022
(212) 872-1133
Fax: (212) 872-1199
E-mail: jweber@wambco.com

Key contact:
Mr. Jeffrey Weber

Founded: 1949

Preferred investment size: $1 million

Preferred stages of financing: Mezzanine, LBO/MBO, Special situations

Industries:
I.04   Broadcasting
I.05   Chemicals
I.06   Communications
I.09   Construction
I.11   Consumer products
I.12   Distribution
I.13   Education
I.14   Electronics
I.15   Energy/natural resources/utilities
I.19   Generalist
I.22   Industrial products
I.28   Media/publishing
I.29   Medical/medical products
I.31   Real estate
I.35   Services (consumer)

Calgary Enterprises, Inc.

Four Park Avenue, Suite 12G
New York, New York 10016
(212) 683-0119
Fax: (212) 683-3119
E-mail: calgary@styx.ios.com

Key contact:
Mr. Steven Insalaco, President

Description: We are a corporate financial advisory investment banking and/or management consulting firm that utilizes its resources on behalf of a client.

Preferred investment size: $5 million and over

Area served: North America

Preferred stages of financing: Start up, First stage, Second stage, Mezzanine, LBO/MBO, Expansion

Industries:
I.19   Generalist

Capital Access Partners

40 Oriole Avenue
Bronxville, New York 10708
E-mail: capital@inch.com
Web: www.inch.com/~capital/

Key contact:
Mr. George C. McKinnis, Chairman
Mr. John Hammer, President
Mr. Allan Gerard, Vice President

Description: We specialize in early stage firms (not seed) with unique technology producing software, electronics, telecommunciations, internet or medical device products in the Northeast U.S.

Preferred investment size: $2.5-3 million

Area served: United States

Preferred stages of financing: Start up, First stage, Second stage

Industries:
I.06	Communications
I.07	Computer hardware
I.08	Computer software
I.14	Electronics
I.20	Healthcare
I.21	High technology
I.22	Industrial products
I.33	Semiconductors

CB Health Ventures

452 Fifth Avenue, Suite 2500
New York, New York 10018
(212) 869-5600
Fax: (212) 869-6418
E-mail: bob@health-ventures.com

Key contact:
Mr. Robert B. Schulz, Manager

Description: We are a group of seasoned professionals investing in early and emerging companies with new products, services or technology addressing large markets in healthcare. We seek to leverage our experience and considerable resources to contribute to the speed of development and market acceptance of our portfolio companies.

Preferred investment size: $2.5-5 million

Area served: Canada, United States

Preferred stages of financing: First stage, Second stage, Mezzanine, Expansion

Industries:
I.03	Biotech/genetic engineering
I.20	Healthcare
I.26	Life sciences
I.29	Medical/medical products

Chase Capital Partners

380 Madison Avenue, 12th Floor
New York, New York 10017-2070
(212) 622-3100
Fax: (212) 622-4606

Key contact:
Mr. John R. Baron, General Partner
Mr. Jeffrey C. Walker, Managing Partner
Mr. Michael R. Hannon, Partner
Mr. Donald J. Hofmann, Partner
Mr. Stephen P. Murray, Partner
Mr. Brian J. Richmand, Partner
Dr. Damion E. Wicker, Partner
Mr. George E. Kelts, III, Managing Director/CAO
Mr. Christopher C. Behrens, Principal
Mr. John Daileader, Principal
Mr. J. Robert Greene, Principal
Mr. W. Brett Ingersoll, Principal
Mr. John M. B. O'Connor, Partner
Mr. Eric Green, Managing Director
Mr. Richard D. Waters, Managing Director
Mr. James D. Kallman, Partner
Mr. Dwight I. Arnesen, Vice President
Mr. Mathew Lori, Principal
Mr. Jonathan R. Lynch, Principal
Ms. Kelly E. Shackleford, Principal
Mr. Jonas L. Steinman, Principal
Mr. Timothy J. Walsh, Principal
Mr. Michael C. Boyd, Associate
Ms. Maeve E. Dempsey, Marketing Associate
Mr. Dorlan Faust, Associate
Mr. Jason Friedman, Associate
Mr. Charles M. B. Goldman, Associate
Mr. Jeffrey J. Logan, Associate

Mr. Paul V. Roberts, Associate
Mr. Brian H. Toolan, Associate

Description: We are a global partnership with approximately $5.5 billion under management. We are a leading provider of private equity and have closed over 550 individual transactions since our inception in 1984. Our sole limited partner is The Chase Manhattan Corporation, the largest bank holding company in the United States with total assets of approximately $340 billion.

Founded: 1984

Amount under management: >$1 billion

Area served: Asia, Europe, North America, Latin America

Preferred stages of financing: Mezzanine, LBO/MBO

Industries:
I.01	Aerospace
I.03	Biotech/genetic engineering
I.04	Broadcasting
I.05	Chemicals
I.06	Communications
I.07	Computer hardware
I.08	Computer software
I.11	Consumer products
I.12	Distribution
I.13	Education
I.14	Electronics
I.15	Energy/natural resources/utilities
I.16	Entertainment
I.17	Environmental services/waste management

I.18	Financial services	I.28	Media/publishing
I.20	Healthcare	I.29	Medical/medical products
I.22	Industrial products	I.31	Real estate
I.23	Information technology services	I.32	Retail
I.25	Leisure/hospitality		

Citicorp Venture Capital, Ltd.

399 Park Avenue
14th Floor, Zone 4
New York, New York 10043
(212) 559-1127
Fax: (212) 527-2496

Key contact:
Mr. Richard Cashin
Mr. William Comfort

Area served: United States

Preferred stages of financing: Second stage, LBO/MBO, Third/later stage

Industries:
I.03 Biotech/genetic engineering
I.06 Communications
I.07 Computer hardware
I.08 Computer software
I.11 Consumer products
I.14 Electronics
I.15 Energy/natural resources/utilities
I.19 Generalist
I.29 Medical/medical products
I.32 Retail
I.36 Transportation

Coleman Venture Group

5909 Northern Boulevard
P.O. Box 244
East Norwich, New York 11732
(516) 626-3642
(516) 626-2722
Fax: (516) 626-9722

Key contact:
Mr. Gregory S. Coleman, President

Description: We have restricted ourselves to only high tech startup positions where we take an equity position. Areas such as semiconductors, specialized circuits and innovative materials are areas which we might consider. Strongly suggest a phone call or executive summary be sent on to us before any business plan.

Amount of capital invested: $700,000

Amount under management: <$10 million

Preferred stage of financing: Start up

Industries:
I.14 Electronics
I.21 High technology

Communications Equity Associates, Inc.

375 Park Avenue, Suite 3808
New York, New York 10152
(212) 319-1968
Fax: (212) 319-4293
Web: www.commequ.com

Key contact:
Mr. J. Patrick Michaels, Chairman/CEO
Mr. Harold Ewen
Mr. Bruno Claude
Mr. George Pollock
Mr. Ming Jung
Mr. Thomas W. Cardy, Executive Vice President
Mr. Scott N. Feuer, Vice President
Mr. Bryan L. Crino, Senior Associate

Description: We have a rich 25-year history of diverse experiences and milestone industry accomplishments which establish us as a worldwide leader. By combining the sophisticated skills of a large Wall Street investment firm with a focus on communications industries, we offer a depth of service that's unparalleled. The experience of our professionals speaks for itself: since our founding, we have completed more than 600 transactions, valued at more than $13 billion. With an extensive network of long-standing relationships and offices on almost every continent, along with our affiliates, we have helped clients in 27 countries successfully pursue their financial and strategic goals.

Founded: 1973

Preferred investment size: No more than 15% of the total fund

Amount under management: $100-500 million

Area served: Worldwide

Preferred stages of financing: LBO/MBO, Growth

Industries:
I.04 Broadcasting
I.06 Communications
I.16 Entertainment
I.23 Information technology services
I.24 Internet services/e-commerce
I.28 Media/publishing

Compass Technology Partners

128 East 31st Street
New York, New York 10016-6848
(212) 685-2763
Fax: (212) 689-5301

Key contact:
Mr. Leon Dulberger

Area served: United States

Preferred stages of financing: Mezzanine, LBO/MBO

Industries:
I.04 Broadcasting
I.06 Communications
I.07 Computer hardware
I.08 Computer software
I.11 Consumer products
I.12 Distribution
I.14 Electronics
I.17 Environmental services/waste management
I.29 Medical/medical products
I.33 Semiconductors
I.35 Services (consumer)

Cornerstone Equity Investors, LLC
717 Fifth Avenue, 11th Floor
New York, New York 10022
(212) 753-0901
Fax: (212) 826-6798

Key contact:
Mr. Robert Getz

Preferred stage of financing: LBO/MBO

Industries:
I.06 Communications
I.14 Electronics
I.18 Financial services
I.28 Media/publishing

Corporate Venture Partners, L.P.
171 East State Street, Suite 261
Ithaca, New York 14850
(607) 277-8024
Fax: (607) 277-8027
E-mail: dsp@cvpventures.com

Key contact:
Mr. Steve Puricelli, General Partner
Mr. David Costine, General Partner

Preferred stage of financing: First stage

Industries:
I.06 Communications
I.14 Electronics
I.20 Healthcare
I.22 Industrial products
I.29 Medical/medical products

CVF Corporation
300 International Drive, Suite 100
Williamsville, New York 14221
(716) 626-3044
Fax: (716) 626-3001
Web: www.cvfcorp.com

Key contact:
Mr. Jeffrey Dreben, Director/President/CEO
Mr. Robert Nally, Director/Secretary/Treasurer
Mr. George Khouri, Director/Consultant
Mr. Lawrence Casse, Vice President

Description: We are a public holding company whose principal business is sourcing, funding and managing emerging companies with proprietary or patented technologies and significant market potential. Founded in 1989, early and continuing shareholders include a number of major institutional investors, insurance companies and corporate pension funds. Our holdings include seven companies in three business areas. The three sectors that we focus on are: process control/industrial automation, information technology/security systems, bio-agriculture/environmental solutions.

Founded: 1989

Preferred stage of financing: Mezzanine

Industries:
I.17 Environmental services/waste management
I.23 Information technology services

Sampling of portfolio companies: Ecoval; SRE Controls; TurboSonic; Dantec Systems Corp.; Gemprint; PetroZyme; Biorem

CW Group, Inc.
1041 Third Avenue, 2nd Floor
New York, New York 10021
(212) 308-5266
Fax: (212) 644-0354

Key contact:
Mr. Walter Channing
Mr. Charles Hartman

Mr. Barry Weinberg

Preferred stages of financing: Seed, Start up

Industries:
I.03 Biotech/genetic engineering
I.29 Medical/medical products

D. H. Blair
44 Wall Street, 2nd Floor
New York, New York 10005
(212) 495-5000
Fax: (212) 269-1438

Key contact:
Mr. Leonard A. Katz
Mr. Martin A. Bell
Mr. J. Morton Davis
Mr. Andrew H. Plevin

Mr. Jonathan Turkel

Preferred stages of financing: First stage, LBO/MBO

Industries:
I.03 Biotech/genetic engineering
I.05 Chemicals
I.06 Communications
I.08 Computer software
I.11 Consumer products
I.12 Distribution

I.14	Electronics	I.29	Medical/medical products
I.15	Energy/natural resources/utilities	I.31	Real estate
I.28	Media/publishing		

East Coast Venture Capital, Inc.

313 West 53rd Street
New York, New York 10019
(212) 245-6460
Fax: (212) 265-2962

Key contact:
Mr. Zindel Zelmanovitch

Area served: Northeast

Preferred stage of financing: Seed

Industries:
I.19   Generalist

Electra Fleming, Inc.

320 Park Avenue, 28th Floor
New York, New York 10022
(212) 319-0081
Fax: (212) 319-3069
E-mail: efinc@electrafleming.com

Key contact:
Mr. Peter A. Carnwath, Managing Director
Ms. Diane M. Smith, Principal
Mr. Barry C. Twomey, Principal
Mr. Scott D. Steele, Principal
Mr. Carl C. Cordova, Principal
Mr. David W. Shorrock, Senior Associate
Mr. Hunter Bost, Senior Associate

Description: We are an international private equity
firm with over 50 investment professionals based in
London, Continental Europe, the USA, Latin
America and Asia. We currently have over $2 billion
under management. Our US office focuses on investment opportunities in North and South America.

Amount of capital invested: $110 million

Preferred investment size: $10-30 million

Amount under management: $100-500 million

Area served: Worldwide

Preferred stages of financing: Second stage, Mezzanine, LBO/MBO, Expansion, Int'l expansion

Industries:
I.01	Aerospace
I.02	Agriculture/forestry/fishing/mining
I.04	Broadcasting
I.06	Communications
I.09	Construction
I.10	Consulting
I.11	Consumer products
I.12	Distribution
I.13	Education
I.16	Entertainment

I.17	Environmental services/waste management
I.18	Financial services
I.19	Generalist
I.20	Healthcare
I.22	Industrial products
I.25	Leisure/hospitality
I.27	Manufacturing
I.28	Media/publishing
I.29	Medical/medical products
I.32	Retail
I.34	Services (business)
I.35	Services (consumer)
I.36	Transportation
I.37	Wholesale

Sampling of portfolio companies: Act III Cinemas
(cinema chain); American Medical Plans (health
maintenance organization); American White Cross
(private label health & personal care products manufacturer); AmSurg (owner & operator of practice-
based surgery centers); Appliance Corporation of
America (manufacturer of kitchen appliances); Auto
Parts Club (chain of retail & commercial stores); The
Benjamin Company (airport bookstores & newsstand
operator); Career Education (operator of private,
post-secondary continuing education schools);
Dakota, Minnesota & Eastern Railroad (regional
railroad operator); Family Christian Stores (christian
prodcuts retailer); International Garden Products
(garden products group); International Wireless
Communications (wireless telecommunications);
Landmark Healthcare (alternative healthcare); Leiner
Health Products (manufacturer of vitamins & nutritional supplements); Lids Corporation (chain of retail
stores & kiosks); Loyalty Management (operator of
travel loyalty programs); North American Health
Plans (managed care organization); O-Cedar Brands
(mop & broom manufacturer); OMNA Medical
Partners (neuromusculoskeletal physician practice
management); Paul Sebastian (fragrance manufacturer)

Elk Associates Funding Corporation

747 Third Avenue
New York, New York 10017
(212) 421-2111
Fax: (212) 421-3488

Key contact:
Ms. Sylvia DiGirolamo
Mr. Gary C. Granoff

Area served: Northeast

Preferred stage of financing: Later stage

Industries:
I.36   Transportation

EOS Partners, L.P.

320 Park Avenue, 22nd Floor
New York, New York 10022
(212) 832-5800
Fax: (212) 832-5815

Key contact:
Mr. Mark L. First, Managing Director
Mr. Steven M. Friedman, General Partner
Mr. Brian D. Young, General Partner
Mr. Douglas R. Korn, Managing Director
Mr. David Lee, Principal

Description: We are a private investment partnership
that seeks to make long term investments in companies where substantial appreciation can be achieved
by bringing our capital and financial expertise into
partnership with management.

Preferred investment size: $3-5 million

Preferred stages of financing: LBO/MBO, Expansion

Industries:
I.15   Energy/natural resources/utilities
I.20   Healthcare
I.23   Information technology services
I.27   Manufacturing
I.34   Services (business)
I.36   Transportation

Esquire Capital Corp.

69 Veterans Memorial Highway
Commack, New York 11725
(516) 462-6946
Fax: (516) 864-8152

Key contact:
Mr. Frederick Eliassen

Mr. Wen-Chan Chin

Preferred stage of financing: Second stage

Industries:
I.19   Generalist

Exeter Group of Funds

10 East 53rd Street, 32nd Floor
New York, New York 10022
(212) 872-1170
Fax: (212) 872-1198

Key contact:
Mr. Keith Fox
Mr. Kurt Bergquist
Mr. Timothy Bradley
Ms. Karen J. Watai
Mr. Jeff Weber

Area served: United States

Preferred stages of financing: Second stage, LBO/
MBO

Industries:
I.12   Distribution
I.15   Energy/natural resources/utilities
I.19   Generalist
I.27   Manufacturing

Exim Capital Corp.

241 5th Avenue, 3rd Floor
New York, New York 10016
(212) 683-3375
Fax: (212) 689-4118

Key contact:
Mr. Victor Chun

Area served: Northeast

Preferred stages of financing: LBO/MBO, Third/later
stage

First County Capital, Inc.

135-14 Northern Boulevard, 2nd Floor
Flushing, New York 11354
(718) 461-1778
Fax: (718) 461-1835

Key contact:
Mr. Orest Glut

Area served: North

Preferred stages of financing: Seed, Start up, First
stage, Second stage

Industries:
I.27   Manufacturing
I.32   Retail
I.34   Services (business)
I.35   Services (consumer)

Flushing Capital Corporation

39-06 Union Street, Room 20
Flushing, New York 11354
(718) 886-5866
Fax: (718) 939-7761

Key contact:
Mr. Frank J. Mitchell

Preferred stage of financing: Third/later stage

JG Fogg & Company, Inc./Westbury Capital Partners, L.P.

400 Post Avenue
Westbury, New York 11590
(516) 333-0218
Fax: (516) 333-2724

Key contact:
Mr. Jeffrey Freed
Mr. John Almeida
Mr. Joseph G. Fogg, III

Mr. Richard Sicoli

Area served: Canada, United States

Preferred stages of financing: Second stage, LBO/MBO

Industries:
I.19   Generalist

Freshstart Venture Capital Corporation

313 West 53rd Street
New York, New York 10019
(212) 265-2249
Fax: (212) 265-2962

Key contact:
Mr. Zindel Zelmanovich

Industries:
I.19   Generalist

Furman Selz SBIC, L.P.

230 Park Avenue
New York, New York 10169
(212) 309-8348
(212) 309-8200
Fax: (212) 692-9608

Key contact:
Mr. Brian Friedman, Manager

Preferred stages of financing: Second stage, Third/later stage

Galen Partners

610 Fifth Avenue, 5th Floor
New York, New York 10020
(212) 218-4990
Fax: (212) 218-4999
Web: www.galen-partners.com

Key contact:
Mr. William R. Grant, General Partner
Mr. Bruce F. Wesson, General Partner
Dr. L. John Wilkerson, General Partner
Mr. Srini Conjeevaram, General Partner
Mr. David W. Jahns, General Partner
Mr. Zubeen Shroff, General Partner

Description: We specialize in private equity, mid-to-late stage investments within the health care sector. Over its eight year history, we have launched three venture funds with $400 million under management. We focus on several sectors of healthcare including unique devices, healthcare services, disease management, healthcare information services and technology.

Amount of capital invested: $35 million

Preferred investment size: $10-15 million

Amount under management: $100-500 million

Area served: United States

Preferred stages of financing: First stage, Second stage, LBO/MBO, Expansion

Industries:
I.20   Healthcare
I.29   Medical/medical products

Sampling of portfolio companies: Affiliated Research Centers, Inc. (clinical trial site management company); Axion HealthCare, Inc. (cancer-focused pharmaceutical company); The Compucare Co. (healthcare information systems for hospitals & MCO's); DAOU Systems, Inc. (computer network systems provider exclusively serving the healthcare industry); Derma Sciences, Inc. (develops, markets & sells wound care products for the management of non-healing skin ulcerations such as pressure & venous ulcers, surgical incisions & burns); DeVilbiss Health Care, Inc. (respiratory equipment: oxygen, nebulizers, humidifiers, vaporizers); EMR, Inc. (medical monitoring & workers compensation management); Fountainhead Water Co., Inc. (bottles & distributes the highest quality pure spring water); Halsey Drug Co., Inc. (manufactures generic drugs in bulk pharmaceutical chemical, solid dosage & liquid forms sold to distributors, wholesalers, drug store chains, institutions, government agencies & other pharmaceutical manufacturers nationwide); Medicode, Inc. (services providers & payors with claims adjudication software & databases); MiniMed Inc. (manufactures & distributes microinfusion pumps & related devices for the management of diabetes); OnCare Inc. (oncology physician practice management); Paradigm Health Corp. (provider of high quality catastrophic rehabilitation services for complex neurologic cases with shared risk, turnkey pricing); Pyxis Corp. (provider of closed loop inventory distribution systems to hospitals & long-term care facilities); qmed, Inc. (manufactures & sells a broad line of medical diagnostic devices including a disease management system for the treatment of coronary artery disease); Stericycle, Inc. (provider of regulated medical waste management services utilizing proprietary technology); Taro Pharmaceutical Industries Ltd. (manufacturer & developer of generic drugs & pharmaceutical compounds); TheraTx, Inc. (sub-acute & long-term care rehabilitation); Vivus, Inc. (provider of therapeutic systems for the treatment of erectile dysfunction); Walsh Int'l., Inc. (sales & marketing systems provider to healthcare companies)

Generation Partners

551 Fifth Avenue, 31st Floor
New York, New York 10176
(212) 450-8500
Fax: (212) 450-8550

Key contact:
Mr. Paul F. Balser, Managing Partner
Mr. John A. Hawkins, Managing Partner
Mr. Mark E. Jennings, Managing Partner
Mr. Lloyd Mandell, Vice President
Mr. Robert M. Pflieger, Vice President
Mr. John S. Schnabel, Vice President/CFO
Mr. Andrew Shinn, Analyst

Description: We are a $165 million private investment
firm focused on providing equity capital for growth
companies. We target investments between $1 and
20 million in private equity transactions including:
buyouts, growth uild-ups, expansion capital and
information technology venture capital opportunities.
Offices are located in New York and San Francisco.
Our partners have made over $200 million.

Founded: 1995

Preferred stages of financing: LBO/MBO, Expansion,
Growth build-ups

Industries:
I.04   Broadcasting
I.16   Entertainment
I.18   Financial services
I.22   Industrial products
I.23   Information technology services
I.28   Media/publishing

Sampling of portfolio companies: Rocky Mountain
Financial Corp. (savings & loan institution in
Wyoming); United New Mexico Financial Corp.
(bank holding company in New Mexico); Scientific
Games Holdings Corp. (world's leading manufacturer
of instant scratch-off lottery tickets); The Carbide/
Graphite Group, Inc. (manufacturer of graphite elec-
trodes used in electric arc steel furnaces & calcium
carbide used to generate acetylene gas); Kansas City
Southern Industries, Inc. (businesses include the
Kansas City Southern Railroad, DST Systems &
Janus Funds); LVI Environmental Services Group,
Inc. (environmental remediation service provider,
focused on asbestos & lead paint abatement projects);
Seaview Petroleum Co. LP (regional asphalt refinery
located in New Jersey); AUNET Corp. (Asia-based
commercial internet service provider); AuraVision
Corp. (developer of video processor integrated
circuits for PCs); Meridian Data, Inc. (designer &
manufacturer of CD-ROM servers); PixTech, Inc.
(developer of field emission display screens); Inter-
Media Capital Partners LP (cable TV operator with
properties in Tennessee & Virginia); Muzak LP
(provider of business music); The Johnny Rockets
Group, Inc. (operator of "Johnny Rockets" restaurants); Jeepers!, Inc. (operator of indoor family entertainment centers); United Retail Group, Inc. (500-
store specialty retailer of large size women's apparel);
Multipoint Networks, Inc. (manufactures & markets
wireless metropolitan area networks); Pacific
Communication Sciences, Inc. (designer, developer
& marketer of telecommunications & data communications equipment for digital wireless applications);
Premisys Communications, Inc. (designs, manufactures & markets integrated access products for telecommunications service providers); P-COM, Inc.
(design, manufactures & markets millimeter wave
radios for the worldwide wireless telecommunications market)

Genesee Funding

70 Linden Oaks, 3rd Floor
Rochester, New York 14625
(716) 383-5550
Fax: (716) 383-5305

Key contact:
Mr. Stuart Marsh

Area served: Northeast

Preferred stage of financing: Later stage

Industries:
I.04   Broadcasting
I.06   Communications
I.08   Computer software
I.12   Distribution
I.14   Electronics
I.29   Medical/medical products
I.35   Services (consumer)

Golub Associates, Inc.

230 Park Avenue, 19th Floor
New York, New York 10169
(212) 207-1575
Fax: (212) 207-1579
E-mail: golub@worldnet.att.net

Key contact:
Mr. Lawrence E. Golub, President
Mr. Gregory W. Cashman, Vice President
Mr. Lionel Leventhal, Vice President

Description: We, along with our affiliates, manage
partnerships with over $75 million available for
equity and subordinated debt investments in middle
market companies. We typically invest in profitable,
privately held businesses with revenues between $10
and $15 million. We look for opportunities with a
management team able to communicate and execute
a demonstrated growth strategy.

Amount under management: $25-100 million

Area served: United States

Preferred stages of financing: Mezzanine, LBO/MBO,
Expansion

Industries:
I.01   Aerospace
I.04   Broadcasting
I.09   Construction
I.11   Consumer products
I.12   Distribution
I.13   Education

I.14 Electronics
I.17 Environmental services/waste management
I.20 Healthcare
I.27 Manufacturing
I.29 Medical/medical products
I.34 Services (business)

Sampling of portfolio companies: Mega Broadcasting Corp. (Spanish language radio network); Country Banc Holding Co. (rural bank rollup); Page One Communications (paging company); Focal Point Products (manufacturer of building products); Long Reach Holdings, Inc. (materials handling equipment manufacturer); Quexco Ltd. (lead recycler); H&W Distributors, Inc. (food distributor)

Greenhaven Capital Associates

90 Park Avenue, Suite 1700
New York, New York 10016
(212) 984-0747

Key contact:
Mr. Norman Kent, Managing Director

Description: We invest in promising information based companies. We prefer to invest in companies that are already established and have proven market acceptance - as well as substantial growth potential.

Amount of capital invested: $15 million

Preferred investment size: $3-5 million

Amount under management: $25-100 million

Area served: North America

Preferred stages of financing: LBO/MBO, Expansion

Industries:
I.10 Consulting
I.23 Information technology services
I.24 Internet services/e-commerce
I.28 Media/publishing
I.30 New media

Hambro International Equity Partners

650 Madison Avenue, 21st Floor
New York, New York 10022-1029
(212) 223-7400
Fax: (212) 223-0305

Key contact:
Mr. Edwin A. Goodman, General Partner
Mr. John L. Cassis, General Partner
Mr. Charles L. Dimmler, III, General Partner

Mr. Arthur C. Spinner, General Partner

Area served: United States

Preferred stages of financing: Mezzanine, Expansion

Industries:
I.20 Healthcare
I.29 Medical/medical products

Hamilton Robinson & Company, Inc.

One Rockefeller Plaza, Suite 1410
New York, New York 10020
(212) 332-1220
Fax: (212) 332-1225

Key contact:
Mr. Scott I. Oakford, Managing Director
Mr. Christopher F. Carmel, Managing Director

Description: Private equity investment firm which seeks long term investments in profitable middle market companies. Central to our strategy is a partnership with operating managers driven by shared objectives and significant incentive.

Founded: 1984

Amount of capital invested: $10 million

Preferred investment size: $5-25 million

Area served: Europe, North America

Preferred stage of financing: LBO/MBO

Industries:
I.01 Aerospace
I.02 Agriculture/forestry/fishing/mining
I.05 Chemicals
I.11 Consumer products
I.12 Distribution
I.15 Energy/natural resources/utilities
I.18 Financial services
I.19 Generalist
I.22 Industrial products
I.27 Manufacturing
I.34 Services (business)
I.35 Services (consumer)
I.36 Transportation

Sampling of portfolio companies: Republic Realty Mortgage Corp. (commercial mortgage banking); Maginnis & Assoc., Inc. (specialty insurance broker); Galveston - Houston (industrial equipment); Maloney Industries Inc. (oil & gas production equipment); Aglo Corp. (farm equipment); DI Industries (oil & gas contract driller); Coca-Cola South Florida (soft drink bottler)

Hammond, Kennedy, Whitney & Company Inc.

230 Park Avenue, Suite 1616
Helmsley Building
New York, New York 10169
(212) 867-1010
Fax: (212) 867-1312

Key contact:
Mr. Ralph R. Whitney, Jr., Chairman

Mr. Glenn Scolnik, President
Mr. Forrest Crisman, Jr., Managing Director
Mr. Andrew McNally, IV, Managing Director

Description: Founded in 1904.

Founded: 1904

Amount of capital invested: $10 million

Preferred investment size: $2-5 million

Amount under management: $25-100 million

Area served: Europe, North America

Preferred stage of financing: LBO/MBO

Industries:
I.27 Manufacturing

Sampling of portfolio companies: Excel Industries Inc. (automotive supplier); Baldwin Technologies Inc. (printing accessories); Control Devices Inc. (automotive sensor supplier); Maine Tire Int'l. (industrial application tires); Grobet File Co. of America (industrial & jewelry tools); Seneco Printing & Label (labels for the bottling industry); Globe Ticket & Label (event tickets); Horton Emergency Vehicles (ambulances); Morehouse Group (publishing specialty)

Hanam Capital Corp.
38 West 32nd Street, Suite 1512
New York, New York 10001
(212) 564-5225
Fax: (212) 564-5307

Key contact:
Mr. Robert Schairer

Area served: Northeast

Preferred stages of financing: First stage, Second stage, Third/later stage

Industries:
I.19 Generalist

Holding Capital Group, Inc.
10 East 53rd Street
New York, New York 10022
(212) 486-6670
Fax: (212) 486-0843

Key contact:
Mr. James Donaghy

Preferred stage of financing: LBO/MBO

Industries:
I.19 Generalist

Ibero American Investors Corp.
104 Scio Street
Rochester, New York 14604
(716) 262-3440
Fax: (716) 262-3441

Key contact:
Emilio Serrano

Area served: Northeast

Preferred stages of financing: Start up, First stage

Industries:
I.06 Communications
I.07 Computer hardware
I.12 Distribution
I.18 Financial services
I.19 Generalist
I.32 Retail
I.34 Services (business)
I.35 Services (consumer)

Inclusive Ventures, LLC
14 Wall Street, Suite 2600
New York, New York 10005
(212) 619-4000
Fax: (212) 619-4001
E-mail: weeden@efin.com

Key contact:
Mr. Charles Weeden, Managing Director

Description: We focus on seed or start-up ventures involving on-line financial documents, trading systems, or on-line document repositories. We typically provide marketing, legal, accounting support for a technical vision.

Amount of capital invested: $1 million

Preferred investment size: $200,000-500,000

Amount under management: <$10 million

Area served: United States

Preferred stages of financing: Seed, Start up

Industries:
I.18 Financial services

InterEquity Capital Partners, L.P.
220 Fifth Avenue, 17th Floor
New York, New York 10001
(212) 779-2022
Fax: (212) 779-2103
E-mail: iecp@aol.com
Web: www.interequity-capital.com

Key contact:
Mr. Irwin Schlass, Chairman/CEO
Mr. Abraham Goldstein, COO/President

Description: Small business investment company licensed by U.S. Small Business Adminsitration.

Amount of capital invested: $1,450,000

Preferred investment size: $1-2 million

Amount under management: $10-25 million

Area served: United States

Preferred stages of financing: Seed, Start up, First

stage, Second stage, Mezzanine, LBO/MBO, Expansion

Industries:
I.01	Aerospace
I.03	Biotech/genetic engineering
I.04	Broadcasting
I.05	Chemicals
I.06	Communications
I.07	Computer hardware
I.08	Computer software
I.09	Construction
I.11	Consumer products
I.12	Distribution
I.14	Electronics
I.15	Energy/natural resources/utilities
I.16	Entertainment
I.17	Environmental services/waste management
I.19	Generalist
I.20	Healthcare
I.21	High technology
I.22	Industrial products
I.23	Information technology services
I.24	Internet services/e-commerce
I.25	Leisure/hospitality
I.26	Life sciences
I.27	Manufacturing
I.28	Media/publishing
I.29	Medical/medical products
I.30	New media
I.32	Retail
I.33	Semiconductors
I.36	Transportation
I.37	Wholesale

Sampling of portfolio companies: LungCheck, Inc. (medical device); Index Stock Photography (stock photography)

International Paper Capital Formation, Inc.

Two Manhattanville Road
Purchase, New York 10577
(914) 397-1578
Fax: (914) 397-1909

Key contact:
John Jepsen, President

Area served: United States

Preferred stages of financing: Second stage, Third/later stage

Industries:
I.19   Generalist

The Jordan, Edmiston Group, Inc.

150 East 52nd Street, 18th Floor
New York, New York 10022
(212) 754-0710
Fax: (212) 754-0337
E-mail: kent@jegi.com
Web: www.jegi.com

Key contact:
Ms. Wilma Jordan, CEO/General Partner
Mr. Kent Hawryluk, General Partner

Description: Our purpose is to maximize capital appreciation through funding and helping to build select expansion-stage emerging communications companies. These target companies are engaged in emerging means of data exchange and electronic commerce that leverage technology, with a particular focus on business applications.

Preferred investment size: $2 million

Amount under management: $25-100 million

Area served: Worldwide

Preferred stage of financing: Expansion

Industries:
I.06	Communications
I.08	Computer software
I.23	Information technology services
I.24	Internet services/e-commerce
I.30	New media

KOCO Capital Company, LP

111 Radio Circle
Mt. Kisco, New York 10549
(914) 242-2324
Fax: (914) 241-7476

Key contact:
Mr. Paul Echausse

Area served: United States

Preferred stage of financing: Later stage

Industries:
I.19   Generalist

The Lambda Funds

380 Lexington Avenue, 54th Floor
New York, New York 10168
(212) 682-3454
Fax: (212) 682-9231
E-mail: lamlamp@aol.com

Key contact:
Mr. Richard J. Dumler, Partner
Mr. Anthony M. Lamport, Partner

Area served: United States

Preferred stages of financing: First stage, LBO/MBO, Expansion

Industries:
I.03	Biotech/genetic engineering
I.06	Communications
I.29	Medical/medical products

LEG Partners SBIC, L.P.
230 Park Avenue, 21st Floor
New York, New York 10169
(212) 207-1585
Fax: (212) 207-1579

Key contact:
Mr. Lawrence E. Golub

Area served: Mid-Atlantic

Industries:
I.27   Manufacturing
I.28   Media/publishing
I.29   Medical/medical products

McCown De Leeuw & Company
101 East 52nd Street, 31st Floor
New York, New York 10022
(212) 355-5500
Fax: (212) 355-6283

Key contact:
Mr. David E. De Leeuw, Managing Partner

Area served: United States

Preferred stages of financing: Second stage, Mezzanine, LBO/MBO

Industries:
I.11   Consumer products
I.18   Financial services
I.23   Information technology services
I.27   Manufacturing
I.34   Services (business)

Medallion Funding Corporation
437 Madison Avenue, 38th Floor
New York, New York 10022
(212) 328-2100
Fax: (212) 328-2121

Key contact:
Mr. Andrew Murstein, President

Description: We are a specialty finance company
serving all of the financing needs of growing
businesses.

Amount of capital invested: $100 million

Preferred investment size: $1 million

Amount under management: $100-500 million

Area served: United States

Preferred stages of financing: Second stage, Mezzanine, LBO/MBO, Expansion

Industries:
I.01   Aerospace
I.02   Agriculture/forestry/fishing/mining
I.03   Biotech/genetic engineering
I.04   Broadcasting
I.05   Chemicals
I.06   Communications
I.07   Computer hardware
I.08   Computer software

I.09   Construction
I.10   Consulting
I.11   Consumer products
I.12   Distribution
I.13   Education
I.14   Electronics
I.15   Energy/natural resources/utilities
I.16   Entertainment
I.17   Environmental services/waste management
I.18   Financial services
I.19   Generalist
I.20   Healthcare
I.21   High technology
I.22   Industrial products
I.23   Information technology services
I.24   Internet services/e-commerce
I.25   Leisure/hospitality
I.26   Life sciences
I.27   Manufacturing
I.28   Media/publishing
I.29   Medical/medical products
I.30   New media
I.31   Real estate
I.32   Retail
I.33   Semiconductors
I.34   Services (business)
I.35   Services (consumer)
I.36   Transportation
I.37   Wholesale

Mercury Capital Inc.
153 East 53rd Street, 49th Floor
New York, New York 10022
(212) 838-0888
Fax: (212) 759-3897
E-mail: pstone@dlfi.com

Key contact:
Mr. David Elenowitz, President
Mr. Chris Stokes, Vice President
Mr. Peter Stone, Senior Associate

Description: We are a private investment firm that
acquires manufacturing, distribution and service
businesses with purchase prices of $15 million to
$200 million. We have in excess of $100 million to
invest in transactions.

Amount under management: $100-500 million

Area served: North America

Preferred stage of financing: LBO/MBO

Industries:
I.01   Aerospace
I.05   Chemicals
I.06   Communications
I.08   Computer software
I.10   Consulting
I.11   Consumer products
I.12   Distribution
I.13   Education
I.14   Electronics
I.15   Energy/natural resources/utilities

I.16   Entertainment
I.17   Environmental services/waste management
I.18   Financial services
I.19   Generalist
I.20   Healthcare
I.21   High technology
I.22   Industrial products
I.23   Information technology services
I.25   Leisure/hospitality
I.26   Life sciences
I.27   Manufacturing
I.28   Media/publishing
I.29   Medical/medical products
I.34   Services (business)
I.35   Services (consumer)
I.36   Transportation
I.37   Wholesale

Sampling of portfolio companies: Wesco (distributor of general merchandise products); Nationmark (importer/distributor of toys, party goods & general merchandise); Tennessee Restaurant Equipment Sales (distributor of food service equipment & supplies); Smith St. John (manufacturer & distributor of food service equipment & supplies); Advantage Merchandise (supplier of toys & general merchandise through catalogs & direct store delivery); Jacks Merchandising (distributor of health & beauty care & general merchandise products); Food Service Supplies (manufacturer & distributor of food service equipment & supplies); Youngs General Merchandise (supplier of pet accessories); The Berton Company (specialty wholesaler & service merchandiser); SIG Holdings (insurance company); Triangle Lighting (lighting products manufacturer & distributor); SKS (manufacturer of blinds & balcony systems); Krings (construction machinery manufacturer); LaSalle-Deitch (distributor of floor coverings, furniture, vinyl siding); Protective Treatments (manufacturer of adhesives & plastics); Hudson/Hines Group (building materials distributor); Hyponex (lawn & garden products manufacturer & distributor)

JP Morgan Capital Corp.

60 Wall Street
New York, New York 10260
(212) 648-9000
Fax: (212) 648-5002
Web: www.jpmorgan.com

Key contact:
Mr. James P. Marriott

Description: We offer clients around the world a full range of integrated capabilities, which include capital raising, strategic advice, market access and asset management. Though we operate in a world that is more complex and faster paced than the one of our founders, our business principles remain those espoused by all three Morgans: integrity, objectivity and judgment.

Industries:
I.03   Biotech/genetic engineering
I.06   Communications
I.08   Computer software
I.11   Consumer products
I.12   Distribution
I.14   Electronics
I.24   Internet services/e-commerce
I.29   Medical/medical products

Morgan Stanley Venture Partners

1221 Avenue of the Americas, 33rd Floor
New York, New York 10020
(212) 762-7900
Fax: (212) 762-8424
E-mail: msventures@ms.com
Web: www.ms.com

Key contact:
Mr. Guy L. de Chazal, General Partner
Ms. Debra Abramovitz, COO
Mr. M. Fazle Husain, General Partner
Mr. David Hammer, Financial Associate
Mr. Aaron Broad, Venture Associate
Mr. Gary Stein, Sr., Venture Associate
Mr. Andrew R. Acker, Venture Analyst
Mr. Philip R. Dur, Venture Analyst
Mr. Arvind Malhan, Venture Analyst

Description: We manage a group of funds which invest primarily in later-stage high growth companies, concentrating on the information technology and healthcare industries. Our goal is to help build successful companies, create wealth for entrepreneurs and generate superior returns for our investors.

Founded: 1968

Preferred investment size: $25 million

Industries:
I.06   Communications
I.08   Computer software
I.20   Healthcare
I.23   Information technology services
I.29   Medical/medical products

Sampling of portfolio companies: Aurum Software (provider of customer relationship management solutions providing client/server sales force automation, marketing & customer support software); Gupta, (software companies); Marcam, (software companies); NovaSoft Systems, Inc. (integrated, rapidly-deployable document & workflow management systems); Precept Software, Inc. (develops & markets standards-based network video applications for the entire enterprise); SPSS (software companies); CSG Systems (providers of customer management solutions for the converging communications markets of cable television, direct broadcast satellite, telecommunications & on-line services industries); interWAVE Communications, Inc. (developing low cost, digital micro cellular network equipment for the global marketplace); PageMart Wireless, Inc. (paging company); Chromatic Research, Inc. (supplier to the PC & consumer electronics industries with a new type of semiconductor technology for the multimedia age); FormFactor, Inc. (founded to take advantage of extraordinary business opportunities in the chaging world of silicon back end); AutoImmune (healthcare products); Cytyc Corp. (develops & markets a sample preparation system for medical diagnostic applications); DentalCo, Inc. (provider of dental practice administration services to dental practices in selected geographic areas); MileStone Healthcare, Inc. (contract management company that provides a range of hospital-based post-acute services); Quintiles (healthcare services & software); U.S. Healthworks (developing an integrated delivery system for occupational medicine through acquisition of workers' compensation clinics); Radius (computer & semiconductor devices & equipment); SemiPower Systems, Inc. (designs & manufactures highly integrated modules & complete drives for controlling AC induction motors used in a wide variety of applications); Visioneer (develops & markets products that provide the fastest & easiest way to get paper into computers & put that paper to work)

Murphy & Partners Fund, LP

45 Rockefeller Plaza, Suite 601
New York, New York 10111
(212) 332-2929
Fax: (212) 332-2920

Key contact:
Mr. John J. Murphy, Jr., Managing General Partner
Mr. Stuart L. Agranoff, General Partner
Mr. Thomas M. Keane, General Partner
Ms. Janet L. Daly, Administrative Partner

Description: Second equity investment fund organized by John J. Murphy, Jr. Focuses on media, healthcare and other service industries (education, distribution). Initial closing in 12/97, final closing 9/98.

Preferred investment size: $2-5 million

Amount under management: $10-25 million

Area served: United States

Preferred stage of financing: LBO/MBO

Industries:
I.04   Broadcasting
I.06   Communications
I.12   Distribution
I.13   Education
I.20   Healthcare

Sampling of portfolio companies: Calendar Broadcasting, Inc. (radio); Calendar Media Corp. (media); American Higher Education Development Corp. (education)

Nazem & Company

645 Madison Avenue, 12th Floor
New York, New York 10022
(212) 371-7900
Fax: (212) 371-2150

Key contact:
Mr. Fred Nazem
Mr. Philip E. Barak
Mr. Jeffrey M. Krauss
Mr. Richard J. Racine

Area served: United States

Preferred stages of financing: Seed, Third/later stage

Industries:
I.06   Communications
I.07   Computer hardware
I.08   Computer software
I.14   Electronics
I.29   Medical/medical products
I.34   Services (business)
I.35   Services (consumer)

Needham & Company, Inc.

445 Park Avenue
New York, New York 10022
(212) 371-8300
Fax: (212) 705-1450
E-mail: kkenny@needham.com
Web: www.needhamco.com

Key contact:
Mr. George A. Needham, General Partner
Mr. John C. Michaelson, General Partner
Mr. John J. Prior, Jr., General Partner
Mr. Glen W. Albanese, CFO
Mr. Jack J. Iacovone, Associate

Description: We are a full service New York-based specialty investment bank, which serves emerging growth companies and their institutional investors with equity trading, sales, research and corporate finance services. Needham Capital Partners II is the long-term equity investment affiliate of Needham & Company. The fund is a long-term investor in the private equities of private "mezzanine" stage companies and smaller public emerging growth companies. The investment focus is on companies in the technology, healthcare and specialty retail industries.

Preferred investment size: $2-4 million

Amount under management: $100-500 million

Area served: United States

Preferred stages of financing: Mezzanine, LBO/MBO

Industries:
I.06   Communications
I.07   Computer hardware
I.08   Computer software
I.11   Consumer products
I.14   Electronics
I.20   Healthcare
I.21   High technology
I.22   Industrial products
I.23   Information technology services
I.24   Internet services/e-commerce
I.27   Manufacturing
I.29   Medical/medical products
I.32   Retail
I.33   Semiconductors

Sampling of portfolio companies: College Enterprises, Inc. (operates a chain of retail copying, duplicating, image processing & communication technology service stores on college campuses throughout the country); Obsidian, Inc. (developing an advanced chemical mechanical polishing tool for semiconductor wafers with demonstrated process advantages & cost effectiveness); Carrier Access Corp.

(develops, manufactures & markets T-1 digital tele-communcations access products for local carrier bypass); Cutter & Buck, Inc. (designs men's sportswear apparel marketed in golf pro shops, resorts & upscale specialty stores); Calileo Technology, Ltd. (designs & markets complex semiconductor devices for high-performance embedded control systems, principally in the area of data communications); IMNET Systems, Inc. (develops, markets, installs & services electronic information & document management systems for the healthcare industry & other document intensive businesses); Lids Corp. (rapidly growing chain of "category-killer" hat stores); SeaMED Corp. (designs & manufactures advanced durable electronic & medical instruments for medical technology companies); WorldGate Communications, Inc. (start-up cable service that allows cable operators to offer low cost, fast & simple access to the internet); U.S. Vision, Inc. (optical retailer, sells prescription eyewear, contact lenses, eye exams & services for fitting custom lenses to eyeglass frames); JT Storage, Inc. (manufactures small, high-capacity disk drives); InterVentional Technologies, Inc. (develops, manufactures & markets invasive disposable microsurgical devices & systems for the treatment of cardiovascular disease);

Zydacron, Inc. (designs, manufactures & markets a family of hardware & software products for low cost, desktop PC videoconferencing); WaferScale Inter-gration, Inc. (designs, develops & produces high-programmable VLSI Products, including an inno-vative portfolio of programmable microcontroller peripherals); Ramp Networks, Inc. (develops & markets connectivity products for small workgroups that allow such groups to seamlessly connect to the internet while establishing a local area network); Rise Technology Co., Inc. (designing high-performance, low-powered X86-compatible microprocessors); Patient Infosystems, Inc. (provides patient-centered healthcare information systems that proactively collect & analyze information to improve patient compliance with prescribed treatments); PACE Health Management Systems, Inc. (develops & markets advanced clinical software which automates the recording, storage & management of patient care information); Digital Arts & Sciences Corp. (develops & distributes graphically oriented software for the management of inventories & collections of objects, where images are an integral element); Rosti (chain of primarily take-out Italian restaurants that is expanding out of the Los Angeles area)

Newfield Capital, Inc.

555 Fifth Avenue, 17th Floor
New York, New York 10017
(212) 599-5000
Fax: (212) 986-5316
E-mail: gcamp@worldnet.att.net

Key contact:
Mr. Gregory T. Camp, Managing Director
Mr. Jerry R. Donatelli, Principal

Area served: Worldwide

Preferred stages of financing: LBO/MBO, Opportu-nistic venture capital & other principal investing

Industries:
I.11	Consumer products
I.18	Financial services
I.20	Healthcare
I.25	Leisure/hospitality
I.28	Media/publishing
I.29	Medical/medical products
I.31	Real estate
I.32	Retail
I.35	Services (consumer)

Northwood Ventures

485 Madison Avenue, 20th Floor
New York, New York 10022
(212) 935-4595
Fax: (212) 826-1093

485 Underhill Boulevard, Suite 205
Syosset, New York 11791-3419
(516) 364-5544
Fax: (516) 364-0879
E-mail: northwdven@aol.com

Key contact:
Mr. Henry T. Wilson, Managing Director
Mr. Peter G. Schiff, President

Description: We are a private equity firm which invests in venture capital opportunities, management buyouts and industry consolidations. We invest across a broad range of industry sectors and work actively in partnership with the management teams of our portfolio companies with the common goal of generating superior returns. We currently manage in excess of $100 million of equity capital through two primary funds, Northwood Ventures LLC and North-wood Capital Partners LLC.

Founded: 1983

Amount of capital invested: $18 million

Preferred investment size: $2-4 million

Amount under management: $100-500 million

Area served: Worldwide

Preferred stages of financing: First stage, Second stage, LBO/MBO, Expansion, Int'l expansion

Industries:
I.03	Biotech/genetic engineering
I.04	Broadcasting
I.05	Chemicals
I.06	Communications
I.11	Consumer products
I.12	Distribution
I.17	Environmental services/waste management
I.18	Financial services
I.19	Generalist
I.22	Industrial products
I.27	Manufacturing
I.28	Media/publishing
I.32	Retail
I.34	Services (business)
I.35	Services (consumer)
I.36	Transportation
I.37	Wholesale

Sampling of portfolio companies: Arcon Coating Mills, Inc. (producer of tapes & edge covering materials used to bind, reinforce, protect & decorate office & school supply products, checkbooks & hard & soft cover books); BizTel Communications, Inc. (network provider of last mile wireless communications using 38 GHz spectrum granted by the FCC); Cincinnati Coca-Cola Bottling, Inc. (bottles & distributes Coca-Cola & its allied products in the greater Cincinnati & Dayton areas); New Dartmouth Bank (the second largest thrift in New Hampshire, was created in 1991 through the acquisition & merger of three failed savings & loans from the FDIC); Nextel Communications, Inc. (wireless communications provider); Office Depot, Inc. (office supply superstore retailer); Redhook Ale Brewery, Inc. (leading microbrewer producing a well-known line of beers including Redhook ESB); Alliance Nat'l., Inc. (operator of executive office suites, a highly fragmented industry); BUCA, Inc. (high growth operator of immigrant Southern Italian family-style neighborhood restaurants named BUCA di Beppo); Caribou Coffee Co., Inc. (operator of coffee gathering places, focusing on midwestern & southeastern markets); Cell Pathways, Inc. (pharmaceutical company focused on the development & commercialization of products to prevent & treat cancer); Commerce Security Bancorp, Inc. (community bank in Southern California); DirecTel Int'l., LLC (start-up paging company operating in Argentina & Brazil); Hygrade Metal Moulding Manufacturing Corp. (manufacturer of aluminum roll-formed products used as components in insulated glass window units); Int'l. Wireless Communications Holdings, Inc. (operator, owner & developer of wireless communications networks in major emerging countries in Asia & Latin Ameirca, including China, Pakistan, Malaysia, Indonesia & Brazil); StoryFirst Communications, Inc. (owns & operates television & radio networks in Russia & the Ukraine); TeleCorp, Inc. (operates mobile wireless communications systems in a number of U.S. markets)

Norwood Venture Corp.

1430 Broadway, #1607
New York, New York 10017
(212) 869-5075
Fax: (212) 869-5331

Key contact:
Mr. Mark B. Anderson, Director
Mr. Robert E. La Blanc, Director
Mr. Mark R. Littell, President/Director
Ms. Hazel Matthews-Forte, Controller/Secretary
Dr. Alfred Saffer, Ph.D., Director

Description: We are a small business investment company licensed by the federal government under the Small Business Investment Act of 1958. We were organized in 1980 as EAB Venture Corp., and operated until early 1988 as a wholly-owned subsidiary of European American Bank (New York). In April, 1988, a group of individual investors, including our management and directors, acquired 100% of the company's common stock and changed our name to Norwood Venture Corp.

Founded: 1980

Preferred investment size: $250,000-1 million

Area served: United States

Preferred stages of financing: Seed, Start up, First stage, Second stage, Mezzanine, LBO/MBO, Expansion, Int'l expansion, Venture leasing, turnaround

Industries:
I.02   Agriculture/forestry/fishing/mining
I.06   Communications
I.07   Computer hardware
I.08   Computer software
I.09   Construction
I.12   Distribution
I.18   Financial services
I.20   Healthcare
I.23   Information technology services
I.27   Manufacturing
I.30   New media
I.32   Retail
I.34   Services (business)

Sampling of portfolio companies: AdTek Information Systems, Inc. (provides proprietary integrated software products & customized software systems to middle market domestic & international banks, as well as foreign banks & U.S. agencies of foreign banks); Ag-Bag Int'l. Ltd. (manufactures & sells patented bulk storage systems for the high moisture storage of silage & grains, as well as for composting); A. H. Harris & Sons, Inc. (distributor of concrete-related construction specialty products & related accessories & tools); American Insurance Management Group, Inc. (active in several areas of insurance, operating as a managing general agent, wholesale broker, issuing carrier & reinsurer); Conner Industries, Inc. (remanufacturer & distributor of lumber products for packaging applications); Datatrac Corp. (provider of software & hardware solutions to the time sensitive delivery business); Devlin Videoservice (providers of video standards conversion, duplication, film-to-tape transfer & related postproduction services); Firecom, Inc. (designs, installs & services sophisticated fire safety systems in high-rise office buildings & hotels); Industrial Services Technologies, Inc. (contract repair & maintenance companies serving the petroleum refining, petrochemical & chemical industries); Interactive Media Worlwide, Inc. (designs, installs & operates interactive video information systems in public facilities such as hotels, airports & municipal centers); Lincoln Services Corp. (developing a network of outpatient rehabilitation centers, both on a free-standing basis & within larger health care facilities); Marco Manufacturing, Inc. (low-cost, rapid turnaround services address new & limited life product cycles, as well as the just-in-time requirements of a variety of high & low technology businesses); NuCo2, Inc. (supplier of liquid CO_2 beverage carbonation systems to food service & recreation businesses); Progressive Strategies, Inc. (provides technology assessment services for both established & emerging companies in the computer industry, using product-specific expertise developed in their technical lab); PJC Technologies, Inc. (designs & fabricates prototype & short run printed circuit boards for the engineering departments of major US manufacturing companies); Quadlogic Controls Corp. (designs & produces electricity meters that are read remotely, via power-line based communication systems); Synergy USA, Inc. (operator of Manhattan-based health clubs); Thermo-Mizer Environmental Corp. (integrating microprocessor-based environmental control systems from this company with certain segments of Laminaire's Corp. equipment line); Walkin Corp. (manufacturer of quality dress shoes, primarily for children)

NYBDC Capital Corporation

41 State Street
P.O. Box 738
Albany, New York 12207
(518) 463-2268
Fax: (518) 463-0240

Key contact:
Mr. Andrew Linehan
Mr. Robert W. Lazar

Area served: New York

Preferred stages of financing: First stage, Second stage, Third/later stage

Industries:
I.19   Generalist

Onondaga Venture Capital Fund, Inc.

714 State Tower Building
Syracuse, New York 13202
(315) 478-0157
Fax: (315) 478-0158

Key contact:
Mr. Irving W. Schwartz, President

Description: We are a private firm investing our own capital. Due to our size, we seek convertible debt with an equity opportunity.

Amount of capital invested: $260,000

Preferred investment size: $200,000

Amount under management: <$10 million

Area served: Northeast

Preferred stages of financing: Second stage, Expansion

Industries:
I.02   Agriculture/forestry/fishing/mining

I.03	Biotech/genetic engineering
I.06	Communications
I.08	Computer software
I.11	Consumer products
I.12	Distribution
I.14	Electronics
I.17	Environmental services/waste management
I.19	Generalist
I.20	Healthcare
I.22	Industrial products
I.23	Information technology services
I.27	Manufacturing
I.29	Medical/medical products
I.34	Services (business)

Sampling of portfolio companies: BioWorks, Inc. (agribusiness); Pathlight Technologies, Inc. (software); Healthway Products, Inc. (air quality); Opto Generic Devices, Inc. (optical encoders); Accuracy Microsensors, Inc. (color measurements); Aether Works, Inc. (telecommunications)

Paramount Capital Investments, LLC

787 Seventh Avenue
New York, New York 10019
(212) 554-4310
Fax: (212) 554-4488

Key contact:
Dr. Lindsay A. Rosenwald, M.D., Chairman/CEO
Mr. Peter Morgan Kash, Senior Managing Director
Mr. Michael S. Weiss, Head of Investment Banking
Mr. Wayne L. Rubin, CFO
Mr. Steve H. Kanzer, Head of Venture Capital

Description: With a track record of successful offerings and start-up companies unparalleled in the biotechnology sector, we are well known as a dynamic industry leader in venture capital, capital raising and mergers and acquisitions.

Preferred stages of financing: Seed, Start up, First stage, Second stage

Industries:
I.03   Biotech/genetic engineering
I.20   Healthcare

Paribas Principal Partners

787 Seventh Avenue
New York, New York 10019
(212) 841-2115
Fax: (212) 841-2502

Key contact:
Mr. Steven Alexander, Partner
Mr. Gary Binning, Partner
Mr. Stephen Eisenstein, Partner

Area served: United States

Preferred stages of financing: LBO/MBO, Expansion

Industries:
I.01	Aerospace
I.04	Broadcasting
I.06	Communications
I.11	Consumer products
I.14	Electronics
I.20	Healthcare
I.22	Industrial products
I.23	Information technology services
I.27	Manufacturing
I.28	Media/publishing
I.29	Medical/medical products
I.34	Services (business)

I.36   Transportation   I.37   Wholesale

Patricof & Company Ventures, Inc.
445 Park Avenue
New York, New York 10022
(212) 753-6300
Fax: (212) 319-6155
Web: www.patricof.com

Key contact:
Ms. Patricia M. Cloherty
Mr. Robert M. Chefitz
Mr. Thomas P. Hirschfeld
Mr. David A. Landau
Mr. Alan J. Patricof
Mr. Salem D. Schuchman
Mr. Laurent C. LePortz
Mr. Marc A. Schwartz

Description: We are a leading international private
equity investment firm that together with our international affiliate, Apax Partners, manages over $3.4
billion on behalf of major institutional investors in
the U.S. and abroad. With over twenty-five years of
direct investing experience, we provide long-term
equity financing to build companies. We have a solid
reputation as a leader in the industry and as an innovative, value-added investor.

Preferred investment size: $5-25 million

Area served: Worldwide

Preferred stages of financing: Start up, First stage,
LBO/MBO, Expansion, Racapitalizations

Industries:
I.06   Communications
I.07   Computer hardware
I.08   Computer software
I.11   Consumer products
I.14   Electronics
I.18   Financial services
I.20   Healthcare
I.22   Industrial products
I.23   Information technology services
I.27   Manufacturing
I.29   Medical/medical products
I.30   New media
I.32   Retail
I.34   Services (business)

Sampling of portfolio companies: Spec Group, Inc.
(provides technicians, specialists, programmers &
professionals for a wide range of staff augmentation,
inspection, training & technical consulting services
for utility, industrial, commercial & government
customers); Medical Arts Press, Inc. (direct marketer
of custom & standard business forms & office &
practice related supplies to healthcare professionals);
Johnny Rockets Group, Inc. (restaurant chain
featuring a 1950's diner concept); Protection One,
Inc. (provides residential monitoring alarm services);
CapMAC Holdings (pioneered the commercial
monoline financial guarantee business); RBMG
Resource Bancshares Corp. (specialty asset gatherer
utilizing a banking depository license in South
Carolina); Centocor Inc. (healthcare company
specializing in the development & commercialization
of therapeutic & diagnostic products to meet critical
human healthcare needs); Dura Delivery Systems,
Inc. (developed a proprietary drug delivery system
called the Dryhaler); Bolder Technologies Corp.
(developed a new generation of rechargeable, sealed,
lead acid batteries); Biocompatibles plc (commercializes a biocompatible coating material for
ophthalmic & medical device coating applications);
Atcom (primary provider to telephone companies &
others of kiosks allowing public access to the internet;
provider of high-speed data ports for travelers who
want T-1 access from their laptops); Bluestone
Software, Inc. (sells enterprise-to-web solutions);
Fore Systems, Inc. (designer, developer & manufacturer of high-performance, networking products
based on asynchronous transfer mode technology);
Tessera, Inc. (semiconductor packaging technology
company); Audible, Inc. (launched its pocket-sized
device that holds up to 2 hours of spoken word audio
& can play it back either over a car radio or headphones); Medscape (internet site for healthcare
professionals); planet U (on-line consumer promotions, including coupons, rebates & sampling);
Sunglass Hut Corp. (mall-based specialty retail
concept selling a variety of fashion eyewear); Office
Depot (retailer of office supplies); Xpedite Systems,
Inc. (provider of enhanced fax services)

Phillips-Smith Specialty Retail Group
7 Locust Lane
Bronxville, New York 10708
(914) 961-0407
Fax: (914) 961-6169
E-mail: Foley10708@aol.com

Key contact:
Mr. Craig Foley, Principal

Description: We are a traditional venture capital firm
which invests in retail businesses with the potential
to become major regional or national retail chains.
We were founded by our managing general partners
Don Phillips and Cece Smith, executives with
successful track records in specialty retailing, restaurants and venture investing.

Founded: 1986

Amount of capital invested: $21.4 million

Preferred investment size: $4-5 million

Amount under management: $100-500 million

Area served: United States

Preferred stages of financing: Seed, Start up, First
stage, Second stage, Mezzanine, LBO/MBO, Expansion

Industries:
I.24   Internet services/e-commerce
I.32   Retail

Sampling of portfolio companies: Bookstop (book
retailer); A Pea In The Pod (maternity apparel); The
Sports Authority (sporting goods superstore);
BizMart (office supply superstore); Petsmart (pet
supply superstore); Gadzooks (teen apparel retailer);
Hot Topic (teen apparel retailer); Canyon Cafes
(southwestern restaurants)

Pierre Funding Corporation

805 Third Avenue, 6th Floor
New York, New York 10022
(212) 888-1515
Fax: (212) 688-4252

Key contact:
Mr. Elias Debbas

Area served: East Coast

Preferred stage of financing: Third/later stage

Industries:
I.19   Generalist

The Pittsford Group, Inc.

8 Lodge Pole Road
Pittsford, New York 14534-4550
(716) 223-3523
Fax: (716) 223-3523
E-mail: lmcheek...@aol.com

Key contact:
Mr. Logan M. Cheek, III, Managing Director

Area served: North America, South/Central America

Preferred stages of financing: Start up, First stage,
Second stage, Mezzanine

Industries:
I.03   Biotech/genetic engineering
I.05   Chemicals
I.06   Communications
I.07   Computer hardware

I.08   Computer software
I.12   Distribution
I.13   Education
I.14   Electronics
I.17   Environmental services/waste management
I.20   Healthcare
I.21   High technology
I.23   Information technology services
I.24   Internet services/e-commerce
I.26   Life sciences
I.28   Media/publishing
I.29   Medical/medical products
I.30   New media

Sampling of portfolio companies: ACC Corp. (telecommunications); Graphite Inc. (materials services)

Poly Ventures

901 Route 110
Farmingdale, New York 11735
(516) 249-4710
Fax: (516) 249-4713

Key contact:
Mr. Robert M. Brill
Mr. Herman Fialkov

Ms. Shelley A. Harrison

Area served: Northeast

Preferred stage of financing: Seed

Industries:
I.06   Communications

Prospect Street Ventures

250 Park Avenue, 17th Floor
New York, New York 10177
(212) 490-0480
Fax: (212) 490-1566
Web: www.prospectstreet.com

Key contact:
Mr. John Barry, Managing Partner
Mr. David Chaney, Associate
Ms. Patricia Blackman, Manager

Description: New York City venture capital firm which
focuses on information technology including software and services, communications and the internet.

Amount of capital invested: $15 million

Preferred investment size: $4-5 million

Amount under management: $100-500 million

Area served: United States

Preferred stages of financing: Seed, Start up, First
stage, Second stage, Mezzanine, LBO/MBO, Expansion, Int'l expansion, Venture Leasing

Industries:
I.06   Communications
I.07   Computer hardware
I.08   Computer software

I.21   High technology
I.23   Information technology services
I.24   Internet services/e-commerce
I.30   New media

Sampling of portfolio companies: Air Media (develops
software for wireless & mobile communications via
internet); All Service Computer Rental (providers of
PC rentals & other services to corporate clients);
Bondnet Trading Systems (provider of electronic
trading platform for fixed inc securities); Helpmate
Robotics, Inc. (manufacturers of robots); New Media
(television programming); Skyline Multimedia Entertainment (entertainment company engaged in
building & operating movie-based simulator &
virtual reality attractions at established tourist sites);
Systron (provides network solutions for large organizations); 24/7 Media (service based business
providing solutions to advertisers & web publishers);
Comet Systems (developed proprietary software that
transforms the cursor from a generic arrow to an
advertising image)

Pyramid Ventures, Inc.
130 Liberty Street
Mailstop 2255
New York, New York 10006
(212) 250-9571
Fax: (212) 250-7651

Key contact:
Mr. Douglas Brent

Mr. Brian Talbot

Area served: United States

Preferred stage of financing: Later stage

Industries:
I.19   Generalist

Rand Capital Corporation
2200 Rand Building
Buffalo, New York 14203
(716) 853-0802
Fax: (716) 854-8480
E-mail: pgrum@randcap.com

Key contact:
Mr. Allen F. Grum, President
Ms. Nora B. Sullivan, Executive Vice President
Mr. Daniel P. Penberthy, CFO

Description: Provide investment banking and capital since 1969.

Amount of capital invested: $2,542,295

Preferred investment size: $400,000

Amount under management: <$10 million

Area served: Northeast North America

Preferred stages of financing: Second stage, Expansion

Industries:
I.04   Broadcasting
I.06   Communications
I.09   Construction
I.11   Consumer products
I.14   Electronics
I.20   Healthcare
I.29   Medical/medical products

Sampling of portfolio companies: American Tactile Corp. (develops equipment & systems to produce ADA signs for the visually impaired); ARIA Wireless Systems, Inc. (markets radio transmission communication equipment); ARS, Inc. (assembles & distributes replacement automotive products); BioVector, Inc. (medical technological sales force company); BioWorks, Inc. (develops & manufactures biological alternative to chemical pesticides); Clearview Cable TV, Inc. (wireless cable television systems operator); Commercial Maintenance Organization, Inc. (maintenance service network for retailers, restaurants & vendors); Comptek Research, Inc. (develops electronic systems for military & non-military applications); Lightbridge, Inc. (provides software based services for wireless telecommunications industry); Fertility Acoustics, Inc. (developer of proprietary methods to diagnose onset of ovulation); HealthWay Products Co., Inc. (manufactures air filters & climate control devices); Heartland Wireless Communications, Inc. (wireless cable television system operator); J. Giardino (owns & leases commercial property); MINRAD, Inc. (developer of laser guided surgical devices); MobileMedia Corp. (provider of paging & other wireless data services); Pathlight Technology, Inc. (develops high technology serial storage architecture for computer industry); Platform Technologies Holdings, LLC (provides sales support & management for unique medical device & diagnostic businesses); Reflection Technology, Inc. (develops & licenses proprietary virtual display technology); Ultra-Scan Corp. (ultrasonic fingerprint scanning technology)

Regent Capital Partners, L.P.
505 Park Avenue, Suite 1700
New York, New York 10022
(212) 735-9900
Fax: (212) 735-9908

Key contact:
Mr. Richard H. Hochman, Chairman
Ms. Nina E. McLemore, President
Mr. J. Oliver Maggard, Executive Vice President

Description: We are a private investment fund formed to make equity and mezzanine investments in companies requiring capital to implement growth strategies or to finance buyouts, acquisitions or consolidations. We target consumer-driven businesses, media and communications, and women-owned businesses.

Amount of capital invested: $12,412,477

Preferred investment size: $3 million

Amount under management: $25-100 million

Area served: United States

Preferred stages of financing: Second stage, Mezzanine

Industries:
I.06   Communications
I.11   Consumer products
I.12   Distribution
I.16   Entertainment
I.27   Manufacturing
I.32   Retail

Sampling of portfolio companies: Adventure Entertainment Corp. (chain of family entertainment centers); Buca, Inc. (full-service, dinner only restaurants); Learningsmith (educationally oriented toys, gift retailer) Medical Asset Management (physical practice management company); Momentum Partners (full service licensing agent for family entertainment practice); Santa Monica Amusements (family amusement park); SuperGraphics (outdoor advertising); Talton Holdings, Inc. (local & long distance telecommunications service provider); EagleQuest Golf Centers (developer, owner & operator of golf

centers); QuietPower Systems, Inc. (active noise &
vibration control technology); Danskin, Inc.
(women's activewear & legwear retailer)

Robertson Stephens-Omega Ventures

590 Madison Avenue
36th Floor
New York, New York 10022
(212) 319-8900
Fax: (212) 407-0488

Description: Late stage venture capital

Preferred investment size: $3-7 million

Amount under management: $100-500 million

Area served: Worldwide

Preferred stages of financing: Second stage, Mezzanine, LBO/MBO, Expansion, Int'l expansion

Industries:
I.03   Biotech/genetic engineering
I.06   Communications
I.07   Computer hardware
I.08   Computer software
I.10   Consulting
I.11   Consumer products
I.12   Distribution
I.13   Education
I.14   Electronics
I.15   Energy/natural resources/utilities
I.17   Environmental services/waste management
I.18   Financial services
I.19   Generalist
I.20   Healthcare
I.21   High technology
I.24   Internet services/e-commerce
I.26   Life sciences
I.27   Manufacturing
I.29   Medical/medical products
I.30   New media
I.33   Semiconductors
I.34   Services (business)
I.35   Services (consumer)

Sampling of portfolio companies: Broderbund
Software, Inc. (software); Insignia Solutions
(software); Voyan Technology (software); Appex
(communications); Metapath Software Corp.
(communications); Radish Communications, Inc.
(communications); Shomiti Systems, Inc. (communications); TeleCruz Technology, Inc. (electronics);
Visioneer Communications, Inc. (electronics); CBT
Group PLC (business services); J3 Learning Corp.
(business services); MemberWorks Inc. (business
services); Abgenix, Inc. (healthcare/life sciences);
COR Therapeutics, Inc. (heatlhcare/life sciences);
Cyto Therapeutics, Inc. (health care/life sciences);
DeVilbiss Health Care, Inc. (healthcare/life
sciences); CompUSA, Inc. (consumer); Dick's
Clothing & Sporting Goods (consumer); Petstuff, Inc.
(consumer); Opta Food Ingredients, Inc. (other)

Rothschild Ventures, Inc.

1251 Avenue of the Americas, 51st Floor
New York, New York 10020
(212) 403-3500
Fax: (212) 403-3652

Key contact:
Ms. Sherri A. Croasdale
Mr. Scott T. Jones
Mr. John D. Miller

Area served: Canada, United States

Preferred stages of financing: Seed, First stage, Second stage, LBO/MBO

Industries:
I.03   Biotech/genetic engineering
I.06   Communications
I.07   Computer hardware
I.08   Computer software
I.11   Consumer products
I.14   Electronics
I.29   Medical/medical products

RRE Investors, LLC

126 East 56th Street
New York, New York 10022
(212) 418-5100
Fax: (212) 355-0330
E-mail: info@rre.com
Web: www.rre.com

Key contact:
Mr. Michael Kaplan, Associate
Mr. James D. Robinson, III, Chairman/CEO
Mr. James D. Robinson, IV, Managing Director
Mr. Stuart J. Ellman, Managing Director

Description: We are a venture capital firm that makes
investments in entrepreneurial information technology companies. Special emphasis is placed on
software, communications and related enterprises
that can become leaders in select technology-driven
markets principally serving the Fortune 500 and their
global equivalents.

Founded: 1994

Preferred investment size: $3-8 million

Amount under management: $100-500 million

Industries:
I.23   Information technology services
I.24   Internet services/e-commerce

Sampling of portfolio companies: BTree; CallWare
Technologies; Connect; Diva Communications;
Finjan; Giga Information Group; Netiva; MagiNet;
Invention Machine

Saunders Karp & Megrue

667 Madison Avenue
New York, New York 10021
(212) 303-6600
Fax: (212) 755-1624

Key contact:
Mr. Thomas A. Saunders, III, General Partner
Mr. Allan W. Karp, General Partner
Mr. John F. Megrue, General Partner
Mr. Christopher K. Reilly, General Partner

Description: Founded in 1990, we are a private equity
investment firm with offices in New York and
Connecticut, seeking investments in a broad spectrum of opportunities, including management-backed
recapitalizations, growth financings, leveraged
acquisitions and joint ventures utilizing our equity
funds.

Founded: 1990

Preferred stages of financing: LBO/MBO, Third/later
stage

Industries:
I.11   Consumer products
I.18   Financial services
I.20   Healthcare
I.23   Information technology services
I.27   Manufacturing
I.32   Retail
I.36   Transportation

Sampling of portfolio companies: Sussex Technology,
Inc. (plastic injection-molding company that manufactures plastic closures & components for companies
in the personal care & medical/dental end-use
markets); Duro Industries (independent dyer,
finisher, printer & coater of apparel fabrics); Hartford
Computer Group, Inc. (authorized assembler for IBM
& an authorized reseller for most major product
manufacturers, offering the products of over 1,100
manufacturers); California Cafe Restaurant Corp.
(operates restaurants in the "casual elegance"
segment of the full-service dining industry); Targus
Group Int'l., Inc. (designer & marketer of computer
luggage for portable PC's); The Children's Place
Retail Stores, Inc. (specialty retailer of high quality,
value-priced children's apparel & accessories for
newborns to twelve-year-olds); Charlotte Russe, Inc.
(operates a chain of mall based women's/junior's
apparel stores under the "Charlotte Russe" name in
California, Arizona & Nevada); Mimi's Cafe (owns &
operates a chain of casual theme, family dining
restaurants in California & Arizona); Souper Salad,
Inc. (owns & operates a chain of over 50 mid-scale
family restaurants in five Southwestern states);
Hibbett Sporting Goods, Inc. (operator of full-line
sporting goods retail stores in small to mid-size
markets in the Southeast); RSI Home Products, Inc.
(manufactures & sells assembled & ready-to-
assemble bathroom & kitchen cabinets to the major
do-it-yourself home center retailers including Lowe's,
Home Depot, Eagle, Home Quarters, etc.); Marie
Callender Pie Shops, Inc. (owns, operates & franchises a chain of over 140 family restaurants in the
Western U.S.); Dollar Tree Stores, Inc. (operates over
850 enclosed mall & strip center variety stores in 26
states that offer all merchandise at a single price
point- $1)

Sentinel Capital Partners

777 Third Avenue, 32nd Floor
New York, New York 10017
(212) 688-3100
Fax: (212) 688-6513
E-mail: webmaster@sentinelpartners.com
Web: www.sentinelpartners.com

Key contact:
Mr. David S. Lobel, Managing Partner
Mr. John F. McCormack, Partner
Mr. Eric D. Bommer, Vice President

Description: We are a private equity firm specializing
in buying and building smaller middle market
companies in partnership with management. We
focus primarily on the consumer sector and pursue
only "friendly" deals.

Amount of capital invested: $10 million

Preferred investment size: $10 million

Amount under management: $100-500 million

Area served: North America

Preferred stages of financing: LBO/MBO, Expansion

Industries:
I.04   Broadcasting
I.11   Consumer products
I.12   Distribution
I.13   Education
I.16   Entertainment
I.18   Financial services
I.24   Internet services/e-commerce
I.25   Leisure/hospitality
I.28   Media/publishing
I.32   Retail
I.34   Services (business)
I.35   Services (consumer)

Sampling of portfolio companies: Hasco Int'l., Inc. (in-
hospital infant portrait services); Border Foods, Inc.
(operator of Taco Bell quick service restaurants);
Floral Plant Growers (produces, markets & sells flori-
culture products to mass merchant retailers); Met
Merchandising Concepts (visual display products &
services for the upscale retail industry)

Situation Ventures Corporation

56-20 59th Street
Maspeth, New York 11378
(718) 894-2000
Fax: (718) 326-4642

Key contact:
Mr. Sam Hollander

Area served: New York metro area

Preferred stages of financing: Start up, First stage, Second stage

Industries:
I.27   Manufacturing

I.32   Retail
I.34   Services (business)
I.35   Services (consumer)

SPP Hambro & Company, LLC

330 Madison Avenue, 28th Floor
New York, New York 10017
(212) 455-4500
Fax: (212) 455-4545
Web: www.spphambro.com

Key contact:
Mr. Neil H. Powell, Chairman
Mr. Stefan L. Shaffer, President
Ms. Amy S. Lazarus, CFO
Ms. Joan M. Blount, Office Manager
Ms. Robin Ellis Busch, Managing Director
Mr. Timothy P. Meyer, Managing Director
Mr. E. Daniel Streeter, Managing Director
Mr. Rana S. Mookherjee, VP-Head of Structured
  Finance

Description: We are an international investment banking firm dedicated exclusively to the private placement market. With the largest collection of private placement professionals practicing today, we have completes over 300 private financings, totaling more than $8 billion and are considered one of the most prolific sources of deal flow in today's market.

Founded: 1989

Amount under management: >$1 billion

Area served: Europe, United States

Preferred stage of financing: Mezzanine

Sprout Group

277 Park Avenue, 21st Floor
New York, New York 10172
(212) 892-8062
Fax: (212) 892-3444
E-mail: pboroian@sproutgroup.com

Key contact:
Mr. Patrick Boroian, General Partner
Mr. Richard Kroon, Managing Partner
Mr. Ben DeRosa, Associate

Description: Venture capital affiliate of Donaldson, Lufkin & Jenrette with more than $1.8 billion of aggregate committed capital. Over our 28 year history, we have made investments in nearly 300 companies whose revenues today exceed $40 billion. We invest in all stages (from start ups through buyouts) in high growth areas such as information technology, medical products and services, business services and retail.

Amount of capital invested: $163 million

Preferred investment size: $5-50 million

Amount under management: >$1 billion

Area served: North America, South/Central America

Preferred stages of financing: Seed, Start up, First stage, Second stage, Mezzanine, LBO/MBO, Expansion

Industries:
I.01   Aerospace
I.03   Biotech/genetic engineering
I.08   Computer software
I.10   Consulting
I.12   Distribution
I.13   Education
I.14   Electronics
I.18   Financial services
I.20   Healthcare
I.21   High technology
I.23   Information technology services
I.24   Internet services/e-commerce
I.26   Life sciences
I.29   Medical/medical products
I.30   New media
I.32   Retail
I.33   Semiconductors
I.34   Services (business)
I.35   Services (consumer)
I.37   Wholesale

Sampling of portfolio companies: Corporate Express (office products, wholesale); Staples (office products, retail); Edison Project (education); SDL (semiconductor laser diodes); Norand (handheld computers); Sequana (genomics); IDEC Pharmaceuticals (biotherapeutics); GTECH (on-line lottery networks)

Stamford Financial Consulting

Stamford Financial Building
Stamford, New York 12167
(607) 652-3311
Fax: (607) 652-6301
E-mail: geo@stamfordfinancial.com

86-19 88th Avenue
Woodhaven, New York 11421
(718) 847-6878
Fax: (718) 847-6994

Key contact:
Mr. George C. Bergleitner, Jr., President

Mr. Alexander C. Brosda, Vice President/Treasurer
Paul J. Madison, Esq., Vice President/Secretary
Mr. Michael J. Reed, Vice President
Mr. William Bunchuck, Vice President
Mr. George C. Bergleitner, III, Chairman of the Board

Founded: 1975

Preferred investment size: $500,000-1 million

Area served: Western Europe, United States

Preferred stages of financing: Second stage, Mezzanine

Industries:
I.06　Communications
I.07　Computer hardware
I.09　Construction
I.14　Electronics

I.18　Financial services
I.20　Healthcare
I.29　Medical/medical products
I.31　Real estate

Sterling/Carl Marks Capital, Inc.

175 Great Neck Road, Suite 408
Great Neck, New York 11021-3313
(516) 482-7374
Fax: (516) 487-0781
E-mail: stercrlmar@aol.com

Key contact:
Mr. Harvey Granat, President
Mr. Harvey Rosenblatt, Executive Vice President
Mr. Robert Davidoff, Vice President

135 East 57th Street
New York, New York 10022
(212) 909-8400

Key contact:
Mr. Howard Davidoff, Vice President

Description: Small business investment company
making equity loans and investments in later stage
companies. Preference: Northeast & Mid-Atlantic.
Level: $500,000 to $3 million.

Amount of capital invested: $4.5 million

Preferred investment size: $500,000-3 million

Amount under management: $10-25 million

Area served: United States

Preferred stages of financing: Mezzanine, LBO/MBO,
Expansion

Industries:
I.04　Broadcasting
I.06　Communications
I.11　Consumer products
I.12　Distribution
I.13　Education
I.16　Entertainment
I.20　Healthcare
I.22　Industrial products
I.23　Information technology services
I.25　Leisure/hospitality
I.27　Manufacturing
I.28　Media/publishing
I.29　Medical/medical products
I.32　Retail

Summit Capital Associates, Inc.

745 Fifth Avenue, Suite 900
New York, New York 10151
(212) 308-4155
Fax: (212) 223-7363

Key contact:
Mr. Richard Messina

Area served: United States

Preferred stages of financing: First stage, Second
stage, Mezzanine, LBO/MBO

Industries:
I.19　Generalist

Ticonderoga Capital, Inc.

535 Madison Avenue, 36th Floor
New York, New York 10022
(212) 906-7100
Fax: (212) 906-8690
E-mail: mromwe@ticondergoacap.com

Key contact:
Mr. Michael J. Cardito, Associate
Mr. Peter A. Leidel, Partner
Mr. Oliver Haarmann, Principal

Description: We are a private equity investment firm
with over $125 million of capital under management.
Our professionals collectively have over 40 years of
private equity investing experience. Having invested
capital in 39 companies since 1991, our professionals
have extensive experience investing in and providing
strategic assistance to rapidly growing companies.

Amount of capital invested: approximately $12 million

Preferred investment size: $5-10 million

Amount under management: $100-500 million

Area served: North America

Preferred stages of financing: Expansion, Late stage
growth

Industries:
I.06　Communications
I.12　Distribution
I.13　Education
I.15　Energy/natural resources/utilities
I.23　Information technology services
I.32　Retail
I.34　Services (business)
I.35　Services (consumer)

Sampling of portfolio companies: Community Rehab
Centers (regional outpatient physical & occupational
therapy services organization); Professional Dental
Assoc. (a dental practice management company
which seeks to partner with successful private
practice dentists throughout the Eastern seaboard in
building practices that deliver exceptional care
service & financial performance); Boots & Coots
(specializes in oil well firefighting & blow-outs);
Concho Resources Inc. (acquires oil & gas properties
in the Permian Basin of Texas & New Mexico & the
onshore Gulf Coast in Texas & Louisiana); Fintube,
LP (manufacturer of precision-welded finned tubes &
derivative products used by the electric industry in
generation plants & by petrochemical & refining
industry processing plants); Interenergy Corp. (diversified energy company which provides natural gas
gathering, processing, distribution & marketing
services in the Rocky Mountain & Mid-Continent

regions); Meenan Oil Co., Inc. (heating oil distributor); Roemer-Swanson Energy Corp. (focuses on three market niches: 1) gas imbalance properties, 2) Section 29 tax credit properties & 3) prospect generation); The Big Party Corp. (party supply superstore with store locations in New England & Florida); Lids Corp. (retail chain of stores positioned as "category killer" by offering the widest possible selection of casual headwear); Metal Supermarkets Ltd. (oversees 41 owned or franchised wholesale metal parts distribution centers in Canada, the U.S. & the United Kingdom); Viking Office Products (mail order direct marketer of office supplies); Radio Movil Digital Americas, Inc. (provider of specialized mobile radio wireless dispatch communications services to businesses in the major countries of South America); CapMac Holdings (monoline financial guaranty insurer specializing in structured asset-backed & other taxable obligations); Carr Separations, Inc. (produces centrifugal separation devices); Cornell Corrections, Inc. (develops, acquires & operates private correctional facilities; private prison management company); Formica Corp. (designs, manufactures & distributes decorative laminates & other surfacing products through most of the world; produces high pressure laminates); Stolper-Fabralloy Co., LLC (fabricator of turbo-machinery components for commercial & military uses for both original equipment manufacturers & overhaul & repair customers); Team Bancshares, Inc. (acquires, recapitalizes & manages commercial banks & related assets in Texas); USI Holdings Corp. (consolidator of small, privately-held commercial insurance brokerage & insurance-related financial services firms)

TLC Funding Corporation

660 White Plains Road
Tarrytown, New York 10591
(914) 332-5200
Fax: (914) 332-5660

Key contact:
Mr. Phillip G. Kass

Area served: Connecticut, Massachusetts, New Jersey,

New York

Preferred stages of financing: Start up, First stage

Industries:
I.27   Manufacturing
I.32   Retail
I.34   Services (business)
I.35   Services (consumer)

Toronto Dominion Capital

31 West 52nd Street, 20th Floor
New York, New York 10019
(212) 827-7760
Fax: (212) 974-8429
E-mail: richb@tdusa.com

Key contact:
Mr. Brian Rich, Managing Director
Mr. Marc Michel, Managing Director

Description: We are a $300 million private equity partnership which is affiliated with Toronto Dominion Bank. We focus on investing in telecommunications and media providers, healthcare servicers, internet services, energy providers and other service businesses. We consider middle stage growth and buyout opportunities and private investments in both private and public companies.

Amount of capital invested: $140 million

Preferred investment size: $5-20 million

Amount under management: $100-500 million

Area served: United States

Preferred stages of financing: Second stage, Mezzanine, LBO/MBO, Expansion

Industries:
I.02   Agriculture/forestry/fishing/mining
I.04   Broadcasting
I.06   Communications
I.10   Consulting
I.12   Distribution
I.15   Energy/natural resources/utilities
I.16   Entertainment
I.20   Healthcare
I.21   High technology
I.23   Information technology services
I.24   Internet services/e-commerce
I.28   Media/publishing
I.29   Medical/medical products
I.30   New media
I.34   Services (business)

Sampling of portfolio companies: American Cellular (rural cellular operator); CellNet Systems (wireless data transmission provider servicing the utilities industry); Charter Communications (cable television operator concentrated in the Southeastern U.S.); Global TeleSystems Group, Inc. (wireless & wireline communication provider in Russia & Europe); Inter-Act (in-store, interactive marketing company providing targeted coupons to customers); Intermedia Communications (TCI affiliated cable operator concentrated in the Southeastern U.S.); Nassau Broadcasting Partners, LP (New Jersey based radio broadcaster); Pathnet, Inc. (facilities-based long distance communications provider); Prime Cable (leading cable operator); Real Time Data (provider of wireless information services to the vending machine industry); TeleCorp (PCS operator & AT&T affiliate); Triton Communications, Inc. (PCS operator & AT&T affiliate); UPC (operator of cable systems in Europe & the Middle East); Western Wireless (cellular communications & PCS provider): Wireless One Network (cellular operator in Southwest Florida); American Mobile Satellite Corp. (wireless communications provider in Southeast Asia & Latin America); American Radio Systems (diversified broadcast radio group); Cablevision (cable tv company); Geotek Communications, Inc. (SMR operator which is implementing a new wireless technology); Sygnet Wireless (independent cellular operator)

Trammell-Shott Capital Management, LLC

19 West 34th Street, Suite 1013
New York, New York 10001
(212) 947-8610
Fax: (212) 947-8641
E-mail: tramshott@aol.com

Key contact:
Mr. Webb Trammell, Member
Mr. Paul Reese, Member
Mr. George Shott, Member

Description: We are focused exclusively on providing
liquidity to private & institutional investors through
the purchase of secondary positions in venture
capital & buyout funds.

Amount of capital invested: $4.5 million

Preferred investment size: $5 million

Amount under management: <$10 million

Area served: Asia, Europe, North America

Preferred stage of financing: Secondaries

Industries:
I.01   Aerospace
I.02   Agriculture/forestry/fishing/mining
I.03   Biotech/genetic engineering
I.04   Broadcasting
I.05   Chemicals
I.06   Communications

I.07   Computer hardware
I.08   Computer software
I.09   Construction
I.10   Consulting
I.11   Consumer products
I.12   Distribution
I.13   Education
I.14   Electronics
I.15   Energy/natural resources/utilities
I.16   Entertainment
I.17   Environmental services/waste management
I.18   Financial services
I.19   Generalist
I.20   Healthcare
I.21   High technology
I.22   Industrial products
I.23   Information technology services
I.24   Internet services/e-commerce
I.25   Leisure/hospitality
I.26   Life sciences
I.27   Manufacturing
I.28   Media/publishing
I.29   Medical/medical products
I.30   New media
I.32   Retail
I.33   Semiconductors
I.34   Services (business)
I.35   Services (consumer)
I.36   Transportation
I.37   Wholesale

Triad Capital Corp. of New York

305 Seventh Avenue, 20th Floor
New York, New York 10001
(212) 243-7360
Fax: (212) 243-7647

Key contact:
Mr. John Tear

Mr. Oscar Figueroa

Area served: United States

Industries:
I.19   Generalist

Trusty Capital Inc.

350 Fifth Avenue, Suite 2026
New York, New York 10118
(212) 629-3011
Fax: (212) 629-3019

Key contact:
Mr. Yungduk Hahn

Area served: Northeast

Preferred stages of financing: Seed, Start up, First
stage, Second stage

Industries:
I.19   Generalist

United Capital Investment Corp.

60 East 42nd Street, Suite 1515
New York, New York 10165
(212) 682-7210
Fax: (212) 573-6352

Key contact:
Mr. Paul Lee

Area served: Northeast

Preferred stage of financing: Later stage

Industries:
I.19   Generalist
I.29   Medical/medical products
I.32   Retail

Vega Capital Corporation

80 Business Park Drive
Armonk, New York 10504
(914) 273-1025
Fax: (914) 273-1028

Key contact:
Mr. Ronald A. Linden, President

Description: We are a small business investment
company (SBIC).

Amount of capital invested: $2 million

Preferred investment size: $500,000-1 million

Amount under management: $10-25 million

Area served: United States

Preferred stages of financing: Mezzanine, LBO/MBO, Expansion, Int'l expansion

Industries:
I.19   Generalist

Vencon Management, Inc.
301 West 53rd Street
New York, New York 10019
(212) 581-8787
Fax: (212) 397-4126
E-mail: vencon@worldnet.att.net

Key contact:
Ms. Julia Lam, Senior Analyst
Mr. Irvin Barash, President

Description: We are one of the world's oldest venture capital firms. Located in the heart of New York City, we specialize in certain technologies. Our advisory division provides venturing and screening services to global businesses.

Founded: 1973

Preferred investment size: $500,000

Amount under management: <$10 million

Area served: Worldwide

Preferred stages of financing: Seed, Start up, First stage, LBO/MBO

Industries:
I.03   Biotech/genetic engineering
I.05   Chemicals
I.14   Electronics
I.15   Energy/natural resources/utilities
I.17   Environmental services/waste management
I.21   High technology
I.26   Life sciences
I.27   Manufacturing
I.29   Medical/medical products
I.33   Semiconductors

Venrock Associates
30 Rockefeller Plaza, Room 5508
New York, New York 10112
(212) 649-5600
Fax: (212) 649-5788
Web: www.venrock.com

Key contact:
Mr. Ted McCourtney, Managing General Partner
Mr. Tony Evnin, Managing General Partner
Mr. Dave Hathaway, Managing General Partner
Ms. Kim Rummelsburg, General Partner
Mr. Mark Bailey, General Partner
Mr. Joe Casey, Associate
Mr. Bryan Roberts, Associate

Description: We are the venture capital arm of the Rockefeller Family, continuing a tradition of funding entrepreneurs that now spans six decades. Our objective is to create long term value by helping build new high technology companies and industries from the earliest stages.

Preferred stages of financing: Seed, Start up, First stage

Industries:
I.03   Biotech/genetic engineering
I.06   Communications
I.07   Computer hardware
I.08   Computer software
I.14   Electronics
I.24   Internet services/e-commerce
I.26   Life sciences
I.29   Medical/medical products

Sampling of portfolio companies: Brightware (internet financial services software); Haystack Labs (develops & markets server software for active intrusion detection & suspicious network activity); Spyglass (develops & markets embedded software components for internet & intranet application development); Airsoft/Shiva (wireless communications software); Int'l. CableTel (develops, constructs & operates broadband communications systems outside the U.S. to provide integrated "last mile" telecommunications services to both businesses & residential customers); XLNT Designs, Inc. (gigabit LAN switching equipment); 3-D/fx Interactive (developing a family of low-cost graphics subsystems aimed at delivering real-time textured-mapped 3-D images for commercial & consumer video game markets); Echelon (low-cost single chip programmable control & communication processor); Award Software (system software including BIOS for PC's); Front-Office Technology (document management system for Microsoft Exchange that fully integrates with Microsoft Windows NT® & Windows 95®); Simba Technologies Software (ODBC middleware tools for database access); Apollo Computer/Hewlett-Packard (workstation class computers & instruments); EP Technologies/Boston Scientific (electrophysiology catheters & systems for minimally-invasive procedures to diagnose & treat cardiac tachyarrhythmias); Caliper Technologies (microanalytical instrumentation); PerSeptive Biosystems (perfusion chromatography for biotechnology research & large-scale biopharmaceutical processing); MedPartners/Mullikin (acquire, develop & operate physician group practices); ThermoLase (laser-based hair removal & skin care); IDUN Pharmaceuticals (discovery of small molecule drugs that would interfere with the programmed cell death processes for the treatment of hyperproliferative & degenerative disorders); SUGEN (biopharmaceuticals from receptor-based approaches to drug discovery); ThermoSpectra (nondestructive analysis instruments that use various energy sources or signals & fast, high-resolution data handling capabilities)

Venture Opportunities Corporation
150 East 58th Street, 16th Floor
New York, New York 10155

(212) 832-3737
Fax: (212) 980-6603

Key contact:
Mr. Jerrold March
Mr. A. Fred March

Area served: Mid-Atlantic, Midwest, Northeast, Southeast

Preferred stages of financing: First stage, Second stage, LBO/MBO, Third/later stage

Industries:
I.06   Communications
I.07   Computer hardware
I.12   Distribution
I.14   Electronics
I.19   Generalist
I.22   Industrial products
I.29   Medical/medical products
I.32   Retail
I.34   Services (business)
I.35   Services (consumer)

Wand Partners

630 Fifth Avenue, Suite 2435
New York, New York 10111
(212) 632-3429
Fax: (212) 307-5599
E-mail: mpa@wandpartners.com
Web: www.wandpartners.com

Key contact:
Mr. Bruce Schnitzer, Founder
Mr. David Callard, Operating Principal
Mr. John S. Struck, Operating Principal
Mr. Malcolm P. Appelbaum, Operating Principal
Mr. Mark L. V. Esiri, Operating Principal

Description: We are a private equity investment firm which is flexible with regard to our role in any given transaction. We presently act as the general partner of Wand Equity Portfolio II on behalf of selected institutional investors including a small group of active capital partners. From an investment standpoint, we look for a balance between sponsored transactions in industries with which our principals are familiar and co-investments facilitating the completion of transactions initiated by others.

Founded: 1987

Preferred stages of financing: Mezzanine, LBO/MBO, Recapitalizations

Industries:
I.12   Distribution
I.15   Energy/natural resources/utilities
I.18   Financial services
I.23   Information technology services
I.27   Manufacturing
I.32   Retail
I.34   Services (business)

Sampling of portfolio companies: Bits & Pieces Inc. (distribution, retailing); Knowledge Base Marketing (business services)

E.M. Warburg, Pincus & Company, LLC

466 Lexington Avenue
New York, New York 10017-3147
(212) 878-0600
Fax: (212) 878-9351
Web: www.warburgpincus.com

Key contact:
Ms. Linda Doherty
Mr. Christopher W. Brody
Mr. Harold Brown
Mr. William H. Janeway
Mr. Sidney Lapidus
Mr. Rodman W. Moorhead, III

Mr. Howard H. Newman
Mr. Lionel I. Pincus
Mr. John L. Vogelstein

Description: Through private investment partnerships, we direct the investment of $7 billion in assets on behalf of well-known institutions and pension funds. Our partnerships represent one of the largest sources of private venture capital financing in the U.S.

Founded: 1939

Area served: Worldwide

Wardenclyffe LLC

370 Lexington Avenue, 19th Floor
New York, New York 10017
(212) 370-3737
Fax: (212) 370-7889
E-mail: shapiro@wclyffe.com

Key contact:
Mr. Mark Shapiro, Managing Director
Mr. Douglas Ellenoff, Managing Director

Description: Micro-Cap public companies (<$150 million mkt. cap.): private placements of equity or debt with equity features, bridge financings, later stage venture funding for private companies: companies should be at or near cash flow breakeven.

Preferred investment size: $1-5 million

Amount under management: <$10 million

Area served: Asia, Europe, United States

Preferred stages of financing: Second stage, LBO/MBO, Expansion, Int'l expansion

Industries:
I.19   Generalist

Wasserstein Adelson Ventures

31 West 52nd Street, 27th Floor
New York, New York 10019
(212) 969-2700
Fax: (212) 969-7879

Key contact:
Mr. Townsend Ziebold, Managing Director
Mr. Perry Steiner, Vice President
Mr. Tom Huang, Associate
Mr. Guanar Aggarwal, Analyst

Area served: United States

Preferred stages of financing: Start up, First stage,
Second stage

Sampling of portfolio companies: Cimabase Software
(software database); Digital River (electronic
software distribution); Parable Corp. (consumer
software); Potomac Group Homes (assisted living);
Venetec (medical devices); Pulse Entertainment
(software developer tools); Total Entertainment
Network (on-line computer gaming)

Winfield Capital Corporation

237 Mamaroneck Avenue
White Plains, New York 10605
(914) 949-2600
Fax: (914) 949-7195

Key contact:
Mr. Paul Perlin
Mr. Stanley M. Pechman

Industries:
I.19   Generalist

North Carolina

The Aurora Funds, Inc.

2525 Meridian Parkway, Suite 220
Durham, North Carolina 27713
(919) 484-0400
Fax: (919) 484-0444
E-mail: afinfo@aurorafunds.com
Web: www.aurorafunds.com

Key contact:
Mr. B. Jefferson Clark, President/Manager
Mr. M. Scott Albert, CEO/Manager

Description: We invest primarily in emerging-based
companies, with a focus on information science and
life science, located in the Southeast United States.
Typical investments range between $250,000 and
$1.5 million in any one company. We prefer to be an
active lead investor but will co-invest with other
firms.

Preferred investment size: $250,000

Amount under management: $10-25 million

Area served: Southeast

Preferred stages of financing: Seed, Start up, First
stage, Second stage

Industries:
I.03   Biotech/genetic engineering

I.05	Chemicals
I.06	Communications
I.07	Computer hardware
I.08	Computer software
I.11	Consumer products
I.14	Electronics
I.17	Environmental services/waste management
I.20	Healthcare
I.21	High technology
I.23	Information technology services
I.24	Internet services/e-commerce
I.26	Life sciences
I.27	Manufacturing
I.29	Medical/medical products

Sampling of portfolio companies: Accipiter (internet
software); All Three Inc. (manufacturing); Injury
Data Corp. (healthcare service); IntraSoft, Inc.
(software management tools); Insect Biotechnology,
Inc. (biotechnology); MicroMass Communications
(communications software); Natus Medical, Inc.
(medical devices); OxiDyn, Inc. (industrial products);
RCS Technologies, Inc. (materials); Solution Technology, Inc. (semiconductor disposables); United
Emergency Services, Inc. (healthcare service); Viro-
Logic, Inc. (biotechnology); Xanthon, Inc. (diagnostics)

Blue Ridge Management Company, Inc.

P.O. Box 21962
Greensboro, North Carolina 27420
(336) 370-0576
Fax: (336) 274-4984

Key contact:
Mr. Edward C. McCarthy, Executive Vice President
Mr. F. James Becher, Jr., President
Mr. Russell R. Myers, Treasurer
Mr. Richard T. Maclean, Vice President

Area served: United States

Preferred stages of financing: Mezzanine, LBO/MBO,
Expansion

Industries:
I.12   Distribution
I.23   Information technology services
I.27   Manufacturing
I.34   Services (business)

Sampling of portfolio companies: The Computer Group
(computer network integration services); Dragon
Corp. (lawn & garden packaged products); SDX
Electronics (electronic manufacturing services); Lors

Medical Corp. (home healthcare provider); Circuit Board Assemblers (electronic manufacturing services); Cherokee Wireless Services (wireless telecom infrastructure services); Tech Resource Group (salesforce automation training & support); Varel Manufacturing (oil field, mining & industrial drill bits); Solar Cosmetic Labs (sun care, cosmetic & health & beauty products)

First Union Capital Partners

301 South College Street
One First Union Center, 5th Floor
Charlotte, North Carolina 28288-0732
(704) 374-4810
Fax: (704) 374-6711

Key contact:
Mr. Pearce Landry
Mr. Kevin J. Roche

Area served: United States

Preferred stages of financing: First stage, Second stage, LBO/MBO, Third/later stage

Industries:
I.06   Communications
I.28   Media/publishing
I.29   Medical/medical products
I.32   Retail
I.35   Services (consumer)

Intersouth Partners

P.O. Box 13546
Research Triangle Park, North Carolina 27709-3546
(919) 544-6473
Fax: (919) 544-6645
E-mail: michelle@intersouth.com
Web: www.intersouth.com

Key contact:
Mr. Dennis J. Dougherty, General Partner
Mr. Mitchell Mumma, General Partner
Mr. D. Gregory Main, Partner
Mr. Jeffrey P. Hoogendam, Associate
Ms. Hazel Cordle, CFO
Ms. Michelle M. Dattellas, Administrative Assistant

Description: We are dedicated to the proven concept that America's entrepreneurial companies, adequately capitalized and professionally advised, are superior investments for institutions and high net worth individuals. Venture capital funds provide the means for such investing.

Founded: 1985

Preferred investment size: Under $5 million

Area served: Southeast, Southwest

Preferred stages of financing: Seed, Start up, First stage

Industries:
I.03   Biotech/genetic engineering
I.08   Computer software
I.14   Electronics
I.17   Environmental services/waste management
I.20   Healthcare
I.26   Life sciences
I.27   Manufacturing
I.29   Medical/medical products

Sampling of portfolio companies: Accordant Health Services (develops & offers disease management for rare chronic diseases); Cardiovascular Diagnostics, Inc. (develops & manufactures diagnostic analyzers & disposable test cards for use in cardiovascular point-of-care patient treatment); Dominion Biosciences (developing biorational pesticides that interrupt the metabolic pathway of insects utilizing patents licensed from Virginia Tech); Insmed Pharmaceuticals (research in therapeutics for Type II, adult on-set, Diabetes); MelanX, Inc. (developing proprietary dermatologic products licensed from the University of Oklahoma); MIST, Inc. (designs, manufactures & markets laparoscopic surgical equipment & instrumentation); Novum, Inc. (provides clinical, analytical, statistical & report writing services for pharmaceutical companies); Sphinx (developed novel therapeutic agents based on a technology known as Cellular Signal Transduction); SunPharm (licensed all the technology from the high profile laboratory of Dr. Raymond Bergeron at the University of Florida); Xanthon (licensed from Dr. Holden Thorpe's laboratory at the University of North Carolina at Chapel Hill, a method for the direct detection of DNA & RNA); Burl Software (designed PC based software tools to quickly examine & repair legacy code like COBOL, still the predominant language for business application program); Digital Recorders, Inc. (manufactures digital audio & visual sign products for use on highways, in mass transit & law enforcement); Integrated Silicon Systems (develops software tools that automate & accelerate integrated circuit design); Legal Network Technologies (provides electronic data interchange between credit grantors & collection attorneys); Trancept Systems, Inc. (design a hardware accelerator for workstations that speeded up mechanical engineering rendering tasks by 100 times); UOL Publishing, Inc. (publisher of high quality, interactive & on-demand educational courseware for the online education & training market through the worldwide web); Vanguard Communications, Inc. (develops & markets multiplexing equipment for use in the subscriber loop of telephone networks); Claw Island Foods (uses a proprietary process for freezing whole crustaceans); IllumElex Corp. (lighting management firm which focuses on maintenance, retrofit & energy services); MPR Services, Inc. (removes comtaminants from gas treating systems utilizing a patented ion-exchange technology)

Key Equity Capital

227 West Trade Street, Suite 1840
Charlotte, North Carolina 28202
(704) 347-1178
Fax: (704) 347-1107

Key contact:
Ms. Shannon G. Smith, General Partner

Description: We invest equity capital in companies that have both exceptional management teams and the potential to achieve significant future growth resulting in long-term equity appreciation. In every portfolio company, we provide the management team with a significant equity participation, reflecting our commitment to appropriate realization of the investment reward.

Amount of capital invested: $42 million

Preferred investment size: $10-25 million

Amount under management: $100-500 million

Area served: United States

Preferred stages of financing: LBO/MBO, Expansion

Industries:
I.01   Aerospace
I.05   Chemicals
I.07   Computer hardware
I.11   Consumer products
I.12   Distribution
I.14   Electronics
I.17   Environmental services/waste management
I.20   Healthcare
I.22   Industrial products
I.27   Manufacturing
I.29   Medical/medical products
I.34   Services (business)
I.37   Wholesale

Sampling of portfolio companies: Advanced Cast Products (cast iron parts); Cardinal Packaging (plastic packaging); Crown Simplimatic (packaging machinery & systems engineering); CSM Industries (molybdenum products); Decatur Aluminum (aluminum sheet); DeCrane Aircraft Holdings (avionics); Family Dental Center Service Co. of America (provider of management services to dental practices); GEO Specialty Chemicals (specialty chemicals); Glasstech (glass processing systems); Jorgensen Forge (large open-die forgings/steel, aluminum & titanium); Laurel Industries (plastic additives); London's Farm Dairy (milk & ice cream processor); S. Madill Ltd. (logging industry equipment); Nat'l. Medical Diagnostics (medical diagnostics equipment servicer); OMEGA Polymer Technologies (plastic products); Ranpak Corp. (packaging materials); Sinter Metals (powdered metal parts); Spectra (computer printer hardware); STERIS (medical sterilization equipment)

Kitty Hawk Capital

2700 Coltsgate Road, Suite 202
Charlotte, North Carolina 28211
(704) 362-3909
Fax: (704) 362-2774
E-mail: khcmain@aol.com

Key contact:
Mr. Walter H. Wilkinson, Jr., General Partner
Mr. W. Chris Hegele, General Partner
Mr. Stephen W. Buchanan, General Partner

Description: We are a private venture capital firm founded in 1980, have approximately $100 million under management and invest our own capital in rapidly growing private companies. Diversified as to industry/stage of company development, we can invest up to $2 million per company. Target transaction size is $1 - $5 million.

Founded: 1980

Amount of capital invested: $4.5 million

Preferred investment size: $1.75 million

Amount under management: $25-100 million

Area served: Southeast

Preferred stages of financing: Start up, First stage, Second stage

Industries:
I.06   Communications
I.07   Computer hardware
I.08   Computer software
I.11   Consumer products
I.14   Electronics
I.17   Environmental services/waste management
I.20   Healthcare
I.21   High technology
I.23   Information technology services
I.24   Internet services/e-commerce
I.29   Medical/medical products
I.33   Semiconductors

Nations Bank Capital Investors

100 North Tryon Street, 10th Floor
Charlotte, North Carolina 28255
(704) 386-8063
Fax: (704) 386-6432

Key contact:
Mr. W. W. (Chet) Walker, Managing Director
Mr. Travis Hain, Managing Director
Ms. Ann Hayes, Managing Director
Mr. Walker Poole, Managing Director
Mr. Trey Sheridan, Managing Director

Description: Risk capital provider for Nations Bank Corp. providing late stage venture investing and equity capital for LBO's, growth financings and acquisitions.

Amount of capital invested: $140 million

Preferred investment size: Varies

Amount under management: $500 million -1 billion

Area served: United States

Preferred stages of financing: First stage, Second stage, Mezzanine, LBO/MBO, Expansion

Industries:
I.01   Aerospace
I.02   Agriculture/forestry/fishing/mining
I.03   Biotech/genetic engineering
I.04   Broadcasting
I.05   Chemicals
I.06   Communications
I.07   Computer hardware
I.08   Computer software
I.09   Construction
I.10   Consulting
I.11   Consumer products
I.12   Distribution

I.13	Education
I.14	Electronics
I.15	Energy/natural resources/utilities
I.16	Entertainment
I.17	Environmental services/waste management
I.18	Financial services
I.19	Generalist
I.20	Healthcare
I.21	High technology
I.22	Industrial products
I.23	Information technology services
I.24	Internet services/e-commerce
I.25	Leisure/hospitality
I.26	Life sciences
I.27	Manufacturing
I.28	Media/publishing
I.29	Medical/medical products
I.30	New media
I.32	Retail
I.33	Semiconductors
I.34	Services (business)
I.35	Services (consumer)
I.36	Transportation
I.37	Wholesale

Sampling of portfolio companies: Johnstown Wire Technologies (steel wire processor); Rite Industries, Inc. (textile & paper dye distributor); Dallas Stars Hockey, LLC (NHL franchise); Litchfield Theaters, Inc. (owner & operator of movie theaters); Q Clubs, Inc. (owner & operator of fitness clubs); Take-out Taxi, Inc. (restaurant delivery service); Affiliated Managers Group, Inc. (provider of asset management services); Costilla Energy, LLC (developer of oil & natural Gas Resources); Reef Chemical (oilfield service company); CallWare Technologies, Inc. (developer of computer telephony software); Empirical Software Inc. (developer of client server performance management software); GX Technology Corp. (developer of oil & gas exploration software); Magnavox Electronics Systems, Inc. (defense communications equipment developer & manufacturer); North American Technologies Group, Inc. (manufacturer of synthetic railroad ties); Classic Communications, Inc. (rural cable systems operator); LCC Corp. (provider of wireless communications engineering & design services); Interim Healthcare, Inc. (home healthcare provider); Serologicals, Inc. (processor of rare human antibodies); Memorial Operations Company (consolidator of cemeteries & funeral homes); Crown-Simplimatic (manufacturer of beverage packaging equipment)

The North Carolina Enterprise Fund, L.P.

3600 Glenwood Avenue, Suite 107
Raleigh, North Carolina 27612
(919) 781-2691
Fax: (919) 783-9195
Web: www.ncef.com

Key contact:
Mr. Charles T. Closson, President/CEO
Mr. Joseph A. Velk, Executive Vice President-Investments
Ms. Nancy P. Owens, Senior Vice President/CFO

Description: We are venture capital fund managing $23 milion of capital that makes equity investments in small to medium-sized private companies based in North Carolina. We invest in businesses which have the potential to become significant enterprises within their chosen markets in a reasonable time frame and do so without the commitment of unrealistic amounts of risk capital.

Amount of capital invested: $4.7 million

Preferred investment size: $1-2 million

Amount under management: $10-25 million

Area served: North Carolina

Preferred stages of financing: Start up, First stage, Second stage, Mezzanine, LBO/MBO, Expansion

Industries:

I.02	Agriculture/forestry/fishing/mining
I.03	Biotech/genetic engineering
I.06	Communications
I.07	Computer hardware
I.08	Computer software
I.11	Consumer products
I.12	Distribution
I.14	Electronics
I.17	Environmental services/waste management
I.20	Healthcare
I.21	High technology
I.22	Industrial products
I.23	Information technology services
I.24	Internet services/e-commerce
I.26	Life sciences
I.27	Manufacturing
I.29	Medical/medical products
I.33	Semiconductors

Sampling of portfolio companies: Aspect Minerals (mining/marketing wet-ground mica); BraodBand Technologies (interactive fiber-to-the-curb systems); Concept Fabrics (fire retardant fabric); Encelle, Inc. (bioartificial pancreas development); EnSys Environmental Products (on-site environmental diagnostic test kits); Genesis Cable (cable television system); Global Software (financial application software); IntraSoft, Inc. (intranet management software); Investment Mortgage Corp. (mortgage/insurance loan product); Microcosm Technologies (MEMS CAD software); NetEdge Systems, Inc. (multi-service access concentrators for telecommunications); Orologic, Inc. (ASIC-based quality of service solutions); PCX Corp. (prefabricated electrical rooms); RF Micro Devices (radio frequency semiconductors); Rostra Precision Controls (automotive aftermarket products); Secant Network Technologies (high-performance network security products); SELEE Corp. (ceramic foam filter manufacturer); Southern Assisted Living (assisted-living provider); SpectraSite Holdings, Inc. (building communication towers for wireless communication); Sphinx Pharmaceuticals (lipid second-messenger drug discovery)

A. M. Pappas & Associates
2222 Chapel Hill - Nelson Highway
Beta Building, Suite 420
Durham, North Carolina 27713
(919) 361-4990
Fax: (919) 361-0497
E-mail: jcollins@ampappas.com
Web: www.ampappas.com

Key contact:
Mr. Arthur M. Pappas, Chairman/CEO
Dr. William McCulloch, Chief Medical Officer
Mr. Peter C. Yorke, Chief Investment Officer
Mr. John M. McPherson, VP-New Business
   Development
Mr. Russell M. Savre, VP-Financial Operations
Mr. Richard E. Widin, VP-Health Info. Systems &
   Technology
Mr. Ford S. Worthy, VP-Staff Operations

Description: We are an international venture development company dedicated to accelerating the
development of life science companies, products and
related technologies. We bring together- under one
roof- risk capital and value-added management,
scientific and technical consulting expertise to help
our clients and our portfolio companies turn great
ideas into commercial successes.

Amount of capital invested: $20 million

Preferred investment size: $2 million

Amount under management: $25-100 million

Area served: Worldwide

Preferred stages of financing: Seed, Start up, First
stage, Second stage, Mezzanine

Industries:
I.03   Biotech/genetic engineering
I.26   Life sciences
I.29   Medical/medical products

Sampling of portfolio companies: SciQuest, Inc.
(operates a scientific vendor website); Maize Genetic
Resources (agricultural biotechnology); Ganymede
Software (computer & network software); Coper-
nicus Gene Systems (focuses on developing &
commercializing products for human gene therapy);
GeneLogic (differential display technology to
identify & quantify novel drug targets from nucleic
acid sequences)

Piedmont Venture Partners
6805 Morrison Boulevard, Suite 380
Charlotte, North Carolina 28211
(704) 365-2575
Fax: (704) 365-9733
E-mail: piedmontventurepartners@compuserve.com

Key contact:
Ms. Pamela Clement, Managing Partner
Ms. Stacy Anderson, Managing Partner
Mr. William Neal, III, Managing Partner

Description: Early stage information technology and
life sciences related companies based in the Southeastern United States.

Amount of capital invested: $10 million

Preferred investment size: $2 million

Amount under management: $10-25 million

Area served: Southeast

Preferred stages of financing: First stage, Second
stage, Expansion

Sampling of portfolio companies: Total Sports (internet
sports content); BuildNet (e-commerce builders &
suppliers); MultiNet (wireless T-1 connections to
internet); Motortrek (NASCAR licensing over
internet); Cortex Vision Systems (advanced surveil-
lance/monitoring); Venture Alliance (technology
transfer from Oak Ridge Nat'l. Labs); Optical Biopsy
(cancer detection with lasers); Ischemia (medical
diagnostics to determine if heart attack or stroke has
occurred); Persimmon IT (software developer,
clinical trials, data base marketing management);
Reprogenesis (tissue engineering); Machine Xpert
(predictive maintenance)

Wakefield Group
1110 East Morehead Street
Charlotte, North Carolina 28204
(704) 372-0355
Fax: (704) 372-8216
Web: www.wakefieldgroup.com

Key contact:
Ms. Anna Spangler Nelson, Managing Director
Mr. Thomas C. Nelson, Managing Director
Mr. Michael F. Elliott, Managing Director

Description: A venture capital firm providing growth
capital for companies located primarily in the
southeast.

Preferred investment size: $1.5 million

Area served: Mid-Atlantic, The Carolinas

Preferred stages of financing: Start up, First stage,
Second stage, LBO/MBO, Expansion

Industries:
I.08   Computer software
I.11   Consumer products
I.12   Distribution
I.18   Financial services
I.20   Healthcare
I.21   High technology
I.22   Industrial products
I.23   Information technology services
I.24   Internet services/e-commerce
I.27   Manufacturing
I.29   Medical/medical products
I.34   Services (business)
I.35   Services (consumer)

North Dakota

InvestAmerica N.D. Management, Inc.
406 Main Avenue, Suite 404
Fargo, North Dakota 58103
(701) 298-0003
Fax: (701) 293-7819
E-mail: jcosgriff@compuserve.com

Key contact:
Mr. John Cosgriff, Manager
Mr. Robert Comey, Vice President
Mr. David Schroder, President
Mr. Kevin Mullane, Vice President

Description: We are the general partner and investment advisor for the North Dakota Small Business Investment Company (NDSBIC). NDSBIC is a licensed SBIC and will invest a majority of its capital in later stage companies.

Amount of capital invested: $2.2 million

Preferred investment size: $500,000

Amount under management: <$10 million

Area served: United States

Preferred stages of financing: Mezzanine, LBO/MBO, Expansion

Industries:
I.01 Aerospace
I.02 Agriculture/forestry/fishing/mining
I.03 Biotech/genetic engineering
I.05 Chemicals
I.06 Communications
I.07 Computer hardware
I.08 Computer software
I.09 Construction
I.10 Consulting
I.11 Consumer products
I.12 Distribution
I.13 Education
I.14 Electronics
I.17 Environmental services/waste management
I.19 Generalist
I.20 Healthcare
I.21 High technology
I.22 Industrial products
I.23 Information technology services
I.24 Internet services/e-commerce
I.25 Leisure/hospitality
I.26 Life sciences
I.27 Manufacturing
I.29 Medical/medical products
I.32 Retail
I.33 Semiconductors
I.34 Services (business)
I.35 Services (consumer)
I.36 Transportation
I.37 Wholesale

NDSBIC
406 Main Avenue, Suite 404
Fargo, North Dakota 58103
(701) 237-6132
(701) 298-0003
Fax: (701) 293-7819

Key contact:
Mr. John Cosgriff

Ohio

Alpha Capital Partners, Ltd.
310 West Monument Avenue, Suite 400
Dayton, Ohio 45402
(937) 222-2006
Fax: (937) 228-0115
Web: www.alphacapital.com

Key contact:
Mr. Orval E. Cook, Senior Vice President
Mr. Curtis R. Crocker, Vice President

Description: We are a venture capital management organization which provides equity financing for promising growth business and buyouts or recapitalizations of established companies. The investment activity of Alpha Capital is concentrated mainly in the greater Midwest. The entrepreneurs whom we have supported have achieved success in a variety of industries.

Founded: 1984

Amount of capital invested: $4,109,377

Preferred investment size: $500,000-3 million

Amount under management: $25-100 million

Area served: Midwest, United States

Preferred stages of financing: First stage, Second stage, LBO/MBO, Expansion

Industries:
I.01 Aerospace
I.02 Agriculture/forestry/fishing/mining
I.03 Biotech/genetic engineering
I.04 Broadcasting
I.05 Chemicals
I.06 Communications
I.07 Computer hardware
I.08 Computer software
I.09 Construction
I.10 Consulting
I.11 Consumer products
I.12 Distribution
I.13 Education
I.15 Energy/natural resources/utilities
I.16 Entertainment

I.17   Environmental services/waste management
I.18   Financial services
I.19   Generalist
I.20   Healthcare
I.21   High technology
I.22   Industrial products
I.23   Information technology services
I.24   Internet services/e-commerce
I.25   Leisure/hospitality
I.26   Life sciences
I.27   Manufacturing
I.28   Media/publishing
I.30   New media
I.32   Retail
I.33   Semiconductors
I.34   Services (business)
I.35   Services (consumer)
I.36   Transportation
I.37   Wholesale

Sampling of portfolio companies: Clear Communications Corp. (software sytems for managing telecom broadband network performance); Color Savvy Systems, Ltd. (systems for precise replication of color); Internet Dynamics, Inc. (internet security system for intranets & extranets); LDMI (switch-based reseller of long distance telecommunications); Shockley Communications Corp. (operator of a group of AM/FM stations in upper Midwest); ½ Off Card Shop, Inc. (specialty retailer of discount cards & party supplies); NorthWord Press, Inc. (publisher of nature theme music, books & other merchandise); Thousand Oaks & Ambassador Lanes (mega centers for bowling & recreation); Vista Restaurants, Inc. (restaurant management company & area franchisee for Perkins); CareCentric Solutions, Inc. (software systems for clinical applications in home healthcare); Glenmark Assoc., Inc. (nursing home facilities & ancillary services); Merge Technologies, Inc. (digital interconnect software & systems for medical imaging equipment); Origen, Inc. (commercialization of veterinary vaccine technologies from universities); Pioneer Laboratories, Inc. (surgical cable & instruments); Somatogen, Inc. (developer of bioengineered blood & other pharmaceutical products); Commercial National Bank (community banking group); Lumitex, Inc. (lighting components for the electronics, medical & automotive industries); Sutton Tool Co. (manufacturer of deburring machines & work holding devices); Vapor Systems Technologies (systems for recovery & control of vapors from fuels)

Banc One Capital Partners

150 East Gay Street, 24th Floor
Columbus, Ohio 43215
(614) 217-1100
Fax: (614) 217-0192
E-mail: laakhamis@bocc.com

Key contact:
Mr. James H. Wolfe, Managing Director
Mr. Donald B. Gardiner, Managing Director
Mr. William P. Leahy, Managing Director
Mr. Michael J. Endres, Chairman

Description: We provide mezzanine, venture capital and financial advisory services to middle-market operating companies in connection with mergers and acquisitions, recapitalizations, corporate divestitures and expansion capital. Such financings are typically in the form of subordinated debt with warrants and/or preferred stock.

Amount of capital invested: $170 million

Preferred investment size: $5-8 million

Amount under management: $100-500 million

Area served: United States

Preferred stages of financing: Mezzanine, LBO/MBO, Expansion

Industries:
I.06   Communications
I.11   Consumer products
I.12   Distribution
I.13   Education
I.14   Electronics
I.17   Environmental services/waste management
I.18   Financial services
I.19   Generalist
I.20   Healthcare
I.22   Industrial products
I.27   Manufacturing
I.28   Media/publishing
I.29   Medical/medical products
I.34   Services (business)
I.36   Transportation
I.37   Wholesale

Sampling of portfolio companies: Compaq Computer Co. (computer manufacturer); Metro Airlines, Inc. (regional commuter airlines); Beauty Control (cosmetic manufacturer); Callaway Golf Co. (manufacturer of golf clubs); First Plus Financial Group (financial services); Plains Resources, Inc. (oil & gas exploration); A&W Brands (soft drink manufacturer); Pronet, Inc. (telephone paging services); Dr. Pepper Bottling Co. (soft drink bottler); Enclean, Inc. (environmental services); Community Health Systems (healthcare facilities & services); Railtex, Inc. (railcar leasing); Kemet Electronics (manufacturer electronic capacitors); Matador Petroleum Corp. (oil exploration & production); DeCrane Aircraft Holdings (manufacturer aerospace products); Argyle Television (operator of television stations)

Battelle Venture Partners

601 West Fifth Avenue
Columbus, Ohio 43201
(614) 424-7005
Fax: (614) 424-4874

Key contact:
Mr. Paul F. Purcell

Area served: United States

Preferred stages of financing: Start up, First stage, Second stage

Industries:
I.15   Energy/natural resources/utilities

Brantley Venture Partners

20600 Chagrin Boulevard, Suite 1150
Cleveland, Ohio 44122
(216) 283-4800
Fax: (216) 283-5324

Key contact:
Mr. Kevin J. Cook, Associate
Mr. Robert P. Pinkas, General Partner
Mr. Michael J. Finn, General Partner
Mr. Paul H. Cascio, General Partner

Area served: United States

Preferred stages of financing: LBO/MBO, Expansion,
Consolidation opportunities

Industries:
I.01   Aerospace

I.05	Chemicals
I.08	Computer software
I.10	Consulting
I.11	Consumer products
I.12	Distribution
I.17	Environmental services/waste management
I.18	Financial services
I.19	Generalist
I.20	Healthcare
I.22	Industrial products
I.23	Information technology services
I.27	Manufacturing
I.28	Media/publishing
I.32	Retail
I.34	Services (business)
I.35	Services (consumer)

CID Equity Partners

312 Elm Street, Suite 2600
Cincinnati, Ohio 45202
(513) 381-4748
Fax: (317) 269-2355
Web: www.cidequity.com

Key contact:
Mr. John T. Hackett, Managing General Partner

The Huntington Center
41 South High Street, Suite 3650
Columbus, Ohio 43215
(614) 222-8184
Fax: (614) 222-8190
E-mail: schou@cidequity.com
Web: www.cidequity.com

Key contact:
Mr. William S. Oesterle, General Partner

Description: We are a venture capital firm with offices
in Indianapolis, Chicago, Cincinnati and Columbus.
Our objective is to invest in companies with potential
for substantial value appreciation. Through long-
term investments of five to seven years, we develop a
partnership, establish a direction for growth, and
build the value of each company. While daily operating decisions are the responsibility of management,
we play an active role in the strategic direction of the
business. The size of the investments are generally
between $1 million and $10 million.

Amount of capital invested: $35 million

Preferred investment size: $3-5 million

Amount under management: $100-500 million

Area served: United States

Preferred stages of financing: Seed, Start up, First
stage, Mezzanine

Industries:

I.03	Biotech/genetic engineering
I.06	Communications
I.08	Computer software
I.12	Distribution
I.18	Financial services
I.20	Healthcare
I.21	High technology
I.22	Industrial products
I.23	Information technology services
I.24	Internet services/e-commerce
I.27	Manufacturing
I.34	Services (business)

Clarion Capital Corp.

1801 East Ninth Street, Suite 510
Cleveland, Ohio 44114
(216) 687-1096
Fax: (216) 694-3545

Key contact:
Mr. Morris Wheeler
Mr. Morton A. Cohen

Area served: Midwest

Preferred stages of financing: First stage, Second
stage, LBO/MBO

Industries:

I.03	Biotech/genetic engineering
I.05	Chemicals
I.06	Communications
I.07	Computer hardware
I.08	Computer software
I.11	Consumer products
I.12	Distribution
I.14	Electronics
I.21	High technology
I.29	Medical/medical products
I.33	Semiconductors

Desco Capital Partners

150 East Campus View Boulevard, Suite 250
Columbus, Ohio 43235
(614) 888-8855
Fax: (614) 888-3779
E-mail: descovc@iwaynet.net

Web: descovc.com

Key contact:
Mr. Roger Bailey, General Partner
Mr. David Siemer, Senior Investment Analyst

Mr. James Shade, Director of Corporate Development
Mr. Paul Kestler, Investment Manager

Description: We are a private investor group who funds enterprises exhibiting exceptional potential for growth. We seek to invest our capital in a 3 to 7 year period. We work in partnership with managers and owners to maximize value.

Founded: 1992

Amount of capital invested: $10 million

Preferred investment size: $1-2 million

Amount under management: $25-100 million

Area served: United States

Preferred stages of financing: First stage, Second stage, Mezzanine, LBO/MBO, Expansion

Industries:
I.01 Aerospace
I.08 Computer software
I.14 Electronics
I.21 High technology
I.22 Industrial products
I.23 Information technology services
I.24 Internet services/e-commerce
I.27 Manufacturing
I.33 Semiconductors

Enterprise Ohio Investment Company

8 North Main Street
Dayton, Ohio 45402
(937) 226-0457
Fax: (937) 222-7035

Key contact:
Ms. Janet White
Mr. Steven Budd

Area served: Ohio

Preferred stages of financing: Second stage, Third/later stage

Industries:
I.19 Generalist

Key Equity Capital

127 Public Square, 6th Floor
Cleveland, Ohio 44114
(216) 689-5776
Fax: (216) 689-3204

Key contact:
Mr. David P. Given, General Partner
Mr. John F. Kirby, General Partner
Mr. Stephen R. Haynes, General Partner

Description: We invest equity capital in companies that have both exceptional management teams and the potential to achieve significant future growth resulting in long-term equity appreciation. In every portfolio company, we provide the management team with a significant equity participation, reflecting our commitment to appropriate realization of the investment reward.

Amount of capital invested: $42 million

Preferred investment size: $10-25 million

Amount under management: $100-500 million

Area served: United States

Preferred stages of financing: LBO/MBO, Expansion

Industries:
I.01 Aerospace
I.05 Chemicals
I.07 Computer hardware
I.11 Consumer products
I.12 Distribution
I.14 Electronics
I.17 Environmental services/waste management
I.20 Healthcare
I.22 Industrial products
I.27 Manufacturing
I.29 Medical/medical products
I.34 Services (business)
I.37 Wholesale

Sampling of portfolio companies: Advaced Cast Products (cast iron parts); Cardinal Packaging (plastic packaging); Crown Simplimatic (packaging machinery & systems engineering); CSM Industries (molybdenum products); Decatur Aluminum (aluminum sheet); DeCrane Aircraft Holdings (avionics); Family Dental Center Service Co. of America (provider of management services to dental practices); GEO Specialty Chemicals (specialty chemicals); Glasstech (glass processing systems); Jorgensen Forge (large open-die forgings/steel, aluminum & titanium); Laurel Industries (plastic additives); London's Farm Dairy (milk & ice cream processor); S. Madill Ltd. (logging industry equipment); Nat'l. Medical Diagnostics (medical diagnostics equipment servicer); OMEGA Polymer Technologies (plastic products); Ranpak Corp. (packaging materials); Sinter Metals (powdered metal parts); Spectra (computer printer hardware); STERIS (medical sterilization equipment)

Morgenthaler Ventures

National City Bank Building
629 Euclid Avenue, Suite 700
Cleveland, Ohio 44114
(216) 621-3070
Fax: (216) 621-2817
Web: www.morgenthaler.com

Key contact:
Mr. David T. Morgenthaler, Managing Partner
Mr. John D. Lutsi, General Partner

Mr. Robert D. Pavey, General Partner
Mr. Theodore A. Laufik, CFO/Partner
Mr. Paul S. Brentlinger, Partner
Mr. Keith M. Kerman, Partner
Mr. Peter G. Taft, Partner
Mr. Steven C. Oliveri, Director-Information Services
Ms. Karen L. Tuleta, Analyst

Description: We are passionately dedicated to being the most valued partner to world-class entrepreneurs building industry-leading enterprises. We have been an active company builder since 1968, funding more than 150 companies, two-thirds of which are now public entities. We focus on early stage investments in information technology and healthcare as well as later stage management-led buyouts.

Founded: 1968

Preferred investment size: $2-8 million

Area served: United States

Preferred stages of financing: Seed, Start up, LBO/ MBO

Industries:
I.03   Biotech/genetic engineering
I.06   Communications
I.08   Computer software
I.11   Consumer products
I.14   Electronics
I.29   Medical/medical products

Sampling of portfolio companies: Aptis (carrier-class concentrators); Premisys (remote access concentrators); Atria (computer-aided software quality); SDRC (mechanical CAD); Think & Do (micro-controller programming); Nuance Communications (call center speech recognition); Vision Software (business automation platform); TimesTen (main memory data management); VeriFone (credit card verification); Chrysalis (formal verification of IC's); Microchip (micro-controller IC's); Synopsys (synthesis of IC's); Calyx Therapeutics (plant-derived pharmaceuticals for human disease); Gliatech (devices for the treatment of the nervous system); Sequana Therapeutics (gene discovery via functional genomics); Inpatient Consultants (hospital-based physician practice management company); Nat'l. Medical Diagnostics (equipment maintenance services for hospitals); Cardio Thoracic Systems (devices for minimally-invasive heart surgery); Menlo Care (specialty catheters for vascular access); SONIC innovations (digital hearing aids)

National City Capital
1965 East Sixth Street, Suite 1010
Cleveland, Ohio 44114
(216) 575-2491
Fax: (216) 575-9965

Key contact:
Mr. Carl E. Baldassarre, Managing Director
Mr. William H. Schecter, President
Mr. Richard J. Martinko, Managing Director
Mr. Todd S. McCuaig, Managing Director

Description: We are the private equity and mezzanine investment subsidiary of National City Corporation, an $80 billion bank holding company based in Cleveland, Ohio with offices throughout the Midwest. We provide financing for buyouts, recapitalizations, expansions and growth equity in a diverse set of industries including manufacturing, distribution, retail, healthcare and specialty services.

Preferred investment size: $5 million

Amount under management: $100-500 million

Area served: United States

Preferred stages of financing: Mezzanine, LBO/MBO, Expansion

Industries:
I.06   Communications
I.11   Consumer products
I.12   Distribution
I.18   Financial services
I.20   Healthcare
I.22   Industrial products
I.27   Manufacturing
I.29   Medical/medical products
I.31   Real estate
I.32   Retail
I.34   Services (business)
I.35   Services (consumer)

Northwest Ohio Venture Fund
300 Madison Avenue
Suite 1525
Toledo, Ohio 43604
(419) 244-9112
Fax: (419) 244-9554
E-mail: BPWalsh@Primenet.com

Key contact:
Mr. Barry P. Walsh
Mr. Curtis D. Crocker

Area served: Midwest

Preferred stages of financing: Seed, First stage, Second stage, LBO/MBO, Expansion, Third stage, turnaround

Industries:
I.03   Biotech/genetic engineering
I.06   Communications
I.14   Electronics
I.15   Energy/natural resources/utilities
I.18   Financial services
I.23   Information technology services
I.27   Manufacturing
I.29   Medical/medical products
I.34   Services (business)

Primus Venture Partners, Inc.
5900 Landerbrook Drive, Suite 200
Cleveland, Ohio 44124-4020
(440) 684-7300
Fax: (440) 684-7342
E-mail: info@primusventure.com
Web: www.primusventure.com

Key contact:
Mr. James T. Bartlett, Managing Director
Mr. Jonathan E. Dick, Managing Director
Mr. Kevin J. McGinty, Managing Director
Mr. William C. Mulligan, Managing Director
Mr. Loyal W. Wilson, Managing Director

Mr. Steven Rothman, CFO
Mr. Scott B. Harper, Investments Manager
Mr. Jeffrey J. Milius, Investments Manager
Mr. Shanti Mittra, Investment Manager
Mr. James S. Farnham, Investment Associate
Mr. C. Ryan Guthrie, Investment Associate
Mr. Craig L. Milius, Investment Associate
Ms. Shelly Snell, Research/Marketing/MIS
Ms. Dawn Martony, Office Manager
Ms. Lynn Fatica, Administrative Assistant
Ms. Kelly McGee, Administrative Assistant

Description: We are flexible in the structure of our
investments, but are always equity investors. We
have no specific percentage ownership requirements,
nor do we insist upon control. Rather, we invest on
the basis of the expected returns if management
meets or exceeds its goals. Our optimum investment
ranges from $5 million to $10 million. We may make
smaller initial investments, but only with the prospect that our ultimate investment will rise to within
the optimum range based on subsequent rounds of
financing.

Preferred investment size: $5-10 million

Amount under management: $100-500 million

Area served: United States

Preferred stages of financing: Start up, First stage,
Second stage, LBO/MBO, Expansion

Industries:
I.04   Broadcasting
I.06   Communications
I.08   Computer software
I.10   Consulting
I.11   Consumer products
I.13   Education
I.18   Financial services
I.20   Healthcare
I.23   Information technology services
I.24   Internet services/e-commerce
I.29   Medical/medical products
I.32   Retail
I.34   Services (business)

Sampling of portfolio companies: Corinthian Schools
(allied health education); HomePlace (houseware &
domestics retailer); Nextec Applications (proprietary
fabric treatments); Point Group (office equipment
distributor); BankVest Capital (equipment leasing
services); Discover Re Managers (commercial
insurance); Larimer Bancorporation (commercial
banking); Western United Insurance (non-standard
automobile insurance); Digital Analysis (network
management software); FlexiInternational Software
(client/server financial software); LCI Int'l. (long
distance telephone services); Wireless Telecom
(wireless product distributor); Bioanalytical Systems
(measurement instrumentation); Isolab (medical
diagnostic kits); NeuroControl (motor function restoration); STERIS (sterilization systems); Transfusion
Technologies (blood processing systems); Amer-
estate (real estate publishing); Astro Metallurgical
(high performance alloys); Tri-City Radio (radio
stations)

River Cities Capital Fund

221 East 4th Street, Suite 2250
Cincinnati, Ohio 45202-4147
(513) 621-9700
Fax: (513) 579-8939
E-mail: rkreiser@rccf.com
Web: www.rccf.com

Key contact:
Mr. R. Glen Mayfield, Principal
Mr. Edwin T. Robinson, Principal
Mr. J. Eric Lenning, Principal
Mr. Frederick C. Kieser, Principal
Mr. Murray R. Wilson, Principal

Description: Our mission is to facilitate the creation
and preservation of capital for our clients and the
realization of their business as well as their personal
financial goals. We listen and work closely with
clients to develop plans and approaches that specifically address their concerns and issues.

Amount of capital invested: $10 million

Preferred investment size: $1-2 million

Amount under management: $25-100 million

Area served: North America, Midwest

Preferred stages of financing: Start up, First stage,
Second stage, Mezzanine, Expansion

Industries:
I.03   Biotech/genetic engineering
I.06   Communications
I.07   Computer hardware
I.08   Computer software
I.13   Education
I.14   Electronics
I.17   Environmental services/waste management
I.19   Generalist
I.20   Healthcare
I.21   High technology
I.22   Industrial products
I.23   Information technology services
I.24   Internet services/e-commerce
I.27   Manufacturing
I.33   Semiconductors

US Medical Resources Corporation

188 Lafayette Circle
Cincinnati, Ohio 45220-1105
(513) 281-3900
Fax: (513) 281-3994
E-mail: usmedres@compuserve.com

Key contact:
Mr. James E. Bowman, Jr., President
Mr. Gary Lee, Vice President
Mr. Yuli Kitaevich, Vice President

Description: Venture capital firm investing our capital
in medical devices and related. Looking for firms
whose products can be sold by us in former Soviet
Union and U.S. Midwest.

Preferred investment size: Varies

Amount under management: <$10 million

Area served: North America, Midwest, Former Soviet
Union

Preferred stages of financing: Start up, First stage

Industries:
I.29   Medical/medical products

Oklahoma

Chisholm Private Capital Partners

5100 East Skelly, Suite 1060
Tulsa, Oklahoma 74135
(918) 663-2500
Fax: (918) 663-1140
E-mail: jbode@chisholmvc.com
Web: chisholmvc.com

Key contact:
Mr. James Bode, General Partner
Mr. Joe Tippins, General Partner

211 North Robinson, Suite 210
Oklahoma City, Oklahoma 73102
(405) 848-8014
Fax: (405) 416-1035
E-mail: jfrick@chisolmvc.com
Web: www.chisolmvc.com

Key contact:
Mr. John B. Frick, General Partner

Description: We are a private equity fund which
invests primarily in Oklahoma. We have over $13
million committed capital which we expect to invest
in approximately ten investments over ten years.
The investment thesis is simply that the area is
underserved by traditional private equity investors,
despite the availability of competitive investment
opportunities. Private equity is particularly difficult
to raise in Oklahoma for companies needing between
$250,000 and $3 million.

Amount of capital invested: $8 million

Preferred investment size: $1 million

Amount under management: $10-25 million

Area served: North America

Preferred stages of financing: Seed, Start up, First
stage, Second stage, Expansion

Industries:
I.01   Aerospace
I.02   Agriculture/forestry/fishing/mining
I.03   Biotech/genetic engineering
I.04   Broadcasting
I.06   Communications
I.07   Computer hardware
I.08   Computer software
I.12   Distribution
I.14   Electronics
I.15   Energy/natural resources/utilities
I.16   Entertainment
I.17   Environmental services/waste management
I.18   Financial services
I.19   Generalist
I.20   Healthcare
I.21   High technology
I.22   Industrial products
I.23   Information technology services
I.24   Internet services/e-commerce
I.26   Life sciences
I.27   Manufacturing
I.28   Media/publishing
I.29   Medical/medical products
I.30   New media
I.34   Services (business)
I.35   Services (consumer)

Sampling of portfolio companies: StadiaNet Sports, Inc.
(media/entertainment); Commodity Capital Group
(financial services); The Rock Island Group (network
services); Dominion (private prisons); DAS Devices
(computer hardware); Infinitec Communications
(telecommunications); OMNA (physician practice
management); AEMT, Inc. (industrial products);
Vertech Systems, LLC (industrial products); Global
Dispatch Technology Corporation (software)

Davis, Tuttle Venture Partners, LP

320 South Boston, Suite 1000
Tulsa, Oklahoma 74103-3703
(918) 584-7272
Fax: (918) 582-3404
E-mail: bdavis@dtvp.com

Key contact:
Mr. Barry Davis, Managing General Partner
Mr. Phil Tuttle, General Partner

Description: We are a third in a series of private equity
funds focused on expansion investments, middle
market buyouts and selected early stage investments
in the Southwest. Our partners have been involved in
continuous venture capital activity over the past 25
years. We are institutionally funded by Fortune 100
pension funds, insurance companies and commercial
banks. We are lead investors and we provide long-
term capital and strategic advice and counsel.

Preferred investment size: $2.5 million

Amount under management: $100-500 million

Area served: United States

Preferred stages of financing: First stage, LBO/MBO,
Expansion

Industries:
I.05   Chemicals
I.06   Communications
I.11   Consumer products
I.12   Distribution
I.13   Education
I.15   Energy/natural resources/utilities
I.17   Environmental services/waste management
I.20   Healthcare
I.22   Industrial products
I.23   Information technology services
I.27   Manufacturing
I.29   Medical/medical products
I.36   Transportation

Intersouth Partners

4045 NW 64th Street, Suite 410
Oklahoma City, Oklahoma 73116
(405) 843-7890
Fax: (405) 843-8048
E-mail: michelle@intersouth.com
Web: www.intersouth.com

Key contact:
Mr. Dennis J. Dougherty, General Partner
Mr. Mitchell Mumma, General Partner
Mr. D. Gregroy Main, Partner
Mr. Jeffrey P. Hoogendam, Associate
Ms. Hazel Cordle, CFO
Ms. Michelle M. Dattellas, Administrative Assistant

Description: We are dedicated to the proven concept
that America's entrepreneurial companies,
adequately capitalized and professionally advised,

are superior investments for institutions and high net
worth individuals. Venture capital funds provide the
means for such investing.

Founded: 1985

Area served: Southeast, Southwest

Preferred stages of financing: Seed, Start up, First
stage

Industries:
I.03	Biotech/genetic engineering
I.08	Computer software
I.14	Electronics
I.17	Environmental services/waste management
I.20	Healthcare
I.26	Life sciences
I.27	Manufacturing
I.29	Medical/medical products

Oregon

Northern Pacific Capital Corp.

P.O. Box 1658
Portland, Oregon 97207
(503) 241-1255
Fax: (503) 299-6653

Key contact:
Mr. Jospeh P. Tennant

Area served: Pacific Northwest

Preferred stages of financing: Second stage, Third/
later stage

Industries:
I.19   Generalist

Olympic Venture Partners

340 Oswego Pointe Drive, Suite 200
Lake Oswego, Oregon 97034
(503) 697-8766
Fax: (503) 697-8863
E-mail: langeler@ovp.com
Web: www.ovp.com

Key contact:
Mr. Gerard H. Langeler, Partner

Description: We are the leading technology-focused
venture capital firm in the Pacific Northwest and the
only firm with offices in both Oregon and Washington. Committed capital under management is over
$160 million sourced from institutional investors
such as endowments, foundations, pension funds and
family trusts.

Preferred investment size: $1 million

Amount under management: $100-500 million

Area served: Western third of North America

Preferred stages of financing: Seed, Start up, First
stage

Industries:
I.03	Biotech/genetic engineering
I.06	Communications
I.08	Computer software
I.14	Electronics
I.20	Healthcare
I.21	High technology
I.26	Life sciences
I.29	Medical/medical products

Sampling of portfolio companies: Cardima, Inc.
(developer of catheter technology for cardiac diagnosis & therapy); Coinstar, Inc. (developer of self-
service coin counting machines); Encoding.com
(optimized encoding of audio & video for the
internet); nth Degree Software, Inc. (developer of
software for printing & publishing); Portland
Software, Inc. (developer of software for secure electronic commerce); Sequel Technology Corp.
(developer of software for internet access
management); Surplus Direct, Inc. (direct marketer of
previous versions of software & hardware); Watch-
guard Technologies, Inc. (developer of low-end
firewall systems & other internet security products);
Cadre Technologies, Inc. (developer of CASE tools
that automate the design, code generation & testing of
software); INTERLINO Software Corp. (developer
of application software for the financial services
industry); Laserscope (manufacturer of high
precision multipurpose surgical lasers); Now
Software, Inc. (developer of workgroup & personal
productivity software); Photon Kinetics, Inc. (manufacturer of optical fiber instruments for laboratory &
field test); Saros Corp. (developer of distributed
network file management systems); Syntellect Inc.
(manufacturer of voice response systems); TView,
Inc. (developer of video processing systems); Seattle
Genetics (developer of therapeutic agents for cancer
& other diseases); Global Mobility Systems
(developer of wireless communication software);
Vascular Solutions, Inc. (developer of medical
devices for vascular sealing); We.bridge, Inc.
(developer of web solutions for channel relationship
management)

Shaw Venture Partners

400 SW Sixth Avenue, Suite 1100
Portland, Oregon 97204
(503) 228-4884
Fax: (503) 227-2471

Key contact:
Mr. Ralph Shaw

Preferred stages of financing: Seed, First stage, Second stage, LBO/MBO, Third/later stage

Industries:
I.03   Biotech/genetic engineering

I.06   Communications
I.07   Computer hardware
I.08   Computer software
I.11   Consumer products
I.14   Electronics
I.27   Manufacturing
I.29   Medical/medical products
I.32   Retail
I.34   Services (business)
I.35   Services (consumer)

Pennsylvania

Adams Capital Management, Inc.

518 Broad Street
Sewickley, Pennsylvania 15143
(412) 749-9454
Fax: (412) 749-9459
E-mail: info@acm.com
Web: www.acm.com

Key contact:
Mr. Joel P. Adams
Mr. William C. Hulley
Mr. William F. Frezza
Mr. Jerry S. Sullivan

Description: Venture capital for applied technology.

Founded: 1994

Amount of capital invested: $60 million

Preferred investment size: $1 million+

Area served: United States

Preferred stages of financing: Start up, First stage, Second stage

Industries:
I.06   Communications
I.08   Computer software
I.29   Medical/medical products

Advanta Partners, LP

Welsh & McKean Roads
Spring House, Pennsylvania 19477-0844
(215) 444-6450
Fax: (215) 444-6499
E-mail: mhollin@advanta.com
Web: www.advanta.com

Key contact:
Mr. Mitchell L. Hollin, Managing Director

Description: We differentiate ourselves by providing the knowledge, resources and experience which comes from industry specialization and the insights of a strategic partner. Specifically, we are looking for companies that can benefit from our expertise in direct marketing, market segmentation, database management, consumer behavior modeling, transaction processing and electronic commerce.

Amount of capital invested: $25 million

Preferred investment size: $5-25 million

Amount under management: $100-500 million

Area served: United States

Preferred stages of financing: Second stage, LBO/MBO, Expansion

Industries:
I.08   Computer software
I.18   Financial services
I.23   Information technology services
I.34   Services (business)
I.35   Services (consumer)

Sampling of portfolio companies: HNC Software (neural network software); Innovative Services of America (sophisticated inbound teleservices); RMH Teleservices (high-volume telemarketer); Brightware (internet-based intelligent software); JDR (accounts receivable management); Great Expectations (video dating service); Harmonic Systems (on-line interactive applications for retail chains); Sky Alland Marketing (relationship marketing firm)

Bachow & Associates, Inc.

Three Bala Plaza East, Suite 502
Bala Cynwyd, Pennsylvania 19004
(610) 660-4900
Fax: (610) 660-4930
E-mail: info@bachow.com
Web: www.bachow.com

Key contact:
Mr. Paul S. Bachow, Senior Managing Director
Mr. Steve Fisher, Managing Partner

Mr. Salvatore A. Grasso, Managing Partner
Mr. Frank H. Nowaczek, Managing Partner
Mr. Jay Seid, Managing Partner
Mr. Samuel H. Schwartz, Vice President
Mr. Noah J. Walley, Vice President
Mr. Robert Ivanoff, Vice President
Mr. Robert V. Anglin, Senior Associate
Mr. Wayne L. Nemeth, Senior Associate
Mr. James Thalheimer, Senior Associate
Mr. Eoin Theobald, Associate

Mr. Tom Lang, Associate

Description: We provide expansion capital to exciting and growing companies. We are actively seeking investment opportunities in selected high growth businesses. We manage over $200 million in investment funds targeting equity transactions of $5 million to $25 million. We invest in private placements and buyout transactions with exceptional growth opportunities.

Founded: 1988

Amount under management: $100-500 million

Preferred stage of financing: LBO/MBO

Industries:
I.06   Communications
I.23   Information technology services
I.27   Manufacturing
I.34   Services (business)

Sampling of portfolio companies: Acme Paging (provider of paging services in Brazil, Argentina & Colombia); Anadigics (manufacturer of microwave frequency integrated circuits for the wireless industry); Bachtel Cellular (owner/operator of cellular systems in several regions); CARE Systems (information technology & services provider for workers' compensation claims administration); Coastel (cellular & wireless communications operator for the Gulf of Mexico); GoCom Communications (owner/operator of broadcast TV stations: KMID-TV, KSPR-TV, KCPM-TV); Discovery Schools (provider of childcare services through 17 locations in the mid-Atlantic states); Genus (manufacturer of semiconductor capital equipment); Innova (manufacturer of very-high-frequency microwave radios); OutSource Int'l. (human resources solutions including employee leasing & temporary staffing services); Paradigm Geophysical (provider of 3-D depth-domain exploration software & services to the oil & gas industry); ProCommunications (nationwide provider of in-bound call-center services); VertiCom (designs, manufactures & sells commercial millimeter-wave radio subsystems for system integrators in wireless communications); VISTA Information Solutions (information database service for the insurance, banking & environmental markets)

Ben Franklin Technology Center of SE Pennsylvania

3625 Market Street
Philadelphia, Pennsylvania 19104
(215) 382-0380
Fax: (215) 387-6050
E-mail: btfc@benfranklin.org
Web: www.benfranklin.org

Key contact:
Ms. RoseAnn B. Rosenthal, President/CEO

Description: We maintain the largest portfolio of seed stage companies in the nation and are the largest source of seed-capital for entrepreneurial development in the Greater Philadelphia region. We currently maintain four funding programs for early stage technology companies and one program for small, local area businesses in Southeastern Pennsylvania. The programs provide a variety of financing options from microloans for small local-area businesses to capital for product commercialization.

Preferred investment size: $50,000-150,000

Area served: Southeastern Pennsylvania

Preferred stages of financing: Seed, Start up, First stage, Second stage

Industries:
I.03   Biotech/genetic engineering
I.08   Computer software
I.11   Consumer products
I.14   Electronics
I.20   Healthcare
I.23   Information technology services
I.29   Medical/medical products
I.35   Services (consumer)

Sampling of portfolio companies: AM Communications Inc. (software & information); Choice One Partners Ltd. (software & information); Datacom Int'l. Inc. (electronics & instrumentation); Global Technology Solutions (consumer); Inflammatics Inc. (biotechnology); Lithium Technology (consumer); Sage Online Inc. (software & information); Selectus Pharmaceuticals (pharmaceuticals); Telefactor Corp (medical instruments & devices)

Berwind Financial Group, L.P.

1500 Market Street
3000 Centre Square West
Philadelphia, Pennsylvania 19102
(215) 575-2400
Fax: (215) 564-5402
E-mail: PGould@Berwind.com

Key contact:
Mr. Peter G. Gould, President
Ms. Linda DeJure, Principal
Mr. Peter M. Askey, Principal
Mr. John E. Schaefer, Principal

Description: We offer merchant banking services and investment banking services through our registered broker-dealer, Berwind Financial, L.P. We specialize in financial advisory services for mergers and acquisitions and all types of financing.

Amount of capital invested: $15 million

Preferred investment size: $5-10 million

Amount under management: $25-100 million

Area served: United States

Preferred stage of financing: LBO/MBO

Industries:
I.01   Aerospace
I.05   Chemicals
I.09   Construction
I.10   Consulting
I.11   Consumer products
I.12   Distribution
I.13   Education
I.14   Electronics
I.17   Environmental services/waste management

I.18   Financial services
I.20   Healthcare
I.22   Industrial products
I.25   Leisure/hospitality
I.26   Life sciences
I.27   Manufacturing
I.29   Medical/medical products
I.34   Services (business)
I.35   Services (consumer)
I.36   Transportation

Sampling of portfolio companies: Tech Services Int'l., LP (provider of full-service support to graphics arts imaging-related equipment); Fypon, Ltd., LP (manufactures polyurethane foam Molded Millwork® for the residential housing market); MII Int'l. Inc. (specialty coater & converter of PVC film for use in signage, marking systems & other products); Classic Kitchens, LP (manufactures custom kitchen & bath cabinetry sold through high-end kitchen dealers & designers under the Heritage, Rutt & St. Charles brand names); Berwind Railway Service Co., LP (provides cleaning, painting & lining, general maintenance & repair to rail freight cars); The Clinipad Corp. (manufactures disposable medical products, primarily applicators coated with a topical antiseptic & procedure-specific kits & trays); Electronic Measurements, Inc. (designs & manufactures high current & high voltage switching power supplies for electronic equipment & instrumentation); McKenzie Sports Products (manufactures foam specialty products for the outdoor sporting industry, including archery targets & taxidermy forms, & distributes taxidermy supplies)

CEO Venture Fund

2000 Technology Drive
Pittsburgh, Pennsylvania 15219
(412) 687-3451
Fax: (412) 687-8139

Key contact:
Mr. Gary G. Glausser, CFO/General Partner
Mr. Glen F. Chatfield
Mr. James Colker
Mr. Gary Golding
Mr. William R. Newlin
Mr. Gene Yost

Preferred stages of financing: First stage, Second stage, LBO/MBO

Industries:
I.03   Biotech/genetic engineering
I.05   Chemicals
I.06   Communications
I.07   Computer hardware
I.08   Computer software
I.14   Electronics

CIP Capital, L.P.

435 Devon Park Drive, Building 200
Wayne, Pennsylvania 19087
(610) 964-7860
Fax: (610) 964-8136

Key contact:
Mr. Joseph M. Corr
Mr. Winston Churchill, Jr.

Area served: East

Preferred stages of financing: First stage, Second stage, LBO/MBO

Industries:
I.03   Biotech/genetic engineering
I.05   Chemicals
I.06   Communications
I.18   Financial services
I.29   Medical/medical products

Communications Equity Associates, Inc.

1235 Westlakes Drive, Suite 245
Berwyn, Pennsylvania 19312
(610) 251-0650
Fax: (610) 251-9180
Web: www.commequ.com

Key contact:
Mr. J. Patrick Michaels, Chairman/CEO
Mr. Harold Ewen
Mr. Bruno Claude
Mr. George Pollock
Mr. Ming Jung
Mr. Thomas W. Cardy, Executive Vice President
Mr. Scott N. Feuer, Vice President
Mr. Bryan L. Crino, Senior Associate

Description: We have a rich 25-year history of diverse experiences and milestone industry accomplishments which establish us as a worldwide leader. By combining the sophisticated skills of a large Wall Street investment firm with a focus on communications industries, we offer a depth of service that's unparalleled. The experience of our professionals speaks for itself: since our founding, we have completed more than 600 transactions, valued at more than $13 billion. With an extensive network of long-standing relationships and offices on almost every continent, along with our affiliates, we have helped clients in 27 countries successfully pursue their financial and strategic goals.

Founded: 1973

Preferred investment size: No more than 15% of the total fund

Amount under management: $100-500 million

Area served: Worldwide

Preferred stages of financing: LBO/MBO, Growth

Industries:
I.04   Broadcasting
I.06   Communications
I.16   Entertainment
I.23   Information technology services
I.24   Internet services/e-commerce
I.28   Media/publishing

CoreStates Enterprise Fund

1345 Chestnut Street
M.S. 1-8-12-1
Philadelphia, Pennsylvania 19107
(215) 973-6519

Key contact:
Mr. Michael Donoghue

Ms. Christine C. Jones

Area served: East Coast

Preferred stages of financing: Second stage, LBO/MBO, Third/later stage

Enertech Capital Partners, L.P.

435 Devon Park Drive, Suite 410
Wayne, Pennsylvania 19087
(610) 254-4141
Fax: (610) 254-4188
E-mail: enertech@enertechcapital.com
Web: www.enertechcapital.com

Key contact:
Mr. David F. Lincoln, Managing Director
Mr. Scott B. Ungerer, Managing Director
Mr. Michael Bevan, Associate
Mr. James C. Biddle, Senior Associate

Description: We were formed in August 1996 to invest in service and technology companies related to utilities and the broader energy marketplace. The principle investors believe that the deregulation in the utility sector- electric, natural gas and water- is creating significantly increased competition and is drastically changing the business model for success.

Amount of capital invested: $18 million

Preferred investment size: $1-5 million

Amount under management: $25-100 million

Area served: North America

Preferred stages of financing: First stage, Second stage, Mezzanine, LBO/MBO, Expansion

Industries:
I.04 Broadcasting
I.06 Communications
I.08 Computer software
I.14 Electronics
I.15 Energy/natural resources/utilities
I.17 Environmental services/waste management
I.23 Information technology services
I.33 Semiconductors

Greater Philadelphia Venture Capital Corp.

351 East Conestoga Road, Room 203
Wayne, Pennsylvania 19087
(610) 688-6829
Fax: (610) 254-8958

Key contact:
Mr. Fred S. Choate

Greystone Capital

P.O. Box 705
Bethlehem, Pennsylvania 18016-0705
(610) 332-5500

Key contact:
Mr. Louis Rodriquez
Mr. Louis P. Pektor, III, President
Mr. Eric J. Ruth, Executive Vice President
Mr. Duane A. Wagner, Research Specialist

Description: We are a full-service financial intermediary with a fifteen year track record of successful negotiation of acquisitions and divestiture of Eastern

Pennsylvania based businesses. We understand the environment of area industry and have been a part of the local business community for over forty years collectively, giving us the ability to provide you with accurate and informative assessments of varied investment opportunities.

Area served: Eastern Pennsylvania

Industries:
I.18 Financial services
I.19 Generalist
I.27 Manufacturing

Howard, Lawson & Company

2 Penn Center Plaza, Suite 410
Philadelphia, Pennsylvania 19102
(215) 988-0010
Fax: (215) 568-0029

Key contact:
Mr. Michael A. Cuneo
Mr. Steve N. Economou

Industries:
I.19 Generalist

Keystone Venture Capital

1601 Market Street, Suite 2500
Philadelphia, Pennsylvania 19103
(215) 241-1200
Fax: (215) 241-1211
E-mail: Jregan@keystonevc.com
Web: www.keystonevc.com

Key contact:
Mr. John R. Regan, General Partner
Mr. Kerry J. Dale, General Partner
Mr. Peter E. Ligeti, General Partner

Description: We focus on equity investments in early to late expansion stage opportunities primarily within the Mid-Atlantic region. Founded in 1982, we manage nearly $60 million of venture capital.

Founded: 1982

Amount of capital invested: $10 million

Preferred investment size: $1.5 million

Amount under management: $25-100 million

Area served: United States

Preferred stages of financing: First stage, Second stage, Expansion

Industries:

I.06	Communications
I.08	Computer software
I.11	Consumer products
I.21	High technology
I.23	Information technology services
I.24	Internet services/e-commerce
I.32	Retail
I.34	Services (business)

Sampling of portfolio companies: U.S. Physicians (physician practice management company); Grand Eagle (acquires under-performing industrial service businesses); Tracking Systems (provides equipment & services used to monitor the location & condition of offenders on probation & parole); Quality Packaging Systems (provides contract packaging services to the pharmaceutical industry); Nat'l. Medical Technologies (provider of sleep disorder testing services); Mothers Work (specialty retailer of maternity clothing); Arnold Palmer Golf Management (acquires, leases & manages golf properties); Hathaway Shirts (oldest men's shirt company in the U.S.); U.S. Vision (optical retailer); Tryum Corp. (manufacturer of baked snack foods on both a private label & branded basis); Security Dynamics (designer & marketer of software & hardware products used to provide secure access to computer systems); Infonautics (develops & markets on-line reference services & products); CDnow (on-line retailer of compact discs & other music-related products over the Internet); Paradigm Software Technologies (develops & markets activity-based costing, project accounting & billing software to the service sector); Intelligent Information (provides real-time, personalized updates & alerts to consumers via wireless devices); Integrated Circuit Systems (designs & markets standard & custom application specific integrated circuits using mixed analog/digital technology); Int'l. Telesystems (provides computer-based outbound call management systems that improve the productivity of telemarketing & telecollection agents)

Mentor Capital Partners, Ltd.

P.O. Box 560
Yardley, Pennsylvania 19067
(215) 736-8882
Fax: (215) 736-8882
Web: www.mentorcapitalpartners.com

Key contact:
Mr. Edward F. Sager, Jr., Partner

Description: We are a regional diversified venture capital & private equity firm, working in partnership with portfolio company management, private or public, to create exceptional value for its investors. We employ our capital to "facilitate a leadership role with company management." It is management's repsonsibility to operate the business. We partner with management to develop the best liquidity alternatives.

Amount of capital invested: $2.5 million

Preferred investment size: $1 million

Amount under management: $10-25 million

Area served: United States

Preferred stages of financing: Mezzanine, LBO/MBO, Expansion

Industries:

I.01	Aerospace
I.06	Communications
I.07	Computer hardware
I.08	Computer software
I.11	Consumer products
I.12	Distribution
I.14	Electronics
I.18	Financial services
I.19	Generalist
I.20	Healthcare
I.21	High technology
I.22	Industrial products
I.23	Information technology services
I.24	Internet services/e-commerce
I.27	Manufacturing
I.29	Medical/medical products
I.32	Retail
I.34	Services (business)
I.35	Services (consumer)

Sampling of portfolio companies: AxSys Corp. (developer & marketer of imaging software for MRI & CT equipment); College Financial Planning Counselors, Inc. (advisors regarding the financing of college tuition & through affiliated financial planners the financing of college costs); CoreCare Systems, Inc. (provider of mental health & behavioral care services in Eastern Pennsylvania & Central NJ); Declaration Holdings, Inc. (provider of administrative services to the mutual fund industry); The Eastwind Group, Inc. (holding company which acquires underperforming businesses in manufacturing & technology); JADE Equipment Corp. (manufacturer of build-to-customer-specification precision automated assembly equipment); KNF Corp. (nylon blown film extruder & bag manufacturers serving the aerospace, chemical, medical, food & electronic industries); North American Cable Equipment, Inc. (distributor of telecommunication products sold to satellite, cable television & wireless industries)

Meridian Venture Partners

259 North Radnor-Chester Road
Radnor, Pennsylvania 19087
(610) 254-2999
Fax: (610) 254-2996
E-mail: mvpart@ix.netcom.com

Key contact:
Mr. Raymond R. Rafferty, Jr., General Partner
Mr. Robert E. Brown, Jr., General Partner
Mr. Bernard B. Markey, General Partner
Mr. Joseph A. Hawke, Associate

Area served: Mid-Atlantic, within 2 hours of office

Preferred stages of financing: Second stage, Mezzanine, LBO/MBO, Expansion, Special situations

Industries:
I.08   Computer software
I.18   Financial services
I.23   Information technology services
I.28   Media/publishing
I.29   Medical/medical products
I.32   Retail
I.34   Services (business)

Mid-Atlantic Venture Funds

125 Goodman Drive
Lehigh University
Bethlehem, Pennsylvania 18015
(610) 865-6550
Fax: (610) 865-6427

Key contact:
Mr. Marc F. Benson
Mr. Frederick J. Beste, III
Mr. Glen R. Bressner

Preferred stages of financing: Seed, First stage, Sec-

ond stage, LBO/MBO

Industries:
I.06   Communications
I.07   Computer hardware
I.08   Computer software
I.14   Electronics
I.27   Manufacturing
I.29   Medical/medical products
I.34   Services (business)
I.35   Services (consumer)

Patricof & Company Ventures, Inc.

Executive Terrace Building
455 South Gulph Road, Suite 410
King of Prussia, Pennsylvania 19406
(610) 265-0286
Fax: (610) 265-4959
Web: www.patricof.com

Key contact:
Mr. Gregory M. Case
Mr. George M. Jenkins
Ms. Tiffany G. Faircloth

Description: We are a leading international private
equity investment firm that together with our international affiliate, Apax Partners, manages over $3.4
billion on behalf of major institutional investors in
the U.S. and abroad. With over twenty-five years of
direct investing experience, we provide long-term
equity financing to build companies. We have a solid
reputation as a leader in the industry and as an innovative, value-added investor.

Preferred investment size: $5-25 million

Area served: Worldwide

Preferred stages of financing: Start up, First stage,
LBO/MBO, Expansion, Recapitalizations

Industries:
I.06   Communications
I.07   Computer hardware
I.08   Computer software
I.11   Consumer products
I.14   Electronics
I.18   Financial services
I.20   Healthcare
I.22   Industrial products
I.23   Information technology services
I.27   Manufacturing
I.29   Medical/medical products
I.30   New media

I.32   Retail
I.34   Services (business)

Sampling of portfolio companies: Spec Group, Inc.
(provides technicians, specialists, programmers &
professionals for a wide range of staff augmentation,
inspection, training & technical consulting services
for utility, industrial, commercial & government
customers); Medical Arts Press, Inc. (direct marketer
of custom & standard business forms & office &
practice related supplies to healthcare professionals);
Johnny Rockets Group, Inc. (restaurant chain
featuring a 1950's diner concept); CapMAC Holdings
(pioneered the commercial monoline financial guarantee business); RBMG Resource Bancshares Corp.
(specialty asset gatherer utilizing a banking depository license in South Carolina); Centocor Inc.
(healthcare company specializing in the development
& commercialization of therapeutic & diagnostic
products to meet critical human healthcare needs);
Total Physician Services, Inc. (physician practice
management company that provides management);
Bolder Technologies Corp. (developed a new generation of rechargeable, sealed, lead acid batteries);
Biocompatibles plc (commercializes a biocompatible
coating material for ophthalmic & medical device
coating applications); Atcom (primary provider to
telephone companies & others of kiosks allowing
public access to the internet; provider of high-speed
data ports for travelers who want T-1 access from
their laptops); Bluestone Software, Inc. (sells enterprise-to-web solutions); Fore Systems, Inc. (designer,
developer & manufacturer of high-performance,
networking products based on asynchronous transfer
mode technology); Rendition, Inc. (fab-less semiconductor company building integrated 2-D/3-D accelerator chips for PCs); Tessera, Inc. (semiconductor
packaging technology company); Audible, Inc.
(launched its pocket-sized device that holds up to 2
hours of spoken word audio & can play it back either

over a car radio or headphones); Medscape (internet site for healthcare professionals); planet U (on-line consumer promotions, including coupons, rebates & sampling); Sunglass Hut Corp. (mall-based specialty retail concept selling a variety of fashion eyewear);

Park 'N View, Inc. (provides cable TV & telephone services to truck drivers in their cabs at truck stops); Xpedite Systems, Inc. (provider of enhanced fax services)

Pennsylvania Growth Fund

5850 Ellsworth Avenue, Suite 303
Pittsburgh, Pennsylvania 15232
(412) 361-0500
Fax: (412) 361-0676

Key contact:
Mr. Barry Lhormer, Partner
Mr. Hal Mendlowitz, Partner

Description: We are a merchant banking company developed for the purpose of managing active investments in established companies that have potential for outstanding investment returns. Our principals are successful entrepreneurs and hands-on investors with diverse backgrounds in manufacturing, distribution, real estate and finance. We have been successfully investing in small companies for over twenty years.

Amount of capital invested: $1 million

Preferred investment size: $1-2 million

Amount under management: <$10 million

Area served: United States

Preferred stages of financing: Mezzanine, LBO/MBO, Expansion

Industries:
I.09   Construction
I.11   Consumer products
I.12   Distribution
I.22   Industrial products
I.27   Manufacturing
I.31   Real estate

Sampling of portfolio companies: Fagens Building Centers (building supplies); Water Mark (real estate development) Raaco Manufacturing (industrial mixer processors); Kennsington Lighting (manufacturing of flourescent lighting); Auto Forge (forgings for automotive)

Plexus Ventures, Inc.

1787 Sentry Parkway West
Building 18, Suite 301
Blue Bell, Pennsylvania 19422
(215) 542-2727
Fax: (215) 542-2288

Key contact:
Mr. John F. Chappell
Dr. Donald E. Kuhla, Ph.D.
Mr. Robert P. Moran

Description: We provide business development advisory services to companies in the biotechnology and pharmaceutical industries. Our clients range in size from emerging therapeutics and drug delivery companies to medium-sized pharmaceutical companies. We help identify and facilitate collaborations among companies worldwide.

Founded: 1990

Area served: Worldwide

Preferred stages of financing: Seed, Start up, First stage

Industries:
I.03   Biotech/genetic engineering
I.20   Healthcare
I.29   Medical/medical products

Sampling of portfolio companies: Aronex (focuses on the development of therapeutic agents against cancer & infectious diseases); Bentley Pharmaceuticals (focuses on improved transdermal, oral & transmucosal drug delivery systems); BioDx (develops instrument, software & informatics technologies in multi-color fluorescence, cell-based screening for high-precision & high-throughput screening in drug discovery); CorBec Pharmaceuticals (develops compounds which modulate macrophage activity in a manner useful against an array of autoimmune diseases); Goldshield Pharmaceuticals (acquires &

aggressively markets well-known but under-promoted ethical & over-the-counter pharmaceutical products); Inhale Therapeutic Systems (develops proprietary device, formulation & packaging technologies for the non-invasive delivery of peptides, proteins & macromolecules); Neurex Corp. (develops neuron specific calcium blockers for the prevention of neurological damage following cardiac arrest); NPS Pharmaceuticals (develops small molecule drugs that target ion regulators of important cell functions with initial applications against hyperparathyroidism & osteoporosis); Polfa Kutno Pharmaceuticals Works S.A. (pharmaceutical company in Poland that markets prescription, OTC & veterinary drugs throughout Poland & the Ukraine); Ribi ImmunoChem Research (develops various vaccine & adjuvant combinations as treatments for melanoma & certain other cancers & as a prophylactic for septic shock); Salix Pharmaceuticals (develops balsalazide sodium for the treatment of ulcerative colitis, Crohn's Disease & radiation-induced colitis); Symphony Pharmaceuticals (develops compounds which regulate CNS receptors & have potential application in neuroprotection, depression, epilepsy & pain); Therion Biologics (develops vaccines & immunotherapeutic products for the prevention & treatment of AIDS, other viral diseases & certain cancers)

PNC Equity Management Corporation
3150 CNG Tower
625 Liberty Avenue
Pittsburgh, Pennsylvania 15222
(412) 768-8661

Key contact:
Mr. Gary Zentner
Mr. David J. Blair
Mr. Peter V. Del Presto
Mr. Paul A. Giusti
Mr. David M. Hillman

Preferred stages of financing: Second stage, LBO/
MBO, Third/later stage

Industries:
I.12   Distribution
I.27   Manufacturing
I.28   Media/publishing
I.29   Medical/medical products
I.34   Services (business)
I.35   Services (consumer)

TA Associates Inc.
One Oxford Center, Suite 4260
Pittsburgh, Pennsylvania 15219-1407
(412) 441-4949
Fax: (412) 441-5784
E-mail: info@ta.com

Key contact:
Ms. Jacqueline C. Morby, Managing Director

Description: For nearly three decades, we have
provided equity capital and knowledgeable assistance to talented entrepreneurs to help them pull
ahead of their competition and build companies of
significant value.

Founded: 1968

Preferred investment size: $10-100 million

Preferred stages of financing: Start up, First stage,
LBO/MBO, Turnaround

Industries:
I.03   Biotech/genetic engineering
I.08   Computer software
I.14   Electronics
I.15   Energy/natural resources/utilities
I.17   Environmental services/waste management

I.18   Financial services
I.20   Healthcare
I.23   Information technology services
I.34   Services (business)

Sampling of portfolio companies: Auto Palace
(consumer products & services); Federal Express
(consumer products & services); Jenny Craig, Inc.
(consumer products & services); Smith Alarm
Systems (consumer products & services); AIM
Management Group (financial services); Affiliated
Managers Group (financial services); Keystone
Group (financial services); Mutual Risk Management
(financial services); Boron LePore (healthcare
services); CompDent Corp. (healthcare services);
Copley Pharmaceutical (healthcare services); Gulf
South Medical Supply (healthcare services);
Preferred Payment Systems (healthcare services);
Bachtel Cellular Liquidity, LP (media & communica-
tions); Continental Cablevision, Inc. (media &
communications); Galaxy Telecom, LP (media &
communications); TSR Wireless (media & communications); ANSYS, Inc. (software & technology);
Axent (software & technology); Hummingbird
(software & technology

TDH
919 Conestoga Road
Building 1, Suite 301
Rosemont, Pennsylvania 19010
(610) 526-9970
Fax: (610) 526-9971
E-mail: JmBuck@aol.com

Key contact:
Mr. J. B. Doherty, Partner
Stephen W. Harris, Partner
Thomas M. Balderston, Partner
James M. Buck, III, Partner

Description: Our management team has experience in
venture capital investing through multiple economic
and portfolio cycles. Since our founding, we have
consistently applied an investment approach directed
towards a diversified portfolio that avoids excessive
concentration in any one industry and is balanced
among early, later stage and acquisition financings.
We prefer to lead our investments and generally
invest between $1 mm to 3 mm.

Founded: 1978

Amount of capital invested: $2.5 million

Preferred investment size: Over $1 million

Amount under management: $25-100 million

Area served: Prefer East of the Mississippi, United
States

Preferred stages of financing: Start up, First stage,
Second stage, Mezzanine, LBO/MBO

Industries:
I.01   Aerospace
I.02   Agriculture/forestry/fishing/mining
I.03   Biotech/genetic engineering
I.04   Broadcasting
I.05   Chemicals
I.06   Communications
I.07   Computer hardware
I.08   Computer software
I.11   Consumer products
I.13   Education
I.14   Electronics
I.18   Financial services
I.20   Healthcare
I.21   High technology
I.22   Industrial products
I.23   Information technology services
I.24   Internet services/e-commerce
I.26   Life sciences
I.27   Manufacturing

I.28   Media/publishing
I.29   Medical/medical products
I.30   New media
I.33   Semiconductors
I.34   Services (business)
I.35   Services (consumer)

Sampling of portfolio companies: Airgas, Inc. (independent distributor of industrial gases & welding equipment); The Aviation Group, Inc. (contract aircraft operator in the overnight package delivery business, serving Emery & Perolator air couriers); Comsell, Inc./Industrial Training Corp. (develops, programs & markets off-the-shelf interactive programs for applications in industrial & technical skills training); ESPN, The Entertainment Sports Programming Network (all-sports cable tv network created for delivery of programming via satellite); Exogen, Inc. (develops products focused on the biophysical treatment of muscoloskeletal injury & disease); Intelligent Electronics, Inc. (franchiser of microcomputer hardware & office equipment stores, distributor of products to the stores which trade under the names of Today's Computer Business Centers, Entre Computer Centers & Connecting Point of America); Staples, Inc. (large format, discount office supply superstore)

Texada Capital Corporation

1255 Drummers Lane, Suite 300
Four Glenhardie Corporate Center
Wayne, Pennsylvania 19087-1565
(610) 527-7170
Fax: (610) 526-0647

Key contact:
Ms. Bluette N Blinoff, Managing Director
Mr. Laurie G. Kolbeins, Managing Director

Description: We are an investment banking firm with a primary focus on clients in the direct response support services industry: telemarketing, direct mail, printing, fulfillment, data base management, electronic transfer and website authoring and management. We offer financial and strategic advisory services for the owners and managers of closely held companies or divisions of public companies.

Amount of capital invested: $500,000

Amount under management: <$10 million

Area served: United States

Preferred stages of financing: Mezzanine, LBO/MBO, Expansion

Industries:
I.06   Communications
I.14   Electronics
I.15   Energy/natural resources/utilities
I.22   Industrial products
I.23   Information technology services
I.24   Internet services/e-commerce
I.27   Manufacturing
I.28   Media/publishing
I.34   Services (business)
I.37   Wholesale

Sampling of portfolio companies: Magnetix Corp. (custom audio duplicator primarily serving spoken word customers: audio books, religious & motivational speakers); Dirextions Division (direct mail & fulfillment company serving the Orlando hospitality & entertainment community); Connextions Int'l., Inc. (inbound & outbound telemarketing company based in Orlando)

TL Ventures

435 Devon Park Drive, 800 Building
Wayne, Pennsylvania 19087
(610) 971-1515
Fax: (610) 975-9330
E-mail: tlv@tlventures.com
Web: www.tlventures.com

Key contact:
Mr. Robert E. Keith, Jr., Managing Director
Mr. Mark J. DeNino, Managing Director
Mr. Gary J. Anderson, Managing Director
Mr. Christopher C. Moller, Managing Director
Mr. Robert Fabbio, Managing Director

Description: We manage over $540 million of private equity capital & focus principally on investments in the information & biotechnology companies. We are associated with Safeguard Scientifics, Inc. Soon to be announcing an office in Austin, Texas.

Preferred investment size: $10 million

Amount under management: $10-25 million

Area served: North America

Preferred stages of financing: First stage, Mezzanine, Expansion

Industries:
I.03   Biotech/genetic engineering
I.06   Communications
I.07   Computer hardware
I.08   Computer software
I.20   Healthcare
I.21   High technology
I.24   Internet services/e-commerce
I.26   Life sciences
I.33   Semiconductors

Sampling of portfolio companies: Cambridge Technology Partners (private equity); Ventix Corp. (enterprise knowledge management software); Neuron Data, Inc. (business rules automation software); Benchmarking Partners (IT analysis & consulting); Coastal Security Systems (electronic security systems & monitoring); Diablo Research (contract research engineering); Masterpack Int'l. (enterprise software); MatchLogic, Inc. (internet advertising); Naviant Technology (database technology & advanced data mining); OraPharma, Inc. (oral/periodontal drug delivery technology); Reliant Data Systems (data migration software); The Reohr Group (information technology consulting & staffing); Whisper Communications (automatic meter reading devices); WiseWire Corp. (internet search & filtering technology)

Yablon Enterprises, Inc.

P.O. Box 7475
Steelton, Pennsylvania 17113-7475
(717) 939-4545
Fax: (717) 939-4545

Key contact:
Mr. Leonard F. Yablon, J.D., President

Description: We exculsively invest in brokers,
finances, re-finances, sells, buys and acts as international intermediaries for resort real estate projects/
properties in Mexico, Canada, Caribbean and South/
Central America's ONLY. Development, bridge,
creative needs of new and/or operating real estate
(resort)/properties/projects.

Founded: 1971

Amount of capital invested: $3.6 million

Preferred investment size: $1.5-25 million

Amount under management: <$10 million

Area served: North America, South/Central America

Preferred stages of financing: First stage, Mezzanine,
Expansion, Int'l expansion

Industries:
I.25   Leisure/hospitality
I.31   Real estate

Puerto Rico

Advent-Morro Equity Partners

206 Calle Tetuan
Edificio Banco Popular, Suite 903
San Juan, Puerto Rico 00902
(787) 725-5285
Fax: (787) 721-1735

Key contact:
Mr. Cyril Meduna, President
Mr. Zoilo Mendez, Vice President
Ms. Carmen Rocafort, Vice President
Ms. Mari Evelyn Rodriguez, Associate

Description: Private venture capital firm investing own
capital.

Amount of capital invested: $6 million

Preferred investment size: $1-1.5 million

Amount under management: $25-100 million

Area served: United States

Preferred stages of financing: First stage, Second
stage, Mezzanine, LBO/MBO, Expansion

Industries:
I.04   Broadcasting

I.05   Chemicals
I.06   Communications
I.07   Computer hardware
I.08   Computer software
I.11   Consumer products
I.12   Distribution
I.13   Education
I.14   Electronics
I.15   Energy/natural resources/utilities
I.17   Environmental services/waste management
I.18   Financial services
I.20   Healthcare
I.22   Industrial products
I.23   Information technology services
I.24   Internet services/e-commerce
I.26   Life sciences
I.27   Manufacturing
I.28   Media/publishing
I.29   Medical/medical products
I.30   New media
I.32   Retail
I.34   Services (business)
I.36   Transportation
I.37   Wholesale

Rhode Island

Domestic Capital Corp.

815 Reservoir Avenue
Cranston, Rhode Island 02910
(401) 946-3310
Fax: (401) 943-6708

Key contact:
Mr. Nathaniel B. Baker

Area served: Northeast

Industries:
I.19   Generalist

Fleet Equity Partners

50 Kennedy Plaza
Providence, Rhode Island 02903
(401) 278-6770
Fax: (401) 278-6387
E-mail: fep@fleetequity.com
Web: www.fleetequitypartners.com

Key contact:
Mr. Robert Van Degna, Managing Partner
Mr. Habib Gorgi, Managing Partner

Description: We are a private equity firm specializing
in telecommunications, media & information, healthcare, manufacturing, business services and consumer

products and services. We also invest in other private equity funds to obtain superior returns and diversification.

Preferred investment size: $10-20 million

Amount under management: $500 million -1 billion

Area served: Europe, North America

Preferred stages of financing: LBO/MBO, Expansion, Consolidations & recapitalizations

Industries:

I.04	Broadcasting
I.06	Communications
I.11	Consumer products
I.12	Distribution
I.13	Education
I.18	Financial services
I.20	Healthcare
I.22	Industrial products
I.23	Information technology services
I.24	Internet services/e-commerce
I.27	Manufacturing
I.28	Media/publishing
I.32	Retail
I.34	Services (business)
I.35	Services (consumer)
I.36	Transportation
I.37	Wholesale

Sampling of portfolio companies: Advanced Materials Technology (semiconductor packaging materials manufacturer) Chemprene Holding (rubber & plastic conveyor belts manufacturer) Dines Industrial Group (manufacturer of truck & trailer suspensions & commercial infrared heating systems); Federated Lithographers-Printers (specialty printer serving commercial & book publishing markets); Florists Transworld Delivery (world's largest floral services organization); Northeast Energy Services (services for energy conservation services firm); Recra Environmental (chemical & environmental testing services); ACC (long distance reseller); Bachtel Cellular (rural cellular operator); Brooks Fiber Properties (competitive local exchange carrier & competitive access provider); Continental Cablevision (CATV owner & operator); Benchmark Communications (radio station operator); CustomMedia (newsletter publisher for apartment communities); Digital Television Services (rural provider of DirecTv services); GMIS (healthcare decision support software); North American Health Plans (managed care organization); Central Tractor Farm & Country (agricultural specialty retailer); Hasco Holdings (in-hospital infant portrait service provider); Pace Fitness, LLC (manufacturer of motorized consumer treadmills); La Petite Academy (nation's second largest childcare center-based chain)

Moneta Capital Corp.

285 Governor Street
Providence, Rhode Island 02906
(401) 454-7500
Fax: (401) 455-3636

Key contact:
Mr. Arnold Kilberg

Area served: Northeast

Industries:
I.19   Generalist

South Carolina

Emergent Business Capital - Equity Group

7 North Laurens Street, Suite 603
Greenville, South Carolina 29601
(864) 232-6198
Fax: (864) 241-4444
E-mail: holly.melton@emergent-group.com
Web: www.bothears.com

Key contact:
Mr. Capers A. Easterby, President
Mr. William A. Litchfield, Senior Vice President

Description: We are a subsidiary of a publicly traded financial services company that provides senior and subordinated debt with equity features to successful small and middle market companies for working capital, acquisition financings, buyouts and recapitalization.

Amount of capital invested: $10 million

Preferred investment size: $1.5 million

Amount under management: $100-500 million

Area served: United States

Preferred stage of financing: Mezzanine

Industries:
I.04   Broadcasting

I.05	Chemicals
I.06	Communications
I.07	Computer hardware
I.08	Computer software
I.11	Consumer products
I.12	Distribution
I.13	Education
I.14	Electronics
I.16	Entertainment
I.17	Environmental services/waste management
I.19	Generalist
I.20	Healthcare
I.21	High technology
I.22	Industrial products
I.23	Information technology services
I.25	Leisure/hospitality
I.27	Manufacturing
I.28	Media/publishing
I.29	Medical/medical products
I.34	Services (business)
I.35	Services (consumer)
I.36	Transportation
I.37	Wholesale

Sampling of portfolio companies: Hunt Assisted Living Center (builds & operates assisted living centers in Southeast US); ILD Teleservices, Inc. (provides operator services & prepaid calling cards); Media Marketing Services (provides businesses with travel award programs for customers & employees); Mentor Dynamics Ltd. (distributor of specialty plastics to transportation industry); Cyrus Corp. (leading reseller of IBM POS equipment); Southern Weaving Co.

(manufacturer of textile webbing & belts for industrial appliances); VAlue Music Concepts, Inc. (operates a chain of value oriented music stores in factory outlets); Network One (provider of long distance services to commercial customers)

Floco Investment Company, Inc.

P.O. Box 1629
Lake City, South Carolina 29560
(803) 389-2731
Fax: (803) 389-4199

Key contact:
Mr. Gregory Fisher
Mr. William H. Johnson

Area served: Southeast

Palmetto Seed Capital Corporation

7 North Laurens, Suite 603
Greenville, South Carolina 29601
(864) 232-6198
Fax: (864) 241-4444

Key contact:
Mr. Capers Easterby

Area served: Southeast

Preferred stages of financing: Seed, Start up, First stage

Industries:
I.06   Communications
I.07   Computer hardware
I.08   Computer software
I.14   Electronics
I.29   Medical/medical products

Tennessee

International Paper Capital Formation, Inc.

International Place II
6400 Poplar Avenue
Memphis, Tennessee 38197
(901) 763-6282
Fax: (901) 763-6076

Key contact:
Mr. Bob J. Higgins

Area served: United States

Preferred stages of financing: Second stage, Third/later stage

Industries:
I.19   Generalist

Massey Burch Capital Corp.

310 25th Avenue North, Suite 103
Nashville, Tennessee 37203
(615) 329-9448
Fax: (615) 329-9237
E-mail: marketing@masseyburch.com
Web: www.masseyburch.com

Key contact:
Mr. Donald M. Johnston, President/Partner
Mr. William F. Earthman, III, Partner
Mr. J. Donald McLemore, Jr., CFO/Partner
Mr. Lucius E. Burch, IV, Partner

Description: We were formed in 1981 as the continuation of the investing activities of Jack C. Massey and Lucius E. Burch, III. We began making venture capital investments in 1968 at Massey Investment Company, and find that the Southeastern's dynamic growth provides us attractive investment opportunities not seized by other venture capital firms.

Founded: 1981

Preferred stages of financing: Seed, Start up, First stage

Industries:
I.06   Communications
I.20   Healthcare
I.23   Information technology services
I.24   Internet services/e-commerce

Sampling of portfolio companies: Digex Business Internet (internet service provider for the commercial marketplace); Intellivoice Communications, Inc. (systems integrator & developer of voice activated service applications for the cellular telephone industry); Criterion Health Strategies (healthcare information service company applying integration warehousing & decision support software & services to the healthcare industry); InterZine Productions, Inc. (provides interactive content for online services, the internet, CD-ROMs & interactive television); PhyCor Management Corp. (formed to service the market of Independent Physicians Associations & operating companion Management Service Organizations); @plan., Inc. (integrated, interactive advertising planning system for the world wide web); CORPHEALTH, Inc. (develops & manages integrated behavioral healthcare delivery systems that are characterized by single-point accountability for services delivery, managed care competencies & business operations); Inforum, Inc.; Corrections Corp. of America; Redgate Communications

Morgan Keegan & Company

50 North Front Street
Morgan Keegan Tower
Memphis, Tennessee 38103
(901) 524-4100

Key contact:
Vicki Douglas

Preferred stages of financing: Second stage, Mezzanine

Industries:
I.04   Broadcasting
I.06   Communications
I.12   Distribution
I.15   Energy/natural resources/utilities
I.22   Industrial products
I.29   Medical/medical products
I.31   Real estate

River Associates, L.L.C.

633 Chestnut Street, Suite 1640
Chattanooga, Tennessee 37450
(423) 755-0888
Fax: (423) 755-0870

Key contact:
Mr. J. Mark Jones, Principal

Description: We are a private equity firm that invests alongside management in profitable niche manufacturing and distribution companies with revenues between $10 and $60 million. Since opening, we have invested in 19 companies operating in a variety of industries located throughout the U.S. Our principals have a variety of operating and financial backgrounds and we gladly provide multiple references. Inquiries from management teams, professional and intermediaries are welcome.

Founded: 1989

Amount of capital invested: $7.5 million equity

Preferred investment size: $2-6 million equity

Amount under management: $25-100 million

Area served: United States

Preferred stage of financing: LBO/MBO

Industries:
I.05   Chemicals
I.12   Distribution
I.19   Generalist
I.22   Industrial products
I.27   Manufacturing

Sampling of portfolio companies: W.R. Case & Sons Cutlery Co. (cutlery manufacturing); United Knitting, Inc. (specialty fabric manufacturing); Cady Industries (specialty packaging manufacturing); Astroturf/S.W. Recreational Industries (synthetic sport surface manufacturing); Capitol Adhesives (floor covering adhesives/accessories); Advanced Photographic Solutions (wholesale photo finishing); Stoneville/ Towne Square Furniture (furniture maufacturing); Tooling Technology (specialty molds/tooling)

Salix Ventures

30 Burton Hills, Suite 370
Nashville, Tennessee 37215
(615) 665-1409
Fax: (615) 665-2912
E-mail: mfelsenthal@salixventures.com
Web: www.salixventures.com

Key contact:
Mr. Christopher Grant, Jr., General Partner
Mr. David A. Ward, General Partner
Mr. Martin R. Felsenthal, Principal

Description: Health care services and health care information technology firm investing in early-stage companies.

Preferred investment size: $5 million

Amount under management: $25-100 million

Area served: United States

Preferred stages of financing: Start up, First stage

Industries:
I.20   Healthcare

Sampling of portfolio companies: Clinical reSearchNet (site management organization); Physician Solutions (pathology services)

Sirrom Capital Corporation

500 Church Street, Suite 200
Nashville, Tennessee 37219
(615) 256-0701
Fax: (615) 726-1208
E-mail: kbennett@sirromcapital.com
Web: www.sirromcapital.com

Key contact:
Mr. George M. Miller, II, President/CEO
Mr. David M. Resha, COO
Carl W. Stratton, CFO

Description: We are a publicly traded company headquartered in Nashville, TN. We are a specialty finance company serving the needs of small businesses in the U.S. and Canada. We have approximately $850 million in committed and available capital to invest in small businesses in the form of secured term loans.

Amount of capital invested: $280 million+

Preferred investment size: $1-5 million

Amount under management: $100-500 million

Area served: North America

Preferred stage of financing: Mezzanine

Industries:
I.03   Biotech/genetic engineering

I.04   Broadcasting
I.06   Communications
I.08   Computer software
I.11   Consumer products
I.12   Distribution
I.14   Electronics
I.18   Financial services
I.20   Healthcare
I.21   High technology
I.22   Industrial products
I.23   Information technology services
I.25   Leisure/hospitality
I.27   Manufacturing
I.28   Media/publishing
I.29   Medical/medical products
I.32   Retail
I.34   Services (business)
I.36   Transportation

Sampling of portfolio companies: Alignis, Inc. (Healthcare); Faxnet (Enhanced facsimile telecommunication services provider); Gulfstream Airlines (Regional airline); MasterGraphics (Consolidator of printing companies); Mobility Electronics (Designer & manufacturer of portable electronics accessories); Multi-Media Data Systems (Multi-media information technology for the healthcare industry); Omni Home Medical (Home medical products & services); One Coast Network (Manufacturer's Representative Organization (MRO) for gifts & home accessories; Orchid Manufacturing (Metal stamping & die casting); Palco Telecom Services (Telecommunications); Caribou Coffee Company (coffeehouses); Pay sys International, Inc. (Software development for consumer finance); Ready Personnel (Staffing); Wolfgang Puck Food Company (Restaurant/food service)

SSM Ventures
845 Crossover Lane, Suite 140
Memphis, Tennessee 38117
(901) 767-1131
Fax: (901) 767-1135
E-mail: rworr@mem.net

Key contact:
Mr. James D. Witherington, Jr., Principal
Mr. C. Barham Ray, Principal
Ms. Ashley M. Mayfield, Principal
Mr. William F. Harrison, Principal
Mr. R. Wilson Orr, III, Principal
Mr. Eric L. Jones, Principal

Description: Our objective is to invest in a diversified portfolio of rapidly growing private companies located primarily in the South. Upon closing of our third fund (May, 1998) we will be one of the larger and more experienced firms based in the South in terms of capital under management and continuity of the principals managing the fund.

Amount of capital invested: $8.2 million

Preferred investment size: $3-10 million

Amount under management: $100-500 million

Area served: United States

Preferred stages of financing: Start up, First stage, Second stage, LBO/MBO, Expansion

Industries:
I.03   Biotech/genetic engineering
I.06   Communications
I.07   Computer hardware
I.08   Computer software
I.11   Consumer products
I.12   Distribution
I.14   Electronics
I.18   Financial services
I.20   Healthcare
I.21   High technology
I.22   Industrial products
I.23   Information technology services
I.24   Internet services/e-commerce
I.32   Retail

Sampling of portfolio companies: DAZEL (client server software); Active Power (kinetic batteries); Motive Software (web-based software); Arch Communications (paging); CONXUS Communications (wireless voice messaging); Direct General (non-standard auto insurance); Kirkland's (specialty retail); Office Furniture, USA (franchiser of office furniture stores); American Pathology (physician practice management); TORCH Health Care (assisted living facilities); Healthcare Innovations (occupational & rehabilitational medicine)

Valley Capital Corporation
100 West Martin Luther King Boulevard
Krystal Building, Suite 212
Chattanooga, Tennessee 37402
(423) 265-1557
Fax: (423) 265-1588

Key contact:
Ms. Faye Robinson
Mr. Lamar J. Partridge

Area served: Southeast

Preferred stages of financing: Second stage, LBO/MBO

Industries:
I.19   Generalist

West Tennessee Venture Capital Corporation
5 North Third Street
Memphis, Tennessee 38103
(901) 522-9237
Fax: (901) 527-6091

Key contact:
Mr. Frank Banks

Industries:
I.19   Generalist

Texas

Alliance Financial of Houston

9130 North Freeway, Suite 203
Houston, Texas 77037
(281) 447-3330
Fax: (281) 447-4222
E-mail: afgalli@usa.net

Key contact:
Mr. Atillio F. Galli
Mr. William M. Berry, Jr.

Description: Venture capital management company.

Amount under management: <$10 million

Area served: North America

Preferred stages of financing: Second stage, Mezzanine, Expansion

Industries:
I.12   Distribution
I.18   Financial services
I.19   Generalist
I.22   Industrial products
I.27   Manufacturing
I.34   Services (business)
I.35   Services (consumer)
I.37   Wholesale

AM Fund

1716 Briarcrest Drive, Suite 507
Bryan, Texas 77802
(409) 846-6072
Fax: (409) 846-9172

Key contact:
Mr. David Mueller

8911 Capital of Texas Highway, Suite 3310
Austin, Texas 78759
(512) 342-2024
Fax: (512) 342-1993

Key contact:
Mr. Cole Dudley

Area served: Southwest

Preferred stage of financing: First stage

Industries:
I.02   Agriculture/forestry/fishing/mining
I.03   Biotech/genetic engineering
I.05   Chemicals
I.06   Communications
I.14   Electronics
I.15   Energy/natural resources/utilities
I.29   Medical/medical products

Austin Ventures

114 West 7th Street, Suite 1300
Austin, Texas 78701
(512) 479-0055
Fax: (512) 476-3952
E-mail: moreinfo@ausven.com
Web: www.austinventures.com

Key contact:
Mr. Joseph C. Aragona, General Partner
Mr. Kenneth P. DeAngelis, General Partner
Mr. Jeffery C. Garvey, General Partner
Mr. John D. Thornton, General Partner
Mr. Blaine Wesner, General Partner
Mr. William P. Wood, General Partner
Mr. Bob Fabbio, Venture Partner
Mr. Marty Fluke, Venture Partner
Mr. Jimmy Treybig, Venture Partner
Mr. James T. Armstrong, Associate
Mr. J. Ross Cockrell, Associate
Mr. Stephn D. Straus, Associate
Mr. John E. Nicholson, CFO/Partner
Ms. Claudia F. Chidester, Director of Research
Mr. David C. Weaver, Director of MIS

Description: We have worked in partnership with talented entrepreneurs to help build some of America's most successful growth companies. Our particular focus on companies in Texas and the Southwest reflects both a confidence in the economic future of the region and a recognition that we can usually add the most value in situations to which we are the closest.

Area served: Texas, Southwest, United States

Preferred stages of financing: Seed, Start up, First stage, Second stage

Industries:
I.06   Communications
I.12   Distribution
I.27   Manufacturing
I.29   Medical/medical products

Sampling of portfolio companies: Active Power (developer of flywheel battery systems); Deja News (developer of services to enable marketing campaign via the internet); GCS (developer of software for the management of pre-clinical trials); Garden Escape (electronics source for home gardening hobbyists); Metasolv (developer of telecommunications software); Outreach Communications (internet electronic commerce payments systems); Smart Technologies, Inc. (enterprise software solutions that leverage the internet as a customer interaction channel); Pervasive Software (developer of database software); Vignette Corp. (developer of content production management software for large-scale web sites); Xtra On-Line (developer of on-line travel software & services); VTel (developer & provider of videoconferencing solutions); Boca Burger (processor & marketer of branded meat alternative products); SynOptics (developer of network communications equipment); Q Clubs (operator of health & fitness clubs); Torch Healthcare (developer & operator of assisted living facilities); Healthcare Innovations (operator of occupational medicine & rehabilitation clinics); Bristol (manufacturer & distributor of insulated copper, wire & cable, plumbing products & plastic pipe); PetStuff (operator of pet food & supplies retail superstores); Dial Page (acquirer of paging & telephone answering services)

Banc One Capital Partners

300 Crescent Court, Suite 1600
Dallas, Texas 75201
(214) 979-4361
Fax: (214) 979-4355
E-mail: sbkriscunas@bocc.com

Key contact:
Ms. Suzanne B. Kriscunas, Managing Director

Description: We provide mezzanine, venture capital and financial advisory services to middle-market operating companies in connection with mergers and acquisitions, recapitalizations, corporate divestitures and expansion capital. Such financings are typically in the form of subordinated debt with warrants and/or preferred stock.

Amount of capital invested: $170 million

Preferred investment size: $5-8 million

Amount under management: $100-500 million

Area served: United States

Preferred stages of financing: Mezzanine, LBO/MBO, Expansion

Industries:
I.06   Communications
I.11   Consumer products
I.12   Distribution
I.13   Education
I.14   Electronics
I.17   Environmental services/waste management
I.18   Financial services
I.19   Generalist
I.20   Healthcare
I.22   Industrial products
I.27   Manufacturing
I.28   Media/publishing
I.29   Medical/medical products
I.34   Services (business)
I.36   Transportation
I.37   Wholesale

Sampling of portfolio companies: Compaq Computer Co. (computer manufacturer); Metro Airlines, Inc. (regional commuter airlines); Beauty Control (cosmetic manufacturer); Callaway Golf Co. (manufacturer of golf clubs); First Plus Financial Group (financial services); Plains Resources, Inc. (oil & gas exploration); A&W Brands (soft drink manufacturer); Pronet, Inc. (telephone paging services); Dr. Pepper Bottling Co. (soft drink bottler); Enclean, Inc. (environmental services); Community Health Systems (healthcare facilities & services); Railtex, Inc. (railcare leasing); Kemet Electronics (manufacturer electronic capacitors); Matador Petroleum Corp. (oil exploration & production); DeCrane Aircraft Holdings (manufacturer aerospace products); Argyle Television (operator of television stations)

C3 Holdings, LLC

5005 LBJ Freeway, LB 119
Dallas, Texas 75244
(972) 233-8778
Fax: (972) 233-0112
E-mail: businessdevelopment@c3holdings.com
Web: www.c3holdings.com

Key contact:
Mr. A. Baron Cass, III, Principal

Description: Our principals bring more than a recognized breadth of experience in capital formation, corporate and joint venture acquisitions, dispositions, investment banking and corporate restructurings. We have all operated businesses on a daily basis. While each principal brings a successful past and a unique perspective to the firm, the combination of individual talents into this highly skilled team truly distinguishes our firm. And because the firm takes a partnership approach to business, business owners gain access to the expertise of all our partners.

Area served: Midwest

Preferred stages of financing: LBO/MBO, Add-ons

Industries:
I.05   Chemicals
I.06   Communications
I.11   Consumer products
I.12   Distribution
I.15   Energy/natural resources/utilities
I.18   Financial services
I.20   Healthcare
I.22   Industrial products
I.23   Information technology services
I.27   Manufacturing
I.31   Real estate
I.32   Retail
I.37   Wholesale

Sampling of portfolio companies: American Safety Razor Co. (manufacturer of brand-name & private brand personal care consumer products); Atlantic Premium Brands, Ltd. (manufacturer & distributor of branded specialty meat products to the retail trade); Bullitt Beverage Co. (wholesale distributor of malt beverage products); Distributive Processes, Inc. (consolidation of wholesale wines & spirits distributors in western Missouri); Nutri/System, LP (developer & provider of assistive weight loss programs); Renaissance Investors, LLC (children's filmmaker & distributor); Standard Brands Paint (manufacturer of coatings for the do-it-yourself market); Tom's Foods, Inc. (manufacturer of a full-line of snack foods for distribution in the over-the-counter & vending machine markets); Cold Jet, Inc. (developer & manufacturer of carbon dioxide cleaning & blasting equipment); Cook Composites & Polymers (int'l. provider of composite systems to the fiberglass reinforced products, coating & ink industries); Cook Paint & Varnish Co. (manufacturer of coatings & related products for residential & commercial uses); Georgia Gulf/Freeman Chenzical (manufacturer of polyester resins & coatings for fiberglass reinforced products); The Warrington Group Ltd. (developer & marketer of safety footwear for firemen); TSI Holdings, Inc. (consolidator of manufacturers of freestanding & chasis mounted tanks); Truswal Systems Corp. (manufacturer of truss plates & provider of engineering services & software systems to the building products industry); Bion, Inc. (developer of therapeutic & diagnostic products for cardiovascular disease); Cry Research, Inc. (statistical developer of predictive models of diseases in infants); Myriad Ultrasound Systems Ltd. (developer & manufacturer of ultrasound diagnostic equipment); Physiologic Diagnostic Services, Inc. (developer & manufacturer of uterine activity monitoring devices); XTL Biopharmaceuticals Ltd. (product developer for treatment of viral & autoimmune diseases)

Capital Southwest Corporation

12900 Preston Road, Suite 700
Dallas, Texas 75230
(972) 233-8242
Fax: (972) 233-7362
Web: www.capitalsouthwest.com

Key contact:
Mr. Howard M. Thomas, Investment Associate
Mr. D. Scott Collier, Vice President
Mr. Tim Smith, Vice President/Secretary/Treasurer
Mr. Patrick F. Hammer, Vice President
Mr. J. Bruce Duty, Senior Vice President
Mr. William R. Thomas, President/Chairman of the Board

Description: We are the nation's largest publicly-owned venture capital investment company. Along with our wholly owned small business investment company subsidiary, we provide capital to support the development and growth of small and medium-sized businesses in varied industries throughout the United States.

Amount of capital invested: $7.5 million

Preferred investment size: $3 million

Amount under management: $100-500 million

Area served: United States

Preferred stages of financing: Start up, First stage, Second stage, LBO/MBO, Expansion

Industries:
I.01   Aerospace
I.03   Biotech/genetic engineering
I.04   Broadcasting
I.05   Chemicals

I.06   Communications
I.07   Computer hardware
I.08   Computer software
I.11   Consumer products
I.14   Electronics
I.20   Healthcare
I.21   High technology
I.22   Industrial products
I.23   Information technology services
I.24   Internet services/e-commerce
I.27   Manufacturing
I.28   Media/publishing
I.29   Medical/medical products
I.30   New media
I.32   Retail
I.33   Semiconductors
I.34   Services (business)
I.35   Services (consumer)
I.36   Transportation
I.37   Wholesale

Sampling of portfolio companies: Alamo Group (manufacturing); Airformed Composites (manufacturing); Denver Technologies (manufacturing); Encore Wire (manufacturing); Palm Harbor Homes (manufacturing); Texas Shredder (manufacturing); Whitmore Manufacturing (manufacturing); Book Stop (specialty retailing); Petstuff (specialty retailing); The Wholesale Club (specialty retailing); All Components, Inc. (technology); Columbia Scientific (technology); Intelligent Reasoning Systems (technology); Maginovox Electronic Systems (technology); Pharmacy Practice Group (health care); SDI Holding Corp. (health care); Cherokee Communications (service); Rewind Holdings, Inc. (service); Steffan Dairy Foods (service); U.S. Funds Express (service)

The Catalyst Group

Three Riverway, Suite 770
Houston, Texas 77056
(713) 623-8133
Fax: (713) 623-0473

Key contact:
Mr. Rick Herrman, Principal
Mr. Ron Nixon, Principal
Mr. Steve Gillioz, Vice President

Description: Four funds; two separate but similar forms of investing: 1) mezzanine debt via two SBIC's, and 2) controlling equity in MBO/LBO activity. Focus is smaller mid-market businesses with revenues $5 - $25 million.

Preferred investment size: $2 million

Amount under management: $25-100 million

Area served: United States

Preferred stages of financing: Mezzanine, LBO/MBO, Expansion

Industries:
I.01   Aerospace
I.02   Agriculture/forestry/fishing/mining
I.04   Broadcasting
I.05   Chemicals
I.06   Communications
I.11   Consumer products
I.12   Distribution
I.14   Electronics
I.17   Environmental services/waste management
I.19   Generalist
I.20   Healthcare
I.22   Industrial products
I.26   Life sciences
I.27   Manufacturing
I.28   Media/publishing
I.29   Medical/medical products
I.32   Retail
I.34   Services (business)
I.37   Wholesale

Sampling of portfolio companies: Lone Star Overnight (intrastate overnight delivery service); Table Toys, Inc. (manufacturer of educational constructive toys); MST COMM. d/b/a KIXZ/KMML (am/fm radio stations); Islander Sportswear (manufacturer of quality leisure & resort wear); Vestec Corp. (manufacturer of scientific laboratory instruments); AG Engineering/Dev. Co. (manufacturer & distributor of agricultural equipment); ACR Group, Inc. (wholesale distributor of HVAC equipment); Flintlock, Ltd. (designer, manufacturer & distributor of candles & home accessories); M&S Restaurants #1, Ltd.; Players Texas Sports, Inc. (wholesale distributor of sports & entertainment trading cards & collectibles); Deck The Walls, Inc. (franchiser of approximately 200 retail locations selling preframed art & providing framing services);Spectracell Labs, Inc. (specialty clinical lab performing nutritional assessments);

Everything Organized, Inc. (retailer of items & systems for home & office organization); AGM Memorials, Inc. (national wholesale designer, fabricator & distributor of granite memorialization products); Summit Moulding & Frame, Inc. (regional wholesale distributor of framing products & supplies); Vulcan Iron Works, Inc. (manufacturer & distributor of pile driving equipment & accessories); Hendee Enterprises, Inc. (manufacturer & distributor of commercial, structural & fabric products); Airbrush Images, Inc. (provider of specialized printing to the outdoor advertising industry); Aluma-Craft Corporation, Inc. (manufacturer & distributor of aluminum & steel screens for windows & patio doors); Elliott Valve Mid-Continent, Ltd. d/b/a Warburton Valve (serves the Mid-Continent & Rockies for valve distribution & repair services)

CCG Venture Partners, LLC
14450 T. C. Jester, Suite 170
Houston, Texas 77014
(281) 893-8331
Fax: (281) 893-2420
E-mail: tybarra@ccgvp.com
Web: www.ccgvp.com

Key contact:
Mr. Rick Davis, Managing Partner/Founder
Mr. John A. Kiltz, Partner
Mr. Mark E. Leyerle, Manager-Leveraged Acquisitions
Ms. Rhonda Kallies, Executive Assistant
Ms. Janine Koch, Controller
Ms. Becky Lee, Administrative Assistant
Mr. David White, IT Manager
Ms. Tracie Ybarra, Executive Administrator

Description: We are a private investment venture capital firm that specializes in two areas: leveraged acquisitions and roll-outs.

Founded: 1995

Preferred investment size: $250,000-2.5 million

Area served: United States

Preferred stages of financing: LBO/MBO, Roll-outs

Industries:
I.15   Energy/natural resources/utilities
I.17   Environmental services/waste management
I.27   Manufacturing

Sampling of portfolio companies: North American Technologies Group, Inc. (engaged in the acquisition & commercialization of technologies in the energy & environmental services industries); DAN-LOC Bolt & Gasket, Inc. (manufactures & sells stud bolts, flanges & metallic ring gaskets for use in a variety of industrial settings); The Flexitallic Group, Inc. (manufacturer of integrated industrial sealing systems); Omni Technology Centers, LLC (provides client server software training & consulting services)

The Centennial Funds
1330 Post Oak Boulevard, Suite 1525
Houston, Texas 77056
(713) 627-9200
Fax: (713) 627-9292
E-mail: davidh@centennial.com

Key contact:
Mr. David C. Hull, Jr.

Area served: United States

Preferred stages of financing: Seed, Start up, First stage, Second stage

Industries:
I.06   Communications
I.07   Computer hardware
I.11   Consumer products
I.14   Electronics
I.35   Services (consumer)

Chen's Financial Group, Inc.
10101 Southwest Freeway, Suite 370
Houston, Texas 77074
(713) 772-8868
Fax: (713) 772-2168

Key contact:
Mr. Samuel Chen

Area served: United States

Preferred stages of financing: Seed, Start up, First stage, Second stage, LBO/MBO, Third/later stage

Industries:
I.25   Leisure/hospitality
I.32   Retail

Cole Capital & Consulting, Inc.
4445 Alpha Road, Suite 110
Dallas, Texas 75244
(972) 503-1516
Fax: (972) 503-1519

Key contact:
Mr. Frank Cole, President
Mr. Pierce Hance, President

Description: We seek companies that need money but not talent. Our primary business is venture capital. We wish to assist our portfolio companies as active board members and advisors but not as participants in daily operations. We can offer assistance in strategic decisions and long range planning, and always provide our network of contacts to promote the portfolio company's efforts.

Amount of capital invested: $3.5 million

Preferred investment size: $750,000-1.5 million

Amount under management: $10-25 million

Area served: United States

Preferred stages of financing: First stage, Second stage, Mezzanine, LBO/MBO, Expansion

Industries:
I.10 Consulting
I.11 Consumer products
I.13 Education
I.16 Entertainment
I.18 Financial services
I.32 Retail
I.34 Services (business)
I.35 Services (consumer)

Sampling of portfolio companies: Archibald Bros. Fine Beverages (manufacturer of beverage & dessert products); Schlutzsky's, Inc. (international business format franchiser); New Florida Markets, Ltd. (area developer of franchise); Deli Keys, Ltd. (area developer of franchise); Springbrook Partners, Ltd. (retail service company)

Columbine Venture Funds

3810 Swarthmore
Houston, Texas 77005-3610
(713) 661-9260
Fax: (713) 661-9265

Key contact:
Mr. Carl S. Stutts

Area served: Rocky Mountains, Southwest

Industries:
I.03 Biotech/genetic engineering
I.05 Chemicals
I.06 Communications
I.07 Computer hardware
I.08 Computer software
I.29 Medical/medical products

Cureton & Company, Inc.

1100 Louisiana Street, Suite 3250
Houston, Texas 77002
(713) 658-9806
Fax: (713) 658-0476

Key contact:
Mr. Stewart Cureton, President
Mr. Robert Antonoff, Executive Vice President

Description: We perform corporate finance and investment banking services for corporate clients in all areas except public market activities. Our focus is to assist the development of growth companies in the Southwest. Sources of funds include substantial individual investors, financial institutions and venture funds.

Founded: 1974

Preferred investment size: $2-10 million

Amount under management: <$10 million

Area served: United States

Preferred stages of financing: First stage, Second stage

Industries:
I.04 Broadcasting
I.05 Chemicals
I.06 Communications
I.07 Computer hardware
I.08 Computer software
I.09 Construction
I.11 Consumer products
I.12 Distribution
I.14 Electronics
I.17 Environmental services/waste management
I.18 Financial services
I.19 Generalist
I.21 High technology
I.22 Industrial products
I.23 Information technology services
I.24 Internet services/e-commerce
I.27 Manufacturing
I.32 Retail
I.34 Services (business)
I.35 Services (consumer)
I.36 Transportation
I.37 Wholesale

Davis, Tuttle Venture Partners, L.P.

8 Greenway Plaza, Suite 1020
Houston, Texas 77046
(713) 993-0440
Fax: (713) 621-2297
E-mail: ptuttle@dtyp.com

Key contact:
Mr. Phil Tuttle, General Partner

Description: We are a third in a series of private equity funds focused on expansion investments, middle market buyouts and selected early stage investments in the Southwest. Our partners have been involved in continuous venture capital activity over the past 25 years. We are institutionally funded by Fortune 100 pension funds, insurance companies and commercial banks. We are lead investors and we provide long-term capital and strategic advice and counsel.

Preferred investment size: $2.5 million

Amount under management: $100-500 million

Area served: United States

Preferred stages of financing: First stage, LBO/MBO, Expansion

Industries:
I.05   Chemicals
I.06   Communications
I.11   Consumer products
I.12   Distribution
I.13   Education
I.15   Energy/natural resources/utilities
I.17   Environmental services/waste management
I.20   Healthcare
I.22   Industrial products
I.23   Information technology services
I.27   Manufacturing
I.29   Medical/medical products
I.36   Transportation

Desco Capital Partners

8029 North MacArthur Boulevard, Box 3112
Irving, Texas 75063
(972) 858-9659
Fax: (972) 858-9660
E-mail: kestlerpd@aol.com
Web: descovc.com

Key contact:
Mr. Paul Kestler, Investment Manager

Description: We are a private investor group who funds
enterprises exhibiting exceptional potential for
growth. We seek to invest our capital in well-
managed companies that can meet objectives in a 3
to 7 year period. We work in partnership with
managers and owners to maximize value.

Founded: 1992

Amount of capital invested: $10 million

Preferred investment size: $1-2 million

Amount under management: $25-100 million

Area served: United States

Preferred stages of financing: First stage, Second
stage, Mezzanine, LBO/MBO, Expansion

Industries:
I.01   Aerospace
I.08   Computer software
I.14   Electronics
I.21   High technology
I.22   Industrial products
I.23   Information technology services
I.24   Internet services/e-commerce
I.27   Manufacturing
I.33   Semiconductors

Essex Woodlands Health Ventures

2170 Buckthorne Place, Suite 170
Woodlands, Texas 77380
(281) 367-9999
Fax: (281) 298-1295

Key contact:
Mr. Don E. Spyrison

Mr. Martin Sutter

Preferred stages of financing: Seed, First stage

Industries:
I.03   Biotech/genetic engineering
I.29   Medical/medical products

First Capital Group of Texas II, LP

750 East Mulberry, Suite 305
P.O. Box 15616
San Antonio, Texas 78212
(210) 736-4233
Fax: (210) 736-5449
E-mail: jpb@texas.net
Web: www.firstcapitalgroup.com

Key contact:
Mr. Jeffrey P. Blanchard, Managing Partner

100 Congress Avenue, Suite 730
Austin, Texas 78701-4042
(512) 494-9754
Fax: (512) 494-9756
E-mail: wwg@texas.net
Web: www.firstcapitalgroup.com

Key contact:
Mr. Ward Greenwood, Managing Partner

Description: We are a private investment firm that
invests our own capital to provide equity financing to
middle-market companies engaged in a variety of
industries throughout Texas and the Southwest. Our
newest partnership, First Capital Group of Texas II,
LP, is a $31 million fund established in 1996 which,
like predecessor funds, will continue to specialize in
supporting expansion financings, management
buyouts and recapitalizations of existing businesses.

Amount of capital invested: $8 million

Preferred investment size: $1-2 million

Amount under management: $25-100 million

Area served: Texas, Southwest

Preferred stages of financing: LBO/MBO, Expansion,
Third stage

Industries:
I.04   Broadcasting
I.05   Chemicals
I.06   Communications
I.07   Computer hardware
I.08   Computer software
I.11   Consumer products
I.12   Distribution
I.13   Education
I.14   Electronics
I.16   Entertainment
I.17   Environmental services/waste management
I.20   Healthcare
I.21   High technology
I.22   Industrial products
I.23   Information technology services
I.27   Manufacturing
I.29   Medical/medical products
I.34   Services (business)
I.35   Services (consumer)
I.36   Transportation

Sampling of portfolio companies: Rewind Productions (touring entertainment industry video projects); Baseball Express (catalog sales); Reef Chemical Co. (specialty chemicals for energy industry); Meyer Machinery (specialized bulk material conveying equipment for food industry); Media Recovery (distribution/manufacturing); Intelligent Technologies (advanced fraud detection); EZ Talk Communications (pre-paid residential telephone service)

Global American Corporation

Bank One Center
1301 South Bowen Road, Suite 440
Arlington, Texas 76013
(888) 795-8981
(817) 795-8981
Fax: (972) 733-4922
E-mail: info@gac-eog.com

Key contact:
Mr. Lewis Pope

Description: Private equity investment firm that engages in financing the capital requirments for a variety of companies, in various industries, through private investors. Industries of interest include: hardware, software, consumer electronics, manufacturing, telecommunications, energy and technology.

Preferred stages of financing: Start up, First stage, LBO/MBO, Expansion

Industries:
I.06   Communications
I.07   Computer hardware
I.08   Computer software
I.14   Electronics
I.15   Energy/natural resources/utilities
I.20   Healthcare
I.23   Information technology services
I.27   Manufacturing

Sampling of portfolio companies: Ciena Corp. (maker of telecommunications equipment)

HCT Capital Corp.

4916 Camp Bowie Boulevard, Suite 200
Ft. Worth, Texas 76107
(817) 763-8706
Fax: (817) 377-8049

Key contact:
Mr. Vichy Woodward Young, Jr.

Area served: Southwest

Preferred stages of financing: Seed, Start up, First stage

Industries:
I.03   Biotech/genetic engineering
I.29   Medical/medical products

G. A. Herrera & Company Investment Bankers

5151 San Felipe, Suite 500
Houston, Texas 77057
(713) 860-1431
Fax: (713) 355-3909
E-mail: g.a.herrera-co@att.net
Web: www.herrera-co.com

Key contact:
Mr. Gilbert A. Herrera, Principal

Description: We are a private investment banking firm with proven expertise in debt and equity placements, merger and acquisition advisory services, valuations, litigation support and expert testimony. We focus on entretreneurial-oriented, well-managed companies seeking experienced, hands-on financial assistance.

Amount of capital invested: $1 million

Preferred investment size: $500,000

Amount under management: <$10 million

Area served: United States

Preferred stages of financing: Second stage, Mezzanine, LBO/MBO, Expansion

Industries:
I.12   Distribution
I.15   Energy/natural resources/utilities
I.20   Healthcare
I.28   Media/publishing
I.34   Services (business)
I.37   Wholesale

Sampling of portfolio companies: Distributors; Service providers; Food (private label & premium label); Energy service

Hook Partners

13760 Noel Road, Suite 805
Dallas, Texas 75240
(972) 991-5457
Fax: (972) 991-5458
E-mail: dhook@hookpartners.com
Web: www.hookpartners.com

Key contact:
Mr. David J. Hook, General Partner
Mr. John B. Hook, General Partner

Description: We are a privately held venture capital firm whose partners have invested in early stage high technology companies. We invest in seed and first round financings of companies located primarily in the West and Southwest, and will act as lead investor or part of a syndicate.

Founded: 1979

Amount of capital invested: under $1 million

Preferred investment size: Under $1 million

Amount under management: $25-100 million

Area served: United States

Preferred stages of financing: Seed, Start up, First stage

Industries:
I.03 Biotech/genetic engineering
I.06 Communications
I.07 Computer hardware
I.08 Computer software
I.14 Electronics
I.20 Healthcare
I.21 High technology
I.23 Information technology services
I.24 Internet services/e-commerce
I.26 Life sciences
I.29 Medical/medical products
I.30 New media

I.33 Semiconductors

Sampling of portfolio companies: Apple Computers (personal computers); Applied Digital Access (network management products); Vitesse Semiconductor (gallium arsenide semiconductors); TriQuint Semiconductors (gallium arsenide semiconductors); Harmonic Lightwaves (fiber optic trancievers); Octel Communications (voice processing systems); Maxtor Corp. (disk drives); Power Integrations, Inc. (smart power semiconductors); VidaMed, Inc. (urology medical devices); Etec Systems, Inc. (semiconductor capital equipment); Clarify, Inc. (customer service & support software); NetSolve, Inc. (data communications services); IC Works, Inc. (semiconductors); Volterra Semiconductors (battery management semiconductors); Spectrian Corp. (communication amplifiers)

Houston Partners, SBIP
401 Louisiana Street, 8th Floor
Houston, Texas 77002
(713) 222-8600
Fax: (713) 222-8932

Key contact:
Mr. Harvard H. Hill, Jr.
Ms. Glenda S. Overbeck
Mr. Kyle Pope

Mr. Roger A. Ramsey

Preferred stage of financing: Third/later round

Industries:
I.03 Biotech/genetic engineering
I.08 Computer software
I.29 Medical/medical products

Hunt Capital Group, LLC
1601 Elm Street, Suite 4000
Dallas, Texas 75201
(214) 720-1600
Fax: (214) 720-1662

Key contact:
Mr. J. R. Holland, Jr., President/CEO
Mr. Peter Stein, Partner
Mr. B. Brad Oldham, Partner
Mr. Tom Fowler, General Counsel

Description: We are a leading private equity investment firm headquartered in Dallas, Texas. Our private equity investments generally range in size from $1 million to $10 million and include a combination of convertible notes, preferred stock, common stock, warrants and related securities

Amount of capital invested: $11.2 million

Preferred investment size: $3-10 million

Amount under management: $10-25 million

Area served: North America

Preferred stages of financing: Second stage, Expansion

Industries:
I.06 Communications
I.12 Distribution
I.16 Entertainment
I.20 Healthcare

Sampling of portfolio companies: Heartland Wireless Communications, Inc. (wireless TV); AMRESCO Note (financial services); Optical Security Group, Inc. (security products); Digital Data Systems, Inc. (CD-Rom Products); Universal Sports America, Inc. (sports event marketing & mgmt.); Sunrise Behavioral Health, Ltd. (health care services); International Radiology Group, L.L.C. (health care services); Specialty Desserts, L.L.C. (specialty desserts); Movies & Games 4 Sale, L.P. (games/video reseller); One-On-One Sports, Inc. (radio networks/stations); Columbus Medical Services, L.L.C. (health care services); Fast Connections, Inc. (telecommunications reseller); Caruth Haven Assisted Living, L.P. (assisted living); Foodstar Restaurant Group, Inc. (restaurant chain); Security Technologies Group, Inc. (security products)

InterWest Partners
Two Galleria Tower, Suite 1670/LB 5
13455 Noel Road
Dallas, Texas 75240-5098
(972) 392-7279
Fax: (972) 490-6348

Key contact:
Mr. H. Berry Cash, Special Limited Partner
Mr. Alan W. Crites, General Partner
Mr. W. Scott Hedrick, General Partner

Mr. W. Stephen Holmes, General Partner
Dr. Gilbert H. Kliman, M.D., Venture Partner
Mr. Robert R, Momsen, General Partner
Dr. Arnold L. Oronsky, Ph.D., General Partner

Description: Since our inception, we've been investing in entrepreneurs - the people who change the way we live and work either by creating an entirely new product or service business, or by transforming an existing one. With over $600 million in committed capital, we are one of the largest venture capital partnerships in the United States. Our business is helping entrepreneurs convert their ideas and ambitions into reality.

Founded: 1979

Preferred stages of financing: Seed, Start up, First stage, Second stage, Mezzanine

Industries:
I.06	Communications
I.07	Computer hardware
I.08	Computer software
I.11	Consumer products
I.12	Distribution
I.13	Education
I.17	Environmental services/waste management
I.20	Healthcare
I.23	Information technology services
I.24	Internet services/e-commerce
I.26	Life sciences
I.27	Manufacturing
I.29	Medical/medical products
I.32	Retail
I.33	Semiconductors
I.35	Services (consumer)
I.37	Wholesale

Sampling of portfolio companies: BenchMarq (integrated circuits for power-sensitive applications); Bridge (communications equipment for ethernet LAN applications); Stratacom (ATM switching equipment for wide area netwroks); Compact Devices (micro-servers for dedicated workgroup applications); MobileWare (client/server communications software); AMX (audio-visual control systems); Acoustic Imaging (diagnostic ultrasound equipment manufacturing); First Medical (point of care diagnostic tests, initially for AMI); American Transitional Hospitals (subacute care within acute care hospitals); Cornerstone Physician Services (management services for physician groups); HBO (hospital information systems); Visteon (application suite for large group practices); Cell Genesys (therapeutic products using homologous recombination); Corixa (immunologically smart vaccines for cancer & infectious diseases); Signal Pharmaceuticals (therapeutic products using small molecule drugs that regulate gene expression); Escalon Packers (tomato canning); Midwest Folding Products (manufacturer of industrial mobile & folding tables); Corporate Express (distribution of office products to medium & large businesses); Cucina Holdings (Java City Bakery-Cafe retail chain & coffee wholesaler)

MESBIC Ventures Holding Company

12655 North Central Expressway, Suite 710
Dallas, Texas 75243
(972) 991-1597
Fax: (972) 991-4770
E-mail: mesbic@gan.net

Key contact:
Mr. Steven E. Martinez, Senior Vice President
Ms. Linda Roach, Senior Vice President
Mr. Donald Lawhorne, President

Description: We are a $62 million SSBIC, specializing in providing long-term venture capital to well-managed growing businesses owned and managed by minority entrepreneurs.

Amount of capital invested: $15 million

Preferred investment size: $1-3 million

Amount under management: $25-100 million

Area served: United States

Preferred stages of financing: Mezzanine, LBO/MBO, Expansion

Industries:
I.04	Broadcasting
I.06	Communications
I.14	Electronics
I.27	Manufacturing
I.33	Semiconductors

Sampling of portfolio companies: Simeus Holdings, Inc. (food processor/manufacturer); McDonald Technologies Int'l., Inc. (electronic engineering design & manufacturing); Biogenex Laboratories (medical diagnostics); Radio One, Inc. (radio broadcasting); Z-Spanish Radio Network, Inc. (radio broadcasting); Buenavision Telecommunications, Inc. (cable tv)

Murphree & Company Inc.

1100 Louisiana, Suite 5225
Houston, Texas 77002
(713) 655-8500
Fax: (713) 655-8503
E-mail: tudor@murphco.com
Web: www.murphco.com

Key contact:
Mr. Dennis E. Murphree, Managing Partner

221 West Sixth Street, Suite 1750
Austin, Texas 78701
(512) 236-1535
Fax: (512) 472-3053
E-mail: tudor@murphco.com

Key contact:
Mr. Geoffrey T. Tudor, Partner

Description: We are an early stage investor with a primary focus in the Southwestern U.S-mainly in Texas, New Mexico and Colorado. Investments are currently being made through Murphree Venture Partners IV, L.P.-a $50 million early stage fund which focuses primarily on high tech opportunities.

Preferred investment size: $1 million

Amount under management: $25-100 million

Area served: United States

Preferred stages of financing: Seed, Start up, First stage

Industries:
I.01	Aerospace
I.03	Biotech/genetic engineering
I.06	Communications
I.07	Computer hardware

I.08   Computer software
I.14   Electronics
I.21   High technology
I.23   Information technology services
I.24   Internet services/e-commerce
I.26   Life sciences
I.29   Medical/medical products
I.33   Semiconductors

Sampling of portfolio companies: Activerse Inc. (software which creates real-time collaboration over the internet); Ensyn Technologies Ltd. (creates biofuel by converting waste wood & wood products into synthetic oil for energy generation & food additives); E-Stamp Corp. (patented PC-based software/hardware system to create postage in lieu of stamps or metering); FFPI Industries Inc. (patented fiber optic/laser-based sensors to detect changes in pressure, deflection, temperature & cavitation); MicroOptical Devices Inc. (VCSEL laser manufacturing utilizing Sandia-developed intellectual property); ModelOffice Inc. (develops software applications that provide shortcuts for writing tasks including sample documents, forms & templates); Physix Inc. (develops medical software systems to provide handheld solutions for doctors & nurses in lieu of written charts, prescriptions, etc.) World.hire Inc. (software for recruiting & screening employment candidates via corporate intranets & the internet); Wintel Inc. (scheduling & routing software for mobile field personnel in industries such as home healthcare, home repair, utilities, etc.); Adaptive Learning Technologies Inc. (educational software which dynamically modifies itself to best suit a child's learning style); Journee Inc. (java based software company developing rapidly-deploying business enterprise software for the $6 billion ERP market)

Nations Banc Capital Corporation

901 Main Street, 22nd Floor
Dallas, Texas 75202
(214) 508-0900
Fax: (214) 508-0985

Key contact:
Mr. Doug Williamson, Managing Director

Description: Risk capital provider for Nations Bank Corp. providing late stage venture investing and equity capital for LBO's, growth financings and acquisitions.

Amount of capital invested: $140 million

Preferred investment size: Varies

Amount under management: $500 million -1 billion

Area served: United States

Preferred stages of financing: First stage, Second stage, Mezzanine, LBO/MBO, Expansion

Industries:
I.01   Aerospace
I.02   Agriculture/forestry/fishing/mining
I.03   Biotech/genetic engineering
I.04   Broadcasting
I.05   Chemicals
I.06   Communications
I.07   Computer hardware
I.08   Computer software
I.09   Construction
I.10   Consulting
I.11   Consumer products
I.12   Distribution
I.13   Education
I.14   Electronics
I.15   Energy/natural resources/utilities
I.16   Entertainment
I.17   Environmental services/waste management
I.18   Financial services
I.19   Generalist
I.20   Healthcare
I.21   High technology
I.22   Industrial products
I.23   Information technology services
I.24   Internet services/e-commerce
I.25   Leisure/hospitality
I.26   Life sciences
I.27   Manufacturing
I.28   Media/publishing
I.29   Medical/medical products
I.30   New media
I.32   Retail
I.33   Semiconductors
I.34   Services (business)
I.35   Services (consumer)
I.36   Transportation
I.37   Wholesale

Sampling of portfolio companies: Knoll, Inc. (office furniture manufacturer); Vermont Castings, Inc. (manufacturer of cast iron stoves & fireplaces); Fresh Fields Markets, Inc. (health food grocer); The Mark Group, Inc. (catalog retailer); StarTime Cinema, Inc. (owner & operator of discount movie theaters); Accordia, Inc. (provider of insurance brokerage services); 3DX Technologies, Inc. (provider of seismic interpretation services for oil & gas exploration); Tigerton Lumber, LLC (owner of hardwood timberlands); Chisholm (manufacturer & distributor of display projectors); Firearms Training Systems, Inc. (developers of small arms training simulators); HAHT Software, Inc. (developer of web based application development tools); Netcom Systems, Inc. (developer & manufacturer of network testing equipment); Performance Awareness Corp. (developer of Load Testing Software); Cumulus Media, LLC (consolidator of small market radio stations); LIN Television Corp. (owner & operator of network affiliated television stations); Prince Communications, LP (provider of real estate publications & on-line services); Behavioral Healthcare Corp. (consolidator of psychiatric hospital facilities); SP Pharmaceuticals, LLC (pharmaceutical manufacturer); Sentry Management Corp. (provider of electronic security services); CSM Industries, Inc. (molybdenum processor)

North Texas MESBIC, Inc.

9500 Forest Lane, Suite 430
Dallas, Texas 75243
(214) 221-3565

Fax: (214) 221-3566
E-mail: alee168@aol.com

Key contact:
Mr. Allan M. Lee, President

Area served: Texas

Preferred stages of financing: First stage, Second stage, Expansion

Industries:
I.22   Industrial products
I.27   Manufacturing
I.32   Retail
I.37   Wholesale

Pacesetter Growth Fund, LP

12655 North Central Expressway
North Central Plaza, Suite 710
Dallas, Texas 75243
(972) 991-1597
Fax: (972) 991-4770
E-mail: mesbic@gan.net

Key contact:
Mr. Steven E. Martinez, Senior Vice President
Ms. Linda Roach, Senior Vice President
Mr. Donald Lawhorne, President

Description: We provide acquisition and expansion capital to firms owned and/or managed by experienced minority entrepreneurs and professional managers.

Amount of capital invested: $9 million

Preferred investment size: $3 million

Amount under management: $25-100 million

Area served: United States

Preferred stages of financing: Mezzanine, LBO/MBO, Expansion

Industries:
I.04   Broadcasting
I.06   Communications
I.14   Electronics
I.27   Manufacturing
I.33   Semiconductors

Sampling of portfolio companies: McDonald Technologies Int'l., Inc. (electronic design & manufacturing); Biogenex Laboratories (medical diagnostics); Vista Stores, LLC (convenience store chain)

Phillips-Smith Specialty Retail Group

5080 Spectrum Drive, Suite 700 West
Dallas, Texas 75248
(972) 387-0725
Fax: (972) 458-2560
E-mail: pssrg@aol.com

Key contact:
Mr. Donald J. Phillips, Managing General Partner
Ms. Cece Smith, Managing General Partner
Mr. G. Michael Machens, General Partner

Description: We are a traditional venture capital firm which invests in retail businesses with the potential to become major regional or national retail chains. We were founded by our managing general partners Don Phillips and Cece Smith, executives with successful track records in specialty retailing, restaurants and venture investing.

Founded: 1986

Amount of capital invested: $21.4 million

Preferred investment size: $4-5 million

Amount under management: $100-500 million

Area served: United States

Preferred stages of financing: Seed, Start up, First stage, Second stage, Mezzanine, LBO/MBO, Expansion

Industries:
I.24   Internet services/e-commerce
I.32   Retail

Sampling of portfolio companies: Bookstop (book retailer); A Pea In The Pod (maternity apparel); The Sports Authority (sporting goods superstore); BizMart (office supply superstore); Petsmart (pet supply superstore); Gadzooks (teen apparel retailer); Hot Topic (teen apparel retailer); Canyon Cafes (southwestern restaurants)

Private Equity Partners

301 Commerce Street, Suite 1600
Ft. Worth, Texas 76102
(817) 332-1600
Fax: (817) 336-7523
E-mail: skleberg@lkcm.com

Key contact:
Mr. Scott M. Kleberg, President
Mr. Jeff Alexander, Vice President

Description: We seek to provide equity capital in partnership with management to facilitate later-stage internal growth, intra-industry acquisitions, recapitalizations and buy-outs, all with the fundamental objective of achieving superior, long-term capital appreciation. We focus our investment activities on manufacturing, distribution and service enterprises that a) have the proven ability to achieve high rates

of return on invested capital, b)possess a sustainable competitive advantage and c) exhibit attractive prospects in light of industry dynamics.

Preferred investment size: $4 million

Amount under management: $25-100 million

Area served: United States

Preferred stages of financing: LBO/MBO, Expansion

Industries:
I.19   Generalist

Retail & Restaurant Growth Capital, L.P.

10,000 North Central Expressway #1060
Dallas, Texas 75231
(214) 750-0065
Fax: (214) 750-0060
Web: www.rrgcsbic.com

Key contact:
Mr. Ray Hemmig, General Partner
Mr. J. Eric Lawrence, General Partner
Mr. Mark Massinter, General Partner
Mr. Joe Harberg, General Partner

Description: We are a private investment partnership
and licensed SBIC providing debt capital and strategic counsel to retail and restaurant businesses that
exhibit a potential for acclerated growth and
expansion.

Preferred investment size: $500,000-3 million

Amount under management: $25-100 million

Area served: United States

Preferred stages of financing: Second stage, Mezzanine, LBO/MBO, Expansion

Industries:
I.32   Retail

Sampling of portfolio companies: Colorado Pen Co.
(fine writing instrument retailer); Quizno's Inc.
(operator & franchisor of quick service sub-sandwich
restaurants); Elizabeth Arden Red (day spa operator,
hair & beauty services); Foodstar Restaurant Group
(fine dining restaurant operator); Texas Land & Cattle
Steak House (Texas themed restaurant operator);
Mobile Car Care (automotive service center
operator); Bikes USA (retailer of bicycles & accessories)

Sevin Rosen Funds

13455 Noel Road, Suite 1670
Two Galleria Tower
Dallas, Texas 75240
(972) 702-1100
Fax: (972) 702-1103
Web: www.srfunds.com

Key contact:
Mr. Kent F. Ekberg, Vice President-Communications &
Research

Description: We are one of the premier venture capital
firms focusing on early stage high technology
projects. Working from offices in Dallas and Palo
Alto, the geographic scope of our investments is
nationwide. The firm has developed a recognized
reputation for helping to build companies. Our most
well known successes to date include Compaq
Computer, Lotus Development, Cyprss Semiconductor, Cyrix, Citrix and CIENA. Since our
founding, approximately $500 million has been
placed under management in six funds. The value of
the equity originally owned by Sevin Rosen Funds is
$4 billion today.

Founded: 1981

Preferred investment size: $5-10 million

Amount under management: $500 million -1 billion

Area served: Europe, North America, Worldwide

Preferred stages of financing: Seed, Start up, First
stage, Second stage

Industries:
I.03   Biotech/genetic engineering
I.06   Communications
I.07   Computer hardware
I.08   Computer software
I.14   Electronics
I.20   Healthcare
I.21   High technology
I.23   Information technology services
I.24   Internet services/e-commerce
I.26   Life sciences
I.30   New media
I.33   Semiconductors

Sampling of portfolio companies: Acuson Corp.;
ArQule, Inc.; Benchmarq Miroelectronics, Inc.;
Borland Int'l., Inc.; Ciena Corp.; Citrix Systems, Inc.;
Compaq Computer Corp.; Convex Computer Corp.;
Corsair Communications, Inc.; Cyberonics, Inc.;
Cypress Semiconductor Corp.; Cyrix Corp.; Elec-
tronic Arts; Landmark Graphics Corp.; Lotus Devel-
opment Corporation; Silicon Graphics Computer
Systems; ViroPharma, Inc.; VTEL Corp.

Southwest Venture Partners

16414 San Pedro, Suite 345
San Antonio, Texas 78232
(210) 402-1200
Fax: (210) 402-1221
E-mail: swvp@aol.com

Key contact:
Mr. Michael Bell

Area served: Southwest

Preferred stages of financing: Seed, Start up, First
stage

Industries:
I.03   Biotech/genetic engineering
I.06   Communications
I.08   Computer software
I.29   Medical/medical products

SSM Ventures

10528 Glass Mountain Trail
Austin, Texas 78750
(512) 258-9429

Key contact:
Mr. Eric L. Jones

Description: Our objective is to invest in a diversified portfolio of rapidly growing private companies located primarily in the South. Upon closing of our third fund (May, 1998) we will be one of the larger and more experienced firms based in the South in terms of capital under management and continuity of the principals managing the fund.

Amount of capital invested: $8.2 million

Preferred investment size: $3-10 million

Amount under management: $100-500 million

Area served: United States

Preferred stages of financing: Start up, First stage, Second stage, LBO/MBO, Expansion

Industries:
I.03   Biotech/genetic engineering
I.06   Communications
I.07   Computer hardware
I.08   Computer software
I.11   Consumer products
I.12   Distribution
I.14   Electronics
I.18   Financial services
I.20   Healthcare
I.21   High technology
I.22   Industrial products
I.23   Information technology services
I.24   Internet services/e-commerce
I.32   Retail

Sampling of portfolio companies: DAZEL (client server software); Active Power (kinetic batteries); Motive Software (web-based software); Arch Communications (paging); CONXUS Communications (wireless voice messaging); Direct General (non-standard auto insurance); Kirkland's (specialty retail); Office Furniture, USA (franchiser of office furniture stores); American Pathology (physician practice management); TORCH Health Care (assisted living facilities); Healthcare Innovations (occupational & rehabilitational medicine)

Stratford Capital Group, LP
200 Crescent Court, Suite 1650
Dallas, Texas 75201
(214) 740-7377
Fax: (214) 740-7340

Key contact:
Mr. Michael D. Brown
Mr. John Fannin
Mr. Darin Winn

Area served: United States

Preferred stages of financing: Second stage, LBO/MBO, Third/later stage, acquisitions

Industries:
I.12   Distribution
I.19   Generalist
I.27   Manufacturing

TGF Management Corp.
100 Congress Avenue, Suite 980
Austin, Texas 78701
(512) 322-3100
Fax: (512) 322-3101
E-mail: tgfmgmt@tgfmanagement.com

Key contact:
Mr. James J. Kozlowski, Principal
Mr. Stephen M. Soileau, Principal
Mr. J. Brent Humphries, Principal

Description: The Texas Growth Fund is a $127 million investment fund. We pursue investments in later-stage venture capital or private equity transactions. We seek investment opportunities in companies that have a substantial operating presence in Texas or are planning to expand their business within the state.

Amount of capital invested: $9.8 million

Preferred investment size: $2-6 million

Amount under management: $100-500 million

Area served: Texas, United States

Preferred stages of financing: Second stage, Mezzanine, LBO/MBO, Expansion

Industries:
I.01   Aerospace
I.04   Broadcasting
I.05   Chemicals
I.06   Communications
I.07   Computer hardware
I.08   Computer software
I.09   Construction
I.10   Consulting
I.11   Consumer products
I.12   Distribution
I.13   Education
I.14   Electronics
I.15   Energy/natural resources/utilities
I.16   Entertainment
I.17   Environmental services/waste management
I.18   Financial services
I.19   Generalist
I.20   Healthcare
I.22   Industrial products
I.23   Information technology services
I.25   Leisure/hospitality
I.27   Manufacturing
I.28   Media/publishing
I.29   Medical/medical products
I.30   New media
I.32   Retail
I.33   Semiconductors
I.34   Services (business)
I.35   Services (consumer)
I.36   Transportation
I.37   Wholesale

Sampling of portfolio companies: Administaff, Inc. (staff leasing company); Argotyche, LP (provides high-tech R&D & systems to the defense industry); Classic Communications, Inc. (owns & operates rural cable TV systems); Coastal Towing, Inc. (provides intercoastal barge transport of petroleum products); Garden Ridge Corp. (big box retailer of craft items & home accessories); Healthway Communications Int'l., Inc.; ICM, Inc. (manufactures clothing for children); Independent Gas Co. Holdings, Inc. (distributes propane gas to residential, commercial customers) Lil'Things, Inc. (big box retailer targeting the infant & juvenile market); QClubs, Inc. (operates large high quality health clubs); Sterling Foods, Inc. (bakes shelf-stable products for military & commercial users); Technology Works, Inc. (makes add-on memory products for PCs); Total Safety, Inc. (provides fire & toxic gas prevention products & services); American Rockwool, Inc. (manufactures mineral fiber insulation); HBW Holdings, Inc. (provides investment banking services); Lofland Acquisition, Inc. (value-added fabricator of rebar that also distributes other construction related products); Rehab Designs of America Corp. (provides orthotic & prosthetic products & services); SimTus Holdings, Inc. (manufacturer & processor of meat & kettle products for restaurants); Sovereign Business Forms, Inc. (manufactures custom business forms)

United Oriental Capital Corporation

908 Town & Country Boulevard, Suite 310
Houston, Texas 77024
(713) 461-3909
Fax: (713) 465-7559

Key contact:
Mr. Jai Min Tai

Preferred stage of financing: First stage

Industries:
I.19   Generalist

Ventex Partners, Ltd.

1001 Fannin Street, Suite 1095
Houston, Texas 77002
(713) 659-7870
Fax: (713) 659-7855

Key contact:
Mr. David Miller
Mr. Richard S. Smith

Area served: Prefer Southwest

Preferred stage of financing: LBO/MBO

Industries:
I.20   Healthcare
I.29   Medical/medical products
I.32   Retail

Ventures Medical Associates

16945 Northchase Drive, Suite 2150
Houston, Texas 77060
(281) 873-5748
Fax: (281) 873-5950

Key contact:
Mr. William T. Mullaney, Managing General Partner

Description: We are focused on achieving substantial capital appreciation through early stage investments in commercially promising new medical technologies, products and services. We manage the Ventures Medical, LP and Ventures Medical II, LP venture capital funds.

Amount of capital invested: $1,012,816

Preferred investment size: $500,000-1 million

Amount under management: $25-100 million

Area served: United States

Preferred stages of financing: Seed, Start up, First stage

Industries:
I.03   Biotech/genetic engineering
I.20   Healthcare
I.26   Life sciences
I.29   Medical/medical products

Sampling of portfolio companies: American Transitional Hospitals, Inc. (transitional hospitals providing subacute care); Aprogenex, Inc. (developer of an in-situ hybridization system); Aronex Pharmaceuticals, Inc. (medicines to treat cancer & life-threatening infectious diseases); Cephalon, Inc. (therapeutics for central nervous system disorders); Cyberonics, Inc. (implantable devices for the treatment of epilepsy); Hepatix, Inc. (technology for treating liver failure); Impath, Inc. (pathology services, primarily in the cancer market)

Woodside Fund

18585 Sigma Road, Suite 100
San Antonio, Texas 78258
(210) 499-5716
Fax: (210) 499-0899
Web: www.woodsidefund.com

Key contact:
Mr. John E. Campion, Special Limited Partner

Description: We are a venture capital firm specializing in start up companies. Each partner has founded and built at least one company, resulting in 80 years of entrepreneurial experience, prior to joining the fund. Our limited partners include some of the nation's most sophisticated institutional and individual investors.

Preferred investment size: $1-5 million

Amount under management: $25-100 million

Area served: Northwest, Rocky Mountains, Southwest, West Coast

Preferred stages of financing: Seed, Start up, First stage, Second stage

Industries:
I.03   Biotech/genetic engineering
I.06   Communications
I.07   Computer hardware
I.08   Computer software
I.13   Education
I.14   Electronics
I.15   Energy/natural resources/utilities
I.20   Healthcare
I.21   High technology

I.23   Information technology services
I.24   Internet services/e-commerce

I.28   Media/publishing
I.30   New media

Utah

First Security Business Investment Corp.
15 East 100 South, Suite 100
Salt Lake City, Utah 84111
(801) 246-5688
Fax: (801) 246-5740
E-mail: jhilton2@fscnet.com

Key contact:
Mr. James Hilton, Vice President/Investment Officer
Mr. Butch Alder, President

Description: SBIC licensed in 1993

Amount of capital invested: $1.5 million

Preferred investment size: $500,000

Amount under management: <$10 million

Area served: United States

Preferred stages of financing: Second stage, Mezzanine, Expansion

Industries:
I.12   Distribution
I.22   Industrial products
I.27   Manufacturing

Sampling of portfolio companies: 10 companies funded to date. 8 follow-on investments.

Wasatch Venture Fund
One South Main Street, Suite 1400
Salt Lake City, Utah 84133
(801) 524-8939
Fax: (801) 524-8941
E-mail: tstevens@wasatchvc.com
Web: www.venture-capital.com/wasatch

Key contact:
Mr. Todd Stevens, Managing Director
Mr. Frank Creer, Partner

Description: Our objective is to finance businesses with extraordinary management that have developed proprietary products and are capable of creating exceptional growth in sales and profits. We will pursue a people-biased, back to basics, early-stage approach to venture capital investing. We intend to invest in information, communication, software and medical product companies based in Utah, California, Arizona, Nevada and other Western states.

Amount of capital invested: $5 million

Preferred investment size: $1 million

Amount under management: $10-25 million

Area served: United States

Preferred stage of financing: First stage

Industries:
I.06   Communications
I.07   Computer hardware
I.08   Computer software
I.21   High technology
I.23   Information technology services
I.24   Internet services/e-commerce
I.33   Semiconductors

Vermont

Green Mountain Capital, L.P.
R.D. #1, Box 1503
Waterbury, Vermont 05676
(802) 244-8981
Fax: (802) 244-8990
E-mail: inq@gmtcap.com
Web: www.gmtcap.com

Key contact:
Mr. Michael Sweatman, Manager

Description: We are a private for-profit small business investment company providing mezzanine finance to companies in Northern New England.

Founded: 1993

Amount of capital invested: $1.5 million

Preferred investment size: $500,000

Amount under management: <$10 million

Area served: New England

Preferred stage of financing: Mezzanine

North Atlantic Capital Corporation
76 St. Paul Street, Suite 600
Burlington, Vermont 05401
(802) 658-7820
Fax: (802) 658-5757
E-mail: gpeters@together.net

Web: www.NorthAtlanticCapital.com

Key contact:
Gregory B. Peters, Vice President

Description: We are a fund manager that provides risk capital to privately owned businesses in the Northeastern United States. Our investment interests support established companies seeking growth through internal expansion or acquisition. We also finance the recapitalization or ownership changes of profitable, well established businesses. Investments range from $1 to 4 million, with the $2 to 3 million level preferred.

Preferred investment size: $2-3 million

Amount under management: $25-100 million

Area served: Northeast

Preferred stages of financing: Second stage, Mezzanine, LBO/MBO, Expansion

Industries:
I.07 Computer hardware
I.08 Computer software
I.10 Consulting
I.12 Distribution
I.14 Electronics
I.17 Environmental services/waste management
I.19 Generalist
I.21 High technology
I.23 Information technology services
I.27 Manufacturing
I.29 Medical/medical products
I.34 Services (business)

Sampling of portfolio companies: Brunswick Technologies, Inc. (industrial reinforcement fabrics); Casella Waste Systems, Inc. (solid waste management); Channel Computing, Inc. (database management software); Commonwealth Care, Inc. (home healthcare services); Community Rehab Centers (physical therapy rehabilitation centers); Contemporary Products, Inc. (home healthcare repsiratory products); Earth's Best, Inc. (organic baby food); Georgetown Collection, Inc. (direct response marketer of collectable dolls); IDEXX Laboratories, Inc. (diagnostic products for veterinary, environmental & food applications); Kitchen Etc. (multi store discount retailer of dinnerware & cookware); Rowena Broadcasting, Inc. (AM/FM broadcasting stations); Steinbrecher Corp. (digital transceivers for cellular communication industry); Transition Technology, Inc. (intelligent PC based controllers); Westminster Craker Co., Inc. (oyster & other specialty crackers); Keyfile Corp. (integrated document management software); Ocean Products, Inc. (atlantic salmon aquaculture); Schiavi Leasing Corp. (modular classroom leasing); Storage Computer Corp. (high speed memory storage devices); Verax Corp. (biotechnology cell culture); Wright Express Corp. (credit & information services for commercial vehicle fleet management)

Virginia

Blue Water Capital, L.L.C.
8300 Greensboro Drive, Suite 1020
McLean, Virginia 22102
(703) 790-8821
Fax: (703) 448-1849
E-mail: barratt@bluewatercapital.com

Key contact:
Mr. Henry D. Barratt

Area served: United States

Preferred stage of financing: Expansion

Industries:
I.05 Chemicals
I.06 Communications
I.08 Computer software
I.18 Financial services

Calvert Ventures
402 Maple Avenue West
Vienna, Virginia 22180
(703) 255-4930
Fax: (703) 255-4931

Key contact:
Mr. John May

Area served: Mid-Atlantic

Preferred stages of financing: Start up, First stage, Second stage

Industries:
I.03 Biotech/genetic engineering
I.11 Consumer products
I.13 Education
I.15 Energy/natural resources/utilities
I.17 Environmental services/waste management
I.29 Medical/medical products
I.35 Services (consumer)

Continental Small Business Investment Corp.
4141 North Henderson Road, Suite 8
Arlington, Virginia 22203
(703) 527-5200
Fax: (703) 527-3700
E-mail: alwetal@erols.com

Key contact:
Mr. Arthur L. Walters, President
Mr. Michael W. Jones, Vice President
Mr. Thomas E. Goodfellow, CFO
Mr. Mark W. Walters, Vice President

Description: We do debt and debt/equity loans- nationally, Europe and South America. Interested in all sectors except pharmaceutical and health care.

Amount of capital invested: $1,425,000

Preferred investment size: $500,000-5 million

Amount under management: $10-25 million

Area served: Europe, North America

Preferred stages of financing: Seed, Start up, First

stage, Second stage, Mezzanine, Expansion, Int'l expansion

Industries:
I.04   Broadcasting
I.06   Communications
I.08   Computer software
I.09   Construction
I.12   Distribution
I.14   Electronics
I.18   Financial services
I.21   High technology

I.22   Industrial products
I.23   Information technology services
I.24   Internet services/e-commerce
I.25   Leisure/hospitality
I.27   Manufacturing
I.31   Real estate
I.34   Services (business)

Sampling of portfolio companies: Television station; dental supplies; retail clothing; construction company; manufacturing; jewelry, retail; software for internet; coffee bean plantation

DynaFund Ventures

1555 Wilson Boulevard, Suite 320
Arlington, Virginia 22209-2405
(703) 841-0990
Fax: (703) 841-8395
E-mail: rwhiting@dynatec.com

Key contact:
Dr. Richard D. Whiting, General Partner

Description: We provide promising technology companies with the investment capital and management support they need to grow their businesses. In addition, we also provide a critical competitive advantage to our portfolio companies by offering access to key engineering, manufacturing and marketing resources in the U.S. and Asia through our own business networks and the complementary networks of our U.S. and Asian Limited Partners.

Amount of capital invested: $5 million

Preferred investment size: $1-3 million

Amount under management: $25-100 million

Area served: United States

Preferred stages of financing: Start up, First stage, Second stage

Industries:
I.06   Communications
I.07   Computer hardware
I.08   Computer software
I.14   Electronics
I.15   Energy/natural resources/utilities
I.16   Entertainment
I.21   High technology
I.23   Information technology services
I.24   Internet services/e-commerce
I.30   New media
I.33   Semiconductors

Sampling of portfolio companies: Arcturus Engineering (medical instruments); New Era Communications (wireless telecommunications); Single Chip Systems (RFID tags); Troika Networks (computer networking); eToys (internet commerce); FreeGate Corp. (multi-server gateway); Synctrix (newtwork devices); Xalti (network-on-a-chip)

Edison Venture Fund

1420 Springhill Road, Suite 420
McLean, Virginia 22102
(703) 903-9546
Fax: (703) 903-9528
E-mail: tasmith@edisonventure.com
Web: www.edisonventure.com

Key contact:
Mr. Gary P. Golding, General Partner
Mr. Thomas A. Smith, General Partner

Description: Since our formation in 1986, we have invested in more than 75 companies. We usually are the sole or lead venture investor. Multiple investments have been complete in our industry specialties, including computer software, communications and other technologies. Our investments are located primarily in the New York-Washington corridor with concentrations in New Jersey, Pennsylvania, Delaware, Maryland and Virginia.

Founded: 1986

Preferred investment size: $500,000-5 million

Area served: Mid-Atlantic

Preferred stage of financing: Expansion

Industries:
I.05   Chemicals
I.06   Communications
I.08   Computer software

I.11   Consumer products
I.13   Education
I.14   Electronics
I.15   Energy/natural resources/utilities
I.17   Environmental services/waste management
I.18   Financial services
I.20   Healthcare
I.24   Internet services/e-commerce

Sampling of portfolio companies: Best Software (PC accounting software sold by direct mail & VARs); Empirical Software (service level management solutions); Incode (manufacturing execution system software, primarily for pharmaceutical companies); Comm Site (manages wireless communications transmission or antenna facilities); Procom (telephone answering, voicemail, alpha paging dispatch, order entry & other messaging services); Versatility (inbound & outbound customer interaction software with sophisticated telephony integration); Visual Networks (network test & management equipment for frame relay & ATM WANs); Yurie Systems (asynchronous transfer mode concentrator & access devices for data telecommunications); Essential Technologies (software for emergency response & integrated environmental management); Optical Data (specialized electronic publisher which produces & distributes laser video disks)

Fairfax Partners

8000 Towers Crescent Drive, Suite 940
Vienna, Virginia 22182
(703) 847-9486
Fax: (703) 847-0911
E-mail: bgouldey@fairfaxpartners.com
Web: www.fairfaxpartners.com

Key contact:
Mr. Stephen W. Ritterbush, Managing General Partner
Mr. Raymond E. List, P.E.
Mr. Bruce K. Gouldey
Mr. Andrew D. Klingenstein, General Counsel

Description: We invest in seed/early stage companies and special situations that look and feel like early stage, including: platform technology and service company roll-ups, technology licensing, corporate technology or divisional spin-outs. Sourcing deal flow through regional networks and on a national basis using our established relationships, we focus on information technology and healthcare from: universities, national laboratories, government agencies, medical societies, engineering and science research organizations.

Preferred stages of financing: Seed, Start up, First stage, Second stage, Mezzanine

Industries:
I.06   Communications
I.07   Computer hardware
I.14   Electronics
I.15   Energy/natural resources/utilities
I.22   Industrial products
I.29   Medical/medical products

Sampling of portfolio companies: CollaGenex Pharmaceuticals, Inc.; Indigo Medical, Inc.; APACHE Medical Systems, Inc.; VanMed, Inc.; MedVest, Inc.

Leachman Steinberg Venture Partners

P.O. Box 316
Markham, Virginia 22643
(540) 364-4830
E-mail: leachman@crosslink.net

Key contact:
Mr. William Leachman, Principal

Description: Focused on companies utilizing the strengths of the internet. Investments have been in small content and entertainment companies, as well as larger enterprises. Liquidation timeframe 5 years via buyout or IPO. To be considered, companies must address rapidly growing market and offer unique competitive advantage.

Preferred investment size: $350,000

Amount under management: $10-25 million

Area served: Europe, North America

Preferred stages of financing: Seed, Start up, Mezzanine

Industries:
I.13   Education
I.16   Entertainment
I.18   Financial services
I.24   Internet services/e-commerce

Sampling of portfolio companies: Lucidmedia; Bottlerocket; Inkombank; University Online

New Enterprise Associates

11911 Freedom Drive
One Fountains Square, Suite 580
Reston, Virginia 20190
(703) 709-9499
Fax: (703) 834-7579
Web: www.nea.com

Key contact:
Mr. Frank A. Bonsal, Jr., Founding Partner
Mr. Ryan D. Drant, Associate
Mr. Ronald H. Kase, General Partner
Mr. Charles M. Linehan, Partner
Mr. Thomas C. McConnell, General Partner
Mr. John M. Nehra, General Partner
Mr. Charles W. Newhall, III, Co-Founder/General Partner
Dr. Sigrid Van Bladel, Ph.D., Partner
Mr. Stewart Alsop, Venture Partner
Mr. Peter J. Barris, General Partner
Mr. Robert T. Coneybeer
Ms. Suzanne Hooper
Mr. C. Richard Kramlich, Co-Founder/General Partner
Mr. Arthur J. Marks, General Partner
Mr. Peter T. Morris, General Partner
Mr. Mark W. Perry, General Partner
Mr. Scott D. Sandell
Ms. Nora M. Zietz, Partner/Director of Research
Ms. Nancy Dorman, General Partner
Mr. Lou Van Dyck, CFO

Ms. Ann Wilson, Director of Administration & HR

Description: We are one of the industry's premier venture capital firms. For 19 years we have practiced classic venture capital by investing in early-stage companies and working with management to nurture and build companies of real and lasting value. We are now the leading start-up venture investor in the country.

Founded: 1978

Preferred investment size: $500,000-6 million

Industries:
I.03   Biotech/genetic engineering
I.06   Communications
I.08   Computer software
I.14   Electronics
I.20   Healthcare
I.23   Information technology services
I.24   Internet services/e-commerce
I.26   Life sciences
I.29   Medical/medical products
I.33   Semiconductors

Sampling of portfolio companies: CaRDiMa, Inc. (medical devices for nonsurgical interventions to study, treat & cure electrophysiological disorders); LocalMed, Inc. (catheters for local drug delivery reducing plaque buildup in the arteries); Transfusion Technologies Corp. (devices to handle blood separation in the operating room); Alkermes, Inc. (products for the treatment of diseases & disorders of the central nervous systems); Neurex Corp. (drugs for a number of therapeutic applications including stroke, epilepsy & migraine headaches); AMERIGROUP Corp. (starts, owns & operates Medicaid HMO's in several states); Surgical Health Corp. (ambulatory surgery centers); Pyxis Corp. (narcotic medication distribution system for hospital use); Big Book, Inc. (internet access to nationwide telephone yellow pages & advertising); Tripod, Inc. (provides digital services on the internet for college students); AVIRNEX Communications Group (a service company utilizing proprietary software for int'l. long distance & enhanced service for both voice & data communications); IndusRiver Networks, Inc. (developing internet-based communications solutions for corporations); Pathnet, Inc. (provides microwave incumbent relocation services required by the emergence of PCS services); Applix, Inc. (advanced UNIX based software for the office automation market); Mission Critical Software, Inc. (systems management product for Windows NT which enables significantly enhanced security administration of NT domains); Software Publishing Corp. (Harvard Graphics & other personal productivity software); Programmer's Paradise, Inc. (publishes a software catalog of programming language packages & software development tools); Convex Computer Systems (high performance super minicomputers based on CRAY architecture & implemented in VLSI technology); Tandon Corp. (disc drives); KOR Electronics, Inc. (digital RF memory subsystems & radar simulators)

SpaceVest

11911 Freedom Drive, Suite 500
Reston, Virginia 20190
(703) 904-9800
Fax: (703) 904-0571
E-mail: spacevest@spacevest.com
Web: www.spacevest.com

Key contact:
Mr. John B. Higginbotham, Chairman
Mr. Frank A. DiBello, Vice Chairman/Managing Director
Mr. Roger P. Widing, Managing Director
Mr. Stephen P. Rochereau, Managing Director
Mr. Ransom J. Parker, Managing Director

Description: We provide expansion capital on an equity basis to small and medium-sized privately held growth companies that are associated with the space industry. We focus on investments in late-stage and established companies positioned fo successful entry and penetration of high-growth commercial markets which supply, support, or depend on space activities.

Amount of capital invested: $9,700,000

Preferred investment size: $1-5 million

Amount under management: $25-100 million

Area served: United States, Worldwide

Preferred stage of financing: Expansion

Industries:
I.01   Aerospace
I.03   Biotech/genetic engineering
I.06   Communications
I.14   Electronics
I.20   Healthcare
I.21   High technology
I.23   Information technology services
I.26   Life sciences
I.29   Medical/medical products

Sampling of portfolio companies: Analytical Graphics, Inc. (producer of the Satellite Tool Kit software suite); Arc Second, Inc. (supplier of advanced, laser-based, position determination systems); Astron Corp. (supplier of advanced antenna & radio frequency products); Harlow Security Systems, Ltd. (European-based supplier of innovative security & access control systems utilizing space-related technologies); Constellation Communications, Inc. (developer of a low-orbit satellite communications system for fixed & mobile telecommunications services); Currie Technologies, Inc. (supplier of innovative electric drive transportation systems utilizing space-related technologies); GER Holdings Corp. (provider of specialized analytical systems & services in the field of remote sensing with specific applications for agriculture & the environment); Global-Net, Inc. (systems integrator with proprietary interconnect software for low-cost, fixed wireless local loop solutions for emerging economies); GlobalCom Int'l., Inc. (provider of fully-integrated telecommunications & information technology services using satellite links); RDL Commercial Technologies Corp. (developer of proprietary optical, code-division-multiple-access transmission & switching technologies which greatly increase throughout capacity of high-speed networks); Thread Technology, Inc. (supplier of unique fasteners & threaded tools utilizing space industry technologies with applications in a variety of industrial & commercial uses)

Strategic Technology Investors, LLC

4001 North 9th Street, Suite 306
Arlington, Virginia 22203
(800) 331-8545
Fax:

Key contact:
Mr. Roy L. Morris, Managing Partner
Mr. Steven Zeerla, Managing Partner

Description: Invests in seed and startup Mid-Atlantic high tech firms.

Preferred investment size: $50,000

Amount under management: <$10 million

Area served: United States

Preferred stages of financing: Seed, Start up, First stage

Industries:
I.06   Communications
I.07   Computer hardware
I.08   Computer software
I.14   Electronics
I.21   High technology

Virginia Capital, L.P.

9 South 12th Street, 4th Floor
Richmond, Virginia 23219
(804) 648-4802
Fax: (804) 648-4809
E-mail: webmaster@vacapital.com
Web: www.vacapital.com

Key contact:
Mr. Fred Russell, Managing Director
Mr. Tom Deardorf, Vice President
Mr. Justin Marriott, Associate

Description: We are a $50 million fund investing $1 million to $5 million for growth or acquisitions.

Amount of capital invested: $15.5 million

Preferred investment size: $3 million

Amount under management: $25-100 million

Area served: United States

Preferred stages of financing: LBO/MBO, Expansion

Industries:
I.06   Communications
I.13   Education
I.17   Environmental services/waste management
I.20   Healthcare
I.24   Internet services/e-commerce
I.25   Leisure/hospitality
I.28   Media/publishing
I.29   Medical/medical products
I.30   New media

Walnut Capital Corporation

8000 Towers Crescent Drive, Suite 1070
Vienna, Virginia 22182
(703) 448-3771
Fax: (703) 448-7751

Key contact:
Mr. Joel Kanter

Preferred stages of financing: Start up, First stage, Second stage, LBO/MBO

Industries:
I.03   Biotech/genetic engineering
I.05   Chemicals
I.06   Communications
I.08   Computer software
I.14   Electronics
I.18   Financial services
I.20   Healthcare
I.29   Medical/medical products
I.32   Retail
I.35   Services (consumer)

Washington

Aabaar Capital

1912 Davison Avenue
Richland, Washington 99352
(509) 946-1050
Fax: (509) 943-7666
E-mail: cew@vcap.com
Web: www.vcap.com

Key contact:
Mr. Charles E. Wilson, III, Principal
Mr. Derrick Marshall, Associate

Description: We work with private and public companies of most all industries looking for growth, expansion and/or acquisition funding partners. Strategically linked with M&A, debt, equity and trade draft partners. We are expanding operations internationally.

Preferred investment size: $5-40 million

Area served: Worldwide

Preferred stages of financing: First stage, Second stage, Mezzanine, LBO/MBO, Expansion, Int'l expansion, Trade draft financing

Industries:
I.01   Aerospace
I.02   Agriculture/forestry/fishing/mining
I.03   Biotech/genetic engineering
I.04   Broadcasting
I.05   Chemicals
I.06   Communications
I.07   Computer hardware
I.08   Computer software
I.09   Construction
I.11   Consumer products
I.12   Distribution
I.14   Electronics
I.15   Energy/natural resources/utilities
I.17   Environmental services/waste management
I.20   Healthcare
I.21   High technology
I.22   Industrial products
I.23   Information technology services
I.24   Internet services/e-commerce
I.26   Life sciences
I.27   Manufacturing
I.29   Medical/medical products
I.31   Real estate
I.32   Retail
I.33   Semiconductors
I.34   Services (business)
I.35   Services (consumer)
I.36   Transportation
I.37   Wholesale

Alexander Hutton Capital, LLC

1325 Fourth Avenue, Suite 535
Seattle, Washington 98101
(206) 382-9961
Fax: (206) 382-1649
E-mail: bankers@ahcapital.com

Key contact:
Mr. Kent L. Johnson
Mr. Jonathan R. Staenberg
Mr. William W. (Chip) Treverton

Description: We pride ourselves on our ability to select only the best companies with the most potential, our ability to achieve reasonable valuations for both sides, our ability to provide knowledgeable management support to the client companies who communicate regularly with their investors and our ability to achieve high rates of return on investor capital within reasonable time frames.

Founded: 1994

Area served: Northwest

Preferred stages of financing: First stage, Second stage, Mezzanine

Arch Venture Partners

1000 Second Avenue, Suite 3700
Seattle, Washington 98104
(206) 674-3266
Fax: (206) 674-3026
E-mail: rtn@archventure.com
Web: www.archventure.com

Key contact:
Mr. Robert Nelsen, Managing Director

Description: We invest in the development of early stage technology companies which have the potential to grow into substantial enterprises. We invest primarily in companies we co-found with leading scientists and entrepreneurs, concentrating on bringing to market technological innovations developed from academics and corporate research.

Amount of capital invested: $20 million

Preferred investment size: $1 million

Amount under management: $100-500 million

Area served: United States

Preferred stages of financing: Seed, Start up, First stage

Industries:
I.03   Biotech/genetic engineering

I.05   Chemicals
I.06   Communications
I.07   Computer hardware
I.08   Computer software
I.13   Education
I.14   Electronics
I.20   Healthcare
I.21   High technology
I.23   Information technology services
I.24   Internet services/e-commerce
I.26   Life sciences
I.33   Semiconductors

Sampling of portfolio companies: Adolor Corp. (biopharmaceutical); Appliant Corp. (software); Apropos Corp. (software); Bell Geospace (oil field services); Caliper Technologies Corp. (microfluidics); DeCode Genetics (genomic information); Genvec (gene therapy); Intelligent Reasoning Systems (electronic test equipment); Internet Dynamics (internet software); Nanophase Technologies (ultra fine ceramic materials); New Era of Networks (applications integration software); Optobionics (opto-electronic retinal implants); R2 Technology (computer-aided diagnosis of mammograms); Siliscape (virtual displays); RWT Corp. (manufacturing execution software)

EnCompass Group U.S. Information Technology Partners Inc.

4040 Lake Washington Boulevard NE, Suite 205
Kirkland, Washington 98033
(425) 558-3624
Fax: (425) 889-2449
E-mail: info@evpartners.com
Web: www.encompassventures.com

Key contact:
Mr. Yasuki Matsumoto, Managing Director
Mr. Craig McCallum, Managing Director
Mr. Scot E. Land, Managing Director
Mr. Wayne C. Wager, Managing Director
Mr. James J. Geddes, Jr., Managing Director

Description: We have focused our investments in information technology companies in the Western U.S. and Canada. We have, and will continue to lead investments in this region. We will also co-invest with other leading U.S. and international venture capital firms and corporations. Our goal is to add value to an information technology company using our unique skills and experience in the Asian markets.

Preferred investment size: $200,000-3 million

Amount under management: $25-100 million

Area served: Canada, Western United States

Preferred stages of financing: Seed, Start up, First stage, Second stage

Industries:
I.06   Communications
I.08   Computer software
I.23   Information technology services
I.24   Internet services/e-commerce
I.29   Medical/medical products

Sampling of portfolio companies: Live Picture (communications)

Fluke Capital Management, L.P.

11400 SE 6th Street, Suite 230
Bellevue, Washington 98004
(425) 453-4590
Fax: (425) 453-4675
E-mail: weston@flukecapital.com
Web: www.flukecapital.com

Key contact:
Mr. Dennis P. Weston, President
Mr. Kevin C. Gabelein, Associate

Description: We are a venture capital firm based in Bellevue, Washington. We invest in early and later stage private companies located in the Pacific Northwest. We invest primarily in companies in information technology and healthcare industries, but are also interested in specialty and innovative service businesses.

Amount of capital invested: $4 million

Preferred investment size: $1-1.5 million

Amount under management: $25-100 million

Area served: Oregon; Washington; Vancouver, BC

Preferred stages of financing: Start up, First stage, Second stage, Mezzanine

Industries:
I.06   Communications
I.07   Computer hardware
I.08   Computer software
I.11   Consumer products
I.12   Distribution
I.14   Electronics
I.17   Environmental services/waste management
I.20   Healthcare
I.21   High technology
I.23   Information technology services
I.24   Internet services/e-commerce
I.26   Life sciences
I.27   Manufacturing
I.29   Medical/medical products
I.32   Retail
I.34   Services (business)
I.35   Services (consumer)
I.37   Wholesale

Sampling of portfolio companies: Starbucks Corp. (specialty roaster & retailer of premium gourmet coffees); Aldus Corp. (develops & markets desktop publishing software); Eagle Hardware & Garden, Inc. (chain of home improvement warehouse centers); Innova Corp. (designs & markets high frequency microwave radios for fixed point wireless communications); Coinstar, Inc. (manufactures & distributes self-service coin processing machines); Redhook Ale Brewery, Inc. (a leading specialty craft brewer of premium ales); Interlinq Software Corp. (develops & markets software for the mortgage banking industry); Lightware, Inc. (develops & markets ultra-portable LCD projectors); Tegic Communications, Inc, (develops a text-entry system for small computing & communications devices); Edmark Corp. (develops & markets educational software for children); Luxar Corp. (designs & markets laser systems for medical & dental surgery); Panlabs International, Inc. (biopharmaceutical company that discovers & profiles therapeutic agents); CareWise, Inc. (distributes healthcare demand management & information services)

Key Equity Capital

700 5th Avenue, 48th Floor
Seattle, Washington 98111
(206) 684-6480
Fax: (206) 684-6301

Key contact:
Mr. Robert S. Wainio, General Partner

Description: We invest equity capital in companies that have both exceptional management teams and the potential to achieve significant future growth resulting in long-term equity appreciation. In every portfolio company, we provide the management team with a significant equity participation, reflecting our commitment to appropriate realization of the investment reward.

Amount of capital invested: $42 million

Preferred investment size: $10-25 million

Amount under management: $100-500 million

Area served: United States

Preferred stages of financing: LBO/MBO, Expansion

Industries:
I.01   Aerospace
I.05   Chemicals
I.07   Computer hardware
I.11   Consumer products
I.12   Distribution
I.14   Electronics
I.17   Environmental services/waste management
I.20   Healthcare
I.22   Industrial products
I.27   Manufacturing
I.29   Medical/medical products
I.34   Services (business)
I.37   Wholesale

Sampling of portfolio companies: Advanced Cast Products (cast iron parts); Cardinal Packaging (plastic packaging); Crown Simplimatic (packaging machinery & systems engineering); CSM Industries (molybdenum products); Decatur Aluminum (aluminum sheet); DeCrane Aircraft Holdings (avionics); Family Dental Center Service Co. of America (provider of management services to dental practices); GEO Specialty Chemicals (specialty chemicals); Glasstech (glass processing systems); Jorgensen Forge (large open-die forgings/steel, aluminum & titanium); Laurel Industries (plastic additives); London's Farm Dairy (milk & ice cream processor); S. Madill Ltd. (logging industry equipment); Nat'l. Medical Diagnostics (medical diagnostics equipment servicer); OMEGA Polymer Technologies (plastic products); Ranpak Corp. (packaging materials); Sinter Metals (powdered metal parts); Spectra (computer printer hardware); STERIS (medical sterilization equipment)

Kirlan Venture Capital, Inc.

221 1st Avenue West, Suite 108
Seattle, Washington 98119-4223
(206) 281-8610
Fax: (206) 285-3451
E-mail: danregis@aol.com

Key contact:
Mr. Daniel P. Regis, President
Ms. Kirsten S. Murbeck, Associate
Ms. Susan L. Preston, Medical Specialist

Description: Private capital venture capital firm founded in 1993 by A. K. Lanterman, chairman & CEO of Holland American Lines/Westours. Invests in early to late stage pre-public companies primarily in technology areas of healthcare, software and telecommunications.

Founded: 1993

Amount of capital invested: $6 million

Preferred investment size: $1-2 million

Amount under management: $25-100 million

Area served: North America

Preferred stages of financing: Start up, First stage, Second stage, Mezzanine

Industries:
I.08   Computer software
I.14   Electronics
I.21   High technology
I.24   Internet services/e-commerce
I.26   Life sciences
I.29   Medical/medical products

Sampling of portfolio companies: Bridgeway Corporation (network management software company which develops software solutions); CareWise, Inc. (a nurse referral service); Columbia Banking System (bank holding company); Diametrics Medical, Inc. (manufactures blood analysis systems for the critical care market); Focal Corp. (develops & commercializes synthetic, absorbable, liquid surgical sealants based on the company's proprietary polymer technology); Health Systems Technologies, Inc. (develops software for the networked managed care organization); Innova Corp. (manufactures a family of high frequency digital microwave radios); Innovation, Inc. (specialty provider to the rapidly growing wireless communications industry); InterNAP Network Services Corp. (internet route management technology company); Lightbridge, Inc. (provider of software-based services); Naiad Technologies, Inc. (develops & commercializes technologies that reduce the cost & increase the safety of handling liquid waste materials); Norian Corp. (produces an injectable & moldable bone replacement material that is biocompatible); Pet's Choice, Inc. (consolidator of the veterinary hospital industry); Sequel Technology Corp. (develops software products which allow users to understand & manage corporate & individual use of internet & intranet usage); Tegic Communications, Inc. (developed text-based communication on wireless cellular handsets & other portable, compact electronic devices)

MDS Capital Corporation

7733 58th Avenue NE
Seattle, Washington 98115
(206) 523-3499
Fax: (206) 525-4082
E-mail: kupor@sprintmail.com

Key contact:
Mr. Bob Kupor, Vice President

Description: We are a division of one of Canada's largest venture capital companies focused exclusively on health care and life sciences investing. Our primary objective is to build significant realizable value for our shareholders, as well as for the management and shareholders of its investee companies. We seek to achieve this by bringing a combination of capital, operating and financial expertise, as well as a network of international contacts within the life science area.

Amount of capital invested: $100 million (Canadian)

Preferred investment size: $3-10 million (Canadian)

Amount under management: $500 million -1 billion

Area served: North America

Preferred stages of financing: Seed, Start up, First stage, Second stage, Mezzanine

Industries:
I.03   Biotech/genetic engineering
I.20   Healthcare
I.26   Life sciences
I.29   Medical/medical products

Sampling of portfolio companies: Anormed Inc. (involved in the discovery & commercialization of therapeutic & diagnostic applications of metal complexes used in diagnosing & treating life threatening diseases); Biostar Inc. (developed novel immunopharmaceuticals that have substantial potenteil markets in cancer therapy, women's health & in food & companion animal sectors); Chiroscience Group PLC (int'l. drug discovery company); Depotech Corp. (California-based drug delivery company); Ellipsis Biotherapeutics Corp. (genomics company located in Toronto); Geron Corp. (biopharmaceutical company exclusively focused on discovering & developing therapeutic & diagnostic products); Life Imaging Systems Inc. (developing proprietary 3-D ultrasound imaging products that will be used for diagnostic purposes); Medtech Partners Inc. (established to access early stage technologies emerging from univesities & research institutions in Quebec); Micrologix Biotech Inc. (focused on developing novel antibiotics based on cationic peptide technology licensed from UBC); Morphometrix Technologies Inc. (develops, manufactures & markets instruments using advanced imaging & algorithmic technologies); Nexia Biotechnologies, Inc. (commercializing transgenic technologies developed at McGill University); Prolinx, Inc. (developing & licensing a novel chemical linking technology used in the development of certain new medical diagnostic & therapeutic products); Redwood Microsystems, Inc. (designing, manufacturing & marketing micromachined actuators which translate signals into motion or force); Seragen Biopharmaceuticals Ltd.

(Canadian operation of Seragen Inc.); Signal Pharmaceuticals, Inc. (integrated target & drug discovery company focused on identifying new classes of small molecule drugs that regulate genes & the production of disease-causing proteins); Systems Xcellence Inc. (software developer, integrator & vendor which has developed a state-of-the-art healthcare software suite of products); Thomson & Nielsen Electronics Ltd. (Ottawa-based manufacturer of instruments for personal radiation protection in medical, industrial & environmental areas); TM Bioscience Corp. (Toronto-based development stage biotechnology company); Ultravision Inc. (involved in the development, manufacturing & distribution of contact lenses & contact lens products); UV Systems Technology Inc. (manufactures & sells ultraviolet disinfection systems for sewage treatment & wastewater)

Olympic Venture Partners

2420 Carillon Point
Kirkland, Washington 98033
(425) 889-9192
Fax: (425) 889-0152
E-mail: info@ovp.com
Web: www.ovp.com

Key contact:
Mr. George Clute, Partner
Mr. Gerard Langeler, Partner
Mr. Charles Waite, Jr., Partner

Description: We are the leading early-stage technology focused venture firm in the Pacific Northwest and the only one with offices in both Washington and Oregon.

Amount of capital invested: $21 million

Preferred investment size: $1-3 million

Amount under management: $100-500 million

Area served: North America

Preferred stages of financing: Seed, Start up, First stage, Second stage

Industries:
I.03   Biotech/genetic engineering
I.06   Communications
I.07   Computer hardware
I.08   Computer software
I.14   Electronics
I.20   Healthcare
I.21   High technology
I.23   Information technology services
I.24   Internet services/e-commerce
I.26   Life sciences
I.29   Medical/medical products
I.33   Semiconductors

Sampling of portfolio companies: Amaze, Inc. (multimedia content software for personal computers); CellPro, Inc. (developer of therapeutic devices utilizing cell separation technology); Logic Modeling Corp. (developer of models for electronic systems simulation); Oculon Corp. (developer of drugs for non-surgical treatment of the eye); ProTools, Inc. (developer of LAN analysis software); Saros Corp. (developer of distributed network file management systems); Spectragraphics Corp. (developer of concurrent engineering software tools); Triconex Corp. (manufacturer of fault tolerant process control equipment); Xilinx, Inc. (developer of field programmable logic devices); CareWise, Inc. (provider of demand management services for the healthcare industry); Corixa Corp. (developer of cancer vaccine & therapeutic products); Elekom Corp. (developer of procurement software for medium to large companies); Global Mobility Systems (developer of wireless communications software); Originet (developer of software & services for electronic music delivery); Rosetta Inpharmatics, Inc. (genomic drug discovery technology); Sequel Technology Corp. (developer of iternet management software); SignalSoft, Inc. (developer of location information software for wireless communications); TView, Inc. (developer of video processing systems); Verity, Inc. (developer of software for advanced multi-protocol content retrieval applications); We.bridge, Inc. (developer of software for sales chain management)

Pacific Horizon Ventures

1001 Fourth Avenue Plaza, Suite 4105
Seattle, Washington 98154
(206) 682-1181
Fax: (206) 682-8077
E-mail: phv@pacifichorizon.com

Key contact:
Mr. Donald J. Elmer, Managing Director
Mr. Matthew J. Mullaney, Research Associate

Description: We are a Seattle-based venture capital firm that invests in technology companies involved in healthcare and information technology. We seek initial investments across three financing stages, from stage I, where proceeds are used to begin commercialization, through mezzanine financing. We take an active role in our earlier stage investments, and for this reason prefer that these companies be located in the Northwest.

Area served: Northwest

Preferred stages of financing: First stage, Second stage, Mezzanine, Third/later stage

Industries:
I.20   Healthcare
I.23   Information technology services

Sampling of portfolio companies: Norian Corp. (developed a synthetic bone paste used to repair fractures); Proxim Corp. (producer of wireless LAN systems); Innova Corp. (develops & sells digital microwave radios used for short-haul data transmission); NeoPath, Inc. (developed an automated Pap smear screening device now in use in clinical & cytology laboratories); Edmark Corp. (develops & distributes a family of educational software products intended for younger children); CareWise Inc. (provides medical information services to large managed care providers & self-insured organizations); Coral Systems Corp. (develops & sells software utilities for the wireless communications market); Diametrics Medical, Inc. (develops & sells portable blood analyzers); Creative Multimedia Corp. (publishes electronic media)

Pacific Northwest Partners SBIC, L.P.
305 108th Avenue NE, 2nd Floor
Bellevue, Washington 98004
(425) 455-9967
Fax: (425) 455-9404

Key contact:
Mr. Theodore M. Wight, General Partner

Area served: Northwest

Preferred stages of financing: Seed, Start up, First stage, Second stage, LBO/MBO

Industries:
I.06   Communications
I.07   Computer hardware
I.08   Computer software
I.19   Generalist
I.29   Medical/medical products
I.32   Retail
I.34   Services (business)
I.35   Services (consumer)

Redleaf Venture Management
800 5th Avenue, Suite 4100
Seattle, Washington 98104
(206) 447-1350
Fax: (206) 447-1351
E-mail: info@redleaf.com
Web: www.redleaf.com

Key contact:
Mr. Russ Aldrich, Principal
Mr. Chris Brookfield

Description: We are a seed & early stage fund engaged with information technology firms developing software solutions for business to business commerce. We are an operationally oriented investment firm & take an active role in all of our portfolio.

Amount of capital invested: $5 million

Preferred investment size: $1-2 million

Amount under management: $10-25 million

Area served: Silicon Valley, CA; Portland, OR; Seattle, WA; Vancouver, BC

Preferred stages of financing: Seed, Start up

Industries:
I.06   Communications
I.07   Computer hardware
I.08   Computer software
I.21   High technology
I.24   Internet services/e-commerce

Sampling of portfolio companies: Netgravity (internet advertising); Wireless Online; Redcreek Communications (data encryption for virtual private nets); Mediaseek Technologies (educational software for teachers/parents); Infoscape (java-based tracking & management applications); Semio (visually-based information retrieval technology); Moai Technologies (business-to-business auction software)

U.S. Venture Partners
777 108th Avenue NE, Suite 1895
Bellevue, Washington 98004
(425) 646-7620
Fax: (425) 990-1595

Key contact:
Mr. Dale Vogel

Description: We focus our investment activity in those areas in which we have greatest expertise. Thus, we will invest principally in companies headquartered in the Western United States in three sectors of industry: medical, technology and retail/consumer.

Founded: 1981

Preferred investment size: $500,000-4 million

Amount under management: $100-500 million

Area served: West Coast

Preferred stages of financing: Start up, First stage, Second stage

Industries:
I.03   Biotech/genetic engineering
I.06   Communications
I.11   Consumer products
I.14   Electronics
I.23   Information technology services
I.29   Medical/medical products

Sampling of portfolio companies: 3Dfx Interactive; Applied Micro Circuits; MMC Networks; NeoMagic; Check Point Software Technologies; Artisan Components; Sun Microsystems; Advanced Cardiovascular Systems

West Virginia

Anker Capital
208 Capital Street, Suite 300
Charleston, West Virginia 25301
(304) 344-1794
Fax: (304) 344-1798

Key contact:
Mr. Thomas Loehr

Area served: Mid-Atlantic

Preferred stage of financing: First stage

Industries:
I.27   Manufacturing

Shenandoah Venture Capital L.P.
208 Capital Street, Suite 300
Charleston, West Virginia 25301
(304) 344-1796
Fax: (304) 344-1798

Key contact:
Thomas E. Loehr

Wisconsin

Capital Investments, Inc.
1009 West Glen Oaks Lane, Suite 103
Mequon, Wisconsin 53092
(414) 241-0303
Fax: (414) 241-8451

Key contact:
Mr. Steven C. Rippl, Executive Vice President
Mr. David E. Mayer, Controller

Description: We are a private mezzanine venture
capital fund which invests in subordinated debt and
equity of privately held companies. We focus on
growing companies in traditional industries with
good management and an ability to expand market-
share rapidly given the capital provided by our
investment.

Amount of capital invested: $3.5 million

Preferred investment size: $1 million

Amount under management: $10-25 million

Area served: United States

Preferred stage of financing: Mezzanine

Industries:
I.06   Communications
I.09   Construction
I.12   Distribution
I.22   Industrial products
I.27   Manufacturing
I.28   Media/publishing
I.34   Services (business)
I.37   Wholesale

Future Value Ventures
330 East Kilbourn Avenue, Suite 711
Milwaukee, Wisconsin 53202
(414) 278-0377
Fax: (414) 278-7321
E-mail: FutureVV@execPC.com
Web: www/~FutureVV@execpc.com

Key contact:
Mr. William P. Beckett, Senior Investment Officer

Description: Provide venture capital and investment
advisory services to minority and women entrepreneurs operating growth-oriented businesses in early-
stages of development.

Amount of capital invested: $300,000

Preferred investment size: $300,000-500,000

Amount under management: <$10 million

Area served: United States

Preferred stages of financing: Mezzanine, Int'l expansion

Industries:
I.19   Generalist

Sampling of portfolio companies: Emerge Magazine
(national magazine); ProStaff Personnel Services
Corp. (staffing services); UNC Media of Milwaukee,
Inc. (FM radio station); Sensor Devices, Inc. (medical
sensors); Think Innovative Media, Inc. (multimedia);
Consolidated Industries, Inc. (engineering & manufacturing); Beauty Concepts, Inc. (full service salons)

Horizon Partners Ltd.
225 East Mason Street, Suite 600
Milwaukee, Wisconsin 53202
(414) 271-2200
Fax: (414) 271-4016
E-mail: hpartners@aol.com

Key contact:
Mr. Robert M. Feerick, Chairman
Mr. Paul A. Stewart, Vice President
Mr. Paul W. Sweeney, Vice President

Description: Founded by over thirty chief executives
(CEO's), we acquire companies which are a good
strategic fit with their respective backgrounds. After
the acquisition, several of these CEO's serve as direc-

tors to the portfolio companies - thus, enhancing
value by consulting with management on critical
issues facing their companies.

Preferred investment size: $2-10 million

Amount under management: $25-100 million

Area served: United States

Preferred stage of financing: LBO/MBO

Industries:
I.11   Consumer products
I.12   Distribution
I.14   Electronics
I.22   Industrial products
I.27   Manufacturing

I.28   Media/publishing
I.34   Services (business)
I.35   Services (consumer)

Sampling of portfolio companies: Gelber Industries, Inc. (distributor of industrial pumps); R.W. Fox & Co. (distributor of industrial pumps); Image Conversion Systems, Inc. (micrographic services); Multiplex Display Fixture Co., Inc. (store fixtures & displays); Orval Kent Food Co., Inc. (refrigerated prepared salads); Byerly Foods, Inc. (refrigerated prepared salads); Mrs. Crockett's Kitchens, Inc. (refrigerated prepared salads); Surface Systems, Inc. (weather information systems); Weather Corp. of America (weather forecasting-utility industry); Xymox Technologies, Inc. (membrane switches)

Mason Wells

770 North Water Street
Milwaukee, Wisconsin 53202
(414) 765-7800
Fax: (414) 765-7850

Key contact:
Mr. John T. Byrnes, Managing Partner
Mr. John J. Riley, Partner
Mr. William G. Krugler, Partner
Mr. Thomas G. Smith, Partner
Mr. Gregory J. Myers, Partner
Ms. Wendy L. Kohler, Partner/CFO
Mr. David L. Kessenich, Associate

Description: We were founded in 1982 as the M&I Capital Markets Group, the merchant banking arm of Marshall & Ilsley Corp., a diversified interstate bank holding company. Today, we are a leading Midwest-based private equity investor with $150 million of capital to invest in growth oriented middle market companies. Since our founding, we have acted as lead investor in over 50 transactions in which we have teamed with entrepreneurial managers to acquire companies in the Midwest with annual revenues between $15 million and $150 million.

Founded: 1982

Area served: Midwest

Preferred stages of financing: Second stage, LBO/ MBO

Industries:
I.08   Computer software
I.22   Industrial products
I.34   Services (business)

Quaestus Management Corporation

111 East Kilbourn Avenue, Suite 2700
Milwaukee, Wisconsin 53202
(414) 615-2800
Fax: (414) 615-2880
E-mail: partners@quaestus.com
Web: www.quaestus.com

Key contact:
Ms. Singari Srivathsa, Investment Analyst

Description: We are a private investment management firm specializing exclusively in the information and media industries, including computer software and services, electronic commerce, information and content, new media and traditional media. Our five professionals possess over 50 years of combined experience in operating, managing, researching and investing in information-related companies.

Founded: 1990

Preferred stage of financing: Third/later stage

Industries:
I.08   Computer software
I.23   Information technology services
I.24   Internet services/e-commerce
I.28   Media/publishing
I.30   New media

Sampling of portfolio companies: Cumulus Broadcasting, Inc. (owns & operates over 60 radio stations in 16 media markets across the country); GEM Radio Network (serves several markets in the English-speaking Caribbean)

Venture Investors Management LLC

565 Science Drive, Suite A
Madison, Wisconsin 53711
(608) 233-3070
Fax: (608) 238-5120
E-mail: vi@ventureinvestors.com
Web: www.ventureinvestors.com

Key contact:
Mr. Roger H. Ganser, Managing Partner
Mr. John Neis, Partner
Mr. Scott Button, Investment Analyst

Description: We manage two early stage venture capital funds focused on opportunities in Wisconsin and contiguous states. We have an established program to help build management teams by matching experienced managers with founding scientists and engineers. We manage a business incubator in the University of Wisconsin Research Park.

Amount of capital invested: $2.5 million

Preferred investment size: $500,000

Amount under management: $10-25 million

Area served: United States

Preferred stages of financing: Seed, Start up, First stage

Industries:
I.03   Biotech/genetic engineering
I.05   Chemicals
I.06   Communications
I.07   Computer hardware
I.08   Computer software
I.12   Distribution
I.14   Electronics
I.17   Environmental services/waste management

I.20   Healthcare
I.21   High technology
I.22   Industrial products
I.23   Information technology services
I.24   Internet services/e-commerce
I.26   Life sciences
I.27   Manufacturing
I.28   Media/publishing
I.29   Medical/medical products
I.30   New media
I.34   Services (business)

Sampling of portfolio companies: Third Wave Technologies, Inc. (DNA diagnostics); Gala Design LLC (recombinant proteins); BioAccoustics, Inc. (medical devices); Promega Corp. (biotech research products); GDXI (medical services); RWT Corp. (industrial software); Synthon Corp. (pharmaceutical intermediates); NorthWord Press (publishing); Gareth Stevens, Inc. (publishing); Extrel Corp. (analytical instruments); Office Solutions, Inc. (software)

CANADA

Alberta

Accolade Capital Inc.

215 10th Avenue SW, Suite 300
Calgary, Alberta T2R 0A4
Canada
(403) 221-0901
Fax: (403) 237-8387
E-mail: accolade@capitalideas.com
Web: www.capitalideas.com/accolade

Key contact:
Mr. Grant Howard, President
Mr. Stace Wills, Managing Partner
Mr. Derek Ball
Mr. Harvey A. Brovald
Mr. Glenn F. McCowan

Description: We are a Calgary-based venture capital firm which provides investments and strategic guidance to private Western Canadian technology companies.

Preferred investment size: $500,000-1.5 million

Area served: Western Canada

Preferred stages of financing: Seed, Start up, First stage, LBO/MBO

Industries:
I.08   Computer software
I.17   Environmental services/waste management
I.23   Information technology services
I.26   Life sciences
I.27   Manufacturing

Western America Venture Group

10205 - 101 Street
1500 Midland Walwyn Tower
Edmonton, Alberta T5J 2Z2
Canada
(403) 496-9171
Fax: (403) 496-9172
E-mail: wag@planet.eon.net

Key contact:
Mr. Richard Caron, President
Mr. Donald P. Caron, Vice President

Description: Specialize in capital investment of less than $10 million and invest primarily in the technology and resource sectors. We also take companies public by venturing with sponsoring investment dealers or act as agents for private placements using securities regulation exemptions.

Preferred investment size: Up to $1 million

Amount under management: $25-100 million

Area served: Worldwide

Preferred stages of financing: Start up, First stage, Second stage, LBO/MBO, Expansion, Int'l expansion, Succession buy outs

Industries:
I.02   Agriculture/forestry/fishing/mining
I.03   Biotech/genetic engineering
I.07   Computer hardware
I.11   Consumer products

I.12   Distribution
I.14   Electronics
I.15   Energy/natural resources/utilities
I.16   Entertainment
I.17   Environmental services/waste management
I.20   Healthcare
I.22   Industrial products
I.23   Information technology services
I.25   Leisure/hospitality
I.26   Life sciences
I.27   Manufacturing
I.29   Medical/medical products
I.37   Wholesale

British Columbia

Business Development Bank of Canada

601 West Hastings Street, Suite 700
Vancouver, British Columbia V6B 5G9
Canada
(604) 666-7814
Fax: (604) 666-7650

Key contact:
Mr. David Bennett, Managing Director

Description: Venture capital division was founded to serve the growing needs of Vancouver high technology companies.

Founded: 1989

Amount under management: $25-100 million

Area served: Canada

Preferred stages of financing: Seed, Start up, First stage, Second stage, Mezzanine, LBO/MBO, Int'l expansion, Third/later stage, turnaround, venture leasing

Industries:
I.14   Electronics
I.22   Industrial products

Flynn Venture Capital Corporation

2795 Beach Drive
Victoria, British Columbia V8R 6K6
Canada
(250) 592-5994
Fax: (250) 592-5094
E-mail: donaldflynn@compuserve.com

Key contact:
Mr. Donald Flynn, Chairman

Description: Private venture capital firm investing in early stage financings primarily in specialty restaurant chains, web sites, communications, horticulture and consumer products in Western United States and Western Canada.

Amount of capital invested: $3 million

Preferred investment size: $50,000-250,000

Amount under management: <$10 million

Area served: North America, Prefer West, Western Canada

Preferred stages of financing: Seed, Start up, First stage, Second stage

Industries:
I.01   Aerospace
I.02   Agriculture/forestry/fishing/mining
I.03   Biotech/genetic engineering
I.06   Communications
I.16   Entertainment
I.23   Information technology services
I.24   Internet services/e-commerce
I.25   Leisure/hospitality
I.30   New media
I.31   Real estate
I.32   Retail
I.34   Services (business)
I.35   Services (consumer)

Sampling of portfolio companies: World Wrapps, Inc. (specialty restaurant chain); World Wrapps Northwest (specialty restaurant chain); Blue Chalk Cafe, Inc. (casual restaurant chain); Left at Albuquerque (casual restaurant chain); Babycenter, Inc. (web site); E-Call, Inc. (communications); Oregon Bulb & Perennial Farms, Inc. (specialty grower & wholesaler); Great Scott, Inc. (toy company)

Pacific Century Group Ventures Ltd.

Suite 309-975, West 13th Avenue
Vancouver, British Columbia V5Z 1P4
Canada
(604) 739-7511
Fax: (604) 739-7447
E-mail: info@pcentury.com
Web: www.pcentury.com

Key contact:
Mr. Harish C. Consul, President

Description: Global investment expertise in fund management, venture capital & corporate finance. Primary focus on information technology, resources, real estate and special situations.

Preferred investment size: $1-5 million

Amount under management: $100-500 million

Area served: Asia, North America

Preferred stages of financing: Seed, Start up, First stage, Second stage, Mezzanine, LBO/MBO, Expansion, Int'l expansion

Industries:
I.03   Biotech/genetic engineering
I.06   Communications
I.07   Computer hardware
I.08   Computer software
I.09   Construction
I.10   Consulting
I.14   Electronics
I.15   Energy/natural resources/utilities
I.16   Entertainment
I.18   Financial services
I.21   High technology
I.23   Information technology services
I.24   Internet services/e-commerce
I.25   Leisure/hospitality
I.26   Life sciences
I.28   Media/publishing
I.30   New media
I.31   Real estate
I.33   Semiconductors
I.34   Services (business)
I.35   Services (consumer)
I.36   Transportation
I.37   Wholesale

Sampling of portfolio companies: Boarkwalk Equities (real estate); CMGI Information (high-tech internet); iZ Technologies (software); amazon.com (internet); Verisign (internet security); Lycos (internet search); Real Networks (high technology); Infoseek (high technology)

Ventures West Management, Inc.

1285 West Pender Street, Suite 280
Vancouver, British Columbia V6E 4B1
Canada
(604) 688-9495
Fax: (604) 687-2145

Key contact:
Mr. Michael J. Brown, President
Dr. Robin J. Louis, Ph.D., Executive Vice President/
COO
Mr. J. Derek Douglas, Vice President
Mr. Sam Znaimer, Vice President

Description: With over $200 million under management in several technology funds, our investment emphasis is on early stage companies in Canada which have the management and product potential to become world leaders in their markets. Our investment experience in knowledge based companies spans a total of over 100 different firms.

Preferred investment size: Over $1 million

Area served: Canada

Preferred stages of financing: Seed, Start up, First stage

Industries:
I.03   Biotech/genetic engineering
I.06   Communications
I.08   Computer software
I.14   Electronics
I.15   Energy/natural resources/utilities
I.17   Environmental services/waste management
I.22   Industrial products
I.29   Medical/medical products

Sampling of portfolio companies: Dees Communications; Ballard Energy & Environmental; The PSC Group; Insystems Technologies; NCompass; Novatel Spectrum

Working Opportunity Fund (EVCC), Ltd.

2901-1055 West Georgia Street
P.O. Box 11170, Royal Centre
Vancouver, British Columbia V6E 3R5
Canada
(604) 688-9631
Fax: (604) 669-7605
E-mail: mike@wofund.com
Web: www.wofund.com/wof

Key contact:
Mr. David Levi, President/CEO
Mr. Michael Phillips, Senior Vice President-
Investments

Description: We are a widely held, private venture capital fund that makes minority ownership investments in a range of business types, with the exceptions of retail, real estate, financial services and resource extraction. Companies can be at any stage of development and syndication is preferred.

Amount of capital invested: $19,491,884

Preferred investment size: $500,000

Amount under management: $100-500 million

Area served: British Columbia

Preferred stages of financing: Seed, Start up, First stage, Second stage, Expansion

Industries:
I.01   Aerospace
I.03   Biotech/genetic engineering
I.05   Chemicals
I.06   Communications
I.07   Computer hardware
I.08   Computer software
I.11   Consumer products
I.14   Electronics
I.15   Energy/natural resources/utilities
I.16   Entertainment
I.17   Environmental services/waste management
I.20   Healthcare
I.21   High technology
I.22   Industrial products
I.23   Information technology services
I.24   Internet services/e-commerce
I.25   Leisure/hospitality
I.26   Life sciences
I.27   Manufacturing
I.29   Medical/medical products
I.33   Semiconductors
I.36   Transportation

Sampling of portfolio companies: Future SEA Farms Inc. (develops & markets enclosed systems for the aquaculture industry); DRI Dehydration Research Inc. (develops & markets vacuum microwave drying systems for food products); Questor Industries Inc. (systems producer of industrial gases); ABC Boat Charters Ltd. (operates a charter vessel business targeted primarily at group tourism); Silvagen Inc. (biotechnology-based reforestation products & services); Chromos Molecular Systems Inc. (research & development of mammalian artificial chromosomes); Mezzaluna Pasta Corp. (produces & markets fresh-frozen, filled & laminated pasta); UWI Unisoft Wares Inc. (develops & sells innovative business forms software for intranet market); SFG Technologies Inc. (municipal & utility company financial software); Epic Data Inc. (data collection information systems); Sonigistix Technologies Inc. (thin film electrostatic transducers); AnorMED Inc. (metal compound pharmaceuticals); NCompass Labs Inc. (internet software designer); Avcorp Industries Inc. (manufacturer of aircraft components); U.V. Systems Technology Inc. (technology for treatment of waste water); StressGen Biotechnologies Corp. (research & development of vaccines); Xillix Technologies Corp. (technology for early detection of cancer); Chancery Software Ltd. (school information & learning systems); Ingenium Technologies Inc. (construction industry data publisher); Stone Electronics Ltd. (underwater scuba communications)

New Brunswick

Working Ventures Canadian Fund, Inc.
133 Prince William Street
St. John, New Brunswick E2L 2B5
Canada
(506) 652-5704
Fax: (506) 652-5706
E-mail: vmillen@workingventures.ca
Web: www.workingventures.ca

Key contact:
Ms. Valerie Millen, Branch Manager

Description: A broadly diversified portfolio of investment in small and medium sized businesses. Our goal is long term capital appreciation for our shareholders. As a result, and providing we do our job well, benefits will accrue to the Canadian economy in terms of job creation, exports and investment in research and development as by-products of successful investment in small and medium sized Canadian businesses.

Founded: 1990

Preferred investment size: $1-7 million

Amount under management: $500 million -1 billion

Area served: Canada

Industries:
I.03   Biotech/genetic engineering
I.06   Communications
I.07   Computer hardware
I.08   Computer software
I.11   Consumer products
I.14   Electronics
I.15   Energy/natural resources/utilities
I.27   Manufacturing
I.29   Medical/medical products
I.36   Transportation

Sampling of portfolio companies: AlarmForce Industries Inc. (developers & installers of residential security systems); Applied Analytics Corp. (develops & markets highly accurate instrumentation used in the rapidly growing geomatics industry); Atlantic Video Lottery Inc. (owner/operator of video lottery machines); CADSOFT Corp. (provider of CAD software solutions targeted to residential home builders, architects & designers); Cary Peripherals Inc. (developer & manufacturer of durable, PC point-of-sale keyboards based on open architecture that become an integral part of end-user's retail system); CrossKeys Systems Corp. (independent software vendor that develops, markets & supports telecommunications management software products & services); Dipix Technologies Inc. (supplier of vision & imaging products to original equipment manufacturers, system integrators & value-added resellers in the fields of industrial inspection, machine vision, biomedical imaging, document scanning & scientific imaging); Envoy Communications Group Inc. (full-service marketing communications agency that develops & implements integrated communications campaigns for nat'l. & regional clients throughout North America); General Wellbeing (retail concept for the growing wellness & self-care market); GlycoDesign Inc. (dedicated to drug discovery & pre-clinical development of novel carbohydrate processing inhibitors); Imperial Rubber & Urethane Corp. (manufacturer & distributor of high quality rubber & urethane products for the oil & gas, petrochemical & pipeline industries); Isolation Systems (engineering, manufacturing, marketing & scale of software & hardware used to create virtual private networks between remote users & their office computer networks); Life Imaging Systems Inc. (established to develop & market a wide range of 3-D ultrasound imaging products used for diagnostic purposes); MDC Corp. (multi-disciplined communications & marketing organization); News Theatre Inc. (provides public & private sector clients with a multi-media theatre for corporate conferences & an audio/visual distribution system which delivers client events live & direct to major newsrooms throughout Greater Toronto & by satellite worldwide); Patheon Inc. (independent provider of commercial manufacturing & packaging services for over-the-counter & prescription drugs); Recreation Services Int'l. Inc. (full-service recreation facility management company); SimEx Inc. (full-service provider of out-of-home entertainment attractions utilizing motion platform simulation for the theme park, museum/science centre & location based entertainment centre markets); TempKraft Canada Inc. (manufactures a recyclable panel insulation product which will initially be for use in the shipment of perishable commodities); Toi-Kinnoir Inc. (medical informatics company which develops healthcare diagnostic & training knowledgeware products)

Nova Scotia

ACF Equity Atlantic Inc.
Purdy's Wharf Tower II, Suite 2106, Box 25
1969 Upper Water Street
Halifax, Nova Scotia B3J 3R7
Canada
(902) 492-5164
Fax: (902) 421-1808
E-mail: acf.equity@ns.sympatico.ca

Key contact:
Mr. Peter Forton, President

Description: We are a venture capital fund formed to make equity and quasi-equity investments in qualifying small and medium-sized businesses in Atlantic Canada. We have over $30 million in committed capital originating from seven chartered banks, one credit union, the four Atlantic Provinces and the Federal Government through the Atlantic Canada Opportunities Agency.

Founded: 1996

Preferred investment size: $250,000-1.5 million

Amount under management: $25-100 million

Area served: Canada

Preferred stages of financing: First stage, Second stage

Industries:
I.03   Biotech/genetic engineering
I.23   Information technology services
I.29   Medical/medical products

Business Development Bank of Canada
Cogswell Tower, Suite 1400
P.O. Box 1656
Halifax, Nova Scotia B3J 2Z7
Canada
(902) 426-7860
Fax: (902) 426-9033

Key contact:
Mr. Peter MacNeil, Senior Manager

Founded: 1983

Amount under management: $25-100 million

Area served: United States

Preferred stages of financing: Seed, Start up, First stage, Second stage, Mezzanine, LBO/MBO, Int'l expansion, Third/later stage, turnaround, venture leasing

Industries:
I.14   Electronics
I.22   Industrial products

Working Ventures Canadian Fund, Inc.
Purdy's Wharf, Tower One
1959 Upper Water Street, Suite 407
Halifax, Nova Scotia B3J 3N2
Canada
(902) 492-2292
Fax: (902) 492-1101
E-mail: slund@workingventures.ca
Web: www.workingventures.ca

Key contact:
Mr. Stephen E. Lund, Branch Manager

Description: A broadly diversified portfolio of investment in small and medium sized businesses. Our goal is long term capital appreciation for our shareholders. As a result, and providing we do our job well, benefits will accrue to the Canadian economy in terms of job creation, exports and investment in research and development as by-products of successful investment in small and medium sized Canadian businesses.

Founded: 1990

Preferred investment size: $1-7 million

Amount under management: $500 million -1 billion

Area served: Canada

Industries:
I.03   Biotech/genetic engineering
I.06   Communications
I.07   Computer hardware
I.08   Computer software
I.11   Consumer products
I.14   Electronics
I.15   Energy/natural resources/utilities
I.27   Manufacturing
I.29   Medical/medical products
I.36   Transportation

Sampling of portfolio companies: AlarmForce Industries Inc. (developers & installers of residential security systems); Applied Analytics Corp. (develops & markets highly accurate instrumentation used in the rapidly growing geomatics industry); Atlantic Video Lottery Inc. (owner/operator of video lottery machines); CADSOFT Corp. (provider of CAD software solutions targeted to residential home builders, architects & designers); Cary Peripherals Inc. (developer & manufacturer of durable, PC point-of-sale keyboards based on open architecture that become an integral part of end-user's retail system); CrossKeys Systems Corp. (independent software vendor that develops, markets & supports telecommunications management software products & services); Dipix Technologies Inc. (supplier of vision & imaging products to original equipment manufacturers, system integrators & value-added resellers in the fields of industrial inspection, machine vision, biomedical imaging, document scanning & scientific imaging); Envoy Communications Group Inc. (full-service marketing communications agency that develops & implements integrated communications campaigns for nat'l. & regional clients throughout North America); General Wellbeing (retail concept for the growing wellness & self-care market); GlycoDesign Inc. (dedicated to drug discovery & preclinical development of novel carbohydrate processing inhibitors); Imperial Rubber & Urethane Corp. (manufacturer & distributor of high quality rubber & urethane products for the oil & gas, petrochemical & pipeline industries); Isolation Systems (engineering, manufacturing, marketing & scale of software & hardware used to create virtual private networks between remote users & their office computer networks); Life Imaging Systems Inc. (established to develop & market a wide range of 3-D ultrasound imaging products used for diagnostic purposes); MDC Corp. (multi-disciplined communications & marketing organization); News Theatre Inc. (provides public & private sector clients with a multimedia theatre for corporate conferences & an audio/visual distribution system which delivers client events live & direct to major newsrooms throughout Greater Toronto & by satellite worldwide); Patheon Inc. (independent provider of commercial manufacturing & packaging services for over-the-counter & prescription drugs); Recreation Services Int'l. Inc. (full-service recreation facility management company); SimEx Inc. (full-service provider of out-of-home entertainment attractions utilizing motion platform simulation for the theme park, museum/science centre & location based entertainment centre markets); TempKraft Canada Inc. (manufactures a recyclable panel insulation product which will initially be for use in the shipment of perishable commodities); Toi-Kinnoir Inc. (medical informatics company which develops healthcare diagnostic & training knowledgeware products)

Ontario

Acorn Ventures Inc.

65 Queen Street West, Suite 1820
Toronto, Ontario M5H 2M5
Canada
(416) 362-9009
Fax: (416) 360-8286
E-mail: robmayer@compuserve.com
Web: www.enterprisefund.com

Key contact:
Mr. Robert Mayer, Vice President

Description: Venture capital fund.

Amount of capital invested: $4 million

Preferred investment size: $1 million

Amount under management: $10-25 million

Area served: North America

Preferred stages of financing: Seed, Start up, First stage, Second stage, Mezzanine, LBO/MBO, Expansion

Industries:
I.06   Communications
I.14   Electronics
I.21   High technology
I.23   Information technology services
I.24   Internet services/e-commerce
I.30   New media
I.33   Semiconductors

J. L. Albright Venture Partners Inc.

145 King Street West, Suite 1100
Toronto, Ontario M5H 1J8
Canada
(416) 943-6109
Fax: (416) 943-6160
E-mail: jprosser@jlaventures.com
Web: www.jlaventures.com

Key contact:
Mr. Jon Prosser, Associate
Mr. John Albright, President
Mr. Gary Rubinoff, Executive Vice President

Area served: Canada

Preferred stages of financing: First stage, Second stage

Industries:
I.01   Aerospace
I.03   Biotech/genetic engineering
I.06   Communications
I.07   Computer hardware

I.08   Computer software
I.13   Education
I.14   Electronics
I.17   Environmental services/waste management
I.20   Healthcare
I.21   High technology
I.23   Information technology services
I.24   Internet services/e-commerce
I.33   Semiconductors

Sampling of portfolio companies: Triple G Corp. (healthcare informatics, laboratory information systems); Isolation Systems Ltd. (virtual private networks); The Descartes Systems Group (supply chain execution software); Inex Corp. (e-commerce software); Indian Motorcycle Co. Inc. (merchandising); Shivasoft Inc. (advanced planning & scheduling systems); Balisoft Technologies Inc. (on-line customer service software)

Bank of Montreal Capital Corporation

302 Bay Street, 7th Floor
Toronto, Ontario M5X 1A1
Canada
(416) 867-7247
Fax: (416) 867-4108
Web: www.bmo.com/bmocc

Key contact:
K. C. Lim, Managing Director
Mr. Mel Margolese, Managing Director
Mr. David H. Pakrul, President/CEO

Description: Recognizing that many entrepreneurial businesses often have difficulty obtaining patient capital funds to finance their growth, we have responded to this need by creating Bank of Montreal Capital Corporation, a specialized financing corporation designed to help small and medium sized Canadian businesses reach their full potential.

Preferred investment size: $500,000-5 million

Amount under management: $100-500 million

Area served: Canada

Preferred stages of financing: Seed, Start up, Expansion, Third/later stage

Industries:
I.23   Information technology services

BCE Capital, Inc.
200 Bay Street, Suite 3120, South Tower
Toronto, Ontario M5J 2J2
Canada
(416) 815-0001
Fax: (416) 941-9494
E-mail: cataford@on.bell.ca
Web: www.bcecapital.com

Key contact:
Mr. Paul Cataford, Vice President-Investments

160 Elgin Street, Suite 1450
Ottawa, Ontario K1G 3J4
Canada
(613) 781-3072
(613) 763-5613
Fax: (613) 237-6262
E-mail: mccarthy@sympatico.ca
Web: www.bcecapital.com

Key contact:
Mr. David McCarthy, Director-Ottawa Operations

Description: Our objective is to generate above-average rates of return through direct investment in small-to-medium size businesses founded on proprietary telecommunications technology. Typically, investments focus on hardware and software products. We are seeking to invest in well-managed companies with a sustainable product advantage in high growth areas of the telecommunications sector.

Amount of capital invested: $12 million

Preferred investment size: $2.5 million

Amount under management: $25-100 million

Area served: North America

Preferred stages of financing: Start up, First stage

Industries:
I.06   Communications
I.08   Computer software
I.11   Consumer products
I.14   Electronics
I.21   High technology
I.23   Information technology services
I.24   Internet services/e-commerce
I.25   Leisure/hospitality
I.28   Media/publishing
I.30   New media
I.33   Semiconductors
I.34   Services (business)
I.35   Services (consumer)

Sampling of portfolio companies: Plaintree Systems (ethernet & giga-bit switches); Faneuil ISG (precision integrated marketing & call centre operations); Switchview (management software for PBX systems); E/O Networks (fiber loop access products for low population density areas); SSIG Holdings (remote sensing value-added information services); The Bulldog Group (multimedia database management software); Impath Networks (video multiplexing solutions for intelligent traffic systems & security monitoring); Sierra Wireless (wide area wireless data modems); VMI Technologies (information management for echocardiology); Vistar Technologies Inc. (data communication solutions for satellites)

Business Development Bank of Canada
280 Albert Street
Ottawa, Ontario K1P 5G8
Canada
(613) 995-8835
Fax: (613) 995-9478

Key contact:
Mr. Richard G. Cornwall, Managing Director

150 King Street West, Suite 100
Toronto, Ontario M5H 1J9
Canada
(416) 973-0034
Fax: (416) 973-5529

Key contact:
Mr. David Russell, Managing Director

Founded: 1983

Amount under management: $25-100 million

Area served: Canada

Preferred stages of financing: Seed, Start up, First stage, Second stage, Mezzanine, LBO/MBO, Int'l expansion, Third/later stage, turnaround, venture leasing

Industries:
I.14   Electronics
I.22   Industrial products

Capital Alliance Ventures Inc.
55 Village Centre Place, Suite 101
Mississauga, Ontario L4Z 1V9
Canada
(905) 272-8443
Fax: (905) 272-2096
E-mail: cavi@istar.ca
Web: www.cavi.com

60 Queen Street, Suite 600
Ottawa, Ontario K1P 5Y7
Canada
(613) 567-3225
(800) 304-2330
Fax: (613) 567-3979

E-mail: info@cavi.com
Web: www.cavi.com

Key contact:
Mr. Richard Charlebois, President
Mr. Ross Dedman, Vice President/CFO
Mr. Denzil Doyle, Chairman of the Board
Mr. Keith Lue, Vice President

Description: We are a labour sponsored investment fund with a two-fold mandate: to provide venture capital investment opportunities with additional tax benefits to the individual investor and to provide venture capital funding to businesses in the high technology, applied science and service sectors. The investor is afforded federal and Ontario tax credits equal to 30% of the first $3500 invested each year; the investment also is eligible for an RRSP deduction.

Founded: 1994

Preferred investment size: $1-3 million

Amount under management: $25-100 million

Area served: Ontario

Industries:
I.06   Communications
I.07   Computer hardware
I.08   Computer software
I.17   Environmental services/waste management
I.20   Healthcare
I.21   High technology
I.23   Information technology services
I.26   Life sciences
I.29   Medical/medical products
I.33   Semiconductors

Sampling of portfolio companies: West End Systems; FRED Systems Ltd.; Milkyway Networks; Tundra Semiconductor Corp.; Chrysalis Information Technology Security Inc.; Comdale Technologies (Canada) Inc.; Consultronics Ltd.; Accelerix Ltd.; Kaval Telecom Inc.; Cadabra Desing Libraries Inc.; Crosskeys Systems Corp.; Formal Systems Inc.; IS2 Research Inc.; Omega Digital Data Inc.; Seprotech Systems Inc.; Int'l. Datacasting; Med-Eng Systems Inc.

CIBC Wood Gundy Capital

161 Bay Street, BCE Place, 8th Floor
Toronto, Ontario M5J 2S8
Canada
(416) 594-7443
Fax: (416) 594-8037

Key contact:
Mr. Alan S. Wearing, Director
Mr. John B. Breen, Director
Mr. Ken Kilgor, Director

Description: Toronto based investment/merchant banking firm providing venture capital to all industries.

Founded: 1989

Preferred investment size: $5-20 million

Area served: Canada, United States

Industries:
I.01   Aerospace
I.02   Agriculture/forestry/fishing/mining
I.03   Biotech/genetic engineering
I.04   Broadcasting
I.05   Chemicals
I.06   Communications
I.07   Computer hardware
I.08   Computer software
I.09   Construction
I.10   Consulting
I.11   Consumer products
I.12   Distribution
I.13   Education
I.14   Electronics
I.15   Energy/natural resources/utilities
I.16   Entertainment
I.17   Environmental services/waste management
I.18   Financial services
I.19   Generalist
I.20   Healthcare
I.21   High technology
I.22   Industrial products
I.23   Information technology services
I.24   Internet services/e-commerce
I.25   Leisure/hospitality
I.26   Life sciences
I.27   Manufacturing
I.28   Media/publishing
I.29   Medical/medical products
I.30   New media
I.31   Real estate
I.32   Retail
I.33   Semiconductors
I.34   Services (business)
I.35   Services (consumer)
I.36   Transportation
I.37   Wholesale

Corporate Growth Assistance, Ltd.

19 York Ridge Road
Toronto, Ontario M2P 1R8
Canada
(416) 222-7772
Fax: (416) 222-6091
E-mail: cgal19yr@netcom.ca

Key contact:
Mr. Millard S. Roth, President

Description: Expansion capital for later stage, closley held mid-market companies supported by active management assistance for corporate strategy; acquisition search and integration; and long term financing. Focus is North America.

Amount of capital invested: $370,000

Preferred investment size: $1.5 million

Amount under management: <$10 million

Area served: North America

Preferred stage of financing: Expansion

Industries:
I.02   Agriculture/forestry/fishing/mining
I.04   Broadcasting
I.05   Chemicals
I.06   Communications
I.12   Distribution
I.13   Education
I.16   Entertainment
I.17   Environmental services/waste management
I.20   Healthcare
I.27   Manufacturing
I.28   Media/publishing
I.29   Medical/medical products
I.34   Services (business)

Sampling of portfolio companies: Carton sealing, pressure sensitive, printed tape processing; Dining & bedroom furniture manufacturing; Direct response relationship marketing services; Fresh carrot & onion processing & fresh potato distributor; Geophysical instrumentation; Multimedia, interactive K-12 courseware development & distribution; Product indentification pressure sensitive labels & license plate stickers; Steel stud, roofdeck, ceiling systems & aluminum soffit & siding manufacturers; suspended scaffold systems manufacturers; Temporary personnel (office, factory, technical) services; Computerized car valutaion data base for insurance industry; Waste water, oil & glycol refining

DGC Entertainment Ventures Corporation

387 Bloor Street East, Suite 401
Toronto, Ontario M4W 1H7
Canada
(416) 972-1158
Fax: (416) 972-0820

Key contact:
Mr. Allan King, President/CEO
Ms. Pamela Brand, Secretary
Mr. Robert Goodwin

Description: Formal venture capital firm serving Ontario based companies in the entertainment, communications and technology sectors.

Founded: 1993

Preferred investment size: $250,000-500,000

Area served: Canada

Preferred stages of financing: Second stage, Mezzanine, Expansion

Industries:
I.06 Communications
I.16 Entertainment
I.21 High technology
I.30 New media

Enterprise Fund

65 Queen Street West, Suite 1820
Toronto, Ontario M5H 2M5
Canada
(416) 362-9009
(800) 563-3857
Fax: (416) 360-8286
E-mail: RobMayer@CompuServe.com
Web: www.EnterpriseFund.com

Key contact:
Mr. Eduard Mayer
Mr. Jeffrey McRae
Mr. Robert Mayer

Description: We are a labour sponsored investment fund corporation making venture capital investments in small-to-medium sized Canadian corporations. We are committed to producing superior long-term returns from investments in developing companies, through careful analysis, active participation and prudent diversification within our portfolio.

Area served: Canada

Sampling of portfolio companies: Image Processing Systems Inc. (computer-based quality control vision inspection systems); CleanSoils Ltd. Partnership (hydrocarbon contaminated soil remediation services); Consultronics Ltd. (telecommunication test & simulation equipment); The Nu-Gro Corp. (fertilizers & horticultural supplies); Engineering Interface Ltd.- Tescor Energy Services (building performance contracting)

ER&D

1 Toronto Street, Box 19, Suite 806
Toronto, Ontario M5C 2V6
Canada
(416) 777-0530
Fax: (416) 368-0430

Key contact:
Mr. Derrick Rolfe, Managing Director

Description: Historically our focus has been to invest exclusively in environmental opportunities. As the perception of the environment by science and the industry has changed so too has our investment scope. The environmental industry has shifted from a reactionary to a process-oriented position. Consequently our focus has expanded to include opportunities that demonstrate degrees of process optimization and resource management. As well, we are particularly interested in biotechnologies and the high potential they hold for the environmental and medical industries.

Preferred investment size: $500,000-3 million

Area served: Canada

Preferred stages of financing: Start up, LBO/MBO

Industries:
I.03 Biotech/genetic engineering
I.17 Environmental services/waste management
I.29 Medical/medical products

Sampling of portfolio companies: AquaNorth Farms Inc. (sustainable forest management company & technology developer); Consolidated Envirowaste Industries Inc. (bio-mass recycling & by-product developer & marketer); Agglo Recovery Inc. (inorganic & organic hazardous waste recycler); Ecoval Inc. (bio-pesticide & natural fertilizer developer, manufacturer & marketer); Uniflo Utilities Management Corp. (pipeline trenchless technology developer & operator & asset manager & systems developer)

GBS Group International

2480 Cawthra Road, #27
Mississauga, Ontario L5A 2X2
Canada

(905) 897-2333
Fax: (905) 897-2334

Key contact:
Mr. Robert Ellis, President Director

Description: Private source of venture capital for established and new businesses in the manufacturing and food industries.

Preferred investment size: $1.5-5 million

Area served: Canada

Preferred stages of financing: Seed, Start up, First stage, Second stage

Industries:
I.11   Consumer products
I.27   Manufacturing
I.35   Services (consumer)

Hargan Ventures

One First Canadian Place, Suite 5100
P.O. Box 24
Toronto, Ontario M5X 1K2
Canada
(416) 643-7182
Fax: (416) 643-7183
E-mail: ifergan@istar.ca
Web: www.cvca.ca

Key contact:
Mr. Sam Ifergan, President
Mr. Harry Hart, Chairman

Description: Private fund. Searching for investments in early stages of growth oriented companies.

Amount of capital invested: $2 million

Preferred investment size: $1 million

Area served: Canada, United States

Preferred stages of financing: Start up, First stage, Second stage

Industries:
I.04   Broadcasting
I.07   Computer hardware
I.08   Computer software
I.11   Consumer products
I.12   Distribution
I.14   Electronics
I.16   Entertainment
I.24   Internet services/e-commerce
I.28   Media/publishing
I.30   New media
I.32   Retail

Sampling of portfolio companies: Brighter Child Interactive (educational software)

Helix Investments (Canada) Ltd.

70 York Street, Suite 1700
Toronto, Ontario M5J 1S9
Canada
(416) 367-1260
Fax: (416) 367-3614
E-mail: rkoturbash@helixvc.com

Key contact:
Mr. D. C. Webster
Mr. J. Wooder
Mr. I. Aiffen
Ms. M. Anis

Description: To provide start-up and seed capital to companies in high-technology industries that have a product at or close to the prototype stage with a demonstrable price/performance advantage over commercially available technology, a proven management team and the potential for significant export sales.

Founded: 1968

Preferred investment size: $1-3 million

Amount under management: $100-500 million

Area served: California, British Columbia, Ontario, Quebec, United States

Preferred stages of financing: Seed, Start up

Industries:
I.03   Biotech/genetic engineering
I.06   Communications
I.08   Computer software
I.14   Electronics
I.23   Information technology services

McLean Watson Capital Inc.

One First Canadian Place, Suite 1410
P.O. Box 129
Toronto, Ontario M5X 1A4
Canada
(416) 363-2000
Fax: (416) 363-2010
E-mail: info@mcleanwatson.com
Web: www.mcleanwatson.com

Key contact:
Mr. Loudon F. Owen, Managing Partner
Mr. John F. Eckert, Managing Partner
Mr. Matthew H. Lawton, Partner
Mr. John R. Stewart, Partner
Mr. Glenn M. Rumbell, Partner

Description: We are a venture capital fund manager. Our investors include institutional investors, private investors and the partners of McLean Watson. We invest in and provide financial and advisory services to information technology companies. Our mission is to invest in a select group of dynamic technology entrepreneurs, to build and maintain long-term relationships, and to actively assist in the growth of the intrinsic value of our investees.

Amount of capital invested: $9 million

Preferred investment size: $2-5 million

Amount under management: $25-100 million

Area served: North America

Preferred stages of financing: First stage, Second stage, Mezzanine, Expansion

Industries:
I.07   Computer hardware
I.08   Computer software
I.23   Information technology services
I.24   Internet services/e-commerce

Sampling of portfolio companies: Alex Informatics, Inc. (developer of "Libra" media server, a software based network multimedia/video delivery & archiving system based on Windows NT); Infrastructures For Information Inc. (developer of document management software for complex information needs); InterNetivity Inc. (developer of Java based software for busineness intelligence applications); IVL Technologies Ltd. (audio digital processing company with applications in the entertainment & education industries); KyberPASS Corp. (security & authentication software for controlled access applications over public networks); Media Synergy Inc. (multimedia authoring tools company providing animated self-extracting e-mail software for internet communications & a range of other consumer authoring tools); Neuma Technology Corp. (software to enable the effective management of the software development process); Pictorius Inc. (internet & intranet enabled client server development tools based on a fully visual,object-oriented development environment); Rhea Int'l. Organization Inc. (Latches product is an access control & user management system for standalone & networked PCs with a high level of in-built security); Rainmaker Digital Pictures Corp. (professional post-production & special effects company with leading compression technology for converting film to digital formats); Softimage Inc. (3-D animation & post-production software)

MDS Capital Corporation

100 International Boulevard
Toronto, Ontario M9W 6J6
Canada
(416) 675-7661
Fax: (416) 213-4232

Key contact:
Mr. Michael Callaghan, Senior Vice President
Mr. Richard Lockie, Senior Vice President
Mr. Frank Gleeson, Senior Vice President
Mr. Ed Rygiel, Senior Vice President

Description: We are Canada's largest venture capital company focused exclusively on health care and life sciences investing. Our primary objective is to build significant realizable value for our shareholders, as well as for the management and shareholders of its investee companies. We seek to achieve this by bringing a combination of capital, operating and financial expertise, as well as a network of international contacts within the life science area.

Amount of capital invested: $100 million (Canadian)

Preferred investment size: $3-10 million (Canadian)

Amount under management: $500 million -1 billion

Area served: North America

Preferred stages of financing: Seed, Start up, First stage, Second stage, Mezzanine

Industries:
I.03   Biotech/genetic engineering
I.20   Healthcare
I.26   Life sciences
I.29   Medical/medical products

Sampling of portfolio companies: Abtox, Inc. (manufactures & develops plasma based sterilization systems, instruments & supplies); Andronic Devices Ltd. (develops & commercializes products arising from the application of concepts in advanced robotics to problems in health care); Apollo Biopharmaceutics, Inc. (early stage biopharmaceutical company focused on the discovery, development & commercialization of neurosteriod drugs for the diagnosis, treatment & prevention of diseases of the central nervous system); Apoptogen, Inc. (discovers & develops novel therapeutics for neurodegenerative disorders & cancer); Centaur Pharmaceuticals Inc. (pharmaceutical technology with broad applications in neurodegenerative diseases, organ transplantation & aging); CME Telemetrix Inc. (designs & manufactures medical instruments for blood analysis & physiological monitoring); Ellipsis Biotherapeutics Corp. (leaders in genetic science for purposes of developing novel diagnostic tests & therapeutic treatments); Gensci Regeneration Sciences Inc. (expertise in innovative bone & tissue regeneration technologies & compounds that have potential of reversing the effects of osteoporosis); Glycodesign Inc. (drug design & development company dedicated to the discovery of novel therapeutics in the field of glycobiology); Hemosol Inc. (developers of a commercially-viable oxygen carrying blood substitute based on human hemoglobin); Inspiration R&D Inc. (technology development company); Microbix Biosystems Inc. (manufactures specialty biological products such as antigens & plasmids & proprietary biologicals such as vaccines, biotechnology educational products & generic biopharmaceuticals); Nanogen, Inc. (combines molecular genetics, microelectronics & nanotechnology in order to develop biopharmaceutical & diagnostics assays); Neurocrine Biosciences Inc. (leading neuroimmunology company focused on the discovery & development of novel therapeutics to treat disease & disorders of the central nervous & immune systems); Neuromotion Inc. (designs, develops & commercializes proprietary & licensed technologies in the functional electronic stimulation area to improve the functionality of motion impaired individuals); Phagetech Inc. (developing a novel approach to new drug discovery); Sparta Pharmaceuticals, Inc. (reformulates existing anticancer drugs, making them more convenient to administer & reducing side effects); Synaptic Pharmaceutical Corp. (develops & uses a proprietary enabling technology to design & develop drugs that modulate the functioning of the nervous system); Terragen Diversity Inc. (explores the biochemistry of microbes); Urocor, Inc. (provider of specialty clinical diagnostic & information services for urologists in the U.S.)

Middlefield Ventures Limited
First Canadian Place, 58th Floor
P.O. Box 192
Toronto, Ontario M5X 1A6
Canada
(416) 362-0714
Fax: (416) 362-7925
E-mail: invest@middlefield.com
Web: www.middlefield.com

Key contact:
Mr. Garth Jestley, President/CEO
Mr. James Parsons, Senior Portfolio Manager
Mr. Don Soane, Vice President-Marketing

Description: Formed in 1984, we are managed by Middlefield Ventures Limited. Investors include pension funds, insurance companies and other major financial institutions. Since inception, we have focused on identifying and investing in early stage companies with excellent earnings growth potential.

Founded: 1984

Area served: Worldwide

Preferred stages of financing: Seed, Start up, First stage

Industries:
I.18   Financial services

Miralta Capital, Inc.
250 Bloor Street East, Suite 301
Toronto, Ontario M4W 1E6
Canada
(416) 925-4274

Key contact:
Mr. Eric E. Baker, President
Mr. Robert Mee, Vice President
Mr. Ronald M. Meade, Chairman

Area served: Canada

Industries:
I.11   Consumer products
I.14   Electronics
I.18   Financial services
I.22   Industrial products
I.23   Information technology services
I.27   Manufacturing

Ontario Limited
Box 23110
Sault Ste. Marie, Ontario P6A 6W6
Canada
(705) 253-0744
Fax: (705) 253-0744

Key contact:
Mr. D. B. Stinson, F.C.A., President/CEO

Description: Act in capacity as funder in correlation with others and as a locater of funding sources experienced in deal structuring and all aspects of mergers, acquisitions, going public and negotiations associated with others who have access to funds, brokers etc. with minimal fees for cost recovery remuneration based on success fees in cash and/or shares depending on type of deal.

Amount of capital invested: $1.5 million

Preferred investment size: $500,000-1 million

Amount under management: <$10 million

Area served: North America

Preferred stages of financing: First stage, Second stage, Expansion

Industries:
I.07   Computer hardware
I.08   Computer software
I.11   Consumer products
I.16   Entertainment
I.21   High technology
I.22   Industrial products
I.25   Leisure/hospitality
I.27   Manufacturing

Sampling of portfolio companies: Hardware/software/security products; Automotive emission reduction; Power/energizing beverage

Priveq Financial Corporation
100 Scarsdale Road, Suite 202
Toronto, Ontario M3B 2R8
Canada
(416) 447-3330
Fax: (416) 447-3331
E-mail: priveq@sympatico.ca
Web: www3.sympatico.ca/priveq

Key contact:
Mr. Bradley W. Ashley, Managing Director

Description: Private equity investor - profitable niche manufacturing and niche services company targets.

Amount of capital invested: $2.5 million

Preferred investment size: $1-3 million

Amount under management: $10-25 million

Area served: Canada, United States

Preferred stages of financing: Second stage, Mezzanine, LBO/MBO, Int'l expansion

Industries:
I.01   Aerospace
I.04   Broadcasting
I.05   Chemicals
I.06   Communications
I.11   Consumer products
I.14   Electronics
I.22   Industrial products
I.23   Information technology services
I.25   Leisure/hospitality
I.27   Manufacturing
I.28   Media/publishing
I.29   Medical/medical products

I.34   Services (business)
I.35   Services (consumer)

Sampling of portfolio companies: Bomar Publishing (consumer electronics trade publication house); Samaritan Air Services (air ambulance operator); C.E. Composites (composite hockey stick manufacturer)

Quorum Funding Corporation

150 King Street West, Sun Life Tower, Suite 1505
P.O. Box 5
Toronto, Ontario M5H 1J9
Canada
(416) 971-6998
Fax: (416) 971-5955
E-mail: quorum.ca

Key contact:
Ms. Wanda M. Dorosz, Managing Director/Partner
Mr. Minhas Mohamed, Partner
Mr. Stephen Li, Partner
Mr. Ted Atkinson, CFO/Partner

Description: We are a navigator of sector-specific, knowledge-based enterprises, broadening their horizons, accelerating their entry into global markets, providing them with strategic operating and capital resources. We are a leading strategic investor in growing, technology-rich businesses. Our portfolio of knowledge-based enterprises is focused on companies with a strong market position, proven technology and proprietary products or services with the potential to become dominant in that market domestically and internationally.

Preferred investment size: $1-3 million

Amount under management: $100-500 million

Area served: North America

Preferred stages of financing: First stage, Second stage, Expansion

Industries:
I.08   Computer software
I.21   High technology
I.22   Industrial products
I.24   Internet services/e-commerce
I.26   Life sciences
I.29   Medical/medical products
I.31   Real estate

Sampling of portfolio companies: Applied Terravision Systems, Inc. (supplier of fully integrated corporate information solutions to the exploration & production sectors of the oil & gas industry); Atlantis Aerospace Corp. (providing unequaled price-performance in broad spectrum of training devices); Boyd Petro-search (formed to meet the growing demand for Geographic Information System technology & services by government agencies & the resource industries); Computer Talk Technology Inc. (seeks to improve customer service, simplify information processing & efficiently automate time consuming functions); Cygnet Storage Solutions, Inc. (developed a complete range of high performance storage solutions); New-View Indutries Inc. (manufacturers of custom window coverings); Neurochem Inc. (unique, significant & demonstrated technology which controls amyloid deposition associated with such disorders as Alzheimer's disease, adult-onset Diabetes & chronic inflammatory disorders); Newstar Technologies, Inc. (software company which provides mission critical e-commerce & financial application software & services to many of the leading Fortune 2000 companies globally); OpTx 2000 Corp. (medical products); Ontario Residential Development Corp. (invests in residential real estate development projects in the Province of Ontario with a mandate to meet certain criteria of affordable housing defined under the guidelines of the Ministry of Municipal Affairs & Housing); PC DOCS Group Int'l. Inc. (vendor of document management software); Pelorus Navigation Systems Inc. (designing, manufacturing, installing & maintaining navigation aids for airports); Positron Fiber Systems Corp. (fiber optic network access); Progressive Solutions Inc. (designs application software for businesses requiring multiple-location solution for complex inventory-control in the forestry products & retail/distribution industries); Promis Systems Corp. (supplier of integrated plant floor management software); Quorum Growth Int'l. Ltd. (represents an ally for Canadian high-tech companies to fast track their entry into one of the world's fastest growing markets & gives Asia access to the modern world of information technology); Technology Launch Initiative (provide the catalyst for global commercialization of Canada's promising technologies); Tecsys Inc. (open systems provider of software solutions to value-added distribution operations)

Retrocom Growth Fund Inc.

89 The Queensway West, Suite 400
Mississauga, Ontario L5B 2V2
Canada
(905) 848-2430
Fax: (905) 848-2869
E-mail: retrocom@inforamp.net
Web: www.rgfjobs.com

Key contact:
Mr. Michael Steplock, Chairman/CEO

Description: Our mandate is to create employment by investing in small and medium-sized Canadian businesses (i.e. companies with less than $50 million in assets and 500 employees or less) engaged in communications and fiber optics, high-tech building technologies, conservation and construction, with objective of achieving long-term capital appreciation.

Founded: 1995

Amount under management: $25-100 million

Area served: Ontario, Nova Scotia

Industries:
I.06   Communications
I.09   Construction
I.17   Environmental services/waste management
I.23   Information technology services
I.27   Manufacturing

Sampling of portfolio companies: The Ice Gardens (a multi-rink sports facility); Baylight Development, Inc. (developed the Sunset Point Condominium Project); The Sarnia Entertainment & Sports Centre (4,000-seat main spectator rink, home of the OHL Sarnia Sting); Lauridon Sports Management, Inc. (provides management & consultancy services for recreation, sports & entertainment facilities); St. Lawrence Co-Operative Housing Corp. Condominium Project (12 storey, 95 unit apartment building); The Kings Gate Condominiums (29 unit, 5 storey condominium building); Centrepoint Project (200,000 square feet of retail space); Midland Park Lake ("cluster" condominium, single family homes); The Canada Sports Gardens (14,000 square-foot restaurant with outdoor patio, food kiosks & a pro shop located in a major sports facility); Parliament Square Co-operative (180 condominium units); Bowling Palace (32 bowling lanes along with other family entertainment services including a restaurant, licensed lounge, billiards, a pro shop & soft-play area for children)

Rothschild Quantico Capital

1 First Canadian Place, Suite 3800
P.O. Box 77
Toronto, Ontario M5X 1B1
Canada
(416) 369-9600
Fax: (416) 864-1261
Web: www.quantico.com

Key contact:
Mr. Gregory Milavsky, President/CEO

Description: We seek companies with prospects for growth internally or through acquisition, export or product line expansion. Preferred companies have proven products or services, a defensible competitive position and operate in industries with favourable dynamics.

Area served: Midwest, Northeast United States; Ontario, Western Canada

Preferred stage of financing: Int'l expansion

Industries:
I.11   Consumer products
I.34   Services (business)
I.35   Services (consumer)

RoyNat Inc.

40 King Street West
Scotia Plaza, 26th Floor
Toronto, Ontario M5H 1H1
Canada
(416) 933-2730
Fax: (416) 933-2783
Web: www.roynat.ca

Key contact:
Mr. Earl Lande, Senior Vice President

Description: We are the leading private term lender in Canada specialising in term financing, merchant banking and leasing services for small and medium size businesses. Funds are provided for acquisition of fixed assets, refinancing existing borrowings, working capital, real estate, equipment financing and mergers and acquisitions.

Area served: Canada

Preferred stages of financing: Second stage, LBO/MBO

Industries:
I.06   Communications
I.11   Consumer products
I.12   Distribution
I.14   Electronics
I.19   Generalist
I.29   Medical/medical products

Toronto Dominion Capital

55 King Street West, 8th Floor
Toronto, Ontario M5K 1A2
Canada
(416) 982-6235
Fax: (416) 982-5045

Key contact:
Mr. John MacIntyre, Managing Director

Description: We are a $300 million private equity partnership which is affiliated with Toronto Dominion Bank. We focus on investing in telecommunications and media providers, healthcare servicers, internet services, energy providers and other service businesses. We consider middle stage growth and buyout opportunities and private investments in both private and public companies.

Amount of capital invested: $140 million

Preferred investment size: $5-20 million

Amount under management: $100-500 million

Area served: United States

Preferred stages of financing: Second stage, Mezzanine, LBO/MBO, Expansion

Industries:
I.02   Agriculture/forestry/fishing/mining
I.04   Broadcasting
I.06   Communications
I.10   Consulting
I.12   Distribution
I.15   Energy/natural resources/utilities
I.16   Entertainment
I.20   Healthcare
I.21   High technology
I.23   Information technology services
I.24   Internet services/e-commerce
I.28   Media/publishing
I.29   Medical/medical products
I.30   New media
I.34   Services (business)

Sampling of portfolio companies: American Cellular (rural cellular operator); American Medical Plans (medicaid focused HMO); Charter Communications (cable television operator concentrated in the Southeastern U.S.); Conxus (provider of two-way paging service); Inter-Act (in-store, interactive marketing company providing targeted coupons to customers); Int'l. Wireless Communications, Inc. (wireless communications provider in Southeast Asia & Latin America); Ortho Net (orthopedics specialty HMO); Pathnet, Inc. (facilities-based long distance communications provider); Real Time Data (provider of wireless information services to the vending machine industry); TeleCorp (PCS operator & AT&T affiliate); Teletrac, Inc. (provider of vehicle location & fleet management services); UPC (operator of cable systems in Europe & the Middle East); Western Wireless (cellular communications & PCS provider); Wireless One Network (cellular operator in Southwest Florida); American Radio Systems (diversified broadcast radio group); Anchor Glass Container Corp. (North America manufacturer of glass containers); Cablevision (cable television company); Geotek Communications, Inc. (SMR operator which is implementing a new wireless technology); Hollinger Int'l. Inc. (int'l. diversified media company); Sygnet Wireless (independent cellular operator)

Trillium Growth Capital Inc.

70 University Avenue, Suite 1450
Toronto, Ontario M5J 2M4
Canada
(416) 977-1450
Fax: (416) 977-6764
E-mail: trillium@ccfl.com

Key contact:
Mr. John Y. Hague, President

Preferred stages of financing: Start up, Expansion

Industries:
I.04   Broadcasting
I.06   Communications
I.07   Computer hardware
I.08   Computer software
I.11   Consumer products
I.14   Electronics
I.22   Industrial products
I.25   Leisure/hospitality
I.27   Manufacturing

Sampling of portfolio companies: BCB Holdings Inc. (communications); Builders' Supplies Ltd. (building materials); Beavertails Canada, Inc. (pastery); Can-Ross Environmental Services, Ltd.; Summit Cosmetics (cosmetics); The Wolf Group (advertising); Magnotta Winery (wines)

VenGrowth Funds

145 Wellington Street West
Toronto, Ontario M5J 1H8
Canada
(416) 971-6656
Fax: (416) 971-6519
E-mail: tim@vengrowth.com

Key contact:
Mr. R. Earl Storie, President
Mr. Allen W. Lupyrypa, Managing Director
Mr. Michael S. Cohen, Managing Director
Mr. A. David Ferguson, Managing Director
Mr. Timothy K. Lee, Investment Associate

Description: Over the past 15 years, we have invested more than $120 million in over 60 companies. We focus on more mature later stage companies which have value-added products or services, sustainable competitive advantages and high growth prospects.

Founded: 1982

Preferred investment size: $2-7 million

Amount under management: $100-500 million

Area served: Ontario

Industries:
I.06   Communications
I.07   Computer hardware
I.08   Computer software
I.11   Consumer products
I.14   Electronics
I.15   Energy/natural resources/utilities
I.17   Environmental services/waste management
I.20   Healthcare
I.22   Industrial products
I.27   Manufacturing
I.29   Medical/medical products
I.30   New media

Ventures West Management, Inc.

181 University Avenue, Suite 1002
Toronto, Ontario M5H 3M7
Canada
(416) 861-0700
Fax: (416) 861-0866

Key contact:
Mr. Mark H. Leonard, Vice President

Description: With over $200 million under management in several technology funds, our investment emphasis is on early stage companies in Canada which have the management and product potential to become world leaders in their markets. Our investment experience in knowledge based companies spans a total of over 100 different firms.

Preferred investment size: Over $1 million

Area served: Canada

Preferred stages of financing: Seed, Start up, First stage

Industries:
I.03   Biotech/genetic engineering
I.06   Communications
I.07   Computer hardware
I.08   Computer software
I.14   Electronics
I.15   Energy/natural resources/utilities
I.17   Environmental services/waste management
I.22   Industrial products
I.29   Medical/medical products

Sampling of portfolio companies: Dees Communications; Ballard Energy & Environmental; The PSC Group; Insystems Technologies; NCompass; Novatel Spectrum

Working Ventures Canadian Fund, Inc.

250 Bloor Street East, Suite 1600
Toronto, Ontario M4W 1E6
Canada
(416) 922-5479
(800) 463-1652
Fax: (416) 929-4390
E-mail: wvid@workingventures.ca
Web: www.workingventures.ca

Key contact:
Mr. Ron Begg, President
Mr. Jim Hall, Senior Vice President-Investments
Mr. Bill Danis, Vice President-Investments
Mr. Jim Whitaker, Vice President-Investments

148 York Street, Suite 202
London, Ontario N6A 1A9
Canada
(519) 645-2120
Fax: (519) 645-3051
Web: www.workingventures.ca

Key contact:
Mr. Richard Jankura

Nine Antares Drive
Nepean, Ontario K2E 7V5
Canada
(613) 225-4775
Fax: (613) 225-4508
E-mail: bwright@workingventures.ca
Web: www.workingventures.ca

Key contact:
Ms. A. Bonnie Wright, Branch Manager

Description: A broadly diversified portfolio of investment in small and medium sized businesses. Our goal is long term capital appreciation for our shareholders. As a result, and providing we do our job well, benefits will accrue to the Canadian economy in terms of job creation, exports and investment in research and development as by-products of successful investment in small and medium sized Canadian businesses.

Founded: 1990

Preferred investment size: $1-7 million

Amount under management: $500 million -1 billion

Area served: Canada

Industries:
I.03   Biotech/genetic engineering
I.06   Communications
I.07   Computer hardware
I.08   Computer software
I.11   Consumer products
I.14   Electronics
I.15   Energy/natural resources/utilities
I.27   Manufacturing
I.29   Medical/medical products
I.36   Transportation

Sampling of portfolio companies: Accelerix Inc. (a fabless semiconductor company involved in the design, manufacture & sale of application specific memory "systems-on-a-chip" products for the PC marketplace); Angoss Software Corp. (provides a family of client/server solutions for decision support, business intelligence & data mining); Base4 Bioinformatics (discipline of employing computer technology to analyze & understand biological information); Certicom Corp., operating as MOBIUS Encryption Technologies (developer & vendor of information security products & services, including hardware & software products, systems integration & cryptographic consulting); DataMirror Corp. (provider of software that moves & transforms data across various hardware & database platforms for analysis & decision support); EDI Communications Networking Inc. (owns & operates a nat'l. data communications network specializing in packet switching technology that enables users to communicate data via intranets connecting multiple locations); Fireworks Entertainment Inc. (engaged in the distribution, production & financing of film & television program); Genesis Microchip Inc. (fabless semiconductor company which specializes in the development & marketing of proprietary, real-time video/image digital signal processing integrated circuits which are used by original equipment manufacturers to scale, resize & de-interlace video images); Hamilton-Douglas Industries Ltd. (operates two subsidiaries Atlantic Reman Ltd. & MFM Industries Ltd.); Imutec Pharma Inc. (biopharmaceutical company engaged in the research, development & commercialization of therapeutic products to treat cancer & other diseases associated with immune system disorders); Jones Packaging Inc. (designs, develops, manufactures & distributes packaging materials that service the pharmaceutical, confectionery, food & healthcare industries); Linmor Technologies Inc. (developer & supplier of network management solutions for multi-vendor, multi-user & high-speed networks); MGI Software Corp. (develops, markets & supports innovative software products in photo & video software markets); Nuvo Network Management Inc. (provides asset management technologies designed to manage PC assets in medium to large-sized corporations); PEI Capital Inc. (community venture capital fund); Research in Motion Inc. (a private Canadian technology company in the emerging market for wireless data communications); SLM Software Inc. (provides transaction management & e-commerce software solutions, primarily to the banking industry); Trentway-Wagar Properties Inc. (provides bus services, concentrating on intercity bus runs, charters, school busing & contracted municipal transit); Virtek Vision Int'l. Inc. (developer & worldwide supplier of machine vision 3-D laser projection technology & machine intelligence systems, principally to the leather goods, aerospace & housing construction industries); Willows Golf & Country Club (golf & recreation complex located strategically at the centre of Western Canada)

Quebec

Accés Capital

1981, avenue McGill College, 9th Floor
Montreal, Quebec H3A 3C7
Canada
(514) 847-5454
Fax: (514) 847-5978
E-mail: accescapital@lacaisse.com
Web: accescapital.lacaisse.com

Key contact:
Mr. Paul Juneau, President
Mr. Pierre-Andre Pomerleau, Director
Mr. Michel Paquette, Assistant Director

Description: We offer capital to companies in all
regions through a variety of financial instruments.
With 11 investment companies at work and capital of
over $90 million, our network is a vital element for
growing companies throughout Québec.

Preferred investment size: $50,000-750,000

Amount under management: <$10 million

Area served: Canada

Preferred stages of financing: Start up, Expansion

Industries:
I.11   Consumer products
I.12   Distribution
I.15   Energy/natural resources/utilities
I.17   Environmental services/waste management
I.18   Financial services
I.19   Generalist
I.22   Industrial products
I.36   Transportation

Argo Global Capital, Inc.

1000 de la Gauchetiere Street West, Suite 2500
Montreal, Quebec H3B 4W5
Canada
(514) 397-8444
Fax: (514) 397-8445
Web: www.gsmcapital.com

Key contact:
Mr. Alan MacIntosh, Vice President/Partner

Description: We are a $137 million fund focused on
investments in wireless technology. One third of the
capital was provided by nine of the world's leading
wireless carriers. Investments are made in companies
located anywhere in the world and at any stage of
their development.

Preferred investment size: $5 million

Amount under management: $100-500 million

Area served: Worldwide

Preferred stages of financing: Start up, First stage,
Second stage, Mezzanine, LBO/MBO, Expansion, Int'l
expansion

Industries:
I.06   Communications

Sampling of portfolio companies: Novatel Wireless
(wireless modem technology); LGC Wireless
(wireless in-building signal distribution)

BCE Capital, Inc.

1000 rue de La Gauchetiere Ouest
Suite 3700
Montreal, Quebec H3B 4Y7
Canada
(514) 397-7171
Fax: (514) 397-7392
E-mail: mboychuk@sympatico.ca
Web: www.bcecapital.com

Key contact:
Mr. Michael Boychuk, President/CEO
Mr. Paul Cataford, Vice President-Investments
Mr. David McCarthy, Director-Ottawa Operations

Description: Our objective is to generate above-
average rates of return through direct investment in
small-to-medium size businesses founded on proprietary telecommunications technology. Typically,
investments focus on hardware and software products. We are seeking to invest in well-managed
companies with a sustainable product advantage in
high growth areas of the telecommunications sector.

Amount of capital invested: $10 million

Preferred investment size: $2-2.5 million

Amount under management: $100-500 million

Area served: North America

Preferred stages of financing: Start up, First stage

Industries:
I.06   Communications
I.07   Computer hardware
I.08   Computer software
I.21   High technology
I.24   Internet services/e-commerce
I.30   New media

Sampling of portfolio companies: Plaintree Systems
(ethernet & giga-bit ethernet switches); Faneuil ISG
(precision integrated target marketing & call centre
operations); Switchview (management software for
PBX systems); E/O Networks (fibre loop access
products for low population density areas); SSiG
Group (remote sensing value-added information
services); MediaLight (high speed modem devices for
internet & work at home); The Bulldog Group (multimedia database management software); RMX Technologies (graphics software for internet); Sierra
Wireless (wide area wireless data modems); Impath
Networks (video multiplexing solutions for intelligent traffic systems & security monitoring)

Business Development Bank of Canada

5 Place Ville Marie, Suite 600
Montreal, Quebec H3B 5E7
Canada
(514) 283-8030
Fax: (514) 283-7675
E-mail: michel.re@bdc.x400.gc.ca
Web: www.bdc.ca

Key contact:
Mr. Michel Re, Vice President

Description: We invest in small businesses that show growth potential in specific markets. The investment structure is determined by the needs and the development stage of the company and can include straight equity options, warrants and debentures. We strongly believe in co-investing with other venture capital funds. This increases the range of financing and of management support skills.

Founded: 1983

Preferred investment size: $1-5 million

Area served: Canada

Preferred stages of financing: Start up, First stage, Second stage, Mezzanine, LBO/MBO, Expansion

Industries:
I.21   High technology

Capimont Inc.

393 Saint-Jacques Street, Suite 258
Montreal, Quebec H2Y 1N9
Canada
(514) 281-0903
Fax: (514) 281-0906
E-mail: capimont@cam.org
Web: www.cam.org/~capimont

Key contact:
Mr. Hubert d'Amours, President
Mr. Roger Fafard, Vice President

Description: We look for situations where we can be an active investor giving small businesses not only financial but also managerial support by providing assistance in monitoring files. We generally favour minority participation in the capital stock of companies. This participation can also be in the form of preferred shares, convertible and equity debentures and equity loans.

Amount of capital invested: $2,453,300

Preferred investment size: $500,000

Amount under management: <$10 million

Area served: North America

Preferred stages of financing: Second stage, Expansion, Int'l expansion

Sampling of portfolio companies: Domotique Secant Inc. (home automation); Les Aliments Leika Inc. (herbal teas, teas & coffees); Silonex Inc. (optoelectronic components); Micro-Électronic CeraTel Inc. (printed circuit board assemblies, complex multilayer & photoengravable products); Bioma Recherche Inc. (medical equipment); Ceres Int'l. Inc. (educational videos); Groupe Covitec Inc. (technical services, equipments renting & shooting teams); Roctest Inc. (geotechnical & structural instrumentation); Touchnet Canada Inc. (electronic self-service counter); Productions Pascal Blais (animation images for cinema, tv & publicity); Kromafibre Inc. (fibre-optic filters utilized in telecommunication); Formulex Canada Inc. (manufacturer of pharmaceutical & natural products); DocImage (software developer of document imaging system); Specialty Sensor Technologies Inc. (manufacturer of sensors for the alarm, security & residential markets)

Capital CDPQ

1981, avenue McGill College, 9th Floor
Montreal, Quebec H3A 3C7
Canada
(514) 847-2611
Fax: (514) 847-2383
Web: capcdpq.lacaisse.com

Key contact:
Mr. Paul Juneau, President
Mr. Charles Cazabon, Director
Mr. Vincent Cerone, Manager
Mr. Gilles Genest, Manager
Mr. Michel Lefebvre, Manager
Mr. Daniel Scheider, Manager
Ms. Louise Theoret, Manager

Mr. Alain Tremblay, Manager
Mr. Jacques Tremblay, Manager

Description: We can provide the financial support needed to launch profitable projects and as a partner, assist in various stages of development. Through our investments of up to $1 million, we seek to promote the growth of profitable companies for the benefit of their shareholders, while contributing to the vitality of Quebec's economy.

Amount under management: $25-100 million

Industries:
I.19   Generalist

Capital Monteregie Inc.

1550 Ampére Street, Suite 300
Boucherville, Quebec J4B 7L4
Canada
(514) 449-2009
Fax: (514) 449-6472
E-mail: srimntrg@total.net

Key contact:
Mr. Jean Matteau, Associate

Description: When we were created, we were given a mandate to invest in businesses in the start-up phase, in the initial stages of development, growth businesses or in exceptional cases, businesses needing final-stage financing. These investments are made with the goal of realizing, with a five to eight year horizon, a superior rate of return on risk capital and contributing to the economic development of the Montérégie area.

Founded: 1993

Preferred investment size: $350,000 (manufacturing); $500,000 (high tech)

Area served: Quebec

Preferred stages of financing: Start up, First stage, Second stage

Industries:
I.06   Communications
I.23   Information technology services
I.27   Manufacturing

Fonds de Developpement Emploi-Montreal Inc.

5703 Sherbrooke Street East, Suite 100
Montreal, Quebec H1N 3M1
Canada
(514) 253-4667
Fax: (514) 253-5128

Key contact:
Mr. Guy Marion, Director General

Description: Our mission is the economic development of Montréal neighborhoods through investments in viable and profitable businesses that have a structural effect on the community and an impact on creating or preserving jobs.

Preferred investment size: $50,000-100,000

Area served: Montreal

Preferred stage of financing: Start up

Industries:
I.17   Environmental services/waste management
I.23   Information technology services
I.27   Manufacturing

Fonds de Solidarite des Travailleurs du Quebec (F.T.Q.)

8717 Berri Street
Montreal, Quebec H2M 2T9
Canada
(514) 383-8383
Fax: (514) 383-2506
Web: www.fondsftq.com

Key contact:
Mr. Richard Bourget, Senior Vice President
Mr. Luc Charron, Vice President
Mr. Roger Giraldeau, Vice President
Mr. Daniel Laporte, Vice President
Mr. Yves Lamarre, Vice President

Description: We are a development capital fund which relies on the savings and support of our members and the Quebec population as a whole to meet the following objectives: to help create and maintain jobs in Quebec by investing in small businesses, to strengthen Quebec's competitive position, to support business development, and to provide workers with economic training.

Founded: 1983

Area served: Quebec

Preferred stages of financing: First stage, Second stage

Industries:
I.19   Generalist

Fonds Regional de Solidarité Gaspésie-Iles-de-la-Madeleine

185 York East Boulevard
P.O. Box 1810
Gaspe, Quebec G0C 1R0
Canada
(418) 368-7346
Fax: (418) 368-4028

Key contact:
Mr. Marc Cayouette, Director General

Description: A limited partnership established in May 1996 with the mission to bring to fruition profitable, sustainable and economically stimulating projects that help create or maintain jobs in the Gaspe and the Magdalen Islands.

Founded: 1996

Preferred investment size: $500,000

Area served: Quebec, in the region of Gaspésie & Ile-de-la-Madelaine

Preferred stages of financing: Seed, Start up, First stage, Second stage, Mezzanine

Industries:
I.02   Agriculture/forestry/fishing/mining
I.03   Biotech/genetic engineering
I.23   Information technology services
I.27   Manufacturing

Fonds Regional de Solidarite Laval

3030, Le Carrefour Boulevard, Suite 1003
Laval, Quebec H7T 2P5
Canada
(514) 978-3344
Fax: (514) 978-3313
E-mail: info@lav.fondsreg.com
Web: www.fondsreg.com

Key contact:
Mr. Guymond Fortin, Director General

Description: Our mission is to invest in business and provide technical support to create, preserve or safeguard local jobs. Through our strategic investments in sectorial and regional development, we stimulate the economy and promote the development of local businesses.

Preferred investment size: $50,000-500,000

Area served: Laval, Quebec

Preferred stages of financing: Seed, Start up

Industries:
I.02   Agriculture/forestry/fishing/mining
I.06   Communications
I.17   Environmental services/waste management
I.23   Information technology services
I.27   Manufacturing
I.37   Wholesale

Le Fonds Regional de Solidarite Chaudiere-Appalaches

5790 Etienne-Dallaire Boulevard, Suite 102
Levis, Quebec G6V 8V6
Canada
(418) 837-1040
Fax: (418) 837-3093

Key contact:
Mr. Rene Bastarache, Director General

Description: Our mission is to invest as a financial partner in businesses in the manufacturing and propulsive industry sector, to create and maintain stable, well-paying and lasting jobs in the Chaudiere-Appalachians region.

Preferred investment size: $50,000-500,000

Area served: Quebec

Preferred stages of financing: First stage, Second stage

Industries:
I.02   Agriculture/forestry/fishing/mining
I.12   Distribution
I.25   Leisure/hospitality
I.27   Manufacturing

Fonds Regional de Solidarité Ile-de-Montréal

255 Saint-Jacques Street, 3rd Floor
Montreal, Quebec H2Y 1M6
Canada
(514) 845-3233
Fax: (514) 845-0625
E-mail: dblanchard@mtl.fondsreg.com
Web: www.mtl.fondsreg.com

Key contact:
Ms. Danielle Blanchard, Managing Director

Description: We invest in companies usually small or start-ups that will realize a project on the Island of Montreal. Those are generally high-tech companies that will export all around the world.

Amount of capital invested: $2,635,000

Preferred investment size: $250,000

Amount under management: $10-25 million

Area served: Canada

Preferred stages of financing: Seed, Start up, First stage, Second stage, LBO/MBO, Expansion, Int'l expansion

Industries:
I.03   Biotech/genetic engineering
I.05   Chemicals
I.06   Communications
I.07   Computer hardware
I.08   Computer software
I.14   Electronics
I.16   Entertainment
I.17   Environmental services/waste management
I.20   Healthcare
I.21   High technology
I.23   Information technology services
I.24   Internet services/e-commerce
I.26   Life sciences
I.29   Medical/medical products
I.30   New media

Sampling of portfolio companies: Stores de bois Montréal inc.; Les Laminés CTEK inc.; Les fumoirs HJS; Signifi.vGR; Cowan Dynamics inc.; Les Productions Prisma inc.; Optima Spécialités Chimiques et Technologie inc.; Les logiciels Govern inc./Govern Softwares inc.; RD6 inc.; Les expertises environnementales Soconag inc.

Fonds Regional de Solidarite Abitibi-Temiscamingue

139, Quebec Boulevard, Suite 101
Rouyn-Noranda, Quebec J9X 6M8
Canada

(819) 762-7422
Fax: (819) 762-8335
E-mail: frsat@sympatico.ca

Key contact:
Mr. André Savar, Director General
Mr. Ghyslain Blanchet, Financial Consultant
Mr. Martin Russel, Financial Analyst

Description: Venutre capital fund with a mission to promote the preservation and creation of jobs, stimulate the local economy and become a partner in the first instance by investing in new businesses, growth businesses, recovering businesses and businesses involved in acquisitions or mergers.

Preferred investment size: $50,000-500,000

Area served: Abitibi-Témiscamingue (Quebec)

Preferred stages of financing: Start up, First stage, LBO/MBO, Expansion

Industries:
I.02   Agriculture/forestry/fishing/mining
I.06   Communications
I.09   Construction
I.13   Education
I.17   Environmental services/waste management
I.20   Healthcare
I.23   Information technology services
I.27   Manufacturing

Fonds Regional de Solidarite Estrie
2100 King Street West, Suite 140
Sherbrooke, Quebec J1L 2E8
Canada
(819) 829-2220
Fax: (819) 829-2263
E-mail: fondsreg-estrie@sympatico.ca

Key contact:
Mr. Luc Pinard, Director General

Description: We complement the traditional financing tools offered by financial institutions and government agencies. Our modes of intervention are

flexible and include equity investment (common or preferred stock), equity loans or any other tool adapted to the needs of your project.

Preferred investment size: $50,000-500,000

Area served: Quebec

Preferred stages of financing: First stage, Second stage

Industries:
I.17   Environmental services/waste management
I.20   Healthcare
I.22   Industrial products
I.23   Information technology services
I.27   Manufacturing

Fonds Regional de Solidarite Monteregie
923, Du Seminaire Boulevard North
Suite 109
Ste. Jean-Sur-Richelieu, Quebec J3A 1B6
Canada
(514) 359-3776
Fax: (514) 359-3363

Key contact:
Mr. Paul-Henri Gagnon, Director General
Mr. Alain Tremblay, Investment Counsellor

Description: We are a development capital fund with $6 million in initial capital. Our mission is to invest sums of $50,000-500,000, as a financial partner, in

manufacturing and propulsive service industries in order to create and preserve stable, well-paying, long-term jobs in the Montérégie area.

Preferred investment size: $50,000-500,000

Area served: Monteregie, Quebec

Preferred stages of financing: Start up, First stage

Industries:
I.02   Agriculture/forestry/fishing/mining
I.27   Manufacturing

Gestion Estrie Capital Inc.
2100, King Street Ouest
Sherbrooke, Quebec J1J 2E8
Canada
(819) 822-4244
Fax: (819) 822-2827

Key contact:
Mr. Mario Beaudoin, Director General

Description: Quebec based formal venture capital firm serving the manufacturing sector of Quebec.

Founded: 1988

Preferred investment size: $50,000-1 million

Area served: Quebec

Preferred stages of financing: Mezzanine, LBO/MBO

Industries:
I.27   Manufacturing

Investissement Desjardins
P.O. Box Succursale Desjardins
2 Complexe Desjardins, Suite 1717
Montreal, Quebec H5B 1B8
Canada
(514) 281-7131
Fax: (514) 281-7808
Web: desjardins.com/id

Key contact:
Mr. Bruno Riverin, President

Founded: 1988

Area served: Quebec

Industries:
I.06   Communications

I.07	Computer hardware	I.20	Healthcare
I.08	Computer software	I.23	Information technology services

Miralta Capital, Inc.
475 Avenue Dumont
Dorval, Quebec H9S 5W2
Canada
(514) 631-2682
Fax: (514) 631-1257
E-mail: bmee@miralta.com

Key contact:
Mr. Robert Mee
Mr. Christopher J. Winn

Founded: 1992

Preferred investment size: $5 million

Amount under management: $25-100 million

Area served: Canada

Industries:
I.06 Communications
I.07 Computer hardware
I.08 Computer software
I.11 Consumer products
I.14 Electronics
I.18 Financial services
I.22 Industrial products
I.23 Information technology services
I.27 Manufacturing
I.35 Services (consumer)

Novacap Investments, Inc.
375 Boulevard Roland Therrien
Bureau 210
Longueuil, Quebec J4H 4A6
Canada
(514) 651-5000
Fax: (514) 651-7585

Key contact:
Mr. Gordon MacFie
Mr. Marc Beauchamp

Mr. Jean-Pierre Chartrand
Mr. Jacques Foisy
Mr. Marc Paiement

Industries:
I.14 Electronics
I.17 Environmental services/waste management
I.27 Manufacturing
I.29 Medical/medical products

Schroders & Associates Canada Inc.
1155 Boulevard Rene Levesque West, Suite 2705
Montreal, Quebec H3B 2K8
Canada
(514) 397-0700
Fax: (514) 861-2495
E-mail: schrodersassocies@sympatico.ca
Web: schroders.ca

Key contact:
Mr. Paul Echenberg, President/CEO
Ms. Cecile Ducharme, Vice President

Description: We act as an advisor to 2 management
buy-out funds investing primarily in Canada. We are
affiliated to Schroder Ventures, an international
network consisting of 25 MBO-VC funds in 10 countries with over $3.5 billion under management.

Amount of capital invested: $35 million

Preferred investment size: $10-15 million

Amount under management: $100-500 million

Area served: North America

Preferred stages of financing: Second stage, LBO/
MBO, Expansion, Int'l expansion

Industries:
I.04 Broadcasting
I.05 Chemicals
I.06 Communications
I.11 Consumer products
I.12 Distribution
I.16 Entertainment
I.17 Environmental services/waste management
I.19 Generalist
I.22 Industrial products
I.23 Information technology services
I.25 Leisure/hospitality
I.27 Manufacturing
I.28 Media/publishing
I.29 Medical/medical products
I.32 Retail
I.33 Semiconductors
I.37 Wholesale

Sampling of portfolio companies: A&W Food Services
(chain of hamburger restaurants); Nova Pb Inc. (lead-
acid battery recycler); Huntingdon Mills (manufacturer of fleece & pile fabrics); GBA Industrial
Equipment (manufacturer of industrial equipment for
the sawmill, paper mill & aluminum industry)

Sofinov, Societe financiere d'innovation Inc.
1981 McGill College Avenue, 7th Floor
Montreal, Quebec H3A 3C7
Canada
(514) 847-2613
Fax: (514) 847-2628
Web: sofinov.lacaisse.com

Key contact:
Mr. Denis Dionne, President
Mr. Claude Miron, Vice President
Mr. Pierre Pharand, Vice President
Mr. Marcel Paquette, Vice President

Description: We are an affiliate of the Caisse de dépôt et placement du Québec, offering strategic financing to technologically innovative companies in the biotechnology, health, information technology and industrial technology sectors. We seek to support the growth of small and medium-sized businesses and to contribute to the province's economic vitality.

Area served: Asia, Canada, Europe, United States

Preferred stages of financing: Seed, Start up, First stage, Second stage, Mezzanine

Industries:
I.03   Biotech/genetic engineering
I.14   Electronics
I.17   Environmental services/waste management
I.20   Healthcare
I.23   Information technology services

Speirs Consultants, Inc.

365 Stanstead
Montreal, Quebec H3R 1X5
Canada
(514) 342-3858
Fax: (514) 342-1977

Key contact:
Mr. Derck Speirs, President

Description: Assists companies find financing. Consulting in finance & general management investing.

Amount under management: <$10 million

Area served: North America

Preferred stages of financing: First stage, Second stage, Mezzanine, LBO/MBO, Expansion, Int'l expansion

Industries:
I.01   Aerospace
I.02   Agriculture/forestry/fishing/mining
I.03   Biotech/genetic engineering
I.04   Broadcasting
I.05   Chemicals
I.06   Communications
I.07   Computer hardware
I.08   Computer software
I.09   Construction
I.10   Consulting
I.11   Consumer products
I.12   Distribution
I.13   Education
I.14   Electronics
I.15   Energy/natural resources/utilities
I.16   Entertainment
I.17   Environmental services/waste management
I.18   Financial services
I.19   Generalist
I.20   Healthcare
I.21   High technology
I.22   Industrial products
I.23   Information technology services
I.24   Internet services/e-commerce
I.25   Leisure/hospitality
I.26   Life sciences
I.27   Manufacturing
I.28   Media/publishing
I.29   Medical/medical products
I.30   New media
I.31   Real estate
I.32   Retail
I.33   Semiconductors
I.34   Services (business)
I.35   Services (consumer)
I.36   Transportation
I.37   Wholesale

Technocap Inc.

4028 Marlowe
Montreal, Quebec H4A 3M2
Canada
(514) 387-1981
Fax: (514) 387-2164
E-mail: mmorency@technocap.com
Web: www.technocap.com

Key contact:
Mr. Martin Morency, Director Business Development
Mr. Richard Prytula, President

Description: We are a private venture company that invests in technology companies and the Net. Our committed capital is $100 million. We have invested over $30 million in twelve companies involved with the Net in enterprise software, web software, networking, semiconductors and telecommunications. Our investments enable total financing of over $60 million and 280 jobs in ten cities.

Amount of capital invested: $10 million

Preferred investment size: $2 million

Amount under management: $100-500 million

Area served: North America

Preferred stages of financing: Seed, Start up, First stage, Second stage, LBO/MBO, Expansion

Industries:
I.06   Communications
I.07   Computer hardware
I.08   Computer software
I.21   High technology
I.33   Semiconductors

Sampling of portfolio companies: Absolu (payphones with intranet servers); Bestseller (multimedia library software); Enterprise (supply chain framework); FreeBalance (year 2000 public sector groupware); Fuseworks (web application framework); GlobalMedic (intranet healthware); Hyperchip (massively parallel semi-conductors); iClassified (voice classifieds platform); NetCorp (voice & video IP switches); OriginalSim (aerospace simulation framework); SatCorp (satellite & wireless telephony); ShowBase (web infobases & infomining)

Telsoft Ventures Inc.
1000 de la Gauchetière Street West
25th Floor
Montreal, Quebec H3B 4W5
Canada
(514) 397-8450
Fax: (514) 397-8451
E-mail: rtalbot@telventures.com
Web: www.telventures.com

Key contact:
Mr. Robert Talbot, President
Mr. François Gaouette, Vice President
Mr. Benoit Hogue, Vice President
Mr. Jean Mayrand, Vice President
Mr. Daniel Lambert, Vice President
Ms. Josee Dumais, Director-Financial Services
Mr. Benoit Beaudry, Analyst-Technology

Description: Since our creation in 1995, we have become the premier source of smart money to Canada's growing software industries. With subscribed capital of $78 million, we are Canada's largest venture-capital fund devoted to the software industry. Our founder sponsors are Telesystem Group and DMR Amdah!

Founded: 1995

Preferred investment size: $1-2 million

Area served: Canada

Industries:
I.08   Computer software
I.23   Information technology services

Sampling of portfolio companies: Focus Automation Systems Inc.; Minacom Int'l., Inc.; Nova Expertise Solutions (1998) Inc.; ObjectQuest Corp.; Raymark Xpert Business Systems Ltd.; Sapling Corp.; Sylvain Faust Inc.; The MEI Group; Virtual Integration Technology

Saskatchewan

The Agri-Food Equity Fund
202 - 3085 Albert Street
Regina, Saskatchewan S4S 0B1
Canada
(306) 787-2346
Fax: (306) 787-0852
E-mail: gconacher@agr.gov.sk.ca
Web: www.agr.gov.sk.ca/afef/index.htm

Key contact:
Mr. Carl Neggers, Executive Director
Mr. Gavin Conacher, Branch Manager

Box 660, 311 Main Street
Humboldt, Saskatchewan S0K 2A0
Canada
(306) 682-6717
Fax: (306) 682-4711
Web: www.agr.gov.sk.ca/afef/index.htm

109-111 Research Drive (Atrium Building)
Saskatoon, Saskatchewan S7N 3R2
Canada
(306) 933-7652
Fax: (306) 933-7668

Key contact:
Mr. Ron Monette, Branch Manager

350 Cheadle Street West
Swift Current, Saskatchewan S9H 4Y7
Canada
(306) 778-8673
Fax: (306) 778-8459

Description: We invest in, promote, and provide information to agri-business enterprises whose activities compliment agriculture in Saskatchewan. We are interested in start-ups and expansions in agri-business companies whose strong management team and markets (market potential) collectively provide good financial returns.

Founded: 1994

Amount of capital invested: $7 million

Preferred investment size: $500,000

Amount under management: $10-25 million

Area served: North America

Preferred stages of financing: Start up, First stage, Expansion

Industries:
I.02   Agriculture/forestry/fishing/mining
I.03   Biotech/genetic engineering
I.05   Chemicals
I.11   Consumer products
I.12   Distribution
I.22   Industrial products
I.27   Manufacturing
I.36   Transportation

Sampling of portfolio companies: TML Foods (meat processing/marketing); Canadian Select Grains (chick pea splitting/processing/marketing); EXL Milling (by-pass protein from canola); Northern Genetics Ltd. (elk genetics services); Schnieders Popcorn (snack foods); Randolf & James Flaxmilling (organic flax processing); Popowich Milling Ltd. (oat milling/processing/retail ready); LLD Care Ltd. (organic deodorants); Melville Seed Ltd. (full feed ration pelleting); Rinkles Ltd. (snack food); Big Quill Resources (phosphate fertilizers); Batco Manufacturing (specialty grain handling equipment)

Saskatchewan Government Growth Fund
1201 - 1801 Hamilton Street
Regina, Saskatchewan S4P 4B4
Canada

(306) 787-2994
Fax: (306) 787-2086

Key contact:
Mr. Gary K. Benson, President
Mr. Rob Duguid, Vice President

Description: Government administered venture capital fund founded in 1989 to serve Saskatchewan businesses in the manufacturing, tourism, IT and mining sectors.

Founded: 1989

Preferred investment size: $1-3 million

Area served: Saskatchewan

Industries:
I.02   Agriculture/forestry/fishing/mining
I.23   Information technology services
I.27   Manufacturing

Ventures West Management, Inc.
410 - 22nd Street East, Suite 880
Saskatoon, Saskatchewan S7K 5T6
Canada
(306) 653-8887
Fax: (306) 653-8886

Key contact:
Mr. Terry Grieve, Vice President

Description: With over $200 million under management in several technology funds, our investment emphasis is on early stage companies in Canada which have the management and product potential to become world leaders in their markets. Our investment experience in knowledge based companies spans a total of over 100 different firms.

Preferred investment size: Over $1 million

Area served: Canada

Preferred stages of financing: Seed, Start up, First stage

Industries:
I.03   Biotech/genetic engineering
I.06   Communications
I.07   Computer hardware
I.08   Computer software
I.14   Electronics
I.15   Energy/natural resources/utilities
I.17   Environmental services/waste management
I.22   Industrial products
I.29   Medical/medical products

Sampling of portfolio companies: Dees Communications; Ballard Energy & Environmental; The PSC Group; Insystems Technologies; NCompass; Novatel Spectrum

---

Working Ventures Canadian Fund, Inc.
830-410 22nd Street East
Saskatoon, Saskatchewan S7K 5T6
Canada
(306) 242-1023
Fax: (306) 242-9959
E-mail: bmunro@workingventures.ca
Web: www.workingventures.ca

Key contact:
Mr. Brad Munro, Branch Manager

Description: A broadly diversified portfolio of investment in small and medium sized businesses. Our goal is long term capital appreciation for our shareholders. As a result, and providing we do our job well, benefits will accrue to the Canadian economy in terms of job creation, exports and investment in research and development as by-products of successful investment in small and medium sized Canadian businesses.

Founded: 1990

Preferred investment size: $1-7 million

Amount under management: $500 million -1 billion

Area served: Canada

Industries:
I.03   Biotech/genetic engineering
I.06   Communications
I.07   Computer hardware
I.08   Computer software
I.11   Consumer products
I.12   Distribution
I.14   Electronics
I.27   Manufacturing
I.29   Medical/medical products
I.36   Transportation

Sampling of portfolio companies: Advanced Car Specialties Ltd. (manufactures specialized exhaust systems for two & four cycle engine applications as well as a large variety of metal fabricated accessories for non-automotive vehicles); A.R.M. Group Inc. (e-commerce solutions provider offering software products for inventory sharing & for electronic purchasing of maintenance, repair & overhaul supplies); Canadian Crude Separators Inc. (provides the oil & gas industry in Alberta & Saskatchewan with a wide range of essential environmental services); CF Hospitality Inc. (owns & operates Super 8 Motels); DC DiagnostiCare Inc. (provider of x-ray, ultrasound, mammography, nuclear medicine & other imaging procedures); Envoy Communications Group Inc. (full-service marketing communications agency that develops & implements integrated communications campaigns for nat'l. & regional clients throughout North America); Gallop & Gallop Advertising Inc. (media company providing customer services to local & nat'l. advertising clients through company-owned billboards, bus shelter advertising panels, airport posters, theater posters & by operating transit vehicle franchises in several major cities); Gest-Accor Inc. (provides wholesale finance services for manufacturers & independent electronics, appliance & furniture retailers across Canada); Indigo! Books & Music Inc. (book & music retailer); Karo Inc. (marketing, design & communication firm developing creative solutions for their clients' products, services & brands); Lower Lakes Towing Ltd. (shipping company); Med-Chem Health Care Ltd. (medical laboratory serving physicians, hospitals, nursing & retirement homes & other laboratories); Mimetix Inc. (pharmaceutical company focused on therapeutics for women's pain management); Nu-Gro Corp. (producer, marketer of fertilizers & horticultural lawn products for the lawn

& garden professional trades); PERLE Systems Ltd. (produces computer products for the network communication industry which facilitate data communication between computers within the same network & between networks); Resolution Pharmaceuticals Inc. (dedicated to research, development & commercialization of radiopharmaceutical compounds); Scintrex Ltd. (developer & manufacturer of scientific instrumentation for the earth science, security, environmental & nuclear energy markets); SoftQuad Int'l. Inc. (vendor of electronic publishing products for use on the internet); Trillium Valley Fish Farms (a trout fish farm operation in the Canadian aquaculture industry); Versus Technologies Inc. (develops electronic trading software & operates as a broker for institutional & retail trading over its proprietary trading network)

MEXICO

Mexico

Advent International

Campos Eliseos 345-4o Piso
Colonia Polanco
Mexico City, Mexico D.F. 11560
Mexico
52 5 202 6770
Fax: 52 5 202 7707
Web: www.adventinternational.com

Key contact:
Mr. Juan Carlos Torres, Director
Mr. Alfredo Alfaro, Director

Description: We are one of the world's largest private equity investment firms, with $3 billion under management and more than 90 professionals in Europe, North America, Asia and Latin America. Our goal is to invest in attractive, growth-oriented companies on a global basis and to provide management teams with the support needed to build businesses of significant value. Through funds managed for both corporate and institutional investors, we are able to invest in companies at all stages of development and in virtually any industry.

Founded: 1984

Amount of capital invested: $250 million

Preferred investment size: Over $5 million

Amount under management: >$1 billion

Area served: Asia, Latin America, Central Europe, United States

Preferred stages of financing: LBO/MBO, Expansion

Industries:
I.03   Biotech/genetic engineering
I.04   Broadcasting
I.05   Chemicals
I.06   Communications
I.08   Computer software
I.11   Consumer products
I.14   Electronics
I.15   Energy/natural resources/utilities
I.18   Financial services
I.20   Healthcare
I.22   Industrial products
I.23   Information technology services
I.27   Manufacturing
I.28   Media/publishing
I.29   Medical/medical products
I.32   Retail

Sampling of portfolio companies: Arris Pharmaceutical Corp. (synthetic small-molecule therapeutics); Ribozyme Pharmaceuticals Inc. (human therapeutics based on ribozymes); Malaysia Steel Works (KL) Sdn. Bhd. (steel bars & rods); Kabelmedia Holding GmbH (cable television); Ching Kuang Chemical Co. (copper-clad laminates); Optical Coating Laboratory Inc. (optical thin-film coated products); Esat Telecom Group PLC (long-distance telecommunications & cellular carrier); Valdor Fiber Optics Inc. (fiber-optic connectors); Latinamericana Duty Free SA de CV (operator of duty-free stores); Vision Express Group Ltd. (superstores offering one-hour optical services); Inframetrics Inc. (thermography systems & thermal imagers); Venture Manufacturing (contract manufacturer of electronic components); Bolder Technologies Corp. (rechargeable sealed lead-acid batteries); Euronet Services Inc. (operator of ATM network in Central Europe); Gaymer Group Europe Ltd. (light alcoholic drinks); Star Foods Polska Sp. z o.o. (snack foods); Curaflex Health Services Inc. (home infusion products & services); Aviron Inc. (recombinant viral vaccines); CV Therapeutics Inc. (discovery & development of cardiovascular drugs); Exelixis Pharmaceuticals Inc. (genomics based on model organisms)

Baring Private Equity Partners, Ltd.

Paseo de la Reforma 509, 7th Floor
Colonia Cuauhtemoc
Mexico City, Mexico 00500
Mexico
52 5 286 5284
Fax: 52 5 286 3396

Key contact:
Mr. Victor Serrato

Preferred stages of financing: First stage, Second stage, Mezzanine

Industries:
I.06   Communications
I.12   Distribution
I.14   Electronics
I.22   Industrial products
I.28   Media/publishing
I.29   Medical/medical products

Ventana Global, Ltd.

Paseo de Los Tamarindos, 400-B, Piso 10
Bosques de Las Lomas
Mexico City, Mexico CP-05120
Mexico
52 5 258 0176
Fax: 52 5 258 0176
E-mail: cderivas@ventanaglobal.com
Web: www.ventanaglobal.com

Key contact:
Mr. Carlos de Rivas

Description: Since our beginning, we have sponsored six private growth partnerships totaling over $180 million in funds under management. With a historical focus concentrated on technology investment in the electronics, medical, biotechnology and environmental sectors, the firm has made a total of 71 investments to date. These investments provide immediate access to a collective base of over 200 world class scientists, engineers, physicians and researchers who work with the portfolio companies of our 6 funds.

Founded: 1984

Amount of capital invested: $4.5 million

Preferred investment size: $1 million

Amount under management: $100-500 million

Area served: South/Central America, United States

Preferred stages of financing: Start up, First stage

Industries:
I.01   Aerospace
I.03   Biotech/genetic engineering
I.05   Chemicals
I.06   Communications
I.07   Computer hardware
I.08   Computer software
I.14   Electronics
I.15   Energy/natural resources/utilities
I.17   Environmental services/waste management
I.20   Healthcare
I.21   High technology
I.22   Industrial products
I.23   Information technology services
I.24   Internet services/e-commerce
I.26   Life sciences
I.29   Medical/medical products
I.30   New media
I.33   Semiconductors
I.34   Services (business)

Sampling of portfolio companies: Advanced Tissue Sciences, Inc. (biotechnology); Canji, Inc. (biotechnology); La Jolla Pharmaceutical Co. (biotechnology); Somatix Therapy Corp. (biotechnology); Fuisz Technologies, Ltd. (biotechnological engineering); Proxima Corp. (computer enhancement products); Consorcio Beta, S.A. de C.V. (environmental); PDGEnvironmental, Inc. (environmental); Safety Storage, Inc. (environmental); CarePartners, Inc. (health services); Medical Imaging Centers of America, Inc. (health services); Escalon Medical Corp. (medical products); MDD, Inc. (medical products); R2 Medical Systems, Inc. (medical products); ETM Entertainment (software applications); United Systems Technology, Inc. (software applications); APTA group, Inc. (solid state/electronics); Dimensional Circuits Corp. (solid state/electronics); SenSys Instruments, Inc. (solid state/electronics); Cellnet Corp. (telecommunications)

INDEX BY INDUSTRIES

I.01 Aerospace

I.02 Agriculture/forestry/fishing/mining

I.03 Biotech/genetic engineering

I.04 Broadcasting

I.05 Chemicals

I.06 Communications

I.07 Computer hardware

I.08 Computer software

I.09 Construction

I.10 Consulting

I.11 Consumer products

I.12 Distribution

I.13 Education

I.14 Electronics

I.15 Energy/natural resources/utilities

I.16 Entertainment

I.17 Environmental services/waste management

I.18 Financial services

I.19 Generalist

I.20 Healthcare

I.21 High technology

I.22 Industrial products

IEG Venture Management
IL, Chicago 108
Indosuez Ventures
CA, Menlo Park 32
InterEquity Capital Partners, L.P.
NY, New York 189
InvestAmerica N.D. Management, Inc.
IN, Cedar Rapids 115
MO, Kansas City 164
ND, Fargo 213
Kansas City Equity Partners
MO, Kansas City 164
Key Equity Capital
NC, Charlotte 209
OH, Cleveland 216
WA, Seattle 256
LaSalle Capital Group, Inc.
IL, Chicago 108
Lawrence Financial
CA, Los Angeles 37
Madison Dearborn Partners, Inc.
IL, Chicago 109
Marwit Capital, L.L.C.
CA, Newport Beach..................... 39
Mason Wells
WI, Milwaukee 261
Massachusetts Technology Development Corp.
(MTDC)
MA, Boston 140
James A. Matzdorff & Co.
CA, Beverly Hills 39
Medallion Funding Corporation
NY, New York 191
The Melbourne Group, Inc.
FL, Melbourne 93
Mentor Capital
CA, San Jose 43
Mentor Capital Partners, Ltd.
NJ, Mt. Laurel 172
PA, Yardley 225
Mercury Capital Inc.
NY, New York 191
Merrill Pickard Anderson & Eyre
CA, Menlo Park 43
MidMark Capital, L.P.
NJ, Chatham........................... 172
Miralta Capital, Inc.
ON, Toronto........................... 273
QE, Dorval............................ 283
MK Global Ventures
CA, Palo Alto.......................... 43
Monosson Technology Enterprises
MA, Boston 141
Morgan Keegan & Company
TN, Memphis.......................... 233
MW Capital Partners
IN, Indianapolis 116
National City Capital
OH, Cleveland 217
National Corporate Finance, Inc.
CA, Newport Beach..................... 45
Nations Banc Capital Corporation
TX, Dallas 244
Nations Bank Capital Investors
NC, Charlotte.......................... 210

Needham & Co., Inc.
CA, Menlo Park 46
MA, Boston 142
NY, New York 193
North American Business Development Co., L.L.C.
FL, Ft. Lauderdale 94
IL, Chicago............................ 110
The North Carolina Enterprise Fund, L.P.
NC, Raleigh 211
North Riverside Capital Corporation
GA, Norcross 99
North Texas MESBIC, Inc.
TX, Dallas 244
Northwood Ventures
NY, New York 194
NY, Syosset 194
Onondaga Venture Capital Fund, Inc.
NY, Syracuse 196
Ontario Limited
ON, Sault Ste. Marie 273
Pacific Mezzanine Fund, L.P.
CA, Emeryville 51
Pacific Mezzanine Investors
CA, Newport Beach..................... 51
Paribas Principal Partners
NY, New York 196
Patricof & Co. Ventures, Inc.
CA, Palo Alto.......................... 53
NY, New York 197
PA, King of Prussia 226
Pennsylvania Growth Fund
PA, Pittsburgh 227
Pfingsten Partners, LLC
IL, Deerfield........................... 111
Priveq Financial Corporation
ON, Toronto........................... 273
Quorum Funding Corporation
ON, Toronto........................... 274
Redwood Partners
CA, Menlo Park 55
RFE Investment Partners
CT, New Canaan 87
Richards, LLC
GA, Atlanta 100
River Associates, L.L.C.
TN, Chattanooga 233
River Cities Capital Fund
OH, Cincinnati 218
Schroder Venture Advisors, Inc.
CT, Stamford 88
Schroders & Associates Canada Inc.
QE, Montreal.......................... 283
Seacoast Capital Partners, LP
CA, San Francisco 57
MA, Danvers 145
Sigma Capital Corp.
FL, Boca Raton 94
William E. Simon & Sons, L.L.C.
CA, Los Angeles 59
NJ, Morristown 174
Sirrom Capital Corporation
TN, Nashville.......................... 233
Solstice Capital
AZ, Tucson............................ 3
MA, Boston 147

I.23 Information technology services

I.24 Internet services/e-commerce

I.25 Leisure/hospitality

I.26 Life sciences

I.27 Manufacturing

I.28 Media/publishing

1.29 Medical/medical products

I.30 New media

I.31 Real estate

I.32 Retail

I.33 Semiconductors

I.34 Services (business)

I.35 Services (consumer)

I.36 Transportation

I.37 Wholesale

INDEX BY PREFERRED STAGE(S) OF FINANCING

Seed

Start up

First stage

Second stage

Mezzanine

LBO/MBO

Expansion

International expansion

Other: See listing for description.

Bradin, B.
Argo Global Capital, Inc.
MA, Lynnfield 126

Bradley, Timothy
Exeter Group of Funds
NY, New York 185

Brand, Pamela
DGC Entertainment Ventures Corporation
ON, Toronto 270

Brandon, Henry J.
William E. Simon & Sons, L.L.C.
CA, Los Angeles 59

Branscum, Chris L.
Hallador Venture Partners
CA, Sacramento 30

Bredt, Thomas H.
Menlo Ventures
CA, Menlo Park 42

Breece, Jr., R. William
Crown Capital Corp.
MO, St. Louis 163

Breen, John B.
CIBC Wood Gundy Capital
ON, Toronto 269

Brener, Harry
Technology Management & Funding, L.P.
NJ, Princeton 175

Brenner, Anthony P.
Omega Ventures
CA, San Francisco 49

Brenner, Tony
Robertson Stephens-Omega Ventures
CA, San Francisco 55

Brent, Doug
BT Capital Partners
NY, New York 180

Brent, Douglas
Pyramid Ventures, Inc.
NY, New York 199

Brentlinger, Paul S.
Morgenthaler Ventures
OH, Cleveland 216

Breshears, Patricia
Western Technology Investment
CA, San Jose 74

Bressner, Glen R.
Mid-Atlantic Venture Funds
PA, Bethlehem 226

Breyer, Jim
Accel Partners
CA, Palo Alto 5

Brill, Robert M.
Poly Ventures
NY, Farmingdale 198

Britt, Chris L.
Marwit Capital, L.L.C.
CA, Newport Beach 39

Broad, Aaron
Morgan Stanley Venture Partners
NY, New York 192

Brody, Christopher W.
E.M. Warburg, Pincus & Co., LLC
NY, New York 207

Broming, Charles
Commonwealth Enterprise Fund, Inc.
MA, Boston 134

Bron, William
Bastion Capital
CA, Los Angeles 12

Brooke, Peter A.
Advent International
MA, Boston 125

Brookfield, Chris
Redleaf Venture Management
WA, Seattle 259

Brooks, Michael C.
JH Whitney & Co.
CT, Stamford 85

Brooks, Todd
JAFCO America Ventures, Inc.
CA, Palo Alto 35

Brosda, Alexander C.
Stamford Financial Consulting
NY, Stamford 202
NY, Woodhaven 202

Brovald, Harvey A.
Accolade Capital Inc.
AB, Calgary 262

Brown, Bernard M.
Insurance Venture Partners, Inc.
CT, Greenwich 85

Brown, Douglas R.
Advent International
MA, Boston 125

Brown, Harold
E.M. Warburg, Pincus & Co., LLC
NY, New York 207

Brown, Jeff
Forrest Binkley & Brown
CA, Newport Beach 26

Brown, Michael D.
Stratford Capital Group, LP
TX, Dallas 247

Brown, Michael J.
Ventures West Management, Inc.
BC, Vancouver 264

Brown, Randy G.
Morgenthaler Ventures
GA, Atlanta 98

Brown, Jr., Robert E.
Meridian Venture Partners
PA, Radnor 226

Brunetta, Frank
Beacon Partners, Inc.
CT, Stamford 81

Buchanan, Stephen W.
Kitty Hawk Capital
NC, Charlotte 210

Buck, III, James M.
TDH
PA, Rosemont 228

Budd, Steven
Enterprise Ohio Investment Company
OH, Dayton 216

Budnick, Victor
Connecticut Innovations, Inc.
CT, Rocky Hill 83

Saffer, Alfred
Norwood Venture Corp.
NY, New York.........................195

Sager, Jr., Edward F.
Mentor Capital Partners, Ltd.
PA, Yardley...........................225

Sandell, Scott D.
New Enterprise Associates
CA, Menlo Park...................... 46
CA, San Francisco.................... 46
MD, Baltimore.......................122
VA, Reston..........................252

Sanders, W. Ferrell
Asset Management Associates, Inc.
CA, Palo Alto....................... 10

Santer, Michael
Platinum Venture Partners, Inc.
IL, Oakbrook Terrace..................111

Santry, Barbara L.
Pathfinder Venture Capital Funds
CA, Menlo Park...................... 53

Sarlo, George S.
Walden Group of Venture Capital Funds
CA, San Francisco.................... 72

Sattich, David A.
Equal Opportunity Finance, Inc.
KY, Louisville.......................117

Saunders, III, Thomas A.
Saunders Karp & Megrue
NY, New York.......................201

Savage, John
Redwood Partners
CA, Menlo Park...................... 55

Savar, André
Fonds Regional de Solidarite Abitibi-Temiscamingue
QE, Rouyn-Noranda 282

Savoldelli, Paul B.
Mandeville Partners
CA, Los Angeles 38

Savre, Russell M.
A. M. Pappas & Associates
NC, Durham..........................212

Schackman, Bruce
The CIT Group/Equity Investments
NJ, Livingston.......................168

Schaefer, John E.
Berwind Financial Group, L.P.
PA, Philadelphia 222

Schaepe, Christopher J.
Weiss, Peck & Greer Venture Partners
CA, San Francisco.................... 72

Schaffer, Jeffrey P.
Marwit Capital, L.L.C.
CA, Newport Beach.................... 39

Schairer, Robert
Hanam Capital Corp.
NY, New York.......................189

Schechter, David
Summit Capital Group, Inc.
KY, Louisville.......................117

Schechter, Jeffrey R.
Grotech Capital Group
MD, Timonium 121

Schecter, William H.
National City Capital
OH, Cleveland 217

Scheider, Daniel
Capital CDPQ
QE, Montreal 279

Schiff, Peter G.
Northwood Ventures
NY, New York.......................194
NY, Syosset 194

Schiffman, Barry
JAFCO America Ventures, Inc.
CA, Palo Alto....................... 35

Schiller, Pieter J.
Advanced Technology Ventures
MA, Waltham........................124

Schindel, Mark D.
Penman Partners
IL, Chicago..........................110

Schlass, Irwin
InterEquity Capital Partners, L.P.
NY, New York.......................189

Schlecht, William R.
The VenCom Group, Inc.
IL, Bannockburn 113

Schlein, Philip S.
U.S. Venture Partners
CA, Menlo Park...................... 69

Schlein, Ted
Kleiner Perkins Caufield & Byers
CA, Menlo Park...................... 36
CA, San Francisco.................... 36

Schmidt, Benno C.
JH Whitney & Co.
CT, Stamford 85

Schmidt, Gerald F.
Cordova Capital
GA, Atlanta 97

Schnabel, John S.
Generation Partners
CA, San Francisco.................... 28
NY, New York.......................187

Schnabel, Rockwell A.
Trident Capital
CA, Los Angeles 67

Schneider, Richard S.
Domain Associates
CA, Costa Mesa...................... 21

Schnitzer, Bruce
Wand Partners
NY, New York.......................207

Schoemaker, Kathleen K.
Domain Associates
NJ, Princeton 168

Schoendorf, Joe
Accel Partners
CA, Palo Alto....................... 5

Schoendorf, Nancy J.
Mohr, Davidow Ventures
CA, Menlo Park...................... 43

Schriesheim, Robert A.
Ameritech Development Corporation
IL, Chicago.........................102